Polling and Survey Research Methods 1935–1979

Polling and Survey Research Methods 1935–1979

An Annotated Bibliography

Compiled by
GRAHAM R. WALDEN

Bibliographies and Indexes in Law and Political Science,
Number 25

GREENWOOD PRESS
Westport, Connecticut • London

Library of Congress Cataloging-in-Publication Data

Walden, Graham R., 1954–
    Polling and survey research methods 1935–1979 : an annotated
bibliography / compiled by Graham R. Walden.
        p.   cm.—(Bibliographies and indexes in law and political
science, ISSN 0742–6909 ; no. 25)
    Includes index.
    ISBN 0–313–27790–7 (alk. paper)
    1. Public opinion polls—Bibliography.   2. Social surveys—
Bibliography.   3. Public opinion—United States—Bibliography.
4. Social surveys—United States—Bibliography.   I. Title.
II. Series.
Z7164.P956.W33   1996
[HM261]
016.3033′8—dc20   96–33127

British Library Cataloguing in Publication Data is available.

Library of Congress Catalog Card Number: 96–33127
ISBN: 0–313–27790–7
ISSN: 0742–6909

First published in 1996

Greenwood Press, 88 Post Road West, Westport, CT 06881
An imprint of Greenwood Publishing Group, Inc.

Printed in the United States of America

The paper used in this book complies with the
Permanent Paper Standard issued by the National
Information Standards Organization (Z39.48–1984).

10 9 8 7 6 5 4 3 2 1

In memory of
my grandmother

Valerie Schroetter Strobach

1893-1985

"Public opinion in this country is everything."

Abraham Lincoln

Speech, Columbus, Ohio
Terrace on the eastern side of the State House

Friday, 8 P.M., September 16, 1859

CONTENTS

PREFACE

This volume provides the reader with bibliographic access to the first forty-five years of polling and survey research utilizing scientific sampling. The volume begins with the work of Gallup, Roper, Crossley, and others in the mid-1930s, and progresses through many stages of development to the end of 1979. The book is to serve as a retrospective to the compilation of entries found in *Public Opinion Polls and Survey Research: A Selective Annotated Bibliography of U.S. Guides and Studies from the 1980s* by Graham R. Walden, New York: Garland Publishing, 1990, 306 pages. The scope, breadth, and depth of the literature compiled in the present bibliography permit an overview of the interdisciplinary subject. Practitioners, researchers, students, librarians, and others are the intended users.

All referenced materials are available from at least one U.S. location from which the item(s) can be examined by using interlibrary loan. Materials which were found to exist only in one location which declined to provide interlibrary loan were not included in this work (occurring in only a few instances from public resources). Documents in private collections or those held by corporate or business interests which do not provide for public perusal are by definition also not part of this compilation.

SCOPE

Primary subject disciplines covered include the following: agriculture, business, economics, education, law, library science, mass media, medicine, political science, psychology, public relations, religion, social work, and sociology. Other subjects are also considered, but at a significantly less frequent rate. Marketing research has been included where considerations pertinent to poll and survey research were undertaken. For readers who wish to pursue the subject holistically, the author suggests an unannotated work by John R. Dickinson titled *The Bibliography of Marketing Research Methods*, Lexington, Massachusetts: Lexington Books, 1990, 1023 pages. Over 14,000 entries are divided into 214 headings and 1,114 subheadings. See also Item No. 13 in Walden's 1935-1979 bibliography.

The major challenge for this compiler was the differentiation of the literature into the categories of those items which were conducted by interview either in person or by using the telephone, and those which were self-administered written questionnaires (SAWQ). This subdivision was not straightforward and frequently required reading the entire document before a categorization was possible. The search involved selecting from in excess of 10,000 bibliographic entries, and actually perusing 3,382 books, journal articles, and other sources. The complete bibliographies of all items were checked, with all potentially useful leads pursued. From these materials 1,013 items were considered appropriate and were annotated. The SAWQ literature of 741 items was separated for consideration in another volume, as these materials constitute a different line of inquiry with somewhat varying challenges to resolve. Readers wishing to pursue the self-administered questionnaire literature primarily from the pre-1980 period can consult the following selections from the broader body of resources available on this topic: Douglas R. Berdie, John F. Anderson, and Marsha A. Niebuhr, *Questionnaires: Design and Use*, 2d ed., Metuchen, New Jersey: Scarecrow Press, 1986, 330 pages (covers materials predominately from the 1970s); Paul L. Erdos, with the assistance of Arthur J. Morgan, *Professional Mail Surveys*, New York, New York: McGraw-Hill, [1970], 289 pages; and Robert Dyer, et al., *Questionnaire Construction Manual. Annex: Literature Survey and Bibliography*, Fort Hood, Texas: U.S. Army Research Institute for the Behavioral & Social Sciences, July 1976, 426 pages (ED 147 359). The reject file grew to 1,628, with subjects ranging from opinion and editorial, to non-U.S. authors and publishers, to those off the topic or too broad, and many other categories. On average the compiler needed to examine at least three items in order to successfully add one to the manuscript – a slow and challenging process requiring seven years to complete.

Books, chapters in books, government documents, and dissertations are covered by 292 citations, or 29 percent of the total. The rest of the entries were found in 721 journal articles representing 71 percent of the citations, with 229 in *Public Opinion Quarterly* (*POQ*) and 492 in non-*POQ* sources. In cases where a work was produced in multiple editions, the last edition prior to 1980 was selected for purposes of inclusion and annotation.

COVERAGE

In broad terms, the following types of materials are annotated: books, journal articles, dissertations, government documents, ERIC documents, book chapters, and articles from the popular press. Research studies, reference works, handbooks and guides, textbooks, histories, and bibliographies from the earliest days of scientifically sampled polls and surveys through to this compiler's earlier annotated bibliography are included. The methods and techniques of the many studies utilizing personal and telephone interviews are presented along with the results of their findings. However, results as such are neither the focus nor the intended content of this volume. Other resources are available which cover poll and survey results, including this author's article titled "Public Opinion Polls: A Guide to Accessing the Literature," in *Reference Services Review (RSR)*, volume 16, number 4, 1988, pages 65-74, which documents where poll and survey data can be located, including results from Gallup, Harris, the National Opinion Research Center, and others. Also considered in the *RSR* article is the *Guide to Resources and Services* by the Inter-University Consortium for Political and Social Research (ICPSR), a repository for the work of 325 colleges and universities located in the United States and fourteen foreign countries.

Materials specifically excluded are the following: book reviews, censuses, computer programs, cross-cultural comparisons, encyclopedia articles, English language publications in foreign countries, editorials, exclusively critical works, foreign authors and publications (non-U.S. authors and non-U.S. publications), letters – comments and replies (published and unpublished), master's theses, newspaper articles, proceedings (with a few exceptions), translations, unpublished papers and data, and privately held materials unavailable via interlibrary loan. [Therefore, articles written by Americans, and others, but appearing in the following well-known examples of foreign publications (as well as others not listed) do not appear in this bibliography: the *International Journal of Opinion and Attitude Research* (Mexico); the *International Social Science Bulletin* (Paris); and these seven publications from the United Kingdom: *International Affairs*, *Population Studies*, *Public Administration*, *Sociological Review*, *Sociology*, *Social Service Quarterly*, and *Social Work*.]

American Association for Public Opinion Research (AAPOR) conferences are excluded. Coverage of these events has been documented in *Public Opinion Quarterly*, along with indexing. In order to create a separate access tool for these materials, a distinct monograph probably would be necessary. Therefore, AAPOR and other proceedings await pursuit in the form of another research project.

A small number of citations discussing self-administered written questionnaires or mail questionnaires have been included when these have been used in a comparative environment with other approaches.

Some notable exceptions to the bibliography parameters include two symposia (Item Nos. 102 and 944), a conference (Item Nos. 105, 109, 164, and 933), and three critical works (Item Nos. 114, 236, and 920). These entries were considered to be of great historical consequence, and were therefore selected.

METHODOLOGY

Print indexes, CD-ROM formats, and online resources were used. Since the retrospective period covered falls well before most CD-ROM availability, and all but a few online files, most of the extensive checking necessary to complete the bibliography was conducted using paper indexes found in the Reference Collection of the Information Services Department, the Reading Rooms, and the Department Libraries at the Ohio State University in Columbus. (See Appendix C for a complete listing of Print and CD-ROM sources searched.)

Dissertation Abstracts International was searched on CD-ROM as the database is available from 1861 forward (with the print resources examined for abstracts not available in the CD-ROM format). Files for which parts of the 1960s and 1970s were available were searched on CD-ROM and then pursued through paper indexes for earlier decades to the mid-1930s.

The following online databases were searched: OCLC's (Online Computer Library Center) PRISM and WorldCat; RLIN (Research Libraries Information Network); and WLN (Washington Library Network). Database vendors DIALOG (owned by Knight-Ridder Information, Incorporated) and BRS (the BRS Online Products division was purchased by CD PLUS Technologies, now called OVID Technologies – with the searchable files known as OVID Online) were used to examine files with time periods not covered by CD-ROMs.

CITATIONS

Book citations include the name of the author(s) or editor(s); title; subtitle, if any; edition, if other than the first; series name, if applicable; editor of the series, if applicable; place of publication; publisher; year of publication; and total number of pages. When the entry item is a book chapter, the inclusive page numbers provided are those for the chapter (the total number of pages for the volume is also included). Journal entries include the name of the author(s); title; subtitle, if any; journal name; volume number; issue number, if applicable; month (season, if quarterly); year; and article page number(s). Citations to congressional hearings include the name of the committee; subcommittee; title; Congress; session; date; place of publication; publisher; publication date; number of pages; and Superintendent of Documents number. The information supplied for doctoral dissertations includes the author's name; title; subtitle, if any; name of the granting institution; year appearing in *Dissertation Abstracts International* (*DAI*); number of leaves; and *DAI* order number and print abstract location.

Each citation appears only once within the text, even though on many occasions it would be useful to exercise multiple postings to more accurately reflect the multifaceted nature of the contents.

The *Chicago Manual of Style* (13th edition) was the reference source for formatting, grammar, and bibliographical form (with a few exceptions such as including the total number of pages after book citations).

ANNOTATIONS

All entries are annotated, descriptive, and nonevaluative. Evaluative observations are found in quoted material only. The entries are designed to be sufficiently in-depth to permit the reader to evaluate whether pursuit of the full text is appropriate, with annotations averaging 133 words.

The debate about appropriate vocabulary – the use of the word "poll" versus the word "survey" – remains one of opinion governed largely by the role the individual has in the industry (that is, whether the person works for a company doing opinion research, or works for a newspaper, or is perhaps in academia). This author has maintained the language of the cited author(s) wherever possible.

The names of various ethnic and special groups have been updated to contemporary usage as of the mid-1990s. Sexist language has been deleted wherever possible, with the s/he, her/him format selected when both sex options occur. Directly quoted material may contain older language formats and appear as such in the Selective Keyword Index.

Upon consultation, and a review of current practice as of the writing of the annotations, this author chose to use the phrase "African Americans." The words "black" and "Negro" are in the Selective Keyword Index when they are included in direct quotes in the annotations, as well as when found in the title citations.

When advanced statistics are used in the work cited, this has been noted in the annotation. Advanced course work or knowledge of statistics will be required in order to adequately understand the content of items so designated.

There are 152 cross-references provided, as well as dozens of reprint references added to the appropriate citations.

Quotations have been used when authors employ unique adjectival qualifiers and select terminology, as well as when succinct communication and special language are utilized. Great effort has been taken to credit the original authors' words.

Where footnotes, references, or bibliographies are included in the original document, the annotation will end with a parenthetical entry or sentence showing the number found.

APPENDIXES

Appendix A, Acronyms, lists all acronyms used in this bibliography, with the full format provided. Terms and phrases for which established acronyms exist, but which were not used in acronym format in citations or annotations, have not been included.

Appendix B, Source Journals, provides a list of the 168 journals used, along with the citation number(s) for each occurrence. The inclusion of these titles is to permit the reader to readily identify the major journals in this field, as well as the obvious benefit of being able to locate an entry by journal name alone. The journals which appear most frequently are the following (with the number of times cited): *Public Opinion Quarterly* - 229; *Journal of the American Statistical Association* - 53; *Journal of Marketing* - 43; *Journal of Marketing Research* - 41; *Journal of Applied Psychology* - 17; *Journal of Advertising Research* - 14; *Business Week* - 13; *American Sociological Review* - 11; *American Journal of Sociology* - 11; *Printers' Ink* - 11; *U.S. News and World Report* - 11; *American Journal of Public Health* - 9; *Journal of Social Issues* - 9; *Sociological Methods and Research* - 9; *Human Organization* - 8; and *Newsweek* - 8.

Appendix C, Print and CD-ROM Sources, lists these formats used for compiling the bibliography. With these resources, and other online files, the core literature was determined. The bibliographies for all items located, both those annotated and those rejected, were searched to expand the research to the maximum degree.

Appendix D, Organizations, is a guide to the names, addresses, and telephone numbers of the major organizations associated with this field. Also included are the names of organizational heads and the year the group was founded.

AUTHOR INDEX

The Author Index lists the names of the 1,054 authors cited in the bibliographic portion of the entries, including multiple authors, editors, compilers, corporate authors, and author(s), editor(s), or compiler(s) of the original source document when the citation is to one chapter or portion of the original. All indexing numbers refer to those of the citations.

An analysis of the frequency of posting of names indicates the following ranking of the most prolific contributors (with the number of publications after the name): Seymour Sudman - 25; Charles F. Cannell - 20; Herbert H. Hyman - 17; George H. Gallup - 15; Stanley L. Payne - 12; Albert B. Blankenship - 11; Philip J. McCarthy - 11; Frederick Mosteller - 11; Eli S. Marks - 10; Norman M. Bradburn - 9; Robert Ferber - 9; and Daniel Katz - 9. An additional twenty-three authors have between five and eight publications each.

SELECTIVE KEYWORD INDEX

The Selective Keyword Index of nearly 7,000 entries is designed to permit access to both the bibliographic citation and the annotation keywords and phrases. On average each entry received twelve postings, with some receiving over thirty. Due to the frequency of occurrence, some individual words have been excluded from the index and appear in the Selective Keyword Index Stop Words list preceding the Selective Keyword Index. However, these terms may appear in phrase format in the index. Names appear in the format in which they were presented in the original text, with the exception of variant formats of the same name and person, which have been combined into one entry using the simplest format. In a select number of cases some enhancements using brackets have been supplied to avoid confusion when dealing with different individuals with the same name. Books and journals cited in the annotations, which are without a referred item number, are indexed by author(s), title, and keywords. The extensive use of phrases is designed to enable the reader to focus quickly and precisely on a given topic. All indexing numbers refer to those of the citations.

The Selective Keyword Index was created manually, with words and phrases selected for relevance and indexing merit. In fewer than one percent of the entries the word order as it appears in the original may have been inverted to create a more useful keyword search capability.

Acronyms appear both in the abbreviated format and in full under separate entries in the Selective Keyword Index, as well as in Appendix A.

In cases where an item has been reprinted, with that citation supplied, the reprinted source words and phrases have not been indexed.

Series titles in full have been posted in the index.

The *Library of Congress Filing Rules* by the U.S. Library of Congress Processing Services, prepared by John C. Rather and Susan C. Biebel, Washington, DC: Library of Congress, 1980, 111 pages, was used for both the Author Index and the Selective Keyword Index.

ACKNOWLEDGMENTS

Special thanks are directed to Distinguished Professor Seymour Sudman, Walter Stellner Chair of Marketing, the University of Illinois at Urbana-Champaign, for writing the Introduction. Dr. James T. Sabin, series editor and executive vice-president of the Greenwood Publishing Group, has been accommodating and generous in all exchanges, for which the author is very grateful.

The author wishes to thank Professor William J. Studer, director, the Ohio State University Libraries, for approving both a one-quarter-length Special Research Assignment, as well as for partial financial assistance in the form of an Advisory Committee on Research grant. Both the Special Research Assignment and the grant mentioned were recommended by members of the University Libraries Advisory Committee on Research. The author thanks all the committee members who reviewed the application.

Additionally, a University Faculty Professional Leave of one quarter was granted. Two committees were responsible for the administration of this program: the University Libraries Faculty Professional Leave Committee and the University Faculty Professional Leave Committee. The author thanks the former for recommending, and the university committee for granting, the request.

Appreciation is extended to the cooperative and responsive members of the Interlibrary Loan Department at the Ohio State University Libraries. Over the years of this manuscript preparation a number of individuals have worked with the requests submitted. The following people processed the 127 items received through the service: Deborah A. Cameron; Brenda L. Goodwin; Orville W. Martin; Instructor Scott H. Seaman (former head, relocated); Instructor David W. Tuffs (former head, relocated); and James R. Whitcomb.

During the many stages of this project, my departmental colleagues were called upon to work extra desk hours that I was unable to attend to during my absences. The Information Services Department has changed dramatically during this period. To all, the author expresses great appreciation. The department members during this research were as follows: Instructor Melvon L. Ankeny; Assistant Professor Emeritus Bernard A. Block; Associate Professor Emeritus Richard R. Centing; Instructor Karen R. Diaz; Assistant Professor Linda A. Krikos; Associate Professor David A. Lincove; Instructor Ralph A. Lowenthal (relocated); Instructor Saragail R. Lynch; Associate Professor Marjorie E. Murfin; Assistant Professor Emeritus Lawrence J. Perk; Instructor Lisa A. Pillow; Instructor Deborah L. Rinderknecht (relocated); Assistant Professor Stephen W. Rogers; and Associate Professor Emerita Carol A. Winchell. The author would like to take this opportunity to thank his colleagues during the last thirteen years for the many learning experiences that have availed themselves from working with a diverse group of knowledgeable reference librarians. Shared know-how has greatly increased this librarian's capabilities to a degree that only an open group experience can foster and encourage. Additionally, the staffs of the many Ohio State University Libraries were helpful, in particular, and beginning with the Information Services Department: Xiang-Ling Dai; Jana R. Murphy; Virginia L. Russell; and Janet M. Wagner. Many of our twenty department libraries and sixteen reading rooms, special collections, and departments in the Main Library were visited during the course of this research. Libraries which were heavily relied upon include the Business, Education, Health Sciences, and Undergraduate department locations, as well as the Main Library.

Assistant Professor John C. Stalker, head, Information Services Department, and Assistant Professor Patricia A. McCandless, assistant director, Main Library Public Services, provided flexibility and understanding of the challenges faced.

Ohio State University electrical engineering student Christopher E. Warren generously assisted with some of the formatting issues, thereby permitting the manuscript preparation to continue on course.

Richard N. Maxwell and Warren L. King from the Ohio State University Office for Disability Services offered suggestions for the current preferred wording usage for people with disabilities. These formats appear throughout this volume, and the author is appreciative for the guidance.

Barbara Kussow, documents reference librarian, the State Library of Ohio, assisted with locating several elusive government documents.

Marlene Bednarz, administrator, the American Association for Public Opinion Research, e-mailed some of the founding dates and addresses for the organizations listed in Appendix D. The author acknowledges the assistance as a useful addition to the publicly available record.

Jane J. Sferra, assistant head, Research Services, Archives/Library Division, the Ohio Historical Society, verified the Abraham Lincoln quotation appearing after the dedication page. The prompt receipt of the sources was welcome assistance. The quotation appears in the *Ohio State Journal*, no. 125, Saturday, 17 September 1859, page 2; and in *The Collected Works of Abraham Lincoln*, edited by Roy P. Basler, vol. 3. The Abraham Lincoln Association, Springfield, Illinois. New Brunswick, NJ: Rutgers University Press, 1953, page 424. 8v.

The preparation of the camera-ready manuscript was conducted by the mother-daughter team of Mary Jo Blevins and Tamara L. Jones (formerly and presently of the Ohio State University). The patience, fortitude, and good humor of these two individuals was certainly put to the test through the many editions, revisions, and alterations requested. Thank you for keying the 1,945,537 characters for a total of 214,621 words.

The author discussed this project with fellow Greenwood Press compiler and Ohio State University colleague, and acknowledges Assistant Professor Martin P. Jamison's contribution as a good listener.

INTRODUCTION

In what has clearly been a labor of love, Graham Walden has now gone backwards in time from the 1980s and extended his annotated bibliography of Polling and Survey Research Methods to the period 1935-1979. A natural question to ask is by whom and how will this bibliography of 1,013 items be used.

One might predict three different types of uses and users. The first use would be by historians and others interested in the development of polls and surveys. It is now sixty years since the early polls of Gallup and Roper in the mid-1930s, and fifty years since the founding of the American Association for Public Opinion Research. One major history has already been published. Jean Converse's book *Survey Research in the United States: Roots and Emergence, 1890-1960*. There is certainly much more to be uncovered. The field has a rich history of triumphs and disasters, and of changing methods and uses all of which are covered in this bibliography. Of course, historians will want to go back to the key primary sources, but the extensive annotation of the references makes it clear to the reader what the major issues were at different times, as well as who were the principal actors.

It is the case that about a quarter of all the references are from the *Public Opinion Quarterly* which since 1937 has been the leading journal in the field of public opinion polling, but the other references are from a highly diverse list of publications that would be unknown to most of us. One limitation to the use of this bibliography for historical purposes is that it restricts itself to the United States. Historians interested in parallel developments in Canada, Western Europe or the rest of the world will need to look elsewhere for references.

A second but related set of researchers who will use this annotated bibliography are sociologists of science. The arrangement of the bibliography by major topics and subtopics facilitates such a use, as do the keyword, author, and source indexes. As one illustration, researchers interested in interviewer effects can go to the section on interviewers and learn who has done work in this area, when it was done, where it was published and what issues were being discussed and what solutions were being recommended at different points in time.

Another use by these sociologists of science, as well as historians, is to trace the interests and productivity of individual researchers. Thus, it was with some surprise that I learned that I was the most frequently cited author in this bibliography. In this role, as well as from reading the abstracts for many well known articles, I can confirm that the annotations are carefully done and highly accurate.

The final use of this bibliography is, of course, to alert researchers in the field to what has already been done so that they do not reinvent the wheel. The computerized bibliographies that I am most familiar with are very useful, but do not extend back to the era covered in this book. I often review papers that limit their references to the last five or ten years, assuming that nothing of consequence was done earlier. As Walden demonstrates, this is clearly not the case.

To sum up, there are multiple uses for a thorough, careful bibliography of the first forty-five years of literature on polling and public opinion research. Few readers will go through from beginning to end, as I did to prepare this Introduction, but those who do will get an accurate and interesting aerial photograph of the development of the field.

Seymour Sudman
Distinguished Professor
Walter Stellner Chair of Marketing
Survey Research Laboratory
University of Illinois at
Urbana-Champaign

Polling and Survey Research Methods 1935–1979

REFERENCE SOURCES

ARCHIVES

1.   Campbell, Angus. "The Archival Resources of the Survey Research Center." *Public Opinion Quarterly* 24, no. 4 (Winter 1960-61): 686-88.

The Survey Research Center (SRC) was established in 1946 at the University of Michigan in Ann Arbor. The SRC's two main goals are to conduct research projects which are in the broad public interest and to assist with the training of students in the social sciences. Research projects come primarily from the center staff, with funding from the federal government, business, private foundations, and the University of Michigan. The SRC also conducts research for private agencies. Over one hundred studies have been conducted to date. Most research projects involve the collection of data from individual respondents (usually by personal interview), and are generally based on samples of some large population. Major findings are often published. Files and data are available for consultation to outside scholars. Six requirements for the use of the SRC archival materials are listed.

2.   Cutler, Stephen J. "Survey Research in the Study of Aging and Adult Development: A Commentary." *Gerontologist* 19, no. 2 (1979): 217-19.

Cutler uses this article to summarize and highlight the papers which appeared on the previous pages of this issue. Attention is drawn to survey research archives and their easy access, low cost, and detailed documentation which frequently accompanies the data. Also noted are the books in this area which provide guidelines for the use of archival data. [See Item No. 795 for Hyman's *Secondary Analysis of Sample Surveys*.] For those seeking to trace question use through time, a publication titled *Survey Data for Trend Analysis: An Index to Repeated Questions in U.S. National Surveys Held by the Roper Public Opinion Research Center* [Item No. 6] is available from the Social Science Research Council. (2 footnotes, 12 references)

3.   Hastings, Philip K. "The Roper Center: An International Archive of Sample Survey Data." *Public Opinion Quarterly* 27, no. 4 (Winter 1963-64): 590-98.

The Roper Public Opinion Research Center celebrated the fifth anniversary of its founding at Williams College, Williamstown, Massachusetts, 1 July 1957. The archive contains a vast collection of social science research data donated by Elmo Roper and Associates, sixteen American survey research groups, and thirty-five research organizations conducting surveys in thirty-nine countries. Over 2,800 studies from the United States and abroad make up the collection which is available for consultation to scholars and research organizations. Both the present and the planned services are explained in detail. Most users come from academe – especially the fields of sociology, political science, and economics. Other users include independent research organizations such as the Brookings Institute, the American Jewish Committee, the RAND Corporation, and various local, state, and federal government agencies. Listed are eight studies based primarily on American sample survey data, eight studies based on cross-national comparisons, and fifteen publications developed entirely or partly on data made available from the Roper Center. Details are provided as to how the archive processes its materials.

4.   Hastings, Philip K. "The Roper Public Opinion Research Center: A Review of Its First Three Years of Operation." *Public Opinion Quarterly* 25, no. 1 (Spring 1961): 120-26.

The Roper Public Opinion Research Center was established at Williams College in Williamstown, Massachusetts, in July 1957. The primary goals of the archive are to assemble, preserve, and organize both retrospective and current survey data; to make these materials available to scholars and others working in the field; and to assist educators in providing social science data for classroom use. The collection originally consisted of studies donated by Elmo Roper and Associates. By mid-1957 seventeen American groups and twenty-six foreign organizations had contributed data to the center. At present nearly two thousand studies have been received. Services include disseminating lists of newly acquired materials, photocopying, supplying copies of interview schedules and questionnaires, lending materials, and providing machine time and work space for qualified users. Examples of topics searched at the center and a list of ten reports based on center data are included. Plans for the expansion of the foreign data section are underway.

5.   Hastings, Philip K. "The Roper Public Opinion Research Center: An International Archive of Social Science Survey Data." *American Behavioral Scientist* 7, no. 3 (November 1963): 9-11.

The Roper Center began in July 1957, but as early as 1947 Elmo Roper and Associates had been placing their data at Williams College. Roper Center Director Hastings observes that this is the first time in history that a "continuing record on changes in the state of public attitudes" is available to scholars and other interested individuals. The article provides an outline of the purposes and services, and examples of some American sample survey data available at the center. The primary users to date have been academicians in the fields of sociology, political science, economics, psychology, and history. Approximately one-third of the studies housed were conducted outside of the United States. In its first six years the center has had over 2,500 users working with the 2,800 studies available.

6.   Hastings, Philip K., ed. Survey *Data for Trend Analysis: An Index to Repeated Questions in U.S. National Surveys Held by the Roper Public Opinion Research Center,* edited by Jessie C. Southwick. [Williamstown, MA]: Roper Public Opinion Research Center in cooperation with the Social Science Research Council, 1974. 567p. Microfiche. (ED 107 542)

The surveys used for this index are from the American Institute of Public Opinion, the National Opinion Research Center, and Roper. The basic data for over 90 percent of the surveys are available only from the Roper Public Opinion Research Center. The earliest survey included is from September 1936, and the most recent is dated October 1973. The database was created to measure and to analyze social change. Each entry contains the question wording, the survey organization responsible, the number and date of the survey, and the number of the question. An essay titled "Trend Studies with Available Survey Data: Opportunities and Pitfalls" (pp. 16-148), by Norval D. Glenn, provides a guide to survey archive research. Services of the Roper Center are described in the next section, followed by a description of the editing procedures, wording policy, entry explanation, and abbreviations used in the index. Appendixes include the sampling procedures and typical demographics for the three organizations represented, as well as sources of marginal distributions for some of the questions cited.

7.   Mendelsohn, Arthur, and Howard Rosenthal. "The Roper Center Automated Archive." *Public Opinion Quarterly* 31, no. 1 (Spring 1967): 107-9.

The Roper Public Opinion Research Center is an international survey archive located at Williams College in Williamstown, Massachusetts. The archive holds six thousand sample surveys covering twelve million interview cards and contains both U.S. and foreign materials (seventy nations are currently represented).

To efficiently store, index, update, and retrieve information for scholars and other users of the center, an RCA 301-3488 computing system was installed. Various hardware and software components are described. Objectives of the system are to reproduce data and codebooks, search indexes for surveys or questions (with Boolean logic), provide cross tabulations, merge surveys into large samples, and perform "cleaning" and error-checking operations. Future uses, refinements, and expansions of the automated system (especially remote console use by members of the International Survey Library Association) are discussed.

8.   Roper Public Opinion Research Center. *Celebrating 25 Years of Service to Research on Human Behavior.* Williamstown, MA: Roper Public Opinion Research Center, 1972. 35p.

This pamphlet reviews the history, outlines the services, and provides information on other relevant topics in commemoration of two-and-a-half decades of service of the Roper Center. The pamphlet is divided into twelve sections: "(1) Background and Development; (2) Data Bank Contents; (3) Services: Types and Procedures; (4) Usage; (5) Operating Staff; (6) Bibliography; (7) Data Processing Facilities; (8) Data Suppliers; (9) Access Classification System; (10) Financial Contributors; (11) 1969 AAPOR [American Association for Public Opinion Research] Awards; and (12) Board of Directors." The holdings of the Roper Center have grown substantially since its founding in 1957 at Williams College in Williamstown, Massachusetts. Beginning with 177 surveys, by 1971 the data bank had original response data from nearly 9,000 surveys, representing 117 survey research organizations in sixty-eight countries. Nearly two thousand requests were addressed in the last year. The center is used by academicians, government agencies, foundations, and nonprofit research organizations. The basic kinds of services provided are search and retrieval, data set reproduction, and analysis. The bibliography section lists twenty-eight publications based on data and services derived from the center. The data suppliers section includes the names of twenty-nine national and eighty-five international data suppliers arranged alphabetically by country. Contributions to the archive during the past twenty-five-year period total $1.6 million. The pamphlet includes photographs, charts, graphs, examples of searches, tables, and information on the fee schedule.

9.   Roper Public Opinion Research Center. *The Roper Public Opinion Research Center at Williams College.* Williamstown, MA: Roper Public Opinion Research Center, 1958. 32p.

The Roper Public Opinion Research Center was founded on 1 July 1957 with Williams College (Williamstown, Massachusetts) serving as the host institution. The center is designed to be a repository or archive for survey data from "recognized opinion research organizations throughout the world," to provide access to scholars to the data, and to make the data available as aids to classroom

teachers. This publication also discusses projects undertaken by Williams College. Eighteen cooperating research groups are described – these incorporate all
of the major organizations of the time. Additionally, twenty-five organizations
from all over the world are listed. Briefly described are the terms of public access, the indexing system used, the services provided, and a selection of four
"endorsements" received by the center.

10.   Roper Public Opinion Research Center Staff. "The Roper Public Opinion
        Research Center." *PROD: Political Research: Organization and Design*
        2, no. 2 (November 1958): 16-18.

Two decades of survey materials from Elmo Roper and Associates, along with
some original survey work by faculty and students at Williams College in Williamstown, Massachusetts, formed the collection of the Roper Public Opinion
Research Center at its founding in July 1957. By the following year the data of
seventeen large American universities and research institutes and that of twenty-
five foreign organizations had been acquired. The center's functions are to assemble, preserve, and organize survey data; to permit scholars accessibility to
the data; and to provide educators with social science data relevant to classroom
teaching. Two indexes, one of questionnaire items and one of face-data information, have been compiled. The center, with a mailing list of over twenty thousand names, processes inquiries from both individuals and institutions. The importance of the archive for primary and secondary research in the social sciences
is outlined.

11.   Rossi, Peter H., and Robert Crain. "The NORC Permanent Community
        Sample." *Public Opinion Quarterly* 32, no. 2 (Summer 1968): 261-72.

The Permanent Community Sample (PCS) includes two elements: the data collection mechanism and a data archive. The comparative community research made
possible via PCS employs a probability sample of two hundred cities in the
United States with populations of fifty thousand or greater. The National Opinion Research Center devised PCS in order to permit "relatively large scale"
community studies. There are four elements to PCS: (1) a social scientist in each
city will be employed on a part-time basis to collect statistics and documents on
community decisions (someone associated with an academic institution); (2) a
part-time interviewer will interview "elites," collect statistics, and work in conjunction with the social scientist; (3) five to ten prominent individuals will be
asked to form a panel to answer questions which "cannot be unambiguously or
economically measured"; and (4) along with census data, the above-gathered
research will be part of a data bank available to community researchers. A series
of nine possible applications for the use of PCS is explored. (27 footnotes)

12.   Ullman, Morris B. "The Records of a Statistical Survey." *American Archivist* 5, no. 1 (January 1942): 28-35.

In the statistical survey the purpose is to gather quantitative facts, to analyze the data, and to present the results in a useful format. Ullman discusses the archivally useful records created during the planning, data collection, and processing phases. The original questionnaire is discussed. The material to be retained should include these components: (1) papers indicating the original objective and plan for the survey; (2) operating records showing the rate of the work of the personnel; (3) the cost of the survey; (4) the equipment used; (5) the questionnaire; and (6) reports, summaries, or evaluations. Written by an employee of the Bureau of the Census, these guidelines have particular pertinence to the census, but also apply in principle to other survey environments.

BIBLIOGRAPHIES

13.   Ferber, Robert, Alain Cousineau, Millard Crask, and Hugh G. Wales., comps. *A Basic Bibliography on Marketing Research.* 3d ed. Bibliography Series, no. 2. [Chicago, IL]: American Marketing Association, 1974. 299p.

This annotated bibliography is divided into five sections covering background materials, techniques, areas of research, communication and administration, and miscellaneous aspects. The volume includes literature from related fields in the social sciences and other disciplines. Inclusion was based on method reliability and broad interest among researchers. Additionally, the physical items must be available in business libraries or "on call" from issuing organizations. The authors strive for pertinence rather than comprehensiveness. Annotations are between one and two sentences, with noteworthy items designated by a plus sign before the authors' names in the bibliographic citation (with journal names abbreviated and a journal code list at the end of the book). Some citations from the second edition [1963] have been deleted, but most titles have been retained to indicate the transition within the field over the last thirty to forty years of research. The techniques chapters cover the following topics (with the number of citation occurrences following each heading): (1) data collection methods - 117; (2) questionnaire construction and design - 57; (3) interviewing - 97; (4) sampling - 178; (5) data processing - 33; (6) attitude and opinion measurement - 172; (7) projective and other psychological methods - 93; (8) behavioral theories - 45; (9) statistical analysis of relationships - 10; (10) model building - 93; (11) systems analysis - 26; and (12) miscellaneous techniques - 88. The total number of references considered in the techniques section is 1,109.

14.   Francis, J. Bruce. "Further Information on Surveying Institutional Con-
       stituencies." In *Surveying Institutional Constituencies*, edited by J. Bruce
       Francis, 95-98. *New Directions for Institutional Advancement: A Quar-
       terly Sourcebook*, editor-in-chief A. Westley Rowland, no. 6. San Fran-
       cisco, CA: Jossey-Bass Inc., Publishers, 1979. 100p.

A sixteen-item annotated bibliography is presented. Two categories cover survey design (five citations) and survey techniques (eleven citations). With the
exception of one *Public Opinion Quarterly* article, all references are to books,
with all but one, a British title, being American imprints. The earliest title cited
is from 1957; the most recent is from 1979, with the balance primarily from the
decade of the 1970s. Nearly all of the titles are of the "textbook" genre designed
for college undergraduates and graduate students.

15.   Sharma, Prakash C. *Public Opinion Polls: A Selected Research Bibliog-
       raphy*. Council of Planning Librarians, Exchange Bibliography, edited
       by Mary Vance, no. 757. Monticello, IL: Council of Planning Librarians,
       March 1975. 11p.

The bibliography has 156 unannotated entries. In the preface, Sharma, a member of the Department of Sociology at the University of Alabama during the
preparation of the publication, advises that the bibliography covers works "published chiefly during 1950-1965." An analysis of the bibliography reveals that
54 items are from the 1960s, and 28 items are from the 1950s, with almost half
of the total entries from earlier decades. There are no entries from the 1970s.
There are 63 book titles and 93 articles and periodicals considered. About 10 percent of the works cited are non-U.S. publications. The bibliography has a number of bibliographic omissions: 23 percent of the book titles do not indicate a
publisher, and 33 percent of the periodical entries do not indicate pagination.
Public Opinion Quarterly is the most frequently cited journal occurring 28
times. Five other journal titles occur three or more times: *American Journal of
Sociology, American Political Science Review, American Sociological Review,
Journal of the American Statistical Association*, and *Journalism Quarterly*.

16.   Spaeth, Mary A. "Recent Publications on Survey Research Techniques."
       Journal of Marketing Research 14, no. 3 (August 1977): 403-9. [A re-
       vised version is reprinted in *Readings in Survey Research,* edited by
       Robert Ferber, 579-602. Chicago, IL: American Marketing Association,
       1978. 604p.]

The 203 citations in this unannotated bibliography are arranged according to the
various stages involved in conducting a survey (with the number of citation occurrences following each section): (1) general - 16; (2) sampling - 17; (3) questionnaire design - 29; (4) data collection - 121; (general - 33); (personnel - 5);

(telephone - 7); and (other - 28); (5) data reduction and processing - 10; and (6) analysis - 10. Most of the books, articles, and book chapters cited in the bibliography were published between 1974 and 1976, with a few entries covering the years 1972 and 1973 (4 items), and some representing the year 1977 (9 items). Approximately 5 percent (12 items) of the material included is foreign, consisting primarily of reports originating from the International Statistical Institute in the Hague-Voorburg. There are twelve studies listed from various branches of the U.S. government, including the U.S. Bureau of the Census. The majority of the journal citations are from three sources: *Public Opinion Quarterly*, the *Journal of Marketing Research*, and the *Journal of the American Statistical Association*. The author states that "selecting was especially necessary for the data processing and analysis sections because of the diversity of methods available and the number of publications discussing them preclude anything other than limited coverage."

17.   U.S. Bureau of the Census. *Indexes to Survey Methodology Literature*. Technical Paper no. 34. U.S. Department of Commerce, Social and Economic Statistics Administration, Bureau of the Census. Washington, DC: U.S. Government Printing Office, April 1974. 225 pages in various pagings. [SuDoc C56.215/2:34]

This unannotated bibliography was developed to assist in identifying relevant sources for staff members of the U.S. Bureau of the Census. The various indexes cover both published and unpublished materials in the field of survey methods and techniques. Although in a developmental mode at the time of publication, the indexes are being issued to satisfy the research needs of those working in the area. Included are citations to books, journal articles, census publications and documents, research reports, and papers emanating from conference presentations. The introduction states that the "subject coverage of the information system emphasizes nonsampling aspects of survey design and operation, particularly the measurement and control of nonsampling errors that occur in the data-collection phase." However, studies focusing on sample design and methods, response error models and theory, and data processing methods have been omitted. Documents dealing with survey techniques applicable to health surveys are included. They come from a database at the Survey Research Center (under the direction of Charles F. Cannell) of the Institute for Social Research at the University of Michigan. The bibliography contains four sections: (1) Bibliographic Index; (2) Personal Author Index; (3) Organization Index; and (4) Key-Word-in-Context (KWIC) Index. The Bibliographic Index is arranged by accession number – that is, the number assigned to the document as it is entered into the Survey Methodology Information System (SMIS). Also provided is information on the document title, volume number, issue number, and date of publication. Both the source document and any individual selections from it are analyzed. The latter includes accession number, author(s) name, title, organizational affiliation, pagination, number of references, and availability. The Personal Author Index provides the names of all authors in the SMIS. Also given is the title and accession number, thereby enabling the full citation to be found in the Bibliographic Index. The Organization Index lists all institutions and organizations with which the authors are affiliated. Document titles are in truncated form in this index as well as in the Personal Author Index. Accession numbers follow the title. The KWIC Index alphabetically lists the significant words from the titles, with natural word order around each significant word. The document accession number appears following each title display. Several paragraphs explain how the documents listed in the bibliography may be acquired by the user.

DIRECTORY

18. Northrop, Ann, comp. "Directory of Major Political Public Opinion Firms in the United States." *National Journal* 3, no. 33 (14 August 1971): 1700-1701.

The directory contains a listing of seventy-four U.S. firms engaged in political public opinion research on a regional or national basis. Each listing contains the name, address, and telephone number, as well as the name and title of the firm's principal officer. (Part-time consultants and firms primarily involved with campaign management have been excluded.) The list also indicates if the company is a member of the National Council on Public Polls, whether the firm is non-profit and /or academic, and if the results are always publicly published.

GLOSSARIES

19. Benson, Dennis K., and Jonathon L. Benson. *A Guide to Survey Research Terms: A BENCHMARK Handbook.* Columbus, OH: The BENCHMARK Program, Academy for Contemporary Problems, April 1975. 23p.

The introduction (pages 1-7) presents a brief overview of the survey research process. Comments are made on sample size, types of surveys, questionnaire construction, interviewing, and the interpretation of the results. Table 1 shows the relationship between sample size and percent error; table 2 compares and contrasts three interview methods: telephone, personal, and mail, showing average costs, response rate ranges, data recovery time, rapport, callback/follow-up, weather, normal length, and types of information collected. Ten book titles and six journal titles, both general and technical, are listed for those seeking additional information on survey research. The glossary lists 200 terms (158 definitions and 42 cross-references) dealing with all phases of survey research. Length of definition ranges from 6 words ("data") to over 240 words ("confidence interval"). A few illustrations accompany the text.

20.   Webster, Richard. "Polls and Commercial Research: Some Definitions and Comments on Terms." *Printers' Ink* 225, no. 7 (12 November 1948): 36f-36h.

Webster begins the article by defining these words: poll, research, opinion research, randomization, the question or questionnaire, and depth interviewing. The word "poll" originally meant head. The article is accompanied by photographs of George Gallup, Elmo Roper, and several pictures of the NBC and ABC network newsrooms during the Truman versus Dewey presidential election.

INSTRUCTIONAL MATERIALS

GENERAL

21.   American Marketing Association. *The Technique of Marketing Research.* Prepared by the Committee on Marketing Research Technique of the American Marketing Association, Ferdinand C. Wheeler, chairman. New York, NY: McGraw-Hill Book Company, 1937. 432p.

The volume, one of the earliest contributions covering techniques in market research in a comprehensive manner, explores the gamut of issues. The chapters cover these areas: (1) analysis of the problem and the purpose for the study; (2) planning, with a review of mail, telephone, and personal interview options; (3) psychological aspects of developing the questionnaire; (4) the "art of asking why" and issues of bias; (5) data collection, considering both developed and undeveloped data; (6) additional aspects of data collection; (7) mail questionnaire, telephone, and personal interview preparation; (8) personnel organization and training; (9) fieldwork preparation; (10) role and training of supervisors in fieldwork; (11) classification of returns, requiring that a classification be articulate, psychologically adequate and pertinent, and logically correct; (12) data organization; (13) review of qualitative data; (14) machine tabulation; (15) aspects of reaching conclusions from the data; (16) interpretation; (17) presentation of results; (18) work beyond conclusion of the research – such as the addition of amendments, and making sure that the results are understood; (19) statistics used in marketing research; and (20) sample size determination. A nineteen-page bibliography is provided, as well as a nine-page index.

22.   Gallup, George. *The Sophisticated Poll Watcher's Guide.* Rev. ed. [Princeton, NJ]: Princeton Opinion Press, 1976. 252p.

13

The question-and-answer format is employed. The questions come from a wide variety of sources including television and radio commentators, magazine editors, and academicians. At the end of the foreword Gallup lists the 178 question contributors. Designed for the lay reader, the guide avoids technical language whenever possible. The book is divided into three sections. Section 1, titled "Polls – What Purpose Do They Serve?" pays particular attention to what Gallup labels the "bandwagon myth." Section 2 deals with poll methodology. Among other concerns the issues of sample size, interviewers and interviewing problems, and the reporting of poll results are considered. The last section, the longest of the three, is devoted to election polls, and provides answers to a number of election poll questions, for example, accuracy, costs of the polls, and why different polls yield different results. There are several items in the appendix which are of particular interest. These include "Highlights of Polling History" and a table titled "Gallup Poll Accuracy in National Elections – 1936 to 1970." There are four pages of suggested readings.

23.   Gallup, George, and Saul Forbes Rae. *The Pulse of Democracy: The Public-Opinion Poll and How It Works.* New York, NY: Simon & Schuster, 1940. 335p.

The beginnings of polls from straw-vote counts to continuous cross-section surveys are described. The lessons derived from the 1936 presidential campaign are enumerated. Poll accuracy, topic selection, question wording, interviewers, and interviewing are discussed. The quantity and quality factors of a poll are considered, along with the issue of the bandwagon vote – if indeed there is such an effect. Gallup and Rae address the concern that polls may "destroy representative democracy." The goal of the book is to describe and defend public opinion polling. The authors note the contribution made by American newspapers that have supported the work of the American Institute of Public Opinion (AIPO) in bringing the results of surveys to the public (even when these disagreed with the editorial columns of the same newspaper). AIPO was founded by Gallup in Princeton, New Jersey, in 1935. Each chapter has a few footnotes. Appendix 1 provides a selection of issues with the questions asked and the "approve," "disapprove," and "no opinion" results. Appendix 2 lists the newspapers which carried the results of the AIPO polls as of May 1940 (118 are listed – divided by political orientation). (46 references)

24.   Gallup, George, James Pollock, and Louis Wirth. "A Radio Discussion of Testing Public Opinion." *University of Chicago Round Table*, no. 86 (5 November 1939): 1-25.

The Round Table is described as the "oldest educational program continuously on the air" for which the entire broadcast is conducted without a script. The radio program is broadcast by NBC. The three participants for this broadcast were George

Gallup, director of the American Institute of Public Opinion; James K. Pollock, professor of political science, University of Michigan; and Louis Wirth, associate professor of sociology, University of Chicago. Questions addressed include the numbers interviewed in Gallup polls, the issue of bandwagon, and how polls are made available to the public. The authors include a nine-item list of suggested readings and two lists of questions – one designed to provide the page number which addresses the issue, the other intended to generate further analysis and discussion. (11 footnotes)

25.   Graeter, Ralph, and Richardson Wood. "Photo Charts of Survey Findings: Some Experiments Made for the Editors of *Life*." *Public Opinion Quarterly* 9, no. 4 (Winter 1945-46): page 430 plus four unnumbered pages.

Graeter and Wood attempt to express survey findings in pictorial format in a 1944 experiment for *Life* magazine. Four pages of drawings and photographs illustrating this effort accompany the text. It is believed that pictures offer only the "roughest approximation" of survey results. However, pictures do have a place in "popularizing" survey findings and might appeal to those who disregard a table of figures. The editors of *Life* ultimately rejected the regular use of this method in favor of "real" pictures.

26.   *Guidelines for Survey Research and Questionnaire Construction: A Topical Paper.* [Gainesville, FL]: Inter-Institutional Research Council, Florida Community Junior College, 1970. 12 leaves.

The introduction is written by Council Associate Director Michael I. Schafer. The volume is divided into two parts. The first, titled "Standards for Statistical Surveys," was prepared by the Executive Office of the President, Bureau of the Budget, Division of Statistical Standards. Part 1 is dated 28 March 1952 and is labeled Circular No. A46. The nine pages cover every aspect of survey research from the purpose of the survey to the preparation and publication of the final report, with a total of twenty-two topics addressed. Part 2, titled "The Design and Construction of Questionnaires," was written by Emerson M. Brooks, Division of Special Farm Statistics, Bureau of Agricultural Economics. The content is from a lecture delivered in the Research and Marketing Course, Graduate School, U.S. Department of Agriculture, 14 June 1948. With fifty headings for topics discussed, Brooks considers a range of subjects from questionnaire color, to memory bias (this occurs when a respondent is asked to recall events a year or more in the past), to interviewer mispronunciation of interview questions.

27.   Lockley, Lawrence C. "Market Description – Quantitative and Qualitative." Part 1, Chap. 2 in *How to Conduct Consumer and Opinion Research; The Sampling Survey in Operation*, edited by Albert B. Blankenship, 11-28. The American Council Series of Public Relations Books, edited

by Rex F. Harlow. New York, NY: Harper & Brothers Publishers, 1946. 314p.

The stages of the planning and conduct of market surveys are outlined, with presentations on the mail questionnaire, the consumer panel, and the personal interview. The usefulness of permanent staffs of mobile interviewers is explored. The chapter describes questionnaire design and offers specific suggestions in a series of short paragraphs. The issue of sampling is addressed, covering both ratio and area sampling. The work of the Census Bureau with area sampling is described. Lockley observes that three types of results can be generated from market surveys, namely information, interpretation of that information, and recommendations. For successful market surveys the author believes that judgment, ingenuity, careful planning, attention to details, and supervision are necessary, along with the appropriate use of survey techniques.

HANDBOOKS AND MANUALS

28.   Backstrom, Charles H., and Gerald D. Hursh. *Survey Research.* Handbooks for Research in Political Behavior, edited by James A. Robinson. [Chicago, IL]: Northwestern University Press, 1963. 192p.

This handbook, designed primarily for political scientists and political sociologists, may also serve as a short manual for student use with field studies. Chapters are devoted to survey planning, sampling, question writing, questionnaire design, fieldwork, and data processing. Fifteen checklists are supplied, including the steps in survey research and interviewing cautions. Each chapter is followed by endnotes. The volume includes a nineteen-page index.

29.   Berelson, Bernard, and Morris Janowitz, eds. *Supplement to Reader in Public Opinion and Communication.* No. 10: *Methods in Public Opinion Research,* 497-611. Glencoe, IL: Free Press, 1953. 611p.

The editors state that the reprints included are "illustrative of some of the central aspects involved in the methodology of opinion research." The ten articles and excerpts are classified under three headings: "Problems of Research Design"; "Problems of Data Collection"; and "Problems of Analysis." The supplement to the 1950 edition has been included in the enlarged 1953 edition. A bibliography appears on pages 603-11. The following entries have been selected from the volume, with individual annotations found at the indicated item number.

"How Surveys Are Made." (Maccoby and Holt - Item No. 136).

"Area Sampling – Some Principles of Sample Design." (Hansen and Hauser - Item No. 157).

"The Controversy over Detailed Interviews – An Offer for Negotiation." (Lazarsfeld - Item No. 476).

"The Interpretation of Survey Findings." (Katz - Item No. 751).

"The Pre-Election Polls of 1948." (Social Science Research Council Committee on Analysis of Pre-Election Polls and Forecasts - Item No. 958).

30.   Boyd, Richard W., and Herbert H. Hyman. "Survey Research." Chap. 6 in *Strategies of Inquiry*, edited by Fred I. Greenstein and Nelson W. Polsby, 265-350. Handbook of Political Science, vol. 7. Reading, MA: Addison-Wesley Publishing Company, 1975. 458p.

A long series of beliefs and behaviors is reviewed in attempting to determine if they can be studied by the survey research method. For example, political effect, attitudes, beliefs, and judgments are considered. The purposes of survey research during different time periods are noted. The categories are divided into the social survey movement, the Great Depression, World War [II], the postwar years, and the cold war. Boyd and Hyman consider the compatibility of commercial and academic uses of surveys. The authors also undertake to determine the effects of surveys on theory. In their conclusion it is acknowledged that the survey technique has "changed the character of the study of politics." A thirteen-page bibliography is provided.

31.   Ferber, Robert, ed. *Handbook of Marketing Research*. New York, NY: McGraw-Hill Book Company, [1974]. (various pagings)

Designed as a handbook and basic reference source for market research, one section of this volume speaks directly to those pursuing survey research using personal and telephone interviews, as well as data collected by mail. In Section 2, Part B, under the heading "Surveys," and in Section 2, Part C, under the heading "Sample Design," the following entries have been selected, with individual annotations found at the indicated item number.

Part B, Chapter 1:   "Survey Design." (Sheatsley - Item No. 140).

        Chapter 4:   "Data Collection Methods: Telephone Surveys." (Payne - Item No. 526).

        Chapter 5:   "Interviewers: Recruiting, Selecting, Training, and Supervising." (Andrews - Item No. 426).

Chapter 7:   "Planning Field Operations." (Hauck - Item No. 470).

Chapter 9:   "Coding." (Sidel - Item No. 761).

Part C, Chapter 1:   "Basic Concepts." (Semon - Item No. 208).

Chapter 2:   "Probability Sampling." (Frankel and Frankel - Item No. 171).

Chapter 3:   "Bayesian Framework for Sample Design." (Sudman - Item No. 159).

32.   Ferber, Robert, ed. *Readings in Survey Research*. Chicago, IL: American Marketing Association, 1978. 604p.

The entries in this volume are reprints from the *Journal of Marketing Research*, August 1977 issue, as well as articles from other sources which deal with sampling, questionnaire preparation, and data collection. There are forty-four chapters divided into the following eight parts: (1) survey research; (2) sample design and nonsampling errors; (3) question design; (4) mail surveys; (5) telephone surveys; (6) personal interview surveys; (7) panels; and (8) other methods. A twenty-two-page revised bibliography titled "Recent Publications on Survey Research Techniques," compiled by Spaeth [Item No. 16], closes the volume. The book includes a one-page author index. The following entries have been selected from the volume, with individual annotations found at the indicated item number.

Part 2, Chapter 3:   "Some Recent Developments in Sample Survey Design." Frankel and Frankel - Item No. 156).

Chapter 5:   "Measurement Errors in Reports of Consumer Expenditures." (Neter - Item No. 772).

Chapter 9:   "Nonresponse Bias and Callbacks in Sample Surveys." (Dunkelberg and Day - Item No. 711).

Chapter 12:   "Sampling a Rare Population: A Case Study." (Ericksen - Item No. 222).

Part 3, Chapter 13:   "Striving for Response Accuracy: Experiments in New Interviewing Techniques." (Cannell, Oksenberg, and Converse - Item No. 462).

Chapter 14: "How to Ask Questions about Drinking and Sex: Response Effects in Measuring Consumer Behavior." (Blair, Sudman, Bradburn, and Stocking - Item No. 279).

Chapter 18: "The Effect of Question Form on Gathering Income Data by Telephone." (Locander and Burton - Item No. 293).

Part 5, Chapter 30: "Relative Efficiency and Bias of Plus-One Telephone Sampling." (Landon and Banks - Item No. 254).

Chapter 31: "Is Random Digit Dialing Really Necessary?" (Rich - Item No. 237).

Part 6, Chapter 32: "Interviewer Bias Once More Revisited." (Boyd and Westfall - Item No. 350).

Chapter 33: "Interview Rapport: Demise of a Concept." (Goudy and Potter - Item No. 423).

Chapter 35: "Measures of Interviewer Bias and Variance." (Bailar, Bailey, and Stevens - Item No. 348).

Part 7, Chapter 37: "A Comparison of Alternative Procedures for Collecting Consumer Expenditure Data for Frequently Purchased Products." (Sudman and Ferber - Item No. 612).

Part 8, Chapter 42: "Compliance with an Interview Request: A Foot-in-the-Door, Self-Perception Interpretation." (Reingen and Kernan - Item No. 459).

Bibliography: "Recent Publications on Survey Research Techniques." (Spaeth - Item No. 16).

33. Hamilton, William R. *Workplan: In-House Polling,* edited by Scot Wolf. Democratic Campaign Guides: Workplans for Winning. Washington, DC: Democratic National Committee, 1975. 27p.

In-house polling has the potential to be a considerable money saver for political campaigns. For example, in 1975 dollars the introduction to this manual compares $500 to $1500 for a volunteer poll versus $6000 to $7000 for a professional telephone survey of four hundred individuals. The first section is designed for the poll director who runs the in-house operation; the second section is used in the training of volunteer interviewers. A model questionnaire is included for interviewer use. The entire manual is divided into steps, concluding with number nine: "Follow the sampling plan provided." Each step has examples. To complete four hundred interviews it is suggested that two hundred hours may be needed by professional interviewers or six days with twenty-five volunteer interviewers.

34.   Newman, Isadore. *Basic Procedures in Conducting Survey Research.* [Akron, OH]: [University of Akron], 1976. 43p.

Divided into eight steps, this procedures volume covers the topic from the intent of the survey research through the writing of the report. In between, the steps suggested include examining the existing resources, defining the population, reviewing the literature, considering the survey instruments (mailed questionnaire, nonmailed questionnaire, telephone surveys, and interviews), studying sampling procedures, and analyzing the results. The introduction provides an eight-step guide for developing the survey instrument. In the report preparation section a dissertation format outline and a rating scale are provided to serve as general guides. (17 references)

TEXTBOOKS

35.   Babbie, Earl R. "Survey Research." Chap. 12 in *The Practice of Social Research,* 315-52. 2d ed. Belmont, CA: Wadsworth Publishing Company, 1979. 596p.

Major areas discussed include questionnaire construction; self-administered questionnaires; interview surveys; a comparison of self-administered questionnaries and interview surveys; strengths and weaknesses of survey research; and secondary analysis. As this volume is intended for textbook use, the chapter is summarized with the main issues outlined in fifteen points. A brief six-entry annotated bibliography is provided. Seven figures are included which primarily illustrate different questionnaire design formats. [See Item No. 37 for the accompanying volume.]

36.   Babbie, Earl R. *Survey Research Methods.* Belmont, CA: Wadsworth Publishing Company, [1973]. 383p.

The logic and skills of survey research are the focus of this textbook intended for undergraduates taking their first research methods course. Other intended users include researchers new to the field and consumers of survey research. The volume is divided into four parts. Part 1 discusses the context of survey research in social science and what constitutes science. Part 2 covers survey research design, including study designs, sampling, instrument design, questionnaires, interviewing, data processing, pretests, and pilot studies. The third part deals with analysis and includes chapters on measurement, tables, index and scale construction, the elaboration model, uses of statistics, complex analysis, and reporting results. Part 4 concerns ethics, uses of results, and the social, scientific, and educational implications of survey research. Additional readings appear at the end of each chapter. Two appendixes are supplied – one for random numbers, the other for binomial estimated sampling error. A four-and-a-half-page subject index is included.

37.　　Babbie, Earl R., and Robert E. Huitt. "Survey Research." Chap. 12 in *Practicing Social Research: Guided Activities to Accompany "The Practice of Social Research,"* 121-69. 2d ed. Belmont, CA: Wadsworth Publishing Company, 1979. 246p.

Survey research is defined as a "method that consists of selecting a sample of respondents and administering a standardized questionnaire to them." Several pages are devoted to summarizing the salient points from the accompanying textbook [Item No. 35]. Key terms are identified, and review questions are posed, followed by discussion questions. Two assignments are provided. The first calls for the examination of an existing survey; the second requires the student to interview ten individuals using the twenty blank interview questionnaires provided (one set is a duplicate to be used for other assignments). The answers to the review questions are found at the back of the volume.

38.　　Cantril, Hadley, and Research Associates in the Office of Public Opinion Research, Princeton University. *Gauging Public Opinion.* Princeton, NJ: Princeton University Press, 1944. Reprint. Port Washington, NY: Kennikat Press, 1972. 318p.

The Cantril volume, designed as a textbook, contains five major parts plus seven appendixes and was written with cooperation and assistance from George Gallup. The work is an early attempt to educate a wide audience on the growing field of polling. Topics covered include question formulation, interviewing, sampling, and "determinants." A complete case study is reported. Appendixes discuss interviewer bias, confidence limits, and intensity of opinion, among other technical note sections. Appendix 7 is a bibliography of about 120 entries covering the years from 1936 to 1943. There are 102 tables, 48 items labeled "figure" (these are not listed in the front of the volume), and a two-and-a-half-page index. The following entries have been selected from the volume, with individual annotations found at the indicated item number.

Part 1,　Chapter 1:　"The Meaning of Questions." (Cantril and Fried - Item No. 269).

　　　　　Chapter 2:　"The Wording of Questions in Public Opinion Polls." (Rugg and Cantril - Item No. 323).

Chapter 3:   "The Measurement of Intensity." (Katz - Item No. 674).

Part 2,   Chapter 5:   "Secret vs. Nonsecret Ballots." (Turnbull - Item No. 544).

Chapter 6:   " 'Trained' vs. 'Untrained' Interviewers." (Rugg - Item No. 435).

Chapter 7:   "The Reliability of Interviewers' Ratings." (Mosteller - Item No. 340).

Chapter 8:   "Interviewer Bias and Rapport." (Salstrom, Katz, Rugg, Mosteller, and Williams - Item No. 359).

Chapter 9:   "Refusals as a Source of Bias." (Harding - Item No. 645).

Part 3,   Chapter 10:   "Some General Principals of Sampling." (Stock - Item No. 151).

Chapter 11:   "How Representative Are 'Representative Samples'?" (Rugg - Item No. 148).

39.   Clover, Vernon T., and Howard L. Balsley. *Business Research Methods.* 2d ed. Grid Series in Management, edited by Steven Kerr. Columbus, OH: Grid Publishing, 1979. 385p.

The Clover and Balsley textbook is intended for use by undergraduates in business research courses. Of particular significance is chapter 5, dealing with survey techniques, which considers the following topics: mail questionnaires; personal interviews; telephone inquiries; recruiting and training interviewers and investigators; motivational research, and the panel. Also included in chapter 5 are a summary, sixteen exercises, seven selected references, and several endnotes. Other pertinent chapters are chapter 7: "Aids in Administering Questionnaire Surveys"; chapter 8: "Constructing and Analyzing Classifications"; chapter 9: "Statistical Inference in Business Research"; and chapter 11: "Correlation, Regression, and Trend Analysis." Each chapter contains a summary, selected references, endnotes, and a set of exercises. The book has a four-page index and five appendixes with tables, including one for five-digit random numbers.

40.   Gallup, George. *A Guide to Public Opinion Polls.* 2d ed. Princeton, NJ: Princeton University Press, [1948]. 117p.

This revision of Gallup's 1944 work is designed to provide answers to frequently asked questions for use by those without technical training. The second edition includes new questions and expanded answers to those previously addressed. The textbook is divided into twelve categories of questions, with a total of eighty-five questions posed. In the foreword Gallup writes about the ten major ways in which public opinion polls have contributed to the democratic process. Quota sampling and area sampling receive considerable attention, with an appraisal of both approaches. Question wording techniques, interviewing methods, and the issue of the record of accuracy of public opinion polls are discussed. Polling activities beyond the borders of the United States are covered for the first time in the second edition. Gallup also deals with sample size, interviewing, accuracy, election predictions, and miscellaneous problems relating to public opinion. Gallup suggests that poll reliability has been demonstrated through success in "completely different circumstances and by different organizations."

41.   Gee, Wilson. "The Survey Method." Chap. 10 in *Social Science Research Methods*, 300-329. New York, NY: Appleton-Century-Crofts, 1950. 390p.

The chapter opens with a consideration of the methodology of surveys. Gee provides a brief historical outline of the survey beginning with William the Conqueror's *Domesday Book* of 1086. This section is followed by a discussion of the procedures used in surveys, covering both the questionnaire and interview formats. Ten rules are suggested for conducting the questionnaire. Fifty "principles" covering the interview are divided into the following sections: interview preparation, the interview proper, interview control, and closing the interview. The last section of the chapter deals with completing the survey. Fifty-two footnotes are provided, along with ten suggested readings. Twenty-one questions for classroom use are supplied.

42.   Jahoda, Marie, Morton Deutsch, and Stuart W. Cook. *Research Methods in Social Relations with Especial Reference to Prejudice*. Part 1. *Basic Processes*. Published for the Society for the Psychological Study of Social Issues. New York, NY: Dryden Press, 1951. Part 1 (pages 2-421) and Part 2 (pages [423]-759) comprise the two-volume set.

Chapters 6, 7, and 9 of part 1 are of specific interest. Chapter 6 covers the questionnaire and interview methods of data collection, comparing the two approaches, discussing question content type, and providing an overview of types of interviews and questionnaires. Chapter 7 discusses projective techniques and other disguised methods of data collection. Chapter 9 considers analysis and interpretation, including categories, tabulations, and statistical analysis. The book has a fifteen-page index. A sixteen-page bibliography is found on pages 391-406.

Part 2 is titled *Selected Techniques*. There are contributions from eleven authors. The same sixteen-page bibliography as in part 1 is found on pages 727-42. The following entries have been selected from part 2, with individual annotations found at the indicated item number.

Chapter 12:   "Constructing Questionnaires and Interview Schedules."
(Kornhauser - Item No. 133).

Chapter 13:   "The Art of Interviewing and a Guide to Interviewer Selection and Training." (Sheatsley - Item No. 436).

Chapter 18:   "The Panel Study." (Rosenberg and Thielens - Item No. 487).

43.   Mark, Mary Louise. *Statistics in the Making: A Primer in Statistical Survey Method.* Bureau of Business Research Publication no. 92. Columbus, OH: Bureau of Business Research, College of Commerce and Administration, Ohio State University, [1958]. 436p.

The purpose of this volume is to serve as an introductory textbook specifically covering the survey or census where the data were collected by interview or questionnaire. The author covers logical, technical, and administrative aspects of the topic in seventeen chapters arranged into four parts. Part 1 is the introduction which provides a historical background. Part 2 covers the logical design. The ten chapters of part 3 deal with tools and their use. Part 4 addresses administration and personnel. Footnotes are located throughout the text, and ninety-nine references appear at the end of the book.

44.   Oscamp, Stuart, in collaboration with Catherine Cameron, et al. "Public Opinion Polling." Chap. 4 in *Attitudes and Opinions,* 73-95. Clinical and Social Psychology Series, edited by Richard Lazarus. Englewood Cliffs, NJ: Prentice-Hall, 1977. 466p.

Written as a textbook for upper-division or graduate students in courses on attitudes, survey research, or public opinion, the volume contains a twenty-two-page chapter on public opinion polling. The chapter, divided into four major segments, covers characteristics, problems, reasons for well-known failures, and the impact on politics. Reviewed are the findings, theories, and practical issues that were known up through the mid-1970s. A separate section contains a photograph and a short biographical sketch of George Gallup. Another section has extracts from a speech by Senator Albert Gore which is critical of public opinion polls (the full text appears in the *Congressional Record* 106 [22 August 1960]: 16958-65.). A list of four suggested readings is provided.

45.   Parten, Mildred. *Surveys, Polls, and Samples: Practical Procedures.* New York, NY: Cooper Square Publishers, 1966. 624p.

In the first of the seventeen chapters in this textbook, Parten traces the historical development of social surveys and polls in the United States, with references to the European forerunners. The development of U.S. government surveys is covered, starting with the census, and outlining other contributions such as current population statistics and agricultural surveys. Public opinion polls, beginning with straw polls, and magazine polls, such as the *Literary Digest*, are reviewed. The *Fortune* Survey receives separate consideration, followed by sections on the Crossley Poll, the Gallup Poll, and the New York City College Poll and other student opinion surveys. Market surveys and radio audience research are discussed. In subsequent chapters Parten outlines practical procedures in each of the significant areas of poll and survey research including planning; sampling; survey personnel; interviewing; bias; editing; coding; tabulation; evaluation; and the preparation of the final report. Four chapters deal with sampling, and another four cover various aspects of data manipulation. Each chapter ends with a list of selected references, where authors' names and reference numbers are given. At the end of the book there are sixty-five pages of bibliographic references with 1,145 entries. A twenty-one-page index is included.

HISTORY

GENERAL

46.   Alderson, Wroe. "Trends in Public Opinion Research." Part 3, Chap. 23 in *How to Conduct Consumer and Opinion Research: The Sampling Survey in Operation*, edited by Albert B. Blankenship, 289-309. The American Council Series of Public Relations Books, edited by Rex F. Harlow. New York, NY: Harper & Brothers Publishers, 1946. 314p.

The origins of public opinion research are briefly traced with separate sections dealing with the works of three national polling organizations lead by Elmo Roper, Archibald Crossley, and George Gallup. The Roper poll, focusing on the measurement of attitudes, began in the spring of 1935 with publication in the May issue of *Fortune,* thus qualifying it as the first among the three to gain a national audience. The first Crossley Poll was conducted in 1936, with the purpose of public opinion polls serving as predictors of elections. The Gallup Organization began in the latter part of 1935 and achieved national recognition with the presidential campaign of 1936. Alderson maintains that the name "Gallup" is the one "universally accepted [as the] symbol for the public opinion polls," primarily due to the "journalistic presentation" of the results. The relationships between public opinion research and social psychology and political science are reviewed, followed by a brief summary of how a public opinion survey is conducted. The future prospects for public opinion polls are explored, with observations concerning quota sampling versus area sampling.

47.   Campbell, Angus. "Measuring Public Attitude: A Summing-Up." *Journal of Social Issues* 2, no. 2 (May 1946): 58-67.

Campbell writes in the concluding article of this issue that "interview surveys" have moved from forecasting election returns to a wider use in the methodology of social science. Described as a uniquely democratic activity (Japan and Germany did not conduct public opinion polls during World War II), the results of surveys cannot supplant the role of leadership in the executive and legislative branches of government. Campbell cites two reservations with current efforts. First, he identifies the danger of taking complex problems and expressing these in "highly simplified terms" in surveys. Second, he notes that all survey opinions are perceived as equal. The equality issues receive considerable discussion, and concern the differing degrees of conviction held by respondents, as well as the fact that the relative influence individuals have translates into different levels of social action. The author cites the need for amateur researchers to enlist the assistance of a survey expert. He believes that sampling error is less likely than interviewing error (because sampling is a well-developed survey procedure). (1 footnote, 11 references)

48.   Childs, Harwood L. "Rule by Public Opinion." *Atlantic Monthly* 157, no. 6 (June 1936): 755-64.

The title stems from the four stages of public opinion developed by James Bryce in 1893. In the fourth stage public opinion not only reigns, but also governs. This occurs when the will of the majority of citizens can be determined and acted upon. Childs observes that while the fourth stage may not have been achieved, today's polling activities are moving in that direction. The activities of the *Literary Digest* are discussed. The *Digest* methodology utilized a list of ten million individuals from telephone directories and automobile registrations. Also covered is the July 1935 issue of *Fortune* magazine's use of the "proportional method of sampling," which involved interviewing three thousand individuals every three months. In October 1935 George Gallup's American Institute of Public Opinion began to publish weekly polls on national issues appearing in seventy-two newspapers nationwide. In 1936 Childs wrote that problem areas include question selection and wording, poll timing, and methods of statistical analysis. Ways of dealing with polls have included a proposed congressional ban or having the Bureau of the Census continuously monitor public opinion.

49.   Costello, Mary. "Public Opinion Polling." *Editorial Research Reports* 1, no. 9 (5 March 1976): 167-84.

Divided into three parts, this article discusses recurrent issues concerning polls in election years, traces the development of techniques used in polling, and considers ways in which pollsters might be regulated. In the first section the variety of poll clientele is reviewed. In particular, George Gallup is quoted as saying that 95 percent of pollsters are private pollers producing work which is not published. The reliability and bias of opinion polls receive attention. In the second part the history of the *Literary Digest* is reviewed, along with an outline of the polling organizations founded in 1935 and 1936. Costello covers congressional involvement with attempts to establish polling standards. The final part deals with proposals to limit or ban preelection surveys, as well as the issue as to whether pollsters should be licensed by the federal government. (21 footnotes)

50.   Crossley, Archibald M. "Early Days of Public Opinion Research." *Public Opinion Quarterly* 21, no. 1 (Spring 1957): 159-64.

At the time this article was written, Crossley was head of Crossley, S-D Surveys, Incorporated, and a past president of the American Institute of Public Opinion (AIPO). He establishes the beginnings of commercial public opinion [CPO] research as occurring in the decade before World War I, a period when it was inextricably bound with marketing research. The mass media stimulated the growth of CPO research in the early years as advertising and space buyers wanted to know more about the buying public. Many of the research techniques that are viewed as recent discoveries or developments had their origins in this early period. Examples include open-ended questions, unstructured interviews, continuing probes, and stratified or quota sampling. The term "scientific sampling" came into use in the mid-1930s with the introduction of national polls on political issues. Important milestones in the development of CPO research were George Gallup's founding of AIPO; the three national presidential polls of 1936; the first *Fortune* Survey of 1935; the first issuance of *Public Opinion Quarterly* in 1937; and, later, the formation of the Roper Organization and the National Opinion Research Center. Crossley states that although CPO research was slow to develop in its first two decades, progress has been rapid since World War II.

51.   Ernst, Morris L., and David Loth. "The Pollsters." Chap. 7 in *The People Know Best: The Ballots vs. the Polls*, 114-35. Washington, DC: Public Affairs Press, 1949. 169p.

The experience of the *Literary Digest* is recounted, along with the major reasons as to why the approach failed in the 1936 election. The chapter discusses the work of Gallup, Roper, and Crossley. The issue of the number of times that the same person is interviewed is considered. Tables are provided comparing the major pollsters' work from 1936 through 1948. Half of the chapter is devoted to quotations and percentage predictions from each of the three major pollsters on the months and days leading up to the 1948 election. The authors make the point that neither the public nor the press or others have gained access to the "secret scientific files" of the leading pollsters.

52.   Gallup, George. "The Changing Climate for Public Opinion Research." *Public Opinion Quarterly* 21, no. 1 (April 1957): 23-27.

The demand for, and acceptance of, public opinion polls has increased dramatically since the first polls were conducted in the fall of 1935. Gallup reviews the *Literary Digest* predictions of 1936. He believes that the false prediction in that year helped bolster the need for scientific sampling procedures. In spite of the incorrect forecasts of 1948 the public continued to support the polls, with most of the criticism coming from academic and government circles. The polling errors made in the 1948 election, however, strengthened the position of polls long term by improving methods and increasing knowledge of the behavior of the American voter. For example, it was found that since voters can change their minds within days of the election, sentiment must be measured at the very end of the campaign as well. The correct forecasts in 1956 are reviewed. Gallup concludes with comments on the words scientific and commercial as applied to polling, and on the faith he has in the American citizen to continue to support public opinion polling and research.

53.   Gallup, George. "Polling Public Opinion: The Director of the Nation's Leading Public Poll Explains Its Functions and Defends It from Critics." *Current History* 51, no. 6 (February 1940): 23-26, 57.

Gallup explains the function of public opinion polling and responds to a variety of critical observations. How polls are conducted, their use, and the contributions they make are each addressed. The straw vote technique of the *Literary Digest* is mentioned, along with the scientifically selected cross-section sampling used by the Gallup Poll, the Crossley Poll, and the *Fortune* Survey. Gallup outlines six controls to ensure that appropriate samples are selected for interviewing. The issue of sample size is discussed, along with concerns about the bandwagon effect, question wording, and ways to measure the direction of opinion intensity. Gallup addresses the criticism that polling is a threat to democracy by saying, among other things, that the people "possess a collective quality of good sense which is manifested time and again."

54.   Katz, Daniel, and Hadley Cantril. "Public Opinion Polls." *Sociometry* 1, no. 1 (July-October 1937): 155-79.

Straw polls are considered first, followed by a classification of polls in which quota control or "weighted sample" polls are included. The Gallup Poll from the American Institute of Public Opinion (AIPO) used the weighted sample type. The accuracy of polls is discussed including that of AIPO, Crossley, *Fortune*, and the *Literary Digest*. An explanation as to why the *Digest's* 1936 prediction was wrong is provided, along with a review as to why other polls (such as Gallup and Crossley) did not produce highly accurate results. The social consequences of polls are considered. Many aspects are outlined, with one suggestion reported that the U.S. Department of the Interior provide polling services to government officials so that they could be up-to-date with public opinion on any issue under consideration. (8 footnotes, 18 references)

55.   Latham, Frank B. "Measuring Public Opinion: The Mechanics of the Polling Systems Refute Charges of Bias." *Scholastic* 35, no. 3 (2 October 1939): 31-32.

Early polling history is reviewed, beginning in 1935 with George Gallup's American Institute of Public Opinion and the *Fortune* Quarterly Survey by Elmo B. Roper, Jr. and Paul T. Cherrington [*sic* Cherington]. The *Literary Digest's* sampling practice of using telephone books and automobile registration lists is described. The timing of when a poll is taken is discussed, with the 1936 examples of Gallup and Crossley cited (the final polls were taken ten to twenty days before the election). Interviewing is seen as preferable to mail ballots since wealthy persons are disproportionately highly represented in their ballot completion. Latham also considers question wording, noting that one or two words can change the response. The bandwagon issue is addressed.

56.   Link, Henry C. "Some Milestones in Public Opinion Research." *Journal of Applied Psychology* 31, no. 3 (June 1947): 225-34.

The early researchers in the commercial arena from 1920 to 1930 are mentioned, with their major contributions being the use of the formal standardized questionnaire, the reliance on face-to-face interviews, and properly distributed large samples. The sample size accuracy issue is addressed. The *Literary Digest* poll, the *Fortune* Survey, the Gallup Poll, and the Crossley Poll are discussed in historical perspective. The beginning of *Public Opinion Quarterly,* financed by the School of Public Affairs of Princeton University, is given as 1937. Also considered in Link's presentation are the development and influence of the questionnaire and question form, early foreign polling organizations, and the founding in 1941 of the National Opinion Research Center at the University of Denver.

57.   Northrop, Ann. "The Rise of the Polls: Bloopers Amid Improving Aim." *National Journal* 3, no. 33 (14 August 1971): 1703.

Scientific survey techniques, which were used first in a poll published in July 1935 by *Fortune* magazine, had been preceded by over one hundred years of straw polling. Beginning with the *Harrisburg Pennsylvanian* reports on the 1824 presidential campaign, the article also notes the first national magazine to conduct a straw poll (the *Farm Journal*). The *Literary Digest* election forecast disaster of 1936 is reviewed. Scientific poll beginnings are discussed, focusing on the pioneering work of three partners (Paul T. Cherington, Elmo B. Roper, and Richardson K. Wood) whose work was published by *Fortune*, followed by Gallup's work in the fall of 1935, and with Archibald M. Crossley working for

King Features in 1936. The 1948 election and the primaries of 1968 are discussed as difficult periods in polling history.

58.   Noyes, Charles E. "Measurement of Public Opinion." *Editorial Research Reports* 2, no. 18 (8 November 1940): 347-60.

Election forecasts prior to 1936, as well as those during that year, are discussed, including a review of the *Literary Digest* experience and mistakes made by the polls. Scientific sampling methods are covered, with the work of Gallup and the *Fortune* Survey highlighted. The measurement of the public's opinion on issues is considered. Examples of question wording are provided, including phrasing which can yield varying interpretations. Opinion intensity questions used by *Fortune* are considered with examples from its preelection surveys. Also included are descriptions of the way Gallup's American Institute of Public Opinion and the *Fortune* Survey conduct their research. (15 footnotes)

59.   "Public-Opinion Polls: An American Tradition That Started in 1824." *Dun's Review* 111, no. 5 (May 1978): 25-26.

A brief review of the history of polling in the United States begins with the 24 July 1824 *Harrisburg Pennsylvanian* straw vote. The *Farm Journal*, in 1912, was the first magazine to conduct a poll. The early high esteem and the 1936 forecast disaster of the *Literary Digest* are chronicled. The problems of the *Digest* sample are discussed, followed by a description of the scientific approach taken by Gallup, Roper, Crossley, and Harris. The 1948 presidential election poll errors are cited. By 1978 polling had become a $500 million industry. The suspected bandwagon effect is discussed.

60.   Schmid, Calvin F. "The Measurement of Public Opinion." *Sociology and Social Research* 34, no. 2 (November-December 1949): 83-90.

The role of "straw voting" in polling history is acknowledged, with the first use occurring before 1900 by the *New York Herald*, and followed by the *Literary Digest* from 1916 until its demise after the failure of the 1936 presidential election prediction. Early polling organizations are listed, including those headed by Gallup, Roper, Crossley, and others, and six university-supported research centers are mentioned. Poll procedures are discussed with the following topics covered: (1) problem formulation; (2) universe or population selection; (3) construction of sample design; (4) questionnaire construction; (5) questionnaire pretesting; (6) interviewing; and (7) results analysis. (15 footnotes)

61.   Spingarn, Jerome H. "These Public-Opinion Polls: How They Work and What They Signify." *Harper's Magazine* 178 (December 1938): 97-104.

Early newspaper mail polls are mentioned, including those of the *Baltimore Sun* and the *Columbus Dispatch* [Ohio]. A short biographical sketch of Gallup is provided, along with an explanation of the methodology used by the American Institute of Public Opinion (AIPO). Also discussed are Roper's work with the *Fortune* Survey and the experience of the *Literary Digest*. Question wording is considered, with examples from *Fortune* and AIPO analyzed. The author suggests that "not too great weight" be placed on the "snap answers" given by respondents to interviewers. Spingarn warns readers to be both "careful and skeptical" when reading poll results. (2 footnotes)

62.   Stephan, Frederick F. "Advances in Survey Methods and Measurement Techniques." *Public Opinion Quarterly* 21, no. 1 (Spring 1957): 79-90.

Some of the first contributors to the quantitative background of the field are identified, beginning in 1928 with Stuart A. Rice. A discussion of the quota method and its use (primarily in market research) follows, along with mention of the *Literary Digest* and the 1936 presidential election. Stephan next provides an outline of the first decade of work in the field. The 1948 presidential election, the failure of the polls, and the consequences for the field are considered. Under the heading "Survey Operations" Stephan discusses problems such as cheating by interviewers, coding, and analysis. In the section titled "Measurement of Attitudes" the author suggests that "testing validity is the greatest problem that confronts opinion research today." The advances in sampling theory and practice are outlined, with random or probability methods seeming to be the direction of choice. Gaps in the literature are cited. Stephan believes the theory of purposive and quota sampling, as well as the theory of sampling items in a universe of attitude content, remain to be addressed. (80 footnotes)

63.   Stephan, Frederick F. "Development of Election Forecasting by Polling Methods." Chap. 2 in *The Pre-Election Polls of 1948: Report to the Committee on Analysis of Pre-Election Polls and Forecasts*, by Frederick Mosteller, Herbert Hyman, Philip J. McCarthy, Eli S. Marks, and David B. Truman, 8-14. Social Science Research Council, Bulletin no. 60. New York, NY: Social Science Research Council, 1949. 396p.

Polling methods are traced (with a consideration of initial informal methods), followed by straw votes (including the experience of the *Literary Digest*), and the employment of standardized field interviews. Also noted is the development in 1935 of polls by Paul Cherington, Elmo Roper, George Gallup, and Archibald M. Crossley, from the fields of advertising, journalism, and marketing. The functions, accuracy, and adequacy of the polls are addressed. The American Association for Public Opinion Research, founded in 1946, is discussed in relationship to the place of polls within the social sciences. The joint Committee on Measurement of Opinion, Attitudes and Consumer Wants, established in 1945 by the

National Research Council and the Social Science Research Council, is mentioned as further evidence of poll use in the social sciences. (3 footnotes)

AMERICAN ASSOCIATION FOR
PUBLIC OPINION RESEARCH

64.   Hart, Clyde W., and Don Cahalan. "The Development of AAPOR." *Public Opinion Quarterly* 21, no. 1 (Spring 1957): 165-73.

The establishment of the American Association for Public Opinion Research (AAPOR), as well as the World Association for Public Opinion Research, grew out of the First International Conference on Public Opinion Research. The conference was held in Denver, Colorado, on 29-31 July 1946. It was organized by Harry H. Field, director of the National Opinion Research Center. Field convened seventy-three leaders in the field of public opinion research. The Second International Conference on Public Opinion Research was held at Williams College in Williamstown, Massachusetts, on 2-5 September 1947. AAPOR was formally "christened" at this time. In this and subsequent conferences many crucial issues were addressed: the role of AAPOR, the nature of its membership, the development of standards, and the writing of a constitution. The Code of Professional Practices is reprinted in *Public Opinion Quarterly (POQ)* (vol. 12, no. 4 and vol. 17, no. 4). *POQ,* entering its second decade of publication, became the official organ of the association. The Research Development Committee inventoried research in progress, offered to help seek funds for the members, and made arrangements for programs on research. Work of the association is geared to the preparation and conduct of the annual meeting. This article, written a decade after the establishment of AAPOR, notes that while membership has grown (to 380 members) the "essential character" remains the same. Current programs focus more on problems of methodology, techniques of analyzing data, political behavior, and the formation of public opinion. (8 footnotes)

65.   Lee, Alfred McClung. "Implementation of Opinion Survey Standards." *Public Opinion Quarterly* 13, no. 4 (Winter 1949-50): 645-52.

Lee centers his discussion of standards around three themes: a summation of the problem to date, an analysis of the nature of codes for sociological research, and a summary of suggestions for the effective implementation of standards. Lee was a member of the Committee on Standards of the American Association for Public Opinion Research (AAPOR) at the time the article was written. The committee, an outgrowth of one of AAPOR's annual conferences, considered code formulation suggestions, and these are summarized to date. Lee then reviews eight steps in drafting a code of professional ethics, some drawn from the codes of other professions such as medicine and law. Implementation can be aided by having a regular section in *Public Opinion Quarterly* for committee contributions; by instigating a monographic series to advance and publicize the goals of the committee; by calling for papers to be submitted to the annual AAPOR meeting; and by establishing an organ for listing and reviewing the reports of opinion research. The author urges that a code for the public opinion research profession be written and implemented in a timely manner. (9 footnotes)

LITERARY DIGEST

66.   Bryson, Maurice C. "The *Literary Digest* Poll: Making of a Statistical Myth." *American Statistician* 30, no. 4 (November 1976): 184-85.

Bryson maintains that the story of the *Literary Digest's* 1936 survey error caused by relying on telephone listings and automobile owners' lists is a myth. There were some twelve million telephones at the time, representing about 40 percent of the households in the United States. Bryson explains that the telephone theory was "incapable of explaining the error" – an error which he attributes to reliance on voluntary response. Ten million ballots were mailed, with "only" 2.3 million replies. Such mail questionnaire samples are "practically always biased." The author cites a variety of writers, including George Gallup, who have perpetuated the myth. Likert partially corrected the story in a 1948 article [Item No. 908]. (9 references)

67.   Cornfield, Jerome. "On Certain Biases in Samples of Human Populations." *Journal of the American Statistical Association* 37, no. 217 (March 1942): 63-68.

The experience of the 1936 *Literary Digest* "poll" is discussed. The use of telephone directories and automobile registrations provided a biased sample. Interestingly, on a strict "scrupulous booking" of returns, the *Digest* erroneously reported that Hoover would win. However, Cornfield indicates that analysis of the data would have made it possible to estimate a Roosevelt majority. Several obstacles to generating an appropriate sample are discussed. One is the need for a complete listing of the units of the population, without which the sampling procedure cannot be devised. Another challenge is the refusal rate, which may be affected by the type of schedule used. Since bias exists in all surveys, it must therefore be adjusted for by weighting. (1 footnote)

PUBLIC OPINION QUARTERLY

68.   Albig, William. "Two Decades of Opinion Study: 1936-1956." *Public Opinion Quarterly* 21, no. 1 (Spring 1957): 14-22.

The author studies the principal trends in public opinion research as reflected by the articles appearing in *Public Opinion Quarterly* over two decades, from 1936 [1937] to 1956. By means of content analysis, articles are classified into one of eleven general categories plus subcategories. The findings are as follows: (1) theoretical-type articles comprised only a small percentage of the total; (2) there was an increase in the number of articles based on empirical quantitative studies; (3) the publication pattern showed a decline in general articles on advertising and publicity, as well as those on propaganda; (4) there was an increase in both qualitative and quantitative content studies; (5) the early years contained no articles on market research methods or results (more recently about 10 percent of the total contents are devoted to this topic); (6) the number of articles on mass media increased; and (7) the majority of articles were on polling and attitude measurement. Albig concludes by stating, "There has been a revolutionary change in the orientation of opinion studies, and the input of attitudes and values is reflected in the output."

69.   Alpert, Harry. *"Public Opinion Quarterly*. Volume 1: A Review." *Public Opinion Quarterly* 21, no. 1 (Spring 1957): 185-89.

Volume 1 of *Public Opinion Quarterly*, published in 1937, is reexamined on the occasion of its twentieth anniversary. Alpert lists and discusses five trends and observations he believes to have taken place: (1) there has been a sense of continuity in terms of the contributors to volume 1 in that they have become the outstanding names in public opinion research at the present time, such as Cantril, Lasswell, Lazarsfeld, Robinson, Roper, and Crossley; (2) much growth and progress has taken place in the area of methodology – for example, scaling techniques, probability sampling, interviewing, validity, and reliability; (3) there has been an expansion of areas of interest and application of survey research to many more disciplines than twenty years ago; (4) there has been "solid progress" through major accomplishments, with many examples provided, and "growth in our understanding of the nature of opinions and attitudes and their relationship to human social behavior"; and (5) some areas have been neglected by public opinion researchers (such as primitive societies, professional ethics standards, communication between researchers and administrators, and the dissemination and utilization of results). (5 footnotes)

70.   Childs, Harwood L. "The First Editor Looks Back." *Public Opinion Quarterly* 21, no. 1 (Spring 1957): 7-13.

Harwood L. Childs, the founder and first managing editor of *Public Opinion Quarterly (POQ),* reviews the history of the journal on its twentieth anniversary. The publication began at Princeton University (Princeton University Press) with volume 1 in 1937. Childs discusses the journal in these terms: (1) the goals of the founders – "a clearing house for contributions from different fields relating to various phases of the study of public opinion"; (2) the attempts to raise financial underwriting, to perfect the editorial staff, to arrange for printing and distribution, and to solicit articles from scholars; (3) the departmental organization is divided into four sections – academic scholarship, government, organized groups, and communications; and (4) the changing nature of the contents of the journal (initially editorially directed, it then tended to reflect actual trends in the field, such as opinion surveys and mass media), and articles became more technical and specialized. In a brief section titled "The Balance Sheet" Childs evaluates the extent to which he believes *POQ* has measured up to the expectations and aspirations of the founding members. He sees the journal as failing "to provide the comprehensive reporting in the various sectors of public opinion which was originally contemplated," and that it "never quite succeeded in bringing about the balanced and comprehensive research attack on the whole broad public opinion front that was originally envisaged." He attributes these failures mainly to budget restrictions.

71.   *"Quarterly*: Princeton Will Ponder Opinion and Policies." *News-Week* 8, no. 25 (19 December 1936): 23-24.

A new periodical titled *Public Opinion Quarterly (POQ)* began publication this week. *POQ* is sponsored by Princeton University's School of Public and International Affairs. The editor, DeWitt Clinton Poole, was a member of the U.S. diplomatic service for twenty years; Harwood L. Childs is the managing editor and originator. *POQ* covers trends in public opinion including "what creates it, what sways it, and how this 'controlling but obscure force' can be used to advantage." Potential readers are government officials, industrial leaders, advertising executives, editors, and public relations personnel. The annual subscription price for the journal is four dollars.

U.S. DEPARTMENT OF AGRICULTURE

72.   Campbell, Albert A. "Attitude Surveying in the Department of Agriculture." Part 2, Chap. 22 in *How to Conduct Consumer and Opinion Research: The Sampling Survey in Operation*, edited by Albert B. Blankenship, 274-85. The American Council Series of Public Relations Books, edited by Rex F. Harlow. New York, NY: Harper & Brothers Publishers, 1946. 314p.

The range of attitude surveys conducted by the Division of Program Surveys at the Department of Agriculture is considered. Numerous procedures are described, such as the planning of objectives and the writing and pretesting of the questionnaire. Campbell reviews the use of the open question in which interview sessions are conducted in a "conversation" format lasting from thirty minutes to one hour. The interviewer records the respondent's replies as accurately as possible. The division uses area sampling, with interviewers receiving instructions as to which houses to visit. In rural areas the Master Sample of Agriculture, consisting of seventy thousand small geographical areas selected from every county in the country, is used to generate either regional or national coverage. At least two attempts are made to reach a respondent before "substitutions" are made. The use of results is highlighted, with the presentation of a specific example involving the problems that farmers would face in post-World War II agricultural production. (1 footnote)

73.   Skott, Hans E. "Attitude Research in the Department of Agriculture." *Public Opinion Quarterly* 7, no. 2 (Summer 1943): 280-92.

In 1939 the Division of Program Surveys became part of the Bureau of Agricultural Economics, which was a unit in the Department of Agriculture. In September 1939 Rensis Likert was named head of the division. Sampling procedures, field methods, the interview form, and analysis are described. The division applies research findings to specific administrative recommendations, as presented in a study of the Forest Service. Various adaptations of standard methodological practice are described, such as going beyond the limitations of quota sampling by introducing stratification to improve the efficiency of the sample. Skott notes the early stage of the new science of "attitude" research and bemoans the "crude hand tools" available at that time.

POLLSTERS AND POLLING ORGANIZATIONS

FORTUNE SURVEY

74.   "The *Fortune* Survey: Its History and Development." *Journal of Educational Sociology* 14, no. 4 (December 1940): 250-53.

In July 1935 *Fortune* magazine began what it described as "a new technique in journalism" – the application of market research techniques to the business of gauging public opinion. Referred to as the "survey," the *Fortune* interviews were conducted by the market research firm of Elmo Roper, with three thousand, then five thousand, personal interviews in eventually up to eighty places. The *Fortune* Survey's success in predicting the 1936 presidential election is discussed. The various stages of the survey are described, including the questions, samples, interviews, tabulations, and mathematical error. The editors of *Fortune* observe that as long as the technique is "honestly applied to finding the truth and not to proving a point," then they see hope for the new approach. (1 footnote)

75.   "The Polls' Unanimous Error Reveals Their Limitations – But They Still Have a Place." *Fortune* 38 (December 1948): 39-40.

The editors of Fortune magazine drafted this statement as a way of addressing the criticisms received over the incorrect prediction for the outcome of the 1948 presidential election. They state that the purpose of the *Fortune* Survey is "to be a mirror reflecting underlying attitudes of the people on the fundamental issues, attitudes that could be discerned and reflected in no other way," and not to serve as a crystal ball. Elmo Roper is quoted from the April 1947 issue of *Fortune* [Item No. 329] as observing: (1) "The answers to all questions cannot be accepted at face value. (2) Conclusions cannot be based invariably on the answers to any *single* question. (3) The importance of the 'don't know' or undecided vote is never to be overlooked. (4) The same question, *differently worded*, might have produced different results." With the limitations noted, the editors reasserted their faith in the survey technique and continued to publish the column.

76.   Wood, Richardson. "How the *Fortune* Survey Is Conducted." *Fortune* 12, no. 4 (October 1935): 58.

The *Fortune* editors select the questions for the survey every three months. The sample consists of three thousand personal interviews in which twenty or more questions may be asked. The survey attempts to proportionally represent classifications found in society – as for example by having 10 percent of the sample from cities of 25,000 to 100,000 as found in the 1930 Census. Wood observes that the three thousand sample size is adequate to reduce probable statistical error to a small percentage. *Fortune* Survey probable error is considered to be less than 1 percent "when the figures are based upon all the people interviewed." Variations may be as great as 6 percent, but to date the survey has checked to "within a negligible percentage." Loaded questions are avoided where possible through the many steps which questions must pass before they become part of the survey. The development of the survey is more a product of "common sense" than of any "mathematical magic."

GALLUP AND THE AMERICAN INSTITUTE OF PUBLIC OPINION

77.   American Institute of Public Opinion. *The New Science of Public Opinion Measurement*. New York, NY and Princeton, NJ: American Institute of Public Opinion, 1939. 16p.

The American Institute of Public Opinion (AIPO), founded in 1935, is briefly described. References are made to the *Fortune* magazine survey and the polls conducted by the *Literary Digest*. Survey conduct as practiced at AIPO is covered, including the selection of sample size and cross section, question wording, timing, and accuracy. The final section of the document discusses the "social value of sampling referenda." The emphasis here is that it is no longer necessary to wait for elections since new results regarding voters' choices can be conducted regularly and at short intervals.

78.   American Institute of Public Opinion. *The Story behind the Gallup Poll*. Princeton, NJ: American Institute of Public Opinion, 1956. 32p.

The American Institute of Public Opinion (AIPO) was founded by George H. Gallup in October 1935. The first release of survey results to newspapers occurred in the same year. The editorial staff of AIPO compiled this publication to explain the growth of polls, the nature of survey sampling, how Gallup Polls are conducted, and Gallup Poll records for presidential election polls from 1936 to 1954. Specific attention is focused on the 1948 presidential election, on presidential popularity, and on what the average person thinks. A list of thirteen countries in which Gallup Polls operate is provided (as well as the names of each organization). An additional partial list of 117 newspapers which publish Gallup Poll results completes the volume.

79.   Bean, Louis H., Philip M. Hauser, Morris Hansen, and Rensis Likert. "Report of the Technical Committee." In U.S. Congress. House. Committee to Investigate Campaign Expenditures. *Campaign Expenditures: Hearings on H. Res. 551*, Part 12, 1293-99. 78th Cong., 2d sess., 2 January 1945. Washington, DC: U.S. Government Printing Office, 1945. 1299p. [SuDoc Y4.C15:C15pt.1-18/3]

A group of four individuals (from the Bureaus of Budget, Census, and Agricultural Economics) was asked to evaluate the data that George Gallup had submitted to the Campaign Expenditures Committee, chaired by Clinton P. Anderson. Bean, et al., determined that Gallup's American Institute of Public Opinion (AIPO) had "sincerely tried to use scientific polling methods" in 1944, but that nonpolling elements had been introduced which involved the use of "judgment and interpretation." The Democratic vote was underestimated in about two-thirds of the states (as was the case in 1940). The technical committee noted a number of issues raised by the Gallup data. These include the following: (1) the reliability of the sampling approach; (2) the sample size (insufficient); (3) the use of judgment when combining data with historical figures; (4) the training and supervisory adequacy of interviewers; (5) the appropriateness of adjustments made for expected voter turnout; and (6) the lack of statements in published reports, indicating the degree to which results are based on judgments. Specifically, the technical committee cites the inadequacy of the quota-sampling method used. The remainder of the report examines each of the six points in detail, with explanations and analyses. The committee contrasts the work of the *Literary Digest* with that of AIPO, and writes that the latter has "made relatively effective use of scientific survey technique." The dual challenges of election polling are observed: the polling organization has first to determine the properties of individuals who will vote for a particular candidate, and the estimate of the voter turnout must be addressed. [See Item No. 97 for Gallup's testimony.]

80.   "Do Polls Tell the Story?...Our Figures Have Pointed to the Winner in 13 of 14 Times." *U.S. News & World Report* 57, no. 14 (5 October 1964): 52-54, 59.

George Gallup is interviewed on a number of topics, including questions concerning methods of sampling and how polls are checked. Poll accuracy and the inaccurate 1948 presidential poll results are discussed. The Gallup polls use a sample of fifteen hundred. Each interview lasts approximately forty minutes and covers many issues such as voting intention, campaign interest, and intensity of preference. The interviewer asks what the respondent believes is the most important problem facing the nation, followed by which political party the respondent believes could best address this problem. The second answer, according to Gallup, provides a "pretty good indicator" as to how the respondent will vote. The refusal rate reported in the United States (and in other countries which have polling) is between 4 and 5 percent.

81.   "Dr. Gallup Closes a Gap between People and Government." *News-Week* 8, no. 20 (14 November 1936): 14-16.

The early days of the American Institute of Public Opinion (AIPO) are described, with the thirty-five-year-old George Gallup managing the organization with thirty-five statisticians and clerks in a single room on the third floor of a building across from Princeton University in Princeton, New Jersey. Gallup's background is briefly reviewed, including reference to his Ph.D. dissertation titled "New Methods for Measuring Reader Appeal" [*sic* "An Objective Method for Determining Reader Interest in the Content of a Newspaper"]. On 20 October 1935 the AIPO poll began as a syndicated feature in thirty newspapers. The total number of papers receiving the poll rose to seventy-eight. The article discusses Gallup's success in forecasting the 1936 presidential election outcome, as well as his prediction as to the result which the *Literary Digest* would suggest (Gallup's numbers were generated four months before the *Digest's* final figures were released – he was off 1 percent with each candidate). In 1936 Gallup could produce a national opinion poll on any subject within a ten-day period.

82.   "Dr. Gallup: Don't Ask Consumers 'Why': Many People Think His Name is Dr. Gallup Poll. The Greeks Use His Name as Their Verb, 'To Poll.' He's One of Marketing Research's Most Devoted Pioneers." *Printers' Ink* 271, no. 13 (24 June 1960): 53-55.

The *Printers' Ink* article traces the life of Gallup, beginning with his birth in Jefferson, Iowa, on 18 November 1901. George Horace Gallup (nicknamed Ted) received his doctorate in journalism [*sic* applied psychology] in 1928 from the State University of Iowa. His dissertation is titled "A New Technique for Objective Methods for Measuring Reader Interest in Newspapers" [sic "An Objective Method for Determining Reader Interest in the Content of a Newspaper"]. Gallup worked for the *Des Moines Register and Tribune* while teaching at Des Moines' Drake University. By 1932 Gallup was a full professor of journalism and advertising at Northwestern University. He then moved to the advertising agency of Young and Rubicam as director of research and stayed fifteen years, the last decade as a vice-president. As a "sideline," he founded the Gallup Poll in 1935. He refers to "why" questions as having a "built-in Chinese wall." He believes that skillful interviewers can lead a respondent to remember past events – in this case events which led a consumer to make purchases. Some outcomes of Gallup's work for newspapers include pictorial journalism, comic strip advertising, and thick Sunday editions. The article includes several photographs of Gallup and was written to acknowledge his thirty-year contribution to market research.

83.   Erwin, Ray. "Gallup Polls Public Opinion for 25 Years." *Editor & Publisher* 93, no. 45 (5 November 1960): 62-63.

Erwin traces the development of the Gallup Poll and advises the reader on the current state of polling with the Gallup Organization. In 1960 about 150 newspapers were reporting results of the Gallup Poll, having purchased the public opinion news service as a syndicated column through the Publishers' Syndicate of Chicago. It is claimed that if all of the Gallup releases (three or four per week) were bound together, they would constitute about sixty-five volumes. Initially, thirty-five newspapers – papers with every political perspective represented – underwrote the costs of the Gallup Poll. Although the present margin of error has been reduced to 3 percent, Gallup acknowledges that the laws of probability indicate with "absolute certainty that in some future election we could be wrong."

84.   Gallup, George. "Guideposts for Poll Readers: Why Election Surveys Differ." *Gallup Opinion Index*, no. 38 (August 1968): 13-14.

Written to address observations made in the mass media concerning differing poll results, Gallup explains the basis for these differences and discusses the record and achievements of the Gallup Poll. In particular, he makes these points: polls measure opinion at a given point in time, disclosure of polling methods should be in full, and disclosure should be required of all published polls. Probability sampling is briefly explained, Gallup Poll interviewing is discussed, and comments are made concerning newspaper subscribers to the service. Gallup observes, "It is worth noting that in no field of social science has human behavior in the aggregate been measured with such a high degree of accuracy."

85.   Gallup, George. "Measuring Public Opinion." *Vital Speeches of the Day* 2, no. 12 (9 March 1936): 370-72.

In a speech delivered before the American Institute of Public Opinion (AIPO) at the Rockefeller Center, New York City, on 16 January 1936, Gallup spoke of five levels of controls utilized by the institute. Ballots must be received from (1) each state in proportion to its voting population, (2) farms and rural areas and from cities in correct proportions, (3) the correct proportions by income levels, (4) the appropriate number of individuals who have reached voting age since 1932, and (5) the proper proportions of those individuals who voted for Roosevelt, Hoover, Thomas, and others in 1932. Most of the speech explains the need for the measurement of public opinion, followed by a reporting of AIPO's results on nine significant issues of the day. Gallup closes by siding with the value of the rule of the majority of the citizens of the nations.

86.   Gallup, George. "Pollsters, Not Prophets." *Society* 13, no. 6 (September-October 1976): 19-23, 25.

Beginning with the 1936 presidential election, Gallup traces his forty years of experience in polling. Using scientific sampling procedures for the first time in 1936, the achievements and errors of the Gallup Poll are noted. In particular, the error of the 1948 election is discussed (the error was caused chiefly by a failure to continue polling up to election day). Gallup refers to these as "lessons." Post-1948 improvements are covered, along with responses to critics, the usefulness of polls, and some observations concerning various consistent findings of the Gallup Poll (such as the public's desire to abandon the present primary system and move to a nationwide primary). A table shows the accuracy of the Gallup Poll in national elections from 1936 to 1974 (in eight-year periods).

87.   "Gallup's Growth." *Newsweek* 14, no. 18 (30 October 1939): 30-31.

George Gallup's career is briefly traced from the University of Iowa experience leading to a doctoral degree, through work measuring reader interest for various newspapers, to Young and Rubicam, a New York firm. In the four years of the American Institute of Public Opinion's (AIPO) operation, over one thousand questions had been asked. Four answers have appeared weekly in the newspapers subscribing to the column. The annual cost is nearly $250,000 in election years. There are seven hundred field-workers. The most significant challenges faced by AIPO are in the areas of phrasing questions that cannot be misunderstood and judging electoral turnouts.

88.   "George Gallup: Mr. Polling." *Journal of Advertising Research* 17, no. 3 (June 1977): 9-12.

As executive head of the Gallup Organization, Incorporated, George Gallup has been the recipient of five awards for outstanding achievement, including the Advertising Gold Medal Award (1964) and the American Marketing Association's Parlin Award (1965). Gallup has received honorary degrees from thirteen colleges and universities. In this interview by Bartos of the *Journal of Advertising Research* staff, Gallup answers a variety of questions dealing with his career

in the advertising world, to issues of poll sampling. He observes that once se-
cretive candidates now boast about their pollsters.

89.   "How Gallup Poll Samples Public Opinion: It Has to Call This Election
        Right – Gallup's Prestige in Market Research Hangs on It." *Business
        Week*, no. 981 (19 June 1948): 39-40, 42, 44, 48-50, 52-53.

The name Gallup is quickly associated with the American Institute of Public
Opinion (AIPO), but not so readily with another organization he heads – namely,
Audience Research, Incorporated (ARI). ARI is a market research firm which
receives considerable attention in this article, with examples of how the company has assisted movie companies with theme selection, title choices, and casting
selection, as well as other companies which are regularly bringing new products
to the market. Gallup's approaches to questioning, pretesting, and sampling are
discussed. Eleven photographs – most showing interviewers at work – accompany the text. One photograph is of Harold H. Anderson, Gallup's partner who
heads the Publishers' Syndicate in Chicago, through which AIPO columns are
bought for a circulation-based fee.

90.   Hubler, Richard G. "George Horace Gallup: Oracle in Tweed." *Forum
        and Century* 103, no. 2 (February 1940): 92-95.

The article on Gallup is both personal and detailed. Although the information
has been widely reported, Hubler has added the human element, writing about
aspects as diverse as Gallup's working day, his family members (three children),
and the salary he earns in each of the roles he fulfills. The highlights of Gallup's
career are traced, along with the number of surveys conducted to date (eight
hundred plus) by the American Institute of Public Opinion (AIPO). Hubler por-
trays Gallup as working for Young and Rubicam from nine o'clock in the morn-
ing to five or six o'clock in the evening, commuting home from New York to
Princeton (one hour), and then spending evenings writing AIPO reports. The
Literary Digest experience is reviewed. It is noted that eighty newspapers subscribe to the Gallup polls.

91.   "Interview with George Gallup: How 55 Million Vote." *U.S. News &
        World Report* 32, no. 21 (23 May 1952): 56-64.

Using the question-and-answer format, Gallup addresses queries from the editors of *U.S. News and World Report*. Topics discussed include the 1948 and
1952 presidential elections; sampling techniques; quota sampling; survey accuracy; income testing; and the determination as to what caused the 1948 survey
error. A total of 125 questions were asked, with most answers in the one-to-two
sentence range. The longest answer (291 words) was in response to the question,

"What public service is fulfilled by polls?" Two graphic designs and one photograph accompany the text.

92.   "A Look inside the Polls: Who Is Asked about What." *U.S. News & World Report* 65, no. 14 (30 September 1968): 44-46.

The way in which the Gallup Poll is conducted is described, and six photographs of Gallup and various phases of polling are provided. George Gallup began his public opinion polling organization in 1935. The failure of the 1948 Gallup Poll is briefly noted. The method of probability sampling is outlined, with the note that Gallup uses 362 voting precincts throughout the United States as the basis for selection. An average of five individuals are interviewed in each precinct (a figure adjusted with each ten-year census). Interviewing is conducted door-to-door, primarily by women working part time. Questionnaires are pretested for understanding and difficulty. Secret ballots are used as a way to deal with respondents who are reluctant to acknowledge orally their voting preferences. The results of a Gallup Poll gathered one weekend are published in newspapers the following weekend. For the poll to be published the day before the election, a sample of six thousand individuals may be used with only the "most likely" voters considered. A table shows the Gallup Poll record in presidential elections.

93.   O'Malley, J. J. "Black Beans and White Beans." *New Yorker* 16, no. 8 (2 March 1940): 20-24.

George Horace Gallup and his American Institute of Public Opinion (AIPO) are the subjects of this biographical essay. The article begins with a discussion of survey sample size. Gallup's early education and life, as well as his early jobs, are stated. The 1936 presidential election poll, the *Literary Digest*, and the *Fortune* Survey are reviewed. Gallup's dual career as a vice-president at Young and Rubicam and as head of AIPO is covered. His private life is mentioned briefly, including comments on his wife, their two sons, and their three-hundred-acre farm outside of Princeton, New Jersey. Gallup is quoted as saying he is "convinced that the voice of the people is right, and that three times a week is not too often to listen to it" in the form of the newspaper-reported Gallup Polls.

94.   Perry, Paul. "Election Survey Procedures of the Gallup Poll." *Public Opinion Quarterly* 24, no. 3 (Fall 1960): 531-42.

The Gallup Poll election surveys, as well as those surveys conducted between elections, use the theory of probability sampling. The sample areas used are those of the election precincts. Further discussion centers on the sampling approach, the late campaign survey, and how the turnout is estimated by using turnout scale scores. The issue of the undecided is addressed, along with a comparison of the survey results with the election results. As a technique to assist in the "unbiased expression of candidate preference," the secret ballot is considered. The Gallup Poll used the secret ballot approach in 1956 and 1958. (2 footnotes)

95.   "Questions Often Asked about Published Polls." *Gallup Opinion Index*, no. 59 (May 1970): 15-23.

Fifteen frequently asked questions concerning public opinion polls, accompanied by answers, are presented. The questions considered are the following: (1) Are the polls scientific? (2) Can a poll predict future outcomes? (3) Is a bandwagon effect present in polls? (4) How many persons are necessary for a sample? (5) How are respondents selected? (6) How can informed opinion be separated from uninformed opinion? (7) Is intensity of feeling capable of being measured? (8) Is too much attention paid to polls by politicians? (9) Can the "why" behind the vote be obtained? (10) Can polls predict the electoral vote? (11) Who is responsible for the selection of questions for the polls? (12) Who supports the Gallup Poll financially? (13) What methods are used by the Gallup Poll? (14) Does the Gallup Poll operate internationally? and (15) Why don't all polls show the same results?

96.   Shannon, Homer H. "Backstage with Dr. Gallup: An Interview with 'the Great Interviewer' Clears Up Many Questions about the Business of Opinion Polling." *Forbes* 51, no. 1 (1 February 1943): 10-11, 28.

The article describes the responses to questions that Gallup is frequently asked. Gallup cites Swiss scientist Bernoulli and the year 1713 for the origin of the mathematics of probability. In explaining how he was able to predict the *Literary Digest* poll outcome, Gallup observes that the *Digest's* methods were unchanged. Gallup simply sent out ten thousand ballots using the *Digest* approach, tabulated them, and compared them with his own methods. A brief biographical sketch is included. Gallup was born in Jefferson, Iowa, in 1901, and earned a B.A., Master's, and Ph.D. in applied psychology from the University of Iowa [State University of Iowa]. He taught journalism at Drake and Northwestern universities, became head of research at a New York advertising agency, and, in 1935, founded the American Institute of Public Opinion and the Gallup Poll.

97.   U.S. Congress. House. Committee to Investigate Campaign Expenditures. *Campaign Expenditures: American Institute of Public Opinion (Gallup Poll), Dr. George Gallup, Witness: Hearings on H. Res. 551*, Part 12, 1235-92. 78th Cong., 2d sess., 28 December 1944. Washington, DC: U.S. Government Printing Office, 1945. 1299p. [SuDoc Y4.C15:C15pt.1-18/3]

Gallup was called to testify in order to explain how polling is an aid to democratic processes, and more particularly how election polling had been conducted by a number of groups – especially by the Gallup Poll. A written report submitted by Gallup is included in the hearing document and contains consideration of the following topics: (1) the 1944 Gallup Poll; (2) funding sources for the Gallup Poll; (3) Gallup's open-door policy; (4) the fallacy of the bandwagon; (5) accuracy; (6) bias; (7) the scientific use of election surveys; (8) sample size; (9) the turnout issue; (10) factors in the 1944 election; (11) 1944 election surveys; (12) national figures; (13) figures for the forty-eight states; and (14) the selection of the final state figures. Campaign Expenditures Committee Chairman Clinton P. Anderson, followed by other committee members, proceeded to question Gallup on the polling methods and techniques utilized in the 1944 election. Gallup also sketches his career from journalism professor at the University of Iowa [State University of Iowa], to the founding of the Gallup Poll in October 1935. He notes that there are 130 newspaper clients who subscribe to the poll. [See Item No. 79.]

ROPER

98.   Anderson, Dale. "Roper's Field Interviewing Organization." *Public Opinion Quarterly* 16, no. 2 (Summer 1952): 263-72.

The Elmo Roper field program to recruit and train field interviewers is described. The field director and staff are responsible for administering the department, outlining the program, and seeing that the program is implemented. Implementation is also the responsibility of the supervisors, each one being responsible for twenty to thirty interviewers. Extensive travel is required of the seven supervisors Roper employed in 1951. Although the supervisors had been interviewers for Roper for at least ten years, additional extensive training was required. The supervisors hire and train all interviewers in their territories. The Roper *Handbook for Interviewers* is used for the trainees. The supervisors' work with the trainees and the role of the New York office in evaluating, planning, and motivating are described. Results of the program can be seen in terms of reduced errors, increased morale, greater efficiency, and less turnover among interviewers. (1 footnote)

99.   McDonald, Donald. *Opinion Polls: Interviews with Elmo Roper and George Gallup, with a comment by William V. Shannon.* Interviews on the American Character. [Santa Barbara, CA]: Center for the Study of Democratic Institutions, 1962. 45p.

On the inside of this four-by-eight-inch publication are three brief biographical sketches of the contributors. The Roper interview appears first and uses just under half of the print space available. Each interview question is separated from the body of the reply. The questions cover a broad array of polling subjects including the following: (1) interviewers; (2) sample size; (3) internal and external polling problems; (4) private polls; (5) the Truman-Dewey campaign; (6) firmness of public opinion; and (7) apathy. Questions addressed to Gallup were also quite diverse and fall into these major topic areas: (1) polling frequency; (2) philosophical inquiries as to the appropriate use of political polls; (3) book readership; (4) continuing polls such as measurements of presidential popularity; (5) poll question avoidance on complex issues where there has been public discussion; (6) Kinsey and moral judgments; and (7) the stimulating effect of poll results generating information that otherwise might not be communicated. Shannon's commentary places polls as they are viewed by traditionalists and liberals. He notes that polls "disclose some astonishing and discouraging depths of ignorance on the part of the people." Misuse of poll data by members of political elite groups is considered. Shannon observes that Roper views polls as assisting citizens to "articulate the character and shading of his views with somewhat greater precision than he can in casting a ballot." Shannon writes that Gallup sees polls as helping to "open up issues and explore 'touchy' areas that leaders are reluctant to enter."

100.   Roper, Elmo. "The Client over the Years." *Public Opinion Quarterly* 21, no. 1 (Spring 1957): 28-32.

Roper provides details on the client-consultant relationship between the firm of Cherington, Roper and Wood and the utility holding company Engineers Public Service, one of the first two clients of the Roper Organization. Roper describes the relationship as being typical of the early days of market research in that most of the contact was with the president of the company. It was the president, rather than middle management, who saw the usefulness of marketing research. Strict confidence existed among the parties. All research was conducted with "action" in mind. A second phase showed the emergence of more marketing consultants, research divisions within companies, and competitive bidding for services. The relationship between pollster and client was far less close, and there was more mistrust and less understanding of the survey process. Survey costs came under scrutiny. Characteristics of the current phase include a return to the close contact with the president enjoyed in the early years. In addition, clients have become more sophisticated about what marketing and attitude research results can produce. Roper categorizes clients as "very intelligent," "moderately intelligent," or "not very intelligent." Those classified in the first group tend to use research in an intelligent manner and show good profits. Those in the latter category have been shown to make less profit.

101.   "Roper: Ask Plain Deceiving Questions. For More Than Two Decades Elmo Roper Has Been Telling U.S. Businessmen What People Think of Them – And Their Products. He Builds Surveys on Common Sense, Absorbs New Techniques and Always Stays at the Top." *Printers' Ink* 263, no. 4 (25 April 1958): 77, 80-81.

A "bio-business" sketch of Elmo Roper, described as "the dean of public opinion researchers" in the United States, is presented. Born Elmo Burns Roper, Jr., on 31 July 1900 in Hebron, Nebraska, he attended the University of Minnesota for one year and the University of Edinburgh, Scotland, for two years. He returned to the United States in 1921 without a degree and opened a jewelry store in the same year. In 1927 he was president of the Iowa Retail Jeweler's Association. After giving up the store in 1928, he went to work for Seth Thomas Clock Company, becoming assistant sales manager in 1933. Roper met Paul Cherington (who helped found the Harvard Business School) and with Richardson Wood formed a company (Cherington, Roper, and Wood) which, with the departure of the others in 1937, became simply Elmo Roper. The article discusses the record of the Roper company, its size, and the approach taken in survey research.

OVERVIEW STUDIES

102.   Blankenship, Albert B. "Public Opinion Polls: A Symposium. The Case for and against the Public Opinion Poll." *Journal of Marketing* 5, no. 2 (October 1940): 110-13.

A series of criticisms levied against polls is considered by Blankenship. Among these are the following: (1) bias in question wording or phrasing; (2) the intensity with which the opinion is held is not measured; (3) sample selection; (4) the reasons for conducting a poll; and (5) that polls destroy the system of democratic government. Each issue is evaluated, with the author providing explanations as to actual polling practices and reasons why some of the criticisms are not justified.

103.   Bogart, Leo. *Silent Politics: Polls and the Awareness of Public Opinion.* New York, NY: Wiley-Interscience, a Division of John Wiley & Sons, [1972]. 250p.

Bogart writes in his preface that the "acceptance of polls by the public have introduced into the political process the notion of an independent criterion of legitimacy in the conduct of government." He closes by saying, "Opinion research is a magnifying mirror of our collective ignorance and perplexities. It gives us cause for introspection." The book deals primarily with what Bogart perceives as the limitations of surveys – the areas of opinion that "elude measurement." Eight chapters cover an array of issues: (1) the relationship of polls and politics; (2) opinion research and public policy; (3) opinion trends; (4) the "how" of opinion changing; (5) opinion inconsistency; (6) unheard opinions; (7) opinions that shock and those that force social changes; and (8) the relationship between opinions and responsibilities. All footnotes are cumulated as twenty-nine pages of endnotes. An eleven-page index is included.

104.   Dodd, Stuart Carter. "Predictive Principles for Polls – Scientific Method in Public Opinion Research." *Public Opinion Quarterly* 15, no. 1 (Spring 1951): 23-42.

Dodd has supplied researchers with a summary of the predictive principles. Prediction from polls includes "foretelling in time, estimating in a population, validating in other behavior, and generalizing in space." Four levels of analysis are discussed: the qualitative, the quantitative, the relative, and the systematic. Objectives statements, variables, and question phrasing are described in a qualitative analysis in polling. Dodd outlines the steps in the polling process in relation to each of the levels of analysis listed above, and then establishes twelve rules for approaching the twelve steps of analysis. The headings used for the rules are as follows: mass behavior, complete listing, operational defining, interviewing, scaling, sampling, reobserving, exactness of hypothesis, correlating, factoring and compounding, and verifying. The *POQ* article closes with a four-page checklist of predictors, with the major headings being behavior, attitudes, and conditions. (11 footnotes)

105.   Gallup, George H., Stuart C. Dodd, Paul F. Lazarsfeld, and Norman C. Meier. "Unsettled Problems of the Sampling Survey Methodology." Chap. 21 in *The Polls and Public Opinion: The Iowa Conference on Attitude and Opinion Research Sponsored by the State University of Iowa, Iowa City*, edited by Norman C. Meier and Harold W. Saunders, 314-34. New York, NY: Henry Holt & Company, [1949]. 355p.

Gallup identifies a number of sampling survey methodology problems, including voters and nonvoters, measuring prestige, and determining intensity. Dodd is concerned with the use of the methodology, namely in the areas of the interaction of human groups, such as in conflicts, competition, and cooperation, or to quote Lazarsfeld, to use the "data to systematically theorize." Lazarsfeld suggests that it is important to keep public opinion research "as close to the social sciences in general as possible." Meier sees one solution to the presidential poll challenge as conducting polls at three-day intervals during the last two weeks of the campaign, and for an additional two weeks after the election. Don Cahalan, the only person to speak during the discussion phase, provides a response to the four papers.

106.   Gergen, David, and William Schambra. "Pollsters and Polling." *Wilson Quarterly* 3, no. 2 (Spring 1979): 61-72.

A review of early prescientific polling is followed by a brief outline of the recent experience since 1935. Political, commercial, and state polling organizations are described, including the names of the significant organizations at each level. Methods of sampling, sample size, types of interviews, and pollsters are discussed. The issue of whether respondents lie to pollsters is considered, along with the possibility that the individuals interviewed want to appear informed. The authors believe that policy planners need to understand the "general sentiments that guide the public," rather than heeding their views on specific problems. Also noted is the usefulness of reading survey results in the context of others conducted in the same area. It is additionally observed that public opinion on many issues is "ill informed or difficult to discern." (2 footnotes)

107.   Ghiselli, Edwin E. "Some Further Points on Public Opinion Polls." *Journal of Marketing* 5, no. 2 (October 1940): 115-19.

Ghiselli addresses three issues, the first of which deals with question format with leading and perfunctory types described. It is reported that as early as 1916 it was recognized that question wording was significant with respect to the nature of the respondents' answers. The second issue concerns polls as measurement devices. Measurement is described as being of two types – counted, and along some scale. Poll respondents are usually asked to choose between two opposite viewpoints. The third issue is whether poll results have an impact on the political behavior of the public, with bandwagon theory, trend analysis, belief versus behavior, and poll readers versus nonpoll readers as the topics covered. (4 footnotes)

108.   Katz, Daniel. "Three Criteria: Knowledge, Conviction, and Significance." *Public Opinion Quarterly* 4, no. 2 (June 1940): 277-84.

Public opinion polls are discussed and evaluated according to three criteria: (1) Knowledge – Are respondents sufficiently informed that they can provide reliable answers? (2) Conviction – Are respondents' beliefs strong enough to produce stability in their responses? and (3) Significance – Are the questions asked of importance to social science? Katz analyzes the "psychological areas" to which questions have been directed: motives, feelings toward social symbols, and ideas and opinions about personal and public problems and issues. The author also discusses the concept of "crystallized" public opinion, the use of filtering questions by the American Institute of Public Opinion, the nature of modern public opinion, and the relevance of polls. The article concludes with this statement: "In the area of opinions and attitudes they [the polls] are decidedly useful, but here they must be interpreted with the greatest caution and supplemented wherever possible by other methods." (6 footnotes)

109.   Meier, Norman C., and Harold W. Saunders, eds. *The Polls and Public Opinion: The Iowa Conference on Attitude and Opinion Research Sponsored by the State University of Iowa, Iowa City.* New York, NY: Henry Holt & Company, [1949]. 355p.

The proceedings of the 10-12 February 1949 Iowa Conference contain three presentations which speak directly to the concerns of this bibliography. The chapters listed are in the form of one or more presenters, followed by discussion. The volume includes a six-page subject index. The following entries have been selected from the volume, with individual annotations found at the indicated item number.

Chapter 15:   "Causes of the Disparity between Poll Findings and Election Returns." (Crossley, Dodd, Bachelder, Gallup, and Kroeger - Item No. 933).

Chapter 18:   "Technical Problems: Methodology as Related to the Requirements of Public Opinion Measurement." (Meier - Item No. 164).

Chapter 21:   "Unsettled Problems of the Sampling Survey Methodology." (Gallup, Dodd, Lazarsfeld, and Meier - Item No. 105).

110.   Mendelsohn, Harold, and Irving Crespi. "The Credibility of Voter-Preference Surveys." Chap. 5.1 in *Public Opinion: Its Formation, Measurement, and Impact*, edited by Susan Welch and John Comer, 362-85. 1st ed. Palo Alto, CA: Mayfield Publishing Company, 1975. 541p.

The Mendelsohn and Crespi entry in this volume has been reprinted from chapter 2 of their book titled *Polls, Television, and the New Politics.* Chandler Publications in Political Science. Scranton, PA: Chandler Publishing Company, [1970]. 329p. [Item No. 111]

111.   Mendelsohn, Harold A., and Irving Crespi. *Polls, Television, and the New Politics.* Chandler Publications in Political Science. Scranton, PA: Chandler Publishing Company, [1970]. 329p.

The first three chapters dealing with polls were written by Crespi. (Mendelsohn wrote chapters 4 and 5 on broadcast media.) Chapter 1, covering the role of polls in the United States, includes discussion of the following topics: (1) use; (2) effect on leaders and voting behavior; (3) relationship to formal party organizations, enactment of law, and foreign policy formulation; (4) polls as "continuing elections"; (5) candidate selection; and (6) the "moderating function" of polls. Chapter 2 examines poll accuracy, result variation caused by the methods used, percentage error, polls as tools to ascertain prospective candidates, and monitoring voter preferences. Chapter 3 explores the political and manipulative uses of polls, such as (1) "leaked" private polls; (2) the effect on party morale and financing; (3) poll reporting standards; (4) the susceptibility of polls to manipulation; (5) the regulation of polls; and (6) the low response rate (but high media attention) received by congressional mail "surveys." A fifteen-entry bibliography on public opinion polls is included at the end of the book. Chapter 1 has seventy-seven endnotes, chapter 2 contains seventy-eight, and chapter 3 includes forty-five.

112.   Shapiro, Leopold J. "The Opinion Poll." Ph.D. diss., University of Chicago, 1956. 202 leaves. [Not available from *Dissertation Abstracts International.*]

The study considers the manner by which opinion polls are initiated, planned, and conducted. Shapiro writes that "an opinion poll is any effort to gain information about a phenomenon by collecting opinion about that phenomenon by polling persons in an interview situation." Some of the questions the research seeks to answer are as follows: (1) "What societal processes give rise to the opinion poll?" (2) "What needs does it serve?" (3) "How does it fit into our society?" (4) "How are the topics of opinion polls determined?" (5) "What gives continuity to opinion polling activity?" (6) "How does the opinion poll secure needed resources from society?" and (7) "Who pays and why?" The research method used was that of participant-observer. A lengthy analysis of the data follows the descriptions of three environments – commercial, government, and nonprofit. The dissertation closes by relating this study to sociological theory. A bibliography is not present; however, there are a few nonconsecutively numbered footnotes, being numbered for each page at a time.

113.   Welch, Susan, and John Comer, eds. *Public Opinion: Its Formation, Measurement, and Impact.* 1st ed. Palo Alto, CA: Mayfield Publishing Company, 1975. 541p.

Chapter 5 considers the measurement of public opinion. The first section is a reprint of chapter 2 of Mendelsohn and Crespi's *Polls, Television, and the New Politics.* Chandler Publications in Political Science. Scranton, PA: Chandler Publishing Company, [1970]. 329p. [Item No. 111]. Also included is a reprint of Wiseman's article "Methodological Bias in Public Opinion Surveys." *Public Opinion Quarterly* 36, no. 1 (Spring 1972): 105-8. [Item No. 565]

114.   Wheeler, Michael. *Lies, Damn Lies, and Statistics: The Manipulation of Public Opinion in America.* New York, NY: Liveright Publishing Corporation, a Subsidiary of W. W. Norton Company, 1976. 300p.

On a separate page preceding the acknowledgments, Wheeler explains the origin of his book title which is attributed to both Benjamin Disraeli and Mark Twain and reads as follows: "There are three kinds of lies – lies, damned lies, and statistics." Topics covered include interviewing, influence, and policing of public opinion polls. Other subjects considered are Nixon, Vietnam, pollster biography, and the Nielsen ratings. Wheeler writes about polls and their influence, but he is particularly concerned with both potential abuse as well as actual instances of misrepresentation. The author sets out to "demystify and demythologize the polling process," with the intent of presenting in jargon-free language the possibilities and the limitations of modern public opinion polling. Wheeler believes that too much power has been concentrated in the hands of the leading polling organizations. He feels a need to both deflate and defuse this power by attacking the credibility and methodological soundness of the polling community. The book has a nine-page index and one page of suggested readings.

115.   Wilson, Elmo C. "The Measurement of Public Opinion." In *Communication and Social Action*, edited by W. Hayes Yeager and William E. Utterback, 121-29. *Annals of the American Academy of Political and Social Science*, edited by Thorsten Sellin, vol. 250. Philadelphia, PA: American Academy of Political and Social Science, March 1947. 183p.

A nine-step outline of the techniques used in conducting a poll opens the article. The need to ascertain how much money is available to be spent on a poll, as well as the speed and precision required, are described as "conditioning" factors. Research organizations in existence in 1947 are discussed, along with the role of polls during World War II. Polling conducted on the consumer, by legislators, and in the political arena in general, is reviewed. Poll accuracy, the practice of weighting or adjustments on polling results, and quota versus area sampling are covered. The article closes with a look to the future, discussing the need for more research in the area of opinion strength or intensity measurement, as well as the need to study the views of opinion framers or leaders whose views "spread in concentric circles among those with whom they come in contact." Complex issues will call for the development of interviewing approaches employing interrelated questions, rather than using a single simple query. (3 footnotes)

116.   Wyle, Clem. "Public-Opinion Polls." *Good Housekeeping* 119, no. 2 (August 1944): 41, 173.

In simple terms Wyle explains the nature of public opinion polls, with consideration given to sample size and composition, question wording, interviewers, income determination, and some of polling's "forerunners." The efforts of the Department of Agriculture are briefly noted. Polls of farmers generated crop estimates in terms of what would be raised where and in what quantities. Market research followed, with the attitudes of consumers and purchasing practices the subject of the investigations.

DESIGN AND PLANNING

ATTITUDE INFORMATION SYSTEM

117.   Francis, J. Bruce. "The Future of Institutional Surveys: New Concepts,
        Techniques, and Technologies." In *Surveying Institutional Constituen-
        cies*, edited by J. Bruce Francis, 89-94. *New Directions for Institutional
        Advancement: A Quarterly Sourcebook*, editor-in-chief A. Westley Row-
        land, no. 6. San Francisco, CA: Jossey-Bass Inc., Publishers, 1979. 100p.

The Attitude Information System (AIS) is described as combining the strengths
of polling, survey research methodology, and management information systems.
Francis suggests seven uses for AIS in institutional advancement: (1) large-scale
samples would be drawn every three years; (2) there would be a questionnaire
item pool; (3) word processors would be used to construct questionnaires in automated environments; (4) fieldwork would be a major portion of survey time; (5)
advanced coding, optical scanning, and computer software for data "cleaning"
would be used; (6) programs would analyze data, and combine, compare, and
contrast with previous findings; and (7) clients should receive data within a few
days. The impact of the "microcomputer revolution" is discussed, as well as heu-
ristic versus algorithmic design approaches. (3 references)

118.   Francis, John Bruce. "Attitude Information System (AIS): A High-Speed
        Survey Technique for University Decision Making." *Journal of Educa-
        tional Data Processing* 11, no. 6 (1974): 1-8.

Three major procedures – management information systems, public opinion polls,
and sample surveys – are discussed, with the advantages and disadvantages of each
highlighted. The preferred alternative is the Attitude Information System (AIS). With

AIS the entire process from the initial meeting with the client to the analyzed data should be completed within fourteen days. The concept is to address university administrators' needs to get specific questions answered from a given sample in order to assist with a pending decision. Francis describes the five steps in AIS: (1) working out the details of the survey in terms of questions, sample size, and the client's timing needs for the data; (2) planning the subsample and the interview schedule (with interviews not to exceed ten to fifteen minutes); (3) using either graduate students or full-time employees to conduct the fieldwork; (4) performing data processing of self-coding and machine-scored forms by computers; and (5) analyzing data with the assistance of computer programs. Francis cites accuracy, credibility, speed, specificity, and easy access as advantages of AIS. (7 references)

COMPUTERS

119.   Abelson, Robert P. "Computers, Polls, & Public Opinion – Some Puzzles & Paradoxes." *Trans-Action* 5, no. 9 (September 1968): 20-27.

The focus of this article is an effort by Abelson, Ithiel de Sola Pool, and others, to computerize public opinion. The first step involved the creation of a large public opinion data bank from archival materials which tabulated voter positions on issues. The second step was to predict the impact Democratic candidates' positions would have on a variety of issues. Abelson maintains that simple computer models are useful because mass public opinion "usually" follows simple patterns. Many caveats are then given to explain why events are difficult to forecast – especially those far into the future. The article addresses six major areas of concern that might be raised by the project: validity, obsolescence, completeness, relative importance, quantitative prediction, and marketing. Two titles are suggested for further reading.

COSTS

120.   Sudman, Seymour. *Reducing the Cost of Surveys*. National Opinion Research Center Monographs in Social Research, no. 10. Chicago, IL: Aldine Publishing Company, 1967. 246p.

Believing that "a detailed understanding of how surveys are conducted and costs generated" will lead to improved cost control and therefore lower costs, Sudman explores the following: (1) probability sampling with quotas; (2) advance listing of special populations; (3) self-administered questionnaires; (4) telephone survey research; (5) interview time in the field; (6) costs and quality of the interviews; (7) use of computers; (8) optical scanning for coding; and (9) the survey schedule.

The preface is by Peter H. Rossi, director of the National Opinion Research Center (NORC). Sudman makes it clear in the acknowledgments that this work is the "combined effort of the entire NORC staff." Eighty-nine tables are provided, along with a six-page index. (61 references)

DECISIONAL APPROACH

121.   Tull, Donald S. "Intentional Bias in Public Opinion Polls for Decisional Purposes." *Public Opinion Quarterly* 39, no. 4 (Winter 1975-76): 552-56.

Decisional (applied) research is compared with basic research. In the latter the goal is to "make the best possible estimate or conduct the best possible hypothesis test" given the limitations of the problem and available resources. In decisional research the aim is to "make the best possible decision under the circumstances." This means that the costs of errors are reviewed, and a design model intentionally incorporating bias may be developed. Tull demonstrates in his article that the "expected value of information is higher for one of the biased designs than for the unbiased one." An example of an incumbent in a national elective office is given. (5 footnotes)

122.   Tull, Donald S., and Gerald S. Albaum. *Survey Research: A Decisional Approach*. The Intex Series in Marketing Research. New York, NY: Intext Educational Publishers, [1973]. 244p.

The decisional approach used is designed to admit the judgment of the investigator in the collection and analysis of data, thereby assisting the decision maker with the provision of information otherwise unavailable. This approach permits value to be weighed against cost when determining methods for gathering the required information. Written from the methodological viewpoint, the authors believe that this volume can be used in a variety of disciplines. Chapters cover the following topics: decision making; inquiry methods; sampling; nonsampling errors; measurement and scaling; scaling techniques and models; objectivist and subjectivist survey research; analysis; and techniques of analysis. Each chapter closes with a selected bibliography. A six-page index included.

DESIGN

General

123.   Alderfer, Clayton P., and L. Dave Brown. "Designing an 'Empathic Questionnaire' for Organizational Research." *Journal of Applied Psychology* 56, no. 6 (December 1972): 456-60.

The researchers consider the challenge of creating a questionnaire which can elicit more information that is threatening to the respondent. The study utilized and compared event-based and theory-based questionnaires. The issue used in the questionnaires dealt with prevalence and characteristics of sarcasm by students and faculty in a private boys' boarding school. The results indicate that when the researchers demonstrated knowledge about key issues in the organization, more information was forthcoming. (8 references)

124.   Alwin, Duane F., ed. *Survey Design and Analysis: Current Issues.* Sage Contemporary Social Science Issues, no. 46. Beverly Hills, CA: Sage Publications, 1978. 156p.

The contributions in this book appeared originally as a special issue of the journal *Sociological Methods and Research*, vol. 6, no. 2 (November 1977). The following entries have been selected from the volume, with individual annotations found at the indicated item number.

"Making Errors in Surveys: An Overview." (Alwin - Item No. 764).

"Question Wording as an Independent Variable in Survey Analysis." (Schuman and Presser - Item No. 325).

"Modest Expectations: The Effects of Interviewers' Prior Expectations on Responses." (Sudman, Bradburn, Blair, and Stocking - Item No. 403).

"The Treatment of Missing Data in Multivariate Analysis." (Kim and Curry - Item No. 775).

"Response Error in Earnings Functions for Nonblack Males." (Bielby and Hauser - Item No. 689).

Two studies from the Alwin collection have been excluded from this bibliography – one by Lloyd Lueptow which is based on a self-administered questionnaire, and the other by Gideon Vigderhous, a foreign author.

125.   Blankenship, Albert B. *Consumer and Opinion Research: The Question-naire Technique.* New York, NY: Harper & Brothers Publishers, 1943. 238p.

The volume, designed for college students as well as for practitioners, presents a critical summary and a discussion of questionnaire techniques. All forms of data collection are covered, including mail, telephone, and personal interview. Subjects discussed include phrasing, testing, sampling, interviewing, processing results, and report writing. The closing chapters review survey validity and reliability, and consider arguments against the survey questionnaire approach. Each of the fifteen chapters lists references, and the book has a six-page index. Two appendixes provide guides to sample size.

126.   Duncan, Otis Dudley. "Measuring Social Change via Replication of Surveys." Chap. 5 in *Social Indicator Models*, edited by Kenneth C. Land and Seymour Spilerman, 105-27. New York, NY: Russell Sage Foundation, 1975. 411p.

The approach Duncan pursues is to replicate studies which have been conducted in earlier years, comparing the findings as a means of estimating the "direction and degree of social change over the intervening period." A replication of the Detroit Area Study (DAS) was undertaken in 1971, the results of which were compared with an earlier 1956 replication. The background for the DAS is reviewed, along with the preliminary steps (including design features) taken for the new replication. Duncan notes that the degree to which change can be adequately determined is based on the comparability of the study design. Specific findings from the two surveys are compared and contrasted, with the author observing that although the replication approach will not "necessarily resolve theoretical issues concerning social dynamics or settle pragmatic issues of social policy," it might allow a more positive consideration of the issues. (21 references)

127.   Finsterbusch, Kurt. "Demonstrating the Value of Mini Surveys in Social Research." *Sociological Methods & Research* 5, no. 1 (August 1976): 117-36.

"Mini" surveys are recommended when funds are limited and for probing value as an accompanying tool with a full-scale survey. Five uses are discussed in detail, including descriptions of populations, collaboration for experts, reexamination of the value of previous findings, probes, and waves in a dynamic survey research study. Finsterbusch discusses the informative value of mini surveys and provides an overview of their uses. (1 footnote, 6 references)

128.   Finsterbusch, Kurt. "The Mini Survey: An Underemployed Research Tool." *Social Science Research* 5, no. 1 (March 1976): 81-93.

Finsterbusch defines "mini" surveys as those which are based on sample sizes of fifteen to fifty respondents. It is suggested that mini surveys be used where time and/or money constraints prevent the completion of a larger sample survey. Four uses for the mini survey are discussed: (1) with Bayesian statistics to combine mini surveys and expert synthesis; (2) to determine the level of comparability between the mini survey and previous findings (the mini survey alignment test); (3) as an estimator of univariate distributions and as a provider of simple cross tabulations or mini survey confidence interval reports; and (4) dynamic mini surveys provide the opportunity to vary the questionnaire construction and to determine how such surveys would be used in relationship to large sample surveys. (4 footnotes)

129.   Fox, Willard M. "How Not to Make Surveys – and Why." *Industrial Marketing* 30, no. 2 (February 1945): 40, 58, 60.

A number of observations are presented for the purpose of advising and warning the prospective survey researcher. Fox notes that respondents use "unconscious rationalization" when answering questions and attempt "to create the impression that he is very well informed." A series of eight points outline the author's suggestions: (1) do not ask a leading question; (2) do not ask opinions; (3) identify respondents by position, occupation, and place of work; (4) avoid loopholes or doubtful entries; (5) limit interview expenses to appropriate sample size; (6) question the use of panels and "country club" samples; (7) analyze all relationships; and (8) do not begin by trying to prove something. Fox states, "Instead, find out what you want to find out and why you want to know it and what you can do about it if you do know it is true, is partially true, or is not true at all."

130.   Goode, Robert V. "How to Get Better Results from Attitude Surveys." *Personnel Journal* 52, no. 3 (March 1973): 187-92.

Goode discusses survey design as needing to be appropriate for the problem at hand, suggests careful treatment of the questionnaire construction, and reviews the use of the personal interview for in-depth analysis. Interviews are appropriate for use in investigating morale issues. The survey administration is to be conducted with confidentiality guaranteed. The author recommends not making the final report available at the first presentation within the organization. When the final report is made, the conclusions, the recommendations, and the plan of action are advised to be included. The study findings should be communicated to affected employees.

131.   Hyman, Herbert. "Interviewing and Questionnaire Design." Chap. 7 in *The Pre-Election Polls of 1948: Report to the Committee on Analysis of Pre-Election Polls and Forecasts,* by Frederick Mosteller, Herbert Hyman, Philip J. McCarthy, Eli S. Marks, and David B. Truman, 119-73.

Social Science Research Council, Bulletin no. 60. New York, NY: Social Science Research Council, 1949. 396p.

A series of interviewing topics is discussed, including the contributions of the
following to the total error in the 1948 preelection polls: (1) empirical measurement of interviewing error in preelection surveys; (2) political sources; (3) ra-
cial/class composition; (4) political composition; (5) administrative procedure; (6)
cheating; (7) performance quality; and (8) conclusions on interviewing and fieldwork. Hyman considers the importance of the comprehensiveness of the questionnaire design. The following topics are also discussed: (1) measures of preference motivation; (2) use of the "telegraphic survey" to deal with "last minute
contingencies"; (3) preference rigidity; (4) latent preferences; (5) likelihood of voting; (6) voting eligibility; (7) question validity; (8) technical features affecting
accuracy; (9) constancy of procedures and trend measurement accuracy; (10)
precoded questions, answer box structure, and data accuracy; (11) standard instructions; and (12) feasibility of the questionnaire. (19 footnotes)

132.   Katz, Daniel. "Survey Technique and Polling Procedure as Methods in
        Social Science." *Journal of Social Issues* 2, no. 4 (November 1946): 62-
        66.

An effort is made to distinguish between survey method and the opinion poll.
Both the field staff and the interviewing techniques are different according to
Katz. Most significantly, Katz states that commercial opinion polls have little
research design, rely on single questions, and obtain all of their data from one
source – namely, the respondents. Survey method, by contrast, seeks data from
all available sources, utilizing the logic of experimental methodology involving
preliminary analysis of the independent, intervening, and dependent variables in
the problem. Two case examples are discussed, one dealing with worker morale
in war industries, the other focusing on German civilian morale in relation to Al-
lied bombing.

133.   Kornhauser, Arthur. "Constructing Questionnaires and Interview Sched-
        ules." Chap. 12 in *Research Methods in Social Relations with Especial
        Reference to Prejudice*, by Marie Jahoda, Morton Deutsch, and Stewart
        W. Cook. Part 2. *Selected Techniques*, 423-62. Published for the Society
        for the Psychological Study of Social Issues. New York, NY: Dryden
        Press, 1951. Part 1 (pages 2-421) and Part 2 (pages [423]-759) comprise
        the two-volume set. [This chapter is condensed from *Training Guide on
        Constructing Questionnaires and Interview Schedules*, prepared by the
        Bureau of Applied Social Research, Columbia University, (195-?). 95
        leaves.]

The presentation is meant to serve as a guide for writing questionnaires. The term questionnaire is used in the chapter to denote both interview schedules and self-administered formats. The major topics considered are question content apart from wording, question wording, response format desired, and question order. A series of questions, designed to assist the questionnaire preparer to ensure that each issue has been duly considered, is posed within each section. The particular focus is on the formulation and ordering of individual questions. The chapter includes an outline of procedures, which has sections on pretesting, reexamination and revision, and editing the questionnaire.

134.   Kornhauser, Arthur, and Paul B. Sheatsley. "Questionnaire Construction and Interview Procedure." In *Research Methods in Social Relations*, by Claire Selltiz, Lawrence S. Wrightsman, and Stuart W. Cook, in collaboration with George I. Balch, Richard Hofstetter, and Leonard Bickman, 541-73. Published for the Society for the Psychological Study of Social Issues (SPSSI). 3d ed. New York, NY: Holt, Rinehart & Winston, 1976. 624p.

In appendix B of this social relations textbook, the authors have provided a basic outline of procedures to follow in constructing questionnaires, the decisions which need to be addressed in the construction phase, and the art of interviewing. Considered are elements such as determining what information is desired, the type of questionnaire to be selected, and writing, pretesting, and editing the questionnaire, along with question content, wording, sequence, and the issue of the form of the response. Issues addressed concerning interviewing deal with "creating a friendly atmosphere," asking questions as worded, obtaining responses, stressing the need of interviewers to follow the sampling requirements established in the design, and investigating the biasing factors introduced by the interviewer. Specific examples are provided for the question construction section. References are in the body of the text, with author last name and year of publication given. A single bibliography for the entire volume appears on pages 583-609.

135.   Lockley, Lawrence C., and Alfred N. Watson. "Some Fundamental Considerations in the Conduct of Polls." *Journal of Marketing* 5, no. 2 (October 1940): 113-15.

Three basic areas are covered: survey design, question wording, and sampling. The authors are concerned that the survey be designed so that those sampled will have information to provide on the topics asked, that the wording of individual questions will be clear and unbiased, and that appropriate sampling will be conducted to ensure that the sampled group truly reflects the views of the entire group under consideration. The challenge for the first of these areas is that "no rules for appraising the surveyability of a question can be formulated." The question, "Can and will people tell me what I want to know?" can be asked to partially address this concern. Again, no rules exist for question writing, with the authors observing that honesty and experienced judgments are the best approaches. Quota sampling is suggested, without using that phraseology. Self-selection by respondents, as in mail surveys, is considered inappropriate.

136.   Maccoby, Eleanor E., and Robert R. Holt. "How Surveys Are Made." *Journal of Social Issues* 2, no. 2 (May 1946): 45-57. [Reprinted in *Supplement to Reader in Public Opinion and Communication*, edited by Bernard Berelson and Morris Janowitz. No. 10: *Methods in Public Opinion Research*, 499-510. Glencoe, IL: Free Press, 1953. 611p.]

The major steps involved in public opinion polling are outlined and discussed for the nonexpert. The work that goes into producing the results which are published regularly in newspapers and elsewhere is described. Maccoby and Holt cover numerous subject areas such as defining survey objectives, the study design choice, sample selection, questionnaire construction, questionnaire pretesting, survey administration, and results analysis. The rules of the scientific method need to be followed, along with the systematic recording of information as part of the basic principles of surveying. The authors refer to these labors as "tortuous and detailed." (1 footnote)

Bibliography

137.   Potter, Dale R., Kathryn M. Sharpe, John C. Hendee, and Roger N. Clark. *Questionnaires for Research: An Annotated Bibliography on Design, Construction, and Use*. USDA Forest Service Research Paper PNW-140. Portland, OR: Pacific Northwest Forest and Range Experiment Station, 1972. 80p. [SuDoc A13.78:PNW-140]

The intended audiences for this annotated bibliography are outdoor recreation researchers and those individuals studying public opinion in the area of natural resources. Each annotation summarizes the content and conclusions of the item, includes a subjective evaluation, and supplies one or more keywords. The average length of the 193 annotations is 104 words, with the evaluations averaging 16 words. There are 16 references to books, book chapters, and papers, with the remainder of the bibliography consisting of journal publications. The journal titles which appear most frequently include the following (with the number of occurrences following the journal name): *Public Opinion Quarterly* - 50; *Journal of Applied Psychology* - 23; *American Sociological Review* - 14; *Printers' Ink* - 11; *Journal of the American Statistical Association* - 6; *Journal of Marketing* - 6; *Sociology and Social Research* - 6; *American Journal of Sociology* - 4; and *Journal of Educational Research* - 4. There are separate author and keyword indexes (three plus pages) provided. The compilers are identified with their job titles on the inside of the front cover.

Instructional Materials

138.   Hyman, Herbert. *Survey Design and Analysis: Principles, Cases and Procedures*, with a foreword by Paul F. Lazarsfeld. Glencoe, IL: Free Press, [1955]. 425p.

The work, designed as a manual for students studying survey analysis, attempts to impart both technical knowledge and experience through the seven survey examples discussed. There are four major parts. The first discusses the orientation of the survey analyst; the second deals with descriptive surveys and the functions of the analyst; the third considers explanatory surveys; and the final section covers the utilization of survey findings with examples. Chapter 1 opens with the following seven case studies: (1) industrial absenteeism; (2) public opinion and the atom bomb; (3) American opinion on commercial radio; (4) prejudice and personality; (5) American sexual behavior; (6) class consciousness; and (7) war bond redemption. The IBM card punchers and sorters are shown as machine processors. Five appendixes provide the questionnaires used in the major surveys described above, examples of procedural materials used throughout the process of survey research, and practice exercises and their answers. The book is footnoted throughout and includes a three-page index of names and studies.

139.   Orlich, Donald C. *Designing Sensible Surveys*. Pleasantville, NY: Redgrave Publishing Company, 1978. 194p.

Data gathering by questionnaire, personal interview, and telephone interview is the focus of this textbook designed for students and practitioners. Orlich discusses designing the items and response modes, coding, conducting the survey, adapting other designs, data analysis, and report writing. Survey research is considered in terms of the decision-making process, with an orientation toward the contributions which might be made in the field of educational theory. The presentation involves both practical and theoretical concerns, as well as the simple and the complex. Thirty-nine tables, figures, and models are provided. (31 references)

140.   Sheatsley, Paul B. "Survey Design." Section 2, Part B, Chap. 1 in *Handbook of Marketing Research*, edited by Robert Ferber, 2/66-2/81. New York, NY: McGraw-Hill Book Company, [1974]. (various pagings)

This is the first chapter dealing with surveys in Ferber's *Handbook*. Sheatsley, with the National Opinion Research Center, begins with a consideration of the amount of time and money that may be involved in a particular survey. A discussion follows of the survey purposes and design, and the issue of sample design. Sampling methods and sample size are reviewed next, along with data collection and the survey questionnaire. (13 references)

PLANNING

141.   Frey, James H. "Problems with Institutional Surveys." In *Surveying Institutional Constituencies,* edited by J. Bruce Frances, 19-25. *New Directions for Institutional Advancement: A Quarterly Sourcebook*, editor-in-chief A. Westley Rowland, no. 6. San Francisco, CA: Jossey-Bass Inc., Publishers, 1979. 100p.

Challenges which hamper the success of surveys are discussed. Overdependence on mail surveys is noted along with nonrepresentative surveys, inattention to design and wording, and superficial analysis. The "piggyback phenomena" (PP) is also mentioned. PP occurs when parties other than the survey researchers attempt to include their own questions or mailings with the survey. A lack of decision makers' interest is also cited (including the assignment of the "least probable personnel" to conduct the survey, providing few resources, and not applying survey results). (7 references)

142.   Hobbs, Walter C. "To Survey or Not to Survey: What Is the Question?" In *Surveying Institutional Constituencies*, edited by J. Bruce Francis, 1-9. *New Directions for Institutional Advancement: A Quarterly Source book,* editor-in-chief A. Westley Rowland, no. 6. San Francisco, CA: Jossey-Bass Inc., Publishers, 1979. 100p.

The benefits and limitations of surveys for use by institutional advancement officers are considered. Hobbs focuses on the need to determine, prior to surveying, what information is being sought and why. Data collection, analysis and interpretation, and the relationship of research to theory are discussed. As the first article in what is referred to as a "Quarterly Sourcebook," Hobbs is setting the stage for subsequent, more specific contributions. The following entries have been selected from the volume, with individual annotations found at the indicated item number.

"An Abecedary of Sampling." (Doyle - Item No. 182).

"Problems with Institutional Surveys." (Frey - Item No. 141).

"Further Information on Surveying Institutional Constituencies." (Francis - Item No. 14).

"The Future of Institutional Surveys: New Concepts, Techniques and Technologies." (Francis - Item No. 117).

"Advantages and Disadvantages of Different Survey Techniques." (Francis, Frey, and Harty - Item No. 559).

143.   Lake County Regional Planning Commission. *Planning Program Survey Research: Volume 3 of a Study of the Structure and Tasks to be Performed in a Long Range Planning Program for the County.* Waukegan, IL: Lake County Regional Planning Commission, 1970. 24 leaves.

The Lake County Regional Planning Commission prepared this volume to serve as "an explanation of survey research objects and methods." The volume is divided into two chapters, with chapter 1 introducing the topic and focusing on interviewing in a modified outline format. Chapter 2 has fifteen checklists covering various topics: steps in survey research; cluster sampling technique; demographic items; occupation and group classifications; identification items; designing schematics; interviewer's materials and code; interviewing details, tactics and cautions; standard answers to respondents; coding manual contents; and coding assistance. (2 footnotes, 19 references).

144.   Whitehead, Ross. "The 'When' and 'How' of Survey-Taking." *Industry Week* 192, no. 1 (3 January 1977): 56-60.

The question as to why a survey should be conducted begins the article. The nature of the problem to be surveyed needs to be defined before planning can begin. A discussion of planning follows, with sample size being the next question addressed, continued by question format and order. Interviewer selection is considered, along with careful record keeping and ways to encourage respondent cooperation. Poll analysis is discussed in a special section titled "Can you be sure you're right?" Another section asks, "Should I do this survey?" and credits the Stanford Research Institute in Menlo Park, California, as the source for the information. Seven questions, designed to test the readiness of the party requesting the survey, are posed. Whitehead states that a complete survey could cost between $20,000 and $30,000.

SAMPLING

GENERAL

145.   Coleman, James S. "Relational Analysis: The Study of Social Organizations with Survey Methods." *Human Organization* 17, no. 4 (Winter 1958-59): 28-36.

The introduction traces the transition from the descriptive use of the word "poll" ("finding out what people think") to the analytical uses in which the "determinants of attitudes" are sought. The movement in sampling from concerns about the individual to those of social organizations begins the discussion. Coleman covers four major types of sampling: snowball, saturation, dense, and multistage. The author advises that these sampling approaches represent only a few from a wide range of possibilities. The second part of the article addresses various analytical methods, including contextual, boundaries of homogeneity, pair analysis, and partitioning into cliques. Two appendixes show examples of "group homogeneity" and "similarity of members of a pair." (12 footnotes)

146.   Hauser, Philip M., and Morris H. Hansen. "On Sampling in Market Surveys." *Journal of Marketing* 9, no. 1 (July 1944): 26-31.

The potentially biased nature of the results from quota sampling is reviewed. Alternatives are presented, starting with complete listings of the population under consideration. As the latter option is usually not available, area sampling is suggested as a viable possibility. The use of census data as the basis for designing examples is outlined. City block information was utilized for locations over fifty thousand inhabitants, and minor civil divisions for smaller ones. A number of examples demonstrating these options are presented. One of the major benefits of area sampling is that the investigator is no longer dependent upon the interviewer for the selection of respondents. (11 footnotes)

147.   Kish, Leslie, and Irene Hess. *The Survey Research Center's National Sample of Dwellings*. ISR no. 2315. Ann Arbor, MI: Institute for Social Research, University of Michigan, 1965. 63p.

This volume updates the 1959 edition. The Survey Research Center's national sample is discussed and described as a "multipurpose, continuous and flexible sample." Dwellings are used to develop the sample (which excludes locations such as dormitories, barracks, and hospitals). The excluded living quarters account for between 5 and 10 percent. Additional topics discussed include the following: (1) primary sampling unit selection; (2) primary area sampling; (3) segment samples; (4) city directory sampling; (5) respondent selection; (6) sample selection; (7) non-sampling errors and biases; (8) estimation procedures; and (9) estimation of the sampling variability. (City directory addresses were not used as part of the sampling frame.) Sections labeled (8) and (9) in this annotation employ advanced statistics. (67 references)

148.   Rugg, Donald. "How Representative Are 'Representative Samples'?" Part 3, Chap. 11 in *Gauging Public Opinion*, by Hadley Cantril and Research Associates in the Office of Public Opinion Research, Princeton University, 142-49. Princeton, NJ: Princeton University Press, 1944. Reprint. Port Washington, NY: Kennikat Press, 1972. 318p.

The degree to which a poll cross section really does represent the larger population is examined by comparing poll samples with census data for the national population. Poll samples seek proportional representation through a number of aspects including "geographical and rural-urban distribution, color, and economic status," as well as age and sex. Comparisons are conducted using the social cross-section sample of the American Institute of Public Opinion and the representative sample of the National Opinion Research Center (NORC). Rural-urban distribution, sex, and "color" sample percentages are "very close" to the census data. There is a bias toward upper-income levels caused by a "reluctance of middle-class interviewers to approach the lowest income groups, who are most likely to be inarticulate and suspicious." The NORC age sample has too many thirty to fifty groups and not enough over fifty. Both samples overrepresent the educated and underrepresent those with less than eight years of schooling. Professionals and managers are overrepresented with "worker groups" underrepresented. (8 footnotes)

149.   Semon, Thomas T., Reuben Cohen, Samuel B. Richmond, and J. Stevens Stock. "Sampling in Marketing Research." *Journal of Marketing* 23, no. 3 (January 1959): 263-73.

This article is a condensation of an item published as number three (*Sampling in Marketing Research*) of the Marketing Research Techniques Series by the American Marketing Association. The following topics are discussed: (1) "target," "frame," and multistage sampling; (2) stratification; (3) probability and nonprobability sampling methods; (4) sampling types; (5) errors in sampling; (6) organizational sampling versus people sampling; and (7) special sample types. Semon stresses that sampling is only one element of surveys – one that cannot make up for deficiencies in other areas (such as the design of the questionnaire or the training of field interviewers).

150.   Stephan, Frederick F., and Philip J. McCarthy. *Sampling Opinions: An Analysis of Survey Procedure*. Wiley Publications in Statistics. New York, NY: John Wiley & Sons, [1958]. 451p.

This study was sponsored by the Committee on Measurement of Opinion, Attitudes and Consumer Wants of the National Research Council and the Social Science Research Council, chaired by Samuel A. Stouffer. The work is divided into three parts, the first being introductory and providing information on the value of samples, answering general questions, and discussing procedures, models, and principles. Part 2 deals with empirical studies undertaken by the authors and summarizes the results from studies conducted by others. Stephan and McCarthy determined that few simple generalizations could be made about sampling procedures, and that "no generally adequate procedures for determining the accuracy of data that result from sampling surveys" exist. Part 3 discusses the problems of actually designing and using a complex sample survey. Each chapter includes endnotes, and two indexes are provided – one for names and organizations, the other for subjects.

151.   Stock, J. Stevens. "Some General Principles of Sampling." Part 3, Chap. 10 in *Gauging Public Opinion*, by Hadley Cantril and Research Associates in the Office of Public Opinion Research, Princeton University, 127-42. Princeton, NJ: Princeton University Press, 1944. Reprint. Port Washington, NY: Kennikat Press, 1972. 318p.

The chapter begins with an overview of the sampling method, followed by the definition of technical terms. Stock continues by further discussing the challenges presented by the need for precision and accuracy. Sources of sampling data are considered, including the use of files, records, lists, city directories, and block and areal sampling. Controlled sampling is described as the "most common" method of sampling used by opinion research organizations. It combines central office controls with instructions to interviewers on the "type" of individual to be interviewed. Samples are controlled using these factors: geographical, level of urbanization, economic status, age, and sex. Random and stratified random sampling are considered. Stratified random sampling is cited as the approach used by most polling organizations. (9 footnotes)

BIAS

152.   Ghosh, Dhirendra N. "On the Selective Nature of Bias." *Public Opinion Quarterly* 43, no. 3 (Fall 1979): 402-4.

Ghosh points out the dangers of concluding that a sample is representative for the variable of primary interest if no significant differences are found on the associated variables under investigation. A study is reported to determine the relationship between blood pressure and a few behavioral variables such as family history, medical history of parents, personal medical history, and data from physical examinations. Four hundred and thirty-nine undergraduate students were divided into two groups – participants in the study and nonparticipants. Samples were drawn from university health records, and t-tests [a statistical test involving confidence limits for the random variable t of a t distribution] were conducted on the variables expected to be associated with blood pressure. In table 1 "no significant differences for mean and variance were found to exist between the participating and nonparticipating groups on any of the related variables." However, highly different conclusions were attained when the same tests were conducted using blood pressure data obtained from health records (table 2). Reasons are offered for possible bias in the sample.

153.   Lowe, Francis E., and Thomas C. McCormick. "Some Survey Sampling Biases." *Public Opinion Quarterly* 19, no. 3 (Fall 1955): 303-15.

The results of a preelection area probability sample of Madison, Wisconsin, were analyzed and compared to those of a previous study conducted by Williams in Elmira, New York [Item No. 177]. The total sample was 947 households for Madison and 1,267 households for Elmira. Specially trained students from the University of Wisconsin were used as interviewers who made as many as five or six calls (home visits) to reach a respondent. These findings are indicated for the Madison group, with comparisons made to the Elmira group: (1) first calls after 6:00 P.M. and weekend calls were most likely to yield interviews; (2) calls placed in the early afternoon were least successful; (3) the final mortality rate was 32.1 percent for Madison and 23.5 percent for Elmira; (4) refusals increased with the age of the respondent; (5) those most often not at home were between the ages of thirty and sixty; (6) more women than men granted interviews in most age groups; (7) there was no consistent trend among the occupations surveyed; and (8) voters versus nonvoters showed no relationship as to whether an interview took place. The authors conclude with a discussion of the impact of nonresponse. They suggest that tests should be developed to determine if the sampling frame will be satisfactory, that weighting of samples be employed, and that respondents be paid for interviews. (19 footnotes)

154.   Williams, W. H. "The Systematic Bias Effects of Incomplete Responses in Rotation Samples." *Public Opinion Quarterly* 33, no. 4 (Winter 1969-70): 593-602.

Rotation designs retain some sampling units and replace others. For example, the U.S. Bureau of the Census conducts the *Current Population Survey* monthly, with one-eighth of the sample replaced each month. The dropped segment is excluded for eight months, and is then returned for four consecutive months. Each rotation group is in the sample for a total of eight months. Williams discusses the observation that there are "systematic changes in the estimate of a characteristic, depending on the frequency of appearance of a rotation group in the sample." Given certain conditions, Williams believes that these changes "must" occur. Incomplete samples and the effects of unknown probabilities are considered. Advanced statistics are used. (14 footnotes)

DESIGN

General

155.   Erickson, W. A. "Optimal Sample Design with Non-Response." *Journal of the American Statistical Association* 62, no. 317 (March 1967): 63-78.

Using Bayesian decision theory, Erickson presents a "simple" model for coping with nonresponse. The following are considered in terms of their impact on sampling nonrespondents: (1) one's opinions; (2) past experience; (3) "objective" evidence with respect to the proportion of nonrespondents; (4) differences among and between respondents and nonrespondents; and (5) the cost of information gathering from nonrespondents. The impact of nonresponse on overall optimal sample design is reviewed. A suggestion is offered as to how to deal with "hard core" nonresponse. Advanced statistics are used throughout the article. (9 references)

156.   Frankel, Martin R., and Lester R. Frankel. "Some Recent Developments in Sample Survey Design." *Journal of Marketing Research* 14, no. 3 (August 1977): 280-93. [Reprinted in *Readings in Survey Research,* edited by Robert Ferber, 41-68. Chicago, IL: American Marketing Association, 1978. 604p.]

The developments discussed, all dealing with probability sampling, are designed for relevancy to marketing research. Among the topics covered are the following: (1) response bias and response variation as elements for controlling total survey error; (2) procedures for the estimation of standard errors based on complex samples, with consideration of the Taylor approximation method, balanced and jackknife repeated replication, and comparisons among the three methods described; (3) manipulation of the sample frame, covering sampling with multiplicity and alphabet segment sampling; (4) methods of using probability selection of telephone households with a variety of directory-assisted selection methods considered; and (5) protection of respondent privacy and confidentiality, including discussions on randomized response and "error innoculation." (4 footnotes, 45 references)

157.   Hansen, Morris H., and Philip M. Hauser. "Area Sampling – Some Principles of Sample Design." *Public Opinion Quarterly* 9, no. 2 (Summer 1945): 183-93. [Reprinted in *Supplement to Reader in Public Opinion and Communication*, edited by Bernard Berelson and Morris Janowitz. No. 10: *Methods in Public Opinion Research*, 546-54. Glencoe, IL: Free Press, 1953. 611p. Also reprinted in *Research Methods: Issues and Insights*, edited by Billy J. Franklin and Harold W. Osborne, 170-79. Belmont, CA: Wadsworth Publishing Company, 1971. 472p.]

The two criteria necessary for sample design, according to Hansen and Hauser, are that the sample must produce reliable information at a minimum cost, and that the reliability of the sample must be measurable. Two sampling designs considered are the quota and area sampling methods. Each is explained and discussed in terms of the above criteria, and the pros and cons of each are explored. The quota method, although widely used, has "difficulties and limitations" and is not seen to meet the second criterion. In area sampling, however, "the reliability of results . . . can be measured and controlled." Examples of area sampling are given, and the basic principles are described. Alternative sampling designs (such as the use of subsampling) are suggested. Also offered are suggestions on how to evaluate alternative designs, increase efficiency, and reduce costs. Comparison costs are made for the two methods, and guidelines are given for appropriate uses of each technique. (8 footnotes)

158.   Houseman, Earl E. "Designs of Samples for Surveys." *Agricultural Economics Research* (USDA) 1, no. 1 (January 1949): 3-10.

Houseman, in nonmathematical language, explains a number of points regarding the design of samples for social science surveys. Starting with survey data error, total error is covered, followed by a discussion of the choice between probability sampling and judgment sampling. The comparative accuracy of the two types of sampling is discussed. Five areas are reviewed regarding sample designs: defining the universe and the units of observation; the sample size; design restrictions; nonresponse; and sample expansion. (3 footnotes)

159.   Sudman, Seymour. "Bayesian Framework for Sample Design." Section 2, Part C, Chap. 3 in *Handbook of Marketing Research*, edited by Robert Ferber, 2/247-2/261. New York, NY: McGraw-Hill Book Company, [1974]. (various pagings)

Three design questions are addressed: (1) What size sample should be selected? (2) What degree of cooperation is needed from respondents? and (3) How does prior information impact the sampling design? Sudman observes that the text discussion is "mainly nonmathematical," and contrasts Bayesian solutions with classical statistical methods. Examples are provided in sections dealing with the value of decisions and the value of information. The optimum sample size for new information is considered, followed by a discussion of stratified sampling which includes six examples. (6 references)

Area

160.   Haner, Charles F., and Norman C. Meier. "The Adaptability of Area-Probability Sampling to Public Opinion Measurement." *Public Opinion Quarterly* 15, no. 2 (Summer 1951): 335-52.

The results of two methods for sampling large populations, quota (stratified, representative quota-control sampling) and area probability, are compared and contrasted. To test the hypothesis that the newer method, area probability, is suited to public opinion research, data were used from the Iowa General Purpose Sample by the Statistical Laboratory of Iowa State College. The quota sample employed was that of the Iowa Poll. The four surveys used approximately fifty experienced interviewers. The methodology and statistical procedures are presented in detail for both household-based items and respondent-based items. Analysis shows that area-probability samples (1) provided 74 to 77 percent coverage, (2) obtained a 22 percent response on callbacks, (3) had more households in upper-socioeconomic brackets, (4) included more Democrats, (5) included fewer well educated respondents, (6) cost no more for fieldwork but more to plan, and (7) obtained about the same answers to opinion questions as for quota sampling. Haner and his colleague conclude that "while probability sampling is sound in theory its practicability for public opinion measurement is open to question." Numerous difficulties with the method are given. (15 footnotes)

161.   Hansen, Morris H., and William N. Hurwitz. "Modern Methods in the Sampling of Human Populations: Some Methods of Area Sampling in a

Local Community." *American Journal of Public Health* 41, no. 6 (June 1951): 662-68.

Good sample survey design strives to achieve "maximum reliability of results per unit of cost." This article discusses the use of stratification, smaller sampling units, and subsampling. Estimation of totals and population or dwelling-unit sampling are considered when a reasonably complete list of addresses is available. Bureau of the Census published block data, as well as unpublished materials for use in sampling, are cited as useful tools. The authors observe that if results of known sampling reliability are needed, it is essential that appropriate supervisory and control organization and procedures are in place to ensure that the work is conducted as specified. (1 footnote, 13 references)

162.   Sharp, Harry, and Allan Feldt. "Some Factors in a Probability Sample Survey of a Metropolitan Community." *American Sociological Review* 24, no. 5 (October 1959): 650-61.

The University of Michigan's Detroit Area Study, conducted in 1956, 1957, and 1958, used an area-probability sample of metropolitan Detroit adults. No limit was placed on callbacks, and substitutions were not permitted. In order to achieve a response rate of 87 percent or 2,313 interviews, 7,743 calls were necessary. Three-fourths of the interviews were achieved after three calls. The results indicate that had the callbacks stopped at two, a biased sample would have been created. The nature of the responses and nonresponses is discussed, along with a detailed explanation of the number of calls placed for the two categories by employment status, age, marital status, sex, and relationship to the head of the household. The socioeconomic characteristics of respondents receiving calls are shown in categories by annual family income, occupation, education, and "subjective social class." Differential response rates which may cause bias are noted for some segments of the population. An analysis of these differentials, incorporating the demographic and socioeconomic characteristics, is presented. Sample bias caused by nonresponse is reviewed, with a comparison of twenty-one items between the actual respondents and the original sample, indicating that in only one case did the bias exceed 2 percent. (34 footnotes)

Area and Quota

163.   Hochstim, Joseph R., and Dilman M. K. Smith. "Area Sampling or Quota Control? – Three Sampling Experiments." *Public Opinion Quarterly* 12, no. 1 (Spring 1948): 73-80.

The article reports on three experiments that were conducted by the Opinion Research Corporation in 1945 and 1946. The tests were designed to determine if area sampling, which is more expensive than quota sampling, is more accurate as well. Also compared is "domal" sampling which is defined as "a sample in which not only blocks but houses and dwelling units within the blocks are predetermined in a systematic way with quotas for one or more characteristics such as sex, age, etc. being assigned." The methodology for the three experiments is given in detail. The authors reach the conclusions that area samples tend to produce a more representative cross section than quota samples, domal sampling makes the cross section more representative and less subject to bias, and callbacks, an extra expense, are sometimes unnecessary. Hochstim and Smith believe each technique has advantages. Selection depends upon the problems presented by the individual survey. Hochstim is chief statistician for Opinion Research Corporation, and Smith is vice-president. (8 footnotes)

164.   Meier, Norman C. "Technical Problems: Methodology as Related to the Requirements of Public Opinion Measurement." Chap. 18 in *The Polls and Public Opinion: The Iowa Conference on Attitude and Opinion Research Sponsored by the State University of Iowa, Iowa City*, edited by Norman C. Meier and Harold W. Saunders, 241-68. New York, NY: Henry Holt & Company, [1949]. 355p.

Introduced by Clyde W. Hart, Meier spoke on the topic of how area methodology can be adapted to the measurement of public opinion. The issue revolves around whether to use quota or area methodology. Meier cites two studies which test the representativeness of each approach, with tables showing income, female/male percentages, educational attainment, political-party affiliation, and percentages voting in the 1944 presidential election. Thirteen pages of discussion follow, with the audience members for the most part criticizing area methodology and defending quota methodology.

165.   Meier, Norman C., and Cletus J. Burke. "Laboratory Tests of Sampling Techniques." *Public Opinion Quarterly* 11, no. 4 (Winter 1947-48): 586-93.

The authors review the pros and cons of the two major types of sampling techniques used in large-scale surveys: quota sampling and area sampling. The former method is used by all public opinion survey groups except the *Washington Post* Poll. Area sampling methods are employed primarily by the Bureau of the Census and the Bureau of Agricultural Economics. The two methods are compared by the use of data from files of a previously conducted survey in Iowa City. The results, viewed as "rather tentative," show that none of the differences were significant at the 5 percent level. Due to the laboratory-constructed samples, both methods faced challenges. It is concluded that "the differences between the results obtained by the two methods are not so great that a clear-cut superiority for one or the other can be easily demonstrated." (6 footnotes)

166.   Peterson, Peter G., and William F. O'Dell. "Selecting Sampling Methods in Commercial Research." *Journal of Marketing* 15, no. 2 (October 1950): 182-89.

Quota sampling and area-probability sampling methods are presented, with suggestions for the commercial researcher as to when each method is appropriate. The authors begin with a definition of terms. It is observed that the challenge lies in deciding when accuracy needs to be favored versus cost and vice versa. The discussion is divided into objectives for selecting sampling techniques, with theoretical and practical issues covered. No single option is selected since specific needs may dictate the approach chosen. Sampling error alone cannot be the deciding factor, as other aspects of the survey may be well suited to the particular option selected – even though it may not be the most efficient statistical approach. (6 footnotes)

167.   "Polls: A Year to Be Wary." *Time* 84, no. 12 (18 September 1964): 31.

In the context of the 1964 presidential election, the article explores the polling techniques used by a variety of organizations. California pollster Mervin Field uses randomization, that is, dividing California into six regions from which Field collects basic social and economic data. Within each region interviewers are assigned several blocks from which they select every third house from the corner. An equal number of both sexes are to be polled. Quota sampling is mentioned as an alternative to the approach described. Gallup, who also uses the randomization technique, avoids the corner house as a possibly higher-priced house with more affluent residents, and selects the youngest voting-age person in each household. Other topics discussed include the difficulty in predicting voter turnout, respondents lying to pollsters, secret ballots, and depth interviews. Also considered are eight-part semantic differential questionnaires in which respondents select one of eight adjectives which best describes their attitude toward an issue or candidate.

Cross Section

168.   Morgan, James N. "How Useful Is the Cross-Section Sample Survey?" *Monthly Labor Review* 95, no. 2 (February 1972): 3-10.

The cross-section sample survey is based on observations of a sample at a point in time, which describes a larger population at that time. The challenge of this approach is the unreliable memory of those interviewed with respect to "attitudes, expectations, plans, and assets held at some past point in time." Morgan explores uses of the cross-section sample such as in the analysis of smaller groups, uncovering trends, studying savings, and mass changes in attitudes. A selection of sixteen cross-section surveys is listed. The low cost of obtaining useful information is discussed as a significant benefit of this approach. (14 endnotes)

Multiple Methods

169.   Barton, Allen H. "Bringing Society Back In: Survey Research and Macro-Methodology." *American Behavioral Scientist* 12, no. 2 (November-December 1968): 1-9.

Barton describes survey research, with random sampling, as producing correlations between individual characteristics (such as age, sex, income, and individual behavior and attitudes). When survey research uses contextual or sociometric samples, it is possible to move analysis to the level of collective units; to compare large numbers of schools, work groups, factories, or communities; and to determine characteristics among those units. The research in this area by Lazarsfeld and his collaborators at Columbia University is discussed, including "(1) measurement of perceived interpersonal environment; (2) use of cluster samples to measure objective social contexts; (3) use of sociometric samples to measure objective interpersonal environments; [and] (4) obtaining survey data on institutional settings and inter-institutional relationships." The article concludes with an analysis of contextual data. (13 references)

170.   Cassady, Ralph, Jr. "Statistical Sampling Techniques and Marketing Research." *Journal of Marketing* 9, no. 4 (April 1945): 317-41.

The sampling techniques addressed include haphazard schemes, and random, stratified, quota, and area methods. The efficiency of the various sampling approaches is discussed. Specific use of these techniques for marketing is covered, such as in the areas of forecasting market behavior and predicting the success of films and fashions. The author reviews a selection of the recent literature in the field. *Public Opinion Quarterly* is cited as "probably the most prolific source of articles on sampling problems." Radio audience measurement is discussed, including the use of mail and telephone surveys and listener diaries. (102 footnotes)

171.   Frankel, Martin R., and Lester R. Frankel. "Probability Sampling." Section 2, Part C, Chap. 2 in *Handbook of Marketing Research*, edited by Robert Ferber, 2/230-2/246. New York, NY: McGraw-Hill Book Company, [1974]. (various pagings)

The authors cite flexibility of sample-selection procedures and the capacity to "make valid statistical probabilistic statements about the reliability of sample estimates" as the reasons the method has endured. Probability sampling is defined, along with other concepts. The role of the simple random sample, as well as the problem of sample design, are discussed. Six sample designs are covered: (1) stratified and unstratified; (2) single-stage or multistage; (3) clustered or unclustered; (4) equal probability or unequal probability; (5) one-phase or two-phase (double); and (6) simple random selection or systematic selection. The estimation of sampling errors is presented. Advanced mathematics is used throughout the chapter. (2 footnotes, 8 references)

172.   Knight, Robert P. *Polls, Sampling and the Voter*. Freedom of Information Center Publication, no. 168. Columbia, MO: Freedom of Information Center, University of Missouri, 1966. (9 numbered pages plus 7 unnumbered pages)

Knight discusses random sampling, modified random sampling, and the "discredited technique" of quota sampling. Pollster accuracy and prediction pressures are covered. The "poll-itician" is described – one who, for example, would "leak" private polls for political gain. The positive ways in which politicians use polls, the bandwagon effect, and congressional concern about polls are also considered. A seven-page appendix is titled "Adjustments or Corrections Sometimes Used by Political Pollsters." There are twenty-six procedures listed with the latest use of each provided, along with a criticism or justification of the adjustment. Appendix B is a thirteen-entry bibliography listing political behavior literature. (10 footnotes)

Pinpoint

173.   Gallup, George. "The Future Direction of Election Polling." *Public Opinion Quarterly* 17, no. 2 (Summer 1953): 202-7.

Gallup describes and discusses a technique referred to as "pinpoint" or "precinct" sampling. The procedure, known since 1940, has been used in six different election environments to date, with an average error of less than 2 percent. The technique was used first on a nationwide basis in 1952. The major features are as follows: (1) election districts are the primary sampling unit; (2) the sampling units are randomly selected within regional city-size strata; (3) within each precinct interviews are conducted with every nth dwelling unit; and (4) a rotation plan is used to maintain age and sex ratios. Data from numerous polls since 1943 are used to demonstrate the effectiveness of the sampling method. Gallup completes the article by listing four reasons why he believes the technique is a useful one for pollsters. (1 footnote)

Probability

174.   Drott, M. Carl. "Random Sampling: A Tool for Library Research." *College and Research Libraries* 30, no. 2 (March 1969): 119-25.

The author describes a method for determining sample size which requires neither special mathematical ability nor statistical background. Accuracy, sample size, how to select a random sample, and the use of a random digit table are discussed. Drott suggests three practical library applications of the procedure. One example deals with library collection size, the second with the opinions of library users concerning library services, and the third deals with shelf space availability.

175.   Sudman, Seymour. "The Multiple Uses of Primary Sampling Areas of National Probability Samples." *Journal of the American Statistical Association* 65, no. 329 (March 1970): 61-70.

When considering special subpopulations, this article reviews the use of existing samples of primary sampling areas. Primary sampling units (PSUs) are used repeatedly as a method of improving interviews and reducing interview costs. A series of possibilities related to this approach are addressed, including a simple cost-variance function, empirical results, procedures when the existing sample is too small or too large, and procedures when the PSUs are too small. Advanced statistics are employed to explain the approaches discussed. (2 footnotes, 8 references)

176.   Wilks, S. S. "Representative Sampling and Poll Reliability." *Public Opinion Quarterly* 4, no. 2 (June 1940): 261-69.

The principles of representative sampling, and the degree to which they can be relied on to reflect the opinions of the whole population, are discussed by a statistician. Among the topics addressed in Wilks's presentation are the components of a statistical population, random and representative sampling, sampling fluctuations, confidence limits, majority, and trend. The summary reiterates these concerns in plain language. (4 footnotes)

177.   Williams, Robert. "Probability Sampling in the Field: A Case History." *Public Opinion Quarterly* 14, no. 2 (Summer 1950): 316-30.

The problems involved in administering a probability sample design in the field under normal survey conditions are highlighted. The area studied was Elmira, New York. [See Item No. 153 for a related study.] Analysis was made of the results of the 1948 Voting Study in terms of individual characteristics, and opinion and action items. Five waves of interviewing took place, the first of which is reported in this article. One respondent was randomly selected from each sample dwelling unit for a total of 1,267 individuals. Interpretation of the data shows the following: (1) 2.8 calls (visits) on average were made per completed interview; (2) a 90 percent success rate was achieved by the third call; (3) three calls were usually sufficient to obtain individual characteristics; (4) household information was obtained in two calls; (5) the sample mortality rate was 18.8 percent of the original sample; and (6) the number of hours spent and the costs involved were about three times that of comparable Roper surveys. Williams discusses the question of how great the mortality of a sample can be without eroding reliability. He concludes with ten observations concerning probability sampling and the discrepancies that can occur between theory and practice. (3 footnotes)

Probability and Quota

178.   "For Better Polls: Probability Samples Are Better Than Quota Samples – But Too Costly. Now Two Ways to Cut That Cost Are Being Tried." *Business Week*, no. 1034 (25 June 1949): 24.

The three leading pollsters (namely Gallup, Crossley, and Roper) were all using quota sampling during the 1948 election miscall. In the quota approach the population is grouped or stratified into classes by age, race, economic level, and so forth. The interviewer is then instructed to interview a certain number of each class – depending upon the proportions called for. Interviewer bias can arise as it is the interviewer who chooses the individuals to interview to fill each quota. In probability sampling (the approach that Gallup and others subscribed to) the sample is randomly selected from the total population under consideration. Gallup introduced a method to reduce callbacks, thereby cutting the cost of surveys utilizing probability sampling. Gallup conducted a two-year survey of thirty-one thousand people to determine who is home and at what time. By calling when the respondent is most likely to be home (that is, the time-place factor), callbacks are reduced. Alfred Politz, head of Alfred Politz, Incorporated, asks each person interviewed whether they were home during five specific times in the previous week. With this information he statistically adjusts his data, correcting for the nonrandom factor of at-homeness to recreate a completely random sample (and eliminate callbacks altogether).

179.   Hansen, Morris H., and William N. Hurwitz. "Dependable Samples for Market Surveys." *Journal of Marketing* 14, no. 3 (October 1949): 363-72.

Quota and probability sampling are discussed, with the latter designated as the method of choice. Cost estimates are part of a presentation of how to plan a survey. The limitations of quota samples are highlighted, while the value of probability samples for prediction is considered. The option possibilities for sampling methodology are discussed. The authors point out that considerable amounts of information already may be available from the Bureau of the Census, including information down to the block level as well as maps, some of which can be quite detailed. Although some of the census material is published and readily available, other unpublished materials can be requested at cost to the user. (1 footnote)

180.   Sudman, Seymour. "Probability Sampling with Quotas." *Journal of the American Statistical Association* 61, no. 315 (September 1966): 749-71.

Sudman's purpose is to demonstrate how quota sampling procedures can be "very close" to traditional probability sampling. His "heretical intent" is to show that quota sampling using "tight geographical controls" (in which the interviewer follows a travel pattern and visits predetermined households) produces bias which is small but where interviewing can be completed quickly, thus rationalizing this procedure even in the light of the failure of the 1948 polls. (Geographic controls represent a change from previous practice.) Data are provided to show the "reasonableness of treating sampling with quotas as a form of probability sampling." Sudman discusses sampling variability of probability samples with quotas, examines the costs of such samples with callbacks and quotas, and compares the survey results of probability callbacks versus quota samples. Bias for quota sampling was found to be between 3 and 5 percent. Cost differentials between quota and callbacks were small. Sudman believes that interviewing speed is the primary advantage of quota sampling. (15 references)

Quota

181.   Carter, Roy E., Jr., Verling C. Troldahl, and R. Smith Schuneman. "Interviewer Bias in Selecting Households." *Journal of Marketing* 27, no. 2 (April 1963): 27-34.

Carter and the other researchers consider the use of quota sampling and the question as to whether there are consistent biases, across interviewers, when the selection of households is controlled by the interviewers. With quota sampling the desired population is identified. Therefore, the interviewed quota consists of individuals in the same proportion as they exist in the entire population. The study results show that interviewers tended to select households which they "liked" and which they perceived as having relatively high income. The authors indicate that the interviewers should not have control of the selection of households, even if sex, age, or other quotas are not met by the interviewer. Quota sampling techniques are used due to low cost and where timeliness is a significant issue. (11 footnotes)

DICTIONARY

182.   Doyle, Kenneth O., Jr. "An Abecedary of Sampling." In *Surveying Insti-tutional Constituencies*, edited by J. Bruce Francis, 27-44. *New Directions for Institutional Advancement: A Quarterly Sourcebook*, editor-in-chief A. Westley Rowland, no. 6. San Francisco, CA: Jossey-Bass Inc., Publishers, 1979. 100p.

As the title states, this article provides the ABCs of sampling, or the vocabulary of the language of the field. Terms defined include population; probability sampling; precision and bias; stratification; simple random sample; quasi-random sample; proportionate stratified random sample; sample size and response rate; cluster sampling; multiphase sampling; snowball sampling; and panel sampling. The terms are defined early in the article and then incorporated into examples of simple sampling designs. (7 references)

ERROR

183.   Bookstein, Abraham. "How to Sample Badly." *Library Quarterly* 44, no. 2 (April 1974): 124-32.

Bookstein deals with three categories of errors which occur when faulty procedures are followed in probability sampling. For purposes of the article, the author restricts the sampling to that which will pick items independently and randomly, and which will "allow each item an equal chance to be selected." The three faults discussed are the misuse of random number tables, the use of a faulty list, and, when a list is not available, the use of a selection procedure that changes the population being sampled. Bookstein demonstrates with nine examples drawn from classroom teaching or from published articles. The author writes in the conclusion that these errors occur with "alarming frequency," and that the steps suggested can help reduce extraneous factors from distorting results. (6 footnotes, 5 references)

184.   Kish, Leslie, and Irene Hess. "On Non-Coverage of Sample Dwellings." *Journal of the American Statistical Association* 53, no. 282 (June 1958): 509-24.

Two major types of nonsampling errors are identified: errors of observation and errors of nonobservation (which are further subdivided into errors of nonresponse and errors of noncoverage). Noncoverage occurs when members of a population are not included in the survey. The noncoverage can be caused by errors in office routine, field instruction, and procedures. Overcoverage takes the error in the opposite direction. The challenges of estimating the noncoverage, block analysis,

analysis by place, and the limitations of these findings are the next areas discussed. Ways to change sampling procedures are considered, along with the use of city directories for sampling. The use of segments is covered, with a segment consisting of some four dwelling units selected from a listing of a larger number of dwelling units. Formulas are devised for computing coverage and response rates. Kish and Hess include a mathematical review of the effects of noncoverage. (20 footnotes)

185.   Sirken, Monroe G. "Household Surveys with Multiplicity." *Journal of the American Statistical Association* 65, no. 329 (March 1970): 257-66.

Multiplicity is an approach in which respondents not only report information concerning themselves, but also report about individuals (such as relatives and neighbors) residing elsewhere. The method does not necessarily produce smaller sampling error for the household reporting, but "in most instances it should be feasible to assure a substantial reduction in sampling error by selecting appropriate multiplicity rules." Response errors will be greater, as self-reports are usually more accurate than proxy respondents. The original use of the multiplicity approach was for estimating aspects of population change. Advanced statistics are used throughout the article. (1 reference)

HISTORY

186.   Bershad, Max A., and Benjamin J. Tepping. "The Development of Household Sample Surveys." *Journal of the American Statistical Association* 64, no. 328 (December 1969): 1134-40.

The early years of sampling practice and theory, beginning with the 1930s, are reviewed. Subsequent years are traced, followed by a consideration of the current practices. Nonsampling error and other problems are discussed. The worldwide use of household sample surveys is covered, with the observation that the expectation is present for greater precision and accuracy. The article is summarized, noting that the quality emphasis of efforts in this area has helped achieve statistical results which have held up over time. The authors believe that in the future household sample surveys will be used in ever greater number and with greater effectiveness. (1 footnote, 19 references)

187.   Johnson, Palmer O. "Development of the Sample Survey as a Scientific Methodology." *Journal of Experimental Education* 27, no. 3 (March 1959): 167-76.

Numerous areas are covered, beginning with the differentiation between an "experiment" and a survey, and followed by the development of the sample survey.

The sample survey as a scientific method is discussed. Johnson writes about general methodology in sampling surveys, sampling and nonsampling errors, basic principles, sample designs, more complex sample designs, and quasi-representative sampling plans. The statistician is described as the individual who designs experimental programs and observational surveys, analyzes results, and determines what has been established and what still needs to be verified. (5 endnotes, 4 references)

188.   Stephan, Frederick F. "History of the Uses of Modern Sampling Procedures." *Journal of the American Statistical Association* 43, no. 241 (March 1948): 12-39.

Early examples of sampling began in Breslau [Poland], with Edmund Halley's selection of mortality statistics to form the basis of his life table. Stephan cites the need for sampling in the areas of agricultural crop and livestock estimates, economic statistics, social surveys, and health statistics, as well as in public opinion polls. Early U.S. newspaper polls included efforts in the *New York Herald* (which prior to 1900 was collecting preelection reports and estimates from all over the country); the *Chicago American* and the *Chicago Journal* (polling a mayoral election in 1905); and the *Columbus Dispatch* [Ohio] (which began a long series of polls beginning with the 1906 election). The development of simpler random and systematic sampling techniques is outlined, followed by a consideration of complex sampling procedures. Judgment, selection, and controls are discussed, including coverage of the work of Cherington, Roper, Gallup, and Crossley. Stephan highlights the impact that World War II had on providing "an even greater accelerating stimulus than the depression of the '30's" on the development of sampling procedures. (77 combined footnotes and references)

189.   Stephan, Frederick F., and Philip J. McCarthy. "Studies in Sampling under the Committee on Measurement of Opinion, Attitudes and Consumer Wants." *Items – Social Science Research Council* 1, no. 2 (June 1947): 1-3.

The first project undertaken by the Committee on Measurement of Opinion, Attitudes and Consumer Wants was to produce bulletins indicating the "fundamental facts and principles" of sampling. The committee was jointly established by the National Research Council and the Social Science Research Council under the chairpersonship of Samuel A. Stouffer of Harvard University. The list of other members included Hadley Cantril, Archibald M. Crossley, George Gallup, Paul F. Lazarsfeld, Rensis Likert, Elmo Roper, and ten other individuals. The Rockefeller Foundation provided a grant for the project which is anticipated to be concluded in just over one-and-a-half years. The article briefly outlines the steps to be undertaken by the committee and describes ten specific studies underway.

The question as to why one should study sampling survey methodology is addressed.

INSTRUCTIONAL MATERIALS

190.   Hansen, Morris H., William N. Hurwitz, and William G. Madow. *Sample Survey Methods and Theory*. Wiley Publications in Statistics. New York, NY: John Wiley & Sons, [1953]. 2 vols. (vol. 1, 638p.; vol. 2, 332p.)

Volume 1 (of a two-volume textbook set on the theory and practical application of sample survey work) covers the following topics: (1) elementary principles; (2) biases and nonsampling errors in survey results; (3) sample designs; (4) simple random sampling; (5) stratified simple random sampling; (6) cluster sampling of the one- or two-stage variety; (7) stratified single or multistage cluster sampling; (8) control of variation in size of cluster in estimating totals, averages, or ratios; (9) multistage sampling with large primary sampling units; (10) estimating variances; (11) regression estimates, double sampling, sampling for time series, systematic sampling, and other sampling methods; and (12) case studies. The volume has an eleven-page index. Volume 2 explains the underlying theory for the above presentations. Initially considered are definitions and fundamental theory, with sample survey design theory a consequence of statistical theory developed over time by a variety of individuals. The volume concludes with a discussion of a theory for response errors. Advanced mathematics is employed throughout. A five-page index is provided. Each chapter ends with a bibliography.

191.   Jessen, Raymond J. *Statistical Survey Techniques*. Wiley Series in Probability and Mathematical Statistics; A Wiley Publication in Applied Statistics. New York, NY: John Wiley & Sons, 1978. 520p.

Designed as a college or university textbook covering the basics of statistical surveys, the material is suitable for use over one or two semesters. Application extends to a wide variety of fields, such as public opinion measurement, sociology, political science, biology, and engineering. Topics covered include, among others: random sampling; estimation; stratification; subsampling; double-sampling; lattice sampling; miscellaneous survey techniques; and analysis and presentation. Advanced level statistical computations are found throughout. Tables are used widely, and each chapter includes references. The book has a three-page subject index.

192.   Kish, Leslie. *Survey Sampling*. New York, NY: John Wiley & Sons, [1965]. 643p.

Kish designed this volume as a textbook for students of the social sciences and as a reference tool for professors and others who are not themselves specialists in statistics. Divided into three parts, part 1 covers the fundamentals, part 2 addresses special problems and techniques, and part 3 deals with related concepts. Part 1 includes information on stratified sampling, systematic sampling, cluster sampling, unequal clusters, selection with probabilities proportional to size measures, and the economic design of surveys. Part 2 examines area sampling, multistage sampling, sampling from imperfect frames, and a number of selection techniques. Part 3 considers biases and nonsampling errors, as well as inference issues from survey data. Five appendixes provide various mathematical explanations and tables. Nine pages of references are included, as well as a four-page index.

193.   McCombs, Maxwell. "Sampling Opinions and Behaviors." Chap. 6 in *Handbook of Reporting Methods*, edited by Maxwell McCombs, Donald Lewis Shaw, and David Grey, 123-38. Boston, MA: Houghton Mifflin Company, 1976. 340p.

Probability samples are differentiated from nonprobability samples, with the discussion explaining representative and nonrepresentative samples. Quota sampling and the *Literary Digest* experience of 1936 are reviewed. Simple random and systematic random samples are discussed, along with multistage sample design, cluster and stratified sampling, and sampling error. The examination of documents for content analysis is described as a time-saver for journalists and behavioral scientists. Sample validation is clarified through a number of examples, and sampling error is presented in mathematical terms. A table lists the sample error for sample sizes from fifty to one thousand in steps of fifty. (5 footnotes)

194.   Scheaffer, Richard L., William Mendenhall, and Lyman Ott. *Elementary Survey Sampling*. 2d ed. North Scituate, MA: Duxbury Press, a Division of Wadsworth Publishing Company, Belmont, CA, 1979. 278p.

Designed as an introductory textbook for students with little mathematical background (a course in elementary statistics is a prerequisite), this volume covers the practical aspects of survey research. The sampling areas addressed are simple random, stratified random, ratio and regression, cluster, systematic, and two-stage cluster. Basic concepts are reviewed, along with a discussion of the elements which constitute the sampling problem. Supplemental topics considered include the random response model, the number of callbacks to be conducted, and the interpretation of subsamples. The book is summarized, various statistical tables are provided in the appendix, answers to chapter problems are given, and a two-page index is included.

195.   Slonim, Morris James. *Sampling: A Quick, Reliable Guide to Practical Statistics*. A Fireside Book. New York, NY: Simon & Schuster, 1960. 144p. [The book was originally published under the title *Sampling in a Nutshell*.]

Business and government executives, accountants, and auditors are the intended recipients of this "light, brief" nontechnical treatment of sampling for "review and reference" purposes. Sociologists, psychologists, market researchers, and public relations personnel will also find the volume useful. Slonim covers these subjects: (1) sample surveys; (2) sampling and nonsampling errors; (3) sampling applications; (4) sampling of accounting data; (5) polls and program ratings; (6) simple random sampling; (7) stratified sampling; (8) cluster sampling; (9) systematic sampling; (10) interpreting replicate subsamples; (11) additional sampling methods; (12) estimating procedures; (13) sample size; (14) quality control; (15) acceptance sampling; and (16) case histories. There are unnumbered footnotes throughout the volume.

196.   Stopher, Peter R., and Arnim H. Meyburg. *Survey Sampling and Multivariate Analysis for Social Scientists and Engineers*. Lexington, MA: Lexington Books, D. C. Heath and Company, 1979. 385p.

The textbook treatment provided discusses the realm where survey design and sampling are united. Broad topics considered include pilot surveys; the definition of the population; ascertaining what information is to be collected; collection methods; choice of sampling frame, unit, and method; nonresponse; and field control and testing. In presenting the sections on the practical aspects of survey completion, Stopher and Meyburg cover administration; survey form design; interviewers; field supervision; the checking of refusal rates and nonresponse; and coding and tabulation. Other chapters of specific interest (which include significant advanced statistical presentations) are titled "Design of Sampling Procedures" (chapter 3, pages 21-44) and "Population Estimates and Sampling Errors" (chapter 4, pages 45-85). (7 references)

197.   Sudman, Seymour. *Applied Sampling*. Quantitative Studies in Social Relations. New York, NY: Academic Press, 1976. 249p.

In the preface Sudman refers to a number of volumes designed for users with advanced levels of statistical knowledge. This textbook is intended for students and researchers who are planning studies, but who possess limited resources and statistical backgrounds. The book is "not intended for use by large governmental agencies for major policy decisions." Less expensive and "relatively sloppy" sampling procedures are presented. Subjects reviewed include the following: (1) small-scale sampling; (2) simple and pseudo-simple random sampling; (3) cluster sampling; (4) stratified sampling; (5) multistage samples; (6) sampling variance estimation from complex samples; and (7) special topics, including these three of sixteen selections: rare populations, snowball sampling, and panel clustering. One hundred two references are provided at the end of the book, along with an eight-page subject index.

METHODOLOGY

198.   Blankenship, Albert B. "The 'Sample' Study in Opinion Research." *Sociometry* 3, no. 3 (July 1940): 271-76.

The article begins with a discussion of the pretest, that is, a limited series of interviews utilizing a variety of questionnaire formats. Although the "sample" or "test-tube" approach is identical to the final large survey, it involves a sample between two hundred and two thousand. Blankenship describes a myriad of benefits to this approach, including the following: (1) assists in determining the cost of the full sample; (2) helps in predicting the type of results on the final study; (3) assists with the determination of the size and nature of the final sample; (4) serves as a check of the interviewers' instructions; (5) aids in the task of adding or deleting questions; (6) measures the reliability and internal consistency of the results obtained; and (7) influences the choice of wording and question sequencing. (6 footnotes)

199.   Booth, Gordon, and J. Sedransk. "Planning Some Two-Factor Comparative Surveys." *Journal of the American Statistical Association* 64, no. 326 (June 1969): 560-73.

Authors Booth and Sedransk provide a statistical examination of sample surveys in which two factors are under consideration, and in which comparisons between "levels" of the factors are very important and where there is "interaction" between the factors. The authors consider both "independent" sampling, where desired sample size is achieved, as well as cases where that is not possible. A double sampling procedure to deal with such cases is discussed. The double sampling procedure can also be "applied to estimation of the (finite) population mean when double sampling with stratification is used." Complex statistical formulas are a large part of the article text. (2 footnotes, 8 references)

200.   Daly, Joseph F. "Some Basic Principles of Statistical Surveys." *Journal of the American Statistical Association* 64, no. 328 (December 1969): 1129-34.

Statistical surveys are designed to provide facts on which judgments, decisions, or administrative activities can be based. Daly would like to see a distinction made between the "statistical program" and the policy decisions which are reached from the program. He maintains that such a distinction exists in the physical sciences, and that it would be wise for the social sciences to follow suit. Daly discusses surveying by sample or subset (providing examples), probability sampling, and multistage sampling of clusters. The author makes a case for survey sponsors to be willing to expend resources to a sufficient degree to ensure that the results are as speculation free as possible. (1 reference)

201.   Deming, W. Edwards. "On Training in Sampling." *Journal of the American Statistical Association* 40, no. 231 (September 1945): 307-16.

Basic principles of efficiency in the planning of surveys are described. Deming identifies three characteristics of a "professional" job of sampling: selection of the respondents is "automatic"; computing procedures should be planned in advance; and sampling error should be computed, with the size of the sample adjusted as needed (with the cost for each error level determined). Deming discusses the need for studies in bias removal. Six steps in the planning of a sample are outlined. Training in sampling is considered, with the value of complete counts noted. In order to obtain better statisticians, he comments that improved training for teachers of statistics will be required. (10 footnotes)

202.   Kish, Leslie. "Selection of the Sample." Chap. 5 in *Research Methods in the Behavioral Sciences,* edited by Leon Festinger and Daniel Katz, 175-239. New York, NY: Holt, Rinehart & Winston, 1953. 660p.

The following topics are considered: fundamentals of sampling; stratification techniques; clustering; practical procedures; various statistics; complex sample designs; and procedures of estimation. Kish observes that the discussion concentrates on the "less mathematical aspects of different procedures of selection." The chapter is divided into twenty-two numbered sections which are further subdivided into the seven topics indicated above. (22 references)

203.   Platten, John H., Jr. "Weighting Procedures in Probability-Type Samples." *Journal of Marketing* 23, no. 1 (July 1958): 47-52.

Procedures for dealing with preselected respondents who are not reached on the first call are considered. Platten suggests that usually no more than 65 percent of the intended respondents are reached with the first call – the balance are not at home when the interviewer visits. Callback costs are high and therefore limited. Techniques to achieve a "complete" sample include weighting, and substitution in the field for missed respondents. Weighting involves the use of "simulated" interviews in the tabulations in order to correct for missing respondents. As the proportion of simulated interviews increases, so does the risk of error or bias. One weighting approach, known as the "nights-at-home technique," is described as being deficient. Platten uses an example to show how the technique failed to

correct a demographic skew. The examples are based on an experiment conducted during a thirty-thousand-interview national study. (3 footnotes)

204.   Roper, Elmo. "Problems and Possibilities in the Sampling Technique."
        Journalism Quarterly 18, no. 1 (March 1941): 1-9.

The elements of a useful sample are discussed, considering both the geography
and the size of the place from which the sample will be drawn. The appropriate
balance of both sexes is important, as well as the age, occupation, and economic
level of the respondents. Roper, director of the *Fortune* Survey, speaks of the
"futility of setting up fixed dollar boundary lines for determining economic levels." One solution reviewed takes into account geographic, income, and size of
place variations in order to approximately classify a respondent, having developed a sliding "scale of living." Pretesting, question wording, and phraseology
are discussed. It is noted that some questions require rewriting as many as
twenty times. Roper observes that advances have been made in quantitative measurements, but that qualitative appraisals need further development. He also
notes that elections, as opposed to public opinion polls, do not provide the voter
with the opportunity to express opinions on the various parts of a candidate's
platform or program.

205.   Roper, Elmo. "Sampling Public Opinion." *Journal of the American Sta-
        tistical Association* 35, no. 210, pt. 1 (June 1940): 325-34.

The following six aspects are discussed as elements to be considered in creating
an appropriate sample: (1) geography; (2) size of the place; (3) sex-proper proportions of females and males; (4) age; (5) occupation; and (6) economic level
(Roper refers to the latter as "the most important single control"). Other critical
areas of concern include question selection and phraseology (ensuring that they
are "perfectly clear"). The issue of interpretation of results is addressed. Roper
believes two areas require further work: how to make qualitative appraisal, and
how to chart all "leading" words and phrases so as to avoid their use. The social
significance of survey methodology is discussed.

206.   Rue, Joseph. "Techniques and Administration of Sampling Projects." *Ari-
        zona Business* 23, no. 8 (October 1976): 3-9.

The introduction explains the advantages of a sample versus a census for the
needs of the business manager. One example cited is the opportunity to ask members of a small sample three hundred questions – an approach which would be
prohibitive via a census. Four sampling approaches are described: simple random, cluster, systematic, and stratified. An example of a multistage survey for
studying urban characteristics is provided. Statistical analysis, the administration
of sampling projects, and the "acceptance" of results from survey procedures are

covered. Sampling is noted to be less expensive, quicker, and more flexible than examining all the members of a population. A brief interview with George Gallup is included in which sample size is discussed in relation to polling methods for political scientists. (5 footnotes)

207.   Sedransk, J. "A Double Sampling Scheme for Analytical Surveys." *Journal of the American Statistical Association* 60, no. 312 (December 1965): 985-1004.

The analytical surveys in the article title refer to "analytical studies of survey data" and appear in the shortened form for the sake of simplicity. In double sampling "a large sample is selected and the group to which each element belongs is identified." Using a predetermined sampling rule, a subsample is selected from each of the groups. The purpose is to determine a specified level of precision which conforms with a given budget (the task being to identify appropriate values for the preliminary and main sample sizes). Sedransk offers several "quick and reliable" solutions for meeting these challenges. He concludes by reviewing the validity of the approximations. Advanced statistics are employed. (10 references)

208.   Semon, Thomas T. "Basic Concepts." Section 2, Part C, Chap. 1 in *Handbook of Marketing Research*, edited by Robert Ferber, 2/217-2/229. New York, NY: McGraw-Hill Book Company, [1974]. (various pagings)

The basic concepts of sample design are reviewed. Among the topics discussed Semon covers the following: (1) quality criteria; (2) sampling errors; (3) design classes; (4) area and cluster sampling and multistage samples; (5) individual sampling unit selection; (6) variance and sampling error; (7) stratification; (8) sample survey result error; (9) imprecision, confidence limits, and statistical power; (10) replicated samples; (11) inaccuracy; (12) sample size; and (13) sample design choice. Factors considered in the choice of sample design were cost, accuracy, the use of the results, the sample size, and the importance of study comparability. (6 references)

SAMPLE SIZE

209.   Corey, Dorothy D., and Rue Corey Pine. "It's the Size of the Sample That Counts." *Western Advertising* 82, no. 23 (May 1964): 23-25.

Primarily concerned with surveys of readership (magazines and newspapers), the authors provide a brief sketch for the justification of statistics, followed by the assertion that a good sample is better than a census. A simple graphic display accompanies an explanation of sample size. Sample results are characterized as being either above or below "the truth" – but rarely coinciding with the truth. Ranges of error are presented. Limitations of small samples are noted, along with a consideration of standard error.

210.   Kilpatrick, Franklin P., and James L. Garard, Jr. "Two Small Sample Opinion Polls." *Public Opinion Quarterly* 18, no. 1 (Spring 1954): 96-98.

Students from a social psychology class at Princeton University conducted polls for several years in the city of Trenton, New Jersey. In 1952 a sample of 300 respondents was polled, followed in 1953 by a sample of 280. The ballot was pretested on a small quota sample. Interviewing was completed about two weeks before election time. The poll results missed the actual vote in the presidential campaign between Eisenhower and Stevenson by less than half of 1 percent, and a similar amount for the gubernatorial race. The authors suggest that while luck may have played a role, researchers can achieve very accurate results by using highly stratified samples on relevant variables with other principles of sample selection followed. Two tables provide percentage breakdowns of the results for the two polls.

211.   King, Harry A. "A Nomogram to Assist in Planning Surveys of Small ($N < 2,000$) Populations." *Research Quarterly* 49, no. 4 (December 1978): 552-57.

A nomogram is developed to show graphically the relationship between population size and maximum error of percentage estimate. King discusses planning the sample survey in consideration of the accuracy of estimation. The statistical theory of small population sampling is presented. The mathematical development of the nomogram is explained, and two examples are given (one involving population stratification). (1 footnote, 6 references)

212.   Link, Henry C. "How Many Interviews Are Necessary for Results of a Certain Accuracy." *Journal of Applied Psychology* 21, no. 6 (December 1937): 1-17.

Link begins with a presentation of the sigma or standard deviation as the formula for determining sample size, with probable error and one, two, and three standard deviations discussed. A study with 5,165 interviews is considered, followed by a section titled "Proof by Samples of 500." The Law of Diminishing Returns is explained. Tables for determining accuracy by size of sample are presented. Four specific examples are detailed with sample and accuracy tables. (3 references)

213.   Lipstein, Benjamin. "In Defense of Small Samples." *Journal of Advertising Research* 15, no. 1 (February 1975): 33-40.

Nine rules for limiting nonsampling errors are identified: (1) simplify the survey; (2) maintain interviewer and respondent involvement in the study; (3) keep the fatigue level low; (4) self-test and pretest the questionnaire to ascertain fatigue level; (5) ask questions that respondents are equipped to answer; (6) limit questions to those essential to the main issue; (7) do not overextend the interviewers; (8) rotate key questions as a means of evaluating fatigue level; and (9) keep the sample to a minimum, rather than what the budget will permit. Lipstein discusses the contributions of others to the issue of errors in sample surveys. Detection bias is examined, the example cited being researchers investigating the relationship between cigarette smoking and lung cancer who assumed that they were causally linked. A review team found that heavy smokers were "much more carefully scrutinized for lung cancer." Interview response bias is considered, and a case is made for small samples. Two-thirds of the article addresses the impact of the interviewer. Lipstein suggests that by eliminating bad interviews a large portion of the interviewers can be "discarded." (16 references)

214.   Reynolds, William, and John H. A. Cross. "Let's Take Some of the Gobbledygook out of Sampling: A Few Research Fundamentals to Help Top Management Understand How Adequacy of Sample Size Is Determined." *Printers' Ink* 230, no. 5 (3 February 1950): 21-23.

Designed as a very basic introduction to some sampling fundamentals, this article is intended for "top management" to grasp the meanings of terms such as "sample," "random," and so forth. The article describes the impact of increasing the sample size, as well as some of the major concepts of sampling. A sample size chart is included. Using a straight edge across the three columns provided (one for percentage of respondents replying "yes," one for sample size, and the third for the limit of error), it is possible to find the sample size necessary to be 99.7 percent certain of the maximum amount of error.

215.   "The Small Sample – How Reliable? Many Laymen Are Still Skeptical but the Experts Say You Can Project the Behavior of Millions from a Sample as Small as 1,000." *Television Magazine* 15 (December 1958): 50-51, 98.

The article content is taken from Gallup's *A Guide to Public Opinion Polls* [Item No. 40]. Several points discussed are as follows: (1) the size of the sample is less important than the accuracy of those interviewed to effect the total group; (2) different sample sizes produce similar results; (3) a comparison of results from the Bureau of the Census versus a sample size of sixteen hundred on a question of religious composition of the population produced "almost identical" results; and (4) carefully selected samples which mirror the entire population can reflect the opinion of the nation with a small margin of error.

216.   Stephan, Frederick F. "Representative Sampling in Large-Scale Surveys." *Journal of the American Statistical Association* 34, no. 206 (June 1939): 343-52.

The *Literary Digest* experience of 1936, as well as the Gallup Poll and the *Fortune* Survey efforts, are reviewed. Three types of sampling discussed are sample tabulations, sampling from a list for a survey, and sampling from a map for a survey. Eight steps involved in sampling are given. The closing section of the article deals with testing sampling methods. Surveys which are other than "complete canvasses" are referred to as "partial" surveys. (15 footnotes)

217.   Woolsey, Theodore D. *Sampling Methods for a Small Household Survey*. Public Health Service Publication no. 480; Public Health Monograph no. 40. [Washington, DC]: U.S. Department of Health, Education, and Welfare, Public Health Service, March 1956. 16p. [SuDocFS2.62:40]

A sampling procedure is described which generated a sample of persons over age forty-five, which was of sufficient size for appropriate analysis, and where only one interview per household could be achieved. To develop the sample a city directory and a city map showing all of the city blocks were used. Sample size was determined by examining the total number of households and calculating the odds of locating someone over age forty-five in each household. Three samples of five hundred were determined to be necessary. Woolsey explains the technique for selecting which person over forty-five would be interviewed in a household with multiple individuals over that age (a sampling table is provided). A discussion of the degree of success achieved through the above steps is included, along with a computation of sampling error. (6 footnotes, 4 references)

SELECTION WITHIN HOUSEHOLDS

218.   Kish, Leslie. "A Procedure for Objective Respondent Selection within the Household." *Journal of the American Statistical Association* 44, no. 247 (September 1949): 380-87.

With increased emphasis being placed on area probability samples of households, Kish discusses a procedure for objectively selecting one member of the household. The procedure involves the interviewer listing each adult person in the household, assigning a serial number to each, and then consulting a selection table for instructions as to which number to select. The results were considered satisfactory. Kish advises that proper interviewer training, and maintenance of interviewer morale, are necessary to sustain good control over the survey data collection. (7 footnotes)

219.   Paisley, William J., and Edwin B. Parker. "A Computer-Generated Sampling Table for Selecting Respondents within Households." *Public Opinion Quarterly* 29, no. 3 (Fall 1965): 431-36.

A sampling procedure developed by Kish is discussed [Item No. 218]. This technique calls for each appropriate person in the household to be listed by both name and order of age. A sampling table is provided to the interviewer to determine which listed person should be interviewed. Troldahl and Carter [Item No. 257] developed a selection technique which requires two questions: (1) "How many (appropriate persons) live in your household – counting yourself?" and (2) "How many of them are men?" Four different sampling tables were used. Selection error may approach 5 percent. To address the situation where more sampling tables are necessary, and to determine how many tables would be needed in order to "maintain equal probabilities of selection for all appropriate persons in households containing from one to five persons," Paisley and Parker calculated that sixty tables would be required. These were generated via IBM key-punched cards for production of regular-sized paper prints for the interviewers' use. Kish noted that about 1 percent of the sampled households had more than five adults. Both respondents and interviewers need a quick, simple, and "least-rapport straining" method for determining who to interview. The authors view the technique as a new use of the computer beyond that of data analyst. (7 footnotes)

220.   Watson, Alfred N. *Respondent Pre-Selection within Sample Areas: A Statistical Method of Selecting Individuals at Random.* Technical Series on Statistical Methods in Market Research, no. 2. Philadelphia, PA: Curtis Publishing Company, February 1947. 7p.

The random selection of individual respondents and the development of "route control sheets" are discussed. Watson is seeking to avoid the bias of having the interviewer select whom to interview, as in the quota method. The respondent preselection process is designed to eliminate the interviewer's discretion in the selection of respondents. The control sheet directs the interviewer to a particular area and designates specific households for interviewing. The questionnaire provides the details as to who should be interviewed in the household. An explanation as to how the households are assigned on the control sheet is given, along with an example of such a sheet and the accompanying instructions. Watson believes the method described is better than relying on the 1940 Census or other out-of-date sources because this approach can take into account new homes as well as homes which have been destroyed. (1 unnumbered footnote)

SPECIAL POPULATIONS

221.   Allen, Irving L. "Selecting an Economic Probability Sample of Negro Households in a City." *Journal of Negro Education* 38, no. 1 (Winter 1969): 4-13.

The selection of a self-weighting, two-stage area probability sample of African-American households in a city is discussed. Problems common to this type of sampling design are covered. The central cities considered are all in Connecticut: Hartford, New Haven, Bridgeport, Waterbury, and Stamford. Selection procedures given varying circumstances are suggested, with several tables showing characteristics of the sampling forms and distribution of the blocks in the sampling frame. (12 footnotes)

222.   Ericksen, Eugene P. "Sampling a Rare Population: A Case Study." *Journal of the American Statistical Association* 71, no. 355 (December 1976): 816-22. [Reprinted in *Readings in Survey Research*, edited by Robert Ferber, 188-201. Chicago, IL: American Marketing Association, 1978. 604p.]

The sampling problem addressed called for a sample of fifteen- through nineteen-year-old females living in households. The fertility practices and expectations were to be studied, with a specified ratio of white to African-American respondents of two to one. A comparison of whites to African Americans was the primary study objective. The estimation of costs and construction of strata, along with the actual stratification procedure, are presented. The results are discussed in terms of the numbers of interviews, the costs per interview, and design effects. The study findings are compared with a more optimal design. Ericksen summarizes the lessons learned from the study into five points. (4 references)

223.   Hubbard, John, Anita Muneta, and Thomas J. Stewart. "Survey Sampling on the Navajo Reservation." *Human Organization* 38, no. 2 (Summer 1979): 187-89.

A health consumer survey was conducted from 1975 to 1976 on the Navajo Reservation in Arizona (the largest Native-American reservation in the United States). Maps were developed between 1973 and 1975 which indicated locations, numbers, and types of dwellings. These maps were used to sample 94 families within one Indian Health Service unit and 140 families within another area. In a three-month period 235 household interviews were conducted by bilingual Navajo staff field researchers who had completed a four-month training program in interviewing techniques. When necessary, the interviewers corrected the existing maps. Prior to this study no formal use of area sampling procedures had been conducted on the reservation. The authors believe they have shown that area sampling can be conducted on the reservation, and that the approach could be extended to other Native-American communities. (6 references)

224.   Reed, John Shelton. "Needles in Haystacks: Studying 'Rare' Populations by Secondary Analysis of National Sample Surveys." *Public Opinion Quarterly* 39, no. 4 (Winter 1975-76): 514-22.

The rare population given as the example in this article is the challenge of locating a representative sample of southern Jews. The fifty-six pooled surveys used were from the Gallup Organization, creating a sample of 85,957 respondents for a total of 166 (0.19 percent) southern Jews. Reed considers the representation of the group in national samples, the challenge of classification error, and the representativeness of the pooled sample of group members. He observes that while this approach will not always provide satisfactory results, it is inexpensive. The surveys used in the secondary analysis measured geographic location, religion, and other variables. (17 footnotes)

225.   Stewart, Frank A. "Some Sampling Problems in Sociometric Surveys." *Sociometry* 11, no. 4 (November 1948): 301-7.

Sociometric surveys deal with the individual or small groups of individuals and only "incidentally" with the total population. Stewart considers sample size, whether to use quota controls or area design, and whether or not callbacks are worth the effort. Centers of interpersonal influence are the focus of this research area, with the range of an individual's influence from five or fewer to perhaps twenty or more. For community sociometric sampling Stewart suggests that in small cities 15 to 20 percent sampling is considered the minimum, and in larger cities samples up to 50 percent are appropriate. In addition, he believes that address assignments should be used, and callbacks are necessary. (7 footnotes)

226.   Sudman, Seymour. "On Sampling of Very Rare Human Populations." *Journal of the American Statistical Association* 67, no. 338 (June 1972): 335-39.

"Very rare" is defined by Sudman to be about 1 percent or less of the total population. The ideas of Wald on sequential sampling are employed and demonstrated to be "highly efficient" in identifying such rare populations (Wald, Abraham. *Sequential Analysis.* New York, NY: John Wiley and Sons, 1947. 212p.). Three examples of rare populations are identified. Appropriate sampling designs are considered for instances in which the screening costs are significant. The use of census data to eliminate clusters which have very few or no members of the sought-after population is discussed. Gatekeeper errors are described in which respondents deliberately answer "no" to questions, thereby eliminating the household from further questioning – even though the "ultimate respondent" might be willing to be interviewed. Techniques to overcome this challenge are provided. Miscalculation errors with rare populations can range from one-third to one-half of the eligible respondents. Sudman maintains that miscalculation errors can be "minimized by careful, thorough screening." Advanced statistics are used throughout the article. (5 references)

227.   Welch, Susan. "Sampling by Referral in a Dispersed Population." *Public Opinion Quarterly* 39, no. 2 (Summer 1975): 237-45.

Because of time and financial considerations involved with other sampling techniques, the "referral" method (sometimes called "snowball sampling") is investigated as a means of locating a small target population. With the referral method one appropriate individual is contacted. This person is then asked to name another person, and so on. The various types of biases present in such a procedure are studied with a group of Mexican Americans living in Omaha, Nebraska. Five census tracts were eventually chosen for the study, yielding a total of 1,218 Mexican Americans. A dual sampling plan (referrals and block screening, and random block screening) was used to determine certain social and economic characteristics of the participants. Comparison of the data for the two groups yielded few significant differences as to age, sex, education, occupation, citizenship, and per capita income. The number of individuals living in the household and the respondents' total family income were higher for the referred group. On seventeen attitudinal measures differences occurred on only two opinions dealing with political questions. Limitations (primarily a small sample size and sample bias) of the study are discussed. The referral method appears "appropriate" for certain types of surveys (especially those with limited resources, and "when circumstances preclude other means." Precautions are discussed. (10 footnotes)

TELEPHONE

City Directory

228.   Smigel, Irwin. "Field Methods and Techniques: A Note on the Use of the City Directory for the Selection of Individual Survey Samples." *Human Organization* 11, no. 4 (Winter 1952): 39-40.

Smigel identifies the following challenges when using the Polk directories for the selection of individual survey samples: (1) the directory includes ineligible individuals either because they live outside of the political limits of the city, they live outside of the community, they are underage, or they are members of the armed forces; (2) transients are not listed, children are excluded (therefore making a random sample of the entire city impossible), and the methods of recording college students in university towns are "inadequate"; (3) the directory is static while the population is dynamic – deaths and name changes cause sample changes; and (4) duplication of names occurs, such as with business owners who are listed alphabetically by personal name with the business name. Assuming the sample desired can fit within these limitations, the directory can save time and money. (10 footnotes)

Random Digit Dialing

General

229.   Cummings, K. Michael. "Random Digit Dialing: A Sampling Technique for Telephone Surveys." *Public Opinion Quarterly* 43, no. 2 (Summer 1979): 233-44.

The use of random digit dialing (RDD) to collect health attitude data is reported. The data were obtained from a survey of adults in Oakland, Michigan, during the swine influenza campaign of 1976 and 1977. Cummings provides information on the results of dialing to sample numbers (tables 2 and 3), the frequency of non-working numbers in the sample, refusals, problems with unanswered calls, and wrong connections, busy signals, answering machines, and so forth. The average cost per fifteen-minute interview was $8.53. These costs are compared to those of prior survey research studies. The two stages of the sample design indicate quite different proportions of working numbers among the numbers generated. There was a 34.4 percent increase in stage two. The costs per interview were also lower ($4.75). Error rate was similar to that of a simple random sample. The author recommends RDD for its low cost, ease of administration, and precision ("at least where the effects of clustering are small"). (2 footnotes, 11 references)

230.   Fletcher, James E., and Harry B. Thompson. "Telephone Directory Samples and Random Telephone Number Generation." *Journal of Broadcasting* 18, no. 2 (Spring 1974): 187-91.

A telephone survey involving audience research for an FM radio station was conducted at the University of Kentucky at Lexington, in 1972. The telephone numbers were derived by combining four-digit-number suffixes derived from random number tables with fourteen telephone prefixes used in Lexington. A total of 666 telephone numbers were generated, with interviewers instructed to place three callbacks to unanswered numbers. The random number approach required three times as much effort in order to incorporate unlisted and recently changed households into the sample. Interviewers spent half of their time actually dialing numbers. Fletcher and Thompson recommend random number use under these circumstances: (1) when the percentage of the unlisted numbers is high; (2) when existing directories are out-of-date; (3) when the cost of acquiring or handling directory data is high; and (4) as a check on directory data. (5 references)

231.   Glasser, Gerald J., and Gale D. Metzger. "Random-Digit Dialing as a Method of Telephone Sampling." *Journal of Marketing Research* 9, no. 1 (February 1972): 59-64.

Telephone sampling methods are briefly described. The impact of noninclusion in telephone directories is outlined, with consideration of the number of telephone households, the number of listed telephone households, and listed versus nonlisted households. Random digit dialing (RDD) is proposed as a way of avoiding the biases of telephone directory listings. RDD is more costly than using a directory and is subject to procedural bias. A survey using RDD is presented, with considerations, procedures, and results discussed. The random numbers are achieved by limiting to specific area codes and working central offices of the telephone company (in March 1970 there were 27,981 such offices). A major challenge is reaching wrong connections (such as nonworking numbers). Another problem is that some households may have multiple lines, thus increasing their probability of selection. The authors note that since RDD provides complete coverage for an area, the additional costs and procedural challenges need to be weighed accordingly. (6 references)

232.   Hauck, Mathew, and Michael Cox. "Locating a Sample by Random Digit Dialing." *Public Opinion Quarterly* 38, no. 2 (Summer 1974): 253-60.

A new application of an existing technique, random digit dialing (RDD), is reported. The Survey Research Laboratory of the University of Illinois, working on a study with the National Opinion Research Center, was assigned the task of obtaining household composition information to form a sample for the study. Procedures were based on those suggested by Sudman [Item No. 259]. Telephone numbers were randomly selected from the Chicago city directory. The last two digits of each number were then dropped and replaced by a random selection of two-digit numbers. Five different methods varying the introduction, the rapport-building questions, and interviewer style were used. Telephone attempts were made with 1,199 numbers of which 323 (26.9 percent) were ineligible. Complete household information was obtained from 501 of the 876 eligible households (57.2 percent). Refusals (34.9 percent) were the primary cause of the low-response rate. Cost per completed interview was $3.20. The authors compare the results of the five interviewing methods. RDD is viewed as a fast, lower-cost way to obtain household data necessary to locate special populations. (12 footnotes)

233.   Klecka, William, and Al Tuchfarber. "The Efficacy of Random Digit Dialing." *Survey Research* 5, no. 1 (January 1973): 14-15.

Telephone interviewing is described as being both less costly and faster than personal interviewing. Random digit dialing (RDD) eliminates most of the problems associated with telephone directories and similar lists. Two surveys conducted using RDD are compared with results from the 1970 Census. Comparisons are made in the areas of African Americans, the poor, sex and age, new enfranchised voters, and race and school enrollment. Both surveys were "quite close" to the census figures (with only a few exceptions). RDD provides an approximately random selection of households, but not individuals. Telephone interviewing is cited as useful when the information needed can be achieved in a fifteen- to twenty-minute interview.

234.   Klecka, William R., and Alfred J. Tuchfarber. "Random Digit Dialing: A Comparison to Personal Surveys." *Public Opinion Quarterly* 42, no. 1 (Spring 1978): 105-14.

The hypothesis tested is that random digit dialing (RDD) is a viable alternative to face-to-face interviewing in terms of cost, accuracy, and efficiency. In this study the results of an RDD survey are compared with data obtained from a personal interview survey. The latter was based on a complex probability sample of Cincinnati, Ohio, households on which the U.S. Bureau of the Census had done a crime victimization study in 1974. One month later the University of Cincinnati, using an RDD sample, replicated the crime study in two surveys. In the census study 9,708 households and 19,903 persons were interviewed; the two RDD studies covered 800 households and 1,639 persons and 662 households and 1,147 persons. The three types of questions asked focused on demographic information, measures of crime victimization, and attitudes toward police and crime. The hypothesis was upheld, as the data generated by the two methods were very similar. Advantages of RDD are discussed and, given the much lower cost of RDD surveys, Klecka and Tuchfarber conclude that telephone surveys will continue to gain popularity. (7 footnotes, 16 references)

235.   Klecka, William R., and Alfred J. Tuchfarber, Jr. "Random Digit Dialing as an Efficient Method for Political Polling." *GPSA Journal* (Georgia Political Science Association) 2 (Spring 1974): 133-51.

Beginning with a discussion of telephone surveys in general, the authors move to the consideration of sampling methods for telephone interviewing. The question as to whether random digit dialing (RDD) produces biased samples is raised. The authors compared RDD-collected data with results from 1970 U.S. Bureau of the Census data. A sample of 1,049 adults in Hamilton County, Ohio, was selected during June 1972. One bias area was detected: renter-occupied households were "significantly under-sampled." RDD is designed to generate random samples of households, rather than individual characteristics. The sample produced a higher percentage of those aged twenty-seven to forty-six (it is believed that young parents are more likely to be at home during the evenings). Another RDD study involved respondents aged eighteen to twenty, which created a random sample of individuals. Males were underrepresented, with no bias against African Americans. The experience of the Ohio Poll Survey using RDD is described. Klecka and Tuchfarber state that RDD samples are "relatively inexpensive, take less time in the field, and [are] not seriously biased for most purposes, and they do have some shortcomings." (22 endnotes)

236.   Kviz, Frederick J. "Random Digit Dialing and Sample Bias." *Public Opinion Quarterly* 42, no. 4 (Winter 1978-79): 544-46.

Kviz criticizes an article by Tull and Albaum [Item No. 242] which attempted to determine bias in a random digit dialing sample. According to Kviz, the authors tested the wrong null hypothesis: "that there is no difference between telephone subscribers and nonsubscribers with respect to the selected demographic variables, housing unit characteristics, and ownership of durable goods." The question – "How well do random digit dialed samples represent the *general population?*" – should have been the basis for the research. Kviz provides numerous examples of how he feels the data presented by Tull and Albaum underrepresent certain households on some of the demographic variables and housing characteristics tested. (1 footnote, 5 references)

237.   Rich, Clyde L. "Is Random Digit Dialing Really Necessary?" *Journal of Marketing Research* 14, no. 3 (August 1977): 300-305. [Reprinted in *Readings in Survey Research*, edited by Robert Ferber, 409-18. Chicago, IL: American Marketing Association, 1978. 604p.]

There are differences in some demographic characteristics between listed and unlisted telephone subscribers. Rich suggests that since these are small, and the number of subscribers listed is large, that the samples created using telephone directories "have virtually the same demographic characteristics" as samples which include unlisted numbers. For categories in which the number of unlisted telephones is high (such as with mobiles, physicians, politicians, and single women), random digit dialing is recommended with the recognition that this approach is costlier. The results are based on a review of surveys conducted by Pacific Telephone over a thirteen-year period. The reasons why subscribers choose to have nonpublished or unlisted numbers are discussed. The demographic characteristics considered include the following: (1) sex; (2) age of head of household; (3) occupation; (4) own/rent; (5) length of residence; (6) number of moves in the last six years; (7) education; (8) number in household; (9) income; (10) life cycle; and (11) type of residence. (3 references)

238.   Sims, J. Taylor, and John F. Willenborg. "Random-Digit Dialing: A Practical Application." *Journal of Business Research* 4, no. 4 (November 1976): 371-81.

The article reports on a study in which random digit dialing (RDD) was successfully used in a statewide attitude survey. The approach eliminates the problem of telephone directory noninclusion and reduces interviewer bias (since a subjective judgment as to whether a directory listing is a business or something other than the desired household number is avoided). The RDD approach can save time and money over other methods. In very small areas where there are a limited number of telephones, RDD will probably not be useful, and therefore it will be more cost and time effective to use directories. Sampling method, interviewing procedures, representativeness, and consistency are discussed in relationship to the use of RDD in this study. (3 endnotes, 8 references)

239.   Tuchfarber, Alfred J., and William F. Klecka. *Random Digit Dialing: Lowering the Cost of Victimization Surveys.* [Washington, DC]: Police Foundation, 1976. 157p.

Written as a handbook, this work is designed to permit the duplication of the random digit dialing (RDD) victimization survey techniques by administrators, planners, or researchers. The historical background of RDD is reviewed, followed by a discussion of the advantages of RDD versus personal interviewing. The testing of the accuracy of RDD in relation to the work of the sixty-thousand household National Crime Panel Surveys conducted by the Law Enforcement Assistance Administration and the Bureau of the Census is presented, with the actual comparison data in the next chapter. In the chapter titled "Using RDD" the following aspects are addressed: (1) planning and administration; (2) sampling; (3) recruiting supervisors and interviewers; (4) training of supervisors and interviewers; (5) questionnaire design; (6) interviewing; (7) screening out ineligible respondents; (8) callback and no-answer procedures; and (9) coding and keypunching. Tuchfarber and Klecka discuss data processing and analysis, along with the creation of the Crime Code and Crime Rates. Five appendixes are included. (18 references)

240.   Tuchfarber, Alfred J., William R. Klecka, Barbara A. Bardes, and Robert W. Oldendick. "Reducing the Cost of Victim Surveys." In *Sample Surveys of the Victims of Crime*, edited by Wesley G. Skogan, 207-21. Cambridge, MA: Ballinger Publishing Company, [1976]. 230p.

Random digit dialing (RDD) is defined as telephone interviewing "coupled with the use of a sample of telephone numbers that has been generated at random." The advantages of telephone interviewing over personal interviewing are covered. The accuracy of RDD is explored with a comparison of demographic characteristics,

RDD, and Bureau of the Census samples. Crime victimization rates are presented with RDD results next to census figures. RDD is shown to be a reliable survey method. Those individuals lacking a telephone do not appear to bias the sample demographically, and in the case of crime data, the information collection is also not adversely affected. The authors describe the option of RDD as an "accurate and efficient method" which, due to its lower cost, can be used by many local criminal justice agencies. (15 notes)

241.   Tuchfarber, Alfred John, Jr. "Random Digit Dialing: A Test of Accuracy and Efficiency." Ph.D. diss., University of Cincinnati, 1974. 163 leaves. [*Dissertation Abstracts International* Order No. 7503375; *DAI* 34A, no. 8 (February 1975): 5492.]

Random digit dialing (RDD) is defined as "telephone interviewing coupled with the random selection of a sample of telephone numbers from ALL possible telephone numbers." Both the accuracy and the efficiency are empirically tested through two large surveys conducted in Cincinnati, Ohio. One survey was of the entire city; the second was of the inner city – an area with few telephones. Demographic data gathered from these surveys, as well as from some conventional surveys, were compared to census data. RDD was found to be as accurate or more accurate than traditional methods for samples of the general population. It was also accurate for samples of subpopulations with high telephone subscription rates. (At the present time about 95 percent of U.S. households have telephones.) RDD was found to be only 15 to 25 percent as costly as face-to-face interviewing. Completion rates were very high. References are provided.

242.   Tull, Donald S., and Gerald S. Albaum. "Bias in Random Digit Dialed Surveys." *Public Opinion Quarterly* 41, no. 3 (Fall 1977): 389-95.

A number of studies are reviewed which concentrate on the effects of excluding unlisted telephone subscribers and nonsubscribers from surveys. The potential for bias resulting from this omission is briefly discussed. Random digit dialing (RDD) is suggested as one method of dealing with the problem. Since over 13 percent of households in 1970 had no telephone service, bias should be considered in RDD surveys. Telephone ownership data were gathered from the Public Use Samples of the *1970 Census of Population and Housing* for the simulated RDD survey, along with demographic and housing characteristics and ownership of durable goods. Results indicate that "the differences between the simulated RDD survey values and the values for the households with no telephone available were significant in all cases at the .001 level." Households with telephones tend to be headed by a white male with higher than average age, income, and educational level, and who is self-employed or who works for a government agency. Those with telephones also live in single homes that they were buying and own more automobiles and household appliances. A criticism of this research appears in an article by Kviz [Item No. 236]. (5 footnotes, 10 references)

243. Waksberg, Joseph. "Sampling Methods for Random Digit Dialing." *Journal of the American Statistical Association* 73, no. 361 (March 1978): 40-46.

Sample selection methods for household telephone interviewing with the use of random digit dialing are presented. With all the units having the same probability of selection, the approach is less costly than surveys which employ the technique of dialing numbers completely at random. Three different cluster sampling variations are discussed. Sample sizes for repeated surveys, cost reductions, and weighting, stratification, and poststratification are considered. Waksberg reviews a series of statistical issues with telephone surveys including the following: (1) the effect of a household with multiple telephone numbers; (2) some "no" answers represent nonworking numbers; (3) a good record-keeping system is necessary for random digit dialing, as the procedure is "in a sense" sequential; and (4) not all surveys can be conducted as telephone interviews (personal interviews are usually used for very long interviews and whenever visual aids are called for). (11 references)

Bibliography

244. Daniel, Wayne W. *The Use of Random Digit Dialing in Telephone Surveys: An Annotated Bibliography*. Public Administration Series: Bibliography no. P-223. Monticello, IL: Vance Bibliographies, 1979. 10p.

Random digit dialing (RDD) was introduced in 1964 by Cooper [Item No. 252] as a method of generating, at random and with equal probability, telephone numbers to be called in a survey. There are 33 annotated citations in this bibliography which lists 4 books, 18 journal articles, 7 conference proceedings, 3 published and unpublished reports, and 1 dissertation. Of the total, 29 references are from the 1970s, 3 are from the 1960s, and 1 is undated. The *Journal of Marketing Research* (7 entries) is the most frequently cited journal, followed by *Public Opinion Quarterly* (4 entries) and *Survey Research* (3 entries). Nearly all references are published in the United States. Annotation length ranges from 17 words to approximately 106 words. All of the entries in the Daniels's bibliography (except for two non-RDD citations) can also be found in a bibliography emanating from the Survey Methodology Information System [Item No. 17].

Random Digit Table

245. RAND Corporation. *A Million Random Digits with 100,000 Normal Deviates*. New York, NY: Free Press, 1955. 600p.

The inclusion of this volume is based on the frequency with which it has been cited in the polling and survey literature. The introduction explains how the random digits were produced, along with tests on the random digits. Normal deviates are discussed, and the last section considers the use of the tables. The subsequent 400 pages consist of the million random digits, followed by 200 pages containing the 100,000 normal deviates (page header – "Table of Gaussian Deviates"). The introduction includes an eleven-entry bibliography.

Unlisted Numbers

246.   Blankenship, A. B. "Listed versus Unlisted Numbers in Telephone Survey Samples." *Journal of Advertising Research* 17, no. 1 (February 1977): 39-42.

In 1977 Blankenship recognized that telephone surveys will be the "method of the future." Citing the increasing resistance to personal interviews in homes as a consequence of fear and resentment, he believes the future lies with the Wide Area Telecommunications Service (WATS) and control facilities which supervise and oversee production at all levels. Fundamental to this approach is the selection of an appropriate sample, which Blankenship maintains can be dependably obtained only through the use of random digit dialing. Data are presented from three research firms (Marketing and Research Counselors, Incorporated; A. C. Nielsen Company; and Trendex, Incorporated) which show similarities and differences between homes with listed and unlisted telephones. The national average for unlisted telephones is cited as 17.8 percent with metropolitan Los Angeles at 33.9 percent and New York City at 26.9 percent. Tables provide breakdowns by geographic region, annual income, age of child(ren), age of male head, and age of female head. (11 references)

247.   Brunner, James A., and G. Allen Brunner. "Are Voluntarily Unlisted Telephone Subscribers Really Different?" *Journal of Marketing Research* 8, no. 1 (February 1971): 121-24.

The issue is whether the population listed in telephone directories is the same or different from those voluntarily unlisted. A study of the Toledo, Ohio, vicinity, conducted in 1967, used personal interviews (688 for listed, and 402 unlisted subscribers from a "confidential source which identified the population of those who requested their numbers to be unlisted"). The hypothesis was that unlisted subscribers are significantly different from those listed. The study demonstrated that there are statistically significant differences in a number of characteristics in households with listed and unlisted numbers. Characteristics compared include the following: (1) education; (2) age; (3) marital status; (4) occupation; (5) residence; (6) group membership; (7) race; (8) corporate or noncorporate residence; (9) single/multiple dwelling unit; (10) size of family; (11) number of children;

(12) number of persons over eighteen years; (13) own or rent; (14) residence at address; and (15) family income. Also examined was a list of product ownership including luxury items and automobiles. Tables 1 through 3 cover these in detail. (2 references)

248.   Glasser, Gerald J., and Gale D. Metzger. "National Estimates of Non-listed Telephone Households and Their Characteristics." *Journal of Marketing Research* 12, no. 3 (August 1975): 359-61.

RADAR [Radio's All-Dimension Audience Research] studies, conducted annually for four years from 1970 to 1974 by Statistical Research, Incorporated, examined telephone directories to estimate the number of non-listed telephone households. The research was funded by four radio networks: ABC, CBS, MBS [the Mutual Broadcasting System], and NBC. While the characteristics of the nonlisted telephone households have been "relatively consistent," there has been "no apparent trend." Almost one in five telephone households is excluded from telephone directories. The two major reasons are that they have elected to be unlisted or that they have moved and are not yet listed. Higher percentages of unlisted numbers appear in households in the western United States, in major metropolitan areas, and among nonwhites. Those individuals between eighteen and thirty-four years of age are also more frequently not listed. Glasser and Metzger advise noting these characteristics when designing sample surveys. (3 references)

249.   Roslow, Sydney, and Laurence Roslow. "Unlisted Phone Subscribers Are Different." *Journal of Advertising Research* 12, no. 4 (August 1972): 35-38.

The Roslows found that samples which are based solely on listed telephones can lead to biased results, both for a behavioral characteristic as well as with demographic factors. The study, conducted by The Pulse, Incorporated, involved 905 individuals in 448 households from three counties in the Toledo Metropolitan Area. The issue being addressed is whether radio listening patterns are different for listed and unlisted telephone users. The data collected reported respondents' listening habits across several radio stations. The study results indicate differences between listed versus unlisted telephone subscribers in the areas of audience share achieved by contemporary music radio stations, by FM stations, and by non-Toledo based stations. (7 references)

250.   Wolfe, Lee M. "Characteristics of Persons with and without Home Telephones." *Journal of Marketing Research* 16, no. 3 (August 1979): 421-25.

Data from the National Opinion Research Center's General Social Surveys from 1973 to 1977 were the basis for this study. A sample of 7,507 respondents was collected from the five-year period. From this group 85.5 percent reported that they could be reached at home by telephone, 10.2 percent reported they could not be reached by telephone in their home, and 4.3 percent declined to answer the question or failed to identify the location of their telephone. The data indicate that less than 2 percent of the responses on a single item in a telephone sample will vary from equivalent responses of a sample from the total population. Wolfe notes that when trying to forecast a close election, such an error margin would not be acceptable. In other types of surveys the results could be adjusted for the bias, or perhaps a personal interview approach may be more advisable. Seventeen characteristics are compared for those with and without telephones. (19 references)

Sample Design

251.   Chilton Research Services. *A National Probability Sample of Telephone Households Using Computerized Sampling Techniques.* Radnor, PA: Chilton Research Services, 1976. (7 numbered plus 4 additional pages of tables and appendix)

A two-stage national sample of all telephone households in the forty-eight continental United States and the District of Columbia is described. As of January 1970, over 90 percent of all U.S. households could be reached by telephone. The first stage of the design was to select the sample of telephone central offices, followed by a computerized random selection of telephone households within these central offices. The procedure for selecting the central offices and then identifying telephone "addresses" is explained. The operating procedures are outlined which describe how callbacks, not-at-homes, and business numbers are dealt with. Refusals are discussed, with the observation that callbacks can stimulate responses in many cases. Several tables and a technical appendix (including projecting to the total United States) are included. (2 unnumbered footnotes)

252.   Cooper, Sanford L. "Random Sampling by Telephone – An Improved Method." *Journal of Marketing Research* 1, no. 4 (November 1964): 45-58.

Cooper identifies and discusses a problem with telephone directories and suggests an alternate procedure. At the beginning of a telephone directory year, between 6 and 9 percent of residential subscribers are not listed, and by the end of the year some 18 percent will be omitted (due to unlisted numbers, individuals who have moved, and errors). Using the appropriate three-digit telephone exchange numbers for an area, plus the next digit as assigned by the telephone company for a particular area, the first four numbers can narrow the range to a particular area. Through utilization of a table of random numbers, the remaining three numbers can be added. Cooper's application of this approach increased the number of interviews by 40 percent over the telephone directory method. The increase in the time required for this new procedure was from 5 to 20 percent. (1 reference)

253.   Groves, Robert M. "An Empirical Comparison of Two Telephone Sample Designs." *Journal of Marketing Research* 15, no. 4 (November 1978): 622-31.

The clustered telephone sample design described by Waksberg [Item No. 243] is compared with a design randomly generating four-digit numbers within working telephone prefixes. Groves describes the two designs, discusses the disposition of sample numbers, and compares the sampling variance of estimates and the variance-cost of the two designs. The clustered sample increases the working household numbers selected from approximately 22 percent to over 55 percent, but the clustered design shows some loss of precision. Groves maintains that the precision loss in the clustered design is offset by the increased number of working household numbers in the sample. (17 footnotes, 7 references)

254.   Landon, E. Laird, Jr., and Sharon K. Banks. "Relative Efficiency and Bias of Plus-One Telephone Sampling." *Journal of Marketing Research* 14, no. 3 (August 1977): 294-99. [Reprinted in *Readings in Survey Research*, edited by Robert Ferber, 298-408. Chicago, IL: American Marketing Association, 1978. 604p.]

Plus-one telephone sampling involves adding one to the last digit of a systematic sample taken from a telephone directory. This approach has been employed because of ease and the inclusion of unlisted telephone numbers. A possible bias may be that not all telephone numbers have an equal chance of inclusion. Non-directory and directory sample designs are discussed. Two approaches are compared in a study, one being random digit design, the other plus-one design. The study shows that the plus-one approach is more efficient, as nonworking numbers are not included. The authors suggest cautious application of the plus-one approach, but warn of "oddities in the way telephone numbers and listings are made by telephone companies." (11 references)

255.   Stock, J. Stevens. "How to Improve Samples Based on Telephone Listings: Simply Weight Households in a Cluster Started from a Telephone Directory by the Reciprocal of the Proportion of Them Listed in It." *Journal of Advertising Research* 2, no. 3 (September 1962): 50-51.

Telephone books are valued as good sources reflecting changes which have occurred in populations for the period up to six months prior to the issuance of the
directory. Stock speaks of probability sampling as one in which "every unit has
some chance [of being included] and that the chance in every case is known."
The Politz-Simmons "nights-at-home formula" [Item No. 617] which uses no
callbacks when the respondent is not at home is discussed. The use of weight
clusters is addressed, beginning with the interviewing of five consecutive households to the left of a randomly selected household listed in the telephone directory. Stock acknowledges that bias exists in the approach although he describes
it as providing an "important statistical gain."

256.   Troldahl, Verling C., and Roy E. Carter, Jr. "Random Selection of Re-
        spondents within Households in Phone Surveys." *Journal of Marketing
        Research* 1, no. 2 (May 1964): 71-76.

The approach is designed to guide the interviewer to randomly select one adult
per household. Two questions are asked, with the interviewer choosing the respondent by examining the intersection of two lines drawn on a chart. The method
has been used in a metropolitan area as well as in a smaller city. The technique
proposed by Kish [Item No. 218] involves the telephone interviewer asking immediately for the ages of all present in the household or their rank order. This
approach leads to "suspicious" respondents simply hanging up the telephone
without having received any explanation of the procedure. The alternative method
suggested here asks, (1) "How many persons eighteen years or older live in your
household . . . counting yourself?" and (2) "How many of them are men?" The
selection process and mechanics of interviewing are further described. A discussion of possible biases follows, along with estimates of bias in the selection procedure. (7 references)

Telephone Directories

257.   Leuthold, David A., and Raymond Scheele. "Patterns of Bias in Sam-
        ples Based on Telephone Directories." *Public Opinion Quarterly* 35, no.
        2 (Summer 1971): 249-57.

Two statewide surveys conducted in the state of Missouri were used as sources
of data on households without telephones and on those with unlisted numbers.
There were 929 respondents in the first sample and 1,924 in the second. Some
of the characteristics for respondents without telephones are as follows: (1) there
was a sharp decline in ownership since 1960 (22 to 10 percent); (2) many tended
to live in rural areas; (3) those with low incomes were not as likely to have a
telephone; and (4) segments of the society considered to be "isolated" were most
likely not to have a telephone. Some of the characteristics for respondents with

unlisted numbers are as follows: (1) about 9 percent (perhaps an underreported figure) had unlisted numbers; (2) there was no correlation with income or occupation; (3) there was a high incidence of nonlisting among African Americans; (4) city dwellers were more likely to have unlisted numbers; and (5) rates were also higher for apartment dwellers, among young, divorced, or separated people, and among labor union members, service workers, and single-parent households. When totaled, the two categories (no telephones and unlisted numbers) represent the percentage which will not be included in a sample based on telephone directories. The authors believe the data indicate the "direction of the biases" that may be inherent in using telephone directories for sample selection. They state that "such samples will exclude one-third or more of the blacks, the separated and divorced, and service workers, and one-fourth or more of the large city-dwellers." Comments are made concerning possible bias, comparative costs with personal interviews, the effect of random digit dialing, and the use of city directories as sources for samples. (15 footnotes)

258.   Perry, Joseph B., Jr. "A Note on the Use of Telephone Directories as a Sample Source." *Public Opinion Quarterly* 32, no. 4 (Winter 1968-69): 691-95.

Although expedient and inexpensive, the telephone book has for some time been regarded as an undesirable source for sample surveys. This view stems largely from the failure of the *Literary Digest* to correctly predict the 1936 presidential election. Data provided by the Bureau of the Census on the number of households with telephones have made it possible to determine the extent of bias introduced through the use of a sample drawn from telephone directories. The Census Bureau's guide *One-in-a-Thousand and the One-in-Ten-Thousand Samples* [(*sic 1/1,000-1/10,000) Samples Description and Technical Documentation.* Washington, DC: U.S. Bureau of the Census, 1964. 1 volume plus supplement.] may be useful to a researcher, or alternatively, cross classification can be generated by the bureau. Cooper's technique for generating a random selection of telephone numbers is recommended for overcoming some of the problems of drawing samples from telephone directories [Item No. 252]. (12 footnotes)

259.   Sudman, Seymour. "Uses of Telephone Directories for Survey Sampling." *Journal of Marketing Research* 10, no. 2 (May 1973): 204-7.

According to the author, the combined use of telephone directories, random digit dialing (RDD), and door-to-door listings is superior to using any single approach, with the further observation that some uses of directories are of higher quality and less expense than the alternatives. Sudman discusses how to determine the percentage of households without telephones or listed telephone numbers. The effect of unlisted telephones is reviewed, citing one community which has 16 percent of the telephones unlisted. A procedure is described for estimating the increase in the number of households by using telephone directories (to compensate for the speed with which census data becomes outdated). Procedures to increase the efficiency of RDD are outlined, as well as the use of telephone directories in face-to-face interviewing. Sudman maintains that developing a file of telephone directories is valuable for a continuing survey. (6 references)

QUESTIONS

BIAS

260.   Hesse, Sharlene J., Ina B. Burstein, and Geri E. Atkins. "Sex Role Bias
in Public Opinion Questionnaires." *Social Policy* 10, no. 3 (November-December 1979): 51-56.

According to the authors, sex role bias has existed during five decades of polling
questions. This bias is exhibited through stereotyped content, by omissions, and
by gender wording. Hesse and her colleagues show that males dominate in frequency of representation as well as in the roles portrayed. They argue that the
choice of polling language serves to "perpetuate differential male and female
behaviors and relationships." Further, it is suggested that the "hierarchies of occupation, income, power, and influence are fixed in favor of men and worded to
prevent rearrangement." The authors call for the use of "they" instead of "she" or
"he" for an increased sensitivity to the problem of sex role bias and for greater
emphasis on poll accuracy and validity. [See Item No. 264 for a related study.]
(12 references)

261.   Kornhauser, Arthur. "Are Public Opinion Polls Fair to Organized Labor?"
Public Opinion Quarterly 10, no. 4 (Winter 1946-47): 484-500.

Three basic questions are addressed: (1) Is the choice of subject matter in polls
one-sided? (2) Are poll questions worded fairly or are they "loaded for or
against labor"? and (3) Are poll results impartially reported? Kornhauser maintains that the evidence indicates that "labor poll material is biased." Topic choice,
question wording, and reporting of results show that "unionism fails to receive balanced and impartial treatment." The author believes that polls are "clearly

not fair to organized labor." A total of 155 poll questions from 1940 to 1945 were examined, of which 8 dealt with positive or favorable aspects of unions, 66 were neutral or doubtful, and 81 dealt with union faults. The section on question wording covers four areas: hidden assumptions, ambiguities, oversimplifications, and suggestive or slanted phraseology. Kornhauser maintains that "painstaking (and time-consuming) work on questions and reports" would significantly reduce the bias noted. Other challenges include the "social-economic pressures upon the opinion polling agencies and, closely associated, the personal social outlook of the agency staffs." (6 footnotes)

262.   Link, Henry C., Albert D. Freiberg, John H. Platten, Jr., and Kenneth E. Clark. "Is Dr. Kornhauser Fair to Organized Pollers?" *Public Opinion Quarterly* 11, no. 2 (Summer 1947): 198-212.

This article is a response to an earlier paper by Kornhauser [Item No. 261]. Four practitioners, each of whom is from a different professional setting, provide their views. Although these authors agree in some respects with Kornhauser's original criticisms, each provides additional alternative perspectives. Link and Freiberg suggest that public opinion research might be called the "science of biases," with the goal of this field being to "measure biases with as little bias as possible." The authors review section by section Kornhauser's primary points, suggesting that standards of fairness are not as simple as described, and that the classification of the questions by Kornhauser is according to a classification of his own making. The issue of question wording is addressed with the observation that the questions are quoted out of context and without the preceding "orienting questions." Link and Freiberg provide specific suggestions for addressing the acknowledged biases. Platten observes that the factual data presented by Kornhauser are open to a number of interpretations, and that individual polling organizations are in the process of challenging the criticisms leveled. Clark raises the issue of the need for research in the area of how readers interpret poll questions. (4 footnotes)

263.   Litwak, Eugene. "A Classification of Biased Questions." *American Journal of Sociology* 62, no. 2 (September 1956): 182-86.

Litwak attempts a systematic classification of biased questions. Five major divisions have been made and appear as these headings: (1) "Bias in Questions as a Function of Purpose"; (2) "Loaded Questions versus Extreme Item"; (3) "Vague Questions versus Exploratory and Projective Questions"; (4) "Double-Barreled Questions versus Preference Scales"; and (5) "Measurement Theory and a Classification of Errors." In tabular form the author illustrates the classification scheme, with errors of dimension across the top and errors of the trace line down the side. Litwak believes that the search for the perfect question is trivial, and that empirical research could systematically classify question structure,

thereby converting questionnaire construction from an art into a science. (6 footnotes)

264.   "Sexist Surveys." *Human Behavior* 8, no. 3 (March 1979): 26-27.

The question of bias in a 1976 Gallup questionnaire is briefly addressed. The
poll on women's social roles concluded that women's attitudes about themselves
"bind them to tradition." Three researchers, Hesse, Burstein, and Atkins, in a
paper titled "Sex Role Bias in Public Opinion Questionnaires" [Item No. 260],
analyzed 3,361 national survey questions used from 1936 to 1973. The study
was undertaken to determine the "extent to which traditional opinions on sex
roles might be reinforced by the content and wording of survey questions." The
study authors conclude that the bias in questionnaires prevents the public from
expressing an unbiased opinion. They state: "The questions offer virtually no opportunity to express equitable attitudes toward men and women. The hierarchies
of occupation, income, power and influence are fixed in favor of men and worded
to prevent rearrangement."

265.   Suchman, Edward A., and Louis Guttman. "A Solution to the Problem
        of Question 'Bias.' " *Public Opinion Quarterly* 11, no. 3 (Fall 1947):
        445-55.

The authors review numerous factors which can cause surveys to yield different
proportions of "favorable" and "unfavorable" responses on the same issues. These
factors include subtle changes in phrasing, the order of the presentation of answer categories, and the position of the question on the questionnaire. Suchman
and Guttman describe an objective method for eliminating the problem of question bias based on scale analysis and intensity analysis. The method attempts to
divide respondents into "pro and con groups which are relatively independent of
question wording." (According to the authors, the theoretical aspects will be
presented elsewhere.) Five steps of the procedure are explained, and two examples demonstrate the technique. The samples concern the opinions of soldiers
toward the army and toward their officers. The method results in an intensity
curve, the middle of which represents decreased intensity of feeling. The lowest
point of the curve stays the same regardless of the particular questions used or
how they were worded. The midpoint divides the population into positive and
negative. The authors conclude by stating that the "study of the shape of curves
may provide leads in developing a theory as to when other behavior can or cannot be predicted from attitudes or opinions." (4 footnotes)

DESIGN

266.   Berdie, Frances S. "To Rile Your Community, Ask Questions Like These." *American School Board Journal* 157, no. 12 (June 1970): 28.

The Exploratory Committee on Assessing the Progress of Education tested average citizens on a number of questions to determine which ones should be omitted as offensive. Eleven areas of concern were identified: (1) invasion of privacy; (2) minority groups; (3) sex; (4) religion; (5) human rights; (6) emotion-arousing terms; (7) violence or cruelty; (8) suggestive words and phrases; (9) censorship; (10) slurs about specific groups or individuals; and (11) inferiority of other nations. The intent of the committee was to enable the National Assessment of Educational Progress to conduct a national survey and to avoid offensive question wording to individuals or groups anywhere in the population.

267.   Borus, Michael E. "Response Error and Questioning Technique in Surveys of Earnings Information." *Journal of the American Statistical Association* 65, no. 330 (June 1970): 566-75.

Two questioning techniques for determining earnings information are compared. The data were gathered initially through three hundred personal interviews conducted in Fort Wayne, Indiana. The second source was data on wages as reported by employers to the Indiana Employment Security Division. Each respondent was asked two broad earnings questions (taken from the 1960 Census), as well as their last three-year work history. For urban low-income neighborhoods the broad question method was as accurate as the work history approach. As the broad question format is less expensive and easier to use, it is recommended for the described setting. The opposite is true for higher-income groups where the work history approach is more accurate. There are four tables provided, with the last being useful in determining how middle-class groups should be addressed, depending upon level of income and years of education. (4 footnotes, 17 references)

268.   Bradburn, Norman M. "Selecting the Questions to Be Asked in Surveys." *Monthly Labor Review* 93, no. 1 (January 1970): 27-29.

Bradburn outlines and discusses what he considers to be five obstacles in the selection of social-psychological survey questions. They are as follows: (1) disagreement among behavioral scientists as to what the relevant variables should be; (2) lack of consensus among behavioral scientists as to the importance of particular variables; (3) lack of interest in methodological research and survey measurement ("the research that is done tends to be fragmented, local, unpublished, and usually specific to particular studies"); (4) underdevelopment of measurement theory ("as compared with the sophistication of sampling theory"); and (5) difficulties arising from shifts in language usage over time, phraseology problems, and wording differences. The author offers some rules of thumb "for use in asking the general questions about what questions to select" to improve the quality of survey research methodology.

269.   Cantril, Hadley, and Edrita Fried. "The Meaning of Questions." Part 1, Chap. 1 in *Gauging Public Opinion*, by Hadley Cantril and Research Associates in the Office of Public Opinion Research, Princeton University, 3-22. Princeton, NJ: Princeton University Press, 1944. Reprint. Port Washington, NY: Kennikat Press, 1972. 318p.

In this chapter Cantril and Fried address some of the difficulties encountered in the writing of questions. These include the following: (1) questions that are too vague and obscure in meaning to permit precise answers; (2) questions "getting at some stereotype or overtone implicit in the questions rather than at the meanings intended"; (3) questions that are misunderstood due to the use of technical or unfamiliar words or whose implications are not understood; (4) questions with alternatives that are too long, or too many alternatives are presented; (5) questions "concerned with only a portion of the population and therefore meaningless to many people"; and (6) questions which get only at surface generalizations and which initiate only stereotyped answers. These points reflect areas which Cantril and Fried maintain must be avoided in order to achieve reliable results from public opinion surveys. (6 footnotes)

270.   Duncanson, J. P. "The Average Telephone Call Is Better Than the Average Telephone Call." *Public Opinion Quarterly* 33, no. 1 (Spring 1969): 112-16.

The article deals with the validity of questions such as "How does this telephone call compare with your usual telephone call? Is it better or worse, or about the same?" Duncanson describes how he believes bias may be present when a respondent is requested to compare a present stimulus with an average of past stimuli or the present item with past items. He suggests that a more appropriate alternative is to ask a respondent to compare a single present stimulus with a usual one. Reported in the article are three studies of telephone transmission quality in which data of the latter variety were collected. The first and second studies involved the use of telephone interviews, while the third used a questionnaire. It was found that "ratings of single, recent telephone calls yield results different from ratings of subjectively averaged, past telephone calls." (1 footnote)

271.   Gallup, George. "The Quintamensional Plan of Question Design." *Public Opinion Quarterly* 11, no. 3 (Fall 1947): 385-93.

In response to numerous criticisms of public opinion measurement, Gallup describes a new system of question design – the "quintamensional" approach. The five-part technique evolved from research by the American Institute of Public Opinion. The design allows "the survey organization to exclude from poll results the answers of any and all persons who are uniformed on any given issue." The five categories consist of these five question types: (1) filter or information questions determine if a respondent has given any thought or attention to the issue; (2) open- or free-answer questions are designed to obtain unstructured opinions; (3) dichotomous or specific issue questions "ask the public to stand up and be counted" on specific issues and usually require a "yes" or "no" answer; (4) "reasons why" questions seek explanations as to why people feel as they do; and (5) intensity questions measure the degree with which opinions are held by the respondent. Examples of each question type, advantages, and possible applications of the system are given. Gallup believes the most important feature of the plan is that it allows the information that is gathered from probing the five aspects to be intercorrelated.

272.   Mosteller, Frederick, and Philip J. McCarthy. "Estimating Population Proportions." *Public Opinion Quarterly* 6, no. 3 (Fall 1942): 452-58.

The limitations of using answers to a single poll question in estimating population proportions in attitude categories are reviewed. For example, researchers may find it difficult to use only one determining question, or the ability and truthfulness of respondents to categorize themselves may be dubious. In this article Mosteller and McCarthy propose a method for the accurate estimation from a set or battery of questions. The number of categories into which the population is being divided for the survey is decided in advance. Questions are constructed so that "there are the same number of possible responses as there are categories." The results of a sample poll focusing on a war-time issue (interventionism versus isolationism position) are given to illustrate the technique. The authors believe that the method proposed may "be readily extended to any number of questions and any number of categories." Advanced statistics are used throughout the article. (2 footnotes)

273.   Nirenberg, Jesse S. "New Study Shows Management the Most Fruitful Way to Question Consumers: A Study by Psychologist Dr. Jesse Nirenberg Compares the Effectiveness of Three Consumer Research Techniques – Direct Questioning, Projective Tests, Depth Probing. The *Printers' Ink*-Sponsored Study Ranks the Three." *Printers' Ink* 265, no. 10 (5 December 1958): 73-74.

Three types of questions are compared: structured, semistructured, and unstructured. The "structure" refers to the degree to which the question limits the answer possibilities. For example, a structured approach might have a "yes" or "no" answer. The semistructured question provides part of a sentence which respondents would then complete using their own words. In the unstructured mode the interviewer simply refers to the topic at issue, thus permitting the respondent to talk about it, with the interviewer drawing out the person on areas in which the respondent chooses to focus. The study used three groups of twenty respondents each. The author maintains the most productive approach is to use unstructured questions on a small sample to uncover attitudes, and then to utilize the findings as the basis for semistructured questionnaires for inclusion in the main sample.

274.   Payne, Stanley L. "Case Study in Question Complexity." *Public Opinion Quarterly* 13, no. 4 (Winter 1949-50): 653-58.

A "tight" question is defined as one in which "the order of stating the alternatives" makes little difference in the choices of respondents, with "loose" questions "more respondents tend to choose the alternative which is stated last." Payne hypothesized that the "extent to which respondents were confused by the question might show up in the degree to which the answers varied as the alternatives were transposed." In a national survey sponsored by the American Petroleum Institute, 6,400 people were divided into two matched cross sections. Sixteen questions, each containing an alternative, were asked. Analysis of the findings indicates that the loose questions' alternative was chosen more frequently when it was presented last, and opinions were held more strongly. Short questions made up of simple words were important elements of a tight question. Payne uses Rudolf Flesch's book *The Art of Plain Talk* to judge the readability of the sixteen survey questions. By this method nine questions were tight at the seventh- to eighth-grade level, and seven were rated as difficult or loose at the late high-school or college level. Payne reiterates the need for straightforward, short, and less complex questions. (2 footnotes).

275.   Payne, Stanley L. "Some Opinion Research Principles Developed through Studies of Social Medicine." *Public Opinion Quarterly* 10, no. 1 (Spring 1946): 93-98.

In 1943 the Opinion Research Corporation (ORC) conducted a poll concerning attitudes toward social medicine, in which 16 percent of the American people approved. The following year a National Opinion Research Center (NORC) poll revealed that 68 percent favored the issue. To determine the reason(s) for the apparently widely differing results, ORC conducted six additional polls. The ballots experimented with question order, choice of words, type of approach, use and order of alternatives, and measures of intensity. Several principles evolved from analyzing the results: "(1) When it is desired to interpret opinion in terms of means, questions should be framed so that respondents can disassociate means from ends. (2) If only one means of achieving a desired end is suggested to respondents, that idea may be expected to receive greater endorsement than when alternative means are suggested. (3) Personalization of questions on issues where opinion is not well crystallized may result in answers which differ strikingly from answers to impersonalized questions." Payne believes the wide variations between the ORC and NORC findings are "reconcilable." (1 footnote)

276.   Payne, Stanley L. "Thoughts about Meaningless Questions." *Public Opinion Quarterly* 14, no. 4 (Winter 1950-51): 687-96.

Payne's observations center around five concerns: (1) respondents answer questions that may be meaningless to them, especially when the question is embedded in the normal course of the interview; (2) answers are not always random, depending upon the respondents' predisposition, and there is a tendency to seek the middle ground and familiarity in making their choices; (3) the proportion of respondents for whom questions are meaningless is "virtually impossible" to determine; (4) the respondents' subsequent behavior which was consistent with their answers does not necessarily reflect a meaningful question; and (5) consistency in replies, "no opinion," or "don't know" answers does not necessarily indicate a meaningful question. Suggestions are given for constructing meaningful questions. These include recognizing the issues or terms that could be meaningless to many respondents; using short questions, clear language, and compact sentences; and employing filter questions, scaling techniques, and pretest questions. (11 footnotes)

277.   Terris, Fay. "Are Poll Questions Too Difficult?" *Public Opinion Quarterly* 13, no. 2 (Summer 1949): 314-19.

The study attempts to determine if the questions asked in U.S. national surveys are too difficult for the lesser-educated segments of the population. The two readability indexes used for the experiment were the Flesch (based on average sentence length and number of syllables), and the Dale-Chall (based on the familiarity of words rather than on the degree of abstraction). A total of 144 questions were drawn from *Public Opinion Quarterly* by the National Opinion Research Center, the American Institute of Public Opinion, and the *Fortune* Survey. Forty-eight questions from each of the three polls were rated by both formulas. Five tables present the results by readability formula, by grade level, and by the name of the poll. It was found that over 90 percent of the questions were too difficult for more than 10 percent of the population. Discrepancies occur in the ratings of the questions between the Flesch and the Dale-Chall formulas. Limitations of the study are noted. Simpler language elements, shorter sentences, and simpler words are suggested, along with the use of open-ended questions and questions adapted for various educational levels. (2 footnotes)

EMBARRASSING AND THREATENING

278.   Barton, Allen H. "Asking the Embarrassing Question." *Public Opinion Quarterly* 22, no. 1 (Spring 1958): 67-68.

Barton uses the question – "Did you kill your wife?" – to illustrate eight different ways of presenting the embarrassing type of question in a nonembarrassing manner. The techniques considered are as follows: (1) the casual approach; (2) the numbered card (the respondent selects an answer on a card); (3) the "everybody" approach; (4) the "other people" approach; (5) the sealed ballot technique; (6) the projective technique (the respondent is asked to choose a relevant picture); (7) the Kinsey technique (the respondent is asked in simple language that assumes "everyone has done everything"); and (8) the placement of the question at the end of the interview. The author believes that asking the embarrassing question is a challenge to pollsters.

279.   Blair, Ed, Seymour Sudman, Norman M. Bradburn, and Carol Stocking. "How to Ask Questions about Drinking and Sex: Response Effects in Measuring Consumer Behavior." *Journal of Marketing Research* 14, no. 3 (August 1977): 316-21. [Reprinted in *Readings in Survey Research*, edited by Robert Ferber, 225-35. Chicago, IL: American Marketing Association, 1978. 604p.]

The study was conducted to determine which question format would be most useful when the content was threatening. A national sample drawn from the National Opinion Research Center's national master sample was used, with 1,172 personal interviews conducted. The level of threatening questions ranged from the lowest being on sports activity to the highest being masturbation. In between were questions on various other sexual activities, drug use, and gambling. To answer the frequency question respondents were given a card with eight options ranging from "daily" at the bottom to "never" on top. The questions were posed in various formats, including open-ended, long, and familiar. The results indicate that threatening questions which simply require a "yes" or "no" answer can be asked using any format. However, when an option is to be selected (such as from the card described above), threatening questions achieve the best results when asked in the open-ended, long format with respondent-familiar wording. (26 references)

280.   Bradburn, Norman M., and Seymour Sudman. *Improving Interviewing Method and Questionnaire Design: Response Effects to Threatening Questions in Survey Research.* The NORC Series in Social Research, National Opinion Research Center; The Jossey-Bass Social and Behavioral Science Series. San Francisco, CA: Jossey-Bass Inc., Publishers, 1979. 214p.

Presented are the results of a jointly conducted survey involving the National Opinion Research Center, affiliated with the University of Chicago, and the Survey Research Laboratory of the University of Illinois. The authors discuss the effects of question threat and interview method, examine the impact of the question structure and length, and detail the interviewers' variations in asking the questions. The "relatively small effects" due to interviewer expectations and the effect of acute and chronic anxiety on response are shown. Also considered are the use of the Marlowe-Crowne Scale as a measure of the social desirability effect, informed consent as related to response and quality, and the impact of the presence of others. The use of data gathered from friends (a relatively new technique in 1979) and the issue of using imprecise quantifying words are discussed. A concluding chapter contains commentary on how these results will relate to survey practice. Two appendixes provide the questions used. Six pages of references are included, along with a five-page index.

281.   Bradburn, Norman M., Seymour Sudman, Ed Blair, and Carol Stocking. "Question Threat and Response Bias." *Public Opinion Quarterly* 42, no. 2 (Summer 1978): 221-34.

The investigation tests the hypothesis that respondent underreporting of socially undesirable behaviors will result from threatening or anxiety-producing questions. The relationship between question structure and length, wording familiarity, and response effects is studied. Data are used from a 1975 National Opinion Research Center survey. In a nationwide sample of 1,172 individuals, threatening questions were asked in the framework of a leisure activity study. During the interview, questions became progressively more threatening (for example, gambling, drinking, smoking, marijuana use, drug use, and sexual behavior). Interviewers, using open-ended questions, rated the respondents as to which questions caused uneasiness. The respondents indicated which question topic was too personal. Respondents could either refuse to answer a question or to distort their answers toward perceived acceptability. Those who reported that questions about an activity would make people uneasy were less likely to report involvement in that activity than those who reported less uneasiness (table 2). The authors believe perceived threat may have acted as a "gatekeeper" to prevent further questions, and since underreporting is associated with perceived threat, "some simple adjustment methods may be used to improve estimates of threatening behavior." (31 references)

282.   Locander, William Bernard. "An Investigation of Interview Method, Threat, and Response Distortion." Ph.D. diss., University of Illinois at Urbana-Champaign, 1974. 190 leaves. [*Dissertation Abstracts International* Order No. 7414574; *DAI* 35A, no. 1 (July 1974): 34.]

The foci of this study are question administration, question threat, and response distortion. Face-to-face, telephone, self-administered, and random response methods, accompanied by varying levels of threat, were tested. The results show that question threat is a major source of response distortion. Of the methods used, telephoning was the "most stable technique" across chronic and acute anxiety groups. Telephoning may be "less affected by differences in population" than the other data collection techniques. The respondent's perception of a question is influenced by a combination of the question method, the level of threat, and the anxiety level of the respondent. Questions in the study dealt with ownership of a Chicago Public Library card, voter registration and voter behavior, bankruptcy, and drunken driving. All of the data were validated. References are provided.

FILTER

283.   Bishop, George F., Robert W. Oldendick, Alfred J. Tuchfarber, and Stephen E. Bennett. "Effects of Opinion Filtering and Opinion Floating: Evidence from a Secondary Analysis." *Political Methodology* 6, no. 3 (1979): 293-309.

The authors investigated changes in opinion filter questions instituted in 1964 in the American National Election Studies. Prior to that year the filter question read, "Do you have an opinion on this or not?" In 1964 the wording was changed to, "Have you been interested enough in this to favor one side over the other?" Previous research has indicated that "respondents who are filtered out on survey questions tend to be significantly less educated and less politically involved than those who are not." "Opinion floaters" are defined as individuals who respond either positively or negatively with respect to political attitudes – especially to leaders or groups. The researchers found that the filtering does make a difference. The magnitude of association among attitudinal items increases when respondents lacking opinion or interest are filtered out. However, the filter question/item content interaction is complex, and as yet not fully explored. The authors suggest that the filter question changes may substantially explain why the Survey Research Center/Center for Political Studies data indicated a rise in issue consistency, issue voting, and so forth, once these changes were instituted. Included is an appendix showing questions using the five-point Likert, the dichotomous-choice, and the seven-point scale formats. (4 endnotes, 21 references)

FORMAT

284.   Blankenship, Albert B. "The Influence of the Question Form upon the Response in a Public Opinion Poll." *Psychological Record* 3, no. 23 (March 1940): 347-422. [This is a reprint of Blankenship's dissertation

completed at Columbia University, 1940. 133 leaves. Not available from *Dissertation Abstracts International.*]

The issue of "leading" or "loaded" questions as a biasing element was raised early in the nation's experience with polling. Blankenship sought to answer seven questions concerning the nature of question wording: (1) Are results influenced by question form? (2) Of five question forms employed, which is the most useful in predicting the results of elections? (3) Given two samples of voters, which question form consistently yields the highest response? (4) Which question form enables the respondent to answer freely without influence or interference from the question wording? (5) Which wording generates the smallest number of "don't know" responses? (6) Does question wording influence the next question asked, and if so, how does it affect consistency and "don't know" answers? and (7) Of the questions used in this study, which one is considered to be the best? A study was conducted in Irvington, New Jersey, with three thousand interviews. A pool of at least fifteen hundred registered voters was sought, and the Irvington registration list indicated 50 percent registration. Blankenship concludes that the only certain indication is that further tests in the same community, using different issues, similar tests elsewhere, and national replication, are necessary before reaching any conclusion. References are provided.

285.   Campbell, Albert A. "Two Problems in the Use of the Open Question." *Journal of Abnormal and Social Psychology* 40, no. 3 (July 1945): 340-43.

The open-question format permits respondents to answer using their own language without specific alternatives from which to select. This format is particularly useful in the pretest stage of questionnaire development. The two problems considered dealt with unfulfilled objectives and varying frames of reference. The first problem concerned the respondents' opportunity to evade, as well as to answer insufficiently. The second problem dealt with the possibility of the respondents to view the question from more than one frame of reference. Campbell sees continued and expanded use of the open-question format even though it can lead to "ambiguity rather than clarity." The technique requires precise and thoughtful preparation of the questions, along with careful interviewing. (3 footnotes)

286.   Dohrenwend, Barbara Snell. "Some Effects of Open and Closed Questions on Respondents' Answers." *Human Organization* 24, no. 2 (Summer 1965): 175-84.

The closed question provides a set of brief answers from which the respondent may select, while the open question calls for the respondent to provide a reply. The format for the systematic examination of the effects of open and closed questions was undertaken using a set of four fifteen- to twenty-minute interviews in which the question form, the subject matter of the questions, and the order of the presentation were systematically varied. The author concludes that well-tested closed questions are more advantageous than open questions. Respondents tend to deviate from the topic with questions about the self. Open questions offer the advantages of costing less and being quicker to undertake. However, it was not found that open questions produced more valid answers than the closed-question format. The article contains six tables and an interviewers' guide. (13 footnotes)

287. Ellenbogen, Bert L., and Robert A. Danley. "Comparability of Responses to a Socially Concordant Question – 'Open End' and 'Closed.' " *Journal of Health and Human Behavior* 3, no. 2 (Summer 1962): 136-40.

The researchers sought answers to two questions: (1) Are answers given to open-end questions comparable to those provided for closed-format questions when asked in the same interview? and (2) Do responses vary when the open- and closed-format questions are varied in terms of proximity in the same interview? The setting was upstate New York, and the subject dealt with availability and use of health services among rural and urban residents. Ellenbogen and Danley found that the same "socially-concordant" question produced greater variety in the open-end format than in the closed format. The closed format, by nature, "constrains" the respondents to items from the checklist. There were inconsistencies between answers provided on the closed format when compared with the previously provided open question. Proximity of the questions neither significantly affected the variety nor the consistency of answers. (8 footnotes)

288. Engel, James F., and Hugh G. Wales. "Spoken versus Pictured Questions on Taboo Topics." *Journal of Advertising Research* 2, no. 1 (March 1962): 11-17.

Six questions, ranging from nonconflicted to socially sensitive, were selected for the study. The issues revolved around the doctor-patient relationship and were addressed to a sample of 304 housewives in Champaign-Urbana, Illinois. The group was divided into two, with one receiving the questions in spoken open-end form, and the other in six cartoons covering the same issues. Four interviewers each conducted seventy-six interviews using the same wording for the questions and introductions for the cartoons. The sensitive questions concerned night house calls, aspirin purchase of brand name products versus alternates, and birth control. Engel and Wales observe that the results indicate that two reactions are recorded – one being the private, personal reactions versus those communicated to another. The authors maintain that in order to obtain a more complete picture, more than one survey methodology may be necessary. In the aspirin example 74 percent chose the known brand when asked, whereas only 48 percent chose the known brand when shown the cartoon. (5 references)

289.   Ghiselli, Edwin E. "The Problem of Question Form in the Measure of Sales by Consumer Interviews." *Journal of Marketing* 6, no. 2 (October 1941): 170-71.

The specific issue discussed is narrowly focused on whether a particular brand was purchased last or whether it was "usually" bought by the consumer. The practice had been to ask, "What brand of X did you buy last?" versus a suggested alternative of, "What brand of X do you usually purchase?" Based on study findings, Ghiselli recommends greater interviewer wording latitude specific to brand purchase.

290.   Guest, Lester. "A Comparison of Two-Choice and Four-Choice Questions." *Journal of Advertising Research* 2, no. 1 (March 1962): 32-34.

A ten-item questionnaire was administered in Lock Haven, Pennsylvania, to two groups of adults, one with ninety-five respondents and the other with eighty-six. Personal interviews were conducted in homes with one sample responding with "agree/disagree" answers, the other with "strongly agree," "agree," "disagree," or "strongly disagree." "Don't know" was not an option. The samples, selected by probability, were not "too dissimilar." Guest maintains that the answers to the four-choice option are more meaningful and permit responses in terms of degree. Majority votes from dichotomous questions might not be different from those obtained from the multiple response questions, but the "relative size of positive and negative responses may be substantially different." Guttman scale analysis was used to compare the results. (3 references)

291.   Hesselbart, Susan. "Education, Ethnic Stereotypes, and Question Format." *Sociology and Social Research* 59, no. 3 (April 1975): 266-73.

This review article examines the findings of past studies in the areas of education, ethnic stereotypes, and question format. The research record indicates that question format "influences relationships between education and stereotyping of minority groups." Education may reduce acquiescence response set which Hesselbart defines as the "tendency to agree with almost any strongly worded or opinionated assertion." The author believes that past research poses many questions as to why and under what conditions those that are better educated are less subject to stereotype than their poorly educated counterparts. The race-relations researchers have used question formats "indiscriminately." "Directly phrased" questions show correlations between education and stereotyping of ethnic groups. However, questions comparing minority and majority group members tend not to exhibit educational differences. (7 endnotes, 23 references)

292.   Hesselbart, Susan. "Racial Stereotypes, Gender Stereotypes and Question Format." *Social Science Quarterly* 59, no. 2 (September 1978): 338-46.

The sample, consisting of 381 adults from Tallahassee, Florida, was 53 percent female and 19 percent African American. Hesselbart found that question format affects the response distributions, as well as the correlations between stereotypes and several other variables. The author suggests that researchers not indiscriminately compile lists of items, that they use more than one type of question format, and that warnings about item phrasing appear in the text of reports rather than in footnotes. A list of five formats used in stereotype research is included. With four tables Hesselbart provides data on the responses, comparative responses by race and gender, responses by trait and question format, and correlations between stereotype indices and other variables. (18 references)

293.   Locander, William B., and John P. Burton. "The Effect of Question Form on Gathering Income Data by Telephone." *Journal of Marketing Research* 13, no. 2 (May 1976): 189-92. [Reprinted in *Readings in Survey Research*, edited by Robert Ferber, 279-86. Chicago, IL: American Marketing Association, 1978. 604p.]

Telephone interviews were conducted with one thousand heads of households in Houston, Texas, in 1975. Two random samples of five hundred adult females and five hundred adult males in separately selected households were generated by the random digit dialing method. Each individual received three callback attempts before being classified as a nonrespondent. Three question forms were used, one with the "more than" language for income level, one using the "less than" format, and one using a "split-point" format (this approach uses a splitting point, for example $10,000, and then brackets up or down from there). The researchers found that the less than and the split-point formats "appeared to reduce the threat to the respondent and therefore did not create the early response tendency of the two more than questions." It is noted that question format should be recognized as an "extremely important" source of response bias. (9 references)

294.   Payne, Stanley L. "Are Open-Ended Questions Worth the Effort?" *Journal of Marketing Research* 2, no. 4 (November 1965): 417-18.

Free-answer or open-ended questions are found to be inefficient and "no more productive of depth or of valid answers than check-box questions are." According to Payne, the problems with this format are found in interviewer variability, coding inconsistency, lack of comparability in trend surveys, tabulating complexity, time required to complete, and added expense. Results from a study in the field of anthropology are cited. The work of Dohrenwend [Item No. 286] is quoted as supporting the above observations. Six "response properties" are identified as length, usability, pertinence, self-revelation, correctness, and reasonableness. Payne recommends deleting open-ended questions from full-scale surveys. (2 references)

295.   Roslow, Sydney, Wallace H. Wulfeck, and Philip G. Corby. "Consumer and Opinion Research: Experimental Studies on the Form of Questions." *Journal of Applied Psychology* 24 (1940): 334-46.

The authors define "form of the question" as "the actual word content or serial order of the words in the sentence." The Psychological Corporation undertook eight studies as part of work connected with advertising and market research problems. Four experimental methods were used: (1) two separate questionnaires were employed, one with alternate forms; (2) forms of the questions changed in successive but similar studies conducted one month apart; (3) free questions were used early in the interview, while answers were checked later against an inventory of products in the home; and (4) free responses were compared with checklist responses. These findings emerged from the studies: (1) the use of stereotypes or emotionally charged words produces "significant changes in the frequencies of positive, negative, or don't know responses"; (2) slight wording changes may or may not adjust the number or responses; (3) free-response questions may produce misleading answers depending upon the memory or familiarity of the respondent; (4) the number and completeness of items provided on a checklist influence the responses; and (5) for survey results interpretation to have validity, the form of the questions used must be considered. (5 footnotes)

296.   Schuman, Howard, and Stanley Presser. "The Open and Closed Question." *American Sociological Review* 44, no. 5 (October 1979): 692-712.

Two reasons for conducting open-attitude questions are to record spontaneous responses and to avoid biases created when providing suggested responses. Both goals are tested as parts of large-scale sample surveys, beginning with a closed question on work values. The authors reach a number of conclusions: (1) not all closed questions have a parallel open form; (2) problems are minimized if the researcher starts with open questions and uses the response wording to construct closed questions; (3) in some cases, where the closed question is properly constructed, the closed question will be more valid than the open question; (4) some findings do remain constant across form; (5) form differences "appear to be smaller" for some; and (6) historians' use of open-question data is likely to be far more valuable than the numerical codes generated through closed questions. (18 footnotes, 26 references)

POSITION

297.   Becker, Sam L. "Why an Order Effect." *Public Opinion Quarterly* 18, no. 3 (Fall 1954): 271-78.

Various hypotheses concerning order effect or "ordinal position effect" are reviewed. Becker believes that prior research has ignored some important factors which may influence response set. For example, some of the studies used students as respondents, and therefore the results may not be generalized to an adult population. Additionally, some studies used multiple-choice questions or used check-list questions alone, rather than checklists buried among other types of questions. The location of the interview, as well as the length of the checklist and questionnaire, must also be considered. The present investigation used data from 16,193 interviews with adults taken from *The 1952 Iowa Radio-Television Audience Survey* and *The Kansas Radio-Television Audience of 1952* survey. A buried check-list question asked, "Of the types of radio programs listed below, which FIVE do you like best? Please name exactly five no more." Sixteen different forms were used, with each program type appearing one time on each form, one time in each ordinal position, and preceding and following every other program type one time. Analysis of the data revealed significant order effects for eight of the sixteen program types. The later on a check-list program type appears, the less likely the respondents will be to choose it as one of their favorites. (15 footnotes)

298.   Bradburn, Norman M., and William M. Mason. "The Effect of Question Order on Responses." *Journal of Marketing Research* 1, no. 4 (November 1964): 57-61.

The authors tested to determine if question order had a bearing on questions of self-report and self-evaluation. A questionnaire concerning self-reports of life satisfaction and presenting four alternative formats was developed. Personal interviews were conducted by the National Opinion Research Center with 2,787 individuals. It was found that interview schedules with systematically rotated questions produced results "relatively unaffected by order of presentation." Bradburn and Mason stress that the nature and extent of the effects of question order can "only be determined by empirical means." The degree to which testing for order effects is conducted is dependent upon the purposes for which the results of each survey are to be used. (12 references)

299.   Carp, Frances M. "Position Effects on Interview Responses." *Journal of Gerontology* 29, no. 5 (September 1974): 581-87.

Research from a number of studies on serial position effects is reviewed. The purpose of the present investigation is to determine whether the order in which stimulus material is presented affects interview responses. The two types of position effects are serial order of response options for an item and the location of items in an interview. Two-hour, in-home, individual interviews were conducted with 899 San Francisco residents aged sixty-five and older. One-half of the respondents received Form A, while the other half received Form B. The forms reversed the order of the response options. Results of the study show that "primacy effect was statistically significant and meaningfully large in regard to evaluative items . . . and either the positive or negative end of the scale drew more responses when it was presented first." For factual items the effect was not evident. Further, no differences were observed in an evaluative item whether it was presented early or late in the interview. (3 footnotes, 16 references)

300.   Carpenter, Edwin H., and Larry G. Blackwood. "The Effect of Question Position on Responses to Attitudinal Questions." *Rural Sociology* 44, no. 1 (Spring 1979): 56-72.

The effect of item position on response was evaluated from data obtained through a nationwide random telephone survey of 2,044 respondents. Twelve different lists were used in a survey of adult attitudes toward wild and domestic animals and their treatment by humans. Four question formats were utilized: (1) five lists asked for measures of acceptability or importance; (2) and (3) six other lists presented the respondent with two different formats in which points totaling one hundred were to be allocated, demonstrating relative importance of each item; and (4) a magnitude estimation scheme was employed to ascertain "degree of affinity" for various wild and domestic animals. Twenty-seven items which had been ranked from zero to ten were tested for order effects. Carpenter and Blackwood found that item position does not affect response. In this study, format, scaling metric, wording, placement in the questionnaire, and substance were varied. It was found that items received "their highest or lowest value when presented first" – a finding which may be more clearly understood in a study focusing on order effects alone, keeping other factors constant. An appendix provides the questions used to test for position effect. (13 references)

301.   Clancy, Kevin J., and Robert A. Wachsler. "Positional Effects in Shared-Cost Surveys." *Public Opinion Quarterly* 35, no. 2 (Summer 1971): 258-65.

In shared-cost surveys, as opposed to custom-designed surveys, clients have little control over the position of their questions in a questionnaire. The two hypotheses tested are that respondents, especially women, are more likely to become bored or tired near the end of an interview, leading them to be more agreeable ("yeasaying"), and that interviewer-respondent rapport is directly related to the length of the interview, with good rapport producing more unbiased responses traceable to social desirability. A telephone survey of four thousand heads of households was conducted inserting six "agree-disagree" questions in two versions of a standard shared-cost questionnaire. In one version the six questions were asked first, while they were positioned last in the second version. Results show little support for either hypothesis: responses to the six questions were similar regardless of their position in the interview. Boredom or fatigue were apparently not factors. This was true for both the main sample and for subgroups based on age, sex, and socioeconomic status. On only one question was there a meaningful difference in response. (11 footnotes)

302.   Gross, Edwin J. "The Effect of Question Sequence on Measures of Buying Interest." *Journal of Advertising Research* 4, no. 3 (September 1964): 40-41.

When asked questions about the disadvantages of a product first, the respondents' subsequent expressed interest in buying the item is lower as compared with those asked about the advantages first. The product in this study was a proposed new writing implement – half pencil and half ballpoint pen. Five groups were interviewed for a total of 175 adults. These Chicagoans were given five varying sequence questionnaires. The emphasis on the negatives produced lower buying interest. Gross cites a standard of 70 percent acceptability for a new product to be further considered by business (the writing implement here averaged approximately 30 percent positive interest – a "dismal failure"). The author recommends conducting a variety of question sequence studies for potential new products, and suggests that this approach be used for food, drug, and cosmetic products as well.

303.   Powers, Edward A., Paula Morrow, Willis J. Goudy, and Patricia M. Keith. "Serial Order Preference in Survey Research." *Public Opinion Quarterly* 41, no. 1 (Spring 1977): 80-85.

The research focuses on the question of whether the order ("rank order location") in which possible answers to attitude questions are presented affects the nature of the responses. Prior literature on the subject is reviewed, and data from the work of Carp [Item No. 299] are reexamined and reanalyzed. Contrary to the Carp report, order effects were found to be not of "substantive significance." In another study, data from a longitudinal survey of 1,332 men in Iowa showed no significant differences in response on either single-item indicators or attitude scales. As part of the research, six attitude scales were also analyzed: Milton Blood's work ethic scale; Vivian Wood's life satisfaction index; Leo Srole's anomia scale; Morris Rosenberg's self-esteem scale; Robert Agger's political cynicism; and Steven Cutler's older person's issues intervention index. Powers and his colleagues found that "less than 1 percent of the variance of any scale could be explained by response option order." The authors conclude that based on the study findings additional attention to serial order preference seems unwarranted. The implications of the findings for survey research are important since longitudinal data would be questionable and difficult to compare if responses are not presented in a consistent manner over time. (2 footnotes, 23 references)

304.   Vicary, James M. "*Gestalt* Theory and Paired Comparisons." *Public Opinion Quarterly* 14, no. 1 (Spring 1950): 139-41.

When paired comparison items are used in public opinion surveys, some of the characteristics of one of the items may sometimes be transferred by the respondent to the other item of the pair. Vicary attributes this "phenomenon" to Gestalt Theory which maintains that people tend to view things as "wholes." Two examples are used to illustrate this "thought transference" process. The cases indicate that open-ended questions can influence the outcome of an order preference survey, and that the order in which alternatives are presented can also affect responses. It is concluded that not enough is known about respondent psychology and Gestalt "error." (2 footnotes)

PRETESTING

305.   Blankenship, Albert B. "Pre-Testing a Questionnaire for a Public Opinion Poll." *Sociometry* 3, no. 3 (July 1940): 263-69.

By way of introducing the need for pretesting questionnaires, Blankenship cites a case in which various question wording formats yielded accuracy differences as great as 14 percent. Paragraph by paragraph, the author reviews steps and considerations which should be undertaken by successful pollsters. These include the following: (1) special attention should be paid to opening questions, as these contribute greatly to the respondent's support, confidence, and interest; (2) ambiguous questions need to be avoided; (3) wording should be suitable to the respondent's level of ability to understand; (4) questions should be reasonable and concrete; (5) personal questions should not be placed at the beginning of the questionnaire; (6) questions which arouse emotional appeal should be phrased in a neutral manner; and (7) the "problem of suggestion" is a challenge. The pretest should be conducted on a small sample similar in characteristics to the final survey. The pretest helps to determine the length of the interview, the question sequencing, and the degree to which success has been achieved in the areas described above. (1 footnote)

306.   Nuckols, Robert C. "A Note on Pre-Testing Public Opinion Questions." *Journal of Applied Psychology* 37, no. 2 (April 1953): 119-20.

Using pretested questions from a well-known polling organization, the author asked nine questions of forty-eight middle-income respondents from Cincinnati and Centerville, Ohio. After the questions had been asked, the respondents were requested to repeat them using their own words (matching the meaning as closely as possible). Of the 430 question interpretations, seventy-three (17 percent) of the responses were either partly or completely incorrect. Nuckols believes that the results indicate that pretesting fails to avoid respondent misinterpretation of many questions. He maintains that a measure of respondent comprehensibility of questions should be undertaken before questions become part of the primary survey. (1 footnote)

RETROSPECTIVE

307.   Fink, Raymond. "The Retrospective Question." *Public Opinion Quarterly* 24, no. 1 (Spring 1960): 143-48.

Fink refers to an article by Kendall and Lazarsfeld (Kendall, Patricia L., and Paul F. Lazarsfeld. "Problems of Survey Analysis." In *Continuities in Social Research: Studies in the Scope and Method of "The American Soldier,"* edited by Robert K. Merton and Paul F. Lazarsfeld, 146-47. [Glencoe, IL]: Free Press, 1950. 255p.) to define the retrospective question. Fink states: "By asking respondents whether or not their attitudes have changed over a specific period of time, these answers can be matched against attitudinal changes recorded on specific items at two or more times." To test the value of the retrospective question, 918 Cornell University students were asked a series of questions about their religious attitudes. The study took place in 1950 and again in 1952. The results indicate that there was a significant tendency for the students whose attitudes did not change on either test item to report change. For respondents whose attitudes did change, their retrospective answers concerning the directions of that change followed the actual direction of change. Three possible explanations for the findings are given. Fink believes panel studies are "especially suited to testing the value of the retrospective question." (3 footnotes)

308.   Morganthau, Tom, and James Doyle. "The Mood of a Nation." *Newsweek* 94, no. 6 (6 August 1979): 26-27.

Appearing in the "National Affairs" section of *Newsweek*, this article's primary value is the manner in which it focuses on the polling technique called "the ladder of life," a technique developed by Hadley Cantril. In the case discussed individuals were requested to rate the state of the nation and how they felt about their own lives on a scale of 1 (worst) to 10 (best). They were then asked how things had been five years earlier, followed by how they thought things would be five years into the future. The article concerns how Jimmy Carter's pollster, Patrick Caddell, interpreted the data, versus the quite different conclusions reached by a wide variety of other survey researchers. Caddell's views were incorporated into a speech by President Carter, frequently referred to as the "Malaise Speech."

309.   Westefeld, Albert. "A Problem of Interpretation in Survey Results." *Journal of Marketing* 17, no. 3 (January 1953): 295-97.

When asked a "hark-back" question (that is, asking the respondent to compare the present with a year ago or some length of past time), respondents favor the present situation with the past viewed as not as good. One explanation may be that the question also measures "general attitudes toward life." Westefeld maintains that the hark-back question is best used to determine "overtones of feeling at the moment, and not to measure trend." Three examples are provided to demonstrate the phenomenon. The first involved personal interviews of seven hundred employees at a machine tool plant. Actual ratings questions showed no improvement, while the hark-back question indicated improvement. The same results were shown with four hundred respondents in a national survey which dealt with attitudes to a basic service industry. The third case involved trend data over a five-year period from "self-administered interviews." A consistent bias toward recent improvements was shown in the hark-back question results.

WORDING

310.   Bishop, George F., Robert W. Oldendick, and Alfred J. Tuchfarber. "Effects of Question Wording and Format on Political Attitude Consistency." *Public Opinion Quarterly* 42, no. 1 (Spring 1978): 81-92.

The year 1964 is viewed by many researchers as the time when the trend lines for "attitude consistency" and "issue voting" in the United States took a sudden upward surge. Some recent studies demonstrate that the American voter has become more ideologically sophisticated, and writers offer various explanations for these trends (such as increased educational attainment and political awareness). The authors, however, hypothesize that alterations in question wording and format play a leading role in the increase of "mass political sophistication." Data are used from a 1973 experiment which was part of a national survey conducted by the National Opinion Research Center (NORC). Three different forms of seven questions were administered by NORC interviewers to random subgroups of about five hundred respondents each. The researchers' hypothesis is upheld. Detailed evidence is presented to explain how wording and format differences can account for much of the change observed during the time period under observation. An appendix gives the issue questions in three formats. (1 footnote, 24 references)

311.   Blankenship, Albert. "Psychological Difficulties in Measuring Consumer Preference." *Journal of Marketing* 6, no. 4, pt. 2 (April 1942): 66-75.

The following principles of question wording are identified: (1) question wording should not be emotional or biased; (2) responses are influenced by the position of the answer alternatives; (3) respondents tend to select the middle alternative between extremes; (4) responses are influenced by the degree of the completeness of the alternatives available; (5) alternatives should be comparable; (6) questions must have meaning to all those asked to respond; (7) questions should ask about behavior instead of hypothetical opinion; (8) respondents should be provided with mechanisms to express their choices; and (9) respondents' pride should not be damaged. Three principles for question order are that the first few questions need to establish the respondents' continued desire for cooperation, question order must seem logical, and question sequence has the potential to bias the results obtained. Blankenship offers two points concerning the interviewing process: the interviewer may not follow the instructions correctly, and interviewer personal bias may be a factor in the results obtained.

312.   Blankenship, Albert B. "The Choice of Words in Poll Questions." *Sociology and Social Research* 25 (September-October 1940): 12-18.

Blankenship reviews words that arouse emotion and prejudice in the respondent. He calls these "danger" words or "emotionally colored" words. Examples include "name calling" words ("dictator," "alien"), names of political parties and figures, and the inclusion or exclusion of terms such as "government spending" or adjectives such as "responsible." It is suggested that questions be clearly stated (thereby avoiding ambiguous terminology), and also that they be appropriate for the respondent. (Language which cannot be understood because of complex vocabulary will achieve incomplete or misleading results.) The author cites a study in which two-fifths of the 3,054 respondents interviewed did not know the meaning of the words "radical," "liberal," and "conservative." Blankenship urges that poll "technicians" exercise discretion in poll word choice. (15 footnotes)

313.   Bradburn, Norman M., and Carrie Miles. "Vague Quantifiers." *Public Opinion Quarterly* 43, no. 1 (Spring 1979): 92-101.

The "vague" quantifiers referred to here are responses to survey questions in terms of "very," "pretty," and "not too." As is noted from an early study, "the meaning of a word varied for each individual and in each context in which the word was used." The theoretical literature from the field of experimental psychology is reviewed. A pilot study is described which attempts to make more precise quantitative estimates for three common vague quantifiers ("not too often," "pretty often," and "very often"). One solution would be to have respondents "make one overall numerical estimate for frequency terms within the context of an interview."

Respondents do seem to have a great deal of difficulty quantifying subjective states and events of modest significance to them. (13 references)

314.   Cantril, Hadley. "Experiments in the Wording of Questions." *Public Opinion Quarterly* 4, no. 2 (June 1940): 330-32.

In response to Elmo Roper's invitation to test alternate wordings for questions suggested to him by *Public Opinion Quarterly* [Item No. 320], two questions were chosen. The first read as follows: "Do you approve of Sumner Welles' visit to European capitals?" The alternate read: "Do you approve of President Roosevelt's sending Sumner Welles to visit European capitals?" The second question was as follows: "Do you think the U.S. should do more than it is now doing to help England and France?" The alternate read: "Do you think the U.S. should do more than it is now doing to help England and France in their fight against Hitler?" Two representative samples of about 1,550 individuals each were selected for the survey of March 1940. Response choices were "approve," "disapprove," and "no opinion." Cantril notes in the presentation of the results that the introduction of President Roosevelt's name had the effect of more people responding and more people disapproving. When Hitler's name was used, 9 percent more people thought the United States should increase its assistance to England and France. Subtleties involved in question wording are discussed.

315.   Hitlin, Robert. "On Question Wording and Stability of Response." *Social Science Research* 5, no. 1 (March 1976): 39-41.

Three items of "conventional wisdom" (CW) are tested and found to be not as "crucial" as once thought. The tests were part of the Georgetown University Poll, conducted in July 1974, using the split-ballot technique. The three CWs are as follows: (1) "Avoid contamination in the order of questions. Do not precede evaluation questions with biasing lead-in questions"; (2) "Do not use official titles in trial heat election questions"; and (3) "Do not include arguments for a proposed action in a question." Using chi square values, Hitlin determined that none of the efforts to manipulate question wording or question order were effective. While in these cases the CWs were not appropriate, they may not necessarily be inappropriate in other settings. The kind of biasing discussed may not apply to all questions. (4 footnotes)

316.   Hubbard, Alfred W. "Phrasing Questions." *Journal of Marketing* 15, no. 1 (July 1950): 48-56.

Questions can be divided into the following three classes according to Hubbard: (1) those that tell the respondent too much; (2) those that do not provide enough information; and (3) questions that are appropriate and permit the respondent to respond. Every effort should be made with the questionnaire to avoid revealing the sponsor's biases. Hubbard discusses a table of objective-subjective direction in questions which he believes may assist question formulators. A figure provides seven different question formats which were successfully used in a survey on the packaging of coffee. Hubbard suggests that much of this article is designed to alert question phrasers to the biases they tend to add to the questions, to sensitize phrasers to feelings that can be aroused by certain words, and to use common sense. He advises that word connotations change and therefore must be monitored. A number of practical suggestions appear throughout the text. (1 footnote)

317.   Payne, Stanley L. *The Art of Asking Questions*. Studies in Public Opin-
         ion, vol. 3. Princeton, NJ: Princeton University Press, 1951. 249p.

This volume is a manual on how to approach the difficult task of wording polling questions appropriately. The "art" of questioning is analyzed by a practitioner. The book discusses the wording of single questions; the nature of open-ended questions; the two-way question; the multiple-choice question; the necessity of brevity and clarity; the concern for the privacy of respondents; and the importance of phrasing good questions. Rules as such are not what the author has steered toward, but rather he attempts to provide observations on human behavior, with exceptions to the rules of wording principles being brought into focus. Oddities and unsolved dilemmas point to additional questions that need addressing. Considerable discussion focuses on how not to formulate many questions. There is a bibliography on pages 239-41.

318.   Payne, Stanley L. "Tricky Words Upset Opinion Polls." *Science Digest*
         30, no. 2 (August 1951): 64-68. [This article is condensed from Payne's
         book *The Art of Asking Questions* - Item No. 317.]

Through a series of examples, Payne demonstrates how changing even a single word in a question can generate completely different outcomes. For example, using the same question and substituting the word "could" or "might" instead of "should" yielded a 19 percent difference. Another question varies the words "allow" and "forbid" with significantly different results. Loaded questions are mentioned – including loaded questions which appeal to the desire for prestige. Techniques of obtaining answers to what would appear to be straightforward questions are suggested. For example, the question, "Do you happen to own a car at present?" generates more reasonable results than the obvious form of the question, "Do you own a car?" Payne warns that little can be taken for granted with respect to the respondents' ability to remember facts and current or important recent events. To demonstrate the point, the article concludes with a ten-question quiz of a factual and personal nature.

319.   Presser, Stanley. "Survey Question Wording and Attitudes in the General Public." Ph.D. diss., University of Michigan, 1977. 156 leaves. [*Dissertation Abstracts International* Order No. 7804796; *DAI* 38A, no. 11 (May 1978): 6980.]

Early studies from the 1940s involved split-ballot experiments on the impact of question wording. Presser maintains that the explanations used for wording effects were circular, and focused on changes in single variable marginals. The current work deals with "relationships" and the use of two types of wording changes: "filtering for no opinion versus not filtering and providing a middle alternative as opposed to not doing so." The study results indicate that wording effects are not "monolithic," and that a "more differentiated view of them is required." Intensity of opinion is the only variable which is related to the middle alternative effect. Education and a "willingness" to say "don't know" (DK) are the best predictors of the change due to the "no opinion filter." Individuals who do not have crystallized opinions (defined as those who are "especially willing to volunteer DK") are "more, not less, resistant to form effect." Presser observes that the "same substantive conclusions" could be drawn from the questions asked even if the filter or offer of a middle alternative were not included even though "proportions moving into such explicitly offered categories are substantial." References are provided.

320.   Roper, Elmo. "Wording Questions for the Polls." *Public Opinion Quarterly* 4, no. 1 (March 1940): 129-30.

Although the problem of sampling in public opinion polls receives much discussion from its critics, Roper believes two other issues merit attention: the measurement of the intensity of an opinion and the wording of poll questions. At the center of the wording problem is the difficulty pollsters have in anticipating the number and types of biases a diverse population might have to particular wording. Caution is also to be used that the specific attitude under consideration is the one that is actually measured. Two differently worded questions are used to illustrate this point. Roper invites the editors of *Public Opinion Quarterly* (*POQ*) to submit to him quarterly four questions with alternative wordings to be tested on a national sample by Roper interviewers. Results will appear in issues of *POQ*. Hopefully, this exercise will lead to the identification of "danger words," as well as to those issues where they might appear. It is stated that many revisions (as high as twenty) are sometimes necessary to achieve "neutral wordings" of questions coming from the Roper Organization.

321.   Roslow, Sydney, and Albert B. Blankenship. "Phrasing the Question in Consumer Research." *Journal of Applied Psychology* 23, no. 5 (October 1939): 612-22.

Nine principles of question phrasing are discussed: (1) the introduction and opening questions must create rapport; (2) questions should not be ambiguous; (3) questions should be concrete, rather than abstract; (4) direct questions are best avoided, allowing respondents a "means of expression"; (5) the context of the question needs to be considered in terms of where it has been placed in the questionnaire; (6) question wording should reflect and be related to the background of the respondent; (7) the impact of extreme alternatives must be considered so as to avoid forcing the respondent to choose one or the other of the extremes; (8) questions should be nonemotional and unbiased; and (9) the impact of items selected for a checklist should be carefully considered, as the presence of these may stimulate responses that might not be identified through free responses. (13 footnotes)

322.   Rugg, Donald. "Experiments in Wording Questions: II." *Public Opinion Quarterly* 5, no. 1 (March 1941): 91-92.

The article summarizes the findings of a second experiment undertaken by the Princeton Public Opinion Research Project [See Item No. 314 for experiment one]. The survey, conducted in September 1940, used questions prepared by *Public Opinion Quarterly* and Elmo Roper. Alternate word forms were submitted by Roper to comparable cross sections of the population, according to criteria used in the *Fortune* Surveys. The questions concerned United States-Brazil-Germany relations and whether the United States should "allow" or "forbid" public speeches against democracy. The subtle changes in question wording produced only some socioeconomic and geographical differences in the first question. In the second question a striking difference in response to the two forms of the question is noted. (1 footnote)

323.   Rugg, Donald, and Hadley Cantril. "The Wording of Questions in Public Opinion Polls." *Journal of Abnormal and Social Psychology* 37, no. 4 (October 1942): 469-95. [A revised version is reprinted in *Gauging Public Opinion*, by Hadley Cantril and Research Associates in the Office of Public Opinion Research, Princeton University, 13-50. Princeton, NJ: Princeton University Press, 1944. Reprint. Port Washington, NY: Kennikat Press, 1972. 318p.]

Previous studies examining question wording are reviewed, with Blankenship's work [Item No. 284] identified as the most complete and carefully controlled. The questions considered in this article are based on results from five surveys conducted during 1941 by the American Institute of Public Opinion (AIPO) and the Office of Public Opinion Research. The treatment of the data is divided into three main headings areas: "Effects of Context"; "The Alternatives Presented"; and "Deviations from 'Objective' Wording." The use of the split-ballot by AIPO and the *Fortune* Survey is discussed. The approach calls for two ballots: one has some of the same questions as the other (the control questions) but also includes some different questions. The design is to enable the study of question wording differences. Some analysis of the type of personality characteristics involved in differing question response is provided. (15 footnotes)

324.   Schuman, Howard, and Otis D. Duncan. "Questions about Attitude Survey Questions." In *Sociological Methodology 1973-1974,* edited by Herbert L. Costner, 232-51. San Francisco, CA: Jossey-Bass Inc., Publishers, 1974. 410p.

The presentation opens with the observation that different question wording – even slight question wording changes – produces different results, perhaps varying from 15 to 20 percent. An example is given in which the Gallup Poll and the Harris poll ask what amounts to the same question, but phrased differently, yielding quite different responses. The question related to speed of U.S. troop withdrawal from Vietnam by President Nixon. The authors seek to highlight the "formidable measurement problems inherent in attitude survey research." The public, responding to questions, may perceive differences between questions which the researcher sees as the same question. Therefore, it may be that what is being measured is different from the purpose for which the question was constructed. The public may be influenced by the social interaction between the interviewer and the respondent, as well as by the "strength and content" of individual questions and their wording alternates. Wording effects, both in type and magnitude, need greater understanding for use in large-scale survey investigations. (22 references)

325.   Schuman, Howard, and Stanley Presser. "Question Wording as an Independent Variable in Survey Analysis." *Sociological Methods & Research* 6, no. 2 (November 1977): 151-70. [Reprinted in *Survey Design and Analysis: Current Issues*, edited by Duane F. Alwin. Sage Contemporary Social Science Issues, no. 46. Beverly Hills, CA: Sage Publications, 1978. 156p.]

Research into question wording and form, first undertaken in the 1940s, is resumed. The authors examine the relationship between education and a host of possibilities. These include whether the investigator should use "agree-disagree" statements or forced-choice items, open or closed questions, "whether and how to balance alternatives offered," the middle alternative, and filter(s) for "no opinion." The sample consisted of random divisions of the 1974 Survey Research Center Omnibus national sample. Schuman and Presser identify these findings: (1) form-resistant correlations appear to be "poor" with the agree-type items, with open/closed items, and for some of the items involving word tone changes; (2) form-resistant correlations occur with formal versus substantive balance and middle alternatives; and (3) the no opinion filter type "occupies a middle ground."

Researchers are warned to be cautious of correlations determined from a single question form. (12 endnotes, 19 references)

326.   Van Dusen, Roxann A., and Nicholas Zill, eds. *Basic Background Items for U.S. Household Surveys*. Washington, DC: Center for Coordination of Research on Social Indicators, Social Science Research Council, [1975]. 63p.

The Center for Coordination of Research on Social Indicators of the Social Science Research Council created a working group, chaired by Philip E. Converse, to reach a consensus as to the basic descriptive information on respondents, families, and households needed for useful comparisons from one survey research organization to another (and for secondary analysis studies). This document is the report of the working group, represented by members from academia, for-profit organizations, and federal survey agencies. Recommended question wordings and coding procedures are included, along with consideration of the following variables: age, sex, marital status, ethnic group, religion, education, employment status, occupation, income, residential characteristics, and political identification. A two-column format is used, with question wording and other elements of the survey on the left, and interviewer instructions, supplementary notes, and references on the right. The items selected are for use in household surveys. (105 references)

MISCELLANEOUS

327.   Cannell, Charles F., and Sally Robison. "Analysis of Individual Questions." Chap. 11 in *Working Papers on Survey Research in Poverty Areas*, edited by John B. Lansing, Stephen B. Withey, and Arthur C. Wolfe, et al., 236-91. Ann Arbor, MI: Survey Research Center, Institute for Social Research, University of Michigan, January 1971. 318 pages plus appendixes.

Respondent and interviewer behavior is coded for purposes of objective evaluation of questions. The approach used is experimental and leaves many challenges yet to be resolved. Statistical analysis is applied, followed by a subjective determination to assess the method. Questions are evaluated based on problems experienced by the interviewer, the respondent, or both. The selection of questions for analysis was based on a review of the coding of interviewer/respondent behaviors which indicated some difficulty. A differentiation of question types was organized along the following scheme: open-closed, simple-difficult, and fact-attitude. A code was developed for each type of problem question. Six pages of potentially problem questions are provided, followed by a diagnosis of the problem questions. A series of tables indicates the question categories by error, such as the questions most frequently omitted by the interviewers, questions asked which should have been skipped by the interviewers, and questions which were refused. Cannell and Robison provide a four-page summary table of problem diagnosis, which is followed by another table showing a subjective analysis of problem questions as caused by aspects such as complex concept, threat, and awkwardness. Nonconsecutively numbered footnotes appear with most of the sixteen tables. Chapters 10, 11, and 12 have a combined seventeen-entry bibliography on pages 317-18.

328.   King, Morton B., Jr. "Reliability of the Idea-Centered Question in Interview Schedules." *American Sociological Review* 9, no. 1 (February 1944): 57-64.

The idea-centered, rather than the word-centered question, is the primary focus of the article. Ideas were conveyed by interviewers in "whatever language was necessary" to communicate with a cross section of the country's population. Therefore, different vocabulary was utilized depending upon the socioeducational background of the respondent. Simple random number sampling was used to select the 426-member sample of heads of households. The method was determined to have a "workable amount of reliability." Analysis was of all question answers together, rather than of individual responses. At least two of the trained interviewers were able to attain "reasonably similar and reliable results." The approach failed to yield quantifiable data. King states that the technique avoids "that spurious exactness which is probably the fate of paper and pencil techniques when administered to non-academic populations." Three tables, a field schedule example, and a figure accompany the text. (2 footnotes)

329.   Roper, Elmo. "The *Fortune* Survey. Survey Pitfalls." *Fortune* 35, no. 4 (April 1947): 6, 12, 16, 25.

Advising the reader of public opinion poll results, Roper expresses four concerns: (1) question answers are not to be taken at face value; (2) conclusions cannot be based on the answers to any single question; (3) "don't know" or undecided votes are to be carefully considered; and (4) wording the same question differently might produce different results. Using results from the *Fortune* Survey, Roper highlights each of these areas of concern by providing specific data, as well as including the month and year of publication.

INTERVIEWERS

ACCURACY, EFFECTIVENESS, AND PERFORMANCE

330.   Axelrod, Morris, and Charles F. Cannell. "A Research Note on an Attempt to Predict Interviewer Effectiveness." *Public Opinion Quarterly* 23, no. 4 (Winter 1959-60): 571-76.

A study was conducted to determine if good interviewers could be distinguished from poor interviewers on the basis of certain demographic and personality measures, and to develop adequate predictors of effective interviewers. Approximately 175 interviewers employed by the Survey Research Center of the University of Michigan comprised the population examined. Age, sex, and education measures were obtained, and three standard tests (the Strong Vocational Interest Inventory, the Kerr-Speroff Empathy Test, and the Guilford-Zimmerman Temperament Survey) were administered. Ratings were also obtained from field supervisors, the office supervisor, and the coders. Findings, though "rather tenuous and sparse," suggest that there was no relationship between demographic variables and performance variables. Of the ten Guilford-Zimmerman factors three (restraint, thoughtfulness-reflectiveness, and personal relations) seemed to be related to the criteria, and the Strong Inventory did not discriminate between good and poor interviewers. The authors cite four factors, which combined, could explain the "failure to discover large differences." These are flaws in the measurements, homogeneity of the population, relatively small size of the sample, and inability of the prediction variables to predict. (11 footnotes)

331.   Cannell, Charles F., Sally A. Lawson, and Doris L. Hausser. *A Technique for Evaluating Interviewer Performance: A Manual for Coding and Analyzing Interviewer Behavior from Tape Recordings of Household*

Interviews. Ann Arbor, MI: Survey Research Center, Institute for Social Research, University of Michigan, [1975]. 138p.

The manual describes a coding technique for use in training and supervising interviewers. The volume is divided into three sections: (A) provides an overview for evaluating interviewers; (B) discusses the interviewer behavior code, tape-recording household interviews, the coding process, interviewer training and supervision, and other applications of the code; and (C) presents a detailed manual of codes and basic reference materials for coders, a sample coded interview, a sample analysis of interviewer performance, instructions to interviewers, and program documentation. Section C also includes information on TIMBO, the computer program employed, as well as details for interviewers on the use of tape recorders.

332.   Church, Helen N., Mary M. Clayton, Charlotte M. Young, and Walter D. Foster. "Can Different Interviewers Obtain Comparable Dietary Survey Data?" *Journal of the American Dietetic Association* 30, no. 8 (August 1954): 777-79.

Data gathered by interviewers in three different locations were compared. The backgrounds of the interviewers were "substantially the same" – all were nutritionists with training in dietary interviewing. The same set of instructions was given to all interviewers. Seven interviewers conducted interviews with 438 randomly sampled respondents. Interviewer differences rarely exceeded 10 percent (the average was 5.4 percent) of the National Research Council allowances for each nutrient. The authors believe that with similar training and backgrounds interviewers working as a team can obtain comparable data. The study was conducted at three state experiment stations participating in the Northeastern Regional Project, including three interviewers in Maine, two in New Jersey, and two in New York. (6 references)

333.   Fisk, George. "Interviewer Ratings of Respondent Interest of Sample Surveys." *Journal of Marketing* 14, no. 5 (April 1950): 725-30.

The question addressed is whether interviewer ratings of respondents can be used to increase the accuracy of a survey. The study covered radio listening as conducted in a survey at the State College of Washington for radio station KWSC. The survey dealt with program policies and was conducted in February 1949. In total 310 students were interviewed, with 238 questioned by six interviewers and the remaining 72 students interviewed by four other interviewers. The findings show that interviewers varied considerably in the way in which interest was assigned on a four-point scale using "excellent," "good," "fair," and "poor" as options, and the variances exhibited may be due primarily to differences among interviewers. Fisk raises the issue that even had the results been "more favorable," the way in which interviewer ratings are to be used in tabulation remains a problem. (8 footnotes)

334.   Hansen, Robert H., and Eli S. Marks. "Influence of the Interviewer on the Accuracy of Survey Results." *Journal of the American Statistical Association* 53, no. 283 (September 1958): 635-55.

The effect of interviewers on survey results is reported on the basis of a large-scale study. The following factors were found when significant interviewer effects were present: (1) interviewer "resistance" to a question (where words are omitted, questions altered, or the answer assumed); (2) cases in which the question contained ambiguity, "subjectivity," or complexity; and (3) the altering of early replies by respondents caused by probing or the asking of additional questions. Further study was conducted relating interviewer performance with interviewer characteristics. Areas considered included test scores; age, sex, occupation, and education of interviewers; and attitudes and expectations concerning respondents' reactions. At least one correlation was found between the number of items omitted and age, some test scores, and expectations about the respondents' cooperation. The data used were from the 1950 Bureau of the Census, Censuses of Population, Housing and Agriculture. Interviewer contribution to the variance of census data ranged from "trivial to highly significant." (7 references)

335.   Hauck, Mathew, and Stanley Steinkamp. *Survey Reliability and Interviewer Competence.* Inter-University Committee for Research on Consumer Behavior. Consumer Savings Project. Studies in Consumer Savings, no. 4. Urbana, IL: Bureau of Economic and Business Research, University of Illinois, 1964. 112p.

The focus of this volume is the role of the interviewer in relationship to the data quality obtained through personal interviews. The ability to validate financial data permitted an evaluation of the effectiveness of the interviewers. The project's background is reviewed, followed by chapters on interviewer variability, selection, training, and supervision – the latter two offering "recommendations for the future." The Consumer Savings Project was established to evaluate the completeness and accuracy of financial survey data and to seek methods to improve such surveys. The approach used employed a series of panel operations in varying geographic locations and at different times. Four different studies were undertaken. Respondents were interviewed five times at three- or four-month intervals. The asset to be validated was the savings account, with a reduced willingness to report amounts held in savings accounts versus those held in checking accounts. Appendixes include the interviewer qualifying examination, the interviewer agreement, the interviewer report form, and the questionnaire (a study of farm family finances). (40 footnotes)

336.   Hochstim, Joseph R., and J. Stevens Stock. "A Method of Measuring In-
        terviewer Variability." *Public Opinion Quarterly* 15, no. 2 (Summer 1951):
        322-34.

Interviewer variability can be a major source of error in sample surveys. Hochstim
and Stock suggest that interviewer variability can be reduced by (1) more intensive training and control of interviewers, (2) more careful question design, (3)
increasing the number of interviewers, and (4) selecting more representative interviewers in relation to the study population. The authors describe a method for
measuring interviewer variability. The environment under examination involves
quota sampling in which the overall number by sex, age, and occupation is specified. Three interviewers conducted 1,015 interviews. Three questions – a fact
question, an information question, and an opinion question – are examined. Question type and interviewer variance are discussed, as well as sample design and interviewer variance. Variance due to interviewer judgment is explored. It is demonstrated that question type has an effect on variance. (3 footnotes)

337.   Kish, Leslie. "Studies of Interviewer Variance for Attitudinal Variables."
        Journal of the American Statistical Association 57, no. 297 (March 1962):
        92-115.

Two studies conducted by the Survey Research Center of the University of Michigan are analyzed. The degree to which interviewer variance contributes to total
survey errors is examined, with observations made concerning the planning and
interpretation of survey statistics. The measurement and magnitude of interviewer
variance are described, followed by a consideration of the effect on research design, subclasses, and comparisons between them. The statistical model used was
simple analysis of variance (ANOVA) for estimating components. Kish suggests
that interviewer errors vary greatly according to characteristics, populations, designs, and resources (such as questionnaires, the nature and training of interviewers, and so forth). (14 references)

338.   Manheimer, Dean, and Herbert Hyman. "Interviewer Performance in Ar-
        ea Sampling." *Public Opinion Quarterly* 13, no. 1 (Spring 1949): 83-92.

The research investigates the effect of interviewer performance on a probability
sample to determine if inaccuracies of the interviewers produced error in the
final sample. Approximately one thousand adult residents of a large eastern city
were selected according to a strict design. Thirteen interviewers and three supervisors were used. It was hypothesized that due to careful recruitment, training, and supervision, interviewer error would be minimal. However, it was found
that area sampling was vulnerable to error due to interviewer performance.
Mistakes were found in the listing of dwelling units, in the selection of a sample
of households, and in the selection of individuals within dwelling units. It is

concluded that even with a carefully designed and supervised survey, successful area sampling is dependent upon field staff accuracy. (5 footnotes)

339.   Mayer, Charles S. "The Interviewer and His Environment." *Journal of Marketing Research* 1, no. 4 (November 1964): 24-31.

Based on three thousand report forms submitted by interviewers for two national studies, the results were analyzed to ascertain the completion rates. The average interview was one hour in length and dealt with economic and related social questions. The interviewer "can in no way affect respondent selection," as the study used a multistage area sample with random selection of respondents within each household. The environmental factors considered include the number of the call, the degree of urbanization, the date and time of the call, the sex of the respondent, and the result of the previous call when considering callbacks. Five calls were placed, with results illustrated in four figures. Mayer maintains that the results of this study will assist field directors to "more accurately quantify" expectations. (8 references)

340.   Mosteller, Frederick. "The Reliability of Interviewers' Ratings." Part 2, Chap. 7 in *Gauging Public Opinion*, by Hadley Cantril and Research Associates in the Office of Public Opinion Research, Princeton University, 98-106. Princeton, NJ: Princeton University Press, 1944. Reprint. Port Washington, NY: Kennikat Press, 1972. 318p.

Techniques are discussed for determining the reliability and validity of controls used by polling organizations. A "control" is defined as a "socioeconomic characteristic which may be used in constructing or in checking the adequacy of a public opinion sample." The first section of the chapter concerns utilizing the same interviewers used on a panel. The same interviewers reinterviewed the same respondents with a three-week separation between the first and second interviews. Tables show the results for economic status (identical classifications - 77 percent); age estimates (classifications in the same ten-year interval - 90 percent); information about ownership of cars (identical classifications - 96.5 percent); and a question rating President Roosevelt's job performance (identical responses - 79 percent). Next, different interviewers classified the same respondents. The results were economic status (identical classifications - 54 percent); age estimates (classifications in the same ten-year interval - 71 percent); information about ownership of cars (identical classifications - 86 percent); and response to the voting question (identical responses - 87 percent). With both the same and different interviewers, the reliability of their ratings on control was high.

341.   Namias, Jean. "Measuring Variation in Interviewer Performance." *Journal of Advertising Research* 6, no. 1 (March 1966): 8-12.

The development of a graphic representation of interviewer performance is reported. In the presentation the interviewer failure number is on the horizontal axis and the success number is on the vertical axis, with each plot representing the total count of a specific characteristic in the sample. The graph shows significant differences in interview results. Supervisors can utilize the graph as a tool to make adjustments with the interviewers. The need for the device stems from the problem of refusals and not-at-homes, whose characteristics may be different from the individuals who do respond to surveys. The statistical method used is designed to separate specific from general causes of variation and can be used for a single survey as well as with a series of surveys. Three different examples are discussed, with the graphic representation shown for each case. (5 references)

342.   Namias, Jean. "A Rapid Method to Detect Differences in Interviewer Performance." *Journal of Marketing* 26, no. 2 (April 1962): 68-72.

A statistical device called the "binomial probability paper" is used to compare graphically the performance of interviewers, thereby permitting the researcher to determine interviewer faults, excellence, and those interviewers who are conducting business according to their own rules. This approach, when conducted early in the survey experience, can assist in indicating which interviewers need retraining and which need to be replaced. Four figures illustrate the approach, with the number of successes on the vertical line, the number of failures on the horizontal line, and a line diagonally with points plotted accordingly. (4 footnotes)

343.   "Quality Control in Survey Research: Interviewers Are Gaining Recognition. While the Science of Choosing the Right Questions Arouses Much Controversy, the Business of Making Sure They're Properly Asked and Reported is Widely Neglected. Some Research Firms Are Recognizing This and Coping with It." *Printers' Ink* 263, no. 6 (9 May 1958): 71-72.

The three main points made about interviewers are that different interviewers get different results, poor interviewers get poor results, and certain types of individuals are good for certain jobs. A profile of a better-educated, near middle age, inexperienced interviewer, who will work exclusively for one firm, who does not need the extra money, and who is female, is suggested by Crossley, S-D Surveys, Incorporated. Various techniques for checking the work of interviewers are considered, including reviewing returns by telephone and writing "cheater" questions in the questionnaire to which response norms have been established. Quota sampling and interviewer selection of the sample are reviewed. The legal status of interviewers, whether employees or independent contractors, is raised (with the federal government drawing the line based on the degree of supervision).

344. Steinkamp, Stanley W. "The Identification of Effective Interviewers." *Journal of the American Statistical Association* 59, no. 308 (December 1964): 1165-74.

A study undertaken at the University of Illinois and conducted in a small metropolitan area in the Midwest in 1960 involved 316 sample addresses. The subject of the interviews concerned "time deposits" at savings institutions. From an applicant pool of one hundred fifty, twenty-one interviewers were selected (from which three were dropped upon discovering falsification in some of their interviews). Much variability was found in the work of the remaining eighteen interviewers. Steinkamp indicates that his study shows that the use of response rates and other frequently used measures of interviewer performance are questionable. "Patterns of performance" are suggested as more suitable measures. (1 footnote, 6 references)

345. Steinkamp, Stanley W. "Some Characteristics of Effective Interviewers." *Journal of Applied Psychology* 50, no. 6 (December 1966): 487-92.

A probability sample of 316 addresses was selected. These represented time deposit records of savings institutions in a small metropolitan area in the Midwest. Twenty-one interviewers conducted from eleven to twenty-four contacts, with individuals contacted at 98 percent of the savings units owning validated accounts. Interviewers conducted sessions (lasting an average of one-and-a-half hours) from which a percentage was validated with the records of the savings institution for that day. Interviewer effectiveness was measured by three means: (1) the pickup rate (the number of responses with validated accounts); (2) the response rate (the interviews obtained); and (3) the account mention rate (the percentage of interviews in which the validated savings account was mentioned by the respondent). The validation of the accounts showed that "a little over two-fifths of the true total amount" had been reported. Personality characteristics as related to interviewer effectiveness showed a positive relationship with self-confidence, higher dominance scores, social skillfulness, social stability, and higher ratings on attention to detail. Steinkamp cautions that since assignments could not be randomized, and considering the small number of interviewers and the nature of the financial data sought, the study should be considered a beginning for future research. The Edwards Personal Preference Schedule is discussed. (14 references)

346. Stock, J. Stevens, and Joseph R. Hochstim. "A Method of Measuring Interviewer Variability." *Public Opinion Quarterly* 15, no. 2 (Summer 1951): 322-34.

By means of the analysis of variance technique, variable error existing among interviewers is measured. The two hypotheses tested are that interviewer variance is affected by the degree of rigidity in the sample design and by the nature and type of the question itself. Four examples are used to show the applicability of the technique: (1) a case study of three interviewers and 1,015 respondents; (2) a study conducted by the Bureau of Labor Statistics involving interviewer judgment; (3) five hundred respondents interviewed by twenty interviewers; and (4) a study done in connection with a revision of the *Consumers' Price Index.* Detailed computations of the results of the four examples follow. The test of the first hypothesis is not conclusive, but the second is deemed "tenable." The conclusion reached is that "interviewer variability amounts to a sizable part of the total statistical error." Five suggestions are offered to reduce interviewer variability: more careful training and supervision; restricting the interviewer in selecting respondents; improving question design; adding interviewing staff; and selecting interviewers representative of the sample studied. (3 footnotes)

347.   Sudman, Seymour. "Quantifying Interviewer Quality." *Public Opinion Quarterly* 30, no. 4 (Winter 1966-67): 664-67.

Traditional subjective methods used by survey organizations to rate the quality of interviewers' work are briefly reviewed, with limitations noted. The article describes a basic statistical technique used by the National Opinion Research Center (NORC) as part of a larger project concerning the reduction of survey costs. Both coders and field supervisors are utilized by NORC. The coders complete error sheets denoting the type of error, such as a missing answer, an irrelevant answer, insufficient detail, "don't know" without a probe, a dangling probe, multiple codes in error, and superfluous questions asked. Error weights are then assigned to each, depending upon the severity of the error. A similar, though more comprehensive list, is filled out by field supervisors who are generally more familiar with the intricacies of the interviewing process. The coders and the field supervisors were found to agree "reasonably well" in their ratings of interviewers. Sudman offers a solution to the problem created by the simple summing or averaging of error points – a method which could lead to misevaluations of interview quality since studies differ in length and complexity. A statistical formula is presented for determining a standard score for each interviewer. The standard scores can then be averaged over a number of studies "to give a meaningful measure of interviewer quality."

BIAS

348.   Bailar, Barbara, Leroy Bailey, and Joyce Stevens. "Measures of Interviewer Bias and Variance." *Journal of Marketing Research* 14, no. 3 (August 1977): 337-43. [Reprinted in *Readings in Survey Research*, edited

by Robert Ferber, 457-69. Chicago, Il.: American Marketing Association, 1978. 604p.]

To test interviewer bias the authors conducted two experiments, one controlled using the National Crime Survey Central Cities Sample, and the other where a controlled experiment was not possible – namely, using the *Current Population Survey*. The studies showed that even with very structured training programs, the interviewers demonstrated "considerable variability" in their data collection on certain items. To some degree nonresponse rates are a function of the interviewer, with interviewer characteristics and attitudes playing a role in variable response rates. High-income interviewers elicited more nonresponses on a variety of income items, and those interviewers who believed it was inappropriate to ask income questions collected higher nonresponse rates in this category. The authors suggest that survey directors stress to interviewers the need and value of the income data as a technique to reduce the documented negative effects. (2 footnotes, 7 references)

349.   Barber, Theodore Zenophon, and Maurice J. Silver. "Fact, Fiction, and the Experimenter Bias Effect." *Psychological Bulletin Monograph Supplement* 70, no. 6, pt. 2 (December 1968): 1-29.

The bias effect is caused by the experimenters' expectations and desires, significantly affecting the experimental outcome. The authors critically analyze thirty-one studies which purport to demonstrate the phenomenon. Most do not achieve that goal. The inadequacies of the studies are highlighted. Barber and Silver note that the effect is more difficult to demonstrate than earlier believed, and that there are other reasons for the effect observed (such as misreported results, verbal reinforcements of respondents, and misleading conclusions from inadequate data). Nineteen studies which did not clearly demonstrate the bias effect, and twelve which "apparently" showed the bias effect, are considered. The authors believe that "more vigorous methodology" is needed, outlining specific suggestions. (63 references)

350.   Boyd, Harper W., Jr., and Ralph Westfall. "Interviewer Bias Once More Revisited." *Journal of Marketing Research* 7, no. 2 (May 1970): 249-53. [Reprinted in *Readings in Survey Research*, edited by Robert Ferber, 420-28. Chicago, IL: American Marketing Association, 1978. 604p.]

This is the third time during a fifteen-year period that Boyd and Westfall [Item Nos. 351 and 352] have examined the literature on interviewer bias. The authors write that little has been added since 1964 to address the overall problem. Some issues have been examined, such as Belson's study on the use of tape recorders (Belson, William A. "Tape Recording: Its Effect on Accuracy of Response in Survey Interviews." *Journal of Marketing Research* 4, no. 3 [August 1967]: 253-60.)

which indicates that recorders may generate bias with upper-class respondents. Steinkamp's use of the Edwards Personal Preference Schedule as a tool in selecting interviewers is discussed [Item No. 345]. However, the authors note that little has been produced since the mid-1960s in terms of knowledge or techniques to avoid large errors due to interviewer bias. The article is divided into sections which deal with respondent selection, data collection, and interviewer selection, training, and control. (32 references)

351.   Boyd, Harper W., Jr., and Ralph Westfall. "Interviewer Bias Revisited." *Journal of Marketing Research* 2, no. 1 (February 1965): 58-63.

The authors surveyed the topic ten years earlier for an article which appeared in the *Journal of Marketing* [Item No. 352]. At that time it was determined that interviewer bias was a major source of error in survey research. The ensuing ten years have seen improvement, but the "same problems still exist to a major degree and relatively little is being done to solve them." Errors caused by the failure to include some respondents (not-at-homes and refusals) are discussed, along with the treatment of nonresponse bias and response selection in probability samples. A consideration of data collection is divided into errors in stimulating responses, respondent perception of the interviewer and vice versa, and interviewer selection, training, and control. Boyd and Westfall maintain that fieldwork is one of the "main sources of error in survey research." (40 references)

352.   Boyd, Harper W., Jr., and Ralph Westfall. "Interviewers as a Source of Error in Surveys." *Journal of Marketing* 19, no. 4 (April 1955): 311-24.

Interviewers are a major source of error in surveys. The errors fall into two main categories: respondent selection errors and data collection errors. Selection errors include failing to obtain data from not-at-homes and refusals, as well as failing to include the proper individuals in the sample. Interviewer bias in data collection occurs when the interviewer influences the respondent's answers, and when the interviewer fails to interpret or record the responses appropriately. The authors advise that "because most of us hear what we want and expect to hear, the results obtained tend to vary with the interviewer's own opinions and expectations." Additionally, it is suggested that expectations may have a greater biasing effect than opinions. Within each of the major categories considered above, many subtopics and areas are discussed in detail. [See Item Nos. 350 and 351.] (82 footnotes)

353.   Cosper, R. "Interviewer Bias in a Study of Drinking Practices." *Quarterly Journal of Studies on Alcohol* 30, no. 1, pt. B (March 1969): 152-57.

As a method of investigating interviewer bias, Cosper questioned twenty-eight interviewers (15 females, 13 males) who had conducted a drinking survey with 321 respondents. The survey had been completed two years earlier. Interviewer characteristics played a role in the level of drinking behavior identified in respondents. Those interviewers who were themselves drinkers found a higher percentage of respondents to be drinkers, and abstainers found a smaller percentage of the respondents to be drinkers. The author determined that male respondents, but not the female respondents, were influenced by the sex of the interviewers. Cosper is concerned with "interviewer influence that takes place during the interview." It is suggested that interviewer training may not be "an effective means of preventing interviewer bias." Interviewer selection may play a large role in reducing interviewer bias, and may in fact be "more important than training." (5 references)

354.   Ferber, Robert, and Hugh G. Wales. "Detection and Correction of Interviewer Bias." *Public Opinion Quarterly* 16, no. 1 (Spring 1952): 107-27.

Two types of interviewer bias are identified: respondent selection bias and answer bias. The former can be detected by comparing characteristics of judgment sample respondents (respondents were selected by the interviewers from the eight areas into which the study area had been divided) with the corresponding probability samples. The survey was conducted in Champaign-Urbana, Illinois, and dealt with prefabricated housing. There was an absence of bias in the overall sample distributions as shown in table 1. The nature of the selection bias was not uniform in direction. Bias can be question specific and not necessarily appear in the aggregate distribution. Answer bias is said to occur if the distribution of answers from respondents differs from those of the interviewers "by a margin too large to be attributed to random variations." Answer bias was found more often on attitude questions, rather than on factual questions. Answer bias may be positive or negative, that is, the bias may agree or disagree with the interviewers' own attitudes. It does not appear to be consistent among the fourteen interviewers used in the study. Interaction between the two types of biases was not very significant. Suggestions are offered for correcting both types of biases. (17 footnotes)

355.   Freitag, Carl B., and John R. Berry. "Interaction and Interviewer Bias in a Survey of the Aged." *Psychological Reports* 34, no. 3, pt. 1 (June 1974): 771-74.

A statewide social indicators survey of the aged was conducted in twenty-nine counties in the state of Georgia. Fifty-four interviewers were selected from seven colleges and one senior citizens' organization. In a rural group 473 respondents were interviewed, with 251 in an urban group. Attitudes toward the aged, race, and the retired status of an interviewer were found to produce interviewer effects. The researchers found that, in general, when interviewer-respondent differences were minimized, the validity of the interview was greater. In order to avoid interviewer effects, the authors suggest not conducting interviews of the aged with young student interviewers. Additionally, African-American interviewers were not as successful as white interviewers in interviewing white respondents. A table provides a breakdown of each characteristic by mean number of responses not ascertained. (11 references)

356.   Hildum, Donald C., and Roger W. Brown. "Verbal Reinforcement and Interview Bias." *Journal of Abnormal and Social Psychology* 53, no. 1 (July 1956): 108-11.

Using the verbal reinforcements "good" and "mm-hmm," the researchers found that the first response biased the results while the latter did not. The interviews were conducted by telephone with forty male students from the Harvard Summer School who had Cambridge telephone numbers. The students were divided into four groups, with two groups for "good" and two for "mm-hmm." The questionnaire subject matter dealt with general education. In each of the two groups, one-half received the reinforcement for pro answers and one-half received the reinforcement for anti answers. Hildum and Brown suggest that pollsters should try having their interviewers intentionally take different sides and note how the respondents react. In order to reduce bias, the authors observe that interviewers ought to be trained to "control their specific reactions to the content received from an informant." (4 references)

357.   Katz, Daniel. "Do Interviewers Bias Poll Results?" *Public Opinion Quarterly* 6, no. 2 (Summer 1942): 248-68.

To test the influence of social status of the interviewer on the results that the interviewer reports, two groups of interviewers were used: nine white-collar middle-class staff from the American Institute of Public Opinion (the control group); and eleven working-class wage earners, most without a college education (the experimental group). About six hundred interviews were completed by each group, using the same instructions and questionnaire, in the same low-rent areas of Pittsburgh. The ballot concerned six questions on labor, war issues, and government ownership. Some of the results from tables 1-4 are as follows: (1) the control group interviewers found a greater number of conservative attitudes among lower-income groups; (2) the experimental group interviewers found more liberal and radical leanings on labor issues; (3) the working-class interviewers found "greater radicalism" among the union group; (4) the experimental group interviewers found more support for isolationist sentiments among lower-income groups; and (5) the differences in the results may be partly due to the level of interviewing experience of the two groups. It appears that the interviewers' social status influences the findings they report, but it might not always be judicious for all studies to select interviewers with "membership-character" in the group to be interviewed. (5 footnotes)

358.   Olmsted, Donald W. "The Accuracy of the Impressions of Survey In-terviewers." *Public Opinion Quarterly* 26, no. 4 (Winter 1962-63): 635-47.

It was hypothesized that interviewers, over repeated interviews, form opinions known as interviewer bias which can influence subsequent respondents' state-ments. Fifteen college students taking a public opinion class (the experimental group) were used as interviewers for a survey on magazine readership — specifi-cally a university publication for faculty and staff. Mail questionnaires, personal interviews, and telephone interviews were conducted. The students were then asked to estimate, in percentages, the results for selected questions from the schedule. During the following term, twenty control students to whom the sur-vey was described were also asked to estimate the results. The study findings indicate the following: (1) the experimental group, as individuals, were no more accurate than the control group members in estimating survey results; (2) the experimental group was collectively somewhat more accurate than the control group; (3) estimates were not random for either group; (4) there were significant individual differences in accuracy for both groups; (5) the grade obtained in the course was related to accuracy; and (6) sex and academic status (undergraduate or graduate) were not related to accuracy. (18 footnotes)

359.   Salstrom, William, Daniel Katz, Donald Rugg, Frederick Mosteller, and Frederick Williams. "Interviewer Bias and Rapport." Part 2, Chap. 8 in *Gauging Public Opinion*, by Hadley Cantril and Research Associates in the Office of Public Opinion Research, Princeton University, 107-18. Princeton, NJ: Princeton University Press, 1944. Reprint. Port Washing-ton, NY: Kennikat Press, 1972. 318p.

The question of the degree to which interviewers may influence respondents is considered. A number of exploratory studies are described, each of which exam-ines a challenge in the face-to-face interview environment. Salstrom found that on some questions reported opinion does correlate with the interviewer's own opinion. Interviewing in small towns is best completed by interviewers from large cities or at least not by local residents. Experienced and inexperienced interviewers generate as much bias. Distortion is created as a result of class and/or race differences between the interviewer and the respondent. To minimize in-terviewer bias Salstrom suggests choosing "an equal number of interviewers who are biased in different directions." Interviewer bias in one direction cancels the biases in the opposite direction "so that the over-all percentage of opinion is not likely to be significantly wrong." (7 footnotes)

360.   Shapiro, Michael J. "Discovering Interviewer Bias in Open-Ended Survey Responses." *Public Opinion Quarterly* 34, no. 3 (Fall 1970): 412-15.

Shapiro describes a study in which unanticipated interviewer bias was discovered. Approximately forty undergraduate student interviewers were used to interview a random sample of 215 voters in Hawaii. Open-ended questions were used to obtain data on the importance to the respondent of four different voting criteria. Factor analysis was performed on all variables used to measure the salience of the different criteria. The seventh factor produced puzzling results, thereby leading the researcher to believe that the questions measured respondent verbosity, rather than salience. Further analysis showed, however, that when the interviews were grouped by interviewer, it was clear that there was an interviewer bias factor at work. Some interviewers had "goaded" respondents to mention more items to the open-ended questions than their less aggressive counterparts. (3 footnotes)

361.   Sheatsley, Paul B. "The Influence of Sub-Questions on Interviewer Performance." *Public Opinion Quarterly* 13, no. 2 (Summer 1949): 310-13.

In this study the field staff of the National Opinion Research Center (NORC) was used to test the hypothesis "that the proportion of answers received on a given question tends to vary in the direction of the interviewers' own opinion on that question." It was also thought that there would be more "don't know" (DK) responses if there were less probing on the part of the interviewer. There were two waves of the study, February and March 1949, involving 1,261 and 1,302 respondents. The question dealt with government spending. A split ballot with four subquestions was used for the second wave. Sheatsley's data in table 1 indicate that the DK vote shrank from 13 percent to 9 percent. The NORC field staff was shown to make no effort to avoid additional work – although there was an opportunity to do so. Some evidence was found to confirm the first hypothesis. Interviewer attitude is seen as more of a source of bias than as a desire to cheat. (3 footnotes)

362.   Smith, Harry L., and Herbert Hyman. "The Biasing Effect of Interviewer Expectations on Survey Results." *Public Opinion Quarterly* 14, no. 3 (Fall 1950): 491-506.

The National Opinion Research Center conducted an experiment to determine whether there was an "observable interviewer error arising from attitude-structure expectations." The results indicate that these expectations distort the answers given by respondents. Certain interviewers may be more prone to such effects than others. Areas covered in the discussion include (1) the perception theory as applied to interviewing problems, (2) the influence of expectation effects on the validity of survey results, (3) the relative influence of interviewer expectations and ideology, and (4) the relation of interviewer characteristics to attitude-structure expectations. (15 footnotes)

363.   Vicary, James M. "The Circular Test of Bias in Personal Interview Surveys." *Public Opinion Quarterly* 19, no. 2 (Summer 1955): 215-18.

A projective device for measuring attitude and detecting interviewer bias in personal interview surveys is described. The Circular Test of Bias consists of a very long summary question placed at the end of a questionnaire. The question focuses on the important elements of the questionnaire and usually requires a "yes" or "no" answer. The respondent is asked to repeat the question verbatim to the interviewer, thereby testing the principles of selective perception and recall. The test indicates the relative importance and impact of different words in the questionnaire, what is remembered, and why it was remembered. Several examples of the technique are given, and other applications are suggested. (3 footnotes)

364.   Williams, J. Allen, Jr. "Interviewer Role Performance: A Further Note on Bias in the Information Interview." *Public Opinion Quarterly* 32, no. 2 (Summer 1968): 287-94.

Bias may occur in the interview when there is social distance between interviewer and respondent, with the latter seeking to "conform to the opinions or expectations of the interviewer." Williams designed an experiment in which two samples of African Americans were selected from two predominately rural areas and two urban areas in North Carolina. Nine white and twelve African-American interviewers were chosen and tested for their objectivity and personal relations scores. The experiment examined the interviewers' objectivity and response bias, personal relations and response bias, and then considered the interviewers' objectivity, personal relations, and response bias. Williams determined that the interviewer's role performance "affects responses when other factors are held constant." As yet unanswered is which approach reduces bias. (19 footnotes)

BIBLIOGRAPHY

365.   Friberg, Justin C. *Survey Research and Field Techniques: A Bibliography for the Fieldworker.* Council of Planning Librarians, Exchange Bibliography, edited by Mary Vance, no. 513. Monticello, IL: Council of Planning Librarians, January 1974. 42p.

According to Friberg, this bibliography is an outgrowth and expansion of a reading list prepared for a graduate field course in geography, but it "only in [a] small degree reflects a noticeable geographical bias." Most entries have been selected from a wider spectrum of the social sciences, with emphasis on research conducted in the field setting. A total of 461 unannotated references are arranged alphabetically by author under these nine headings (with the number of occurrences following each heading): (1) "An Orientation to Survey Research" - 67; (2) "Sampling" - 68; (3) "Methods of Observation" - 60; (4) "Interviewing" - 105; (5) "Questionnaires" - 48; (6) "Scaling Data" - 25; (7) "Photography" - 15; (8) "Fieldwork in Foreign Areas" - 50; and (9) "Ethical Issues of Fieldwork" - 23. Included are citations to books, chapters in books, journal articles, conference proceedings, and others. Analysis of the dates of the published works shows the following (with the number of occurrences following the year): 1919 - 1; 1920s - 5; 1930s - 9; 1940s - 44; 1950s - 149; 1960s - 207; 1970s - 44; and undated - 2. All references are in English and are primarily published in the United States. Frequently cited journals include the *American Anthropologist*, the *American Journal of Sociology*, the *American Sociological Review, Human Organization*, the *Professional Geographer*, and *Public Opinion Quarterly*.

CHARACTERISTICS

Age

366.   Benney, Mark, David Riesman, and Shirley A. Star. "Age and Sex in the Interview." *American Journal of Sociology* 62, no. 2 (September 1956): 143-52.

When examining the sex and age of interviewers and respondents participating in interviews concerning sensitive areas of communication, the authors' research indicates the following: (1) high responses were achieved by (a) young men talking to young men, and (b) young women talking to young women; and (2) low responses occurred when (a) young men were talking to young women, and (b) older women were talking to older men. Male interviewers obtained fewer responses than female interviewers. Female interviewers received their highest responses from women, except as noted above. From a sample of 3,531 respondents in a Mental Health Survey, 9.4 percent referred to sex as a answer to one question, and 2,036 respondents, 58 percent, listed sexual habits as a possible cause of mental disturbances in response to a second question. This "Interview Project" was conducted at the University of Chicago. (16 footnotes)

367.   Ehrlich, June Sachar, and David Riesman. "Age and Authority in the Interview." *Public Opinion Quarterly* 25, no. 1 (Spring 1961): 39-56.

Approximately one hundred middle-class female interviewers, ranging in age from the early twenties to the late sixties, were used in a study to determine if the "age and bearing" of the interviewers might influence the responses. It was hypothesized that the younger interviewers would be less likely to remind the girls of their parents, and that, regardless of age, some interviewers would appear more authoritative than others. Data were used from a nationwide sample survey of teenage girls concerning, among other aspects, their attitudes toward parents and peers. The survey, the Adolescent Girls Study, was conducted by the Survey Research Center for the Girl Scouts of America. The findings are presented in tables 1 through 13. In general, the younger interviewers received slightly more "peer-oriented" answers. The same is true for the less authoritarian interviewers. Interviewers in the oldest group (over age fifty-three), perhaps perceived as authority figures, received more "adult-oriented" answers. Interviewer effects were greatest among girls whose responses were judged less independent on the four questions used to measure this characteristic and among those girls "presumably subjected to strong cross-pressures, and almost nonexistent among those for whom parental demands in all probability far outweighed peer demands." The authors believe that more attention should be given to matching interviewers and respondents – once information is available about the qualities that make a difference. (21 footnotes)

368.   Kravitz, Sanford, and Camille Lambert, Jr. "Volunteer Interviewers among the Elderly." *Gerontologist* 3, no. 2 (June 1963): 55-60, 90.

A group of seventeen volunteers completed orientation sessions for would-be interviewers. The median age was sixty-eight, with ages ranging from sixty-five to eighty. All of the group members had experience as interviewers during their careers. Potential respondents were sent letters advising them that an interviewer would call. Previous work patterns emerged, with some former sales representatives making five to fifteen calls a day. The researchers initially sought to have three hundred interviews conducted in four weeks, at fifteen to twenty interviews for each volunteer. However, illness on the part of the interviewers or their spouses prevented this schedule. Refusal rates averaged from 5.3 to 22.2 percent. The Newton, Massachusetts, survey was "part of a demonstration project to determine the feasibility of channeling the skills, capacities, and interests of older persons into the health and welfare community in behalf of the chronically ill and aged." The interviewers were paid $1.50 per completed interview for travel expenses, an amount viewed to be insufficient by the volunteers. The authors found that this test group was able to serve as interviewers for fact-gathering surveys, but that there was considerable reluctance to volunteer due to a preference to commitments toward other activities. (3 references)

Appearance

369.   Robinson, Duane, and Sylvia Rohde. "Two Experiments with an Anti-Semitism Poll." *Journal of Abnormal and Social Psychology* 41, no. 2 (April 1946): 136-44.

One experiment examined the impact of having a Jewish-appearing interviewer ask the anti-Semitic poll questions; the second was concerned with whether respondents' answers showed differences when they were asked direct versus indirect questions. In the first experiment four samples were interviewed: (1) 384 by Jewish-looking interviewers; (2) the same number by non-Jewish-looking interviewers; (3) 189 by Jewish-looking interviewers who introduced themselves with Jewish names; and (4) 210 non-Jewish-looking interviewers who introduced themselves with non-Jewish names. The following results were found: (1) respondents express anti-Semitic opinions "more readily" with non-Jewish-appearing interviewers than with those who appear Jewish; (2) prejudicial responses are withheld to a greater degree when Jewish-appearing interviewers introduce themselves with Jewish names; (3) greater differences occur with a general question as compared with a more specific question; (4) lower economic and educational groups respond to a greater degree to the differences in appearance of the two interview modes; (5) direct questions illicit more anti-Semitic responses than do indirect questions; (6) the authors hypothesize that respondents are more willing to agree with anti-Jewish statements when made, rather than attack "on any occasion"; and (7) lower economic and educational groups are "more willing to agree" with anti-Semitic statements. (6 footnotes)

370.   Skelly, Florence R. "Interviewer-Appearance Stereotypes as a Possible Source of Bias." *Journal of Marketing* 19, no. 1 (July 1954): 74-75.

The "bias of interviewer appearance" is discussed in terms of the influence that an interviewer who fits a certain stereotype can have on the survey results. Described is a survey conducted by S-D Surveys, Incorporated, concerning incidence of liquor use – specifically "hard liquor." The company found that respondents reacted to interviewers whom they perceived as stereotypical of individuals holding strong anti-liquor feelings. The author recommends that surveys concerning controversial subjects or products "around which stereotypes have arisen" should have the interviewers screened to remove those whose appearance resembles the stereotype.

Race

371.   Axelrod, Morris, Donald R. Matthews, and James W. Prothro. "Recruitment for Survey Research on Race Problems in the South." *Public Opinion Quarterly* 26, no. 2 (Summer 1962): 254-62.

As part of a larger study undertaken by the University of North Carolina of the
changing role of African Americans in society, sampling and interviewing tasks
were contracted out to the Survey Research Center (SRC) of the University of
Michigan. The article focuses on the special administrative problems encountered by the SRC in recruiting and training an African-American interviewing
staff to survey select areas in the South. The topic concerned African-American
political participation. Desiring a biracial staff for this particular assignment, the
SRC first contacted known African-American scholars and leaders throughout
the South for recommendations. Advertisements were placed in newspapers in
the primary sampling areas. Problems arose in locating interviewers for rural
areas, in acquiring interviewers who were available between March and June,
and in selecting appropriate African-American interviewers (no "race men" or
"Uncle Thomas" types for example). Twenty interviewers were eventually selected and sent to intensive four-day training sessions. Interviewers were told to
stress the southern sponsorship of the study and to de-emphasize the political
nature of the project. The special field problems involved in collecting the data
are noted. Although the quality of the interviews gathered was not available at
the time of the writing of this article, it is stated that no African-American interviewers were threatened or beaten, rapport with respondents was normal, the
level of response was good, and performance, in general, equaled that of regular
SRC professionals. (11 footnotes)

372.   Hatchett, Shirley, and Howard Schuman. "White Respondents and Race-
of-Interviewer Effects." *Public Opinion Quarterly* 39, no. 4 (Winter 1975-
76): 523-28.

Most previous research on cross-racial interviewing has focused on the effect of
white interviewers on African-American respondents [Item Nos. 373, 377, 378,
and 443]. According to the authors, the "problem [of African Americans interviewing whites] deserves to be investigated because of the theoretical light it
may throw on the nature and dynamics of interviewing bias in general." To determine if white respondents show race-of-interviewer effects on sensitive racial
issues as do African-American respondents, 106 of 1,485 whites living in Detroit were selected. They were assigned, randomly, to nine African American
and seven white interviewers – some graduate students involved in the Detroit
Area Study and some professionals from the Survey Research Center. Results
show that on all four items dealing with personal racial attitudes of the questionnaire, whites gave more favorable opinions of African Americans when

the interviewer was African American, the difference being very significant for three of the four items. Although the experimental group was small, Hatchett and Schuman believe the findings can be applied to a large white population. They discuss the use of the Racial Liberalism Index. The authors conclude that "white respondents are at least as susceptible to race-of-interviewer effects as black respondents." It also appears that the more educated a white respondent is, the stronger the need to appear tolerant in the eyes of African Americans. (9 footnotes)

373.   Schuman, Howard, and Jean M. Converse. "The Effects of Black and White Interviewers on Black Responses in 1968." *Public Opinion Quarterly* 35, no. 1 (Spring 1971): 44-68.

Racial effects in interviewing northern urban African-American respondents, dealing with both racial and nonracial topics, is the focus of this article. The authors seek to ascertain the type of question and the type of respondent most affected by race-of-interviewer effects. Such effects were shown to be present in 1968, but were "limited primarily to questions dealing with militant protest and hostility toward whites." Effects are higher for African Americans at the lowest status levels and are not noticeable at a lower level among young African Americans or those born in the North. The largest effects are noted when the question asked the respondents to name their favorite entertainers. The authors observe that "black entertainers are mentioned much more to black interviewers, white entertainers to white interviewers." Schuman and Converse explain this as the "frame-of-reference phenomenon." (31 footnotes)

374.   Skelton, Sharon Scott Barnhart. "The Effects of Race and Sex of the Interviewer on Automated Interview Behavior." Ph.D. diss., University of Alabama, 1973. 131 leaves. [*Dissertation Abstracts International* Order No. 7327381; *DAI* 34B, no. 5 (November 1973): 2318.]

Fifty white male and female students in psychology courses at the University of Alabama were used in a study of the effect of race and sex of the interviewer on noncontent verbal behavior. The students were shown thirteen videotapes via the Standardized Video Taped Interview (SVTI), which presented thirteen African American and white, male and female interviewers. Students were asked to rate each interviewer on "likability" according to the Adjective Check List. There were "highly significant" differences in likability among the interviewers, and a "significant difference between the extreme interviewers in each race-sex group." Female students rated the interviewers "more likable" than did males. An additional study is reported which involved four of the same interviewers, one from each sex and race group. All had received similar likability ratings in the first study. Here, the SVTI was used with thirty-two males and thirty-two females to observe the interaction between them and the four interviewers. References are provided.

375.   Wardrip, Jon Paullin. "A Comparison of the Susceptibility of Black versus White Respondents to Race-of-Interviewer Effects on Racial and Nonracial Questions in Both Personal and Self-Administered Questionnaire Interviewing Situations." Ph.D. diss., University of Texas at Austin, 1979. 195 leaves. [*Dissertation Abstracts International* Order No. 8009950; *DAI* 40A, no. 11 (May 1980): 6038.]

The research compares the degree to which African-American and white respondents are affected by two types of response effects. Personal interviews and self-administered questionnaires were used to present both racial and nonracial questions. Investigated were the "susceptibility" of race-of-interviewer effects on the African-American and white respondents, if and how much the respondents reacted to the two methods of administration, the effect of the questionnaire format in overcoming response bias, and which method (interview-respondent effect or method-of-administration) produced more response bias. Analysis of the data reveals the following: (1) major sources of response bias were due to race-of-interviewer effects for both races; (2) whites tended to provide more "socially accepted" answers on racial questions to opposite-race interviewers in personal interviews; (3) questions of a racial nature produced more response bias; (4) self-administered questionnaires were more effective at overcoming biasing effects on racial questions for whites but not for African Americans; and (5) interviewer-respondent effects produced more response bias on racial questions than did the method of administration; however, there was little difference between the two on nonracial items. Wardrip suggests that African Americans may interview whites if the questionnaire format is used and privacy is assured, and that while African Americans should interview African Americans on both racial and nonracial questions, the "use of self-administered questionnaires may help reduce the tendency among blacks to answer more 'militantly' to other blacks." References are provided.

376.   Williams, Frederick, and Hadley Cantril. "The Use of Interviewer Rapport as a Method of Detecting Differences between 'Public' and 'Private' Opinion." *Journal of Social Psychology* 22, 2d half (November 1945): 171-75.

Four questions, three concerning the 1944 presidential election and one focusing on World War II, were asked of two comparable cross sections of approximately eight hundred African Americans in Harlem, New York. One group was interviewed exclusively by white interviewers, while the other was interviewed entirely by African-American interviewers. No significant differences were found among the responses obtained from white versus African-American interviewers on the three political questions. However, African Americans somewhat tended to hide their opinions from the white interviewers as to who was our chief enemy – the Japanese or the Germans. It is noted that while 55 percent of the national population ranked Japan, rather than Germany, as our chief enemy in April 1944, only 26 percent of the Harlem African Americans reflected this opinion. (1 footnote)

377.   Williams, J. Allen. "Interviewer-Respondent Interaction: A Study of Bias in the Information Interview." *Sociometry* 27, no. 3 (September 1964): 338-52.

This article is a summary of Williams's dissertation [Item No. 378]. A sample of 840 African-American respondents was created from two urban and two rural areas in North Carolina. Thirteen African American and nine white females were given a full-day training course in interviewing. Issues concerning the measurement of social distance (race and social rank) and threat potential in the interview schedule were explored. Williams determined that "race of interviewer, social distance between respondent and interviewer, and the threat potential of interview questions are related to interview bias." The race of the interviewer is a biasing issue only when the social distance is high and the interview question is very threatening. An appendix includes questions from the interview schedule arranged in order of threat potential. (19 footnotes)

378.   Williams, James Allen, Jr. "Interviewer-Respondent Interaction: A Study of Bias in the Information Interview." Ph.D. diss., University of North Carolina at Chapel Hill, 1963. 158 leaves. [*Dissertation Abstracts International* Order No. 6409446; *DAI* 25, no. 8 (January 1967): 4857.]

The issue addressed by Williams is whether interviewer characteristics influence the information provided by respondents in surveys. Three possible variables were examined: (1) social distance, as measured by the race of the interviewer and an index of social position; (2) role performance, identified through fifteen indicators including the three main items of objectivity, agreeableness, and the use of good interviewing techniques; and (3) threat potential of the interview questions, which are divided into the categories of "irrelevant," "relevant verifiable," and "relevant-nonverifiable." The sample consisted of 870 African-American respondents from rural and urban areas. Area sampling was utilized, and nine white and thirteen African-American interviewers were employed. Williams found that social distance and threat potential are "highly associated with bias" in survey interviews. Role performance was not as clear in outcome, but while objectivity is necessary for reducing bias on its own, it cannot overcome other interviewer characteristics (such as race). References are provided.

Sex

379.   Colombotos, John, Jack Elinson, and Regina Loewenstein. "Effect of Interviewers' Sex on Interview Responses." *Milbank Memorial Fund Quarterly* 47, no. 1, pt. 2 (January 1969): 227-32. (Adapted from *Public Health Reports* 83, no. 8 [August 1968]: 685-90.)

The investigation found that there was "essentially no difference" in the reporting of psychiatric symptoms to twenty-one white male and ten white female interviewers in a community survey. The sample consisted of 2,300 housing units. A total of 1,713 respondent forms were completed. Of these, 86 percent or 1,479 were completed by the interviewers described above, each of whom completed fifteen or more forms. The authors observe that response patterns for other subjects and specific other questions may produce different results, but at least for psychiatric symptoms questions, the need to hire either male or female interviewers must be "critically reexamined." (12 references)

380.   Kirsch, Arthur D., Carol H. Newcomb, and Ira H. Cisin. *An Experimental Study of Sensitivity of Survey Techniques in Measuring Drinking Practices*. George Washington University, Social Research Project, Report no. 1. Washington, DC: Social Research Project, George Washington University, March 1965. 20p.

The two goals of the study were to determine if the techniques developed by the California Drinking Practices staff were "sufficiently precise to classify persons into appropriate quantity-frequency groups in large-scale sample surveys," and to compare male and female interviewers with respect to male and female respondents in terms of their ability to determine patterns of drinking habits. The experimental group consisted of eighty-one interviews of individuals "listed on the rolls of an alcoholic clinic in a southern metropolitan area as having sought help (or having been referred by others for help) but who failed to follow through on treatment." The control group was composed of eighty-one persons who were members of the same sex, race, and age level living in the same neighborhoods as the above. Male interviewers yielded less "under-statement" of drinking versus female interviewers. The first goal was validated in that the researchers determined that the set of questions used can classify the respondents as needed. (4 footnotes)

Speech

381.   Blair, Edward Allen. "Non-Programmed Speech Behaviors in a Household Survey." Ph.D. diss., University of Illinois at Urbana-Champaign,

1978. 216 leaves. [*Dissertation Abstracts International* Order No. 7820903; *DAI* 39A, no. 5 (November 1978): 3108.]

Nonprogrammed speech includes interviewer supplied probes, feedback, and variations from the written questions. Blair wanted to know if this form of speech has an impact on respondents' feelings and answers in a personal interview for a household survey. The three effects investigated were favorable feedback, improper probing behaviors or coding errors, and additional reading errors and "speech disfluencies." It was believed that as the questioning became more threatening, interviewers' behaviors would cause respondents to "become uneasy and distort their answers." The study results show "little or no systematic effects on respondents." Since over forty thousand speech records were in the data set, it is unlikely that the results were due to measurement problems. Blair offers several possible explanations as to why the effects did not occur, including that "extralinguistic anxiety cues had no effects." References are provided.

382.   Collins, W. Andrew. "Interviewers' Verbal Idiosyncrasies as a Source of Bias." *Public Opinion Quarterly* 34, no. 3 (Fall 1970): 416-22.

This study explores the effect of interviewers' verbal habits on the validity of survey data. Interview schedules from two California cities were used. Measures were vocabulary, or how often certain words appeared in recorded responses, and verbosity, or how long the recorded response lasted. Data presented in tables 1 and 2 suggest that both vocabulary and verbosity habits of the interviewer "pose a serious double threat to the validity of much survey data." Even statistical controls for situational and respondent effects (such as time of interview, type of call, number of calls, and sex of the respondent) did not reduce the significant main effects. Collins concludes that while random error may balance out over the course of a study, systematic error probably does not. The author emphasizes the need for better training procedures, the careful use of openended questions, and specifying precisely what constitutes an adequately recorded response. Questions for future research are posed. These concern the nature and direction of the effects of interviewer error, and how and under what conditions the idiosyncratic verbal behavior of interviewers affects study conclusions. (10 footnotes)

Voice

383.   Barath, Arpad, and Charles F. Cannell. "Effect of Interviewer's Voice Intonation." *Public Opinion Quarterly* 40, no. 3 (Fall 1976): 370-73.

Interviewers have a tendency to drop their voices while asking a long series of "agree-disagree" or "yes-no" list items (instead of raising their voices as is usual in asking questions). Two issues are investigated in this study: (1) whether voice-dropping versus voice-raising intonation would have any effect on the frequency of "yes" responses; and (2) whether intonation of a question would have any effect on the respondents' motivation to complete a task. Nine female interviewers were used to interview a total of 228 women between ages eighteen and sixty-five in Toledo and Detroit. Respondents were divided into two groups (interviewer voice rising or interviewer voice dropping) and given a list of health-related questions. It was found that the number of affirmative responses was significantly higher for the voice-rising group. The interest level of this group was maintained at a much higher level as well. Four explanations are offered for the outcome. It is concluded that interviewer intonation can have a powerful effect on response behavior. Further investigation is needed to determine if there are implications for task-related motivation. (5 references)

384.   Blair, Ed. "More on the Effects of Interviewer's Voice Intonation." *Public Opinion Quarterly* 41, no. 4 (Winter 1977-78): 544-48.

Blair criticizes the findings of a previous study by Barath and Cannell [Item No. 383]. He believes the literature cited by those authors neither supports nor contradicts the hypothesis that raising the interviewer's voice will elicit more positive responses. The effect on response of naturally occurring interviewer's voice intonations (where the interviewer has not been coached to raise the voice) is studied. Of an original sample of 1,172 interviews, 1,048 were taped-recorded, and 483 were selected to receive a twelve-item and a nine-item checklist on leisure and sports activities. The fifty-nine interviewers were judged on their intonation. The data in tables 1 to 3 show sharply contradictory results to those of Barath and Cannell, in that in Blair's research rising intonations are associated with lower reporting. Blair suggests several reasons which may account for the differences between the two studies. However, he does not suggest that dropping intonations cause higher reporting. (10 references)

385.   Wechsler, James. "Interviews and Interviewers." *Public Opinion Quarterly* 4, no. 2 (June 1940): 258-60.

One challenge that the interviewer faces is that the person being interviewed may not know what the interviewer is talking about. As individuals do not like to reply "no opinion," answers may be forthcoming about which they have no understanding. Wechsler raises the question of bias, noting that an interviewer may ask a question in "belligerent, positive tones, with the obvious inference that he won't take no for an answer." The author continues by observing that the interviewer "can make his victim extraordinarily uncomfortable." Voice tone and presentation method are two of the ways the interviewer can influence the responses. Wechsler believes that careful attention to detail by polling organizations can help achieve the goal of appropriate interviewing techniques.

CHEATING, FRAUD, AND MISREPRESENTATION

386.   Allen, I. L., and J. D. Colfax. "Respondents' Attitudes toward Legitimate Surveys in Four Cities." *Journal of Marketing Research* 5, no. 4 (November 1968): 431-33.

The issue addressed here is the impact that salespeople have who start their presentations with an interview as a means of getting the door opened. In Chicago, 60 percent of respondents had experienced interviews which led to sales attempts. Two hundred fifty communities in thirty-four states have imposed either registration of interviewers with police or a ban on door-to-door calling. For this study surveys were conducted in four Connecticut cities: Hartford, New Haven, Bridgeport, and Waterbury. Respondents were asked five questions concerning salespersons posing as interviewers, the prohibition of the approach, and their views on legitimate surveys. Of those who granted interviews, legitimate surveying seemed to be well regarded and not an area which respondents felt should be restricted. Allen and Colfax observe that how the interview sales approach impacts overall refusal rates, and access to respondents in cities in general, remains to be explained. (7 references)

387.   Baxter, Richard. "An Inquiry into the Misuse of the Survey Technique by Sales Solicitors." *Public Opinion Quarterly* 28, no. 1 (Spring 1964): 124-34.

Two approaches were used to determine the level of misuse of surveys by sales solicitors. The first dealt with public awareness of the deceptive use of surveys; the second was a survey of researchers and their perceptions of the problem. Using its California Poll, the Field Research Company of San Francisco questioned 589 individuals. The results show that significant proportions of the adult public had been approached by individuals using deceptive surveys. The article analyzes the different experiences of women and men, city and rural, telephone and in-person interview, geographic area, and type of product being sold with respect to the California Poll results. The second approach of surveying the directors of research organizations showed that by a two-to-one margin these individuals did not see refusal as problematic. Additionally, maintaining rapport during interviews did not seem to be a problem. (2 footnotes)

388.   Bennett, Archibald S. "Toward a Solution of the 'Cheater Problem' among Part-Time Research Investigators." *Journal of Marketing* 12, no. 4 (April 1948): 470-74.

A number of steps are suggested to deal with the "cheater problem." These include paying interviewers to read the instructions twice, and paying them an appropriate rate in a timely manner. Additionally, the questionnaire form should be kept as simple as possible. A grading sheet for supervisors is recommended – a check-off sheet which permits an evaluation of how effective the supervisor has been. A "Thanks for the Interview" card is used which, among other purposes, permits the survey organization to determine if someone was really interviewed. The card has a place for the name, date, length of interview, and subject discussed. Bennett reasons that these methods will adjust existing problems and allow organizations to identify errant interviewers. (1 footnote)

389.   Crespi, Leo P. "The Cheater Problem in Polling." *Public Opinion Quarterly* 9, no. 4 (Winter 1945-46): 431-45.

The "cheater" problem on the part of the interviewer is of growing concern to pollsters. Most research has highlighted the role of the morality of the interviewer. However, Crespi believes cheating problems "lie as much in the structure of ballots and the conditions of administration as in the personal integrity of the interviewer." He sees the problem as one of morale, rather than of morals. Ways of analyzing cheating through an examination of the ballot, and tests to detect fabrication, are given. Demoralizing factors for the interviewer include unreasonable length of the ballot; too many questions demanding "why" and "what for" answers; lengthy wording; and complex, antagonizing, and repetitive questions. Administrative demoralizers for interviewers consist of little personal contact between themselves and the office; part-time positions; very difficult samples; and unfavorable conditions (such as the weather). Suggestions are offered to alleviate the situation, but the ultimate solution is the institution of a national professional interviewing organization. This group would set standards and initiate a code of ethics for the profession. (2 footnotes)

390.   Evans, Franklin B. "On Interviewer Cheating." *Public Opinion Quarterly* 25, no. 1 (Spring 1961): 126-27.

The problem of cheating, although rarely addressed in the literature, is perhaps more widespread than is realized. Two factors that may increase cheating on the part of interviewers are the difficulty of locating and interviewing preselected respondents and telephoning them for appointments, and allowing hired interviewers to recruit their friends or acquaintances. A case is cited in which four of thirteen experienced married female interviewers, working part-time, were caught cheating. The four interviewers were all close friends. After contacting a respondent by telephone and acquiring some information, the interviewers then faked (or filled out themselves) vital parts of the survey (in this case a psychological schedule) without contacting the respondent in person as was required. Some brief suggestions are made as to how to better control the cheater problem. (1 footnote)

391.   Hauck, Mathew. "Is Survey Postcard Verification Effective?" *Public Opinion Quarterly* 33, no. 1 (Spring 1969): 117-20.

The use of a thank-you letter with a return postcard asking about some aspect of an interview has been widely used to reveal falsified interviews. In an attempt to test the validity of this method, four geographic areas in Illinois were selected. A previously interviewed sample of 587 people and a matching noninterviewed sample of 580 were sent thank-you letters with return postcards. Some thank-you letters and postcards identified the study and others did not. The following are some of the study findings: (1) about 50 percent of the interviewed sample returned the postcard, as opposed to only 10 percent of the noninterviewed sample (table 1); (2) the return rate was greater in rural than in urban areas for the interviewed sample, but geographic area had little effect on the noninterviewed sample; (3) for the interviewed sample, identification of the study had little effect on return of the postcard, but this was opposite for the noninterviewed sample; (4) six respondents said they had not been interviewed when they had, and eight said they had been interviewed when they had not (table 2); and (5) older respondents, those better educated, and more whites than African Americans returned the postcards. Implications of the findings are discussed. Hauck concludes that the postcard method "should not be used as a primary form of quality control on surveys." (3 footnotes)

392.   Hofstetter, C. Richard. "Salesmen as Survey Researchers: A Note on Fraudulent Interviews." *Social Science Quarterly* 52, no. 4 (March 1972): 991-94.

The effect of unethical misrepresentation by salespersons making sales pitches may lead to what Hofstetter refers to as "dampened public receptiveness to legitimate research endeavors." In a 1970 study 557 Ohio residents with home telephones were interviewed by the staff of the Polimetrics Laboratory of the Department of Political Science at the Ohio State University. The completion rate was a little less than 60 percent, with the most frequently stated reason for refusal due to prior sales misrepresentation. Over half of all the survey contacts in Ohio were phony sales gimmicks. Hofstetter observes that refusal rates, respondent "reactivity," and the possibility of restrictive legislation are all areas for concern for the professional survey researcher. (4 footnotes)

393.   Rugg, W. Donald. "Interviewer Opinion on the 'Salesman as Interviewer' Problem." *Public Opinion Quarterly* 35, no 4 (Winter 1971-72): 625-26.

In response to a letter from the American Association for Public Opinion Research, the Opinion Research Corporation (ORC) investigated the problem of salespersons posing as interviewers. These pseudo-interviewers were most frequently trying to

sell magazines, encyclopedias, and home furnishings. A total of 747 ORC interviewers were polled. The results indicate that 51 percent said they had been refused an interview because the respondent believed it was a sales pitch. Nearly
half of the interviewers had heard of cases where salespersons had used the survey approach while attempting to sell a product. The major source of survey
abuse information came from the respondents. Approximately 45 percent of the
interviewers offering an opinion thought there were survey abuses by salespersons and that this was a serious problem.

EFFECTS

394.   Blankenship, Albert B. "The Effect of the Interviewer upon the Re-
        sponse in a Public Opinion Poll." *Journal of Consulting Psychology* 4,
        no. 4 (July-August 1940): 134-36.

The issue of whether the interviewer may influence the way in which individuals respond was recognized early in polling. A study of three experienced interviewers is discussed. In the summer of 1939 the three interviewers asked ten
questions for a total of three hundred interviews. The results were tabulated,
with an asterisk indicating the attitudes of the interviewers for each of the questions. The study found that interviewers secured more answers in line with their
own views in three of seven categories which showed reliable differences; in
four other categories some interviewer effect was noted in seven of thirty-one
questions. In a large national poll the variety of interviewers would probably not
lead to such a constant bias. Polling agencies repeatedly discard an interviewer's
work which is "entirely out of line" with the results of others. (5 footnotes)

395.   Bridge, R. Gary, Leo G. Reeder, David Kanouse, Donald R. Kinder, Viv-
        ian Tong Nagy, and Charles M. Judd. "Interviewing Changes Attitudes
        – Sometimes." *Public Opinion Quarterly* 41, no. 1 (Spring 1977): 56-64.

Several prior studies on interviewer effects are reviewed in detail. Interviewer
effects are seen to present important ethical and methodological problems, especially for panel or "wave" studies – those conducted over a period of time.
The respondent's desire to "maximize self-esteem" and to "master the environment, to be competent" are two factors to be taken into account in explaining
interview effects. For this experiment 376 UCLA staff members were randomly selected and randomly assigned to different treatment conditions. All were
asked questions about either cancer or crime. About one week later one-half
received either relevant information or no information. Five weeks later all were
reinterviewed. Interviews were conducted by telephone by sixteen experienced
interviewers. It was found that asking questions about cancer changed the respondent's attitudes toward the importance they attached to good health. However,

interviewing about burglary prevention showed no similar interview effects. It is suggested that interview effects occur "when the respondent's attitudes and information are unfocused or ambiguous *and* the topic is important." (3 footnotes, 14 references)

396.   Cannell, Charles Frederick. "A Study of the Effects of Interviewers' Expectations upon Interviewing Results." Ph.D. diss., Ohio State University, 1954. 164 leaves. [*Dissertation Abstracts International* Order No. 5800679; *DAI* 18, no. 3 (1962): 1092.]

Intensive personal interviews lasting from one to one-and-a-half hours were conducted in the homes of 462 respondents. Each interviewer conducted between seventeen and thirty-five interviews. The questions asked were of the "open" variety which required more than a single-word answer (thereby forcing interviewers to use various techniques to "stimulate" the respondent to provide complete responses). Cannell found that "interviewers' personal expectations or attitudes did not effect the results of interviews," and that there were "few differences" among interviewers. Subject matter had a greater bearing with regard to interviewer differences than did interviewer expectations. Interviewer differences can be overcome through appropriate interviewing techniques and interviewer training. Factual questions were "relatively free" from interviewer differences, by contrast with impersonal or abstract questions which showed significant differences among interviewers. Cannell was unable to ascertain the cause of these interviewer differences. References are provided.

397.   Dohrenwend, Barbara Snell, John Colombotos, and Bruce P. Dohrenwend. "Social Distance and Interviewer Effects." *Public Opinion Quarterly* 32, no. 3 (Fall 1968): 410-22. [An adapted version of this article appears in *Milbank Memorial Fund Quarterly* 47, no. 1, pt. 2 (January 1969): 213-26.]

A model was developed to address the question as to which types of interviewers bias what types of respondents. The first hypothesis tested was that white middle-class interviewers, with negative attitudes toward individuals of lower status, bias the responses of African Americans and white lower-class respondents more than do white middle-class interviewers without negative attitudes. A sample of 1,713 adults from the Washington Heights Health District of New York City were interviewed by fifty-seven male and female interviewers. The respondents were divided into three income levels. The results were consistent with the hypothesis, except that no difference was found among low-income African Americans by type of interviewer. The second hypothesis addressed dealt with status similarity as a likely generator of biased answers. No evidence was found that "embarrassed" interviewers recorded more biased answers from respondents of like sex or age than those received from respondents whose sex or age were different. (19 footnotes)

398. Feldman, J. J., Herbert Hyman, and C. W. Hart. "A Field Study of Interviewer Effects on the Quality of Survey Data." *Public Opinion Quarterly* 15, no. 4 (Winter 1951-52): 734-61.

Data for the study were drawn from a 1949 survey on civic problems and voting practices in Denver, Colorado. The survey had two "hidden" purposes, the second of which, and the basis for the present article, was to examine the variations in respondents' replies to questions of both a factual and an opinion nature "obtained by interviewers of known characteristics." Equivalent assignments were given to five groups of nine interviewers, with Denver being divided into five matched sectors of 270 respondents each. The results were as follows: (1) few important differences were found among individual interviewers on questions of the closed type and on questions of fact; (2) there were very significant differences in interviewers' field ratings of certain respondent attributes; (3) on open-ended questions there were wide interviewer differences both in the kind and number of responses; and (4) there were wide variations in the proportion of invalid responses gathered by individual interviewers to questions of a factual nature. Interviewer effects on the validity of study results are discussed. Approximately four pages review prior literature on the topic. (24 footnotes)

399. Hyman, Herbert. "Isolation, Measurement, and Control of Interviewer Effect." *Items – Social Science Research Council* 3, no. 2 (June 1949): 15-17.

The project described is part of a two-year study sponsored by the joint Committee on Measurement of Opinion, Attitudes and Consumer Wants of the National Research Council and the Social Science Research Council. Several approaches were undertaken in the study: (1) case studies and phenomenological interviewing; (2) quantitative methods; (3) common effects with relationship to validity; (4) end effects; and (5) dynamics of the interviewing process. The actual research was conducted by the National Opinion Research Center with the assistance of an advisory committee composed of Frederick F. Stephan (chair-person), Archibald M. Crossley, W. Edwards Deming, George Gallup, Paul F. Lazarsfeld, Rensis Likert, and Elmo Roper. (2 footnotes)

400. Hyman, Herbert. "Problems in the Collection of Opinion-Research Data." *American Journal of Sociology* 55, no. 4 (January 1950): 362-70.

The primary challenge in the collection of survey research data is the effect of the interviewer on the quality of the results This article explores the work of the National Opinion Research Center in the isolation, measurement, and control of this phenomenon. Hyman introduces an idea, then presents examples. Variations may arise from one or more of the following reasons: (1) the recording method might be changed from previous practices; (2) the interaction between interviewer and respondent; (3) the way the interviewer perceives the respondent; and (4) the interviewer wishes to avoid asking tedious, embarrassing or difficult questions. Experiments are described which are designed to determine the role of situational factors in the interview setting. The validity of interview data is discussed. (11 footnotes)

401.   Shosteck, Herschel. "Respondent Militancy as a Control Variable for Interviewer Effect." *Journal of Social Issues* 33, no. 4 (Fall 1977): 36-45.

The challenge created by interviewer effect is discussed, and the shortcomings of the standard procedure of trying to match interviewers and respondents on ethnic and, where possible, socioeconomic characteristics, are described. These problems include the difficulty of finding ethnic interviewers, the high dropout rate of ethnic interviewers, the high turnover among African-American interviewers, and the significant increase in research costs due to the challenges described. Interviewer effects are described in terms of their subtlety, specific results of a study, and how to interpret their impact. One way of dealing with the effect is to utilize militant African Americans for respondents since the "answer patterns which blacks give blacks and those which militants give whites are virtually the same." The author suggests "extreme caution" in utilizing the approach, given the "limitations of our data." (2 endnotes, 6 references)

402.   Stember, Herbert, and Herbert Hyman. "Interviewer Effects in the Classification of Responses." *Public Opinion Quarterly* 13, no. 4 (Winter 1949-50): 669-82.

As part of a larger study by the National Opinion Research Center, tests were made to determine if there would be different results if responses were classified into precoded answer boxes in the field, rather than recorded verbatim and classified centrally. The work was based on the hypothesis that the results would be different and that more interviewer effects, or bias, would be noted when the field coding procedure was utilized. The authors consider two factors that might introduce bias under conditions of field classification: judgmental problems and motivational factors. The study design used a questionnaire with identical questions on international affairs. Each interviewer received forms with answer boxes and forms to be recorded verbatim. A comparison of the two samples under the varying recording conditions is shown in table 1. For the most part the field classification method did not affect the overall results. However, it was found that attitudinal biases affected the classification of answers of inexperienced interviewers more than experienced interviewers (table 6). (17 footnotes)

403.   Sudman, Seymour, Norman M. Bradburn, Ed Blair, and Carol Stocking. "Modest Expectations: The Effects of Interviewers' Prior Expectations on Responses." *Sociological Methods & Research* 6, no. 2 (November 1977): 171-82. [Reprinted in *Survey Design and Analysis: Current Issues*, edited by Duane F. Allen. Sage Contemporary Social Science Issues, no. 46. Beverly Hills, CA: Sage Publications, 1978. 156p.]

A national sample of 1,172 respondents to a 1975 National Opinion Research Center survey was the basis for this study. In each of fifty primary sampling areas the best interviewers were selected (two or three from each area, all female, and mostly between the ages of thirty-five and fifty). A self-administered questionnaire was completed by the selected interviewers prior to conducting the interviews. Six questions concerning expectations about the survey appeared in the questionnaire. The actual survey dealt with leisure activities, with threatening questions following questions about bowling, golfing, and so forth. The threatening questions concerned drinking, drugs, and sexual behavior. The study results indicate "small effects" as a product of interviewer prior expectations – which in most practical situations are trivial and "can be ignored." The research does suggest that "interviewers who expect a study to be difficult should not be hired for that study," and that interviewers "should not be trained to expect underreporting." (9 references)

404.   Udow, Alfred B. *The "Interviewer-Effect" in Public Opinion and Market Research Surveys.* In *Archives of Psychology*, edited by R. S. Woodworth, no. 277. New York, NY: n.p., 1942. 36p. [This is a reprint of Udow's dissertation completed at Columbia University, 1942. The original dissertation is unavailable for borrowing and therefore has not been included in this bibliography.]

The first of two surveys was conducted by interviewers who did not know who the sponsor was, and a second was undertaken by interviewers who had been provided with false information regarding sponsorship. Prior to conducting each survey, interviewers gave their own answers to the survey questions. Twenty-two interviewers conducted 660 interviews. Udow found that neither the interviewers' own opinions nor the knowledge of sponsorship affected the survey results. The "common belief" is that interviewers affect data in "ways favorable to the opinions they themselves hold." Two areas not addressed are personal involvement by the interviewers in the questions and interviewer training. (12 references)

405.   Venkatesan, M. "Laboratory Experiments in Marketing: The Experimenter Effect." *Journal of Marketing Research* 4, no. 2 (May 1967): 142-46.

The discussion begins with a review of the work of social psychologists investigating the experimenter effect. Sources of bias include the following: (1) experimenter expectancy and outcome-orientation; (2) effects of early data returns; (3) desirability of data; (4) modeling effects of the experimenter; (5) personality; (6) sex; and (7) other attributes of the experimenter. Studies are reported on experimenter expectation, modeling, and attributes, as well as on early data returns. The results show that the experimenter is unaware of the biases, and they are not generated with intent. Both verbal and visual cues transmit bias. Venkatesan observes that experimenter bias must be reduced if a true science of marketing is to be developed. (33 references)

ERROR

406.   Case, Peter B. "How to Catch Interviewer Errors." *Journal of Advertising Research* 11, no. 2 (April 1971): 39-43.

In 1968 the Advertising Research Foundation offered an interview verification service to market research firms. The system used nine items in a telephone reinterview with the respondent to verify that the interview occurred as it had been planned, and to determine the performance of the interviewer. Field Audit and Completion Test (FACT) data indicate that one of four interviews may contain serious errors. Most of the errors are committed by a small group of interviewers and usually occur when the respondent is difficult to reach. Four tables provide FACT error data.

407.   Hansen, Morris H., and Joseph Steinberg. "Control of Errors in Surveys." *Biometrics* 12, no. 4 (December 1956): 463-74.

The errors considered here involve those occurring in the collection process. The authors begin with a discussion of the general approaches to controlling errors. The *Current Population Survey* (*CPS*) is addressed, including a review of procedures for selection, training, and supervision. (The *CPS* is conducted monthly for purposes of estimating labor force characteristics, as well as for other information requirements on an as-needed basis.) Field operations of the *CPS* constitute the focus of the article, with consideration of the "control and quality check procedure." Reinterviews and reconciliation procedures are also discussed. Hansen and Steinberg note that more attention needs to be directed toward respondent errors.

408.   Neely, Twila E. "A Study of Error in the Interview." Ph.D. diss., Columbia University, 1937. 150 leaves. [Not available from *Dissertation Abstracts International.*]

The dissertation is divided into two parts: chapters 2 through 7 concern the errors of the respondents, and chapters 8 through 10 discuss the errors of the interviewer. Part 1 includes consideration of withholding of facts; distortion as a result of interest, emotion, and memory; inadequate factual knowledge to answer questions; and memory difficulties as related to the areas of employment history, earnings and income, and cost of living and consumption. Part 2 reviews interviewer problems caused by inadequate communication skills, by difficulty in describing the required data, and through carelessness. The concluding chapter delineates four types of questions and gives specific categories for each. These are the questions which are the most difficult for the respondents, followed by moderately difficult, least difficult, and those for which the accuracy is not yet known. Yearly earnings fit in the most difficult category, and age and education are examples from the least difficult category. The accuracy of the respondent-supplied data concerning injuries in automobile accidents is described in an appendix. References are provided.

INSTRUCTIONAL MATERIALS

409.   Adams, J. Stacy. *Interviewing Procedures: A Manual for Survey Interviewers.* Chapel Hill, NC: University of North Carolina Press, [1958]. 56p.

Basic general principles and procedures of interviewing are presented, with explanations of both the "hows" as well as the "whys" of interviewing techniques. The physical format of the publication is designed to be small enough to enable easy use in the field. Although the section on sampling is specifically focused on the procedures used in the Survey Operations Unit at the University of North Carolina, the principles employed are also presented. In a brief history of surveys the 1790 Census is cited as one of the first "systematic surveys." The chapters in the manual include the introduction, the phases of an interview survey, interviewing, sampling, and interviewer bias. A forty-eight-item, brief-entry glossary is provided, along with an eight-entry suggested readings list.

410.   Bader, Carolyn F. *The Interviewer's Guide.* St. Louis, MO: Institute of Market Research, 1947. 110p.

The basics of market research interviewing are covered, with emphasis on the qualifications needed and the techniques used by successful interviewers. The volume opens with a foreword titled "Survey Susy" by Frances T. Kirkwood (reprinted from *Family Circle Magazine*). This places the interviewers' role in the context of post-World War II – the mid-1940s. The purpose and function of various aspects of market research are explained, along with other information that Bader believes the interviewer needs to know (such as techniques for interviewing persons from a variety of social classes, interviewing farmers, and pretesting). The final chapter deals with the issue of memorizing answers to questions (the author suggests that the interviewers take notes). Nine cartoons by Walter H. Sudfeld are included. A twelve-item glossary completes the volume.

411.   *A Guide to Survey Research for Interviewers.* Rev. ed. [Chicago, IL]: Elrick and Lavidge, 1967. 26p.

The volume is divided into two parts: "The Theory and Purpose of Marketing Research" and "The Practice of Survey Research." Part I provides an introduction to market research, examines how to define the problem which is to be addressed, reviews planning the questionnaire, and offers suggestions for selecting the respondents. Sampling accuracy, probability sampling, sample size, and the need for callbacks are described. Part II considers the preparations necessary for interviewing, such as familiarity with the sampling instructions. The next section provides specific techniques to be used during interviewing, for example asking and reading every question exactly as it appears in the questionnaire. In the following section there are ten points which describe how to obtain responses. The final two sections deal with processing the interview information and analyzing, interpreting, and reporting the data. A summary statement highlights the steps involved in a market research survey.

412.   "An Interviewer Tells How to Avoid Getting Wrong Answers from Research." *Printers' Ink* 262, no. 2 (10 January 1958): 73-74.

Questions which are "ambiguous, stilted, wordy, over-formal" lead to diluted and adulterated answers according to Samuel Katz, an interviewer with a large consumer research firm. Katz provides a number of examples to illustrate his points. He also believes that the communication distance between the research analyst and the interviewer is large. Although each new questionnaire is accompanied by a clarification sheet, these sheets usually simply state the obvious. The challenge – "take down everything the respondent says" – is discussed with the inference that not everything can always be recorded, as this could be over one hundred words. Katz believes that (1) interviewers should be more thoroughly briefed, (2) survey goals need to be explained, (3) survey question writers should have to periodically work at interviewing to see how their efforts work in practice, (4) every question ought to be pretested, and (5) more space should be provided on questionnaires.

413.   University of Michigan. Survey Research Center. *Interviewers' Manual: Survey Research Center.* Rev. ed. Ann Arbor, MI: Survey Research Center, Institute for Social Research, University of Michigan, 1976. 143p.

The sample survey is explained by means of the kinds of questions which are asked, how the results will be used, the types of surveys available, and how surveys are conducted. The interviewing procedure is introduced in terms of how the initial contact is made and the interview is secured. Questionnaire use is discussed, followed by an outline of interviewing techniques including probing and nondirective probing. The chapter on recording and editing discusses notetaking strategies and provides examples of tape-recorded interviews. Call and callback strategy, sampling principles and procedures, and identifying the respondents' locations are covered. Forms, records, and administrative procedures are described. Many illustrations accompany about half the chapters. Appendixes include a table for computing percentages, pretesting, a letter to authorities, and a tape-recorded interview evaluation code. The book includes a three-page subject index.

414.   Williams, Douglas. "Basic Instructions for Interviewers." *Public Opinion Quarterly* 6, no. 4 (Winter 1942): 634-41.

The "basic instructions" are those used by the National Opinion Research Center for their interviewing staffs. The following are some of the topics covered: (1) the selection of respondents, for example what a proper "spread" should be, and correct distribution; (2) how to approach a potential respondent using a proper introduction; (3) the manner and attitude desired during the interview; (4) how to process certain types of answers; (5) matters relating to completing the questionnaire; and (6) how to obtain more sensitive data from a respondent. Interviewers are cautioned against taking interviews over the telephone, having friends take their place, and sharing the results of their efforts with others.

INTERVIEWER-RESPONDENT INTERACTION

415.   Atkin, Charles K., and Steven H. Chaffee. "Instrumental Response Strategies in Opinion Interviews." *Public Opinion Quarterly* 36, no. 1 (Spring 1972): 69-79.

Two experiments were conducted to test the hypothesis that some respondents attempt to have their opinions influence the behavior of the interviewer. Respondents whose motivation is that they believe they can gain something (for example, advice, power, prestige, and so forth), will consciously distort their answers, thereby possibly invalidating the data. The respondents might try to ask the interviewer questions or try to control the interviewer's feelings toward them, perhaps through "ingratiation" tactics. The interviewer's self-identification was systematically varied in the two field studies. The first experiment involved fifty-six Madison, Wisconsin, residents who were questioned by Firefighters Union officials. Ingratiation effects were found on the fire-fighting items, but anti-ingratiation effects were noted on questions dealing with a public policy issue. In the second experiment the respondents were 225 mothers in Middleton, Wisconsin. The subject was television violence. There was little difference between the experimental and control groups in their support for federal action on television violence. The authors believe that the two field studies uphold the above-stated hypothesis, and that the essential problem in personal interviews "is one of interpretation and not of data collection." (21 footnotes)

416.   Bradley, Joseph E. "Survey Bias as a Function of Respondent-Interviewer Interaction." Ph.D. diss., Pennsylvania State College, 1953. 90 [13] leaves. [*Dissertation Abstracts International* Order No. 0007404; *DAI* PSU 16, 530.]

The respondent-interviewer interaction study undertaken sought to determine if the sex of the interviewer had an impact on the ease of the interview and the degree to which rapport was achieved with the respondent. Additionally, Bradley investigated whether the respondent's interest in the content is connected to susceptibility to interviewer effects. The results indicate the following: (1) "few major deviations [exist] between the sample of respondents interviewed by men and those interviewed by women"; (2) male interviewers average more refusals than female interviewers; (3) respondents have better rapport with male interviewers at the end of the interview; (4) male interviewers' approach is about as successful as female interviewers, but are more feared by female respondents who therefore are not as likely to permit entrance to the home for the interview; (5) females tend to be more truthful with interviewers; and (6) "some questions may show the least interested respondents most subject to interviewer bias and other questions may show the least and most interested respondents least subject to interviewer bias." Appendix A contains the directions given to the interviewer, as well as a copy of the questionnaire. References are provided.

417.   Brown, J. Marshall. "Respondents Rate Public Opinion Interviewers." *Journal of Applied Psychology* 39, no. 2 (April 1955): 96-102.

This article is a summary of Brown's dissertation [Item No. 418]. The Respondent Rating Scale (R.R. Scale) used is shown in full. Three tables are included, the first of which relates interviewing criteria with interviewers' ratings; the second compares the answers respondents gave with how the interviewers were rated; and the third shows the percentages of respondents by age, educational level, and economic level who answered the identical question the same way or differently on the questionnaire and the R.R. Scale. Brown found a significant positive relationship between interviewers' ratings of behaviors during the interview with respondents' indications thereof. (3 footnotes, 24 references)

418.   Brown, John Marshall. "The Development and Testing of a Respondent Rating Scale for Opinion and Market Research Interviewers." Ph.D. diss., Pennsylvania State College, 1951. 194 leaves. [*Dissertation Abstracts International* Order No. 0003301; *DAI* PSU 14, 435.]

The purpose of this dissertation was to "develop and test a new method of evaluating interviewer-respondent relationship." The approach used was to have the respondents rate the interviewers. The Respondent Rating Scale (referred to as the R.R. Scale) is provided in appendix A. Brown found that the R.R. Scale was useful for measuring interviewer work characteristics, aspects of the questionnaire, and the feelings of the respondents during the interview. Respondents who gave better answers on the scale provided fewer "don't know" answers and contributed more useful answers to free-response questions. The scale answers did not increase when respondents were interviewed by persons with high supervisory ratings, greater experience, lower refusal rates, or were among the last three interviewed by one interviewer. Brown determined that the R.R. Scale is useful as an evaluation device for opinion and marketing research interviewers. References are provided.

419.   Cannell, Charles F., and Morris Axelrod. "The Respondent Reports on the Interview." *American Journal of Sociology* 62, no. 2 (September 1956): 177-81.

Three different methods of investigation were used to collect data to determine respondents' perception of interviews and what their attitudes were toward having been interviewed. Survey A used the *Survey of Consumer Finances* conducted by the Survey Research Center (SRC). The three thousand respondents were heads of families. About three-fourths of the interviewers were female. Survey B, conducted jointly by the Scripps Foundation for Research in Population Problems and the SRC, involved questions on plans for family size. The interviewers and the respondents were female. The third, Survey C, used approximately eight hundred interviews, was conducted in the Metropolitan Detroit area, and concerned decision making within the family. Results of the three studies show that a high proportion of respondents reacted favorably to being interviewed, and a high proportion were willing to be reinterviewed. These findings varied only slightly from study to study. The authors conclude that a major element was pleasure in the relationship with the interviewer, and that respondents will provide information, even of a very personal nature, "as a means of maintaining the enjoyable personal connection with the interviewer." Cannell and Axelrod note that the proportion of respondents who found the interview interesting varied only slightly among the three studies, even though the types of questions asked (factual versus attitudinal) differed greatly. (2 footnotes)

420.   De Koning, Thomas Lewis. "Interviewer and Respondent Interaction in the Household Survey Interview." Ph.D. diss., University of Michigan, 1969. 196 leaves. [*Dissertation Abstracts International* Order No. 7014498; *DAI* 31A, no. 2 (August 1970): 824.]

The different types of verbal activities engaged in by interviewer and respondent are studied, with particular attention given to the impact that race and age have on these activities. Four sample groups of employed male respondents (African Americans and whites, age groups 18-34 and 35-64) were interviewed by four white, middle-class, middle-aged, female interviewers. In total 181 interviews were conducted and tape-recorded. Using a specially devised coding scheme, all verbal behavior was coded. Approximately 40 percent of all interviewer behavior is outside of question asking and probing (and therefore not controlled for in interviewer training). The most frequent uncontrolled interviewer behavior is feedback, accounting for 23 percent of all interviewer behavior. Question type produced different results by race and age. African-American respondents "manifested more behaviors before an adequate answer was obtained" to open questions, and older respondents "showed more behaviors before an adequate answer" was provided to closed questions. Older respondents exhibited a larger proportion of all behaviors than younger respondents. Young respondents were more task-oriented, had lower rates of inadequate answers, and asked more frequently for clarification. Young African-American respondents were more likely to get feedback, and African Americans and older respondents were more likely to receive clarification after making requests. A theoretical explanation for the interview environment is explained by the respondents ingratiating themselves with the interviewer by providing a response that they believed will meet with the interviewers' approval. By contrast, interviewer ingratiation was established by the social-emotional use of feedback. References are provided.

421.   Fowler, Floyd Jackson, Jr. "Education, Interaction, and Interview Performance." Ph.D. diss., University of Michigan, 1966. 257 leaves. [*Dissertation Abstracts International* Order No. 6614520; *DAI* 27A, no. 7 (January 1967): 2195.]

The research seeks to identify and investigate the reasons for the "consistent" tendency of less-educated respondents to provide less accurate and more incomplete answers in sample surveys. Four hundred twelve Health Interview Survey (HIS) interviews were used as the basis for the study. The relationship between thirty-five HIS interviewers and respondents was observed in four different ways. Four variables were investigated which might account for the relationship between respondent education and respondent performance. The analysis showed significant differences by education in the skill level the respondent had toward the task, the knowledge they had concerning the interview, their feelings toward the task, and their relationship with the interviewer. The

author concludes that "(1) the factors affecting the quality of respondent performance differ by respondent education; (2) respondent attitudes have little
power in explaining performance differences in this particular interview; [and]
(3) developing an effective interviewer-respondent relationship is a critical
problem in obtaining good performance from less educated respondents." References are provided.

422.   Freeman, John, and Edgar W. Butler. "Some Sources of Interviewer Var-
          iance in Surveys." *Public Opinion Quarterly* 40, no. 1 (Spring 1976): 79-
          91.

Some prior research studies on interviewer variance as linked to response error
are reviewed. The present study investigates the possible influence of interviewer-respondent interaction as a contributing factor to interviewer variance.
The data used came from a survey of "housewives" in California and was based
on 2,600 interviews conducted by thirty-three interviewers. All but one were
schoolteachers without previous survey interviewing experience, but who had
taken a three credit university course in interviewing. The subject was mental
retardation. Items included in the analysis were age, sex, socioeconomic status,
social mobility, and interviewer ratings. Results are as follows: (1) interviewer
variance was found to differ across interview schedule items; (2) variance was
influenced by combinations of age and sex of interviewers and respondents; (3)
comparisons on socioeconomic status produced inconsistent results; (4) interviewer ideology schedules proved less useful than expected; and (5) interviewer
ratings provided no grounds for a hypothesis. The authors conclude that selecting interviewers and assigning respondents is complex, and that matching interviewers to respondents on "fact sheet" characteristics may cause error in some
cases and reduce it in others. (19 footnotes)

423.   Goudy, Willis J., and Harry R. Potter. "Interview Rapport: Demise of a
          Concept." *Public Opinion Quarterly* 39, no. 4 (Winter 1975-76): 529-
          43. [Reprinted in *Readings in Survey Research,* edited by Robert Fer-
          ber, 429-43. Chicago, IL: American Marketing Association, 1978. 604p.]

Much of the prior research which examines the concept of rapport in interviewing is reviewed. Particular attention is paid to the work of Weiss (Weiss, Carol.
"Interaction in the Research Interview: The Effects of Rapport on Response."
Proceedings, Social Statistics Section, American Statistical Association, 1970, 18-
19.). Weiss suggests that the idea of rapport, as a meaningful component in the
interview situation, be abandoned. She believes that the measures of rapport are
different, thus making the entire concept ambiguous, and in one case, directly in
conflict. The present paper focuses on the relationship between rapport and the
variables often suggested as being influential to the interview situation. Using
Hill and Hall's rapport scale (Hill, Richard J., and Nason E. Hall. "A Note on

Rapport and the Quality of Interview Data." *Southwestern Social Science Quarterly* 44, no. 3 [December 1963]: 247-55.), Goudy and Potter conducted 619 interviews as part of two community studies in urban and rural areas of a midwestern state. The scale included rapport items, interviewer characteristics, and interview variables. Generally, the interviewers with extensive experience reported higher rapport scores than those of the inexperienced interviewers. Several factors appearing to correlate with rapport are noted. The authors advocate adopting Weiss's suggestions and concentrating on the problems involved in recording and coding interview data. Further empirical research on the topic may be without merit "unless agreement on a conceptual and operational definition can be reached, and unless elements in the interviewing situation purporting to constitute rapport can be isolated and tested." (38 footnotes containing 70 references)

424.   Marquis, Kent H., and Charles F. Cannell. *A Study of Interviewer-Respondent Interaction in the Urban Employment Survey.* Ann Arbor, MI: Survey Research Center, August 1969. 94 leaves plus appendixes. (This final report was submitted to the Manpower Administration, U.S. Department of Labor, Contract No. 81-24-68-26, and is available as technical report PB 188 456 through the National Technical Information Service.)

The survey, a revised version of the Urban Employment Survey, was designed to ascertain employment and income difficulties for individuals in urban slum areas. Four sample groups, totaling 181 interviews, were conducted with employed males (white and African American, age groups 18-34 and 35-64). The interviewers were white, female, and middle-class. Each interview was tape-recorded and "discrete items of verbal behavior of both respondent and interviewer were coded for analysis," with an average of five hundred "verbal acts" coded per interview. Of these, 44 percent were by the respondents and 56 percent were by the interviewers. Interviewers' behavior consisted of question asking, probing, and feedback. Approximately one-third of all verbal behaviors occurred after an "adequate" response had been obtained. The effect of race on verbal behavior was "not great (compared to age)." Older respondents had a "high 'behavior activity level' " – responding to a much greater degree than younger respondents. Using the greater verbal responses to open-ended questions as an example, the researchers note that "the type of question is an important variable in determining the outcome of the interview." A number of the incorrectly asked questions contained "ambiguous parenthetical statements" or used awkward syntax. Questions which required recall of past events or where the goal was not clear to the interviewers generated inadequate answers. Additionally, questions requiring many verbal exchanges, detailed answers, and difficult forced-choice answers produced inadequate answer rates. (14 references)

425.   Marquis, Kent Hammond. "Effects of a Household Interview Technique Based on Social Reinforcement." Ph.D. diss., University of Michigan, 1967. 151 leaves. [*Dissertation Abstracts International* Order No. 6717813; *DAI* 28A, no. 7 (January 1968): 2776.]

The interview format discussed concerns the household health variety in which respondents fail to provide all the information requested. An underreporting bias exists for chronic and acute conditions. A study was undertaken to test whether changes in the behavior of the interviewer would adjust the frequency of reporting health information. In the experimental group the interviewer provided a reinforcing statement after each instance of morbidity reported by the respondent, gave longer introductions to sections of the survey, asked longer questions, looked at the respondent when the interviewer was speaking, and smiled. In the control group none of the above behaviors were used by the interviewers. The social reinforcements, and other behaviors described, increased the reports of symptoms and conditions by about 25 percent. Physician visit reports were not increased in the experimental group. Marquis notes that complex interactions account for the behavior exhibited, primarily between approval motivation and awareness, and among approval motivation, item embarrassment, opportunity for social reinforcement, and if the respondents are reporting for themselves or for others. References are provided.

SELECTION AND TRAINING

426.   Andrews, Lee. "Interviewers: Recruiting, Selecting, Training, and Supervising." Section 2, Part B, Chap. 5 in *Handbook of Marketing Research*, edited by Robert Ferber, 2/124-2/132. New York, NY: McGraw-Hill Book Company, [1974]. (various pagings)

The selection of interviewers section considers the following characteristics deemed appropriate: good health, extroversion, and "favorable personal appearance." The observation is made that opportunities exist for both sexes. Race, nationality, and sex are covered, and it is noted that "blacks do better with black respondents, and whites with whites." Personnel recruitment and basic training for the field are also discussed. A list of "dos and don'ts" is provided under the category of working procedure. The role of the supervisor is seen as making certain that the instructions are followed and that the surveys are delivered on time. A discussion follows as to how the supervisor should meet these goals. (4 references)

427.   Barioux, Max. "A Method for the Selection, Training, and Evaluation of Interviewers." *Public Opinion Quarterly* 16, no. 1 (Spring 1952): 128-30.

The role of the interviewer in the effectiveness of a polling organization is viewed as crucial. Barioux describes several methods for the successful selection, training, and evaluation of the interviewer. Traits and qualifications consistent with a good interviewer are a pleasant manner, an ability to exude confidence, an ability to follow instructions, accurate work habits, an honest personality, and perseverance, as well as intelligence, meticulousness, and a belief in the value of polls. A questionnaire, personal references, and perhaps a trial interview are used to detect desirable physical and social qualities. An interviewer's work is judged primarily by the lack of refusals gathered and technical errors made. By means of an "Observation Chart" and other evaluation techniques, feedback is provided to the interviewer as to her/his performance alone and in relation to the other interviewers. (1 footnote)

428.   Converse, Jean M., and Howard Schuman. *Conversations at Random: Survey Research as Interviewers See It*. New York, NY: John Wiley & Sons, [1974]. 111p.

The work presented is based on the thoughts of 150 graduate students who, over a ten-year period, were trained in survey research, specifically through the University of Michigan's Detroit Area Study. The issues covered include how interviewers solve – and also how they fail to solve – practical field situations, as well as how researchers and respondents are viewed by the interviewers. The intended audience includes students, social scientists, and individuals interested in "interviewing as a way of life." A fifty-five-entry annotated bibliography on interviewing and seventy-one footnotes are provided. The volume closes with an appendix in which the authors discuss fourteen points concerning the training of interviewers. An author index and a brief subject index are supplied.

429.   Dvorak, Beatrice J., Frances C. Fox, and Charles Meigh. "Tests for Field Survey Interviewers." *Journal of Marketing* 16, no. 3, pt. 1 (January 1952): 301-6.

The U.S. Bureau of Labor conducted a standardized battery of aptitude tests for use in selecting the Field Survey Interviewers. Twelve hundred individuals were to be hired in ninety-one locations across America for positions lasting from six weeks to four months. The U.S. Employment Service was responsible for the aptitude battery. Job analysis and criterion were conducted. The following measures of aptitude were determined: (1) intelligence – general learning ability; (2) verbal; (3) numerical; (4) spatial; (5) form perception; (6) clerical perception; (7) aiming or eye-hand coordination; and (8) motor speed. An experimental group of 130 Field Survey Interviewers was administered the tests. The General Aptitude Test Battery results were analyzed, with intelligence, verbal and numerical ability, and clerical perception deemed the most important for survey interview performance. Potential interviewers were interviewed, and if hired, received job evaluations based on their success. The bureau filled twelve hundred positions in one week using the above techniques. (2 footnotes)

430. Guest, Lester. "A New Training Method for Opinion Interviewers." *Public Opinion Quarterly* 18, no. 3 (Fall 1954): 287-99.

The training method utilized was to have simple discussions of the schedule to be employed. The categories used were discussion, schedule discussion and the use of practice interviews, and schedule discussion and some experience in coding. Sixty interviewers were involved in the experiment (some others were also included as substitutes were needed). Error reduction was higher as a result of the coding experience, rather than as a result of the practice interviews. The results do not indicate that fatigue or "good expectations" played a role in error rate as the assignment approached the end. (16 footnotes)

431. Lienau, C. C. "Selection, Training and Performance of the National Health Survey Field Staff." *American Journal of Hygiene* 34, no. 3, section A (November 1941): 110-32.

During the winter of 1935-36, the National Health Survey employed over 4,000 individuals to conduct over 800,000 schedules for families covering sixty-four demographic all-illness items. The project was funded by the federal government through the Works Progress Administration and was supervised by the U.S. Public Health Service. Numerous tests covering abilities and special achievement in completing the schedule were given to the field staff. Information about the "enumerator" was attached to the records collected. Interviewer error information was maintained. The article is divided into three sections: (1) organization, selection, training, and records of the field staff; (2) differences of household size and illness reporting related to the sex, age, education, and occupation of the enumerator; and (3) psychological examination, training test, and field performance of the staff. (8 footnotes, 1 reference)

432. Menefee, Selden. "Recruiting an Opinion Field Staff." *Public Opinion Quarterly* 8, no. 2 (Summer 1944): 262-69.

The article details the author's experiences in organizing a nationwide field staff of interviewers as part of a program of the Office of Public Opinion Research at Princeton University. As an initial step, interviewing was conducted in fifty-nine "sample points" around the country. Key personnel were contacted by letter in each of the areas. The letters asked for recommendations for possible interviewers. Good sources for these recommendations are school superintendents, teachers, librarians, heads of social work agencies, YMCA and YWCA secretaries, newspaper editors, labor union officials, and so forth. Desirable traits for interviewers are stability, honesty, dependability, a pleasant personality, intelligence, an interest in polling, objectivity, and preferably, some interviewing experience. In wartime, especially, good sources for interviewers are "housewives," teachers, librarians, social workers, free-lance writers, students, and retirees. Some of the main categories to be avoided are salespersons, those already employed full time, those working for another poll, those of foreign birth, and the wealthy. Seven steps for training the newly hired personnel are given.

433.   Morgan, Elizabeth Gregory. "The Right Interviewer for the Job." *Journal of Marketing* 16, no. 2 (October 1951): 201-2.

Interviewers may be more appropriately utilized with certain types of respondents. A case is described in which the "expensive ensemble and perfect grooming" of an interviewer biased the responses to questions concerning luxury cosmetics. Further examples are provided, one in which the interviewer appears "stupid" – an appearance Morgan describes as being readily seen as a cause for a study to be invalidated. Assigning an interviewer to respondents which creates "unrest and dissatisfaction" is to be avoided. Training supervisors are advised to classify interviewers carefully and to send them on assignments for which they are "best suited."

434.   Reed, Vergil D., Katherine G. Parker, and Herbert A. Vitriol. "Selection, Training and Supervision of Field Interviewers in Marketing Research." *Journal of Marketing* 12, no. 3 (January 1948): 365-78.

Sponsored and developed by the American Marketing Association Committee on Marketing Research Techniques, this article is intended to provide the fundamentals in a nontechnical format. In discussing interviewer selection the following areas are considered: (1) sources; (2) letters of application; (3) academic sources; (4) women's organizations and key individuals in the community; (5) newspapers and other market research organizations; (6) full-time versus part-time resident interviewers; and (7) qualifications. Training is reviewed in terms of the planning stage, manuals or handbooks, individual survey instruction, and other aids. In the supervision section the authors discuss validation, the new interviewer, the experienced interviewer, new surveys, and the need for standards. (2 footnotes)

435.   Rugg, Donald. " 'Trained' vs. 'Untrained' Interviewers." Part 2, Chap. 6 in *Gauging Public Opinion*, by Hadley Cantril and Research Associates in the Office of Public Opinion Research, Princeton University, 83-97. Princeton, NJ: Princeton University Press, 1944. Reprint. Port Washington, NY: Kennikat Press, 1972. 318p.

Individuals who received personal instruction in interviewing techniques are referred to as "trained"; individuals who received training by mail are called "untrained." The National Opinion Research Center (NORC) provided interviewers with instruction booklets, as well as personal instruction. The American Institute of Public Opinion (AIPO) secured, trained, and supervised interviewers by mail. Fifty-five NORC interviewers and a corresponding number of AIPO interviewers were compared on the quality of their work as judged by four independent raters. Rugg reports that there was "no significant difference between the quality of work turned in by the trained and untrained interviewers." The NORC interviewers were, however, better at following instructions and obtaining complete data, while the AIPO interviewers recorded more "spontaneous comments" and were considered to be "really well trained." AIPO has decided to send representatives to personally supervise the training of interviewers. (5 footnotes)

436. Sheatsley, Paul B. "The Art of Interviewing and a Guide to Interviewer Selection and Training." Chap. 13 in *Research Methods in Social Relations with Especial Reference to Prejudice*. Part 2. *Selected Techniques*, by Marie Jahoda, Morton Deutsche, and Stuart W. Cook, 463-92. Published for the Society for the Psychological Study of Social Issues. New York, NY: Dryden Press, 1951. Part 1 (pages 2-421) and Part 2 (pages [423]-759) comprise the two-volume set.

Sheatsley, of the National Opinion Research Center, offers suggestions on effective ways to select interviewers and to improve their skills through proper training. He first discusses six general rules of interviewing procedure, including how to establish rapport with the respondent, how to ask a question, and ways to efficiently obtain and report a response. The important considerations in selecting an interviewer are also discussed. These include choosing personnel with traits such as intelligence, accuracy, adaptability, temperament, health, appearance, interest, and so forth. Several additional pages are devoted to the issues of how to motivate and train interviewers.

437. Snead, Roswell P. "Problems of Field Interviewers." *Journal of Marketing* 7, no. 2 (October 1942): 139-45.

The climate under which interviewers operated in the early 1940s is described. Snead observes that while attention has been focused on how the data are analyzed, little effort has been directed toward interviewers and how they perform their functions. It is noted that most interviewers are married women who have other jobs, and conduct interviews in their off-hours. The method of notifying interviewers of an impending assignment is described. Snead suggests that the notification is usually extremely brief with little informational value. Many organizations view their interviewers as "contractors," and, when compared with others in such roles, are not adequately apprised in advance of their tasks. A number of other suggestions are made which are designed to promote the relationship between interviewers and the organizations for which they work. It is observed that advances in the supervision and training of a widespread part-time workforce are likely to be slow. (8 footnotes)

438.   Womer, Stanley, and Harper Boyd. "The Use of a Voice Recorder in the Selection and Training of Field Workers." *Public Opinion Quarterly* 15, no. 2 (Summer 1951): 358-63.

The successful use of the tape recorder for screening qualified interviewers and for assisting in their training is reported. The authors describe the construction of a model which incorporates the typical field problems that an interviewer will be likely to encounter. A hidden recording machine records the trial interview or "script" which is then scored by the project supervisor. The advantages and disadvantages of the technique are outlined. As an aid in training programs, details are given for projects designed to handle a single project, rather than to train field-workers in general. Womer and Boyd describe the composite interview, the making of the script, the job sample interviews, the role of the project supervisors, and the possibilities for training field interviewers assisted by a recorder.

INTERVIEWING

GENERAL

439.   Cannell, Charles F., and Robert L. Kahn. "The Collection of Data by In-
        terviewing." Chap. 8 in *Research Methods in the Behavioral Sciences*,
        edited by Leon Festinger and Daniel Katz, 327-80. New York, NY: Holt,
        Rinehart & Winston, 1953. 660p.

The chapter begins with a consideration of the potentialities and the limitations
of the interview. The psychological basis of the interview is explored, as well as
the motivation of the respondent. A discussion of questionnaire design covers
the following points: (1) purpose; (2) language; (3) frame of reference; (4) information level; (5) social acceptance; (6) leading questions; (7) the single idea;
(8) question sequence; (9) question form; and (10) the pretest. Interviewing principles are highlighted, including asking the questions, stimulating complete responses, and recording the responses. A forty-six-entry sample interview is included (with complete interviewer and respondent observations). Some principles of interviewer training are provided. The chapter has a one-page summary and
an eighteen-entry bibliography.

440.   Cannell, Charles F., Kent H. Marquis, and Andre Laurent. *A Summary
        of Research Studies of Interviewing Methodology*. In *Vital and Health
        Statistics: Data Evaluation and Methods Research*. Public Health Ser-
        vice Publication No. 1000, Series 2, No. 69. U.S. Department of Health,
        Education, and Welfare, DHEW Publication No. (HRA) 77-1343. Rock-
        ville, MD and Washington, DC: U.S. Department of Health, Education,
        and Welfare, Public Health Service, Health Resources Administration,

National Center for Health Statistics, March 1977. 78p. [SuDoc HE20. 6209:2/69]

The interviewing process is examined to identify aspects which can be improved in order to achieve greater success in data collection. The data presented show that when the length of the interview question is substantially increased, with the information demand held the same, "no appreciable increase" is obtained in response duration, the response contains more information, and the information reported is more valid. A possible explanation is that lengthening the question adds redundancy which may impair the clarity of the question. Broad areas of discussion include the following: (1) a review of studies of underreporting of health events in household interviews; (2) interview behavior; (3) interviewer performance differences and the impact on supervision and training; (4) verbal reinforcement and data accuracy; (5) memory and information retrieval; and (6) question length and reporting behavior in the interview. (75 references)

441.   Caplow, Theodore. "The Dynamics of Information Interviewing." *American Journal of Sociology* 62, no. 2 (September 1956): 165-71.

Six principles of interviewing, which Caplow suggests are generally agreed upon, are outlined. The author maintains that interviewers are inadequately trained. Among the principles is the notion that the interviewer should remain neutral in order to "facilitate the self-expression of the respondent." Caplow notes that when dealing with areas of behavior which are condemned by all, respondents misreport and suppress facts no matter how unobtrusive the interviewer tries to be. The interview is defined as a "two-person conversation, conducted by one of the participants in accordance with a definite program." Long survey interviews can be successfully concluded, even though there may be no benefit to the respondent. Only in cases of interviewer strain or confusion is a respondent likely to seek to discontinue the interview once it is underway. Pretests of interview schedules, through trial and error, may reduce some of the challenges faced by interviewers, but individual reaction may not fit predetermined categories. (27 footnotes)

442.   Getzels, J. W. "The Question-Answer Process: A Conceptualization and Some Derived Hypotheses for Empirical Examination." *Public Opinion Quarterly* 18, no. 1 (Spring 1954): 80-91.

Most of the previous investigations in the field have focused on the process of responding to visual stimuli. Getzels believes that the process of responding to verbal stimuli is more complex since it involves social interaction. He maintains that more research needs to be directed toward the underlying processes of observed response, instead of simply focusing on the observed response itself. The analytic steps in a three-step model of the question-answer process are described (the model was based on recent theoretical and experimental studies in the field of perception). Also discussed are the effect of interviewer characteristics on responses to the same question, how respondents bias their answers to reflect what they perceive to be "correct" behavior, and the effect of the situational context or settings in which a question is asked. Getzels concludes by enumerating eleven derived hypotheses for empirical examination. These have been tested elsewhere with "generally positive" results. (15 footnotes)

443.   Hyman, Herbert H., with William J. Cobb, et al. *Interviewing in Social Research*, with a foreword by Samuel A. Stouffer. A Phoenix Book. Chicago, IL: University of Chicago Press, 1954. 415p.

The National Opinion Research Center, commissioned by the Social Science Research Council and the National Research Council joint Committee on Measurement of Opinion, Attitudes and Consumer Wants, conducted a study (beginning in 1947) to systematically investigate the sources of error which occur when interviewing using the data collection approach. The study required almost six years. The book is both a report of these findings and a "treatise on interviewing." The first of seven chapters begins with a consideration of the reliability of interviewing. Other chapters define the interview situation; consider interviewer effects; discuss reactions of the respondent; review the situations in which interviewer effect occurs; and investigate interviewer effects under "normal" operating conditions and how these effects can be measured and reduced. Thirty pages of endnotes are included.

444.   Schwartz, Alvin. "The Public Relations of Interviewing." *Journal of Marketing* 27, no. 3 (July 1963): 34-37.

The main reasons governing why those who consent to be interviewed and those who refuse are addressed. Schwartz begins with willing respondents and quickly moves to refusals, where suspicion that the interviewer is trying to sell something, and suspicion that there are other motives for the interview, are the basis for the behavior. Community regulation of interviewers is noted, with six states cited, for a total of 117 communities with regulations in place. Other topics discussed include the perception of the respondent, the quality of the interviewer, and the factors which build interviewer acceptance. Schwartz notes the need for greater understanding of market research, as well as the need to deal with misrepresentation on the part of salespersons.

ADMINISTRATION

445.   Bevis, Joseph C. "Management of Field Staffs in the Opinion Research Field." *Journal of the American Statistical Association* 40, no. 230 (June 1945): 245-46.

The practices of the Opinion Research Corporation (ORC), with whom Bevis is associated, are described. ORC has two kinds of interviewers: those who travel the country, and resident interviewers. The resident staff, which numbers 851 interviewers in 566 locations, is almost entirely part time, with two-thirds female and one-third male. ORC deals directly with field interviewers. Instructions to interviewers are generally brief. Upon employment, each new interviewer receives a training manual and guidance from a supervisor. ORC pays by the hour, believing this approach will assure careful completion of entries by the interviewer. Most interviewers are hired by mail.

446.   Sheatsley, Paul B. "Some Uses of Interviewer-Report Forms." *Public Opinion Quarterly* 11, no. 4 (Winter 1947-48): 601-11.

The uses of interviewer report forms by the National Opinion Research Center (NORC) are reported. The applications of the forms fall into the categories of questionnaire wording and construction, analysis of polling results, and supervision and maintenance of the field staff. In 1943 the NORC forms were improved and standardized. Seven questions are given which all NORC field staff are asked to complete. Factors listed for making a survey difficult include questionnaire design, public reaction to issues, size and type of quota, and weather and season. "Uninteresting" surveys are ones in which there are problems with the subject of the survey or the questionnaire design, as well as other factors (such as busy or uninformed respondents). Additional uses of interviewer reports are as measures of public interest and knowledge, and as guides to misunderstandings and motivation. The forms' usefulness in establishing and maintaining rapport between the supervisor and the field staff is discussed. (3 footnotes)

447.   Sudman, Seymour. "Time Allocation in Survey Interviewing and in Other Field Occupations." *Public Opinion Quarterly* 29, no. 4 (Winter 1965-66): 638-48.

Time records, submitted by survey research interviewers, are used as a basis for an analysis of interviewing costs. Data were drawn from studies emanating from the National Opinion Research Center, the Census Bureau (the 1960 Census and the *Current Population Survey*), and the Survey Research Center of the University of Michigan. Tables 1 through 3 illustrate the percentage of time spent by the three organizations' interviewers on various tasks such as study time, clerical time, editing time, travel, and interviewing. Despite differences in methodology, similarities among the studies were significant. Interviewers in all studies were found to spend approximately one-third of their time interviewing and the rest of the time addressing associated tasks. The second part of the article is devoted to a comparison of payment method and interviewing time among four groups: the interviewers, social workers, public health nurses, and salespersons. Payment for interviewers is usually on an hourly basis, while the others work for a fixed salary or commissions. Allocation of interviewing time shows strong similarities among all groups except the nurses. Method of payment, education, age, or family status were not significant variables. Stressful, uninvited, and tense personal contact with the respondent (a feature common to interviewers, social workers, and salespersons) is offered as a reason for the similarities. (7 footnotes)

BIBLIOGRAPHIES

448.   Kinton, Jack F. *Interviewing: A Comprehensive Social and Behavioral Science Bibliography*. Aurora, IL: SSSR [Social Science and Sociological Resources], 1974. 15 leaves. Photocopy.

This unannotated bibliography contains citations to 218 books and journal articles. It is arranged in six sections (with the number of citation occurrences following the title of the section): (1) "Textbooks on Social Research Interviewing" - 28; (2) "Interviewing Books 1968-1973" - 49; (3) "Interviewing: Selected Journal Articles Bibliography 1955-1968" - 41; (4) "Interviewing: Selected Journal Articles Bibliography Pre-1955" - 15; (5) "The Field Research Interview: A Selective Journal Article Bibliography" - 30; and (6) "Interviewing: A Journal Articles Bibliography 1968-1973" - 55. There is minimal duplication of titles among the categories. Thirty-three entries are marked with an asterisk (denoting a valuable addition to the literature), and twenty-seven entries are marked with a double asterisk (denoting a crucial addition to the literature). The entry dates range from 1932 to 1973 with the following percentage breakdown by decade: 1930s - 10 percent; 1950s - 23 percent; 1960s - 38 percent; and 1970s - 29 percent.

449.   Sharma, Prakash C. *Interview and Techniques of Interviewing: A Selected Research Bibliography (1930-1966)*. Council of Planning Librarians, Exchange Bibliography, edited by Mary Vance, no. 715. Monticello, IL: Council of Planning Librarians, December 1974. 28p.

The bibliography contains a listing of 379 unannotated references to books, chapters in books, and journal articles in the field of interviewing. Part 1 lists 92 books and 124 articles published from 1930 to 1955. Part 2 lists 58 books and 105 articles published from 1956 to 1966. Citations are arranged alphabetically by author within these time periods. All are English-language titles and "are by no means definitive nor are they meant to be, but they represent many of the publications which may be used as guides for further research." Frequently cited journal titles include the following in alphabetical order: *American Sociological Review*; *Journal of Abnormal and Social Psychology*; *Journal of Social Psychology*; and *Public Opinion Quarterly*. There are misspellings and numerous omissions of bibliographic data in the Sharma compilation.

COMPUTER ASSISTED

450.   Honomichl, Jack J. "Computers Speed Up Interviewing Process, Also Can Supply Instant Survey Results." *Advertising Age* 48, no. 7 (14 February 1977): 14, 78.

Computerized interviewing using the cathode ray tube (CRT) is discussed. Honomichl observes that this approach is both fast and accurate. The interviewer reads the question from the computer screen and types in the reply, moving through the process in rapid order. When an answer calls for subsequent questions to be skipped, the next appropriate question is immediately made available as a product of the advanced programming which went into the development of the questionnaire for computer application. The companies noted which are currently using CRTs for interviewing are all large organizations working for major corporations. The cost of a bank of CRTs and appropriate staffing are cited for one company as $200,000. The average cost for median-size projects is about $30,000 (using as many as twenty-four CRTs).

451.   Shure, Gerald H., and Robert J. Meeker. "A Minicomputer System for Computer-Assisted Telephone Interviewing." *Behavior Research Methods & Instrumentation* 10, no. 2 (1978): 196-202.

The use of computer-assisted telephone interviewing (CATI) is discussed in each of the areas where it has been demonstrated to be useful: in the preinterview questionnaire schedule design stage; in the interactive interviewing stage; and with postinterview processing programs. CATI is credited with being capable of assisting in dealing with the challenges of reliability, validity, and cost of telephone interviews. CATI offers improved control through response coding, error checking, and "contingency branching based on prior response patterns." Consistency checks can also detect discrepancies provided by respondents to different items throughout the interview. Interviewers can add comments during the session and record them in the computer. In addition, order effects can be systematically monitored, open-ended questions can be recorded and coded by using systematic procedures, and random digit dialing procedures can be incorporated. Interview timing data can be automatically collected. (7 references, 2 endnotes)

COSTS

452. Mayer, Charles S. *Interviewing Costs in Survey Research: A Computer Simulation Study.* Michigan Business Reports, no. 46. Ann Arbor, MI: Bureau of Business Research, Graduate School of Business Administration, University of Michigan, [1964]. 114p.

Using computer simulation, Mayer seeks to develop probable cost options for alternate field interviewing plans. One advantage of this approach is that a variety of plans can be tested without disturbing the status quo. Assumptions and limitations of this model are discussed. Interviewers' behavior patterns are considered. Response and nonresponse are analyzed, with patterns of response examined. Also explained are probability assumptions used in the simulation models and other input parameters. The computer simulation model is presented, followed by a demonstration of an actual case. The author concludes that this approach is an effective way for a field manager to "pretest the cost implications of alternate plans of sample design and field procedure." Three appendixes are provided, including a glossary of terms and a sample page computer printout. A seven-and-one-half-page bibliography is included, with footnotes throughout the text.

453. Mayer, Charles S. "Pretesting Field Interviewing Costs through Simulation." *Journal of Marketing* 28, no. 2 (April 1964): 47-50.

As an alternative to the former approaches of judgment or experiment, Mayer suggests that with the use of computers a simulation can be developed. He discusses the function performed by the interviewers as they would be viewed in a model of interviewing, the structure of the model, and the parameters for various aspects such as report forms, area maps, and the probability that an interview will be completed. A simplified flowchart is shown which traces how the computer simulates field interviewing. The validity and use of the simulation model are considered. The model is designed to assist the decision maker as to which approach to use in field interviewing. Mayer describes the model as being a useful training device, as well as an aid to "trouble areas." (3 footnotes)

454. Sudman, Seymour. "New Approaches to Control of Interviewing Costs." *Journal of Marketing Research* 3, no. 1 (February 1966): 56-61.

The usual way to pay interviewers, including those working door-to-door, has been by the hour. Sudman reasons that this is not in line with other hourly workers who are "generally under tight supervision and control through supervisors and time clocks." The approach used in the last thirty years is described as having the following flaws: (1) inefficient and the less experienced interviewers are rewarded; (2) accuracy in time reports may be in doubt; (3) advance field cost estimation is very difficult; and (4) time sheet checking is expensive and "generally accomplishes little." Sudman reviews the Bureau of the Census solution to this challenge – namely, the establishment of controls. These are detailed, with the observation that individuals working at 80 percent or less from the standard receive bonuses, while those "substantially above standard may be fired." A pay formula developed at the National Opinion Research Center (NORC) is described. The interviewers who participated in the experimental use of the program responded positively to a mail questionnaire seeking reactions. There are two tables and three appendixes showing the forms used to explain the NORC formula. (1 reference)

EFFECTS

455.   Crespi, Leo P. "The Interview Effect in Polling." *Public Opinion Quarterly* 12, no. 1 (Spring 1948): 99-111.

Crespi urges that the "interview effect" must be faced by pollsters as part of the "notion of 'poll wisdom.' " The present paper investigates the impact of a public opinion interview on a number of respondents. Through the use of an interview-reinterview scenario, 350 cases in Trenton, New Jersey, were tested to determine if respondents would change their "no opinion" views between the two interviews. The twenty-seven questions asked, as well as the number of shifting opinions both to and from a no opinion response, are shown in table 1. In all but three questions (with slight differences) a very significant interview effect is noted (table 2). The author believes the results show that "one of the component elements in the impact of an interview upon a respondent is an appreciable mental stimulation – an incitement to either information seeking, thought, or both, to the end that individuals develop opinions where formerly they had none." Crespi discusses the social implications of the drift in opinions, possible biases in the interview effect, and various types of biases. Pollsters must consider not only what biasing factors may do to them, but also the effect biasing may have on the respondent. Pollsters must not adopt a "respondent-be-damned" policy in questionnaire and interviewing practices. (12 footnotes)

456.   Stember, Charles Herbert. "The Effect of Field Procedures on Public Opinion Data." Ph.D. diss., Columbia University, 1955. 148 leaves. [*Dissertation Abstracts International* Order No. 0015751; *DAI* 16, no. 3 (October 1972): 590.]

Data from the American Institute of Public Opinion and the National Opinion Research Center are compared. The same questionnaire was used by the two organizations, interviewing equivalent samples of about 2,500 adults. The interviewer instructions and the codes used were also the same. The results for the "free answer questions" had about the same number of no opinion responses in each data set. Results of precoded questions were significantly different. The organization which "encouraged" fuller answers did succeed in obtaining longer replies, and these replies were found to have "greater amounts of meaningful material." Quality analysis revealed a "relationship between question reliability and situational difficulty induced by the question." Probing and recording differences produced variations in response distribution. Ideological differences between the two staffs produced no measurable effects on results. When considering northern and southern African-American groups, it was found that African Americans spoke more "freely and frankly" to African-American interviewers. References are provided.

FOOT-IN-THE-DOOR

457.   DeJong, William, and David Funder. "Effect of Payment for Initial Compliance: Unanswered Questions about the Foot-in-the-Door Phenomenon." *Personality and Social Psychology Bulletin* 3, no. 4 (Fall 1977): 662-65.

A study was undertaken to test the theoretical explanation of the foot-in-the-door effect, namely, that "persons offered a monetary payment for their compliance to an initial, small request would not be more likely to comply with a subsequent demand." The experiment involved promising two dollars to some telephone survey respondents for participating in a telephone survey, and comparing them with a control group which did not receive payment. The compliance rate for a subsequent no-payment survey request was not higher for those who initially received no payment. The payment recipients were more compliant with a follow-up request. Factors beyond reward are cited as explanations for the behavior of the payment category. These include the desire to remove a guilty feeling for having received two dollars for five-minutes work. Further, after the first study, the payment recipients received a letter labeling them as "doers." The second study failed to demonstrate the foot-in-the-door effect. The size of the initial request and the similarity with the follow-up request, as well as yet undetermined variables, are deciding elements as to whether the effect will be demonstrated. (4 footnotes, 5 references).

458.   Freedman, J. L., and S. C. Fraser. "Compliance without Pressure: The Foot-in-the-Door Technique." *Journal of Personality and Social Psychology* 4 (1966): 195-202.

Two experiments tested the proposition that if respondents agree to a small request, then they are more likely to respond to a larger one at a later time. The initial request involved answering a number of questions – specifically eight questions on household soaps – posed via the telephone. A second variation included asking if the interview could be conducted, but not asking the questions – simply advising respondents that their names were being added to a list. The third alternative involved the interviewer advising potential respondents about the organization and the questions to be asked, without actually requiring any feedback. The longer request involved a telephone request for five or six people to go to a household and enumerate all household products. The request was never fulfilled nor were the consents or denials recorded. The second experiment involved a request to put up a small sign or to sign a petition. The follow-up larger request involved posting a large yard sign reading "Drive Carefully." The first request "tended to increase the degree of compliance" with the second request. If the same person made both requests, the likelihood of second request compliance increased. When a different requester made the larger request, the effect was still "quite strong." (8 references)

459.   Reingen, Peter H., and Jerome B. Kernan. "Compliance with an Interview Request: A Foot-in-the-Door, Self-Perception Interpretation." *Journal of Marketing Research* 14, no. 3 (August 1977): 365-69. [Reprinted in *Readings in Survey Research*, edited by Robert Ferber, 541-48. Chicago, IL: American Marketing Association, 1978. 604p.]

The foot-in-the-door approach stems from a salesperson getting a foot in the door by asking a simple request in order to get the individual to respond to a larger request. In survey usage the approach refers to getting the respondent to answer a few questions initially, to be followed later by a much larger request (with the view that compliance will be greater with this approach). The authors devised an experiment using a 2 x 2 design in which one group received thirty-five initial questions (approximately half received a five-dollar gift certificate and the other half received no incentive), followed by twenty additional questions seven to nine days later. The other group received five questions initially (and were divided the same way as above). The authors found that the foot-in-the-door approach works "as well as money and it has no more disabilities than dollar incentives." A direct application of the approach already in use is the telephone calling of potential respondents who are to receive mail questionnaires. Bem's theory of self-perception (Bem, Daryl J. "Self-Perception Theory." In *Advances in Experimental Social Psychology*, vol. 6, edited by Leonard Berkowitz, 1-62. New York, NY: Academic Press, 1972. 310p.) holds that "a person infers his attitudes from self-observation of his behavior." (15 references)

460.   Seligman, Clive, Malcolm Bush, and Kenneth Kirsch. "Relationship between Compliance in the Foot-in-the-Door Paradigm and Size of First Request." *Journal of Personality and Social Psychology* 33, no. 5 (May 1976): 517-20.

The foot-in-the-door technique involves asking the respondent a small request initially, and then later asking the same person a much larger request. The paradigm holds that once individuals view themselves as complying, they are then more likely to agree with the later request. To test this paradigm 119 adults were randomly selected from a suburban telephone directory. In the first request answers to five, twenty, thirty, or forty-five short-answer ("yes/no") questions were surveyed. The time required for these questions ranged from fifteen seconds to three minutes. The control group did not receive the initial request. The follow-up call occurred two days later and involved a request to answer fifty-five survey questions. The results show that the larger requests in the first call had a significant effect on future compliance, while the two smaller initial requests were not effective in generating future compliance. In other words the initial request must be of a large enough magnitude to gain the commitment of the individual. (7 references)

461.   Snyder, Mark, and Michael R. Cunningham. "To Comply or Not Comply: Testing the Self-Perception Explanation of the 'Foot-in-the-Door' Phenomenon." *Journal of Personality and Social Psychology* 31, no. 1 (January 1975): 64-67.

To test the foot-in-the-door phenomenon ninety-two individuals were randomly chosen from the telephone directory and randomly assigned a small initial request (eight questions) or a large initial request (fifty questions). The self-perception explanation being investigated holds that if individuals can be induced to comply with an initial request, then they are more likely to comply at a later time with a larger and more substantial demand. The study was conducted in Minneapolis, Minnesota, with both female and male interviewers. The first calls were made on a Wednesday afternoon, followed two days later with Friday afternoon calls. The experimental results support the self-perception interpretation of the phenomenon. (3 footnotes, 7 references)

HEALTH FIELD

462.   Cannell, Charles F., Lois Oksenberg, and Jean M. Converse. "Striving for Response Accuracy: Experiments in New Interviewing Techniques." *Journal of Marketing Research* 14, no. 3 (August 1977): 306-15. [Reprinted in *Readings in Survey Research*, edited by Robert Ferber, 205-24. Chicago, IL: American Marketing Association, 1978. 604p.]

A total of 921 white female respondents between eighteen and sixty-four years of age were interviewed on health and health-related matters. The research was conducted in Detroit and Toledo. The questionnaire employed was administered using three interview techniques: instructions, feedback, and commitment. The authors found that the use of these three techniques improves the quality of reporting. Additional advantages are that (1) the variability of behavior among interviewers is reduced, (2) the greater specificity of the interview techniques places greater control in the hands of the researcher, rather than the interviewers, and (3) by incorporating these techniques into the questionnaire and providing interviewer training, the researcher can reduce biasing effects and increase information validity. The authors maintain that survey data are "more subject to invalidity than generally is recognized," and that the use of these techniques "can markedly improve the quality of survey data." (2 footnotes, 25 references)

463.   Cannell, Charles F., Lois Oksenberg, and Jean M. Converse, eds. *Experiments in Interviewing Techniques: Field Experiments in Health Reporting, 1971-1977.* NCHSR Research Report Series; DHEW Publication no. (HRA) 78-3204. Hyattsville, MD: U.S. Department of Health, Education, and Welfare, Public Health Service, Health Resources Administration, National Center for Health Services Research, 1977. 447p. [SuDoc HE20.6512:In 8/971-77]

The following seven experiments were undertaken: (1) interviewer style and questionnaire form; (2) the effects of instructions and verbal modeling on health information reporting in household interviews; (3) the impact of commitment to being a good respondent on interview performance; (4) the effects of feedback and reinforcement on the report of health information; (5) the influence of instructions, commitment, and feedback on reporting in personal interviews; (6) the effects of interviewer voice intonation on reporting; and (7) personal versus telephone interviews: the effects of telephone reinterviews on the reporting of psychiatric symptomatology. The authors maintain that their findings indicate that problems of bias related to the survey interview are "even greater than many investigations assume." The experiments were, however, not conducted using representative national samples, and also lack validation data. The authors suggest that the primary value of the experiments may lie in their contribution to the "development of greater conceptual clarity" and in the design of the later experiments. Each chapter has two or more authors. The appendix has 223 pages and covers all forms and interview schedules used in each experiment, as well as letters, procedures, and objectives. (85 references)

464.   Gleeson, Geraldine A. *Interviewing Methods in the Health Interview Survey.* In *Vital and Health Statistics: Data Evaluation and Methods Research.* Public Health Service Publication, Series 2, No. 48. Washington, DC: U.S. Department of Health, Education, and Welfare, Public Health Service, National Center for Health Statistics, 1972. 86p. [SuDoc HE20.2210:2/48]

Two approaches to data collection are considered. The first, known as the "condition approach," refers to questions seeking information about illnesses and injuries. The second method, called the "person approach," deals with short- and long-term disability and/or the receipt of medical care. Gleeson discusses the use of these two approaches in the national Health Interview Survey between July 1967 and June 1968. Topics considered include the following: (1) data collection; (2) the reevaluation of the survey; (3) a comparison of the two samples used; (4) the study of chronic limitation of activity information gathered; (5) the incidence of acute conditions; and (6) the determination of disability days as reported in relation to school or work days lost due to a specific condition. It is concluded that the person approach is feasible, and "no drastic changes in levels and relationships in health measures have resulted from the adoption of the person approach in the collection phase of the ongoing survey." Three appendixes include technical notes on methods, definitions of certain terms used, and the complete questionnaires used for the condition and person approaches. (10 references)

465.   Loewenstein, Regina. *Two Approaches to Health Interview Surveys.* [New York, NY]: School of Public Health and Administrative Medicine, Columbia University, 1969. 455p.

The two approaches referred to in the title are the following: (1) the "conditions approach" in which fifty-four probe questions addressed specific illnesses, conditions, and services used during the year before the interview; and (2) the "facilities approach" in which fifty probe questions asked about specific types of facilities used in the year before the interview. Information was sought on all types of health care with the exception of dental care. Data were obtained from 1,862 individuals with the conditions schedule and from 1,943 respondents with the facilities schedule. The interviews were conducted in the Washington Heights Health Center District of New York City between 1965 and 1966 as part of the Community Master Sample Survey. Sixty-two individuals, mostly white males, with a median age of twenty-nine, were trained as interviewers. Random assignments and reassignments were used. The median interview length was thirty- to thirty-five minutes depending upon the approach. Slight differences were found in the yield and accuracy of the two methods, but because the facilities schedule is "easier and cheaper to execute," Loewenstein recommends this approach. The appendixes include 296 pages of detailed tables, the interview schedules, the sampling plan and procedures, a glossary, and other statistical tables. References are located at the end of each chapter.

466.   Marquis, Kent H., and Charles F. Cannell. *Effect of Some Experimental Interviewing Techniques on Reporting in the Health Interview Survey.* In *Vital and Health Statistics: Data Evaluation and Methods Research.* Public Health Service Publication No. 1000, Series 2, No. 41. Rockville,

MD and Washington, DC: U.S. Department of Health, Education, and Welfare, Public Health Service, Health Services and Mental Health Administration, National Center for Health Statistics, 1971. 62p. [SuDoc HE 20.2210:2/41]

The purpose of the study was to investigate various aspects of the questionnaire design, as well as the interviewing techniques, as a means to improve reporting of health events in a modified Health Interview Survey household interview. Three modifications were employed: (1) the reinforcement technique in which expressions of approval, extra words, and facial-postural cues were used after respondents recalled health events; (2) the sensitization technique in which the list of symptoms is read at the beginning of the interview to sensitize respondents to the task ahead; and (3) the control technique in which respondents experienced no reinforcements, and the symptoms list was placed near the end of the interview. The sample consisted of 429 females from within the city limits of Detroit who were white, native born, between the ages of seventeen and sixty-five, and of low to middle income. The length of the interview averaged twenty-two minutes – several minutes longer for the reinforcement technique, as more information was being reported. The researchers found that the reinforcement technique generated about 29 percent more reports of symptoms than did the sensitization technique. Symptoms classified as "highly embarrassing" experienced the highest increase using the reinforcement technique. The sensitization technique did not significantly increase the reporting of chronic and acute conditions and produced essentially the same results as the control technique of other health data. Also considered are the effects of respondent attitude and personality on reporting. The appendix contains the full text of the questionnaires used for each technique. (10 references)

INSTRUCTIONAL MATERIALS

467.   Bingham, Walter Van Dyke, and Bruce Victor Moore. *How to Interview.* 4th rev. ed., prepared with the collaboration of John W. Gustad. New York, NY: Harper & Brothers Publishers, [1959]. 277p.

The first four chapters of this textbook deal with general principles of the interview, discussing the interview participants, guideposts to the interview, and selection and training of interviewers. Chapter 7, titled "Public Opinion Polls and Commercial Surveys," is found under the general heading for Part 3: "Interviewing for Facts and Opinions." Bingham and Moore cover the preparation of the schedule of questions, the types of interviewing to be used (questionnaires and informal interviews), and the issue of obtaining confidential information. A "straight forward manner of telling the precise object of the visit" is the best approach for gaining valuable and frequently confidential data, according to the authors. Chapter 7 has thirty-five references. All other chapters include references as well.

468.   Blankenship, A. B. *Professional Telephone Surveys.* New York, NY: Mc-Graw-Hill Book Company, 1977. 244p.

Intended for the generalist market researcher, the book is useful for the market research teacher to accompany other textbooks. It also has reference value for students. The three initial chapters cover how telephone surveys became part of survey research, how professional telephone surveys emerged, and an evaluation of the option. In chapters 4 through 8 Blankenship discusses technique, including coverage of sampling, questionnaire construction and testing, the interview and interviewing, data processing, and the reporting of results. The book closes with a consideration of special uses of telephone surveys, suggestions on how to purchase a professional telephone survey, and a look to the future development of professional telephone surveying. References are found at the end of each chapter. The volume includes a six-page index.

469.   Cannell, Charles F., and Robert L. Kahn. "Interviewing." Chap. 15 in *The Handbook of Social Psychology*, edited by Gardner Lindzey and Elliot Aronson. Vol. 2. *Research Methods*, 526-95. 2d ed. Reading, MA: Addison-Wesley Publishing Company, 1968. 819p.

The chapter opens with a discussion concerning the nature of the research interview, and then moves to a consideration of the quantitative and qualitative aspects of interviewing. Through a series of subheadings the authors address the following topics: (1) conditions for successful interviewing; (2) reliability and validity studies; (3) content, technique, and invalidity; (4) interviewer and respondent characteristics as sources of bias; (5) bias avoidance; (6) question formulation; (7) open and closed questions; (8) direct and indirect questions; (9) interviewing technique; and (10) selection, training, and supervision of interviewers. Interviewer costs are discussed in 1968 dollars, with specifics provided in terms of time, costs, and percentages. Question sequence is addressed with six suggestions outlined. Similar suggestions can be found in a number of sections, including training and indirect questions. References appear in the text by author last name and publication year. (113 references)

470.   Hauck, Matthew. "Planning Field Operations." Section 2, Part B, Chap. 7 in *Handbook of Marketing Research*, edited by Robert Ferber, 2/147 -2/159. New York, NY: McGraw-Hill Book Company, [1974]. (various pagings)

The chapter opens with a review of preparations required for field operations, followed by aspects involved in the conduct of the field plans, including issues concerning a time schedule and cost and quality control. Planning for personal interviews, telephone interviews, and data collection by mail is discussed. Hauck's suggestions on controlling nonsampling errors cover sources of bias, how to avoid bias, and bias detection and correction. (6 references)

471.   Kahn, Robert L., and Charles F. Cannell. *The Dynamics of Interviewing: Theory, Technique, and Cases.* New York, NY: John Wiley & Sons, [1957]. 368p.

Discussing both the theoretical and the applied aspects of interviewing, this textbook is designed for survey and market researchers, as well as for individuals in the disciplines of medicine, journalism, law, and social work. Part 1 covers the communication elements of the interview; the psychological considerations (including ways to motivate respondents); the manner by which objectives of the interview are determined; the development of questions; and the questionnaire design. Interview measurement, probing, and learning close the first part. Part 2 provides transcripts of recorded interviews in the areas of medicine, personnel, supervisor-subordinate relations, and social work. A six-page bibliography is provided, along with an eight-page subject index.

472.   National Opinion Research Center. *Interviewing for NORC.* Rev. ed. Denver, CO: National Opinion Research Center, University of Denver, 1947. 154p.

The purpose of this volume is to outline the steps, concerns, and issues which must be understood in order to be a National Opinion Research Center (NORC) interviewer. The book, containing sixteen chapters, begins with an explanation of what NORC is, how a survey is planned, and what earnings expectations a NORC interviewer should have. The rest of the book is divided into three categories: how to achieve a good interview, how to deal with a particular assignment, and how to manage special problems which might be encountered. Issues addressed cover the following: (1) asking the questions; (2) obtaining responses; (3) reporting the answers; (4) quotas; (5) stratified random sampling; (6) gathering specific factual data; (7) interviewing in a rural area; and (8) pretesting. A nine-entry bibliography is provided, along with a list of nineteen periodicals to consult for further reading.

473.   Richardson, Stephen A., Barbara Snell Dohrenwend, and David Klein. *Interviewing: Its Forms and Functions.* New York, NY: Basic Books, [1965]. 380p.

Interviewing for polls and surveys is considered under the index heading "schedule interview" (that is, where questions are asked in a "prescribed" sequence and where the interviewer records "verbatim" or in specially precoded spaces). Areas covered include the reasons for choosing this format; the combination of this format with other interview formats; the costs and coverage of the approach; examples; the primary uses; question antecedents; question scope; use with sensitive topics; and the nature of the task of the interviewer. The book is divided into four main parts: (1) "The Interview as a Research Instrument"; (2) "Respondent Participation"; (3) "The Question-Answer Process"; and (4) "Interviewer and Respondent." The volume has a thirteen-page index. (139 references).

474.   Wilson, Earl B. *How to Make Money Interviewing for Surveys and Polls: A Complete Marketing Research Home Study Course.* 3 vols. Santa Barbara, CA: Vector Press, [1972]. 379p.

Part 1, "How to Make Money Conducting Interviews" (lessons 1-7, pages 1-134), introduces the topic, provides answers to basic questions, suggests ways to start an interviewing service, and discusses the tax advantages of this business. Also covered are how to operate an interview service, techniques for obtaining interviewing assignments by mail, and how to begin making money with interviews. Part 2, "How to Make Money Conducting Your Own Surveys and Polls" (lessons 8-18, pages 136-310; there is no page 135), explains the "whys and hows" of surveys and polls, the techniques of making prospects into steady clients, how to conduct polls and surveys, the use of market research methods, test marketing techniques, questionnaire design, sampling techniques, store audits, marketing forecasts, money-making in new product marketing, and report writing. Part 3, "How and Where You Can Get Free Publications to Learn More about the Interviewing Business" (chapters 1-18, pages 311-79), provides selections of free publications to be used in conjunction with lessons 1 through 18 in the first two parts of this self-study course. There are items which the user would request by mail, with a delay time of four or more weeks until receipt. Most of the documents listed are from various federal agencies or departments.

OPEN

475.   Campbell, Angus. "Polling, Open Interviewing, and the Problem of Interpretation." *Journal of Social Issues* 2, no. 4 (November 1946): 67-71.

Campbell reviews public opinion poll shortcomings which he believes leaves the public with a "flavor of superficiality." One problem is the use of terms such as "free speech" in poll questions without knowing what the phrase means to respondents. The author sees polls as useful in "measuring the simple division of public opinion on clear-cut and with understood issues." A technique called "open interviewing" is defined as using a fixed schedule of questions in a fixed order, with the answers provided entirely with the respondent's own wording. One advantage cited is that the interviewer can quickly determine if the respondent has understood the question (which is not the case on "yes/no" and "true/false" answer options). The open interview also yields information on the meaning and intensity of the respondent's answer. Campbell cites the recently organized Survey Research Center of the University of Michigan as continuing open-interview surveys, a technique developed in the Division of Program Surveys of the U.S. Department of Agriculture (which conducted surveys for the Office of War Information during World War II). (4 footnotes)

476.   Lazarsfeld, Paul F. "The Controversy over Detailed Interviews – An Offer for Negotiation." *Public Opinion Quarterly* 8, no. 1 (Spring 1944): 38-60. [Reprinted in *Supplement to Reader in Public Opinion and Communication*, edited by Bernard Berelson and Morris Janowitz. No. 10: *Methods in Public Opinion Research*, 555-70. Glencoe, IL: Free Press, 1953. 611p.]

Lazarsfeld defines and discusses the development of two philosophies of public opinion research: one view supporting depth or open-ended interviews (OI), and the other supporting more objective means of research (for example, an answer of "yes," "no," or "don't know"). Six main functions of OI are listed and described: (1) clarifying the meaning of a respondent's answer; (2) singling out the decisive aspects of an opinion; (3) identifying what factors have influenced an opinion; (4) determining complex attitude patterns; (5) interpreting motivation; and (6) clarifying statistical relationship. Six possible objective alternatives of OI are, respectively: (1) an interlocking system of poll questions; (2) checklists; (3) none; (4) scales and typologies; (5) projective tests; and (6) none. Lazarsfeld compares and contrasts the value of both techniques. He believes that OI is invaluable, both at the beginning and at the end of a study. He briefly discusses the problems involved in converting OI into sets of specific poll questions, and concludes that sometimes a combination of the two techniques is desirable and necessary, depending upon the specific research task. (23 footnotes)

PANEL

477.   Bailar, Barbara A. "The Effects of Rotation Group Bias on Estimates from Panel Surveys." *Journal of the American Statistical Association* 70, no. 349 (March 1975): 23-30.

Results from a number of surveys have demonstrated that repeated interviewing of the same individuals can frequently change response patterns. Bailar reports that many survey organizations have witnessed this phenomenon. The *Current Population Survey (CPS)*, conducted by the Bureau of the Census and designed to collect data on labor force participation and other items, is the focus of this article. Findings of the study indicate that respondents report several characteristics at higher levels during the first interview than during successive interviews. Sections of the presentation cover the rotation group bias (RGB) in the *CPS*, the estimation procedure, the effect of RGB on ratio and composite estimators, an estimation of the data, and an estimate of the total mean-square error of selected *CPS* statistics. An appendix of statistical formulas follows. (1 unnumbered footnote, 13 references)

478.   Evan, William M. "Cohort Analysis of Survey Data: A Procedure for Studying Long-Term Opinion Change." *Public Opinion Quarterly* 23, no. 1 (Spring 1959): 63-72.

Evan describes a method of analysis which "combines the long-run perspective of the trend study with the panel-study focus on process." The panel analyst interviews the same respondents over time. S/he can study not only net change, but also "turnover." The trend analyst is restricted only to the study of net change. A "cohort" is defined as the "analogue of a group of specific panel respondents in successive cross-sectional surveys" (that is, a group of persons born in a particular year, or five-year period, or at any interval). The cohort technique, or generational analysis, is used to examine a series of three cross-sectional polls conducted by the American Institute of Public Opinion over a sixteen-year period. The polls covered three historical situations: the [Great] Depression, World War II, and the postwar period. In tabular form Evan shows how opinion changes (by age breakdowns) of a cohort can be studied. Methodology is explained and limitations of the study are outlined. (21 footnotes)

479.   Ferber, Robert. *Collecting Financial Data by Consumer Panel Techniques: A Pilot Study.* Inter-University Committee for Research on Consumer Behavior. Consumer Savings Project. Studies in Consumer Savings, no. 1. Urbana, IL: Bureau of Economic and Business Research, University of Illinois, 1959. 177p.

The initial sample for the pilot study consisted of 8,300 names from the Chicago metropolitan area in 1956. Four out of five people interviewed were willing to provide information on their savings behavior. The interviewers perceived the great majority of those interviewed to be "sincere, accurate, and comprehensive" with respect to the information requested. Respondents in managerial occupations tended to be less accurate and comprehensive than those in other occupations. About one-third of all the individuals interviewed declined to provide information on their total assets. Survey dropouts occurred during the first two waves of the five-wave panel. Refusals were due to disinterest or lack of time and an unwillingness to reveal personal financial information. Interviewers had considerable variability with older respondents, with female interviewers being the most successful. Ferber believes that the most efficient means of collecting information on consumer financial behavior may be through a combination of the panel technique and the securing of data from financial institutions. Ninety-eight pages of appendixes include interviewer instructions and questionnaires used. (24 footnotes).

480.   Glock, Charles Young. "Participation Bias and Re-Interview Effect in Panel Studies." Ph.D. diss., Columbia University, 1952. 295 leaves. [*Dissertation Abstracts International* Order No. 0004185; *DAI* 12, no. 5 (November 1966): 756.]

The panel technique is defined as a method which involves "repeated interviews with the same individuals at different points in time." Glock believes it is "one of the most promising for obtaining a more complete understanding of social change of a short term nature." He discusses two "operational difficulties" inherent in panel studies which social scientists must overcome. The first is referred to as "participation bias"– a situation in which some panel members refuse to be a follow-up or cannot be located. The dissertation focuses on this problem by examining data collected from sixteen panel studies. The effect of repeated interviewing on panel responses comprises the second problem which is examined through the use of two experimental panel studies. Results indicate that the individuals who become panel members and who participate on a continuing basis have different characteristics, attitudes, behavior, and opinions from those who do not (other than age, sex, education, and family size characteristics). Concerning the problem of reinterview effect, the data indicate "no evidence of a re-interview effect on level of interest in amount of exposure to information about, or level of knowledge of the panel topic." There was evidence of reinterview effect on consistency of response under certain conditions. References are provided.

481.   Goldstein, Jacob. "The Relative Advantages and Limitations of the Panel and Successive-Sample Techniques in the Analysis of Opinion Change." *Journal of Social Psychology* 50, 2d half, (November 1959): 305-20.

The opinion change under consideration deals with "overall changes, or changes within subgroups, or with the interrelationships over time of two or more variables." One limitation of the panel method is the problem of mortality, that is, the withdrawal of respondents interviewed at an earlier time. A challenge with the successive-sample technique is that the composition of the samples may be different, and that imperfections in the sampling procedures may bias the results. Most of the successive samples on opinion change deal with short-range changes, with a few covering intervals of forty years. Panel studies had no more than a four-year interval. Goldstein suggests that successive-sample data can be supplemented by the analysis of mail on particular issues which has been received by "prominent" persons. The viewpoint of the "self-selected sample of letter-writers" would be garnered. Another suggestion is to use voting statistics to supplement poll studies. The latter two approaches are designed to enhance fragmentary poll data for secondary analysis. (33 references)

482.   Lazarsfeld, Paul F. " 'Panel' Studies." *Public Opinion Quarterly* 4, no. 1 (March 1940): 122-28.

Lazarsfeld uses several prior studies to highlight the advantages and disadvantages of the panel technique. In the first, a poll was taken in Irvington, New Jersey, by A. B. Blankenship of the Psychological Corporation. The question concerned legalizing parimutuel betting. The poll was taken two weeks before a state referendum on the subject. During the week following the election, 358 respondents were reinterviewed by the Princeton Office of Radio Research. Data in tables 1 and 2 illustrate that 160 people voted the same, 32 reversed their opinions, and 121 who originally had an opinion did not actually vote. Other examples include polls by the American Institute of Public Opinion, America's Town Meeting of the Air, and the Chicago Round Table. Advantages of the panel technique are that it is less expensive (due to one-time selection and a smaller sample), cumulative changes can be measured over time, and the same degree of statistical reliability (as compared to a series of poll samples) is present. Difficulties include locating the same respondents for reinterview, obtaining and retaining the cooperation of respondents from one interview to the next, estimating the effect of "self-selective bias," and determining whether repeated interviews, in themselves, influence opinions. (7 footnotes)

483.   Lazarsfeld, Paul F. "Repeated Interviews as a Tool for Studying Changes in Opinion and Their Causes." *American Statistical Association Bulletin* 2, no. 1 (January 1941): 3-7.

Repeated interviews are referred to in the article as the "panel technique" – a method designed to permit the researcher to determine how opinions form over a period of time. In the first example described a sample of six hundred people was exposed to the panel technique and received seven interviews. Lazarsfeld was interested in studying those individuals who changed their minds between two interviews. The major challenge is what Lazarsfeld refers to as "mortality" or "drop-out." The greatest difficulty is between the first and the second interviews, as some individuals refuse to continue to participate. The study discussed had a drop-out rate of 13 percent. The other challenges cited include people being out of town, sick, or deceased. These three categories amounted to between 6 and 7 percent. (1 footnote)

484.   Lazarsfeld, Paul, and Marjorie Fiske. "The 'Panel' as a New Tool for Measuring Opinion." *Public Opinion Quarterly* 2, no. 4 (October 1938): 596-612.

Lazarsfeld and Fiske define the panel technique as "repeated interviews with the same group of people." The authors list and discuss six advantages and several disadvantages of using the procedure in sample surveys. The rest of the article is devoted to three reports of various uses of the technique. The first reported is an experiment conducted by the editors of the *Woman's Home Companion* who attempted to use the panel method as a means to become closer to their readers. A total of 1,500 women from about three million readers were selected to participate. The results of the questionnaire were used to shape editorial and advertising policies. The editors found the panel technique to be "admirably flexible." The use of the panel method in the cultural field is reported next. In the interests of time and money, the technique was used by the National Board of Motion Picture Review for recruiting volunteers to review new movies for child and family appropriateness. A final example of a "sociological use" is outlined. It involved a British nationwide sociological experiment called "Mass Observation." The panel was used as a practical means of collecting the detailed information desired. Lazarsfeld concludes that "all of these studies have been much too experimental in form to permit concrete generalization as to the efficacy of the panel method as a tool for research." Further investigation is needed before a "theory of panel application" can be established. (13 footnotes)

485.   Neter, John, and Joseph Waksberg. "Conditioning Effects from Repeated Household Interviews." *Journal of Marketing* 28, no. 2 (April 1964): 51-56.

The effect of repeated interviews on the behavior and reporting patterns of respondents is referred to as the "conditioning effect." The authors undertook a study to test the effect by conducting four separate interviews with the same households, with the sample selected in the form of area segments from a set of seventy sample areas. The first three interviews were one month apart, while the fourth interview was three months following the third. The second and third interviews were conducted in the same manner using the same recall period. The conditioning effect was determined primarily by comparing the alteration and repair expenditures reported during the second and third interviews. The conditioning effect was found in reports of jobs, expenditures, and size of jobs. In each case the conditioning effects decreased from the second to the third interviews. Interview length, when varied, did not have a noticeable effect. Changes in the designated respondent also failed to change the success rate. (6 footnotes)

486.   Powers, Edward A., Willis J. Goudy, and Pat M. Keith. "Congruence between Panel and Recall Data in Longitudinal Research." *Public Opinion Quarterly* 42, no. 3 (Fall 1978): 380-89.

The research attempts to determine whether responses to recall items differ from previously obtained self-reports. In a 1964 study 1,870 employed males, age fifty or older, were questioned on matters of health, income, family, work, and general attitudes. All who could be located from the original sample (1,332) were reinterviewed in 1974. Respondents were asked to recall what their situations and attitudes had been ten years earlier. Analysis of the data indicates the following: (1) most respondents gave inconsistent responses between the retrospective and present measures; (2) their recall responses tended to present them in a more favorable light than did the information obtained a decade before; and (3) the answers to both attitudinal and factual questions lacked "congruence." The research also examines the question, "To what extent are variable relationships different when using recall and concurrent measures?" Data indicate that recall techniques had "little utility for descriptive purposes but may be used cautiously in correlational studies." (3 footnotes, 29 references)

487.   Rosenberg, Morris, and Wagner Thielens, with Paul F. Lazarsfeld. "The Panel Study." Chap. 18 in *Research Methods in Social Relations with Especial Reference to Prejudice*, by Marie Jahoda, Morton Deutsch, and Stuart W. Cook. Part 2. *Selected Techniques*, 587-609. Published for the Society for the Psychological Study of Social Issues. New York, NY: Dryden Press, 1951. Part 1 (pages 2-421) and Part 2 (pages [423]-759) comprise the two-volume set.

The panel study involves repeating the research design at least twice with the same set of respondents. Lazarsfeld has previously used the technique in election campaigns. Rosenberg and Thielens were Lazarsfeld students who assisted with methodological challenges. The primary use of the panel study is to examine behavior and attitude changes. Several examples are provided, namely, a community panel survey in Sandusky, Ohio, in 1940 in which seven "waves" were conducted before the nominating convention, to near the election day. A similar study occurred in Elmira, New York, during the 1948 political campaign [Item No. 177]. Determining which respondents are likely to change their attitudes, as well as what their experiences have been, are evaluated. The authors discuss creating "indexes of change" as a way of deciding when a respondent becomes labeled a "cheater." The issue of the reinterview effect is discussed, with the possibility that the respondent may develop a "professional or critical attitude." Additionally, the panel experience may generate a "freezing effect," thereby causing the respondents to retain the same attitude throughout. In the last section dealing with panel study administration, the following topics are addressed: (1) the time period between successive waves; (2) sample size; (3) sample type; (4) whether financial or other forms of incentives should be offered; (5) how to deal with the challenge of keeping respondents interested in the questions without simultaneously introducing bias as a result of changing the question format; (6) interviewer selection; (7) whether interviewers are best served by awareness of respondents' previous responses; and (8) some drawbacks of conducting panels by mail self-administered written questionnaires. The last category includes the problem of receiving complete responses in a timely manner or with possible biasing through discussion with family, friends, and neighbors.

488.   Ruch, Floyd L. "Effects of Repeated Interviewing on Respondent's Answers." *Journal of Consulting Psychology* 5, no. 4 (July-August 1941): 179-82.

Existing research concerning repeated interviewing effects on respondents' answers is reviewed, with Ruch being unable to draw any conclusions other than to suggest that further research is needed. In the earliest study in the area of repeated interviews, conducted by Hollingworth (Hollingworth, H. L. "Judgments of the Comic." *Psychological Review* 18 [1911]: 132-56.), ten individuals evaluated the funniness of thirty-nine jokes. The jokes were to be ordered in "degrees of funniness," – a procedure which was repeated once a week for five weeks. The findings indicate that the repetition "markedly" altered the respondents' estimates of the jokes' humor. Other studies cited include those by Link (Link, H. C. *The New Psychology of Selling and Advertising.* New York, NY: Macmillan Company, 1932. 293p.) who showed that the same questions from short and long interviews cannot be compared because long formats generate boredom and irritation on the part of the respondent, thus causing errors by both the respondent and the interviewer. Other research is reviewed, with the advantages and disadvantages of repeated interviewing considered. (9 references)

489.   Wax, Murray, and Leopold J. Shapiro. "Repeated Interviewing." *American Journal of Sociology* 62, no. 2 (September 1956): 215-17.

The practice of repeatedly interviewing the same individuals is considered from a theoretical standpoint, as well as from the point of view of an actual study. In the survey design discussed, respondents were interviewed from two to five times. The initial interview, conducted using "standard survey procedures," was followed by the selection of a subsample of 120 individuals who were to participate in an intensive case study. The authors maintain that the multiple-interview technique permitted low-cost instruction changes and data gathering. The issue of the heightening of respondents' awareness of their conduct as a product of interviewing is reviewed. (3 footnotes)

PERSONAL

490.   Bauman, Karl E., and Charles L. Chase. "Interviewers as Coders of Occupation." *Public Opinion Quarterly* 38, no. 1 (Spring 1974): 107-12.

Traditionally, interviewers gather occupational data and then give it to office coders for assignment. The article reports a study to explore the feasibility of having interviewers assign the codes in the field so that more complete information can be obtained. Five possible drawbacks are listed for the latter method. As part of a larger study of family planning in nine U.S. cities, 846 white and 851 African-American women in low-income areas were interviewed, respectively, by white and African-American interviewers. Some returns were coded in the field while others were coded in the office. Correlations were made between occupational status and both education and family income in two designs. The data show that the correlations of the white interviewers performing coding in the field were as high as for the office coders for white respondents. However, the African-American field interviewers failed to produce correlations as high as the office coders. The authors could not explain this last finding and urge further research. (7 footnotes)

491. Dohrenwend, Barbara Snell. "An Experimental Study of Directive Interviewing." *Public Opinion Quarterly* 34, no. 1 (Spring 1970): 117-25.

The term "directive" is used in this paper to refer to "questions that imply the answer." The study tests Kinsey's hypothesis that directive interviewing will increase the accuracy of reports of socially unacceptable behavior (in this case illegal abortions). A subsample of 219 previously interviewed females living in New York City was interviewed by fourteen female interviewers (slightly less than 70 percent of the sample was available for interviewing). There were four experimental interview schedules using questions which were either directive or nondirective. Other questions were used to lead up to the abortion issue. Dohrenwend, in table 1, details the characteristics and refusals of the group. Data in tables 2 and 3 show that directive questions significantly increased reports of knowledge about some of the abortion questions by higher-educated respondents. Less well educated respondents tended to deny knowledge of abortions including their own, whether the questions were directive or nondirective. The role of social desirability ratings in the outcome is explored. Further research is required "to learn how to bring the accuracy of reports by less well educated respondents about highly controversial topics up to the level of those with more education." (14 footnotes)

492. Mayer, Charles S. "The Overlooked Ingredient in Survey Research." *Business Horizons* 9, no. 3 (Fall 1966): 75-82.

The focus is on personal interviews conducted in the home for the purpose of completing consumer surveys. Mayer addresses the issue of what constitutes "quality interviewing," beginning with the fact that interviewing is a part-time occupation and that most interviewers are female. The nature of the role is described. A number of challenges are identified: (1) fabricating, that is, cheating;

(2) falsifying work records to increase hours worked and distances traveled; (3) working simultaneously on multiple surveys, with respondents asked to respond to two questionnaires back-to-back, thus creating fatigue problems; (4) asking only the key questions and filling in the rest later; (5) changing the procedure – such as switching a personal interview to the telephone; (6) asking questions of an inappropriate respondent; (7) improvising questions; (8) forcing or expanding responses; (9) using untrained interviewers; and (10) employing supervisors who do not appropriately supervise interviewers or who do not supervise whatsoever. Mayer suggests requirements for quality interviewing, including some available controls which can be instituted (such as validating interviewer visits by telephone). Other safeguards include the use of cost data, call records, and listing sheets by the supplier. Another suggestion is to have a consolidated field service, permitting professional management and permanent local resident supervisors. (7 footnotes)

493.   Vaughn, Charles L., and William A. Reynolds. "Reliability of Personal Interview Data." *Journal of Applied Psychology* 35, no. 1 (February 1951): 61-63.

The investigators sought to evaluate the reliability of survey reports of respondents' age, education, and socioeconomic level. Respondents were selected at random from city directories, thereby obtaining a "pre-designated" sample of individuals. Interviews were conducted with 888 adults in Des Moines, Iowa, and 430 adults in Springfield, Massachusetts. About three months later reinterviews were scheduled. Interviews took place in homes, with the interviewer asking questions concerning age, education, and socioeconomic level at the end of fifteen minutes of questioning. When the results were compared with those previously obtained by Cantril and Research Associates in the Office of Public Opinion Research [Item No. 38] (even though different methods were used), the age reports are considered reliable, education levels are satisfactory but less reliable, and socioeconomic level results are the least reliable of all three. (5 footnotes)

PROJECTIVE

494.   Greenberg, Arthur L. "Argumentative Role Playing: A New Projective Technique for Use in Survey Research." Ph.D. diss., Pennsylvania State College, 1953. 128 leaves. [*Dissertation Abstracts International* Order No. 0007407; *DAI* PSU 16, 548.]

The projective device used involved the presentation of an argument situation to the respondent by the interviewer. The respondents were asked to project themselves into the situation, and then to take a position and provide reasons as to why it is correct. Systematic probe remarks were made, such as "You're doing fine. Give me some more reasons." Greenberg found that the approach "is a more effective instrument for securing information concerning the motivation of respondents than is the free response question." The author believes that through the use of the projective technique a "larger number of respondents will answer the questions asked them and will be more likely to give multiple answers to the questions, and that at least 20 percent more reasons, many of which are non-stereotyped and personally revealing, will be secured." The dissertation includes summary, problem analysis, procedure, and results chapters. There are twenty tables with the text. An eighteen-page appendix provides the text of the questionnaire employed, as well as interviewer instructions. References are provided.

495.   Greenberg, Arthur L. "Respondent Ego-Involvement in Large-Scale Surveys." *Journal of Marketing* 20, no. 4 (April 1956): 390-93.

One reason individuals respond to interviewers is because they are "flattered" to be asked their opinion, that is, "what they have to say." According to Greenberg, this level of ego-involvement, while useful, can be increased by employing the technique of argumentative role playing. Such a "friendly argument," it is suggested, is closer to reality than standardized interviews. The interviewers used for the study were twenty-eight college students who conducted a total of 827 interviews. A probability sample of adult residents of Altoona, Pennsylvania, was divided into two groups – the control group received open-ended and dichotomous questions, while the experimental group was asked three role-playing questions instead. Respondents in the experimental group gave a larger number of reasons for their opinions. Greenberg maintains that the role-playing approach is useful for large-scale studies, and that the additional expense and effort required are not substantial (about twenty minutes of additional interviewer instruction). Only a few questions need to be in the role-playing mode for an impact to be seen in the rest of the interview. (3 footnotes)

496.   McCord, Hallack. "Discovering the 'Confused' Respondent: A Possible Projective Method." *Public Opinion Quarterly* 15, no. 2 (Summer 1951): 363-66.

For various reasons some respondents reply to survey questions with "confused" answers which are not strictly "fact." In an experiment in Denver, Colorado, student interviewers were used to gather 166 usable interviews. The preferences for one visual form or another (circles with the tops or bottoms left open) were compared with responses to five "confusion" questions. These were designed so that a respondent could not respond affirmatively and still be replying "factually" and/or "truthfully." The questions were loaded so as to exert pressure on the respondent to answer "yes." The outcome of the experiment shows that from 8 to 53 percent of the respondents gave affirmative answers on the five confusion questions. For example, some respondents said that they had voted in an election which was never held, or that they had heard of a nonexistent word, famous writer, magazine, or an imaginary piece of legislation. Further, there is some indication that the more likely individuals are to give confused answers, the more likely they are to show a preference for the circles with the bottom section left open. (This finding supports the view of some handwriting experts that "insincere" persons often leave some letters open at the bottom.) The author believes that a limited sample size prohibits concrete conclusions, and further research is warranted. (1 footnote)

497.   Sanford, Fillmore H. "The Use of a Projective Device in Attitude Surveying." *Public Opinion Quarterly* 14, no. 4 (Winter 1950-51): 697-709.

The projective device referred to in the title is a cartoon-like drawing designed to gather opinions about matters which may be "socially or psychologically touchy" to a respondent. Six such drawings and two direct questions were used in an experiment (part of a larger study) with 963 respondents in Philadelphia to elicit information on what they "worried about." A comparison of the three stimuli shows the following: (1) the drawings tended to elicit responses in the interview situation; (2) respondents seemed to enjoy the use of the pictures; (3) the answers given were more specific, personal, and intimate than those for the direct questions; (4) reliability for the picture answers was about the same as for the direct questions; and (5) some evidence indicates that answers were also more valid. The author cites the results of a study on the relationship between authoritarianism and the content of worries. It is suggested that the projective device may be appropriate for large-scale interviewing, and that it may succeed in gathering data unobtainable through the use of more conventional techniques. (8 footnotes)

SCHEDULING

498.   Brunner, G. Allen, and Stephen J. Carroll, Jr. "Weekday Evening Interviews of Employed Persons Are Better." *Public Opinion Quarterly* 33, no. 2 (Summer 1969): 265-67.

The study tests the effect on completion rates of interviewing employed people on weekdays, as opposed to Saturdays. Homes in a section of Hyattsville, Maryland, were randomly selected for the May 1966 study. Another section of the same area was used for replication in the winter month of December 1966. Included were 993 persons for the Saturday interviews and 823 persons for the weekday interviews. All interviews were conducted by members of a marketing research class who used identical opening statements and questionnaires (relating to employee attitudes toward supervision). The authors' hypotheses that there would be more refusals for weekday evening hours than for Saturday, and that there would be more not-at-homes during Saturday daytime hours, were upheld. Although the completion rate was not very high in either study, it was much higher for the weekday interviews. The authors believe the low completion rate was due to the requirement that only the employed head of household be interviewed. Seasonal differences were not evident. Some of the evidence suggested that, as expected, refusals increased during the Christmas holiday. (1 footnote)

499.   DeLamater, John, and Patricia MacCorquodale. "The Effects of Interview Schedule Variations on Reported Sexual Behavior." *Sociological Methods & Research* 4, no. 2 (November 1975): 215-36.

The authors consistently found that interview schedule variations did not affect reported sexual behavior. Reports of sexual and other "threatening" behaviors "may be relatively uninfluenced by methodological variations." The research undertaken is placed in context through a review of the literature. The study involved three aspects of the interview schedule: (1) whether or not the interviews or self-reports were able to assess the lifetime sexual behavior of the respondents; (2) the placement of questions regarding sexual behavior in the middle or at the end of a lengthy survey; and (3) the order in which other questions were asked. Information is provided concerning the selection of the respondents, the basic measures used, the interview schedule, and the interviewers. The results are presented with six tables and followed by a discussion. (9 footnotes, 15 references)

SPECIFIC POPULATIONS

Low Income

500.   Weinberg, Eve. *Community Surveys with Local Talent: A Handbook.* NORC Report no. 123. [Chicago, IL]: National Opinion Research Center, [1971]. 294p.

This handbook provides guidelines for conducting field interviewing for sample surveys in low-income areas. The surveys gathered data on the extent and patterns of health care as a way to assist newly established neighborhood health centers. The areas where the National Opinion Research Center undertook the work were Bedford-Crown Heights, Brooklyn, New York; Red Hook, Brooklyn, New York; and Atlanta, Georgia. Probability samples of one thousand to fifteen hundred households were used. Thirty to sixty interviewers were hired, based on the needs of the community. Residents from the target areas were selected as interviewers, with preference given to the unemployed or underemployed. Specific chapters cover initial preparatory survey business, interviewer selection, sampling, interviewer training, fieldwork supervision, and the role of the supervisor at the conclusion of the survey. Eight appendixes contain examples of the paperwork and form used during the procedures (these cover 216 pages or about three-fourths of the handbook). (1 reference)

Mexican Americans

501.   Freeman, Donald M. "A Note on Interviewing Mexican-Americans." *Social Science Quarterly* 49, no. 4 (March 1969): 909-18.

In 1966 a survey was conducted in South Tucson, Arizona, a predominately Mexican-American enclave in the southwestern corner of Tucson. Using a thirty-five-page questionnaire, 188 interviews were completed. The cost of conducting the survey was greater than usual because of translating the questionnaire, hiring bilingual interviewers, and training special field-workers. Freeman found that (1) Mexican Americans are willing to be interviewed, (2) with appropriate measures language differences are not unmanageable, (3) marginal communities pose enumeration and sampling challenges, (4) the same interview schedules for Anglos can be successfully used with Mexican Americans, and (5) noncitizens did not object to being interviewed. Freeman suggests that Mexican Americans be surveyed in other areas of the country to evaluate if different levels of ethnic acceptance impact the author's findings. (20 footnotes)

502.   Welch, Susan, John Comer, and Michael Steinman. "Interviewing in a Mexican-American Community: An Investigation of Some Potential Sources of Response Bias." *Public Opinion Quarterly* 37, no. 1 (Spring 1973): 115-26.

The research evaluates the influence of three different aspects of the interview situation on response consistency. The three aspects were the language used for the interview, the ethnicity of the interviewer, and the location where the respondent was born and raised. The survey sample was 178 Mexican Americans living in two predominately rural counties in Nebraska. Three hypotheses were tested: (1) responses of Mexican Americans interviewed in English differ from responses of those interviewed in Spanish; (2) responses of Mexican Americans interviewed by Anglos differ from responses of Mexican Americans interviewed by Mexican Americans, and by Anglos and Mexican Americans working together; and (3) responses of Mexican Americans born and raised in the United States differ from responses of Mexican Americans who were born and raised in Mexico. A fourteen-page questionnaire concerning health care and political participation was administered. Analysis of the results shows the following: (1) initial differences between respondents interviewed in English or Spanish on the health-related questions disappear when education and age are controlled; (2) in general, there was little difference in response concerning the political questions regardless of the language used; (3) ethnicity of the interviewer seemed to have little influence on the nature of the responses, and initial differences disappear with education and age controls; and (4) respondents' country of origin results are less clear, but when age and education were controlled, differences in responses to health questions disappear and were noted in only one of the political questions. Other variables affecting the results are discussed. The authors reach the conclusion that "interview data can be obtained from Mexican-Americans with about the same degree of reliability as from any other group." (10 footnotes)

503.   Zusman, Marty E., and Arnold O. Olson. "Gathering Complete Response from Mexican-Americans by Personal Interview." *Journal of Social Issues* 33, no. 4 (Fall 1977): 46-55.

Complete response is seen to be comprised of three factors: sample mortality, item nonresponse, and detail given to open-ended questions. To investigate the quality of response to the personal interview, 166 Mexican-American farm migrants (95 parents and 71 children) were selected as part of a larger study conducted in Indiana. The migrants were given two different schedules of thirty to forty questions. Study findings are as follows: (1) the sample mortality was 5 percent as compared to approximately 20 percent among a stable population; (2) overall nonresponse for parents to only one or no items was 33 percent of the sample; (3) differences in completeness of response were found for demographic as opposed to perceptual items; (4) there was a much higher response rate among the children interviewed; and (5) parents provided far more detail when responding to a positive rather than to a negative question, while the reverse was true for children. The authors conclude that serious problems (such as incomplete response) may result from the use of the personal interview findings for social action research projects. (13 references)

Minorities

504.   Myers, Vincent. "Survey Methods for Minority Populations." *Journal of Social Issues* 33, no. 4 (Fall 1977): 11-19.

Nineteen Job Corps centers in seventeen states were the locations for 1,797 interviews conducted primarily with minority youth. Myers suggests that "respondents who are poor and/or of racial or ethnic minority backgrounds require unconventional rules of survey procedure." It is further suggested that the real issue is the degree of distance which may exist between the interviewer and the respondent. During the first twenty minutes of an interview, "close to a mundane conversation could occur and interviewers simply checked appropriate categories as the responses evolved." The approach of penetrating and understanding the respondents' experience before formal interviews begin poses many challenges. The information sought during the survey was data on illegal drug use. (1 end-note, 26 references)

505.   Myers, Vincent. "Toward a Synthesis of Ethnographic and Survey Methods." *Human Organization* 36, no. 3 (Fall 1977): 244-51.

The author used "unconventional survey procedures" in a national survey involving young minority females and males from lower-socioeconomic backgrounds, as well as their nonminority counterparts. The procedures are compared with conventional procedures in the several pages comprising table 1. The sample was Job Corps enrollees in nineteen centers in seventeen states, for a total of 1,797 interviews. The respondents were young African Americans, Hispanics, from the Caribbean, and whites, as well as Job Corps staff. The U.S. Department of Labor and the National Institute on Drug Abuse were seeking information on "drug-related sentiments and cognitions" from the sample described above. Myers is unsure if conventional procedures were improved upon. However, he states that the approach "brought us to, and past the threshold of our respondents' experience." (13 references).

506.   Schwartz, David A. "Coping with Field Problems of Large Surveys among the Urban Poor." *Public Opinion Quarterly* 34, no. 2 (Summer 1970): 267-72.

Some problems and solutions involved in conducting large opinion research surveys among urban minorities are reviewed. The study is based on the experiences of Behavioral Research Survey Services (BRS), a division of Audits and Surveys, Incorporated. The challenge is in interviewing large numbers of people within a small geographic area, within a short time period. Generating community support, primarily through community leaders, is a necessary first step. Mechanisms are discussed for hiring and training interviewers and for supervising and controlling fieldwork by establishing local field offices within the area. These should be staffed by a full-time supervisor. The BRS office hired, trained, and supervised new interviewers – all residents of the area being surveyed and of the same race as the community under investigation. Interviewers were given an extensive training session, complete with at least one practice interview with actual respondents. The high level of attrition among interviewers has been a continuing problem for BRS. Ongoing interviewer supervision and payment are discussed. Finally, it was found to be judicious to set up a separate local field organization which functioned independently of the main office of BRS, as local residents often did not accept or respond to the supervisory team from New York. (1 footnote)

507. Word, Carl O. "Cross Cultural Methods for Survey Research in Black Urban Areas." *Journal of Black Psychology* 3, no. 2 (February 1977): 72-87.

This article addresses the shortcomings of current survey research methods with regard to polling urbanized African-American populations. According to Word, the following are major sources of error in survey data: (1) attitude models; (2) design of questions; (3) problems of measurement in multicultural settings; (4) problems concerning African-American linguistics and sociolinguistic aspects of speech; (5) inability of English speakers to understand the subtleties of African-American language and nonverbal cues; and (6) high refusal rates. Alternative strategies (figure 1 lists the sources of error and control procedures) and implications for survey data in public and private settings are also considered. Six specific suggestions for improving interviewing success are included. These deal with sensitivity to respondent answers (for example, "don't know" may mean the respondent is contemplating an answer), and ways in which the interviewer can pace the interview to establish appropriate rapport. (2 footnotes, 40 references)

Navajo

508. Streib, Gordon F. "The Use of Survey Methods among the Navajo." *American Anthropologist* 54, no. 1 (January-March 1952): 30-40.

The first setting was near Fruitland, New Mexico, on the Navajo Reservation, followed by Many Farms, Arizona, a location near the geographical center of the Reservation, one hundred miles from the nearest town of Gallup, New Mexico. The survey covered questions about farming, the Korean War, and the Navajo Ten-Year Program. The questionnaire was translated into Navajo. Interviews were conducted in English; otherwise an interpreter was used. Systematic sampling procedures were not employed. Respondents were interviewed wherever they could be located – in their homes and on their farms. English-language interviews lasted from thirty-five to ninety minutes, while bilingual sessions ranged from forty to one hundred eighty minutes. With adaptations, Streib found that survey techniques could be implemented in a semiliterate society. Lengthy questionnaires which pose both factual and attitudinal questions can be used. The author maintains that there are no impediments to employing representative sampling methods. (8 references)

Poverty Areas

509.   Lansing, John B., Stephen B. Withey, and Arthur C. Wolfe, et al., eds. *Working Papers on Survey Research in Poverty Areas.* Ann Arbor, MI: Survey Research Center, Institute for Social Research, University of Michigan, January 1971. 318 pages plus appendixes.

The authors' report is the product of work undertaken by the Survey Research Center (SRC) of the University of Michigan serving as a subcontractor to the Urban Institute in Washington, D.C. The institute was developing a survey research project to evaluate the Model Cities Program which was also under contract with the Department of Housing and Urban Development. The SRC was to assist in project planning. The report is designed to be of assistance to others conducting surveys in the central portions of large cities. The report is divided into a review of problems, a pilot survey in eight urban areas, and an analysis of tape-recorded interviewer-respondent interaction in three urban areas. Four appendixes covering 152 pages provide the codes, procedures, questionnaire, and codebook used. A three-page summary of the report appears at the front of the volume and highlights seven specific problems, states the report findings, and then provides a recommendation. The following questions are raised: (1) Should the respondent be paid? (2) Do interviewer and respondent have to be of the same race? and (3) Who should be the chosen respondent within a family? References follow each chapter. The following entries have been selected from the volume, with individual annotations found at the indicated item number.

Chapter 2:   "The Problem of Non-Response in Sample Surveys." (Benus and Ackerman - Item No. 699).

Chapter 10:   "Purpose and Procedures of the Tape Recording Analysis." (Marquis - Item No. 518).

Chapter 11:   "Analysis of Individual Questions." (Cannell and Robison - Item No. 327).

Chapter 12:   "Effects of Race, Residence, and Selection of Respondent on the Conduct of the Interview." (Marquis - Item No. 627).

Senior Citizens

510.   Dean, Laura Lee, Jeanne A. Teresi, and David E. Wilder. "The Human Element in Survey Research." *International Journal of Aging and Human Development* 8, no. 1 (1977-78): 83-92.

The actual project upon which the experiences described in this article are based is called the U.S.-U.K. Cross-National Project. The interviewing discussed deals with individuals who were sixty-five years of age and over, and lived in New York City. The community survey employed a stratified random sample. The article considers the various people involved in operating this type of survey, including the locator, the project coordinator, and the interviewers. Logistics are covered, such as needing a translator for 16 percent of the interviews and needing an "escort" for 20 percent of the calls in neighborhoods evaluated as dangerous. Six approaches to gaining access to households are discussed: (1) gimmicks (personal touches such as greeting cards); (2) scientific-oriented approach (newsclippings introducing the research group); (3) service-oriented approach (pamphlets with telephone numbers of service agencies); (4) endorsements (religious leaders); (5) payment of respondents; and (6) eclectic approach (whatever approach best suits the individual to be interviewed). Interviewer selection, training, and the challenge of maintaining these individuals on the staff are outlined. Each interview for the study discussed averaged six hours including time for travel, interviewing, rating, and summarizing. The University of Michigan is reported to need seven hours to obtain each one-hour interview. (3 references)

511.   Havighurst, Robert J. "Problems of Sampling and Interviewing in Studies of Old People." *Journal of Gerontology* 5, no. 2 (April 1950): 158-67.

In a "typical" midwestern community Havighurst found that approximately 75 percent of the persons over sixty-five years of age can be interviewed concerning their adjustment problems. About 10 percent are too ill or are unable to be interviewed, with an additional 10 to 15 percent who refuse to be interviewed. Groups exhibiting the greatest resistance to be interviewed include "lower-middle class women and men" and "upper-class women." Havighurst observes that personal interviewing is more effective than mail questionnaires with "older" people. Individuals from "middle class professional backgrounds" can be almost as effectively surveyed by mail. Warners' Index of Status Characteristics was used with a sample which began as a list of approximately 670 names. Various approaches including letters, telephone calls, appointments, and doorbell ringing, were taken by the interviewers in order to secure the personal interview. The study findings are compared with four other studies, two of which involved teachers, one dealt with secretaries, and the last concerned retired Methodist ministers and their widows. (8 references)

512.   Scaff, Alvin H. "Interviewing the Aged." *Claremont Quarterly* 2, no. 1 (December 1952): 23-30.

The seventeen-page interview questionnaire used contained 158 items and generally required from thirty minutes to one hour to complete. The questions concerned both personal and private matters, such as religion, income, and political affiliation. Interviewer selection was conducted by seeking "mature" and intelligent individuals who would work for relatively little money and who would be willing to be away from home for as long as two weeks at a time. Eleven women and one man were selected. The training of the interviewers involved four full days and used a thirteen-page instruction manual. Practice interviews were conducted in a community not far from the sample area. As the interviews were completed, the contents were checked daily for mistakes which were corrected with revisits as necessary. Second interviewers were sent back to clarify points. Using this approach, interviewers continued to be trained throughout the process. (No professional interviewers had been selected for this project.) To increase accuracy and completeness, callbacks were placed as many as nine times in order to locate not-at-homes. The largest number of nonrespondents had "strong feelings of independence," followed by those who perceived the questions to be too personal, with most of the rest claiming to be too busy.

513.   Zelan, Joseph. "Interviewing the Aged." *Public Opinion Quarterly* 33, no. 3 (Fall 1969): 420-24.

From a 1963 study undertaken by Brandeis University and the National Opinion Research Center, 1,847 males were sampled (1,678 were actually interviewed as some had died). All were veterans of the Spanish-American War (these were known as Spancos). When the research began in 1964, there were 18,564 Spancos in the United States. The author wanted to determine if cooperation and rapport could be obtained with an aged population (the late seventies and above), as well as to study the effect of respondent and interviewer characteristics on the interview. The following are some of the findings which emerged from the study: (1) Spancos were remarkably healthy for their ages; (2) they were easy to locate; (3) they willingly completed a lengthy schedule (sixty-four questions, thirty-two pages) administered by the interviewers; (4) they appeared eager to be interviewed; (5) there was a completion rate of 92 percent; (6) 75 percent of the interviewers thought this assignment was easier than others; and (7) most of the aged respondents had an active life as judged by the "Role Index." Zelan concludes that aged persons can be readily surveyed if they are reasonably healthy, have a personal interest in the research, and are fairly mobile. (6 footnotes)

TAPE RECORDERS

514.   Bevis, Joseph C. "Interviewing with Tape Recorders." *Public Opinion Quarterly* 13, no. 4 (Winter 1949-50): 629-34.

Bevis reports on a study that he believes is the first to make exclusive use of tape recorders for an entire survey. The main advantage of using tape recorders is the faithful representation of the respondents' words, thereby eliminating certain types of bias. More refined analysis is also possible. Disadvantages include the fact that most tape recorders require electricity, converters emit an interfering hum, the microphone is indiscriminate, and transcription is tedious and expensive. A survey which used hidden recorders is reported in detail. The survey involved four hundred interviews with gasoline station attendants who were questioned for about four minutes by interviewers after they had purchased gasoline. The tape recorder was concealed under the interviewer's shirtsleeve. The ethical and legal ramifications of recording respondents' words unknown to them are explored. For example, respondents unaware of the tape recorder may speak or act more freely, their words could possibly be used against them, and the record of what they say is permanent and indisputable. A similar issue, that of telephone recording devices, has been brought before the Federal Communications Commission (FCC). The FCC approved the use of telephone recorders provided they emit a soft beep every fifteen seconds. Counsel has advised Bevis that no liability exists in using tape recorders for interviewing "so long as there is no way for a third party to trace the replies to any individual respondent."

515. Bucher, Rue, Charles E. Fritz, and E. L. Quarantelli. "Tape Recorded Interviews in Social Research." *American Sociological Review* 21, no. 3 (June 1956): 359-64.

The reported research is based on nearly one thousand nondirective interviews conducted by the National Opinion Research Center (NORC). Conducted over a four-year period, the interviews were part of NORC's Disaster Project. The advantages of tape recording include the following: (1) verbalizations are not lost in significant proportions as they are when written; (2) interviewer bias is reduced since the interviewer no longer selects what to write down and what to delete; (3) recordings permit the evaluation of the interviewer's effect on the data; (4) interviewers can devote complete attention to respondents; and (5) recording eliminates the time and effort spent editing and adjusting written notes. In addition, tape recorders do not seem to increase refusal rates, nor do they decrease interviewer-respondent rapport. The data do not show response alteration as a consequence of the presence of tape recorders. The authors believe that tape recorders are useful in three interview settings: exploratory, pretest, and intensive unstructured or nondirective. Interdisciplinary research provides another area, with the possibility that tape recorders can also be used to select and train interviewers. Time-cost factors are discussed. Costs associated with the technique are high if the data are to be transcribed. The approach is noted for greater precision in the development of interview data. (12 footnotes)

516. Bucher, Rue, Charles E. Fritz, and E. L. Quarantelli. "Tape Recorded Research: Some Field and Data Processing Problems." *Public Opinion Quarterly* 20, no. 2 (Summer 1956): 427-39.

The problems involved in gathering data by machine in the field are reported, based on the experiences of members of the Disaster Project of the National Opinion Research Center of the University of Chicago. The project studied the psychological and sociological reactions to disaster situations. The Disaster Team conducted approximately one thousand nondirective type interviews, of which seven hundred were tape-recorded. Interviews averaged about one-and-a-half hours. Transcribed, they averaged about twenty-nine typed pages per interview. Some of the field problems encountered concerned (1) approaching the respondent and gaining rapport, (2) setting up the recording equipment, (3) maintaining recording quality, (4) interrupting the interview to change tapes, (5) concluding the interview, (6) identifying tapes, and (7) monitoring and controlling quality. Further problems arose in transcribing the recordings for data analysis. The author discusses factors such as the fatigue of the transcriber; errors in grammar, phrases, and punctuation; and the problem of nonverbal indicators. Checking the transcription for accuracy is best done by the original interviewer. (13 footnotes)

517.   Engel, James F. "Tape Recorders in Consumer Research." *Journal of Marketing* 26, no. 2 (April 1962): 73-74.

This article is aimed specifically at market research interviews although the thoughts expressed have broader applicability. The study undertaken involved 304 interviews as well as approximately 40 pretest interviews. The author outlines both positive and negative issues. Positive aspects include the following: (1) recorded responses reveal "behavioral cues" which may assist in an understanding of response patterns; (2) interviewer honestly is maintained since a record of the interview is on tape as well as in written format; (3) omissions or errors in the written report can be detected; (4) interviewer bias can be discovered; and (5) recorders are useful in pretesting questionnaires. Negative aspects include the following: (1) reviewing the tapes is costly; (2) response bias may arise because of the presence of the recorder; and (3) interviewers may resist the requirement of conducting interviews with the recorders. (2 footnotes)

518.   Marquis, Kent H. "Purpose and Procedures of the Tape Recording Analysis." Chap. 10 in *Working Papers on Survey Research in Poverty Areas*, edited by John B. Lansing, Stephen B. Withey, and Arthur C. Wolfe, et al., 219-35. Ann Arbor, MI: Survey Research Center, Institute for Social Research, University of Michigan, January 1971. 318 pages plus appendixes.

The interview environment in which tape recorders were used sought information concerning residents of model neighborhood areas. Subsamples in suburban Baltimore and Detroit, and in Worcester, Massachusetts, were used for purposes of tape recording. After the study was introduced and the appropriate respondents

were selected, permission was sought to tape-record the interviews. Many mechanical challenges were experienced – from broken tapes to poor sound quality. A total of 164 interviews were successfully recorded. A behavior coding
scheme was adapted from a previous work by Marquis and Cannell (reproduced
by mimeograph). A five-page appendix provides a brief description of the scheme,
with entries such as "refuses," "laughs," and "don't know." Three sections cover
interviewer behavior codes (questions, probes, and other interviewer behavior);
respondent behavior codes (answers and feedback); and respondent and interviewer behavior codes (social behavior). The interviews were coded by eight
members of the Survey Research Center coding staff. The "overall code-by-code/
interview reliability was 75 percent," a number considered to be acceptable when
compared with other complex behavior coding schemes. (5 footnotes) Chapters
10, 11, and 12 have a combined seventeen-entry bibliography on pages 317-18.

519.   Payne, Stanley L. "Interviewer Memory Faults." *Public Opinion Quarterly* 13, no. 4 (Winter 1949-50): 684-85.

The "reconstructed" interview is defined as an interview "during which the interviewer takes no notes but later makes a supposedly complete report." Although the technique is seen as relaxing to the respondent, it places greater burden on the memory abilities of the interviewer. Three experienced interviewers
were asked to tape-record their conversations (in this case interviews with gasoline station attendants). They were then asked to reconstruct from memory,
within a few minutes, the content of those conversations. The conversations were
short, on the average of five minutes. Compared with the tape recordings, the interviewers made errors in about 25 percent of the three hundred "recapitulations."
The experiment raises questions concerning the reliability of reconstructed interviews, especially if the interview is lengthy. Caution is to be used in such
cases.

TEAM

520.   Kincaid, Harry V., and Margaret Bright. "The Tandem Interview: Trial
of the Two-Interviewer Team." *Public Opinion Quarterly* 21, no. 2 (Summer 1957): 304-12.

The word "tandem" in the title refers to the use of two interviewers per respondent in the interview setting. Kincaid and Bright made up the interviewing team
in this case. The authors' experiences in team interviewing of forty-seven business executives form the basis for the research. Average length of the interview
was one-and-a-half hours. In the female-male team both asked the questions
although the former generally recorded the notes. The team members appeared as
colleagues, rather than as secretary and interviewer. Advantages of the technique

are these: (1) greater efficiency in recording; (2) increased precision, range, and sensitivity of questions; (3) greater probability of rapport; and (4) greater efficiency and accuracy in reconstructing, reporting, and analyzing responses. Team interviewing can be used with "high status" respondents, for exploratory studies, as an adjunct to other sample surveys, for reinterviewing a portion of a larger sample, and for interviewing respondents on taboo or sensitive topics. Several problems with the use of the tandem technique are outlined. These include a limited pool of full-time trained interviewers, an insufficient number of tasks for both members of the team, possible friction between interviewers, and additional administrative problems in large-scale surveys of the general population. While the authors believe the technique merits "serious consideration," its use is limited to certain types of studies at the present time. (11 footnotes)

TELEPHONE

General

521.   Coombs, Lolagene, and Ronald Freedman. "Use of Telephone Interviews in a Longitudinal Fertility Study." *Public Opinion Quarterly* 28, no. 1 (Spring 1964): 112-17.

A telephone survey was selected as the method of follow-up for a group of women previously interviewed as part of the Detroit Area Study, a University of Michigan-Survey Research Center continuous program. The subjects were the social and economic correlates of fertility, and whether the families achieved their expectations regarding family planning. The original sample was 1,304 white females, interviewed in January and February 1962, who were told that they would be contacted again. From October to December the second interviews were conducted. A prior letter reminded the participants of the upcoming interview. All respondents were to be reached by telephone. Those who could not were contacted by house calls or a mailed interview. Results reveal a 97.6 percent response rate, with 91.3 percent contacted by telephone. Of this group 8.3 percent required house calls; less than 1 percent were contacted by mail. In December 1963, 98 percent of those interviewed in the follow-up were interviewed a third time (87 percent of the original sample). The authors provide reasons for the unusually high response rate and details of how the respondents were tracked. The telephone is seen as an economical method for longitudinal studies – even those involving sensitive personal issues. Although the tracing of respondents was extensive, and there were many long-distance and toll telephone calls, Coombs and Freedman estimate that telephone interviewing was about 60 percent less costly than personal interviewing. (7 footnotes)

522.   Eastlack, J. O., Jr., and Henry Assael. "Better Telephone Surveys through Centralized Interviewing." *Journal of Advertising Research* 6, no. 1 (March 1966): 2-7.

The use of Wide Area Telephoning Service (WATS) for a major survey research application is discussed. The researchers found that WATS permitted testable estimates of sample reliability and interviewer performance. The telephone universe can be defined, and evaluation and control of interviewer performance are simplified. WATS use requires the researcher to more carefully preevaluate the questionnaire and interviewing procedures. The costs involved would suggest that the approach be reserved for studies requiring extreme precision and control. Additional thought and planning are called for when using WATS as compared to other current approaches. (12 references)

523.   Falthzik, Alfred M. "When to Make a Telephone Interview." *Journal of Marketing Research* 9, no. 4 (November 1972): 451-52.

A study to determine the most appropriate days and time of day to complete telephone interviews with "housewives" or female heads of households was undertaken. The communities selected were Wheaton, Viers Mill, North Bethesda, and Rockville, Maryland. The locations were approximately the same size and representative of all income groups. Days were divided into three time periods: 9:00 A.M. to 12:00 Noon; 2:30 P.M. to 5:30 P.M.; and 7:00 P.M. to 10:00 P.M. The survey was conducted over three weeks, seven days per week, with twenty calls per time period. In total 1,260 interviews were conducted. These were divided almost equally among the four communities. The study found that Monday, Tuesday, Wednesday, and Thursday are the best days, and that 9:00 A.M. to 12:00 Noon is the best time. (6 references)

524.   Lucas, William A., and William C. Adams. *An Assessment of Telephone Survey Methods.* RAND Report R-2135. Santa Monica, CA: RAND Corporation, 1977. 65p. Microfiche. (ED 187 299).

The methodology used in a study conducted for the National Science Foundation by the RAND Corporation is reported. The investigation examined the relationship between local television news viewing and local knowledge – specifically the effects of local media in seven western Pennsylvania cities. Information is provided on the strengths and weaknesses of telephone surveys for studying political and communication behavior. Prior literature indicates that the telephone is the "preferred" means of collecting data on citizen media use and political knowledge. (This article was written at a time when the authors maintain that "social scientists in academic circles continue to doubt the validity of data collected by telephone.") Lucas and Adams discuss sampling issues, telephone survey response reliability, and issues of quality in survey administration. The appendixes present data from the Pennsylvania cities and the questionnaire used in the study. (47 references)

525.   Mitchell, Glen H., and Everett M. Rogers. "Telephone Interviewing Used as a Research Tool." *Journal of Home Economics* 52, no. 2 (February 1960): 108-10.

The advantages and limitations of telephone interviewing for surveys are expressed. The advantages are as follows: (1) lower cost as compared with mail questionnaires or personal interviews; (2) higher response rate, with lowest refusal rate as compared with mail and face-to-face approaches; (3) greater control over interviewers, who are centrally located and can easily be monitored; and (4) bilingual interviewers can be called on as necessary, and biases created in personal interviewing such as the effects of appearance, facial expressions, and mannerisms (other than vocal) are not present. The limitations are as follows: (1) bias in using telephone directories (such as unlisted numbers, individuals who have changed addresses and are not yet listed, and those who do not have a telephone); (2) interview length (must be of limited duration in order to maintain rapport); and (3) visual materials cannot be used. The authors believe that telephone interviewing is highly useful when appropriately applied. (2 footnotes)

526.   Payne, Stanley L. "Data Collection Methods: Telephone Surveys." Section 2, Part B, Chap. 4 in *Handbook of Marketing Research*, edited by Robert Ferber, 2/105-2/123. New York, NY: McGraw-Hill Book Company, 1974. (various pagings)

The limitations of telephone surveys are discussed first, followed by a section on the advantages of telephone surveys. The purposes for which telephone surveys can be used are outlined, along with a presentation of sampling and questionnaire designs for telephone surveys. Payne also covers interviewer selection and etiquette. A chapter summary is provided, along with an eleven-entry bibliography.

527.   Payne, Stanley L. "Some Advantages of Telephone Surveys." *Journal of Marketing* 20, no. 3 (January 1956): 278-81.

The reticence to use the telephone in surveys is attributed to the disastrous outcome of the 1936 *Literary Digest* poll which relied on, among other things, telephone subscriber lists. Payne maintains that the environment twenty years later is quite different – with Evanston, Illinois, cited as an example where 97 percent of all households have telephones. Telephone interviews are described as the "most statistically efficient method," as well as the most economical (as long as the universe of telephone subscribers is adequate). Five examples of successful telephone surveys are used to show the variety of subject disciplines which can be covered. Payne notes that the term "survey" has been usurped by salespeople conducting phony surveys, and he recommends describing the project as a "research study." (2 footnotes)

528.   Sudman, Seymour. "New Uses of Telephone Methods." *Journal of Marketing Research* 3, no. 2 (May 1966): 163-67.

The new uses described by Sudman serve to reduce the cost of interviewing. Travel expenses are reduced by making appointments by telephone. Several studies involving such appointments are described, including a national sample of adolescents and the "happiness" studies in Prince Georges County, Maryland. The use of the telephone for the screening of rare populations is discussed, with the focus on people who are visually impaired or blind. Long-distance telephoning of physicians in New York City and Orange County is also covered. Sudman found the results from the telephone interviews to be not "less satisfactory than those obtained from personal interviews." It is noted that other approaches will be necessary when the respondent must examine a card or view a visual stimuli. (12 references)

529.   Tyebjee, Tyzoon T. "Telephone Survey Methods: The State of the Art." *Journal of Marketing* 43, no. 3 (Summer 1979): 68-78.

The major methodological issues of telephone survey research are identified, with the study conclusions presented. The areas for review are categorized into five sections: research management, validity of data, response rates, sampling, and questionnaire design. Subheadings under research management include cost, control, and time. Nonresponse caused by refusals and persons not-at-home is considered. The effects of excluding nontelephone households, sampling from telephone directories, and the use of random digit dialing are reviewed. Tyebjee describes the "near saturation of telephones in American households," but observes that persons at the poverty level and in rural areas may be excluded as they may not have telephones. (5 footnotes, 58 references)

530.   "Using the Telephone in Sampling." *Printers' Ink* 282, no. 5 (1 February 1963): 52-53.

Robert E. Riordan, vice-president of marketing and research with D. P. Brother and Company of Detroit, Michigan, is interviewed by *Printers' Ink* on the merits of telephone interviewing (in this case dealing primarily with industrial research). The article is presented in the question-and-answer format. Riordan observes that the telephone interview has "immediacy" and permits the questions to be revealed one at a time. Some of the questions addressed concerned these topics: (1) sampling; (2) level of cooperation; (3) survey planning time; (4) costs; (5) challenges of long interviews; (6) reaching the "captains of industry";

and (7) "double-interview techniques" (interviewing secretaries first, and then persuading them that the questionnaire would be of interest to their supervisors in order to achieve interview opportunities with high-level management personnel).

531.   Weller, Tom. "Telephone Interviewing Procedures." *Survey Research* 5, no. 1 (January 1973): 13-14.

Telephone interviewing is described as more convenient and less expensive by 20 to 30 percent over field interviewing. As manager of operations at the Public Opinion Center in Dayton, Ohio, Weller discusses the use of touch-tone telephones, head sets, silent monitoring systems, tape-recording of interviews, and random digit dialing (RDD). Weller also describes two additional sampling methods: (1) systematic sampling of voter registration lists; and (2) as number one, except that prospective respondents who could not be located are sought via field methods. The data in several tables show the types of response to RDD and provide a breakdown by the sex of the respondents.

532.   Wilshaw, Donn R., and Rose Mary Hardick. "Instant Survey: New Answer to an Old Problem." *School Management* 17, no. 9 (November-December 1973): 30-32.

The methodology and organizational details of how one school in Greece, New York, conducts its telephone surveys are described. The benefits of telephone surveys over mailed questionnaires are outlined. In 1973 refusal to participate on the part of individuals reached in a telephone survey was not a problem as few people refused. Four hundred people were randomly sampled in a community of seventy thousand people. The surveys conducted with this approach dealt with a single issue, asked a minimal number of questions, and provided for virtually immediate use of the results. The survey instructions and a sample budget survey are included.

Completion Rates

533.   Brunner, G. Allen, and Stephen J. Carroll, Jr. "The Effect of Prior Telephone Appointments on Completion Rates and Response Content." *Public Opinion Quarterly* 31, no. 4 (Winter 1967-68): 652-54.

Two samples were generated using a random sampling procedure. One unit, called the College Park sample, had a sample size of 270 each for the experimental and the control groups. The Bethesda sample had an experimental group of 107 and a control group of 79. Although the prior telephone call did not greatly affect the response pattern, it did have a negative impact on the overall completion rate. The authors note that there is a much higher refusal rate for telephone requests than for interview requests received in person at home. Additionally, the plan to reduce the not-at-homes by the prior telephone call was not very successful. Prior notification of respondents will probably significantly increase the cost of conducting the survey. (2 footnotes)

534.   Gates, Roger, and Carl McDaniel. "Improving Completion Rates by More Efficient Scheduling of Telephone Interviews." *Viewpoints: The Journal for Data Collection* 16 (May 1976): 8-10.

A study was conducted to determine the optimal time to conduct telephone interviews with female heads of households. A sample of fifteen hundred numbers randomly selected from Tarrant County (Fort Worth is located here), Texas, was called in three time periods: 9:00 A.M. to 12:00 Noon; 1:30 P.M. to 4:30 P.M.; and 6:30 P.M. to 9:30 P.M. No callbacks or additions were made. The results show that weekday mornings are the most productive times to call. Refusals were highest on the weekends, with the numbers of not-at-homes high for the weekends, Tuesdays, and Fridays. Not-at-homes accounted for almost half of the afternoon calls. Monday had the highest rate of completion, and Saturday the lowest. As of the date of this study, 93 percent of homes had telephones. Three tables provide the dispositions of the calls, and the completions, refusals, and not-at-homes by day of week and time of day.

Equipment

535.   " 'Call-Girl' Console Speeds Opinion Polling: New Device Designed for Broadcast Journalism Using Phone and Tape Cassettes Makes Large, Same-Day Opinion Polling Possible." *Broadcasting* 89 (1 September 1975): 43.

Designed primarily as a marketing tool for television stations, the "call-girl" console is produced by Key Marketing and sells for $3,995. A single operator can work three stations and conduct public opinion surveys on what are usually local issues. One user reports that in a three-hour period four hundred calls can be placed, recorded, and the results tallied. Each station has two cassette recorders, one for outgoing messages and the other for recording incoming responses. The operator places the call, and when answered, the machine is connected with the taped message (usually produced by the station's news director). A limited time tape recording is made of the responses. The console is designed to allow the operator to handle 100-125 calls an hour. The article reports sales to thirty-seven stations, primarily in major metropolitan locations.

536.   Hynes, Robert D. " 'Out-Call Logging' Keeps Tabs on LA Times Polling Operation." *Communications News* 15, no. 10 (October 1978): 32-33.

The Rockwell-Collins ACD Telephone System used by the *Los Angeles Times* records or logs outgoing calls. This "out-call logging" technique was utilized to provide cost information for in-house polling. Previously, telephone surveys had been conducted by outside agencies. The telephone surveys conducted in-house sought to complete one thousand interviews, each taking about fifteen minutes. With the computer-generated list of ten thousand telephone numbers (using prefixes based on census tracts), geographical, economic, and ethnic cross sections were achieved. A typical survey can be completed in three days and, on an annual basis, saved $50,000 over the previous arrangement. *Los Angeles Times* Editor Bill Thomas was seeking a polling approach which would serve as a reporting tool to accompany significant stories.

Refusals

537.   Dillman, Don A., Jean Gorton Gallegos, and James H. Frey. "Reducing Refusal Rates for Telephone Interviews*.*" *Public Opinion Quarterly* 40, no. 1 (Spring 1976): 66-78.

Three experiments are reported which examined three factors which might influence refusal rates. The factors are variations in the introductory message, notice by letter of an impending telephone interview, and sex of the interviewer. Experimental samples were selected from all published telephone directories for the state of Washington (92 percent of the households have telephones). Interviewers were trained university students working under supervision of a centralized telephone laboratory. Results of the first experiment, involving four different treatments, showed response rates in all of the approaches to be relatively consistent. Refusals ranged from 17 to 22 percent. Experiment number two, a continuation of the first, introduced new features such as usefulness of the study and rewards. These incentives did not increase response rates. In the third experiment three forms of a prior letter were sent to different groups. The refusal rate was 7.6 percent, thereby indicating that the letter did make a difference. Sex of the interviewer had very little effect on refusal rate in all three studies. Implications of the study are given for mail questionnaires and random digit dialing. (23 footnotes)

MISCELLANEOUS

538.   Alexander, Cheryl S., and Henry Jay Becker. "The Use of Vignettes in Survey Research." *Public Opinion Quarterly* 42, no. 1 (Spring 1978): 93-104.

The authors define the word "vignettes" as "systematically elaborated descriptions of concrete situations," or, more simply, as "short descriptions of a person or a social situation which contain precise references to what are thought to be the most important factors in the decision-making or judgment-making processes of respondents." Alexander and Becker discuss these advantages of the vignettes technique: (1) the researcher can vary the characteristics and variables used in a description of a situation to evoke a response to a question; (2) as compared to direct questioning, it is more difficult for respondents to bias their answers; (3) the social stimulus is standardized across respondents; and (4) the decision-making situation is more realistic. A fractional replication experimental design is reported which maximized the number of different vignette versions that the research instruments can manipulate. To illustrate the applicability of the vignette technique to survey research, the results of a study of the reactions of 368 police officers and 312 nurses to crime victims are given. Findings support the use of the method. (3 footnotes, 13 references)

539.   Cataldo, Everett F., Richard M. Johnson, Lyman A. Kellstedt, and Lester W. Milbrath. "Card Sorting as a Technique for Survey Interviewing." *Public Opinion Quarterly* 34, no. 2 (Summer 1970): 202-15.

An experiment in the use of card sorting (a method related to the Q-technique) in a large-scale survey is reported. With the card-sorting technique the respondent is asked a question and then presented with a deck of stimulus cards, each containing different content. The respondent reads the cards, sorts them into standard response categories, and places them on a board. The subject was political participation. Two waves of interviewing took place with over one thousand respondents in each wave. The location was Buffalo, New York, but the technique has also been used in the thirteen-state Comparative State Election Project and in Ontario, Canada. Data quality was judged in terms of reliability, validity, and response bias. Results show that the method produces data that are as reliable as that of other large-scale surveys. Validity was assessed by face and construct validity methods and produced acceptable results. Card sorting appeared to have counteracted some biasing effects. It was both quick and easy for the respondents, even for the nonliterate. Card sorting is recommended to other researchers as a data-gathering device for large-scale survey studies. (10 footnotes)

540.   Dohrenwend, Barbara Snell, and Stephen A. Richardson. "Directiveness and Nondirectiveness in Research Interviewing: A Reformulation of the Problem." *Psychological Bulletin* 60, no. 5 (September 1963): 475-85.

The authors review the literature on directiveness and nondirectiveness, consider the impact on interviewing of the two alternate approaches, and discuss the way in which the interviewers' questioning can affect the length of response, the topic selection, and the direction of the informants' responses. Three interview designs are studied: limited-response, free-response, and defensive-responsive. Also discussed are the purposes of each type and the reliability and validity of the responses achieved through the approaches. Dohrenwend and Richardson maintain that "any of the three interview designs can be considered for collecting standardized data." (2 footnotes, 31 references)

541.   Hogue, Gerald. "Directional Probe Symbol 'X' as an Aid in Interview Control." *Public Opinion Quarterly* 20, no. 4 (Winter 1956-57): 718-19.

A technique is described and recommended as a way to improve field interviewers' communication with the home office. In the past an X usually has been used on the form to denote difficulty (or an interruption or a breakdown) in securing a response to a free-answer question. The conventional X probe is used instead of requiring the interviewer to record verbatim the respondents' words. In one study interviewers were instructed to use a circled X when the probe is a directional one. This procedure assisted in judging the interviewers' performance, in locating weak spots in the form, and in clarifying the interview situation. A circle without the X could be used to indicate any interruption in the interview.

542.   Myers, Vincent Henry. "Unconventional Techniques for Collecting Survey Data: A Reassessment of Conventional Theory and Practice." Ph.D. diss., University of California, Los Angeles, 1974. 242 leaves. [*Dissertation Abstracts International* Order No. 7424605; *DAI* 35A, no. 5 (November 1974): 3133.]

Myers maintains that verbally standardized interviews are "deficient" in the views of phenomenological sociologists, minority social scientists, and minority populations at large. Unconventional assumptions and techniques were tested in a study. Interviewers were involved in the planning of the instrument and were "taught to tailor dynamic, natural, and fluctuating interviewing styles to respondents within the contingencies of each exchange." The interviews were functionally rather than verbally standardized. Myers concludes that the use of unconventional techniques produces "parity" between validity and reliability, reduces biases occurring in conventional interviews, and addresses recent criticisms against conventional survey methodology. Phenomenological theory is the foundation for the alternate procedures described. References are provided.

543.   Perrine, Mervyn W., and Alden E. Wessman. "Disguised Public Opinion Interviewing with Small Samples." *Public Opinion Quarterly* 18, no. 1 (Spring 1954): 92-96.

A number of relatively inexperienced interviewers participated in this study of "disguised" interviewing (that is, interviewing in which the identities of the interviewers are not revealed to the respondents). The study attempted to predict the outcomes of the congressional and gubernatorial races in Union County, New Jersey, using a "rough quota-control" sampling method, with emphasis on "proportional geographic and representative socio-economic distribution." The investigation employed a small sample of 214 respondents. The interviewers usually posed as strangers and initiated casual conversations to establish rapport with potential respondents. Voting intentions were eventually gleaned and recorded. About five interviews per hour were conducted. Between 60 and 70 percent of the contacts yielded insufficient information due to lack of rapport with the interviewer, inclement weather, hurried respondents, after-dark hours, and poor locations. Among those most difficult to contact were women, African Americans, proprietors, and municipal employees. The average error rate was 2.64 percent. Small sample techniques and disguised interviewing are recommended. (3 footnotes)

544.   Turnbull, William. "Secret vs. Nonsecret Ballots." Part 2, Chap. 5 in *Gauging Public Opinion* by Hadley Cantril and Research Associates in the Office of Public Opinion Research, Princeton University, 77-97. Princeton, NJ: Princeton University Press, 1944. Reprint. Port Washington, NY: Kennikat Press, 1972. 318p.

The secret ballot was utilized to counter the possibility that the respondent might be "suspicious, embarrassed, nervous, inarticulate, irritated, hostile or patronizing." The second-ballot technique was employed with ten questions based on their controversial content. Conventional interviewers were used in 302 cases, with 300 responding by secret ballot. When the secret ballot was used, the interviewer carried a padlocked ballot box prominently marked "SECRET BALLOT." The respondent could mark the ballot privately and deposit the completed ballot in the box. Turnbull found that the ballots do "produce marked differences in answers under certain conditions." Answers are different when the respondent is of the view that their "prestige" is involved. Turnbull suggests that the secret ballot be employed when questions deal with "high social prestige" and/or they involve highly controversial topics. The author noted that it was possible that the differences found between "privately" and "publicly" expressed opinions may have been exaggerated. (6 footnotes)

MIXED MODE DATA COLLECTION METHODS

MAIL AND PERSONAL

545.   Cannell, Charles F., and Floyd Fowler. *Comparison of Hospitalization Reporting in Three Survey Procedures: Study of Alternative Survey Methods for Collection of Hospitalization Data from Household Respondents, 1963.* In *Health Statistics from the U.S. National Health Survey*, Series D, No. 8. Washington, DC: U.S. Department of Health, Education, and Welfare, Public Health Service, January 1963. 48p. [SuDoc FS2.85:D-8] [Reprinted in *Vital and Health Statistics: Data Evaluation and Methods Research*. Public Health Service Publication No. 1000, Series 2, No. 8. Washington, DC: U.S. Department of Health, Education, and Welfare, Public Health Service, National Center for Health Statistics, July 1965. 48p.] [SuDoc HE20.6209:2/8]

The Survey Research Center of the Institute for Social Research at the University of Michigan prepared the report. Cannell and Fowler discuss the following three procedures: (1) the standard Health Interview Survey questionnaire and procedures were employed; (2) the revised interview schedule was followed with a mail form in which the respondent was to indicate hospitalization information which had been overlooked; and (3) hospitalization questions were eliminated from the interview, and were to be completed on a self-administered form provided at the close of the interview and mailed to a regional office of the Bureau of the Census. The purpose was to determine "over-all net effectiveness" of the procedures. Cost comparison was not undertaken. The results show that the percentages of hospital episodes not reported in each procedure from above were, respectively, 17 percent, 9 percent, and 16 percent. When overreporting was removed, the percentages declined by 2 to 3 percent in each case. In all three procedural approaches, the greater the degree of perceived social threat or embarrassment, the greater the degree to which the hospitalization was not reported. The researchers explain the success of the second approach to motivating respondents by "encouraging and directing increased effort to report." The number of respondents interviewed by procedure was, respectively, 448, 526, and 471. The appendixes contain sampling errors, an analysis of interview assignments, and the questionnaires used. (3 footnotes)

546.   Cannell, Charles F., and Floyd J. Fowler. "Comparison of a Self-Enumerative Procedure and a Personal Interview: A Validity Study." *Public Opinion Quarterly* 27, no. 2 (Summer 1963): 250-64.

To compare the validity of the two field measuring techniques, data were obtained from a sample of hospitals in the Detroit area. The topic was hospitalizations. Six hypotheses were developed and tested. Twenty interviewers were hired and trained for the personal interviews. They interviewed all at-home adults in the family and took proxy statements for others for a total of 462 respondents. In the self-enumerative procedure some of the data were gathered by personal interviewers, but the hospitalization data were collected by questionnaire, returned by mail by the respondent. The sample size was 465 individuals. Analysis of the data shows the following: (1) when medical records were available, or in proxy reporting, the self-enumerative procedure was more accurate; (2) facts on diagnosis and type of surgery were reported more accurately in the interview setting; (3) personal interviews were better when problems arose as to what constitutes an adequate response or when questions concerned threatening or embarrassing surgery; (4) respondents' education was found to be more important in the interview procedure; and (5) respondents' motivation was found to be more important in the self-enumerative procedure, and was, in general, the most significant variable in reporting. (16 footnotes)

547.   Ellis, Albert. "Questionnaire versus Interview Methods in the Study of Human Love Relationships." *American Sociological Review* 12, no. 5 (October 1947): 541-53.

For research investigating love and marital relations of college students, it was found that the questionnaire approach is as satisfactory as the interview method. As questions become more ego-involving, the questionnaire may produce more self-revealing data than the interview approach. Eighty-nine female undergraduate students from three New York colleges were interviewed in the spring of 1944. One year later an anonymous mailed questionnaire, containing many of the same questions used in the interview, was sent to the original respondents. Usable, completed returns were received from sixty-nine individuals, with an average age of 20.5. A six-page table compares each question asked with the responses provided to the interviewer and on the questionnaire. Sixty questions are presented. (5 footnotes) [See Item No. 548 for a follow-up study.]

548.   Ellis, Albert. "Questionnaire versus Interview Methods in the Study of Human Love Relationships. II. Uncategorized Responses." *American Sociological Review* 13, no. 1 (February 1948): 61-65.

This is a follow-up study to the one reported in the *American Sociological Review* in October 1947 which dealt with categorized responses [Item No. 547]. The present study is concerned with responses to six questions requiring uncategorized responses. The questions are listed in the article, along with a table which provides the responses to interviewer and questionnaire. About half the respondents changed their answers from interview mode to questionnaire mode on most of the questions. More unfavorable changes were made from interview to questionnaire format, and of the changes made on the questionnaire, twice as many were less favorable to the respondents. As before, Ellis concludes that the questionnaire method of data gathering in this case seems to be as satisfactory as the interview method. (1 footnote)

549.   Ferber, Marianne A., and Bonnie G. Birnbaum. "Retrospective Earnings Data: Some Solutions for Old Problems." *Public Opinion Quarterly* 43, no. 1 (Spring 1979): 112-18.

This pilot study investigates the use of the recall method to collect salary data in longitudinal or panel research. Three questions were posed for the research: (1) Will the response rate be high? (2) Will the information from respondents for past years be less accurate? and (3) Will selective recall produce biased results? From a group of female clerical employees (age thirty-five or older) at the University of Illinois, Urbana-Champaign, 238 were randomly selected for telephone interviews. Mail questionnaires were sent to 697 others. Salary information, available through university records, allowed the respondents' reports to be validated. The findings indicate a high refusal rate and the inability or unwillingness of respondents to provide complete information on salary questions. Through the use of the recall method, the authors found that retrospective information was not much less accurate than current salary information. The method is seen as a cheaper and quicker alternative to panel studies. (10 footnotes, 5 references)

550.   Ferber, Robert. "Which – Mail Questionnaires or Personal Interviews? – A Reconciliation of Opposing Views on the Basis of Available Factual Data." *Printers' Ink* 222, no. 7 (13 February 1948): 44-47, 61, 64, 66.

Mail questionnaires are compared with personal interviews on the following points: (1) sample control and geographic distribution; (2) costs; (3) response frankness; (4) the nature of mail questionnaire respondents; and (5) a variety of other points including the relative approachability of each option and nonrespondent omissions in mail questionnaires. A table comparing the two approaches with advantages and disadvantages lists six positive entries for the mail option and seven negatives. An additional disadvantage with mail questionnaires is that they require more time to organize and to conduct than personal interviews (Ferber cites at least two weeks for the mail option versus just over one week for personal interviews). Ferber believes that the comparison indicates that neither technique is superior, but depends upon the needs of the particular environment. In many instances using both techniques together may be the best approach. (15 references)

551.   Gibson, Frank K., and Brett W. Hawkins. "Interviews versus Questionnaires." *American Behavioral Scientist* 12, no. 1 (September-October 1968): NS-9 - NS-11.

Members of the Georgia General Assembly were the respondents in a study which attempted to determine their attitudes regarding the effects of reapportionment. Of the two hundred fifty-nine members of the 1967 session of the assembly, seventy-three were interviewed, with the remaining members receiving essentially the same interview schedule as a mail questionnaire. For this study forty-one interview and forty-eight questionnaire responses were compared. The authors found that when surveying a relatively homogeneous group, asking questions on matters about which the respondents are aware, and promising response anonymity, the questionnaire "may produce substantially the same results" as interviews and at considerably less expense. (3 footnotes, 1 reference)

552.   Jackson, Robert M., and J. W. M. Rothney. "A Comparative Study of the Mailed Questionnaire and the Interview in Follow-Up Studies." *Personnel and Guidance Journal* 39, no. 7 (March 1961): 569-71.

The Wisconsin Counseling Study, begun in 1948, involved 890 students. The experimental group received "intensive counseling" from members of the University of Wisconsin during the three years of high school. The control group received the usual services offered by the high-school guidance department. All 685 graduates received a four-page mail questionnaire five years after high-school graduation. Fifty students were selected for follow-up interviews. The sample was generated by selecting every fourteenth name from the alphabetic lists of the control and experimental groups. These individuals received a personal letter seeking their consent. The fifty who agreed were tape-recorded during the follow-up interview. The interviewer memorized the question wording and order exactly as they appeared in the mail questionnaire. The study found that the interviewers generated "significantly more complete answers" as compared with the mail format. Each approach yielded information not found in the other. Two of three respondents answered "consistently" to items in both formats. Factual questions received higher responses than evaluative types. With each successive page of the mail questionnaire the number of responses declined significantly. Even though mail questionnaires require less time and are more cost effective, the authors believe that interviews are justifiable due to the "greater insight into the respondents," as well as to the more complete responses generated. (6 references)

553.　Magid, Frank N., Nicholas G. Fotion, and David Gold. "A Mail-Questionnaire Adjunct to the Interview." *Public Opinion Quarterly* 26, no. 1 (Spring 1962): 111-14.

Long interviews can generate reliability difficulties in terms of the data gathered near the completion. One way to address this problem is through the use of a mail questionnaire in addition to the interview. The challenge is to achieve a sufficient number of returns from the mail questionnaire. The authors believe that rapport, engagement, and a sense of commitment generated during the interview can lead to high mail response rates. The rate of return can also be used to evaluate the degree of success achieved by various interviewers. An additional value of the mail questionnaire format is that it can be used to ask possibly embarrassing questions or those in which an anonymous situation might be more useful. As a means of checking reliability, the same question can be asked in both formats. (4 footnotes)

554.　Nuckols, Robert C. "Personal Interview versus Mail Panel Survey." *Journal of Marketing Research* 1, no. 1 (February 1964): 11-16.

The personal interview sample contained 3,286 heads of "complete husband-wife families"; the mail panel included 800 participants. The task was to determine the validity of life insurance ownership through a comparison of survey data with company records and census distributions. The study "favored" the mail panel, with the finding that respondents "could handle a relatively long and complex questionnaire." Additionally, the mail panel members "report life insurance ownership information more accurately and with less bias than do personal interview respondents, even when those personally interviewed check their records." Nuckols discusses free-response questions, the willingness to admit embarrassing behavior, inter-item relationships, and cost issues. (5 references)

555.　O'Dell, William F. "Personal Interviews or Mail Panels?" *Journal of Marketing* 26, no. 4 (October 1962): 34-39.

Mail panels are defined as "consumer panels used for the gathering of information on a particular subject or group of subjects in single surveys." If the decision as to which mode of data collection is not clear from the onset, then issues of cost and data accuracy become the deciding factors. O'Dell considers sampling bias, response error, sequence, interviewer bias, and specificity of response. Costs are compared for the two approaches. Sampling validity and response validity are covered. In making the final choice cost factors and previous experience should be taken into consideration. (1 footnote)

MAIL, PERSONAL, AND SELF-ADMINISTERED

556.   Zusman, Marty Evan. "The Nature of Method Effects: A Comparison of the Personal Interview, Personal Questionnaire and Mail Questionnaire." Ph.D. diss., Indiana University, 1973. 224 leaves. [*Dissertation Abstracts International* Order No. 7409450; *DAI* 34A, no. 10 (April 1974): 6768.]

The personal questionnaire environment is described as one in which "an administrator contacted a respondent who was then given the questionnaire to read and record" her/his own responses. Three types of data collection methods are compared and contrasted: the personal interview, the personal questionnaire (a scenario in which a respondent, contacted by an administrator in a noncaptive situation, reads and records his own responses), and the mailed questionnaire. The investigation attempted to assess the relative efficacy of the three methods, to identify the kinds of items which impact data quality, and to pinpoint the primary factors of the data collection methods which affect quality differences. The major criteria studied were completeness, and reliability and validity of the information gathered, as well as demographic, attitudinal, and behavioral items, sample mortality, item nonresponse, internal consistency, and others. The role of the administrator was also investigated. Analysis of the data shows significant quality differences among the methods. The personal interview showed the least sample mortality and item nonresponse. The personal questionnaire had the highest consistency and reliability of response in the test-retest situation, and had the least "measurement effect upon the response." The most detailed answers to open-ended questions were found in the responses to the mailed questionnaire. Based on these findings, Zusman recommends the personal questionnaire as the technique of choice for sociological research. References are provided.

MAIL, PERSONAL, AND TELEPHONE

557.   Banas, Paul A., and Rene V. Davis. "Identifying the Physically Handicapped through Survey Methods." *American Journal of Public Health* 52, no. 3 (March 1962): 443-49.

Simply worded questionnaires performed adequately when compared with complex forms. Approximately 70 percent of those identified as people with disabilities were found through survey methods. It is shown that telephone interviews and mail questionnaires are as effective as personal interviews when identifying people with disabilities. These results are from a survey conducted in Minnesota, by the University of Minnesota's Industrial Relations Center. Four different formats were developed for the questionnaire used during the telephone interviews. These formats were tested on a small sample before the final format was selected for statewide survey use. In a metropolitan area the telephone approach proved the most economical, with mail questionnaires useful for widely dispersed rural respondents, and personal interviews used only if greater depth of information is sought. About one-third of known people with disabilities were missed through the survey approaches. Banas and Davis observe that "ease of identification varied with the nature of the disability." (8 references)

558.   Blankenship, Albert B., Archibald Crossley, Myron S. Heidingsfield, Herta Herzog, and Arthur Kornhauser. "Questionnaire Preparation and Interviewer Technique." *Journal of Marketing* 14, no. 3 (October 1949): 399-433.

As chairperson of a subcommittee of the Marketing Research Techniques Committee, Blankenship and four other members prepared a set of "principles" or general rules of procedure. Although the title uses the term "questionnaire," not only is the mail questionnaire considered, but also the telephone interview, the personal interview, the formal questionnaire, and the qualitative interview. The document is divided into three main parts: (1) "Summary of Principles"; (2) "Selecting the Method of Obtaining the Information"; and (3) "Structural Design of the Method Selected" (which individually considers the categories specified above). (30 footnotes)

559.   Francis, J. Bruce, James H. Frey, and Harold Harty. "Advantages and Disadvantages of Different Survey Techniques." In *Surveying Institutional Constituencies*, edited by J. Bruce Francis, 11-18. *New Directions for Institutional Advancement: A Quarterly Sourcebook*, editor-in-chief A. Westley Rowland, no. 6. San Francisco, CA: Jossey-Bass Inc., Publishers, 1979. 100p.

The personal interview, the telephone interview, and the mail questionnaire are compared and contrasted. Particular attention is directed to the mail questionnaire, with cost, convenience, and bias reduction discussed as positive aspects. Disadvantages with the mail format are highlighted, including low response, question shortcomings, and "questionnaire haters." Cost-benefit analysis is suggested as a way of aiding the method selection process. A chart is provided with a column for each type of survey approach, with advantages listed first and disadvantages below. (16 references)

560.   Hinkle, Andrew Lee, and Glen D. King. "A Comparison of Three Survey Methods to Obtain Data for Community Mental Health Program Planning." *American Journal of Community Psychology* 6, no. 4 (August 1978): 389-97.

The three methods compared are the telephone survey, the mail questionnaire, and the face-to-face interview. Two hundred twenty-four people were randomly seleted using a telephone directory, 1,000 randomly selected individuals were mailed questionnaires with returns requested, and 449 face-to-face interviews were completed from a random sample. Response confidentiality was assured. The mail questionnaire proved to be the most costly per completed unit and tended to sample only upper-socioeconomic-status individuals who expressed dissatisfaction with their community mental health program. The face-to-face and telephone interviews yielded comparable data, with telephone surveys being the most economical. The completion rates were telephone, 57 percent; mail questionnaire, 19 percent; and personal interview, 70 percent. (15 references)

561.   Hochstim, Joseph R. "A Critical Comparison of Three Strategies of Collecting Data from Households." *Journal of the American Statistical Association* 62, no. 319 (September 1967): 976-89.

The study was conducted between 1961 and 1962 in Alameda County, California, with a sample of 2,148 housing units. Hochstim compared the personal interview, the telephone interview, and the mail questionnaire. Area probability sampling and identical questionnaires were used in all three data collection modes. The responses to each strategy were highly comparable, and the "substantive findings were virtually interchangeable." Validity differences were small. The cost per interview varied a great deal, with substantial cost savings reported by using mail questionnaires and telephone interviews. Follow-up of nonrespondents is essential, with persistent telephone calling and personal interviews necessary. Subsampling procedures are suggested in the final stages of data collection as a means of reducing the high cost per respondent. (2 footnotes, 8 references)

562.   Krueck, Thomas George. "A Comparison of Three Alternative Methods of Conducting a Follow-Up Study Based on Cost, Rate of Response, and Nature of Information Obtained." Ph.D. diss., University of Wisconsin-Madison, 1975. 120 leaves. [*Dissertation Abstracts International* Order No. 7519075; *DAI* 36A, no. 7 (January 1976): 4355.]

The research compares and contrasts three data collection methods – the mailed questionnaire, the personal interview, and the telephone interview – in order to identify which methods, or combination of methods, would be most efficient in a follow-up study. The population surveyed involved 492 graduates of a vocational school in Dallas, Texas. Items studied included response rate, differences in the nature of the responses, comparative costs, and relevance to particular ethnic groups. The major findings include the following: (1) the telephone interview produced the highest response rate; (2) the mailed questionnaire had a significantly higher rate of nonresponse, particularly to open-ended questions; (3) the personal interview approach was twice as costly as the other two; (4) response rates were higher for Anglos than for African Americans or Mexican Americans; (5) the telephone interview method showed the highest response rate for all ethnic groups; and (6) no significant differences were found based on the method used. The author concludes that a response rate of at least 70 percent would be ensured by a clerical personnel-conducted telephone interview survey, combined with mailed questionnaires, for "subjects living outside the immediate community or those not having telephones." References are provided.

563.   Payne, Stanley L. "Combination of Survey Methods." *Journal of Marketing Research* 1, no. 2 (May 1964): 61-62.

The survey methods referred to are those of the personal interview, the telephone interview, and the mail questionnaire. Payne suggests that the use of all three approaches with the same respondents can generate results which none of the three methods used alone could produce. One example is where a test item is personally delivered, but the follow-up to determine responses was conducted by telephone. Further approaches include the following: (1) personal placement of products in the market research test, self-administered questionnaires, and return envelopes; (2) mail returns of the respondents' completed forms; and (3) follow-up through telephone interviews – with each of the steps employed in every household under study. Payne presents data showing an 82 percent return rate for the mailed returns and a 97 percent completion rate for telephone follow-up. Another possible suggestion is to reverse the order of the above three options. The use of two-method combinations by the Bureau of the Census in 1960 is cited. Payne suggests that the technique described above is the first application combining three approaches. (5 references).

564.   Thornberry, Owen Thomas, Jr. "An Evaluation of Three Strategies for the Collection of Data from Households." Ph.D. diss., Brown University, 1976. 340 leaves. [*Dissertation Abstracts International* Order No. 7714202; *DAI* 38A, no. 1 (July 1977): 511.]

Combinations of three data collection strategies – the personal interview, the telephone interview, and the self-administered mail questionnaire – are compared and contrasted in a sample of households previously not contacted in person. Pros and cons of each method are reviewed, and the lack of empirical research in the use of combinations of the methods is noted. The interviews concerned the health of family members and how the family utilized health services in the state of Rhode Island. The three methods were evaluated according to response rate, method of completion, cost, completeness of returns, and comparability of findings. Results include these points: (1) the personal interview and the telephone interview had the highest response rates; (2) the rate of completion differed significantly by the main method of collection; (3) the personal interview costs were about twice as much as the telephone method or the mail questionnaire; and (4) nonresponse was very low for all strategies. Intrastrategy and interstrategy comparisons are also shown. The use of combinations of the three methods is viewed as the "optimal" approach for collecting data for many sample surveys. References are provided.

565.   Wiseman, Frederick. "Methodological Bias in Public Opinion Surveys." *Public Opinion Quarterly* 36, no. 1 (Spring 1972): 105-8. [Reprinted in Chap. 5.2 in *Public Opinion: Its Formation, Measurement, and Impact*, edited by Susan Welch and John Comer, 386-90. Palo Alto, CA: Mayfield Publishing Company, 1975. 541p.]

Three data collection methods (the mail questionnaire, the telephone interview, and the personal interview) are compared and contrasted to determine if sample survey responses are influenced by the methods used to gather the data. Residents of a suburban Boston community were divided into three experimental groups, each receiving one of the three options. Nine questions concerning local and national issues were posed to all groups. Analysis of the data shows the following: (1) the mail questionnaire retrieved the largest number of completed interviews (a result partially attributed to a prior telephone notification); (2) statistically significant differences were not found for age, sex, marital status, occupation, income, or religion; (3) a significant amount of bias due to the data collection methods was found on only two of the questions; and (4) the mail questionnaire retrieved the largest number of socially undesirable responses (these were related to the religious preference of the respondent). The author concludes that response bias "is likely to be a problem" in both telephone and personal interviews when a question involves a socially undesirable response. Warner's randomized response model [Item No. 739] is offered as a possible solution to the problem. (6 footnotes)

566.   Zelen, William F. "A Comparative Analysis of Three Data Collecting Methodologies." Ph.D. diss., Kent State University, 1975. 279 leaves. [*Dissertation Abstracts International* Order No. 7614372; *DAI* 37A, no. 1 (July 1976): 36.]

Zelen employs face-to-face, telephone, and mail questionnaire methodologies to determine if the approaches "differentially affected respondents' answers." The survey topic related to the respondents' perception of the internal communication system in their university. Zelen used three separate studies, one for each method. Each study had a random sample of one hundred respondents from four categories in the university (administration, faculty, students, and nonacademic personnel). The author found that it would be best to select the method based on the needs of the respondents sought for participation. Generally speaking, the three methods are interchangeable. Even though each has shortcomings, these can be overcome through researcher accommodation. (72 references)

MAIL, PERSONAL, TELEPHONE, AND THE RANDOMIZED RESPONSE MODEL

567.   Locander, William, Seymour Sudman, and Norman Bradburn. "An Investigation of Interview Method, Threat and Response Distortion." *Journal of the American Statistical Association* 71, no. 354 (November 1976): 269-75.

Four types of interview techniques are compared: face-to-face, telephone, self-administered, and the random response model (RRM). The level of threat ranged from ownership of a library card and voting behavior at the low end, with bankruptcy in between, and drunken driving at the high end of the threat scale. Interviews were conducted with 941 individuals, with an overall completion rate of 72.2 percent. The study found that as the threat level increases, the response distortion increases sharply. No single data collection technique proved to be superior for all the varieties of threat-level questions posed. The authors suggest that convenience of the researcher should dictate which method to use. The RRM provides the best performance when dealing with "socially undesirable acts," but nevertheless showed a 35 percent understatement of drunken driving. Telephone interviewing gained the highest degree of cooperation for this city setting (Chicago). Even when privacy is maintained, the manner of questioning did not vary high response bias for high threat items. There are four tables, one figure, and an appendix of validation questions and the context in which they were asked. (46 references)

MAIL AND TELEPHONE

568.   Dillman, Don A. *Mail and Telephone Surveys: The Total Design Method.* A Wiley-Interscience Publication. New York, NY: John Wiley & Sons, 1978. 325p.

The purpose of this book is to provide someone who already knows the procedural basics of survey research with step-by-step details of how to conduct mail and telephone surveys. Dillman maintains that the great shortcomings of non-face-to-face interview formats – such as low response rates and the need to have short questionnaires – have been largely surmounted. The approach used is called the "total design method" (TDM). TDM calls for attention to every detail which might affect how the respondents react to the survey. The author found that for the general public a consistent 75 percent response rate can be achieved with mail surveys, and an 80 to 90 percent consistent response rate through telephone surveys. Beginning with a discussion of the facets of TDM, Dillman examines the pros and cons of mail, telephone, and face-to-face surveys. Further chapters are devoted to the general principles of question writing; the construction of mail questionnaires and their use; the construction and implementation of telephone questionnaires and surveys; and finally, a look toward the future beyond TDM. Each chapter ends with a conclusion, and notes or references from the text. A bibliography includes references to over 340 articles; 35 book titles are in a separate list.

569.   Hughes, George Edward. "A Comparative Analysis of the Mailed Questionnaire, the Telephone Interview, and a Combined Survey Approach as Techniques for Conducting Follow-Up Studies of Graduates." Ph.D. diss., Southern Illinois University at Carbondale, 1977. 203 leaves. [*Dissertation Abstracts International* Order No. 7724465; *DAI* 38A, no. 5 (November 1977): 2587.]

Three data collection methods are compared and contrasted: the mail questionnaire, the telephone interview, and a combination approach (a mail questionnaire followed by a telephone call to obtain the response). The study population was a group of six hundred graduates of the Teacher Education Program at Southern Illinois University at Carbondale. Areas of inquiry cover cost of the three methods, response rate, sample mortality, nature and usefulness of the data gathered, and the characteristics of both the respondents and the nonrespondents. Among the findings of the follow-up study are the following: (1) mail questionnaire costs per response were lowest of the three; (2) comparable response rates were found for the three methods; (3) sample mortality was lowest for the mail questionnaire method; (4) mail questionnaire respondents showed the greatest consistency in responding; (5) more telephone respondents provided answers to the free-response question; (6) no differences were found in the direction of the responses; (7) the mail questionnaire produced more item nonresponse; (8) the number of nonusable responses was about the same for all methods; and (9) no meaningful differences were found in the characteristics of the groups. References are provided.

PERSONAL AND CLINICAL EXAMINATION
OR MEDICAL RECORDS

570.   Bahr, Howard M., and Kathleen C. Houts. "Can You Trust a Homeless Man? A Comparison of Official Records and Interview Responses by Bowery Men." *Public Opinion Quarterly* 35, no. 3 (Fall 1971): 374-82.

The investigation compares the extent of reliability and validity (or, as the authors prefer, the "discrepancy" or disagreement) between information gathered from personal interviews to that obtained from other sources (in this case agency records). Four factors are viewed as affecting discrepancy: recency of the respondents' behavior in question; the social desirability effect; the length and complexity of the question; and the rapport established between interviewer and respondent. The sample population consisted of 203 Bowery men in Manhattan, and 199 residents of Camp LaGuardia, an institution near New York City for "skid-row" men. Data obtained by interview were compared to client records of the Municipal Men's Shelter. The highest discrepancy rates occurred for those questions requiring the respondent to recall specific dates – especially those occurring at an earlier time. Respondents were influenced by social desirability factors, but perhaps no more so than similar groups. The simpler the item, the higher the consistency between interview and records. The nature of the question was found to be more influential on discrepancy rates than was the extent of rapport with the interviewer. It is concluded that homeless aged men are no more likely to be "consciously untruthful" than are members of similar disadvantaged groups. (13 footnotes)

571.   Balamuth, Eve, Sam Shapiro, and Paul M. Densen. *Health Interview Responses Compared with Medical Records.* In *Health Statistics from the U.S. National Health Survey*, Series D, No. 5. Washington, DC: U.S. Department of Health, Education, and Welfare, Public Health Service, June 1963. 74p. [SuDoc FS2.85:D-5] [Reprinted in *Vital and Health Statistics: Data Evaluation and Methods Research.* Public Health Service Publication No. 1000, Series 2, No. 7. Rockville, MD and Washington, DC: U.S. Department of Health, Education, and Welfare, Public Health Service, Health Services and Mental Health Administration, National Center for Health Statistics, July 1965. 74p.] [SuDoc FS2.85/ 2:2/no.7]

The sample was drawn from families enrolled in the Health Insurance Plan of Greater New York. The plan provides care through a group practice of thirty-one medical groups. The physician reports for services received in the last year were obtained. The Bureau of the Census conducted the interviews for the National Health Survey, and all conditions described in the interviews were coded according to the International Statistical Classification - Public Health Service codes. The objectives of the study were to determine which conditions were reported in the household interviews (and which were not), to explain the nature and causes of the discrepancies, and to recommend means of improving the methodology. Completed interviews were achieved with 3,937 persons from 1,388 households. Findings reported cover chronic conditions, nonchronic conditions, and hospitalizations. The study found that the survey information "does not conform even moderately well to the universe of conditions inferred from physician reporting." Even some serious chronic conditions were not reported during interviews. A secondary summary document created by the physician was used, rather than the physicians' direct clinical notes. It is suggested that using the latter might prove more desirable. There are thirty-two tables, with the appendixes providing the questionnaire, detailed diagnostic tables, and one page explaining the sampling methodology. (19 footnotes)

572.   Elinson, Jack, and Ray E. Trussell. "Some Factors Relating to Degree of Correspondence of Diagnostic Information Obtained by Household Interviews and Clinical Examinations." *American Journal of Public Health* 47, no. 3 (March 1957): 311-21.

The authors compare the findings of characteristics evaluated through clinical means with interviewer-reported diagnostic information. Findings are reviewed in terms of the following: (1) sex, age, family income, and educational level; (2) differential verification of hospitalized conditions; (3) self-report versus other family members' reports; (4) clinicians' diagnostic variations; and (5) classifications of chronic disease, arthritis, and heart disease is possible (in two studies). Interview return rates are now commonly reported at 85 to 90 percent, with one of the studies cited here at 91 percent with four thousand families interviewed from the predesignated probability sample (a census study experienced 98 percent). For an overview of disease prevalence, self-report generated a higher yield than when another family member reported. Underreporting appears to be a larger problem than overreporting. Clinically diagnosable disease is more likely to be inadequately or incompletely reported in the household interview. High-school graduates generated interview data that were "less likely to be adequate" than those who had not graduated. High-income family interview reports were less adequate than lower-income families. (5 references)

573.   Krueger, Dean E. "Measurement of Prevalence of Chronic Disease by Household Interviews and Clinical Evaluations." *American Journal of Public Health* 47, no. 8 (August 1957): 953-60.

The methods used included interviews with a sample of 3,700 Baltimore households having 11,574 members. A subsample of 809 persons had their medical histories taken and were given physical examinations at Johns Hopkins Hospital. A sample of households was selected by the U.S. Bureau of the Census for the Commission on Chronic Illness. The interviews were conducted by the bureau using a questionnaire developed by both agencies. Interviews were conducted for 98 percent of the occupied dwellings, with one respondent providing information for all household members. Differential samples ranged from 6 percent for the no-illness group to 100 percent for the most diseased group. The author concludes that the "lay interview is not new, or likely soon to become, a valuable tool for measuring the prevalence of diagnosable chronic disease." (4 references)

574.   Madow, William G. *Net Differences in Interview Data on Chronic Conditions and Information Derived from Medical Records.* In *Vital and Health Statistics: Data Evaluation and Methods Research.* Public Health Service Publication Series 2, No. 57. DHEW Publication No. (HSM) 73-1331. Rockville, MD: U.S. Department of Health, Education, and Welfare, Public Health Service, Health Services and Mental Health Administration, National Center for Health Statistics, June 1973. 58p. [SuDoc HE20.2210:2/57]

Completeness and accuracy of reported chronic conditions in health interviews were compared with information from medical records. The Stanford Research Institute conducted the study for the National Health Survey. The sample population of 5,027 respondents was selected from members of the Kaiser Foundation Health Plan which covered both outpatient and hospital care. Interviews were conducted after physician records covered a twelve-month period. Interview underreporting of conditions was estimated at 46.8 percent, with overreporting estimated at 40.4 percent. Conditions were categorized into low and high indexes for under/overreporting. These conditions are identified. Conditions which might cause "embarrassment or reluctance" on the part of the respondent were underreported in the interview. The more frequently a patient sees a physician for a condition, the more likely that it will be reported in the interview. Additionally, the regular use of medication for a condition will increase the probability that it will be reported during the interview. Women have a "greater tendency to overreport their conditions." Persons age sixty-five and older of both sexes exhibited "substantially higher" accuracy and completeness of reporting. (2 footnotes)

575.   Mooney, H. William. *Methodology in Two California Health Surveys: San Jose (1952) and Statewide (1954-55).* U.S. Public Health Service. Public Health Monograph No. 70; Public Health Service. Publication No. 942. [Washington, DC]: U.S. Government Printing Office, 1962. 143p. [SuDoc FS2.62:70]

The 1952 San Jose Survey was an investigation of alternate household survey methods. The results from the San Jose Survey were used in the planning and design of a statewide survey. The surveys were conducted with technical assistance from the Bureau of the Census. The volume is divided into two parts, the first presenting the household survey methods, with the second considering uses of the record data. In the methodology portion Mooney discusses the following topics and associated results: (1) the incomplete reporting of illness and chronic conditions; (2) depending upon the severity, the further back in time that an illness occurred the less likely it is to be reported; (3) to accommodate recall problems, the selected recall time was for the four weeks before the interview; (4) as a memory aid, a health calendar was mailed prior to the interview to be completed by the respondent before the interview; (5) repeat interviews "generally" lowered the reported incidence of illness and the days of restricted activity due to illness; (6) reinterviews were conducted by supervisors, with the "striking" finding that the quality (as determined by the number of additional conditions reported) varied "markedly" among interviewers; and (7) the interviews were randomly assigned to the interviewers in the San Jose Survey, with a small positive relationship between performance and aptitude test scores (the statewide California Health Survey did not use randomized assignments, and sizable differences in interviewer performances were noted). In the uses of the record data section Mooney discusses data validation and how to estimate for rare characteristics. The appendixes provide forty-nine pages of reliability estimates, definitions of terms, statistical design, general qualifications, and the forms used. (20 references)

576.   Thompson, Donovan J., and Joseph Tauber. "Household Survey, Individual Interview, and Clinical Examination to Determine Prevalence of Heart Disease." *American Journal of Public Health* 47, no. 9 (September 1957): 1131-40.

Three approaches are presented for calculating the prevalence of heart disease in the Arsenal Health District of Pittsburgh. The first was determined by analyzing the answers to a question included in a general household morbidity survey, the second from answers to a question in a study directed exclusively toward diseases of the heart, and the third from physician examinations looking specifically for cases of clinical heart disease in the sample members. A sample of three thousand households with 7,130 persons, fifteen years of age or older, was selected. Using a five-page questionnaire, nonprofessional interviewers conducted interviews lasting from twenty to thirty minutes. The researchers did not find the "lay" interviewers to be satisfactory. The interview procedures were not "adequate" for determining the prevalence of clinical heart disease in a general population. Mild cases of heart disease were missed in the interview procedures. Thompson and Tauber note that tense and wording changes in the survey questions used on different occasions were responsible for some of the survey data variances. (2 references)

PERSONAL AND SELF-ADMINISTERED

577.   Alderfer, Clayton P. "Convergent and Discriminant Validation of Satisfaction and Desire Measures by Interviews and Questionnaires." *Journal of Applied Psychology* 51, no. 6 (December 1967): 509-20.

This article states that when interviews are used along with questionnaires it is possible to reduce respondent-interviewer alienation, thereby increasing the validity of the questionnaire data. Alderfer is attempting to address the "either/or" spheres within psychology – those who criticize interviewing alone, and those who see questionnaires as the "agonizing repetition of trivial questions in the misguided quest of science." The results of the study lead Alderfer to maintain that the struggle between the two approaches is not necessary. The study used the Campbell-Fiske multitrait-multimethod framework (Campbell, Donald T., and Donald W. Fiske. "Convergent and Discriminate Validation by the Multitrait-Multimethod Matrix." *Psychological Bulletin* 56 [1959]: 81-105.). Relatively high discriminant and convergent validity for the satisfaction scales, and low convergent and moderate discriminant validity for the desire scales, were indicated in the results. (4 footnotes, 9 references)

578.   Enterline, Philip E., and Katherine G. Capt. "Validation of Information Provided by Household Respondents in Health Surveys." *American Journal of Public Health* 49, no. 2 (February 1959): 205-12.

The experimental design called for interviews with adult males. When these individuals were unavailable, one group of households received a written questionnaire to be completed when the male returned; the other group received repeated visits until the male was found at home (the group assignments were random). An additional portion of the sample consisted of interviews gathered from another eligible household respondent (usually the wife), if the male, thirty-five years or older, was unavailable. The samples were composed of 307 self-reporters and 310 reported by others; 302 questionnaires were received. When using the North Dakota Health Survey, the authors found that no less disease was reported than if each adult had reported for themselves. Consistent underreporting was noted in the self-administered written questionnaires for those items which in terms of health are "considered by many to have a bad connotation." One-third of the sample were farmers by occupation, with comparisons made with this group to those individuals with other diseases (such as heart and stomach problems). (4 references)

579.   Horan, John J., Thomas B. Westcott, Carolyn Vetovich, and John D. Swisher. "Drug Usage: An Experimental Comparison of Three Assessment Conditions." *Psychological Reports* 35, no. 1, pt. 1 (August 1974): 211-15.

Advanced undergraduate and graduate students at a major university were "strongly urged" to participate in a "survey of student opinions on the use of various products." Sixty-six respondents were randomly assigned to one of the following three drug usage assessment conditions: anonymous group-administered questionnaires, anonymous interviews, and interviews where the respondents' names had been verified from the beginning. Self-report is the most widely used method for evaluating the extent of illegal drug usage in a particular population. No differences were noted among the study methods when legal drug use was addressed; however, when illegal drugs were the issue, differences did occur. Respondents whose names are known may substantially minimize the reporting of their drug use. The researchers suggest that because of this factor "much descriptive and experimental drug abuse research may be quite invalid." (3 footnotes, 7 references)

580.   Kahn, Robert Louis. "A Comparison of Two Methods of Collecting Data for Social Research: The Fixed-Alternative Questionnaire and the Open-Ended Interview." Ph.D. diss., University of Michigan, 1952. 255 leaves. [*Dissertation Abstracts International* Order No. 0003776; *DAI* 12, no. 4 (July 1968): 382.]

Two data collection methods – the personal, nondirective interview and the fixed-alternative questionnaire – are compared in an industrial setting. Personal interviews which identified the respondent and anonymous questionnaires were used to ask identical questions concerning the work situation. The study group was 206 employees. Of the five hypotheses tested, three were confirmed, one was unconfirmed, and one was unclear. Kahn's investigation showed the following: (1) the mean agreement between the two collection methods varied from 82 percent for safe, factual, "low-threat" items, to 37 percent for "high-threat," attitudinal questions; (2) responses to the questionnaire format were much more critical and hostile; (3) the rate of nonresponse was less for the questionnaire but not significantly so; (4) the incidence of extreme responses was greater for the questionnaire; and (5) the ability to predict criterion scores were in the predicted direction (that is, greater) for the questionnaire than for the interview, but there was not enough evidence to support "a rigorous test of the hypothesis." Kahn concludes that the questionnaire format has some advantages in certain situations, and that the "unwillingness to communicate" is responsible for "measurable distortions of response." References are provided.

581.   Knudsen, Dean D., Hallowell Pope, and Donald P. Irish. "Response Differences to Questions on Sexual Standards: An Interview-Questionnaire Comparison." *Public Opinion Quarterly* 31, no. 2 (Summer 1967): 290-97.

The study compares interviewer versus questionnaire response differences on questions of a sexual nature. Three groups of white females in North Carolina, all who had become pregnant before marriage, consisted of (1) a sample of 150 private patients, from over 125 white physicians, who anonymously completed questionnaires in the doctor's office, (2) a sample of 311 females whose names were selected from birth certificates as having had an illegitimate child and who were interviewed in person, and (3) a sample of 77 respondents in maternity homes who filled out a questionnaire while the interviewer was present. Four questions regarding premarital sex were asked of each respondent in each sample. Among the results are the following: (1) sample 2 respondents were more likely to support what they thought the public and interviewer views were; (2) sample 3 had the lowest number who said that premarital sex was never appropriate; (3) sample 1 respondents more often answered to subcultural norms; and (4) respondents from lower-socioeconomic levels deferred to the norms represented by the higher-status interviewers. The authors believe these findings have implications "for situations that involve determining attitudes toward deviant behavior among persons aware of their deviance from societal norms." (11 footnotes)

582.   Metzner, Helen, and Floyd Mann. "A Limited Comparison of Two Methods of Data Collection: The Fixed Alternative Questionnaire and the Open-Ended Interview." *American Sociological Review* 17, no. 4 (August 1952): 486-91.

A fixed-alternative questionnaire was administered to all the employees of an electric utility, with personal interviews subsequently given to those employees who were classified in extremely high- and low-morale groups. The questions concerned personal and background characteristics, as well as feelings about three aspects dealing with job satisfaction. The questionnaires and interviews were all conducted within three months of each other in 1948. The interview results indicate a greater percentage of employees satisfied than did the questionnaire results. The article compares and contrasts the results from white-collar respondents with those from blue-collar respondents. The role of different perceptions of these two groups as to whether the questionnaire format was really anonymous is discussed. (2 footnotes)

583.   Ragonetti, Thomas J. "The Social-Psychology of Survey Techniques: An Examination of the Influence of Personal Confrontation and Interviewer's Sex upon Survey Results." *Cornell Journal of Social Relations* 5, no. 1 (Spring 1970): 41-49.

A sample of first-year male students at Cornell University was asked an emotionally loaded controversial question about their frequency of sexual intercourse. Three different formats were employed: a group-administered questionnaire, a male interviewer, and a female interviewer. The level of personal contact seems to have a direct bearing on the way in which the question is answered. The personal interview yielded significantly higher estimates of frequency of sexual intercourse, irregardless of the sex of the interviewer. The author concludes that questionnaires seem "more effective in eliciting honest answers to questions having emotional overtones for the subject." Three tables compare the results of each format for three questions from the questionnaire. The full text of the ten-item questionnaire is included. (2 footnotes)

584. Walters, James. "Relationship between Reliability of Responses in Family Life Research and Method of Data Collection." *Marriage and Family Living* 22, no. 3 (August 1960): 232-37.

The question considered is whether interviews, which are frequently composed of closed-end questionnaires, should be used in studies of family behavior. Seventy-two mothers were selected – all from a similar socioeconomic class, and all residing in Tallahassee, Florida. Seventy-two interviews and seventy-two questionnaires were completed. The sample was divided into three groups. One group was interviewed twice, one group received the questionnaire twice, and one-half of the third group was interviewed first and then received the questionnaire, while the other half of group three received the questionnaire first and was then interviewed. Walters found that the questionnaire would be appropriate for this sample since the data generated is as "reliable" as the interview method, and more economical. Questions dealt with weaning, thumbsucking, feeding, ignoring, marital conflict, inconsiderateness of the husband, and rejection of homemaking. The complete questions are provided with percentages of agreement for each of the groups described above. (15 footnotes)

PERSONAL, SELF-ADMINISTERED, AND TELEPHONE

585. Field, Donald R. "The Telephone Interview in Leisure Research." *Journal of Leisure Research* 5, no. 1 (Winter 1973): 51-59.

The use of telephone interviewing as a viable alternative to personal interviewing is explored. The major advantage is that telephone interviewing is less expensive (in this case eleven dollars per interview versus thirty-five to fifty dollars for personal interviews). Field presents a discussion of methodological alternatives, including self-administered questionnaires and personal interviews, followed by the pros and cons of telephone interviews. Sample selection and ways to deal with unlisted telephone numbers are covered. Interviewer-respondent rapport is discussed, noting that a small number of interviewers were used throughout the study, and that these individuals were closely monitored. Superficiality of telephone data is cited as a criticism of the approach. "Depth within a specific focus" is, however, an achievable goal. Field cites the following as criteria for selecting telephone interviewing: a large geographic area of study population, time, and budget constraints. (4 footnotes, 24 references)

PERSONAL AND TELEPHONE

586.   Cahalan, Don. "Measuring Newspaper Readership by Telephone: Two Comparisons with Face-to-Face Interviews." *Journal of Advertising Research* 1, no. 1 (September 1960): 1-6.

The issue addressed by Cahalan is whether the results of telephone and face-to-face interviews produced "roughly the same answers." New car owners in and around New York City were asked questions about readership of a newspaper. Several studies were conducted. In the first group seventy-one respondents were interviewed first by telephone, and then face-to-face the same evening. Seven New York City newspapers were shown to the respondents in the evening. The respondents were then asked to identify what they had looked through "yesterday." Percentage consistency is reported. Another group of ninety-eight persons was first interviewed face-to-face, then later shown the newspapers face-to-face. A second study involved a larger sample of two hundred respondents, all of whom first received telephone calls, and approximately 44 percent received follow-up interviews in the respondent's homes. The study showed the following: (1) a measure of "yesterday" readership can be determined for less money and time using telephone interviews as compared with personal interviews; (2) results can be expected to be the same in 95 percent of the cases; (3) percentages will differ no more than a few percentage points; and (4) the results represent newspaper readership only, and may not be transferable to other media. (4 references)

587.   Colombotos, John. "Personal versus Telephone Interviews: Effect on Responses." *Public Health Reports* 84, no. 9 (September 1969): 773-82.

The experience of previous studies and the placement of telephone interviewing in relation to mail questionnaires and personal interviews are discussed. A sample of 1,600 physicians was interviewed between 1964 and 1967. From this sample 1,007 were interviewed twice, before and after Medicare. All but a small selected sample were interviewed by telephone; the small sample was interviewed in person for comparative purposes. The interviews took about one hour and covered attitudes toward "participation of government" in medical care and feelings toward certain political issues. Background questions (such as age, religion, and income) were also asked. The National Opinion Research Center did the fieldwork in the physicians' opinion study. Colombotos found that there were "essentially no differences between the responses." The telephone approach is more cost effective, and the data gathered are comparable to the personal interview. The level of precision of "socially acceptable responses" is comparable for both survey methods. (21 references)

588.   Cureton, Robert Dennis. "A Methodological Comparison of Telephone and Face-to-Face Interviewing for Political Public Opinion Polling." Ph.D. diss., Southern Illinois University at Carbondale, 1976. 111 leaves. [*Dissertation Abstracts International* Order No. 7706210; *DAI* 37A, no. 9 (March 1977): 5437.]

The approach used by Cureton was to employ a ten- to twenty-minute questionnaire either by telephone or in person, followed by a one- to two-minute debriefing questionnaire. In the summary and conclusions chapter it is stated that "telephone interviewing generally produces results as useful for measurement of political attitudes and prediction as does face-to-face [interviewing]." Several areas in which the face-to-face interview may be sought are those involving long interviews and those requiring any kind of visual aid. This dissertation was written at a time when the Gallup Organization used the face-to-face technique "almost exclusively" for nationwide polls. Cureton writes that telephone interviewing in political polling had become "quite popular." References are provided.

589.   French, Charles E., and Douglas C. Kranz. "Telephone Interviews as a Means of Surveying Farmers." *Journal of Farm Economics* 39, no. 1 (February 1957): 153-55.

A sample of ninety-seven dairy farmers received personal interviews to be followed-up by telephone interviews six months later. Three refused further questioning. The farmers were located in eighteen counties in northeastern Indiana, three in Ohio, and one in Michigan. Sixteen farmers were Amish and did not have telephones, leaving a sample of seventy-eight for telephone surveying. Those who could not be reached by telephone were sent mail surveys. After three follow-up letters, the mail survey completion rate was "only" 82 percent. The authors believe that the telephone survey provided the most satisfactory results. The response was greater by telephone than by mail, and less costly than personal interviews which averaged forty-five miles of travel per usable survey. Interviewer time for personal interviews was much greater. (1 footnote)

590.   Groves, Robert M. "Actors and Questions in Telephone and Personal Interview Surveys." *Public Opinion Quarterly* 43, no. 2 (Summer 1979): 190-205.

The term "actors" in the title refers to interviewers in the interviewer-respondent situation. This paper concentrates on some of the differences between personal and telephone interviews in the actors' behavior and in the form of questioning.

Also studied are the respondents' reactions both to the request for an interview and to the process itself, and the properties of questions using response cards for personal interviews and then adapting the questions for telephone use. Data came from a project in which two national telephone surveys were conducted with 1,734 individuals. One survey used a stratified random sample with telephone numbers from across the United States; the other used seventy-four counties and metropolitan areas in the Survey Research Center's national household sample. The same questions were used for both groups. Groves indicates in tables 1 through 5 and in figures 1 through 3 that the achieved response rates show that few respondents preferred the telephone as compared to face-to-face interviews. Subsequent national surveys support this finding. Most personal interview respondents preferred the face-to-face technique. Telephone respondents showed more uneasiness in answering sensitive questions, more refusals to questions concerning financial matters, and more impatience to the length of the interview. Comments on the adaptation of "show-card" questions for telephone use and suggestions on ways to improve telephone questioning techniques complete the article. (6 footnotes, 6 references)

591.   Groves, Robert M. "Comparing Telephone and Personal Interview Surveys." *Economic Outlook USA* 5, no. 1 (Summer 1978): 49-51.

Groves begins with several reasons as to why telephone interviewing has become attractive: approximately 90 percent of the population have telephones, the costs of face-to-face interviews are increasing (primarily due to travel costs), and random digit dialing enables the pollster to access the 25 percent nationally that have unlisted telephone numbers (40 percent in some metropolitan areas). The results of two concurrent national surveys conducted by the Survey Research Center at the University of Michigan are compared. One was a face-to-face interview environment, the other was by telephone. The same questions were used for both collection techniques. Depending upon the components included, the telephone mode cost 45 to 65 percent of the personal interview, but response rates for the telephone interviews were "somewhat below" the personal interviews. The two modes "generally yielded similar distributions." A major advantage of telephone interviewing is the ability to monitor and control interviewer error to a significantly greater degree and with much greater ease.

592.   Groves, Robert M. "On the Mode of Administering a Questionnaire and Responses to Open-Ended Items." *Social Science Research* 7, no. 3 (September 1978): 257-71.

The study undertaken at the Survey Research Center (SRC) during April and May 1976 was designed to compare the sampling, field, and measurement properties of telephone and personal interview surveys. Personal interviews with respondents age eighteen and over in 1,548 sample households were collected by 132 interviewers in the seventy-four primary areas of the SRC national sample. Simultaneously, thirty-eight interviewers at the Ann Arbor, Michigan, SRC office collected telephone interviews in 1,734 households using random digit dialing sampling. Telephone interviews led to greater speed of questioning as there were fewer requests for question repetition. Shorter answers were provided to open-ended items in the telephone interviews. Younger and higher-income respondents showed the greatest tendency to fewer question repetition requests on the telephone. Sex and education were insignificant factors. Age and income are suggested as the keys to which mode to select in terms of collecting quality data. (10 footnotes, 5 references)

593.   Groves, Robert M., and Robert L. Kahn. *Surveys by Telephone: A National Comparison with Personal Interviews*. Quantitative Studies in Social Relations, edited by Peter H. Rossi. New York, NY: Academic Press, a Subsidiary of Harcourt Brace Jovanovich, Publishers, 1979. 358p.

Sampling and interviewing by telephone are experimentally evaluated and compared with results from personal interviewing. The first several chapters discuss measuring populations using both approaches, and review sample designs. The next chapter covers the administration of the surveys, followed by response differences between the two collection modes. Method effects are discussed along with measurable sources of error. Costs of both approaches are compared. The authors believe that the random generation of sample telephone numbers and current work in telephone interviewing are two of the most important developments in the field during the last fifty years (the third being areal probability sampling in the 1940s). Telephone surveys are described as easy and inexpensive to generate samples, and quick and economical to conduct interviews, with the added advantage of immediate entry of data into computers. Four appendixes are included, the first of which provides the text of the telephone questionnaire used. (45 references)

594.   Henson, Ramon, Aleda Roth, and Charles F. Cannell. *Personal versus Telephone Interviews and the Effects of Telephone Reinterviews on Reporting of Psychiatric Symptomatology*. Prepared for the National Center for Health Services, NCHSR 76-300: PB-248 863. Springfield, VA: Distributed by the National Technical Information Service, 1974. 92 leaves.

The study examined the impact of a variety of interviewing procedures. The sample was drawn from blocks selected from the 1970 census tract data for Kansas City. There were 961 completed interviews in the personal interview group and 206 for the telephone control group (a series of fourteen tables explains the number of respondents in a series of categories – including marital status, race, and income level). The results indicate that there are few differences between telephone and personal interviews in the reporting of psychiatric symptoms. (However, no studies compare the transmission of private or personal information via telephone and personal interviews.) The presence of the interviewer does not lead to "higher or lower reporting" of private symptoms. Telephone interviewers generally achieved lower responses than personal interviews. Varying the interviewers from the first to the second interview produced greater differences. Response rates and costs were examined for the two approaches. Overall, the personal interviews generated "considerably higher" response rates, but the telephone interview costs were "considerably smaller." The authors suggest that the telephone technique is a "viable alternative" to personal interviewing. The following seven appendixes complete the volume: (1) Ramon Henson, "A Smallest Space Analysis of the Lubin Depression Adjective Checklist"; (2) Ramon Henson, "A Smallest Space Analysis of the Langner Psychiatric Symptoms Scale"; (3) Aleda Roth, "A Factor Analysis of the Lubin Depression Adjective Checklist"; (4) Aleda Roth, "A Factor Analysis of the Langner Psychiatric Symptoms Scale"; (5) Ramon Henson, "Embarrassment Ratings of the Lubin Scale Items"; (6) Ramon Henson, "Relationships between Demographic Characteristics and Selected Dependent Variables"; and (7) Aleda Roth, "An Analysis of Survey Costs."

595.   Henson, Ramon, Charles F. Cannell, and Aleda Roth. "Effects of Interview Mode on Reporting of Moods, Symptoms, and Need for Social Approval." *Journal of Social Psychology* 105, 1st half (June 1978): 123-29.

The interview modes considered in this investigation are those of the personal interview versus the telephone interview. The subject was the reporting of moods and symptoms indicative of mental health status and social desirability. The researchers used indices derived from the Lubin Depression Adjective Checklist, the Langner Psychiatric Symptoms Scale, and the Crowne-Marlowe Social Desirability Scale. For the study 961 respondents received personal interviews, and 206 received telephone interviews. The personal interviews achieved a greater reporting of mental health symptoms and less reporting of need for approval than did the telephone interviews. The authors note the loss of nonverbal communication cues and face-to-face contact as the major differences between the modes. They suggest that telephone interviewers should use more positive verbal cues. (2 footnotes, 19 references)

596.   Herman, Jeanne Brett. "Mixed-Mode Data Collection: Telephone and Personal Interviewing." *Journal of Applied Psychology* 62, no. 4 (August 1977): 399-404.

In a study of voting in union representation elections, a combined telephone and personal interview approach to data collection was pursued. Thirty-one different elections involving 1,239 employees were reviewed. The background of these individuals was heterogeneous by socioeconomic considerations, as well as by race, age, income, and urban and rural background. Individuals who could not be reached by telephone or who refused to be so interviewed were interviewed in person. The data quality for telephone and personal interviews was similar. Telephone respondents were more likely to refuse to state their vote and were less likely to report unlawful campaign practices. The major advantage with the telephone mode is the higher contact rate. Cost reduction is the primary benefit of employing the mixed-mode format. The approach used in this study saved $10,746 in interviewer wages. The sensitivity of the data requested needs to be evaluated when selecting the collection method. (11 references)

597.   Karol, J. J. "Measuring Radio Audiences." *Public Opinion Quarterly* 1, no. 2 (April 1937): 92-96.

The following advantages of telephone surveys are noted: (1) they are cheaper than personal interviews in urban areas; (2) they produce quick results; (3) most telephone households have radios; and (4) since telephoning is conducted from one location, checking for standardized questions and data is easier. Problems cited include the following: (1) about 43 percent of American homes in towns over 2,500 have telephones; (2) telephone surveys are not workable in rural areas; and (3) it is difficult to determine the income groups in a sample. Personal interviews are similarly reviewed. Positive aspects are that careful control of samples is possible, the amount of information gathering is less limited, respondent reactions can be closely monitored, and details concerning radio equipment can be determined. The salaries and travel expenses of interviewers are perceived as negative aspects. Karol distinguishes between aided recall questions (those where the respondent is asked to report when and what was listened to) versus unaided recall questions (being advised of a station's programming and then being asked about it). A third alternative – automatic recorders that monitor radio use – is discussed. (4 footnotes)

598.   Kegeles, S. Stephen, Clinton F. Fink, and John P. Kirscht. "Interviewing a National Sample by Long-Distance Telephone." *Public Opinion Quarterly* 33, no. 3 (Fall 1969): 412-19.

The usefulness of the telephone in surveying a national sample of 744 persons in the United States is explored. The group was about half of an original sample which had been interviewed in person about sixteen months earlier. The issues considered in the interviews were respondent's beliefs and health practices concerning dental disease, tuberculosis, and cancer. A total of 805 telephone calls were made; 454 interviews resulted over the four-week period. Calls were made from 1:00 to 5:00 P.M. Monday through Saturday and 7:00 to 10:00 P.M. on weekdays. Data in table 1 show the costs of the survey broken down by salaries, telephone calls, and other expenses (installation, materials, supplies, rent, and so forth). The total cost for the survey was $4,882, or $10.75 per completed interview. Coding and analysis brought the costs to $8,537. The response rate was 79 percent (this figure includes some difficult-to-contact respondents who were sent mail questionnaires). Responses were consistent with prior responses in a face-to-face interview. The problem of sample bias is discussed since certain groups (for example, people with lower-socioeconomic status and those living in rural areas) were underrepresented. Although "direct evidence" of the validity of the data from the follow-up study cannot be provided, there is evidence that the telephone interviews produced responses that were consistent with those from the personal interviews. The telephone is highly recommended for obtaining personal and social information. (6 footnotes)

599.   Mitchell, Glen H., and Everett M. Rogers. "Telephone Interviewing." *Journal of Farm Economics* 40, no. 3 (August 1958): 743-47.

The advantages and limitations of telephone interviewing are discussed. Two studies were conducted. The first involved telephone interviews with over eight thousand urban households in nine major Ohio cities from 1954 to 1956. The subject was the consumption of dairy products. Personal interviews were conducted with two hundred households which did not have telephones (these were used for comparison with the telephone sample). In the second study of 1956, telephone interviews concerning the purchase of Christmas trees were conducted with three thousand "housewives." Eight midwestern states were surveyed with personal interviews conducted in Columbus, Ohio. The following advantages are discussed: (1) cost – in 1958 dollars, telephone interviews averaged forty-four cents, mail questionnaires fifty-four cents, and personal interviews $2.72; (2) time – telephone surveys averaged twelve minutes, personal interviews thirty-two minutes; and (3) rate of response – the dairy consumption telephone survey had 93 to 99.6 percent as compared with a 9 to 16 percent refusal rate for personal interviews (a figure that includes not-at-homes, with three callbacks). Additional advantages are that supervising telephone interviewers can help address concerns of dishonesty and deviation from prescribed questions, multilinguists can be used more effectively and efficiently when conducting telephone surveys, and biases caused by appearance, facial expressions, and nonvocal mannerisms are avoided. The limitations discussed include biases (such as reaching only those households with telephones and unlisted numbers), respondent unwillingness to continue long interviews, and the impossibility of using visual aids. The authors note that combinations can be made utilizing telephone surveys and other formats. (6 footnotes)

600.   Newhouse, Dean, and Franklin Kilpatrick. "Polling Student Opinion by Telephone." *Journal of Higher Education* 20 (1949): 211-12, 225-26.

Newhouse, director of the Office of Student Affairs at the University of Washington, reports on the use of polls as tools for college administrators. A series of five polls were conducted using samples of 130 to 300 students. These proved useful and productive. A comparative test of face-to-face interviews to telephone interviewing, each with two hundred students, was conducted. The conclusions drawn from each data set were the same, with the speed, economy, and simplicity of the telephone approach noted. One telephone poll was initiated and completed within twenty-four hours, while several others were concluded in less than seventy-two hours each. A number of successful poll uses by the Office of Student Affairs are cited. (3 footnotes)

601.   Oakes, Ralph H. "Differences in Responsiveness in Telephone versus Personal Interviews." *Journal of Marketing* 19, no. 2 (October 1954): 169.

Using a "free response question," Oakes sought to determine if there were differences in responsiveness to the two types of interviews. This question was posed: "Have you any suggestions for changes in the service, the food or beverages, or anything else in the Loyola cafeteria?" The respondents included 216 students at Loyola University of the South. Sixty-five personal and forty-four telephone interviews were obtained. Twice as many suggestions were offered during the personal interviews as compared with the telephone interviews. Oakes explores possible explanations for the differences and concludes that people "express their attitudes or opinions more fully, when they are approached in person, than when interviewed over the telephone." (3 footnotes)

602.   Rogers, Theresa F. "Interviews by Telephone and in Person: Quality of Responses and Field Performance." *Public Opinion Quarterly* 40, no. 1 (Spring 1976): 51-65.

The study measures the effects of two interviewing strategies – telephone and in person – on the quality of data and field performance. Quality of response is measured by respondents' ability to answer complex knowledge and attitudinal items, validity of response, and willingness and consistency in supplying data of a personal nature. Measures of field performance include response rate, length of the interview, number of contacts required, preferable times for interviewing, preferences for interviewing strategy, and interviewer effects. The follow-up sample (ninety-five whites, ninety-five African Americans, and fifty-seven Hispanics) was drawn from a larger study in Washington Heights in New York City and the Grand Concourse in the Bronx. The groups were randomly assigned to be interviewed by telephone or in person. The interview schedule was thirty-five pages and contained both open and closed questions. Results show that the data retrieved by telephone on both complex attitudinal and knowledge questions, as well as questions on personal items (such as income), were as complete and accurate as that of face-to-face interviews. Field techniques were also success-ful. It is additionally noted that among those respondents randomly assigned to be interviewed in person or by telephone (1) there was an 82 percent response rate, (2) there were minimal requests from respondents to change the interview-ing method assigned to them, (3) the evening hours were the best time to con-duct either type of interview, (4) Monday through Thursday were the most pro-ductive days, and (5) for respondents who were contacted by telephone, and who had previously been interviewed in person, either mode was acceptable to 50 percent: 50 percent had no preference, 26 percent favored the face-to-face interview, and the remaining 24 percent preferred the telephone interview. (26 footnotes)

603.   Schmiedeskamp, Jay W. "Reinterviews by Telephone." *Journal of Market-ing* 26, no. 1 (January 1962): 28-34.

In 1959 the Survey Research Center of the University of Michigan undertook a telephone reinterview study. The average personal interview which preceded the telephone reinterview call lasted between sixty and seventy-five minutes. The average telephone reinterview call lasted eleven minutes. These were so-called "hot" telephone interviews (as compared with "cold" calling), in that the person receiving the call would not mistake it for a "disguised selling effort," and had already provided personal data during the personal interview. The telephone re-interviews were less expensive and took less time than the personal interviews. The purpose of the study was to "investigate change in consumer attitudes from one time to the next." In 1962, 26 percent of the families in the United States did not have telephones, a factor which is discussed relative to biases created through the presence or absence of certain socioeconomic groups from the sam-ple. (4 footnotes)

604.   Shapiro, Sam, Richard Yaffe, Robert R. Fuchsberg, and Helen C. Cor-peno. "Medical Economics Survey-Methods Study: Design, Data Collec-tion, and Analytical Plan." *Medical Care* 14, no. 11 (November 1976): 893-912.

A sample of one thousand households distributed between Baltimore City and Washington County was selected. One adult in each household was interviewed following Health Interview Survey procedures. Respondents were asked to keep a diary of health expenses. Four experimental modes were established for the collection of follow-up information over the next six months. Each group had 250 households. The design included monthly telephone calls, bimonthly tele-phone calls, monthly telephone calls and in-person visits, and bimonthly in-person visits. The final session for all groups involved an in-home visit. The authors recommend extending the time to one year to reduce recall problems, and to use third-party payers as sources for insurance payment information. In total, 802 households completed the initial interview, with the authors noting that "only broad categorizations and limited crosstabulations" are possible. The initial response rate was 77.5 percent – a figure which declined to 13.6 percent after six months. Record access was permitted by 84.9 percent of individuals who completed the entire survey. The monthly in-person contact resulted in the lowest participation rate. (21 references)

605.   Sudman, Seymour. "Optimum Cluster Designs within a Primary Unit Using Combined Telephone Screening and Face-to-Face Interviewing." *Journal of the American Statistical Association* 73, no. 362 (June 1978): 300-304.

Telephone samples are used to locate special subgroups which will receive personal interviews. This article consideres when this practice is more efficient than face-to-face screening. Sudman discusses telephone screening and a personal interview, and cost functions for alternative procedures. He provides examples and reviews the use of nongeographic lists. Telephone screening is the optimum approach unless (1) "The homogeneity within the cluster is small; (2) The density of interviews is low; [and] (3) Locating and screening costs are small relative to interviewing costs." (6 references)

606.   Yaffe, Richard, Sam Shapiro, Robert R. Fuchsberg, Charles A. Rohde, and Helen C. Corpeno. "Medical Economics Survey-Methods Study: Cost-Effectiveness of Alternate Survey Strategies." *Medical Care* 16, no. 8 (August 1978): 641-59.

The study was designed to determine the most cost-effective approach for a national survey. Over a period of seven months health care use and costs were recorded from 691 households in Maryland. The effectiveness of monthly versus bimonthly interviews, and in-person versus telephone contacts, were considered. Completeness and accuracy were evaluated through record verification. The results showed "substantial deficiencies" in the household reporting. Interview frequency did not affect accuracy. The bimonthly schedule was less expensive and did not have as high a rate of attrition. In the Baltimore portion of the study the in-person contact achieved "significantly better reporting." In rural Washington County no difference was noted. The authors suggest that for the 10 percent cost increase for in-person contact, the approach "may well be justified by the improved accuracy of the data obtained for certain types of populations." (8 references)

SELF-ADMINISTERED AND MEDICAL RECORDS

607. Madow, William G. *Interview Data on Chronic Conditions Compared with Information Derived from Medical Records.* In *Vital and Health Statistics: Data Evaluation and Methods Research.* Public Health Service Publication No. 1000, Series 2, No. 23. Rockville, MD and Washington, DC: U.S. Department of Health, Education, and Welfare, Public Health Service, Health Services and Mental Health Administration, National Center for Health Statistics, 1967. 84p. [SuDoc FS2.85/2:2/no. 23]

Respondents underreported chronic conditions to the extent that only 90 percent of chronic conditions were reported as compared with medical records. Many cases of chronic conditions were reported for which there were no medical records. The sample consisted of 5,988 individuals seventeen years of age and over, with approximately the same number of females as males. Three different forms of questionnaire were used: (1) one comparable to that used in the Health Interview Survey; (2) a format where the checklist was changed (the purpose of which was to help the respondent remember physician visits); and (3) a version essentially the same as format number one, except checklists were self-administered instead of being read by the interviewer. The study found that the questionnaire format differences did not "seriously affect the reporting of chronic conditions by the respondents." There are twenty-one pages of detailed tables, with the appendixes providing the questionnaires, the diagnostic recode number 3, and the sampling design. There are noncumulated footnotes throughout the report.

SELF-ADMINISTERED AND TELEPHONE

608. Wheatley, John J. "Self-Administered Written Questionnaires or Telephone Interviews?" *Journal of Marketing Research* 10, no. 1 (February 1973): 94-95.

Two random samples of University of Washington students were selected from the student directory and, as part of a longer interview, were asked their opinions and attitudes concerning a nationally advertised and recognized brand of beer. A total of 74 students were given a written questionnaire, and 148 were contacted by telephone with the same question. The two data-gathering methods showed no significant differences in the nature of the response to the same set of questions. Wheatley believes that either method is feasible depending upon cost and time considerations. The absence or presence of an interviewer was not a significant factor in this study. (1 footnote, 2 references)

MISCELLANEOUS

609.   Benson, Lawrence E. "Studies in Secret-Ballot Technique." *Public Opinion Quarterly* 5, no. 1 (March 1941): 79-82.

Several studies conducted by the American Institute of Public Opinion (AIPO) are reported. In an experiment in the state of Maine, half of the respondents were interviewed face-to-face and the other half by secret ballot. The question concerned which candidates were favored for certain state offices and for president. The number of undecided voters was reduced from 21 percent on the personal interview to 9 percent on the secret ballot. Democrats, rather than Republicans, were found to be more reluctant to express a choice. In the 1940 presidential contest there was a drop in the undecided vote from 16 percent to 2 percent. A drop in the undecided vote (about one-third) also occurred in Erie County, Ohio (a political "barometer" area), in a poll taken prior to the national election. A modified random sampling method rather than controlled sampling was used in this study. Willkie, as opposed to Roosevelt, was shown to be the preferred candidate for president. This finding disagreed with those of AIPO's nationwide surveys. With only one exception, it was the first time in over fifty years that Erie County's vote had deviated more than 4 percent from national surveys and the first time it had ever favored the losing candidate. The reason given was that Erie County's population was composed of many foreign-born or first-generation Germans and Italians who had shifted their votes from Democratic to Republican. (3 footnotes)

610.   Bromer, Richard Frank. "A Comparison of Three Methods of Opinion Polling." Ph.D. diss., Purdue University, 1948. 109 leaves plus 13 numbered appendix pages. [*Dissertation Abstracts International* Order No. 0013812; *DAI* 16, no. 1 (August 1971): 171.]

The author compares and contrasts three methods of opinion polling: the depth interview, the straight interview, and the secret ballot. The depth interview, as explained by Bromer, is an in-person interview in the respondent's home in which the respondent is encouraged to speak at length on the questions asked. The interviewer "copies down the gist of what the respondent has to say." The straight interview is one in which the respondent is given a choice of two or three answers to each question. Bromer uses the form "agree," "disagree," and "undecided." The secret ballot spoken of here is one which the respondent completes in private. The respondent can then drop the ballot in a "locked ballot box" carried from house to house by the interviewer. The telephone format is not considered here, as all interviews were conducted at the respondent's home. In the Bromer study only one question yielded a highly significant difference between the total results through each of the three approaches – and this may have been generated

by who the respondents thought the interviewer represented. References are
provided.

611.   Kemper, Raymond Alfred. "Secret Ballots, Open Ballots, and Personal
        Interviews in Opinion Polling." Ph.D. diss., Columbia University, 1951.
        148 leaves. [*Dissertation Abstracts International* Order No. 0002540;
        DAI 11, no. 3 (October 1979): 765.]

The methodology for this dissertation consisted of using a sample of fifteen
hundred adults. The sample was divided into three comparable subsample groups:
one subsample was interviewed face-to-face, a second group used secret ballots
and sealed ballot-boxes, and the third group was polled employing open ballots
which were returned to the field-worker once the respondent had completed the
form. Twenty fact questions and thirteen opinion questions were used. Three
comparisons were then made based on the results. The face-to-face data were
compared with the secret-ballot and open-ballot data, and the open-ballot results
were compared with those of the secret ballot. When the three methods of polling were examined, differences were found with seven of the twenty fact questions and with nine of the thirteen opinion questions. References are provided.

612.   Sudman, Seymour, and Robert Ferber. "A Comparison of Alternative
        Procedures for Collecting Consumer Expenditure Data for Frequently
        Purchased Products." *Journal of Marketing Research* 11, no. 2 (May
        1974): 128-35. [Reprinted in *Readings in Survey Research*, edited by
        Robert Ferber, 487-502. Chicago, IL: American Marketing Association,
        1978. 604p.]

The method used to date has been recall, with the alternative being the use of diaries. Some individuals are either unwilling or unable to maintain written diaries.
A study undertaken by the Survey Research Laboratory (SRL) of the University
of Illinois in cooperation with the U.S. Bureau of the Census explored some
other options. The primary one was the use of daily telephone calls to the household. A further alternative was giving the respondent a choice of weekly diaries,
daily telephone calls, or the use of a tape recorder. From the city of Chicago and
surrounding suburbs, 409 households were selected. In city households, for
those which were compensated for their record keeping, there was an 85 percent
cooperation level. Uncompensated households in the city were at the 68 percent
level. Suburban areas did not register much difference. When identified as being
conducted under the auspices of the Census Bureau and SRL, city results were
the same, whereas census auspices in the suburbs produced higher results. While
daily telephone calls to households are useful supplements, they are not as
complete or as accurate as diary data. Sudman and Ferber recommend further
experimentation in the use of telephone calls for inner cities. The authors express
concern over the low level of initial cooperation – 60 percent. The effective rate

of participation, given dropouts during the two-week trial, amounted to 47 percent. Since the sample is small, the authors suggest caution as to whether the sampling variations would exist in a large-scale survey. (5 references)

RESPONDENTS

ACCURACY AND CONSISTENCY

613. Cahalan, Don. "Correlates of Respondent Accuracy in the Denver Validity Survey." *Public Opinion Quarterly* 32, no. 4 (Winter 1968-69): 607-21.

The Denver Validity Survey of 1949, nineteen years later, continues to be the "only probability sample survey designed specifically for the purpose of measuring against official records the relative accuracy of responses on a range of questions of fact." In total, 920 interviews were conducted using an area probability sample of adults taken from a current city directory. Forty-five interviewers were given randomly selected assignments, and were themselves selected to represent a range of variables (sex, age, socioeconomic status, and interview experience). Five tables provide a summary of overall accuracy of respondent reports, the relationship of performance to claims by sex, age, and socioeconomic status, and the interaction of socioeconomic status of respondents and interviewers. Cahalan concludes that "certain questions on past behavior simply do not lend themselves to accurate measurement through survey research approaches." The explanation provided is that it is not that people do not want to tell the truth to interviewers, but rather that "they sometimes cannot tell the truth to themselves." (7 footnotes)

614. Dakin, Ralph E., and Donald Tennant. "Consistency of Response by Event-Recall Intervals and Characteristics of Respondents." *Sociological Quarterly* 9, no. 1 (Winter 1968): 73-84.

The study found that respondents exhibit considerable inconsistency in the answers they provide to specific survey questions dealing with past conditions. Fifty-nine respondents were consistent with only 63.6 percent of their answers when asked the same questions one year apart. (The respondents were first interviewed in June 1959, then again in June 1960.) The nature of the question was the most important determining factor with respect to consistency. Place of residence was almost perfectly consistent (98.3 percent) versus little consistency on income (24.1 percent). The authors note that because of the small number of respondents and the fact that some of these were atypical, the data should be considered suggestive. The selection of the sample did not follow probability sampling procedures. (19 footnotes)

615.   Gutek, Barbara A. "On the Accuracy of Retrospective Attitudinal Data." *Public Opinion Quarterly* 42, no. 3 (Fall 1978): 390-401.

Several prior studies of retrospective attitudinal and behavioral data are reviewed. The present study tests the hypothesis that attitudes in the recent past will be recalled by respondents more accurately than those occurring some years in the past. Data used for the study were taken from a 1973 nationwide sample of 1,431 adult residents of the United States. The subject concerned experiences with, and feelings about, government bureaucracies. The dates of the bureaucratic encounter were divided into five time periods, six properties of the episode were measured, and correlations were made and examined. The above hypothesis was not supported by the data. Individuals generally showed the same pattern of relationships concerning aspects of the bureaucratic encounter whether they were recalling events which occurred only several months before the interview or as long as fifteen to forty years in the past. The passage of time did not seem to produce more error variance on the part of the respondents. Gutek discusses underreporting, the point at which inaccuracy begins, the "generalizability" of the findings, and the implications for survey researchers. (4 footnotes, 19 references)

AVAILABILITY

616.   Hilgard, Ernest R., and Stanley L. Payne. "Those Not at Home: Riddle for Pollsters." *Public Opinion Quarterly* 8, no. 2 (Summer 1944): 254-61.

The article examines the characteristics of people whom interviewers cannot find at home. The authors believe distortion of survey findings can occur when only stay-at-home characteristics are taken into account. Characteristics of those not at home were identified from a division of the War Production Board in November 1943. The quota control system of sampling and the specific assignment method are defined. The second method, in which the interviewer is told precisely where and when to interview, was chosen to collect interview data for this study. A national sample of 3,265 interviews was obtained: 2,072 on the first call, 726 on the second, and 467 on the third or later call. The amount of distortion that can result when relying only on first-call respondents is shown in table 1. Hilgard and Payne conclude that significant differences exist between people reached on the first call and those reached on subsequent calls. Repeated calls must be made in order to represent second and third callers in sample surveys. The importance of the results to market research, as well as the pros and cons of the two data collection systems, are discussed. (4 footnotes)

617.   Politz, Alfred, and Willard Simmons. "An Attempt to Get the 'Not-at-Homes' into the Sample without Callbacks." Part 1. *Journal of the American Statistical Association* 44, no. 245 (March 1949): 9-16.

Each respondent in the sample is visited only once. Each person is asked about specific times – if they were at home or not. Including the interviewing hours, a picture is created of the times that the respondent was home. The questionnaires were divided into six groups, divided by the time individuals were at home (1/6, 2/6 . . . , 6/6 of the time). The sample estimate, for any variable under study, is "produced by weighting the results for each group by the reciprocal of the estimated per cent that persons are at home." The authors show that under certain conditions this approach is unbiased. A comparison is made between this technique and callbacks. (5 footnotes)

618.   Ross, H. Laurence. "The Inaccessible Respondent: A Note on Privacy in City and Country." *Public Opinion Quarterly* 27, no. 2 (Summer 1963): 269-75.

In order to determine reasons for inaccessibility (the failure of the interviewer to reach the respondent and perform the interview), mailed questionnaires and in-person interviews were conducted. Interviewers for the National Opinion Research Center and the American Institute of Public Opinion were asked to discuss inaccessibility problems for three areas: rural, single-family, and apartments. The three main sources of respondent inaccessibility are as follows: (1) absence from home (especially in urban areas and in apartment-house areas); (2) the problem of the "gatekeepers" (that is, friends, relatives, servants, and apartment-building personnel) who refuse to allow the interviewer access to the prospective respondent; and (3) entrance devices (for example, buzzers and locked front doors) on multiple dwelling units. The author offers suggestions for coping with each of these challenges. He cites Simmel's research (Simmel, Georg. "The Metropolis and Mental Life." In *The Sociology of Georg Simmel*, edited by Kurt Wolff, 409-24. Glencoe, IL: Free Press, 1950. 445p.) in helping to account for the lack of accessibility on the part of the city dweller (such as an attitude of reserve, the preservation of privacy, and so forth). (3 footnotes)

619.   Simmons, Willard R. "A Plan to Account for 'Not-at-Homes' by Combining Weighting and Callbacks." *Journal of Marketing* 19, no. 1 (July 1954): 42-53.

A mechanism is described which reduces the cost and time of callbacks in attempts to reach respondents who are not at home on the first call. The weighting plan described is discussed in terms of reliability and also in combination with callbacks. The effect on reliability is considered, and the application of this approach to an actual survey is presented. The appendix contains an explanation of the method used to compute tolerances, a derivation of the weights used to account for the not-at-homes, and a presentation of the variances of the estimates (the final two sections employ advanced mathematics). (16 footnotes)

620.   Weaver, Charles N., Sandra L. Holmes, and Norval D. Glenn. "Some Characteristics of Inaccessible Respondents in a Telephone Survey." *Journal of Applied Psychology* 60, no. 2 (April 1975): 260-62.

To investigate biasing effects, 514 city employees in San Antonio, Texas, were asked questions on birth date, employment, seniority, salary, occupation, and whether eighteen-year-olds should have the right to vote. Of the respondents, 140 were female and male African Americans holding various city jobs, and 374 (117 Mexican Americans and 257 white Anglo-Saxons) were males in the police and fire departments. Study findings indicate that (1) the highest rate of refusals occurred in the oldest age group, (2) overall rates and patterns of refusals were similar to those of face-to-face interviews, (3) there was a very high inaccessibility rate for African-American respondents, and (4) neither refusals nor inaccessibility resulted in large differences between the distributions of contacted participants and the participants interviewed. The authors conclude that the chance of biasing survey responses from refusals or inaccessibility are minimal. (2 footnotes, 7 references)

621.   Weber, Dean, and Richard C. Burt. *Who's Home When.* U.S. Bureau of the Census, Working Paper, no. 37. [Washington, DC]: U.S. Bureau of the Census, 1973. 15p. [SuDoc C56.229:37]

A sample of about six thousand households was surveyed by the U.S. Bureau of the Census as part of the *Current Population Survey.* In order to assist researchers with cost estimates, the study undertook to determine when people of various characteristics were at home by time of day. The most difficult to find at home were people living in urban areas, with those in farm areas being the least difficult to locate. As the day progressed into the evening, the proportion of those at home increased, even for individuals over sixty-five who already have the highest at-home rates. The interviewing day began at 8 A.M. and ended at 8:59 P.M. The tables have breakdowns by sex, race, Standard Metropolitan Statistical Areas (SMSAs above and below 250,000, and Non-SMSAs-Nonfarm). The data show the proportion of persons at home during the interviewer's first visit by type of area and time of day. The tables are divided into poverty, above poverty, farm and nonfarm. Age categories are 14-19; 20-24; 25-34; 35-44; 45-54; 55-64; and 65 and over.

BIAS

622.   Krause, Merton S. "Role-Deviant Respondent Sets and Resulting Bias, Their Detection and Control in the Survey Interview." *Journal of Social Psychology* 67, 1st half (October 1965): 163-83.

The term "bias" is defined as anything which diverts the respondent's answers from being "maximally responsive, recordable, honest, understandable, considered, and complete." Krause defines "role-deviant" respondent sets as biases caused by "ulterior-motivational determinants." Set-detection methods are discussed, followed by control of respondent sets. The latter section covers politeness, honesty, self-expression, saving face, foresight, and motivation to enact the respondent role. Bias detection and bias control are considered. Krause notes that in order to eliminate poor sampling procedures, question ambiguity, or uncontrolled respondent bias, "prior studies for set detection" which are more demanding than the final survey may have to be undertaken. (15 footnotes, 68 references)

623.   Summers, Gene F., and Andre D. Hammonds. "Toward a Paradigm for Respondent Bias in Survey Research." *Sociological Quarterly* 10, no. 1 (Winter 1969): 113-21.

Five major elements involved in respondent bias are identified: "(1) Visual Cues of the Investigator (present vs. absent), (2) Type of Enumeration (investigator vs. self), (3) Identifiability of Respondent (anonymous vs. identified), (4) Nature of the Content (threatening vs. non-threatening), and (5) Statuses of Investigator and Respondent [SIR] (similar vs. dissimilar)." SIR could also be called Investigator Respondent Social Distance. The paradigm suggested revolves around a discussion of each of the above elements. The paradigm is illustrated in a figure, with eight possible formats included (ranging from a signed mail questionnaire, to standardized interviews, to street-corner interviews). The authors stress that the paradigm serves to provide order in the area of respondent bias but should not be construed as a theory of respondent bias. (5 footnotes)

CHARACTERISTICS

Age

624.   Friedman, Monroe, and Ira M. Wasserman. "Characteristics of Respon-
        dents and Non-Respondents in a Telephone Survey Study of Elderly Con-
        sumers." *Psychological Reports* 42, no. 3, pt. 1 (June 1978): 714.

Using a voter registration list for Ann Arbor, Michigan, 524 names were randomly selected and sent letters advising them that they would be contacted.
Telephone interviews were conducted with the respondents, all of whom were
sixty years of age or over. The age, sex, and socioeconomic status of all respondents and nonrespondents were determined using the voter registration list, as
well as the results of a 1975 study by the Ann Arbor Recreation Department which
examined socioeconomic status. The results indicate no variation in response by
sex or socioeconomic status. Nonrespondents were approximately two years older than respondents, with poor health cited as the reason for refusals. (3 footnotes, 3 references)

625.   Gergen, Kenneth J., and Kurt W. Back. "Communication in the Interview
        and the Disengaged Respondent." *Public Opinion Quarterly* 30, no. 3
        (Fall 1966): 385-98.

The term "disengaged" is used to mean the "diminutions in the variety, density,
and number of social interactions" of the aged population. Cumming and Henry's
theory of disengagement and aging (Cumming, Elaine, and William E. Henry.
Growing Old. New York, NY: Basic Books, 1961. 293p.) suggests that aged respondents may have less contact with societal norms, be out of touch with important issues, and be freer to express alternative opinions. The effect on survey
results of the personality of aged respondents is the focus of this study. Data
from four Gallup surveys were analyzed, that is, all items where the "no opinion" response was an option in relation to increasing age. The surveys were
conducted over a fifteen-year period. Analysis shows that the number of no opinion responses was greater for the "old group" (at a significant level for two of
the four surveys). In general, results were seen to uphold the disengagement
theory. The authors conclude with a discussion of the implications of the study
for the interviewer. (15 footnotes)

Race

626.   Hare, A. Paul. "Interview Responses: Personality or Conformity?" *Public
        Opinion Quarterly* 24, no. 4 (Winter 1960-61): 679-85.

Some of the recent additions to the literature on conformity are briefly reviewed, noting in particular the work of Cronbach (Cronbach, L. J. "Response Sets and Test Validity." *Educational and Psychological Measurement* 6 [1946]: 475-94.), and that of Couch and Keniston (Couch, A. S., and K. Keniston. "Yeasayers and Naysayers: Agreeing Response Set as a Personality Variable." *Journal of Abnormal and Social Psychology* 60 [1960]: 151-74.). The present study is part of a larger five-year investigation of the responses of lower-class urban-area mothers who had delivered premature babies. One of the ten interviews administered to each mother concerned personality and social variables. These scales were included to measure "personality" differences between African-American and white mothers. Sample 1 used ten African-American mothers and ten white mothers of premature babies. Sample 2 used eight African-American women and eight white women to further examine if conformity had a role in the results. Items were given both in their original form and reversed for sample 2. African Americans were found to have a tendency to agree more frequently, even when the item content was reversed. In addition, African Americans provided more inconsistent responses in the "agree-agree" direction and more in the "can't answer" category. The conformity hypothesis is upheld. The author believes that the lower the socioeconomic and educational levels of the African-American respondents, the more they have a tendency to misunderstand the questions and "because their social status moved them to agree more with a high status interviewer." (15 footnotes)

627.   Marquis, Kent H. "Effects of Race, Residence, and Selection of Respondent on the Conduct of the Interview." Chap. 12 in *Working Papers on Survey Research in Poverty Areas*, edited by John B. Lansing, Stephen B. Withey, and Arthur C. Wolfe, et al., 292-316. Ann Arbor, MI: Survey Research Center, Institute for Social Research, University of Michigan, January 1971. 318 pages plus appendixes.

The chapter is divided into three main areas: a general description of the interview, a discussion of the "effects on behavior of matching and not matching interviewer-respondent race," and a presentation of the results of two multiple regression analyses. Marquis found that the research suggests that "better data might be obtained if blacks interviewed blacks." When whites are interviewed by African Americans, the "total behavior per question decreases significantly." The study indicates that better data would be generated by white interviewers and white respondents. The "amounts and kinds" of interviewer behavior do not seem to be related to place of residence. However, the model neighborhoods were being compared with suburbs composed mostly of whites in late 1969 and 1970. Some doubt is expressed as to the certainty of the data on residence effects. For households with a husband and wife, a random selection procedure was used to select one respondent to be interviewed. Husbands' interviews contained "lower amounts of behavior per question for the interviewer and respondent." Marquis states that "interviews with the husband, compared to the wife, appear very business like and to the point" with more task behavior and "proportionately less of the other kinds of behavior." Chapters 10, 11, and 12 have a combined seventeen-entry bibliography on pages 317-18. (2 footnotes)

Sex

628.   Ballweg, John A. "Husband-Wife Response Similarities on Evaluative and Non-Evaluative Survey Questions." *Public Opinion Quarterly* 33, no. 2 (Summer 1969): 249-54.

A total of 179 couples were interviewed for a study to assess response similarities on so-called "hard" (nonevaluative) and "soft" (evaluative) survey questions. Husband and wife were interviewed simultaneously in separate rooms using questions concerning income (hard) and child discipline (soft). Each couple had a twelve-year-old child at home. The major findings show that there was a 60.3 percent consensus for husbands and wives responding to the hard data question, but only 22.9 percent of the husband-wife pairs responded the same to the question concerning who was responsible for disciplining their child. The authors conclude that consensus between husbands and wives can be enhanced when a fixed numerical value can be assigned to the data. For those responses requiring evaluation there is a greater likelihood that either the husband or the wife will stress the importance of her/his role over that of the spouse. The limitations involved in interviewing only one family member on family behavioral patterns are pointed out. (7 footnotes)

ERROR

629.   Smith, Edward M., and Joseph Barry Mason. "The Influence of Instructions on Respondent Error." *Journal of Marketing Research* 7, no. 2 (May 1970): 254-55.

The issue as to whether respondents "inadvertently give false information or deliberately conceal lack of knowledge, or attempt to 'help' the researcher" is examined. A study involving a random sample of 148 respondents interviewed at home is reported. Four groups were established: two experimental and two control. The first experimental group and the first control group members were shown a set of forty trademarks and asked to identify those which they recognized. The second experimental group and the second control group members were shown twenty existing and twenty bogus trademarks. Both groups were told that there might be some bogus trademarks in the set. Approximately 13 percent of the bogus trademarks were erroneously identified by the second experimental group and the second control group. It is concluded that alerting respondents to the inclusion of bogus trademarks did not reduce the recognition error. (1 footnote, 5 references)

FOREWARNED

630. Nuckols, Robert C. "A Study of Respondent Forewarning in Public Opinion Polls." *Journal of Applied Psychology* 37, no. 2 (April 1953): 121-25. [This study is part of a dissertation - Item No. 631.]

Two community surveys which used a letter to forewarn respondents were conducted in Altoona and Williamsport, Pennsylvania. The questionnaire used by the interviewers had nineteen opinion questions concerning the transportation service, the city government, and the housing situation. Of the forewarned respondents in Altoona 68 percent reported prior knowledge of the survey; 63 percent of the forewarned respondents in Williamsport reported prior knowledge. The author describes the forewarning letter as having had a "general lack of effectiveness." The forewarned respondents gave only slightly more answers to open-ended questions than did the nonforewarned. Nuckols partly explains the results by the fact that the letter was mimeographed and was therefore perhaps not attractive enough for recipients to choose to read the contents. One benefit of forewarning may be that interviewers believe that the process is helpful, which in turn makes the interviewing process more pleasant for them.

631. Nuckols, Robert C. "A Study of Respondent Forewarning in Public Opinion Research." Ph.D. diss., Pennsylvania State College, 1951. 126 leaves + [25 unmarked]. [*Dissertation Abstracts International* Order No. 0003308; *DAI* PSU 14, 468.]

The purpose of the dissertation was to determine the effects of forewarning the respondents of a public opinion poll of the nature of the interview to follow. Nuckols hypothesized that if respondents were forewarned (by letter), they would have more time to "recall and organize bits of information" and be prepared to give "more detailed and thought-out answers." He also suggests that the level of cooperation will be increased, and that the entire experience will be more "enjoyable" for all concerned. It had been only fifteen years since the advent of modern polling, with much of the interviewing still conducted with in-person visits. The results of the test Nuckols devised did not show a significant difference for those forewarned. References are provided.

INFORMANTS

632.   Singer, Eleanor. "Agreement between 'Inaccessible' Respondents and Informants." *Public Opinion Quarterly* 36, no. 4 (Winter 1972-73): 603-11.

Informants are used in survey research when respondents themselves are unavailable or when data obtained from the respondents are questionable. This research investigates the issues surrounding the use of informants, a technique
often used for interviewing the aged and the chronically ill, in a longitudinal
study of the social and economic consequences of therapy with the drug levo-
dopa. The study was conducted on a number of patients (the respondents) with
Parkinson's disease by the Center for Policy Research. "Soft" questions centered
around a patient's daily functioning; "hard" questions asked for information
about the patient's social functioning. "Informant interviews" were taken for every
fourth patient in the sample of 169 who was judged by her/his physician as being unable to function as a respondent. Responses of nineteen respondent-in-
formant pairs were compared. Findings indicate a high level of agreement on
most items. Differences among the items were small and random. It is concluded that there is likely to be consensus between informant and respondent
responses when the questions asked are relatively objective, the informants have
close contact with the respondents, the population is somewhat homogeneous,
and the interview setting "provided no clear-cut motivation to distort responses
in one direction or another." Limitations of the sample and applicability of the
data to other similar studies are discussed. (16 footnotes)

633.   Star, Shirley A. "Obtaining Household Opinions from a Single Respondent." *Public Opinion Quarterly* 17, no. 3 (Fall 1953): 386-91.

In an attempt to combine the views of individual members of a household into a
composite household opinion, three alternative approaches are offered: (1) asking respondents for their own opinions (in areas where their views would be
representative of the household); (2) asking respondents to state the household
or family view (the respondent weighed conflicting views to arrive at a family
consensus); and (3) asking respondents to give their own views as well as those
of the other adults and children in the household (these answers were then
combined into a family type). The respondents were regarded as informants in
the last approach. Traditionally, the sampling scheme selected either husband or
wife as head of household, alternately, as respondents. Three questions concerning recreational preferences, attitudes toward television, and interest in subscription television were used, with 345 males and 364 females participating.
Overall, results show little difference in opinion between male and female respondents to the questions, irrespective of which of the three questioning formats was used. Areas in which differences did occur are indicated. The author

believes the one respondent per household scheme proved "relatively success-ful" for the subject matter dealt with in the survey. (92 footnotes)

634.   Sudman, Seymour, Ed Blair, Norman Bradburn, and Carol Stocking. "Estimates of Threatening Behavior Based on Reports of Friends." *Public Opinion Quarterly* 41, no. 2 (Summer 1977): 261-64.

An approach to improve data obtained about illegal or threatening topics is re-viewed. The technique involves asking the respondent questions about the be-havior of the respondent's three closest friends. Advantages are anonymity (there-by reducing invasion of privacy), reduced underreporting, and smaller sampling error. Three questions on intoxication and marijuana use were asked of 1,172 respondents as part of a larger study on response effects. The National Opinion Research Center conducted the interviews. Comparisons of self reported behav-ior and that reported by the respondent about their three closest friends show the reported behavior for the friends is higher than for oneself. More accurate data were obtained from reports concerning friends' behavior in the past year. How-ever, the authors note that estimates based on reports of closest friends ever en-gaging in an activity are not as useful since many friendships are of shorter du-ration. The level of respondent uneasiness while being interviewed apparently was not a factor. Further, it was found that the "sampling variances of estimates based on friends are reduced even when the correlation of behavior among friends is sizeable." (1 footnote, 13 references)

PAYMENTS

635.   Dohrenwend, Barbara Snell. "An Experimental Study of Payments to Re-spondents." *Public Opinion Quarterly* 34, no. 4 (Winter 1970-71): 621-24.

An experiment was conducted to determine if a five-dollar honorarium would increase response rates. The money could be donated to a charity if the re-spondents desired, providing them with an "altruistic motive." The honorarium might also highlight the importance that the researcher attaches to the respon-dents' contribution. As part of another study undertaken in the Washington Heights section of Manhattan, a sample of households was chosen from two cen-sus tracts – one composed primarily of African Americans and one primarily of whites. Income level varied between tracts. The panel survey took place in two parts, approximately one year apart. Both graduate students and professional interviewers were used. Results show that on both waves of the study overall refusal rates were high (41.1 and 42.2 percent). Completion rates were unaf-fected by the offer of an honorarium. Neither race, sex, income, nor level of expe-rience of the interviewer affected outcomes. Although payment may be helpful in some cases with some groups of respondents, results of this study show "that to improve completion rates in general population surveys we should put our money elsewhere." (4 footnotes)

RECALL

636.   Gottfredson, Michael R., and Michael J. Hindelang. "A Consideration of Telescoping and Memory Decay Biases in Victimization Surveys." *Journal of Criminal Justice* 5, no. 3 (Fall 1977): 202-16.

Victimization data from the National Crime Survey were used to determine the relationship between memory biases and characteristics of incidents and respondents. The authors found that there is no evidence that memory biases are "substantially related to respondent and incident characteristics." Victimization reports are affected by memory biases, with respondents tending to report to interviewers "a relatively high percentage of victimizations occurring in months nearest to the interview." Victimization surveys are retrospective studies in which the person interviewed reports about criminal victimization they have "personally experienced within a specified period of time." Telescoping refers to "misplacing events in time" and can be either forward or backward. Memory decay may lead to a respondent forgetting an event entirely. The data used in the Gottfredson and Hindelang study were derived from surveys conducted by the Law Enforcement Assistance Administration and the Bureau of the Census, with 22,000 interviews conducted in eight cities with respondents twelve years of age and older. (12 endnotes, 13 references)

637.   Morgenstern, Richard D., and Nancy S. Barrett. "The Retrospective Bias in Unemployment Reporting by Sex, Race, and Age." *Journal of the American Statistical Association* 69, no. 346 (June 1974): 355-57.

The official measure of unemployment is based on the *Current Population Survey* which is administered monthly to 50,000 households. Females, more than males, and youths of both sexes significantly understate their unemployment when recall observations from up to a year ago are compared with statements from the previous week. The understatement can be as high as 50 percent. White males, aged twenty-five and over, and females, aged forty-five and over, "all evidence some tendency to overstate their unemployment in the Wage Experience Survey relative to current reporting." The authors observe that the biases exhibited in the study described need to be considered in relation to the retrospective reporting as collected in the decennial census or in the *Survey of Economic Opportunity*. (7 footnotes, 6 references)

638.   Spanier, Graham B. "Use of Recall Data in Survey Research on Human Sexual Behavior." *Social Biology* 23, no. 3 (Fall 1976): 244-53.

Error sources with retrospective accounts of human sexual behavior are explored. The use of recall data is discussed, with the main challenges identified as "faulty recall" or unintentional false reporting, and "falsified accounts" in which intentionally false reporting is offered due to a variety of reasons including fear of honesty and ego problems. Earlier research in the area is reviewed. Under the heading "faulty recall," poor memory and sexual identity are identified. Spanier suggests that if the interviewer is able to establish rapport with the respondent, falsified replies are "less likely" to be a problem. While the problems of recall data are acknowledged, the author points out that respondents are being asked questions about their sexual experiences. Recalling one's own experience is less subject to error than recalling the behavior of others. (1 footnote, 32 references)

639.   Sudman, Seymour, and Norman M. Bradburn. "Effects of Time and Memory Factors on Response in Surveys." *Journal of the American Statistical Association* 68, no. 344 (December 1973): 805-15.

Several approaches were employed to test the effects of time and memory on survey responses by using records and aided recall. The use of records controls overstatements but has little or no effect on errors of omission. Aided recall ("where the possible answers are explicitly presented to the respondent") reduces omissions but does not reduce telescoping effects (the time compression error in which the event is thought to have occurred closer in time than it did). Records are useful when dealing with major events; aided recall is successful when less important events and longer recall times are called for (diaries are suggested under some conditions of extended recall periods). Other factors considered include age, face-to-face interview versus self-administered questionnaire, perception of threatening question or study, question position in the questionnaire, and the question structure. (1 footnote, 14 references)

640.   Withey, Stephen B. "Reliability of Recall of Income." *Public Opinion Quarterly* 18, no. 2 (Summer 1954): 197-204.

Withey reviews the difficulties in obtaining accurate figures from respondents concerning income, as well as the methodological problems involved in measuring income for various uses. A study is reported in which a national sample of urban adults was queried in January 1948 about their January 1947 income. Six hundred fifty-five of the respondents were reinterviewed in January 1949 about their January 1947 income. The purpose was to determine if annual income was reliably recalled over the time period under consideration and, if not, whether errors in recall were of a random nature. Detailed analysis shows that only about 25 percent of the respondents made reports that were within 5 percent of each other. The correlation between amounts reported on the two dates was high. The magnitude of income change and the magnitude of unreliability were related. Approximately 25 percent reported a false direction of income change greater than 5 percent. Since recall of income was inaccurate and nonrandom, it is concluded that "considerable error may be introduced by recall and a false picture is likely to be drawn in the analysis." (3 footnotes)

REFUSALS

641.   Dohrenwend, Barbara Snell, and Bruce P. Dohrenwend. "Sources of Refusals in Surveys." *Public Opinion Quarterly* 32, no. 1 (Spring 1968): 74-83. [An adapted version of this article appears in *Milbank Memorial Fund Quarterly* 47, no. 1, pt. 2 (January 1969): 201-10.]

A probability subsample of ninety-four married couples and twenty-six single household heads for a combined total of 214 individuals were reinterviewed. The previous survey, undertaken an average of two years earlier, was conducted in the Washington Heights section of Manhattan. The ethnic groups represented in the subsample were limited to Irish, Jewish, African Americans, and Puerto Ricans between the ages of twenty-one and fifty-nine and living in households headed by a male. Respondents in 19 percent of these households refused to be reinterviewed. The authors determined that potential respondents who refused to participate, when faced with competent interviewers, "differ in some respects from those that do cooperate." Additionally, the Dohrenwends found cases of both interviewers and respondents who were responsible for refusals. (15 footnotes)

642.   Dommermuth, William P., and Philip R. Cateora. "Can Refusals by Respondents Be Decreased?" *Journal of Marketing* 27, no. 3 (July 1963): 74-76.

The authors sought to determine if contact by telephone or by letter prior to an interview would reduce the refusal rate. The methodology involved three groups. Group one received no contact prior to the interviewer appearing at the door, group two received a telephone call a few days before the interviewer's visit, and the third group received an individually typed letter a few days before the interviewer appeared. Group one had 192 households, group two had 158 households, and there were 134 households represented in the third group. Results indicate that neither experimental approach reduced the rate of total refusals. Greater acceptance of the interviewer by those who agreed to respond may be achieved through prior contact. (1 footnote)

643.   Gaudet, Hazel, and E. C. Wilson. "Who Escapes the Personal Investiga-
        tor?" *Journal of Applied Psychology* 24, no. 6 (December 1940): 773-77.

A sample of 2,800 individuals was selected as representative of an Ohio county,
and in May 1940 were interviewed concerning their radio and reading habits,
political opinions, and personal characteristics. During the following summer,
1,800 individuals were to be reinterviewed. From the 1,794 attempted contacts,
about 9 percent were not successful, 3 percent refused, and 6 percent were unavailable. The refusals tended to be "housewives" and persons of "little education." The unavailables were mostly male, with a greater proportion of industrial
workers. They also tended to be in the lower economic strata. Gaudet and Wilson maintain that since the refusals and the unavailables were from opposite
groups, and since the percentages in both groups were small, with a sufficient
sample size their impact will not "seriously" bias the final results. (1 footnote)

644.   Gorman, Benjamin. "Respondent Accessibility and Respondent Surfeit:
        Refusal Rate Bias in Sampling." *Rural Sociology* 34, no. 1 (March 1969):
        75-79.

The study undertaken dealt with rural and small-town residents in the southwest
plains. The content of the study is not specified. The sample consisted of 349
dwellings of an estimated universe of 21,800. All interviewing was conducted
by two interviewers. Once contact was made, all interviewing was completed
on the spot or by later appointment. Gorman hypothesized that refusal rates are
related to the frequency of being approached by survey interviewers, or "respondent surfeit." The dwellings in the sample were categorized by degree of accessibility in the following scheme: town, outlying areas and state highways, main
farm roads, secondary farm roads, and isolated. It was found that refusal rate
does vary with geographic accessibility. The more accessible the dwelling, the
higher the refusal rate, with the social classes "elite" and "poor but respectable"
having a high rate of response. (8 references)

645.   Harding, John. "Refusals as a Source of Bias." Part 2, Chap. 9 in *Gaug-
        ing Public Opinion* by Hadley Cantril and Research Associates in the Of-
        fice of Public Opinion Research, Princeton University, 119-23. Prince-
        ton, NJ: Princeton University Press, 1944. Reprint. Port Washington, NY:
        Kennikat Press, 1972. 318p.

In two surveys conducted in March and July 1942 by the Office of Public Opinion
Research, interviewers recorded all refusals or discontinuations of the interview
process. It was found that 14 percent of all individuals approached for interviews
were refusals, with 429 in March and 476 in July. Refusals were "most frequent
among poor people, women, and in large cities." Harding determined that refusals
did not "greatly affect" the degree to which the sample was a representative cross

section of the population. The suggestion is made that the opinions of refusals are "often more superficial and unstable than those of more cooperative respondents." (2 footnotes)

646.   Mercer, Jane R., and Edgar W. Butler. "Disengagement of the Aged Population and Response Differentials in Survey Research." *Social Forces* 46, no. 1 (September 1967): 89-96.

Just over one-tenth of the housing units of a city constituted the sample, with interviews completed in 90.7 percent of approximately three thousand occupied housing units. A refusal rate of 7.9 percent resulted. The survey was described as a study of chronic handicaps with an emphasis on mental retardation. The researchers found that the disengagement framework for the aged population fit the results of higher than usual refusal rates of older people in social surveys. Mercer and Butler believe that their findings tend to "support the hypothesis that older persons who refuse may be more disengaged than those who cooperate." Refusers tended to live in small multitype units where there were no children. (12 footnotes)

647.   Ohlsten, Jerome W. "How Survey Researchers Meet Public Resistance." *Advertising Age* 47, no. 28 (12 July 1976): 67-68.

The issue addressed is the increasing rate of refusals, or individuals declining to be interviewed. In the late 1960s the percentage cited in this category is 3 to 4 percent; in the mid-1970s the number has reportedly reached as high as 12 percent. A series of contributing factors is cited: (1) towns/cities barring interviewing; (2) high-rise units with security doors and/or door personnel; (3) fear of permitting someone to enter the home; (4) high crime areas where interviewers fear to tread; and (5) refusal based on perceived invasion of privacy grounds. Another problem is that interviews are getting much longer – as long as two-and-a-half hours. W. R. Simmons and Associates is presented as having gone to great length to overcome refusals, including (1) providing letters of introduction, (2) presenting gifts to interviewers, (3) offering money incentives to successful interviewers and supervisors, (4) allowing up to six evening calls per respondent to establish contact, (5) making long-distance calls, and (6) hiring bilingual interviewers. Even with these caveats, 9.8 percent still could not be reached, and an additional 13.1 percent refused to be surveyed.

648.   "The Public Clams Up on Survey Takers: W. R. Simmons Pulled Its People Out of the Field, and Its Report Will Be Late." *Business Week*, no. 2297 (15 September 1973): 216, 220.

Both ghetto and wealthy areas pose challenges for survey research firms. Ghettos pose problems because residents are suspicious of interviewers. Affluent areas are problematic due to residents who "don't want to be bothered" or are frequently not home. Unless it is necessary, many firms are resorting to mail questionnaires or telephone surveys instead of face-to-face interviewing. Springtime is considered better for personal interviews because daylight time is increasing and people are not away as much as in the summer. Boredom on the part of both interviewers and respondents is considered, as well as the problem of salespersons posing as survey researchers. Incentives, such as gifts of electrical gadgets, are discussed as ways to induce respondent cooperation.

649.   Skelton, Vincent C. "Patterns behind 'Income Refusals'." *Journal of Marketing* 27, no. 3 (July 1963): 38-41.

Nonresponse is significantly higher for income questions than for those concerning education or age. Several techniques of dealing with income nonresponse are suggested, such as placing the income question at the end of the questionnaire. Another approach is to provide ranges of income from which to select. A variation on this theme is to offer one income range at a time. If the respondent still refuses, s/he should be asked if the income level is above or below a certain designated point. In 1962 a survey of 2,507 telephone households was conducted from which the data were tabulated by age, education, and relationship to the household head. The overall refusal rate was 31 percent on the range of income questions. Females were less likely than males to answer income questions. Female refusal rates were 17 percent for the income question, 6 percent for the education question, and 2 percent for the age question. Male refusal rates were 12 percent for the income question, 4 percent for the education question, and 1 percent for the age question. Two primary reasons – lack of knowledge and personal reticence – are suggested for income question refusal. (1 footnote)

RELUCTANT

650.   Pomeroy, Wardell B. "The Reluctant Respondent." *Public Opinion Quarterly* 27, no. 2 (Summer 1963): 287-93.

Based on his experience at the Institute for Sex Research, Pomeroy discusses some of the ways to help respondents become less reluctant to relate personal information (prior sexual experiences in this case) to interviewers. The three basic requirements are to tell the respondent of the importance and usefulness of the research, to convince her/him that the information imparted will be strictly confidential, and to assure the respondent that interviewers do not morally evaluate or judge experiences. Several methods of overcoming respondent resistance and conducting fruitful interviews are described: (1) interviewers must be highly trained; (2) female interviewers can be effective; (3) the more poorly educated respondents pick up nonverbal cues very quickly; (4) group sampling is more productive than taking histories of single individuals; (5) the interviewer must control the interview; and (6) the interviewer must be cognizant of sex taboos and idioms at various social and economic levels. The primary factors in respondent reluctance, however, are poorly trained interviewers and faulty interviewing practices.

651.   Robins, Lee N. "The Reluctant Respondent." *Public Opinion Quarterly* 27, no. 2 (Summer 1963): 276-86.

"Reluctant" respondents are described as both those individuals who refuse to be interviewed as well as those who "stall" – they postpone the interview, cancel appointments, or fail to decide whether or not to participate. The possible biasing effects on the sample are considered. Respondents were 465 former patients (about thirty years ago) of a child guidance clinic, and 100 normal controls. A variety of records were available from which researchers could obtain social and personality variables. Because of the antisocial personal histories of the experimental group, it was hypothesized that there would be a higher rate of refusal on the highly sensitive interview questions than for the normal population or for the former patients whose subsequent lives had improved. Included in the results are the following: (1) refusers were found more often among respondents with routine white-collar occupations, low education, foreign-born parents, and local residencies; (2) stallers differed from other respondents in that there were more local residents included; (3) social or personality variables were about the same for refusers who were eventually persuaded to participate from those who could not be persuaded; (4) local versus out-of-town residency distinguished easy-to-interview from difficult-to-interview respondents; (5) the difficult-to-interview respondents were about as honest as others; and (6) past antisocial behavior was unrelated to the willingness to be interviewed. (6 footnotes)

RESPONSE LATENCY

652.   LaBarbera, Priscilla A., and James M. MacLachlan. "Response Latency in Telephone Interviews: It Was Correlated with How Certain the Respondents Said They Were." *Journal of Advertising Research* 19, no. 3 (June 1979): 49-55.

"Response latency" (RL) is defined as the amount of time a respondent takes to think about a response before the answer is provided. Psychological literature indicates the more certain the respondent is, the quicker will be the answer. Certainty values (CV) of respondents in relation to their RL in the telephone interview are studied. The authors demonstrate that CV can serve as "an index of strength of preference when two alternatives are presented." Additionally, CV indicates the resistance of an attitude to change. It is suggested that RL data can be used to cut survey costs by reducing the number of questions needed in order to achieve the client's purposes. (17 references)

653. MacLachlan, James, John Czepiel, and Priscilla LaBarbera. "Implementation of Response Latency Measures." *Journal of Marketing Research* 16, no. 4 (November 1979): 573-77.

The amount of time a respondent contemplates before answering a question is defined as "response latency" (RL). RL can serve as an indicator of the respondent's certainty. In this research a voice-operated relay system was used which activated an electronic stopwatch. A digital readout provided the exact RL. The study results indicate that RL is not "appreciably influenced by the serial position of questions, practice effects, or respondent boredom." The study also found that if RL exceeded two seconds, the respondent was probably supplying "helpful guessing" behavior, rather than knowledge. The approach of RL measurement is shown to be useful for both high- and low-involvement questions. (1 footnote, 8 references)

TRACKING

654. Crider, Donald M., and Fern K. Willits. "Respondent Retrieval Bias in a Longitudinal Survey." *Sociology and Social Research* 58, no. 1 (October 1973): 56-65.

The initial study was conducted in 1947 with 2,344 respondents who were high-school sophomores in rural schools in Pennsylvania. Another contact was made in 1957. The present study took place eleven years later in 1968-69. The individual characteristics considered were the sex of the respondent, marital status and family size, the type and prestige of occupation, respondent education level, and participation in formal organizations. Three approaches were used to locate the respondents: mail, telephone calls, and community visits. Cards requesting current name and address were sent, with follow-up occurring one month later. Telephone numbers were sought through long-distance operators. When a listing could not be found, people with the same surname were called. The procedure was successful, with addresses for 80 percent of the respondents being found by telephone. Beginning with a subsample of 320 to track, 64 were not located by telephone and were pursued via visits (which were limited to the Middle Atlantic States). Overall, 97 percent of the respondents were able to be tracked and current addresses identified. Success was found to be higher in more rural areas. The individual characteristics were not found to be significant during the variety of tracking procedures used. Five tables provide an analysis of data by rurality, respondent attributes, and relationships to the original sample. (8 endnotes, 13 references)

655.   Crider, Donald M., Fern K. Willits, and Robert C. Bealer. *Locating People in Longitudinal Studies: A Research Report and Suggested Guidelines.* Bulletin 778. University Park, PA: Pennsylvania Agricultural Experiment Station, Pennsylvania State University, May 1972. 32p. Microfiche. (ED 072 332)

The challenge discussed, and ways to approach the question, concern how to track respondents over long periods of time. The study sought to follow up a subsample of 320 individuals from a 1947-57 longitudinal study. The subsample was stratified by sex, marital status, and migrant status (had respondents moved across a state line during the initial ten-year study). The tracking methods used included mail, telephone, community visits, and public records. First-class letters yielded just less than 50 percent return; telephone calls, 80 percent; and community visits (for example, post offices, neighborhoods, schools, and last-known employer) retrieved almost all the rest. Public records (marriage licenses and real estate transfers) yielded only 19 percent. The above approach achieved current addresses for all but 2 percent of the subsample. (17 references)

656.   Crider, Donald M., Fern K. Willits, and Robert C. Bealer. "Tracking Respondents in Longitudinal Surveys." *Public Opinion Quarterly* 35, no. 4 (Winter 1971-72): 613-20.

Four different tracking methods used to locate respondents over time are compared and contrasted: mail, long-distance telephone, community visitation, and public records. A study of 2,810 high-school sophomores had taken place in 1947 in Pennsylvania. Contact had occurred several times, the last being in 1957 (at which time 2,344 individuals were located). In 1966 researchers wanted to contact this group again. An initial stratified sample of 320 persons was subjected to one of the four tracking procedures. The following are the results: (1) two mailings retrieved 48 percent of the addresses for the sample or 153 people located; (2) the telephone method yielded 80 percent or 264 people located using the 1957 residence area, and 85 percent with the 1947 area; (3) visits to the 1947 post offices tracking 157 individuals achieved an 82 percent success rate, while the 1957 post offices yielded 57 correct addresses or 38 percent; (4) using the last known employer in 1957 produced 55 correct addresses or a 60 percent success rate; (5) visits to the 1947 high school tracking 79 individuals produced a 75 percent correct address rate; and (6) tracking 140 individuals using public records yielded 27 or 19 percent for marriage licenses, 8 percent for real estate records, and 4 percent for wills. Comparisons in tracking success are made to the 1947 group, and suggestions for tracking respondents in longitudinal surveys are offered. Costs by procedure are also given. It is concluded that most cases can be retrieved with time and effort on the part of the investigator. (13 footnotes)

657. Eckland, Bruce K. "Retrieving Mobile Cases in Longitudinal Surveys." *Public Opinion Quarterly* 32, no.1 (Spring 1968): 51-64.

The increased use of longitudinal surveys is attributed to two factors. First, more complex models for the basic analysis of social processes are being developed. Second, applied research requires a longitudinal approach by social scientists for use by both public and private organizations. Eckland lists ten recent successful longitudinal studies which show high retrieval rates for respondents. A major criticism of follow-up studies is lost respondents. Five resources are described that may be used to retrieve mobile cases: (1) postal services; (2) telephone services; (3) local and regional coordinators; (4) public records (that is, utility companies, high schools, alumni associations, and tax rolls); and (5) private services. These sources have been based on the personal experiences of a number of investigators, by correspondence or in person, as no experimental research is known to have tested the alternative methods. Eckland states at the beginning of the article: "Because published materials are scarce, this review is based largely upon the personal commentaries and references supplied by other investigators." Twenty-seven names are listed. Some special difficulties common to panel studies are addressed. (31 footnotes)

658. McAllister, Ronald J., Edgar W. Butler, and Steven J. Goe. "Evolution of a Strategy for the Retrieval of Cases in Longitudinal Survey Research." *Sociology and Social Research* 58, no. 1 (October 1973): 37-47.

Success in longitudinal research is dependent upon following through with a "specified sequence" of information sources. The original interview was conducted in 1963 and involved 10 percent of a southern California city of some 100,000 inhabitants. Interviews were conducted with 2,661 households with the topic being the epidemiology of mental retardation. In 1972 a sample of 600 persons was selected (these were individuals aged nine to fifteen in 1963), a portion of whom had exhibited symptoms of physical, intellectual, or behavioral impairment. The remainder was selected from the "normal" population aged nine to fifteen in 1963. The authors proceed to discuss several methods and techniques for gathering current name and address information: (1) design original surveys with longitudinal efforts in mind, thereby including appropriate biographical information with the surname spelled out by the respondent; (2) include the date of birth; (3) ascertain the respondent's and the spouse's place of employment; (4) note ethnicity; and (5) complete the name and address of a friend or relative who will know where the respondent is. The search process should include the following: (1) check marriage records for marriages and remarriages and therefore possible surname changes; (2) contact the respondent by the U.S. Postal Service; (3) use current telephone directories, out-of-date directories, and directories from a twenty- to-thirty-mile radius; (4) utilize telephone operators for follow-up searches; (5) consult crisscross directories, county voter registration files, school transfer records, collection billings from water, power, and sewage companies, police records, and welfare files; (6) contact public utilities' credit offices, employers, and state departments of motor vehicles, as well as neighbors; (7) call other individuals with the same unusual last name, as the person contacted may be familiar with the respondent; and (8) contact county probation offices. A great deal of patience is needed to sustain searching for an individual. Other challenges include the possibility that the respondent will have forgotten the original survey; that males are on average "much more difficult to contact" than females; that there is a high marital rate for a sample aged eighteen to twenty-five; that parents attempt to "insulate" young adults from others outside; and that neighborhoods may change significantly – with formerly residential areas now exclusively business. A two-page flowchart depicts the recommended sequence and procedures. (3 endnotes, 12 references)

659.   McAllister, Ronald J., Steven J. Goe, and Edgar W. Butler. "Tracking Respondents in Longitudinal Surveys: Some Preliminary Considerations." *Public Opinion Quarterly* 37, no. 3 (Fall 1973): 413-16.

According to the authors, this "research note" is written to serve as an addendum to an article by Crider, et al., [Item No. 656] in which four different tracking methods used to locate respondents over time were compared. The present article offers a number of suggestions for the researcher who is undertaking a longitudinal survey. It is urged that the execution of a panel design take place before the first-wave interviews begin, and that longitudinal data be collected even if such a study is perhaps unintended. If one is planning to reinterview, the following suggestions are made: (1) all biographical information should be accurately recorded (that is, spelling of all names, making certain all children's surnames in a household are the same as the parents, and so forth); (2) all information collected should be complete (for example, middle initials, date of birth, and possible social security number); (3) the complete names and addresses of friends and/or relatives should be obtained at some point in the interview; and (4) the place of employment and ethnicity should be verified. By following these and Crider's guidelines, the retrieval of longitudinal cases can be greatly facilitated. (4 footnotes)

660.   Parnes, Herbert S. "Longitudinal Surveys: Prospects and Problems: Surveys Which Follow the Same Workers through Time Are Yielding New Insights into Their Labor Market Behavior." *Monthly Labor Review* 95, no. 2 (February 1972): 11-15.

The National Longitudinal Surveys of labor market behavior are described. Parnes outlines the study design and reviews the data generated. The unique contributions of these surveys are discussed, as well as some of the methodological problems. The purpose of the present study is to "explain individuals' labor force behavior and experience." Using Census data, four groups were selected, utilizing 235 sample areas. Each sample had five thousand respondents. Each person was interviewed approximately annually over the course of five years. One advantage of the approach is that it permits the collection of data which would be difficult or impossible to do retrospectively – such as "characteristics which are subject to change over time." Additionally, longitudinal surveys reduce errors in response which are the result of faulty recall. (10 endnotes)

TRUTHFUL

661.   Allen, Irving L. "Detecting Respondents Who Fake and Confuse Information about Question Areas on Surveys." *Journal of Applied Psychology* 50, no. 6 (December 1966): 523-28.

The research described revolves around the belief that those individuals who respond to nonexistent survey items provide invalid answers to other questions. This study examines the verbal behavior of 625 respondents. The data from those individuals who claim knowledge of the phony item are comparatively analyzed. The author sought to determine if the use of meaningless questions "effectively increases the validity of the distribution of responses and whether it does . . . designate respondents who are more apt to fake or confuse information." The other question addressed is whether demographic traits of respondents play a role in the way bogus questions are answered. Allen found that respondents who claimed knowledge of the fictitious item are also more likely to indicate awareness of the genuine item and to express positive attitudes toward items. The author concludes that the bogus question technique is an effective approach to identify those likely to confuse and fake information. Removal of the suspect respondents had "little effect" on the frequency distribution. The suspect respondents are more likely to have low education. (8 references).

662.   Clancy, Kevin J., Lyman E. Ostlund, and Gordon A. Wyner. "False Reporting of Magazine Readership." *Journal of Advertising Research* 19, no. 5 (October 1979): 23-30.

The study results indicate that between 27 and 37 percent of the respondents claimed to have read items which had not yet been published. The authors describe this phenomenon as being the "guilt of overclaiming." Further evidence of overclaiming is provided in a table showing false reports across three reading-material categories of articles and advertisements. The sample consisted of approximately one thousand subscribers to a magazine which appeals to middle- and upper-income households. Personal interviews were conducted, with the respondent being shown the most recent cover of the magazine and asked if they had looked at or read that issue. About 50 percent responded "yes." These "readers" were then shown a set of eight full-length articles, eight brief articles, and eight advertisements. Of the latter categories half were actually in the most recent issue and half were to run in future issues. The researchers found that social desirability has only a "modest relationship" to false reports of readership. Additional research should explore the role of understatement and the entire issue of bias in self-report surveys. (27 references)

663.   Dean, John P., and William Foote Whyte. "How Do You Know If the Informant Is Telling the Truth?" *Human Organization* 17, no. 2 (Summer 1958): 34-38.

The simple answer to the question as stated is "no" – you cannot tell. However, the authors observe that "the informant's statement represents merely the perception of the informant, filtered and modified by his cognitive and emotional reactions and reported through his personal verbal usages." The respondent's report of subjective data is examined, with a number of concerns addressed: (1) Are there any ulterior motives which might cause the replies to be modified? (2) Do "bars to spontaneity" exist? (3) Does the respondent seek to please the interviewer so that the opinions voiced will be well received? and (4) Are there conditions which would motivate the respondent to show only one aspect to the interviewer? Major elements in the distortion of objective data are outlined. Dean and Whyte note that the more appropriate question to consider is this: "What do the informant's statements reveal about his feelings and perceptions and what inferences can be made from them about the actual environment or events he has experienced?"

664.   Hyman, Herbert. "Do They Tell the Truth?" *Public Opinion Quarterly* 8, no. 4 (Winter 1944-45): 557-59.

Three surveys are reported in an attempt to respond to the question, "Do the answers of people really give a true picture of their behavior?" Records from the Division of Surveys of the Office of War Information's Bureau of Special Services were used as an objective measure of a respondent's behavior. The subjects of the questions were the redemption of war bonds, the displaying of government posters by storekeepers, and absenteeism among workers in an industrial plant. The questions all dealt with behavior to which high prestige is attached. The "distortions" from the actual records were 17, 42, and 23 percent, respectively. Even though the statistics are significant, at least with respect to behavior having a "prestige character," caution must be used when interpreting the results of surveys. Other factors (such as characteristics of the respondents) must be taken into account. (1 footnote)

UNDECIDED

665.   Marks, Eli S. "Processing, Estimating, and Adjustment of Survey Data: Treatment of Undecided Responses." Chap. 8 in *The Pre-Election Polls of 1948: Report to the Committee on Analysis of Pre-Election Polls and Forecasts*, by Frederick Mosteller, Herbert Hyman, Philip J. McCarthy, Eli S. Marks, and David B. Truman, 190-210. Social Science Research Council, Bulletin no. 60. New York, NY: Social Science Research Council, 1949. 396p.

Crossley, Gallup, and Roper faced the challenge of what to do with individuals who were "undecided." This section defines the term, discusses what proportion of voters were undecided, reviews how these were handled, and ascertains whether a better allocation of the number of undecided voters could have been made. Allocation options based on economic or demographic factors are considered, as well as those based on expressed opinions on the issues. Specifically, a determination is made as to what degree the undecided voters could have been allocated to Truman. After a review of the data, Marks writes that "the maximum error attributable to the allocation of the 'undecided' did not exceed 1.5 percentage points in any case where 'leanings' of the undecided were obtained and used in allocations." (1 footnote)

666.   Marks, Eli S. "The Undecided Voter." Chap. 11 in *The Pre-Election Polls of 1948: Report to the Committee on Analysis of Pre-Election Polls and Forecasts*, by Frederick Mosteller, Herbert Hyman, Philip J. McCarthy, Eli S. Marks, and David B. Truman, 263-89. Social Science Research Council, Bulletin no. 60. New York, NY: Social Science Research Council, 1949. 396p.

The role of the undecided voter in polls is explored. The number and characteristics of the undecided are considered. The survey results for fourteen questions are provided, indicating the percentages of "agree/disagree" responses by Dewey supporters, Truman supporters, and the undecided. The undecided voter as "apathetic" is discussed, as well as the use of "don't know" as a means to evade a "stigmatized situation." The undecided respondent as one "in conflict" is considered. This category is one in which there is an "overt discrepancy between the candidate favored and opinion on issues or class interest." Marks calls for planned and organized research guided by hypotheses in order to avoid "chaos" in undecided voter research.

MISCELLANEOUS

667.   Bishop, George D., David L. Hamilton, and John B. McConahay. *Attitudes and Non-Attitudes in the Belief Systems of Mass Publics: A Field Study.* Institute of Policy Sciences and Public Affairs Working Paper, no. 4772. [Durham, NC]: Center for Policy Analysis, Institute of Policy Sciences and Public Affairs, Duke University, 1977. 27p.

The assumption that survey respondents have stable and meaningful attitudes has been questioned by Philip E. Converse. The field study described by Bishop and his coauthors is designed to examine the issue. The results indicate that respondents in both college-educated and noncollege-educated groups had "quite stable attitudes on specific issues." In the discussion portion the authors caution survey researchers in the interpretation of a shift on a single issue, or the election outcome of one focused on a single issue, as not necessarily meaning that a general shift in the electorate has occurred along the liberal-conservative continuum. (5 footnotes, 18 references)

668.   Cory, Christopher T. "The Prevalence of 'Pseudo-Opinions' on Polls." *Psychology Today* 13, no. 6 (November 1979): 21.

Psychology Today provides a brief summary of an article which appeared in full in *Public Opinion Quarterly* [44, no. 2 (Summer 1980): 198-209]. George F. Bishop, a psychologist at the University of Cincinnati, and three colleagues designed a poll to measure the uninformed opinion factor in poll research. Their findings show that people who were most likely to volunteer opinions were also those with the least education. With education considered as a constant, African-American respondents were more likely to answer than white participants. It was also found that well-informed opinion holders should not be assumed to know nothing about a subject simply because they answer "don't know" to the details of a particular issue.

669.   Ferber, Robert. "The Effect of Respondent Ignorance on Survey Results." *Journal of the American Statistical Association* 51, no. 276 (December 1956): 576-86.

By random number selection, 647 individuals were chosen from the city directory for Champaign-Urbana, in 1955. The interviewers asked for opinions on four issues. After each opinion was expressed, the interviewer "by repeated questioning" determined the respondent's knowledge on each subject. Each response was labeled "informed," "don't know," or "misinformed." Fewer than 50 percent of those questioned were informed on any of the issues dealing with minimum hourly wages, guaranteed wage, government bond rates of returns as purchase inducement, and the principles of fair trade laws. The misinformed answered to the same degree as the informed. The opinions of the informed differed significantly from the opinions of all the other respondents. Ferber recommends that on issues and topics where ignorance and/or misinformation may be a strong factor, the knowledge level of the respondents should be determined. (9 footnotes)

670. Roper, Elmo. "Classifying Respondents by Economic Status." *Public Opinion Quarterly* 4, no. 2 (June 1940): 270-72.

For this article Roper, who conducts the *Fortune* Surveys, was asked to describe the methods used by the Roper Organization to classify respondents according to economic level. Determining this particular breakdown is as important as the age or sex of the respondent and much more difficult to classify. Roper briefly cites two examples to illustrate the problems involved. Experienced Roper interviewers have, for the past six years, used an economic level designation which accommodates not only geographic variations in average income, but also size of place variations. The divisions are based on a sliding "scale of living" classification ranging from the most affluent at the top to those at the poverty level at the bottom. Roper describes the four categories used when only whites are considered in a survey. Although "rather arbitrary," the definition of income level is viewed as having served satisfactorily.

RESPONSES

ATTITUDE MEASUREMENT DEVICES

671.   Carper, James, and Leonard W. Doob. "Intervening Responses between
        Questions and Answers in Attitude Surveys." *Public Opinion Quarterly*
        17, no. 4 (Winter 1953-54): 511-19.

Carper and Doob investigate the effect on overt responses to six attitude items
of three independent variables. Overt responses are defined as "the objective
ratings on attitude and certainty scales." The statements dealt with equal opportunity and the role of government. The three variables were (1) asking respondents to write down their reasons for agreement or disagreement ("intervening
responses"), (2) ranking the statements by order of acceptance, and (3) giving
respondents a brief communication which stated that "consistency is a virtue" or
"inconsistency is a virtue." The respondents were 120 college students taking an
undergraduate course in psychology. The students were randomly distributed into the twelve groups according to the experimental design. Detailed results are
given and analyzed in terms of the effect of the six variables on overt responses,
intervening responses, and patterning effects. The variables "had essentially no
important or consistent effects upon the overt responses of the subjects in this
experiment." (8 footnotes)

672.   Crespi, Irving. "Use of a Scaling Technique in Surveys." *Journal of Mar-
        keting* 25 (July 1961): 69-72.

The use of a ten-point scaling device, devised by Jan Stapel, is discussed as a
means to determine qualitative aspects such as attitudinal structure. The Stapel
scale features a ten-point nonverbal rating scale ranging from minus five to plus

five, designed to simultaneously determine direction and intensity. The scale is to be used with an adjective list prepared for the particular topic. Crespi compares this approach with semantic differential – a technique in which pairs of contrasting adjectives are tested. The scaling device and the adjective list can be used in personal interviews, as well as through self-administration. Interviewer expenses and skills needed are modest. The approach, which can be used to determine the "social image" of designs, brands, or corporations, quantifies factors which had previously been treated as "qualitative." (4 footnotes)

673.   "Gallupmeter." *Newsweek* 41, no. 26 (29 June 1953): 26.

The American Institute of Public Opinion (AIPO) began to use the Scalometer in 1953. The device, developed by Jan Stapel of the Netherlands, was designed to assist in determining the approximate intensity of approval and disapproval. The Scalometer ranges from minus five to plus five, with the respondent placing a finger on the square which most nearly represents her/his feelings (each number has its own square, for a total of ten squares). The first test by AIPO of the Scalometer was with reaction to President Eisenhower, Secretary of State John Foster Dulles, and Senator Joseph R. McCarthy.

674.   Katz, Daniel. "The Measurement of Intensity." Part 1, Chap. 3 in *Gauging Public Opinion*, by Hadley Cantril and Research Associates in the Office of Public Opinion Research, Princeton University, 51-65. Princeton, NJ: Princeton University Press, 1944. Reprint. Port Washington, NY: Kennikat Press, 1972. 318p.

The issue addressed is how to determine whether an expressed attitude is superficially held or whether it will change only under special circumstances. The techniques used for measuring intensity by the American Institute of Public Opinion are analyzed, with comparisons of self-rating versus interviewer's rating, and the thermometer as a measure of intensity of voting intention. The use of the graded scale to measure intensity is described. An experiment is discussed in which the effectiveness of the various devices for measuring intensity are compared. The four approaches are verbal self-rating, thermometer or self-rating on a graphic numerical scale, the four-step scale, and verbal self-rating on "certainty or sureness of the correctness of one's opinion." Sureness of rating and the thermometer approaches were found to be the "most effective" devices. Katz observes that both the intensity and the direction of an opinion are needed in order to achieve an accurate understanding and to make predictions. (3 footnotes)

BIAS

675.   Adams, J. Stacy. "An Experiment in Question and Response Bias." *Public Opinion Quarterly* 20, no. 3 (Fall 1956): 593-98.

The hypothesis under review is that respondents "tend to inhibit" expression of strongly unfavorable responses. For the investigation Adams considered the responses of 341 individuals. Respondents answered comparative judgment questions on items such as parking facilities, stores, and shopping prices between Winston-Salem and other shopping environments. In varying a question in which the last portion is worded differently ("or worse in Winston-Salem than in other places?" versus "or better in other places than in Winston-Salem?"), it was found that there was "no general tendency for respondents to inhibit the expression of strongly unfavorable responses." In one case, the opposite was observed. Bias occurred as a result of question wording and question topic. Bias was found to stem from socially conflicted subjects, favorably and unfavorably "loaded" response alternatives, and respondents' efforts to provide the "expected" answer. (7 footnotes)

676.   Frankel, Lester R. *The Role of Accuracy and Precision of Response in Sample Surveys*. Modern Marketing Series, no. 7. [New York, NY]: Audits & Surveys, 1971. 14p. [Reprinted from *New Developments in Survey Sampling*, edited by Norman L. Johnson and Harry Smith, Jr. New York, NY: John Wiley & Sons, 1969. 732p.]

Using a statistical presentation, Frankel discusses response bias, reliability of response, response variation, and the amount of information elicited by a question in sample surveys. At issue are the relationships between the questions and the responses and what the implications of these are in terms of the design of the sample survey. The author notes two categories of interest with response, namely, response bias and response precision. Response precision can be subdivided into response error (a function of the measuring instrument, also known as the interviewing procedure), and response variation. Response bias and response error can be minimized, and the costs of achieving these goals can be determined. Response variation can be modified by selecting alternate question formats. (A one-paragraph biographical note and a photograph of Frankel appear on page fourteen.) (4 references)

677.   Gove, Walter R., and Michael R. Geerken. "Response Bias in Surveys of Mental Health: An Empirical Investigation." *American Journal of Sociology* 82, no. 6 (May 1977): 1289-1318.

A probability sample of 2,248 respondents, aged eighteen and over, from the forty-eight contiguous states was interviewed. At the time of the screening interview,

8.8 percent were refusals, and at the time of the interview, there was a 14.5 percent refusal rate. The study was designed to investigate the relationship between sex and marital roles, and mental health. Three types of response bias examined are the tendency to yeasay or naysay, the "perception of the desirability or undesirability of the trait in question," and the need for social approval. Gove and Geerken found that the response bias variables "did not affect the relationships between the demographic variables and the mental health scales." The authors also found that controlling for age diminishes the "already minimal effects" of response bias. Other demographic variables considered include sex, race, education, income, marital status, and occupation. A review of existing literature on response bias is presented. (43 references)

CONSISTENCY

678.   Jaeger, Carol M., and Jean L. Pennock. "An Analysis of Consistency of Response in Household Surveys." *Journal of the American Statistical Association* 56, no. 294 (June 1961): 320-27.

The Jaeger and Pennock investigation sought to determine the degree of respondent accuracy in recalling the type, condition, and model year of their washing machines. As a supplement to the *Current Population Survey* of the Bureau of the Census, the sample consisted of approximately 17,500 households, and was conducted nationwide. The identical questions were asked in two national surveys one year apart from the identical households. The questions were direct, simple, and factual in nature. Of the responses 75 percent were two years or less apart. While there was some inconsistency, there was very little impact for the sample as a whole. The authors note that the "net effect of all inconsistencies in these data is not appreciable." Three tables, one figure, and one chart accompany the text. (6 footnotes)

DON'T KNOW AND NO OPINION

679.   Berger, Philip K., and James E. Sullivan. "Instructional Set, Interview Context, and the Incidence of 'Don't Know' Responses." *Journal of Applied Psychology* 54, no. 5 (October 1970): 414-16.

Berger and Sullivan's research examines a 1966 hypothesis formulated by Webb, et al., (Webb, E. J., D. T. Campbell, R. D. Schwartz, and L. Sechrest. *Unobtrusive Measures: Nonreactive Research in the Social Sciences*. Chicago, IL: Rand McNally, 1966. 225p.) which proposes that emphasizing the respondent's importance to the results of an attitude survey would result in fewer "don't know" responses. A group of 180 college students was administered a twenty-item questionnaire relating to campus life using face-to-face interviews, telephone interviews, and anonymous classroom administration. The experimental group was told that they had been selected through an elaborate scientific process, while the instructions for the control group contained no statement on their importance as part of a scientifically selected sample. The results of this study fail to confirm Webb's "experting" hypothesis. In two of the three contexts (telephone and group administration) there were significantly more "don't know" responses in the experimental group. In the face-to-face context there were no differences between the two instructional set conditions. (4 footnotes, 8 references)

680.   Converse, Jean M. "Predicting No Opinion in the Polls." *Public Opinion Quarterly* 40, no. 4 (Winter 1976-77): 515-30.

Using questions from the *Gallup Opinion Index* 1969-71 and the *Harris Survey Yearbook of Public Opinion 1970*, Converse found that as respondents' education decreases, the number of "no opinion" responses increases. The education level is considered the "single best predictor" of "don't know" (DK) or no opinion answers. A measure of the language complexity of the questions does not show a relationship with DK. Question content, on the other hand, does have predictive value. The nationwide samples were between 1,500 and 1,600 respondents. Using only nonrepeated questions which also provided the researchers with the respondents' education and question characteristics, 198 questions were selected from the Gallup index and 114 from the Harris yearbook. Flesch's "ease-of-reading" formula (Flesch, Rudolf. "A New Readability Yard-stick." *Journal of Applied Psychology* 32 [1948]: 221-33.) was used for the language complexity measure. Task difficulty and question form were two other question characteristics which were examined. These characteristics show effects on no opinion to a greater extent in the Harris data. (9 footnotes, 15 references)

681.   Faulkenberry, G. David, and Robert Mason. "Characteristics of Nonopinion and No Opinion Response Groups." *Public Opinion Quarterly* 42, no. 4 (Winter 1978-79): 533-43.

The results from a 1975 nationwide survey of 1,551 people were used for this study. The topic was the use of windmills for generating electric power. Interviewers were trained to categorize equivocal responses as nonexistent ("don't know") [DK] or ambivalent ("no opinion") opinion states. The respondents were classified into four opinion groups: "DK," "no opinion," "oppose," or "favor." An "among-groups discriminate analysis" was employed using six variables: level of education, awareness, exposure to mass media, familiarity with the subject, city size, and wind energy potential of her/his state of residence. Analysis demonstrates that two groups, DK and no opinion, not only differed from the other two groups, but also from each other. Those individuals whose responses had been classified as nonexistent opinions were less educated, reported less media exposure, and had less knowledge of the topic than those classified as ambivalent. The distinction between these two opinion states must be noted in sample surveys. The authors state near the end of the article: "The data clearly suggest that nonexistent and ambivalent opinion groups should be distinguished from one another empirically and that both opinion states should be allowed to play their respective roles in social science models." (4 footnotes, 9 references)

682.   Francis, Joe D., and Lawrence Busch. "What We Now Know about 'I Don't Knows.' " *Public Opinion Quarterly* 39, no. 2 (Summer 1975): 207-18.

The researchers hypothesized, contrary to existing assumptions, that nonsubstantive responses (NSRs) such as "don't know" [DK] and "no opinion" are not random. The data used to test the hypothesis were the 1960, the 1964, and the 1968 presidential election studies produced at the University of Michigan's Survey Research Center. From these studies a number of questions were selected, and a simple index was created by counting the number of questions for which a DK or a no opinion response was provided by the respondent. The researchers believed that female, nonwhite, low-educated, low-income, and noninvolved respondents with a "feeling of low political efficacy" would provide a predictably high number of DK responses. The hypothesis was substantiated, with NSRs found to be other than random. The authors provide a review of prior research on the topic. (11 footnotes)

683.   Rapoport, Ronald B. "What They Don't Know Can Hurt You." *American Journal of Political Science* 23, no. 4 (November 1979): 805-15.

The use of correlational techniques excludes "don't know" (DK) respondents, which Rapoport argues has had an important effect on many findings regarding attitude stability and constraint. The challenge arises because the results represent only those persons who expressed opinions, which may cause difficulties when generalized to the full sample. Rapoport believes researchers should investigate "to what extent diffidence or discomfort in the interview situation" underlie DK responses. A solution considered is to randomly assign DK respondents. One possibility is that DK respondents would select all possible response categories with equal probability, and alternatively that these individuals would select response categories approaching those of the non-DK respondents. Using the random assignment approach, the author found that "education is as strongly related to attitudinal constraint in 1968 as in 1956," and that "expected relationships between knowledge and attitude stability, among adolescents are substantially strengthened." (8 references)

684.   Schuman, Howard, and Stanley Presser. "The Assessment of 'No Opinion' in Attitude Surveys." Chap. 10 in *Sociological Methodology 1979*,

edited by Karl F. Schuessler, 241-75. The Jossey-Bass Social and Behavioral Science Series. San Francisco, CA: Jossey-Bass Inc., Publishers,
1978. 388p.

One response to the "don't know" (DK) challenge is not to provide the option as
an explicit choice, but rather to record DK only when it is offered by the respondent. A repeated finding is that the DK response correlates with low education. The use of filter questions is discussed. These permit the respondent to make
a "legitimate" response of DK. The former type is referred to as the "standard"
question format. Schuman and Presser experimentally compared the two forms
of the questions in six survey items; five replications of the experiments; one
panel-type follow-up; and a single comparison of two different types of filters.
The experiments were conducted face-to-face and by telephone by a variety of
organizations. The researchers wanted to determine if the availability of the DK
filter increased the number of individuals choosing the option, and if the proportions of individuals choosing the option changed. The study results indicate
that the DK filters can "substantially" increase the proportion of respondents
who select DK responses, and that the increase is related to the filter employed.
Increased DK selection does not seem to be related to the content of the question. The term "floaters" is introduced for individuals who provide an answer to
the standard format, but who provide a DK response when offered a filtered version of the same question. Efforts were undertaken to ascertain the identity of
the floaters, with the observation that floating was the product of "less than average interest or knowledge" concerning the public issues addressed in the survey question. (21 footnotes, 23 references)

EFFECTS

685.   Crane, Ben Michael. "The Silence Effect in Public Opinion." Ph.D. diss.,
        University of Wisconsin, Madison, 1979. 268 leaves. [*Dissertation Ab-
        stracts International* Order No. 8001133; *DAI* 40A, no. 8 (February 1980):
        4284.]

The "silence effect" referred to here concerns the "tendency of individuals to
refrain from publicly expressing their views when those views are perceived to
be in the minority or losing support." Crane's study considers the "quasi-statistical sense" mechanism by which individuals are suspected of gaining awareness of public opinion. The author tested the effect with a cross-sectional telephone survey of Madison, Wisconsin, residents and found that the silence effect
was "consistently observed across three types of dependent measures and two
different public issues." Chapter 1, a review of the literature, contains sections
dealing with the quasi-statistical sense, conformity pressures, the silence effect,
the spiral effect, the unshakable minority, and the notion of involvement. The

rest of the dissertation includes chapters on theory, method, results, and conclusions. Crane repeatedly credits Elisabeth Noelle-Neumann's empirical research into the individual basis of public opinion as the foundation for his efforts, which he suggests are to "seek to inspect, clarify, replicate, and extend her work." Appendixes supply the interviewer with instructions and the research instruments. References are provided.

686.   Johnson, Weldon T., and John D. DeLamater. "Response Effects in Sex Surveys." *Public Opinion Quarterly* 40, no. 2 (Summer 1976): 165-81.

The authors review the two main sources of nonsampling error in survey research: the refusal to be interviewed and the intentional reporting of false information. These factors may be even more problematic when the topic is of a sensitive nature. Two studies which pertained to human sexual behavior are reported. One used a probability sample of 857 unmarried undergraduate students from the University of Wisconsin and a systematic random sample of 504 non-college youth in Madison, Wisconsin. The other study involved face-to-face interviews and self-administered questionnaires with over 2,000 adults and 700 teenagers. The topic was erotic materials. The research was conducted for the Commission on Obscenity and Pornography. Included in the findings are that (1) respondent cooperation in the sex surveys was about the same as in surveys dealing with less sensitive topics, (2) response to sexual topics was not related to gender, sexual experience, rapport, or competence of the interviewer, and (3) self-reported respondent truthfulness also was not associated with interviewer characteristics, or demographic or sexual characteristics of the respondents. The basic problem in sex surveys may lie not with the respondent but with the interviewers' and researchers' feelings toward sex research as evidenced by the high rate of interviewer turnover or refusal. (30 footnotes)

687.   Smith, Tom W. "In Search of House Effects: A Comparison of Responses to Various Questions by Different Survey Organizations." *Public Opinion Quarterly* 42, no. 4 (Winter 1978-79): 443-63.

Differences between the Harris Survey and the General Social Survey on the confidence in leaders questions led the researcher to wonder whether surveys which were both conducted at different times and by different survey organizations (houses) could be used in trend analysis. Smith examines a number of questions and the responses received by different houses (with the date indicated). The author states that the available data suggest that "house effects are not a large and systematic problem." It is recommended that when two surveys are compared, house and other response effects should be checked for. An appendix provides the actual question wording from the surveys compared. (11 footnotes, 21 references)

688.   Sudman, Seymour, and Norman M. Bradburn. *Response Effects in Surveys: A Review and Synthesis*. National Opinion Research Center Monographs in Social Research, no. 16. Chicago, IL: Aldine Publishing Company, [1974]. 257p.

The conceptual framework is discussed, along with a model of the interview, and dependent and independent variables. The main chapters cover task variables, the effects of time and memory factors on response, the effects of respondent and interviewer characteristics on response to attitudinal questions, and what the findings suggest for further research. The results are based on coding studies found in over ninety-five sources, beginning with doctoral dissertations and followed by journals, proceedings, and unpublished manuscripts. Included in the Sudman and Bradburn volume is a 935-item bibliography on the response effects literature from the United States, Britain, France, Germany, and Sweden. Neil Shover, Said Atamna, and Dan Waung compiled the bibliography and coded the items found. A ten-page subject index to the bibliography is included. Two appendixes contain the coding instructions and full distribution of responses from a table presented in the chapter on task variables.

ERROR

689.   Bielby, William T., and Robert M. Hauser. "Response Error in Earnings Functions for Nonblack Males." *Sociological Methods & Research* 6, no. 2 (November 1977): 241-80. [Reprinted in *Survey Design and Analysis: Current Issues*, edited by Duane F. Alwin. Sage Contemporary Social Science Issues, no. 46. Beverly Hills, CA: Sage Publications, 1978. 156p.]

The authors used data from the Income Supplement Reinterview program of the March 1973 *Current Population Survey (CPS)* and from the remeasurement program of the 1973 Occupational Changes in a Generation-II survey. In 1973 the *CPS* data represented about fifty-three million males (civilian noninstitutional) between ages twenty and sixty-five. The authors were surprised at the relative accuracy with which earnings were reported in the *CPS*. It was determined that race affects the reliability of obtained survey data to a considerable degree. In terms of accuracy personal interviews are more so than telephone, which in turn are more accurate than self-administered questionnaires. Bielby and Hauser state in the conclusion that "if CPS respondents do indeed understate the consistency between their schooling and earnings, then the unmediated effects of schooling are understated by as much as twenty percent." Further, they observe that "the degree to which ignoring measurement error leads to understatement of the transmission of social inequality by schooling is neither trivial nor overwhelming." (12 endnotes, 28 references)

690.   Borus, Michael E. "Response Error in Survey Reports of Earnings Information." *Journal of the American Statistical Association* 61, no. 315 (September 1966): 729-38.

Three questions are addressed for individuals dealing with survey data on earnings: (1) "Does response error in the estimation of earnings vary significantly with the characteristics of the samples studied, so that sampling error techniques will not be able to establish a range of values which has a given probability of containing the population parameters?" (2) If there is a positive answer to the first question, which population characteristics would significantly affect the sample values? and (3) What adjustments are necessary to deal with this bias? The study data are based on a sample of 342 respondents who were taking government retraining courses between November 1962 and April 1963. Including the author, a staff of four interviewers was used. The author found that earnings data acquired through sampling a population will not be subject to the sampling error above since the bias of response error is also present. Using regression analysis, Borus found that response error in earnings data "regressed" significantly upon sex, age, education, training status, the amount of earnings reported, interviewer familiarity with the schedule, and the number of hours employed. Borus concludes that adjustments will be required to survey earnings data in order to remove the bias of response error. (20 footnotes, 80 references)

691.   Dutka, Solomon, and Lester R. Frankel. *Let's Not Forget about Response Error.* Modern Marketing Series, no. 12. New York, NY: Audits & Surveys, 1976. 16p.

A number of techniques are described: (1) the detection of response errors (RE); (2) the statistical measurement of RE; (3) ways to eliminate or reduce RE; and (4) minimizing the effects of RE. Statistical procedures are provided to address the various points described above. The RE discussed deals with the replies to questions from interviewers. Specific topics reviewed include detecting response bias, balancing RE and statistical sampling error, weighting responses by degrees of certainty, and "does 'always' mean always."

692.   Haberman, Paul W., and Jill Sheinberg. "Education Reported in Interviews: An Aspect of Survey Content Error." *Public Opinion Quarterly* 30, no. 2 (Summer 1966): 295-301.

The research investigates the differences, at a three-year interval, in the level of educational attainment as reported for the same persons. Two studies are cited: the Master Sample Survey (Study A) and the National Council on Alcoholism (Study B). Study A obtained education information (answered by a family informant) for 7,276 residents of the Washington Heights Health District of New York City in 1960-61. Study B reinterviewed 430 of these people in 1963-64:

alcoholics and their spouses, along with two control groups. Table 1 indicates the response deviations were nearly the same whether the respondent reported for herself/himself or was reported by a family informant. In both studies the responses of approximately "2/5 (37.9 percent) of the total sample varied between the two studies as to educational level attained." Table 3 indicates that males and older respondents had the most discrepancies. Only small discrepancies were found among race and comparison-group status. Comparisons of the data are made with several other studies. Ways of reducing the number of inconsistencies are suggested. (7 footnotes)

693.   Hansen, Morris H., William N. Hurwitz, Eli S. Marks, and W. Parker Mauldin. "Response Errors in Surveys." *Journal of the American Statistical Association* 46, no. 254 (June 1951): 147-90.

Response error is used to mean "non-sampling errors introduced during the course of data collection" which may be caused by the questionnaire design, the interviewing approach, the characteristics, attitudes, or knowledge of the respondent, as well as by a variety of other causes. Hansen, et al., seek the explicit formulation of a mathematical model for response error. The statistical analysis presented applies only when the conditions are those of the specified mathematical model. Considerable experimental evidence is needed to determine whether the model can serve the needs of a given survey. An appendix is titled "Variance of a Sample Mean." Complex statistics appear throughout the article. (8 footnotes, 4 references)

694.   Ito, Rikuma. "An Analysis of Response Error: A Case Study." *Journal of Business* 36, no. 4 (October 1963): 440-47.

The data used in this study are based on a consumer finance survey conducted by the Federal Reserve Board. Questions concerned the amount of consumers' monthly payments and the gross and net amount of their loans on new cars. Ito discusses response bias, the size distribution of response errors, the elements involved in the response errors, and the occupation and financial indebtedness of the head of the responding unit. The author notes the importance of response errors, observes the need for interviewer training and education, and comments on the fact that respondent characteristics cannot be controlled by survey design, but a "system of correction procedures to adjust the deviate estimate" can be developed. (11 footnotes)

695.   Lansing, John B., Gerald P. Ginsburg, and Kaisa Braaten. *An Investigation of Response Error*. Inter-University Committee for Research on Consumer Behavior. Consumer Savings Project. Studies in Consumer Savings, no. 2. Urbana, IL: Bureau of Economic and Business Research, University of Illinois, 1961. 300p.

The Survey Research Center of the University of Michigan conducted a series of studies known as the Consumer Savings Project of the Inter-University Committee for Research on Consumer Behavior. The authors consider the magnitude and direction of response error when conducting financial surveys on savings accounts, loans, and automobile debt. "Response error" is defined as the difference between the reported value of a statistic as compared with the actual value provided in the interview. Lansing, et al., consider only the errors made during the interview and the write-up by the interviewer. The authors attempted to "measure and manipulate" response error. The work is divided into four parts with the first two covering the introduction and preliminary studies, followed by three field experiments in the financial areas described above, and closing with the formulation of a theory of response error. It is suggested that a "psychology" of response error needs to be developed. Ninety-three pages of appendixes provide the information on sampling error, the questionnaires used, split sample study results, and some supplementary tables.

696.   Neter, John, E. Scott Maynes, and R. Ramanathan. "The Effect of Mismatching on the Measurement of Response Errors." *Journal of the American Statistical Association* 60, no. 312 (December 1965): 1005-27.

Two models are developed for dealing with the implications of matching errors which may occur when comparing responses to existing records. The authors found that even "relatively small imperfections" in the matching could lead to "substantial bias in estimating the relationship between response errors and 'true' values." The example studied by Neter, et al., deals with bank accounts, with the sources and frequency of mismatching explained. An appendix contains the derivations for a model. (12 references)

697.   Neter, John, and Joseph Waksberg. *Response Errors in Collection of Expenditures Data by Household Interviews: An Experimental Study.* U.S. Bureau of the Census. Technical Paper No. 11. [Washington, DC]: U.S. Department of Commerce. Bureau of the Census, 1965. 107p. [SuDoc C3.212:11]

The work on this assignment began in 1959 and involved the desire on the part of the Department of Commerce to have a quarterly statistical series on residential maintenance, repairs, additions, and alterations, along with other construction statistics. Residential alterations and repairs expenditures data were collected using household interviews. Neter and Waksberg found that unbounded recall (ordinary recall where expenditures might be included by the respondent which actually occurred in another time period) for the preceding one month, and for the preceding three months, generated an unsatisfactory result due to bias. For large expenditures the three-month recall period may work as satisfactorily as the one-month period. Using a designated respondent is "no more effective than the use of any knowledgeable adult as respondent." If small expenditures are sought, the authors recommend a detailed, probing questionnaire. Panels were used in the study, with each panel consisting of a probability sample of fifty area segments which were selected within a fixed set of seventy primary sampling units. The fifty segments contained 300 households, with 192 resident owners of one to four housing unit properties and 108 renters. (68 references)

INTENSITY

698.   Clover, Vernon T. "Measuring Firmness with Which Opinions Are Held." *Public Opinion Quarterly* 14, no. 2 (Summer 1950): 338-40.

Ten questions, asked of ninety-five respondents, were used in a repeat survey to determine the accuracy of the replies or the firmness with which respondents held opinions. A detailed analysis of the interviewer-completed questionnaires showed very small overall net changes in percentages answering each question in a given manner. However, there were significant differences in the percentages of respondents who changed their answers between the interviews. It was found that changes from "yes" to "no" and vice versa offset one another in the total results. The author concludes that caution must be used in the interpretation of repeat interview results, and that a question-by-question and respondent-by-respondent tabulation of responses is required.

NONRESPONSE

General

699.   Benus, Jacob, and Jean C. Ackerman. "The Problem of Non-Response in Sample Surveys." Chap. 2 in *Working Papers on Survey Research in Poverty Areas*, edited by John B. Lansing, Stephen B. Withey, and Arthur C. Wolfe, et al., 26-59. Ann Arbor, MI: Survey Research Center, Institute for Social Research, University of Michigan, January 1971. 318 pages plus appendixes.

Respondent refusals and absences, along with illness, "mental incapacity," language barriers, and unavailability due to travel, pose the larger portion of nonresponse. Benus and Ackerman explore the consequences of these factors in single-wave studies, followed by consideration of multiwave panel studies. Nonresponse in poverty areas is examined, with a discussion of mobility rates in these areas. The impact of respondent payments on nonresponse is discussed, including the panel study environment. In the studies conducted refusals amounted to approximately one-half of the total nonresponse, with movers between one-fourth and one-third of the total number of respondents lost. The authors state that "in the reported panel studies losses have tended to cumulate to about four out of ten of the original respondents in successive waves over three or four years." One bias which was demonstrated was that individuals with less than a college education "tended to be underrepresented in later waves of a panel." The researchers suggest that respondent payment is a "promising approach" to improving response. (6 footnotes)

700.   Daniel, Wayne W. "Nonresponse in Sociological Surveys: A Review of Some Methods for Handling the Problem." *Sociological Methods & Research* 3, no. 3 (February 1975): 291-307.

Sources of nonresponse include individuals who are not-at-home, refusals, those unable to respond, and respondents who cannot be located. Daniel presents eight techniques for dealing with the problem of nonresponse: (1) the Hansen-Hurwitz method; (2) the Politz-Simmons method; (3) the Kish-Hess replacement procedure; (4) Bartholomew's two-call technique; (5) the Hendricks's extrapolation method; (6) a Bayesian approach; (7) Dalenius's method for dealing with not-at-homes; and (8) Dillman's personalization technique. It is reported that nonrespondents may range from 10 to almost 28 percent of the total sample. Completion rates for private survey companies during the 1960s were between 80 and 85 percent, whereas during the mid-1970s the rate was between 60 and 65 percent. Explanations for the decline include these factors: (1) it is more difficult to find people at home; (2) there are more working women; (3) higher crime rates lead to suspicion of strangers; and (4) there is a growing sensitivity to invasions of privacy. (43 references)

701.   Hawkins, Darnell Felix. "Nonresponse in Detroit Area Study Surveys: A Ten Year Analysis." Ph.D. diss., University of Michigan, 1976. 221 leaves. [*Dissertation Abstracts International* Order No. 7619152; *DAI* 37A, no. 2 (August 1976): 1261.]

Data from ten surveys conducted by the Detroit Area Study of the University of Michigan from 1956 to 1974 are used as a basis for this study. Four questions concerning survey nonresponse are posed and investigated: (1) In what ways does nonresponse (interim) affect the distribution of respondent demographic characteristics? (2) In what ways does nonresponse influence the "calculation of substantive variable values"? (3) How do the demographic characteristics of terminal nonrespondents differ from those of respondents? and (4) What is the impact of nonresponse on the "inferences and conclusions" of current social researchers? Hawkins concludes that nonrespondents, whether interim or terminal, are not "random samples of the larger sample of the surveyed population," and that the nonresponse group is likely to differ in important ways. Also considered is the effect of bias due to nonresponse on social surveys. References are provided.

702.   Hawkins, Darnell Felix. *Nonresponse in Detroit Area Study Surveys: A Ten Year Analysis.* Working Papers in Methodology, no. 8. Chapel Hill, NC: Institute for Research in Social Science, University of North Carolina, 1977. 186p.

Until the mid-1960s academic-based surveys generally reported nonresponse rates of not more than 20 percent. By the mid-1970s surveys in major metropolitan areas were reporting 50 percent nonresponse rates. This study considers nonresponse as a form of measurement error in social surveys. Social survey sampling theory, past nonresponse studies, and an overview of the current study are provided in the introduction. The study methodology is presented, along with chapters on interim distributional bias, interim substantive bias, terminal distributional bias, and estimation of terminal substantive bias. In conclusion Hawkins observes that the "increasingly higher rates of nonresponse add to the possibility of bias due to nonresponse." Six appendixes are provided. (59 references)

703.   Houseman, Earl E. "Statistical Treatment of the Nonresponse Problem." *Agricultural Economics Research* (USDA) 5, no. 1 (January 1953): 12-19.

The response rate for personal interview surveys ranges from as low as 30 percent and often less than 90 percent when only one call per household is made. For mailed questionnaires the response rate can be 5 percent or less or above 80 percent from a single mailing. Houseman recommends three to four visits to a household depending upon the nature of the population and study undertaken. Additionally, it is observed that a 90 percent response is "adequate without attempting to make adjustments for nonresponse." When high precision is necessary, a response rate of over 90 percent may be required. The article addresses the following areas: (1) definition of bias due to nonresponse; (2) substitution and weighting; (3) analysis of successive responses; (4) subsampling of nonrespondents; (5) determination of the optimum number of callbacks; (6) weighting by the reciprocals of the pis; and (7) costs. (7 footnotes)

704.   Loewenstein, Regina, John Colombotos, and Jack Elinson. "Interviews Hardest-to-Obtain in an Urban Health Survey." *Milbank Memorial Fund Quarterly* 47, no. 1, pt. 2 (January 1969): 195-200.

Nonresponse bias was studied by the staff of the Master Sample Survey in the Washington Heights Health District. The characteristics of a subsample of a "hard-to-obtain" sample were investigated. In 1961 a sample of 340 households was selected for intensive field efforts. Two hundred characteristics were investigated, with the researchers finding that very few of those characteristics would have been affected if interviewing had stopped after the initial round with no intensive efforts conducted. Two tables are provided which show the field status of the dwelling units, and the size of the families and the ages of the individuals sampled. (4 footnotes)

705.   Lundberg, George A., and Otto N. Larsen. "Characteristics of Hard-to-Reach Individuals in Field Surveys." *Public Opinion Quarterly* 13, no. 3 (Fall 1949): 487-94.

The study attempts to determine the extent to which those individuals, uncooperative or unavailable during an initial survey, might have affected the outcome of the survey. From a follow-up sample of two hundred people, data on approximately two-thirds of them still could not be obtained – even after repeated efforts. The follow-up took place three months from the original interview in the small town of Mount Vernon, Washington. The follow-up study used two female and three male graduate students as interviewers who located 169 households and obtained personal interviews with forty-four respondents. Mailed questionnaires were also used to test the feasibility of collecting data in that manner. Of the two hundred questionnaires mailed to the sample under investigation, fifty-five were returned. The figures in table 1 illustrate the reasons people could not be reached (such as refusals), those who had relocated, the aged, those not available, and some already interviewed. Analysis of the group finally contacted indicated no real differences in personal characteristics or in response patterns from those of the original survey. It was necessary to make sixty-eight calls to obtain forty-four interviews. More females than males were interviewed in both cases; the percentage of females interviewed in the hard-to-reach category was also considerably greater. (2 footnotes)

706.   Wiseman, Frederick, and Philip McDonald. "Noncontact and Refusal Rates in Consumer Telephone Surveys." *Journal of Marketing Research* 16, no. 4 (November 1979): 478-84.

The objectives of the study were to determine "current levels of the major components of nonresponse" and to identify the procedures and techniques most significantly correlated with the components of the nonresponse rate. Data for the research were provided from a consumer telephone survey of the Marketing Science Institute and the Council of American Survey Research Organizations. The data collection period was for six weeks beginning in March 1978. Noncontact occurs when the respondent (1) is not at home, (2) does not get to the telephone in time, (3) is speaking to someone else, (4) has an unlisted, unpublished, or disconnected number, (5) does not have a telephone, and (6) is not contacted due to a household member(s) refusal to participate. Two factors are seen to influence response rates: many designated respondents are not contacted, and, if contact is made, there is a better than one in four chance of refusal. The authors explore the controllable factors (for example, the number of attempts made to contact an individual), as well as the methodological procedures which can improve telephone response rates. Table 1, "Selected Survey Response Studies and Papers," lists ten of the "more salient" studies dealing with nonresponse. Information provided in the table includes the name of the researcher/sponsor, their affiliation, the source of information, the purpose(s) of the research, and conclusion(s) of the study. There is also a list of the thirty-two firms which agreed to participate in the study. Areas needing further research are addressed. (4 footnotes, 17 references)

707.   Wiseman, Frederick, and Philip McDonald. *The Nonresponse Problem in Consumer Telephone Surveys*. Marketing Science Institute, report no. 78-116. Cambridge, MA: Marketing Science Institute, 1978. 78p.

The study considers noncontact rates, refusal rates, and response rates in telephone surveys. Results indicate that a large percentage of designated respondents/households are not contacted, and even "when contact is made, there is more than a one in four chance that a refusal will result." The findings are based on 182 telephone surveys which attempted one million telephone interviews. The data were supplied confidentially by market research firms and manufacturers conducting surveys. Response rates are often below 40 percent in consumer telephone surveys. Chapters include an introduction; a presentation of the major findings; a review of the literature; a description of the research undertaken; the database created; the noncontact, refusal, and response rates; and conclusions. Appendixes include the tally sheet for telephone interviews and the reporting procedures and guidelines. (18 references)

Bibliography

708.   Hawkins, Darnell Felix. *A Bibliography of Studies of Nonresponse in Survey Research*. IRSS Technical Papers, no. 2. [Chapel Hill, NC]: Institute for Research in Social Science, University of North Carolina at Chapel Hill, 1978. 34p.

The 177 references listed in this bibliography are grouped into five sections (with the number of citation occurrences following the title of the section): (1) descriptive studies - 43; (2) substantive bias studies - 11; (3) remedial studies (field oriented) - 57; (4) remedial studies (statistics oriented) - 39; and (5) general and miscellaneous studies - 27. Most of the studies included deal with ways to reduce nonresponse rates, especially those involving mail questionnaires. The nonresponse literature focuses on the personal interview and mailed surveys in journals, books, and monographs during the past thirty years. There are 3 references from the 1930s, 30 from the 1940s, 33 from the 1950s, 62 from the 1960s, and 49 from the 1970s. A few of the entries are foreign publications. Annotation length varies from one sentence to 105 words; 81 (45 percent) of the entries have no annotation. *Public Opinion Quarterly* is the most frequently cited journal with 48 entries. Other frequently cited journals are the *Journal of Marketing*, the *Journal of the American Statistical Association*, the *Journal of Marketing Research*, and the *International Journal of Opinion and Attitude Research*.

NONRESPONSE BIAS

General

709.   Birnbaum, Z. W., and Monroe G. Sirken. "Bias Due to Non-Availability in Sampling Surveys." *Journal of the American Statistical Association* 45, no. 249 (March 1950): 98-111.

An approach is presented for dealing with the errors caused by nonavailability of respondents. The technique discussed is considered in terms of the sample size used, as well as the number of callbacks conducted. Variance and survey costs are related to the preceding factors. The authors then demonstrate how precision can be optimized at a certain cost by "playing sampling error against the bias" resulting from unavailable respondents. The article uses advanced statistics. (12 references)

710.   Deming, W. Edwards. "On a Probability Mechanism to Attain an Economic Balance between the Resultant Error of Response and the Bias of Non-Response." *Journal of the American Statistical Association* 48, no. 264 (December 1953): 743-72.

The nonresponse discussed here includes individuals not at home, as well as those who refuse to respond. Refusals can be permanent or temporary. The time spent at home and the "firmness" of the temporary refusal comprise Deming's graded series of classes. He states: "The bias of nonresponse arises from the variation of any characteristic from one class to another. The variance of response arises from the variation of any characteristic from one member to another within a single class, and from the random variation in the number of responses therefrom." Increasing the initial sample size will not have an effect on the bias of nonresponse. Successive recalls will decrease the response bias. Without recalls, no matter the sample size, the results are questionable. The first two recalls in this study reduced the bias by 50 percent. A complete count often "represents an extreme waste of effort." Deming proposes a mechanism for determining the most useful level for balancing response error with nonresponse bias. The Politz plan is discussed [Item No. 617]. (12 footnotes)

711. Dunkelberg, William C., and George S. Day. "Nonresponse Bias and Call-backs in Sample Surveys." *Journal of Marketing Research* 10, no. 2 (May 1973): 160-68. [Reprinted in *Readings in Survey Research*, edited by Robert Ferber, 154-68. Chicago, IL: American Marketing Association, 1978. 604p.]

Callbacks are conducted to contact individuals who were not reached in the first or subsequent attempts. The first attempt in a personal interview sample survey yields between 25 and 30 percent, with about the same results on the first call-back. With the third and subsequent attempts, the number of completed interviews declines rapidly. A callback policy balances the reduced yield from further callbacks versus the advantages of a more representative sample. The study indicates that it is possible to calculate the number of calls necessary in order to achieve a certain level of accuracy. The article includes nine tables showing the impact of a variety of variables such as occupation, income, sex, the number of earners in the family, marital status, and race. The results show that for most of the above, the variables were found to "converge on their population values after two or three callbacks." The value of callback effort in relation to accuracy can be determined in terms of cost estimates per additional call. (4 footnotes, 12 references)

712. Hawkins, Darnell F. "Estimation of Nonresponse Bias." *Sociological Methods & Research* 3, no. 4 (May 1975): 461-88.

A review of past studies dealing with nonresponse is presented, followed by a discussion of wave analysis and the problem of interim nonresponse. The 1973 Detroit Area Study (DAS) was used in the analysis of the interviewing process. The article also considers the estimation of terminal nonresponse bias. Hawkins notes that his presentation will need to be duplicated by others to determine if the approach is reliable for estimating nonresponse bias. The Race Discrimination item in the DAS receives considerable attention. It is observed that more middle-aged and older individuals' opinions were missing from the data, with younger respondents' opinions included because they are "inclined to accept interviews." The older respondents who do participate may have views "vastly different" from the older individuals who do not participate. Hawkins suggests greater persuasion efforts for middle-aged respondents, as well as using subsampling and oversampling. Four tables, six endnotes, and eighteen bibliographic entries are provided.

713. Kish, Leslie, and Irene Hess. "A 'Replacement' Procedure for Reducing the Bias of Non-Response." *American Statistician* 13, no. 4 (October 1959): 17-19.

The procedure is to include, with survey addresses, some nonresponse addresses from previous surveys in which the sampling approach was similar. The authors state that "interviews from the former nonresponse addresses became 'replacements' for survey addresses which result in nonresponses." Kish and Hess suggest that this procedure is particularly valuable to organizations which frequently use similar sampling methods. The Survey Research Center at the University of Michigan has used the replacement procedure for the "not-at-home" group of nonresponses, and plans to use the approach with refusals as well. The authors hope to see this research tested further, at margin cost, with a number of field projects conducted by other investigators. (8 references)

714.   Lagay, Bruce W. "Assessing Bias: A Comparison of Two Methods." *Public Opinion Quarterly* 33, no. 4 (Winter 1969-70): 615-18.

Two techniques, the check data method and the dependent variable method, were used to estimate the influence of nonresponse on several variables. The first approach explored the comparison of response and nonresponse groups by using selected demographic data. Registries, census materials, and field visits were used to gather information. The second method attempted to locate and interview a subsample of persons who had been originally excluded, and then to compare that group with the original group with reference to the major dependent variable (family social functioning) under consideration. Extensive tracking methods, using informants, involved the telephone, the postal service, and field visiting. The sample consisted of 118 families, 59 for each method. Results suggest no significant differences between families in the bias study subsample and respondents in the originally interviewed subsample on race, birth legitimacy, type of dwelling, type of neighborhood, and so forth. The two samples differ significantly in dependent variable score distributions, demonstrating "the existence of a significant positive sampling bias." A limitation of the study is noted. (9 footnotes)

715.   O'Neil, Michael J. "Estimating the Nonresponse Bias Due to Refusals in Telephone Surveys." *Public Opinion Quarterly* 43, no. 2 (Summer 1979): 218-32.

O'Neil reviews some of the recent studies on the problem of nonresponse, noting that many fail to observe the nature of the differences between respondents and nonrespondents. Further, respondents who are never reached must be distinguished from those who refuse to be interviewed. The latter can have an effect of "unknown magnitude" on sample estimates. The present research attempts to show comparable data for telephone surveys and to identify the characteristics and effects of refusals. Data were derived from a random-digit-dialed general population survey of 1,209 households in Chicago. Extensive callbacks and follow-up letters were used. With these procedures the completion rate increased from 74.5 percent to 86.8 percent. Two measures for "quantifiable nonsubjective assessment" were introduced and applied under a wide range of conditions. Findings indicate the following: (1) resistors were disproportionately blue-collar and service workers; (2) resistors tended to have less education and lower incomes; (3) whites, Poles, Germans, and the Irish were overrepresented among resistors, while African Americans and Scandinavians were more likely to be amenable; (4) religion was not a factor; (5) respondents over age sixty-five were especially likely to be resistors; (6) homeowners exhibited the strongest tendency to be resistors; and (7) resistors may be less socially active than other respondents. The author states that "comparing these findings with other research provides strong evidence that the effects of nonresponse on sample estimates do depend on whether nonresponse is due to insufficient numbers of callbacks or to explicit refusals." Implications of the study for future research are explored. (8 footnotes, 32 references)

716.   Wilcox, James B. "The Interaction of Refusal and Not-at-Home Sources of Nonresponse Bias." *Journal of Marketing Research* 14, no. 4 (November 1977): 592-97.

The major sources of nonresponse bias are refusals and not-at-homes. Refusals decline to cooperate and the not-at-homes are unavailable when the interviewer calls. The methodology used to examine the interaction of the two sources described above involved a sample of 1,125, with 947 (84 percent) reached after three telephone calls, and 52 (29 percent) of 178 refusers responding to at least one question dealing with education, family size, and income. The results show that "less well-educated respondents were easier to find at home, but were more hesitant to cooperate," and that "it was slightly easier to find adult members of larger families" at home. Wilcox suggests that both sources of nonresponse bias be considered in the "design of corrective techniques and in estimates of nonresponse effects." (27 references)

Bibliography

717.   Daniel, Wayne W. *Statistical Adjustment for Nonresponse in Sample Surveys: A Selected Bibliography with Annotations*. Public Administration Series: Bibliography no. P-339. Monticello, IL: Vance Bibliographies, 1979. 11p.

This annotated bibliography is concerned with techniques for dealing with the problem of nonresponse, specifically the "statistical adjustment for nonresponse bias after the data have been calculated." The 47 references, arranged alphabetically by author, consist of these categories: 31 journal articles, 11 books, 4 papers and proceedings, and 1 report. The bibliography includes works from the following time periods: 4 from the 1940s; 12 from the 1950s; 8 from the 1960s; 22 from the 1970s; and 1 undated. Journals cited most frequently include the *Journal of the American Statistical Association* (6 entries); *Public Opinion Quarterly* (4 entries); and the *Journal of Marketing Research* (3 entries). A few are foreign citations. Annotations range in length from 7 words to approximately 148 words. One annotated bibliography by Hawkins [Item No. 708] is listed. A number of studies are by, and deal with, the work of Politz and Simmons [Item No. 617] and Hansen and Hurwitz [Item Nos. 161 and 179]. (4 footnotes)

Weighting

718.   Mandell, Lewis. "When to Weight: Determining Nonresponse Bias in Survey Data." *Public Opinion Quarterly* 38, no. 2 (Summer 1974): 347-52.

Two examples are used to illustrate how differential nonresponse can introduce bias in population estimates since response rate is not uniform across all segments of the population. The researcher must decide if there is enough bias present to develop weights. Mandell examines the criteria which he feels are important considerations in determining how and when to weight for nonresponse. He states: "The Omega [statistic] does not vary with the dependent variable that is being considered; it states the bias as a proportion of the difference in subgroup means of any variable in the study. It allows the researcher to establish one criterion for maximum allowable nonresponse bias and weight only for those subgroups where the value of [the Omega symbol] exceeds that criteria." The symbol in the quotation refers to the "bias in the estimate of a population mean expressed as a proportion of the difference between subgroup means." Advanced statistics are used throughout the article. (3 footnotes)

OVERREPORTING AND UNDERREPORTING

719.   Cannell, Charles F., Gordon Fisher, and Thomas Bakker. *Reporting of Hospitalization in the Health Interview Survey.* In *Health Statistics from the U.S. National Health Survey*, Series D, No. 4. Washington, DC: U.S. Department of Health, Education, and Welfare, Public Health Service, May 1961. 71p. [SuDoc FS2.85:D-4]

The report was prepared by the Survey Research Center of the Institute for Social Research at the University of Michigan. The main focus of the study was to examine the problem of underreporting of hospital episodes, to determine which types of hospitalizations were underreported, and to investigate response errors. The sample consisted of individuals with one or more hospital discharges from twenty-one facilities from 1 April 1958 through 31 March 1959. Interviewers were not told the purpose of the study out of concern for more vigorous probing for hospital episodes. Interviews were conducted with 1,505 individuals. Cannell and his coauthors determined that forgetting and respondent motivation were important factors in underreporting. Respondents with a "low level of motivation" did not try very hard to recall hospitalizations. Reported hospital episodes are compared with hospital records, with underreporting based on length of stay, diagnosis, and time between the interview and the hospital stay tabulated. Follow-up interviews were conducted with individuals who did not report one or more hospital episodes. Persons with low family income were more likely to underreport, as were "nonwhites," and as the time between episode and interview increased. Individuals who did not "enjoy" the interview tended to be less consistent in reporting hospitalizations. Misreporting of the characteristics of hospitalization is examined, with attention to the reported length of stay and the diagnoses and operations causing hospitalization. Four appendixes provide data on sample errors; nonresponse; diagnoses and operations rated by degree of embarrassment or threat; the hospitals involved in the study; and the forms and questionnaires utilized. (3 footnotes)

720.   Haberman, Paul W., and Jack Elinson. "Family Income Reported in Surveys: Husbands versus Wives." *Journal of Marketing Research* 4, no. 2 (May 1967): 191-94.

For this research 645 marital pairs were included in a survey of 2,118 respondents. Identical interviews were conducted with husbands and wives, thereby providing the researchers the opportunity to compare how annual family income was reported. The results show that "three fifths of the pairs reported the same income, using thirteen intervals. The ratio of husbands to wives reporting higher income was about three to two." Generally, the inconsistencies that were reported reflected wives' underreporting family income. Haberman and Elinson suggest that for most purposes income reports from either spouse are adequate. Two other studies are cited (University of Illinois, 1951 and 1952, and the National Council on Alcoholism, 1963 and 1964) in which reports were obtained from husbands and wives. Their data are comparable, with 71 percent of the pairs agreeing on family income. (4 references)

721.   Levine, James P. "The Potential for Crime Overreporting in Criminal Victimization Surveys." *Criminology* 14, no. 3 (November 1976): 307-30.

Methodological weaknesses of survey research are responsible for a range of distortions and the production of "overblown crime rates out of proportion to the real level of crime," according to Levine. He maintains that "undue faith" has been placed in victimization surveys. Respondent concealment and provision of fake information are discussed. The results of ten studies are cited in which incorrect information was given, with the percentage in each case specified. Memory problems as well as outright lying are considered. Also reviewed are interviewer biases, coding unreliability, and measuring response error. Levine believes an index should be established which averages the official crime records with survey results. It is suggested that the notion that massive amounts of crime go unreported to the police should be viewed skeptically. The author is concerned about the proliferation of unsound data as harmful to the field of criminology and to what is known about the "characteristics of victims, perpetrators, and crimes." (1 footnote, 50 references)

722.   Mandell, Lewis, and Lorman L. Lundsten. "Some Insight into the Underreporting of Financial Data by Sample Survey Respondents." *Journal of Marketing Research* 15, no. 2 (May 1978): 294-99.

In 1973 the Survey Research Center of the University of Michigan conducted a study designed to test various methods which would increase the degree of reporting of financial data by sample survey respondents. A list of 150 addresses was provided by a local bank for savings accounts with over $10,000. No names were supplied. Seventy-six respondents completed all or part of the interview; a total of forty-nine completed the additional resource form. The latter respondents each received twenty-five dollars or an equal gift to a charity of their choice for agreeing to complete the resource book. The authors believe that the additional survey costs to complete the study were "not justified by the gains in reported balances." The more detailed the questions asked, as well as the financial motivation provided, did somewhat improve the reporting of financial assets. (3 footnotes, 11 references)

723.   Parry, Hugh J., Mitchell B. Balter, and Ira H. Cisin. "Primary Levels of Underreporting Psychotropic Drug Use." *Public Opinion Quarterly* 34, no. 4 (Winter 1970-71): 582-92.

The research, part of a larger long-term study, examines the validity of respondents' reporting of their own use of psychotropic or psychotherapeutic drugs (that is, sedatives, stimulants, and tranquilizers). The respondents were white residents of low-socioeconomic status from a midwestern city. The interviewers, who worked "blind," administered the questionnaire. The complex methodology involved three experimental groups and three comparison groups of approximately 150 to 200 persons each. Antibiotic use was obtained as a comparison since these drugs do not have social stigma attached to them. A special color photo-chart showing the antibiotics was used. The findings were as follows: (1) tranquilizer users were most likely to give valid responses; (2) stimulant users were most likely to provide only partially valid answers; (3) valid levels for psychotropic drug users were about 10 percent higher than for the antibiotic users; (4) visual aids and more intensive questioning appeared to reduce levels of invalidity; (5) certain factors such as low education, uncooperative attitude, sex (males), and language problems were found to be associated with invalid responses; and (6) antibiotic users had a significantly lower validity of response. Explanations for the findings are offered. (13 footnotes)

RANDOMIZED RESPONSE MODEL

724.   Abul-Ela, Abdel-Latif A., Bernard G. Greenberg, and Daniel G. Horvitz. "A Multiproportions Randomized Response Model." *Journal of the American Statistical Association* 62, no. 319 (September 1967): 990-1008.

An extension of a technique developed by Warner [Item No. 739] is presented. At issue is the problem that respondents will either not reply or will lie if they believe that the answer will "stigmatize" them in front of the interviewer. The authors expand the randomized response model to a trichotomous technique. As respondents may lie with any interviewing technique, comparisons of different approaches are shown. The approach was found to "work only with highly skilled interviewers and on more intelligent respondents." Suggestions are provided for improvements in field technique. Advanced statistics are used throughout the article. (6 references)

725.   Folsom, Ralph E., Bernard G. Greenberg, Daniel G. Horvitz, and James R. Abernathy. "The Two Alternate Questions Randomized Response Model." *Journal of the American Statistical Association* 68, no. 343 (September 1973): 525-30.

The model described moves the randomized response model to another mode, one in which two nonsensitive alternative questions are asked in conjunction with the sensitive questions. The approach was field-tested in 1971 by the Research Triangle Institute. The probability sample consisted of persons sixteen years of age and older from Mecklenburg County, North Carolina. Individuals who drink alcohol were the sought-after population. The format and questions asked are presented, along with the instructions which respondents received on the randomizing technique. The efficiency of this approach is mathematically compared with Moors's optimized version of the standard two-sample single-alternate question model (Moors, J. J. A. "Optimization of the Unrelated Question Randomized Response Model." *Journal of the American Statistical Association* 66, no. 335 [September 1971]: 627-29.), as well as with the one-sample single-alternative question model. Advanced statistics are used throughout the article. (13 references)

726.   Liu, P. T., and L. P. Chow. "A New Discrete Quantitative Randomized Response Model." *Journal of the American Statistical Association* 71, no. 353 (March 1976): 72-73.

The randomized response technique (RRT) is expanded to include gathering discrete quantitative data on sensitive problems. The authors maintain that RRT is simple and more efficient than existing models. The device used contains a number of red and white colored balls. The ball-shaped object has a small "window" protruding from the surface which will accommodate one ball. The unit is shaken and turned upside down so that one ball appears in the window. The authors also suggest an alternative approach – namely, dice with colored and numbered faces. The estimation of the parameters is presented (employing advanced statistics). (6 references)

727.   Maceli, John C. *How to Ask Sensitive Questions without Getting Punched in the Nose.* Modules in Applied Mathematics, no. 35. [Washington, DC]: Mathematical Association of American, 1976. 16 leaves.

The random response model (RRM) is presented as an approach to use in survey research. The model permits the researcher to determine the properties of a human population possessing a sensitive characteristic without being able to identify a particular respondent's answer. In RRM the respondent provides answers that "furnish information only on a probability basis." This module in applied mathematics is intended for use in a one-hour college classroom presentation, and requires the knowledge of elementary probability. The module provides examples of RRM. Examples are also given for the unrelated question model (UQM). The uses of RRM and UQM are discussed, followed by classroom suggestions and problems. An appendix contains a short randomized response survey. A fifteen-entry annotated bibliography is provided.

728.   Wiseman, Frederick, Mark Moriarty, and Marianne Schafer. "Estimating Public Opinion with the Randomized Response Model." *Public Opinion Quarterly* 39, no. 4 (Winter 1975-76): 507-13.

In October 1974 sensitive questions covering racial, political, and moral topics were asked through both direct personal interviews and self-administered questionnaires. The randomized response model (RRM) was then implemented to "estimate public sentiment" on these issues. There were 340 respondents for the RRM group and 198 each for the personal interview and questionnaire formats. The results were compared. The authors found that the results using RRM were "similar" to the personal interview data, but "dissimilar" to the questionnaire results. The authors believe that this is the first use of RRM to gauge public opinion. Explanations for the variance are covered, including discussions of the interviewers, the samples, time lapse, questions of confidence in the randomizing device (white, blue, and red poker chips), and confusion on the part of respondents concerning the method. (8 footnotes)

RANDOMIZED RESPONSE TECHNIQUE

General

729.   Barksdale, William Benjamin. "New Randomized Response Techniques for Control of Non-Sampling Errors in Surveys." Ph.D. diss., University of North Carolina at Chapel Hill, 1971. 221 leaves. [*Dissertation Abstracts International* Order No. 7210689; *DAI* 32B, no. 9 (March 1972): 5053.]

The research "extends and applies" randomized response techniques to situations in which the joint frequencies of two attributes (of which one or both may be "stigmatizing") must be located. Methods examined include the following: (1) a direct question is asked, the randomized response technique is utilized, or a standardized version of the alternate question technique is employed (in the latter a respondent is simply asked to answer "yes" or "no" as indicated by a randomizing device); and (2) the randomizing device "chooses between the two attributes" and the respondent is requested to tell if the trait the device has chosen is one that she/he possesses. Another device is used to repeat the procedure, again producing two answers. The results of a small field trial involving method 2 are presented. A definition of a "generalized mean square error measure" is given and determined for each method. Also considered are bias, variance, sample size, randomizing proportions, nonresponse, and/or untruthfulness of the responses "using mean square error efficiency for the comparison of methods." References are provided.

730.   Boruch, Robert F. "Assuring Confidentiality of Responses in Social Research: A Note on Strategies." *American Sociologist* 6, no. 4 (November 1971): 308-11.

The question investigates how a researcher can gain a truthful answer when that answer might lead to "social or legal sanctions against the respondent or the researcher." The randomized response technique (RRT) is presented as one means to address this challenge. Simplification of the RRT is suggested, as well as an extension for longitudinal data. Another alternative discussed employs administrative models in which longitudinal data are consolidated. The respondent is given this data and a sheet with the question of primary interest on which the answer(s) is marked. The sheets are returned with identification. (3 footnotes, 8 references)

731.   Fligner, Michael A., George E. Policello II, and Jagbir Singh. "A Comparison of Two Randomized Response Survey Methods with Consideration for the Level of Respondent Protection." *Communications in Statistics: Theory and Methods* A6, no. 15 (1977): 1511-24.

Warner's randomized response technique [Item No. 739] and the unrelated question method are compared. Both techniques are designed to improve accuracy and honesty in surveys dealing with sensitive questions. The level of protection provided to the respondent is considered. Estimations for both approaches are compared, with the observation that "what previous authors have claimed to be the maximum likelihood estimators of the population proportion with the sensitive characteristics, are in fact not the maximum likelihood estimators." The authors conclude that parameters can be selected for the unrelated question scheme which will provide the same protection as found with Warner's technique. (12 references)

732.   Greenberg, Bernard G., James R. Abernathy, and Daniel G. Horvitz. "A New Survey Technique and Its Application in the Field of Public Health." *Milbank Memorial Fund Quarterly* 48, no. 4, pt. 2 (October 1970): 39-55.

A survey was conducted in five metropolitan areas of central North Carolina in which a randomized response device was used to ensure that the respondents' personal situation was not revealed. Three different survey samples were employed; the sizes used were 750, 1,300, and 1,600 females. Most of the respondents believed that the approach was legitimate. The topic dealt with induced abortion, oral contraceptive use, emotional problems, and the views of the respondents regarding the random response procedure. The authors were "generally satisfied with the findings." Three tables are presented, providing responses to each of the survey question areas, and broken down by race, age, education, and number of pregnancies. (8 references)

733.   Greenberg, Bernard G., Roy R. Kuebler, Jr., James R. Abernathy, and Daniel G. Horvitz. "Application of the Randomized Response Technique in Obtaining Quantitative Data." *Journal of the American Statistical Association* 66, no. 334 (June 1971): 243-50.

The randomized response technique (RRT) is extended from categorical responses to quantitative responses. RRT is designed to "eliminate evasive answer bias in sensitive questions." The theory of the use of RRT for quantitative applications is presented. The example discussed involved the estimation of induced abortion rates as part of the North Carolina Abortion Study. Four probability samples of adult females were selected from five urban areas in North Carolina. The results from the study indicate the estimates and variances of the mean number of abortions induced during a lifetime, as well as the mean income of heads of households. Advanced statistics are used throughout the article. (10 references)

734. Hochberg, Yosef, Jane C. Stutts, and Donald W. Reinfurt. *The Randomized Response Technique: A Review and Application.* Prepared for the U.S. Department of Transportation, National Highway Safety Administration. Chapel Hill, NC: Highway Safety Research Center, University of North Carolina, 1976. 92p.

The authors seek to determine the applicability of the randomized response technique (RRT) to highway safety research. The report is divided into five chapters beginning with a brief introduction, and followed by an outline of the theoretical development of the technique employing advanced mathematics. Chapter 3 considers field application of RRT. Chapter 5 contains discussion and recommendations. The original 1965 article on RRT by Warner [Item No. 739] is cited. As of 1977, the authors conclude that "much additional field research is needed before the technique can be of any great value to highway safety researchers." The authors note that RRT might be more appropriately named "randomized question technique." Four appendixes, including the cover letter and questionnaire form for several randomized response pilot studies, are provided. (24 references)

735. Lamb, Charles W., Jr., and Donald E. Stem, Jr. "An Empirical Validation of the Randomized Response Technique." *Journal of Marketing Research* 15, no. 4 (November 1978): 616-21.

The randomized response model (RRM) is reported to be successful in minimizing measurement error. The model also provides more accurate estimates of sensitive behavior than do conventional interview techniques. A convenience sample of 312 students was used for this study. The sensitive item was failure of college courses. This proved not to be a sensitive issue; however, frequency of failure was. Three different techniques using the RRM were employed: qualitative, quantitative, and ratio estimates. Lamb and Stem write that the improved estimation provided by the three techniques described should be useful for marketing studies on sensitive issues – such as in consumption and shopping behavior studies. Advanced mathematics is utilized to show the calculations for the various RRMs. (14 references)

736. Liu, P. T., L. P. Chow, and W. H. Mosley. "Use of the Randomized Response Technique with a New Randomizing Device." *Journal of the American Statistical Association* 70, no. 350 (June 1975): 329-32.

Previous randomizing devices have consisted of tossing a coin or coins and using different colored balls in a box, a deck of cards, and tables of random numbers. The device considered here consists of a container in the shape of a flask with a "body" and a long "neck" with colored balls inside. The technique is intended to produce both discrete quantitative and qualitative data on sensitive questions. The colored balls represent different sensitive characteristics. The efficiency of estimates is discussed, as well as a numerical example dealing with the question of how many times the respondent has had sexual relations other than with their legally married spouse. The study shows that the accuracy of the randomized response technique can be increased through the improvement of the randomizing device. The authors observe that a drawback of the approach is that the device is complicated. Advanced statistics are used throughout the article. (16 references)

737.   Pohl, Barbikay Bissell, and Norval Frederick Pohl. "Random Response Technique for Reducing Non-Sampling Error in Interview Survey Research." *Journal of Experimental Education* 44, no. 1 (Fall 1975): 48-53.

Three variations of the randomized response technique (RRT) are discussed. The Warner technique [Item No. 739] permits the person being interviewed to make a "random" selection of one of a pair of directly opposite questions. Simmons developed an approach known as "unrelated question RRT" in which the respondent selects from unrelated questions rather than the dichotomized Warner method (Greenberg, B. G., A.-L. A. Abul-Ela, W. R. Simmons, and D. G. Horvitz. "The Unrelated Question Randomized Response Model: Theoretical Framework." *Journal of the American Statistical Association* 64: [1969]: 520-39.). Simmons's approach is designed to avoid respondent confusion with the opposite question choice. A third alternative suggested by Greenberg [see above reference] involves a single question with the respondent able to select the three possible answers. All the variations are designed to avoid both refusal bias and response bias and to maintain the privacy of respondents. Randomizing mechanisms used to date include spinners, plastic boxes filled with colored balls, decks of cards, and random number tables. (4 footnotes, 14 references)

738.   Shimizu, Iris M., and Gordon Scott Bonham. "Randomized Response Technique in a National Survey." *Journal of the American Statistical Association* 73, no. 361 (March 1978): 35-39.

The randomized response technique (RRT), using two unrelated questions in separate half-samples (with a coin as the randomizing device), was employed in the 1973 National Survey of Family Growth. The purpose of the study was to produce an estimate of the number of females having abortions during a twelve-month period. There were 9,797 respondents, with 98.5 percent providing "yes" or "no" answers. The results indicate higher estimates for abortions than had been reported previously. The authors caution against placing too much confidence in any one estimate, as survey errors may be a factor. Although RRT has been used for about ten years, field administration and analysis still require further refinement. (3 footnotes, 11 references)

739.   Warner, Stanley L. "Randomized Response: A Survey Technique for Eliminating Evasive Answer Bias." *Journal of the American Statistical Association* 60, no. 309 (March 1965): 63-69.

Responses to questions which call for personal or controversial information may be met with no answer or with incorrect answers. Warner proposes an environment in which the answers are provided on a probability basis, thereby permitting the respondent to reveal less or nothing to the interviewer. A mathematical model for random responses for proportions is presented. Several tables are provided which compare the randomized and regular estimates for two different levels of true probability. (2 footnotes, 5 references)

740.   Zdep, S. M., Isabelle N. Rhodes, R. M. Schwarz, and Mary J. Kilkenny. "The Validity of the Randomized Response Technique." *Public Opinion Quarterly* 43, no. 4 (Winter 1979-80): 544-49.

The validity of the randomized response technique (RRT) is examined. Developed by Warner in 1965 [Item No. 739], the technique is used to obtain reliable data when dealing with sensitive issues on surveys (in this case marijuana use). RRT offers an alternative to direct questioning although it is costly and difficult to administer. A national probability sample of 2,084 adults was involved in the research. Using a randomizing device, results were compared for the question, "Have you at any time used marijuana?" with results obtained independently by using one of two nonsensitive direct questions. Estimates of marijuana use were slightly greater for the RRT group (24 percent versus 21 percent), supporting the authors' hypothesis. Also, as predicted, the discrepancy between RRT and direct questioning varied by age groups, with the youngest group yielding similar results. For the three groups over age twenty-six RRT found greater marijuana use than did direct questioning. Neither sex nor race comparisons showed significant differences between techniques. Implications of the research for studies involving even more sensitive topics are discussed. (17 references)

Bibliography

741.   Daniel, Wayne W. *Collecting Sensitive Data by Randomized Response: An Annotated Bibliography.* Research Monograph no. 85. Atlanta, GA:

Publishing Services Division, College of Business Administration, Georgia State University, 1979. 113p.

Both the theoretical and the application aspects of the randomized response technique are the focus of this bibliography. Daniel's nine-page introduction provides a background on nonresponse and explains Warner's 1965 effort [Item No. 739] to overcome the difficulties associated with gathering sensitive data. The bibliography contains 145 annotated entries and 17 unannotated entries (with the number of citation occurrences following the title of the section): various published and unpublished reports and studies - 58; journal articles - 56; conference proceedings and papers - 33; theses and dissertations - 8; and books and chapters in books - 7. The chronological arrangement shows the following breakdown: 1965-69 (10 entries); 1970-79 (146 entries); and undated (5 entries). Of the journal entries, 18 are from the *Journal of the American Statistical Association*, with the rest from a wide variety of journals such as the *International Statistical Review* and *Social Science Research*. The author uses alternative sources for the same or similar study (for example, research issued originally as a report might also have been published as a journal article). Approximately 40 items are from foreign countries, primarily Sweden. An author index is included. (5 footnotes)

RESPONSE RATES

742.   Carroll, Stephen J., Jr., and Alfred M. Falthzik. "Research Note on Some Factors Related to Completion Rates in Surveys of Employed Persons." *Psychological Reports* 35, no. 1, pt. 2 (August 1974): 377-78.

Carroll and Falthzik review five studies which consider completion rates. In each case Carroll was one of the researchers. The research discussed in this article involves the effect on response rate when interviewers claim they are from Marketing Facts, Incorporated (a fictitious firm), as compared with claiming they are from a local university. Eighty salespersons were randomly selected using a Polk directory. The subject of the survey was the incentive compensation received by salespersons. The results indicate that those interviewed by the university representative achieved a "significantly higher" response rate. The authors maintain that the "better known and more trustworthy source" led to the higher rate. (8 references)

743.   Hill, Stuart L. "Increasing the Response Rate for Structured Interviews in Community Research." *American Behavioral Scientist* 11, no. 3 (January-February 1968): 47-48.

With the increasing rate of refusals, Hill tested an alternative method of getting the attention of potential respondents. By reproducing a copy of the local newspaper story about the research activities of the community poll, and sending a newspaper photograph of the investigator two to three days before the interviewer arrived, a completion rate of 98 percent was achieved. A pretest without the mailing produced a refusal rate of four out of twelve homes. The newspaper used was the community weekly mailed free to residents of the area. The topic of the poll covered community development and membership in local associations. A random sample of 175 residents received the mailings. A personally addressed typed letter using university letterhead – assuring anonymity – was sent. Successful responses were achieved in 172 households. Hill believes the approach used was instrumental in establishing the credibility and integrity of the researcher, but that perhaps the technique will work best in small communities with a widely read local paper. (2 footnotes)

744.   Kviz, Frederick J. "Toward a Standard Definition of Response Rate." *Public Opinion Quarterly* 41, no. 2 (Summer 1977): 265-67.

Survey researchers use differing estimates of response rate, leading to methodological difficulties in interpreting and comparing data. Kviz defines response rate as "the proportion of all sample members who are eligible to participate in the survey from whom a complete and usable set of data is collected." Response rate equals the number of completed interviews or questionnaires divided by the number of eligible sample members. Briefly addressed are the problems of low response rates (refusals, ill respondents, those who cannot be located, or those whose language is unknown to the interviewer) and the temptation of some researchers to exclude selected categories of nonresponse. The author provides a definition for completion rate: "the proportion of completed interviews/questionnaires obtained from a sample." Until a standard definition of response rate is adopted, survey researchers are urged to state clearly how they have used the term in their research. (2 references)

745.   Singer, Eleanor. "Informed Consent: Consequences for Response Rate and Response Quality in Social Surveys." *American Sociological Review* 43, no. 2 (April 1978): 144-62.

A national probability sample of 2,084 potential respondents was asked "presumably" sensitive questions in the areas of marijuana use, drinking, mental health, and sexual behavior. The overall survey response rate was 67 percent. Three major findings are reported: (1) about 8 percent of those asked to sign a consent form refused to do so, but were willing to be interviewed; (2) those who declined to sign the consent form tended to refuse to respond to individual questions within the interview and also provided "poorer" data when they answered; and (3) confidentiality assurance increases the willingness to answer questions and "enhances the quality of response." Singer recommends providing respondents with a "more detailed, informative, and truthful introduction." If consent signatures are deemed necessary, it is recommended that they be sought after the interview has been concluded (in order to avoid adverse quality impacts). The study results are for a general population survey responding to generally sensitive content. (21 footnotes, 58 references)

ANALYSIS

GENERAL

746.   Bailer, Barbara A., and C. Michael Lanphier. *Development of Survey Methods to Assess Survey Practices: A Report of the American Statistical Association Pilot Project on the Assessment of Survey Practices and Data Quality in Surveys of Human Populations.* Washington, DC: American Statistical Association, [1978]. 117p.

Survey Research Methods, a subsection of the American Statistical Association, developed a proposal in 1975 to assess survey practices. The document provides a discussion of the events which led to the perceived need for such a study, as well as the purposes, the design, and summary of the results. The major findings are presented along with recommendations. A twenty-four-page section titled "Interview Schedule for Survey of Surveys" is included. In a pilot study a questionnaire was devised which tested thirty-six surveys. The sponsor of twenty-six of these surveys was the federal government, with the rest divided among state governments, academic institutions, or professional associations. Each survey was for a population of 250 or more respondents. The results show that twenty-two of the thirty-six surveys failed to meet their objectives, samples were "for the most part, poorly designed," survey response rates were difficult to collect and compare, and there were no "generally agreed upon" standards for the presentation of survey data. (41 endnotes)

747.   Bielby, William T., and James R. Kluegel. *Simultaneous Statistical Inference and Statistical Power in Survey Research Applications of the General Linear Model.* Institute for Research on Poverty Discussion Papers:

326-75. Madison, WI: University of Wisconsin at Madison, 1976. 43p. Microfiche. (ED 129 836)

The issues of simultaneous statistical inference and statistical power in survey research applications of the general linear model are explored. The authors suggest techniques in which these approaches can be incorporated into the statistical analysis of survey data. A number of examples are provided which demonstrate these techniques. Advanced statistics are used throughout. (18 references)

748.   Blau, Peter M. "Determining the Dependent Variable in Certain Correlations." *Public Opinion Quarterly* 19, no. 1 (Spring 1955): 100-105.

Several procedures are reviewed which attempt to determine the time sequence of the occurrence of two variables. When the chronological order of variables is unknown, the dependent variable in a correlation "can be determined by establishing that the partial relations between it and a common antecedent factor disappear when the other variable in the original correlation is held constant." Blau provides an example of the method which he describes as being "a new application of Lazarsfeld's schema for testing the validity of theoretical interpretation" (Kendall, Patricia L., and Paul F. Lazarsfeld. "Problems of Survey Analysis." In *Continuities in Social Research: Studies in the Scope and Method of "The American Soldier,"* edited by Robert K. Merton and Paul F. Lazarsfeld, 147-58. [Glencoe, IL]: Free Press, 1950. 255p.). Tables 1 and 2 illustrate the results of a study of elderly people and how the individual's conception of her/his age is related to how s/he feels others think about it. If the respondent feels s/he is old, s/he is five times as likely as those who consider themselves middle-aged to believe that others think of herself/himself as old. S/he is likely to think of herself/himself as old once s/he reaches age seventy (regardless of the perceptions of others). Blau believes it is often possible to obtain data about common antecedents even when it is impossible to date crucial variables. (6 footnotes)

749.   Curtis, Richard F., and Elton F. Jackson. "Multiple Indicators in Survey Research." *American Journal of Sociology* 68, no. 2 (September 1962): 195-204.

The article explains the use of multiple indicators in survey research in which the effect of one underlying conceptual variable influences another. This approach would be useful when studying the relationship between variables such as integration, morale, prejudice, adjustment, and similar topics. Curtis and Jackson attempt to test a hypothesized causal relationship between two underlying conceptual variables. The authors suggest that certain patterns of findings using multiple indicators lead to clear interpretations, while others lead only to confusion. It is stated that the multiple indicator method produces more information than single indicators or single-composite indexes. (15 footnotes)

750. Goodman, Leo A. "A General Model for the Analysis of Surveys." *American Journal of Sociology* 77, no. 6 (May 1972): 1035-86.

Goodman discusses applying direct estimation methods and indirect testing procedures to survey research analysis. This approach replaces the "causal system" diagram which is considered first, followed by the presentation of a model that corresponds to the causal model, and then by a general model. These follow a series of methods which can help researchers determine if their survey data support or negate a given hypothesized causal system. The methods are illustrated by reanalyzing data which were analyzed in 1971. The relationship between two given dichotomous variables is considered, along with the impact of introducing additional variables. (53 footnotes, 26 references)

751. Katz, Daniel. "The Interpretation of Survey Findings." *Journal of Social Issues* 2, no. 2 (May 1946): 33-44. [Reprinted in *Supplement to Reader in Public Opinion and Communication*, edited by Bernard Berelson and Morris Janowitz. No. 10: *Methods in Public Opinion Research*, 573-83. Glencoe, IL: Free Press, 1953. 611p.]

A number of errors in the interpretation of survey findings are identified: (1) the confusion between people's judgments and the objective facts; (2) inappropriate samples; (3) the failure to sufficiently distinguish between crystallized versus uncrystallized public opinion; (4) ill-defined context for interpretation, including the failure to ask related and dependent questions, the failure to evaluate the respondent's own frame of reference, and the error of imputing absolute value to a single percentage; (5) the portrayal of single cases as "typical"; and (6) "quota-control" sampling weakness. Katz believes that polls and surveys "may well constitute the most significant recent development in social science." The criticisms are designed to foster greater use of survey findings and to make the advances in survey research more widely known. (1 footnote)

752. Lurie, Walter A. "Statistics and Public Opinion." *Public Opinion Quarterly* 1, no. 4 (October 1937): 78-83.

This early article in the new public opinion research field relates the search for answers about public opinion to the application of standard statistics. To each of a number of questions that a hypothetical hat manufacturer poses, Lurie provides the statistical solution, starting with simple direct questions and progressing to questions of a greater analytical nature. The multiple-choice question is discussed, as well as variance and factor analysis. (10 footnotes)

753. Rosenberg, Morris. *The Logic of Survey Analysis*. New York, NY: Basic Books, Inc., Publishers, [1968]. 283p.

The following constitute the main areas of interest in this volume: (1) the substantive and theoretical significance of survey data; (2) the explication; (3) the actual process of data analysis; and (4) simplicity – as in answering the following question: "Given a relationship between two variables, what can be learned by introducing a third variable into the analysis?" The theme of the work concerns the analytic procedure referred to as "elaboration." Rosenberg considers the range of possible meanings between two variables, followed by why the relationship exists. The conditions under which the relationship appears are explored next, leading to the issue of conjoint influence. The two remaining chapters cover the "strategy" of survey analysis, and deal with general issues underlying the approach to survey data. Two appendixes are titled "Basic Principles of Table Reading" and "The Arithmetic of Controls." Each of the nine chapters ends with references. The book has a ten-page index.

754.   Selvin, Hanan C. "A Critique of Tests of Significance in Survey Research." *American Sociological Review* 22, no. 5 (October 1957): 519-27.

Problems raised by the applications of tests of significance to explanatory empirical studies are considered. These fall into two categories: problems of designing appropriate procedures for testing hypotheses, and problems with interpreting the results of those tests. Selvin concludes that it is "almost impossible to design studies to meet the conditions for using the tests," and that the circumstances in which the tests are used make it difficult to draw correct inferences. The author states that "in design and in interpretation, in principle and in practice, tests for statistical significance are inapplicable in nonexperimental research." (30 footnotes)

755.   Sonquist, John A., and William C. Dunkelberg. *Survey and Opinion Research: Procedures for Processing and Analysis.* Englewood Cliffs, NJ: Prentice-Hall, 1977. 502p.

The authors view their work as being a handbook for use by both university undergraduate and graduate students seeking to conduct manual and computer-based processing operations. Topics covered include the following: (1) scheduling the data processing steps; (2) data structures; (3) editing; (4) coding and code construction; (5) data quality control; (6) variable generation, discussing the Guttman, Thurstone, and Likert models; (7) statistical analysis; and (8) administration. A ninety-four-page section provides the questionnaire, the editors' instruction book, the card layout form, the card codes, the editors' decision book, and the data listing. ASCII and EBCDIC Codes appear at the end of the volume. A four-page index and a twenty-seven-page bibliography are included.

CAUSAL ANALYSIS

756.   Goodman, Leo A. "A Brief Guide to the Causal Analysis of Data from Surveys." *American Journal of Sociology* 84, no. 5 (March 1979): 1078-95.

Causal analysis of qualitative variables is discussed. The utility of the more recently developed methods is illustrated by application to the data obtained from two previously conducted surveys. The first involved 3,392 schoolboys, each interviewed at two successive points in time. The questions concerned the boys' self-perceived membership in the "leading crowd" and their feelings about their status. The second survey involved 266 adults, each reinterviewed at two successive points in time, concerning their voting intentions. Two tables cross-classify the responses of the two groups. Causal analysis and the analysis of marginal tables follow. One section of the article is devoted to Reynolds's [Item No. 757] criticism of the methods of analysis presented in a previous article by Goodman (Goodman, Leo A. "Causal Analysis of Data from Panel Studies and Other Kinds of Surveys." *American Journal of Sociology* 78, no. 5 [March 1973]: 1135-91.). The author responds to the "irrelevant" criticisms in detail and deals with the magnitude of the effects among the variables. The purpose of the final section, labeled "appendix," "is to clarify why the structure of a system of quantitative variables will usually be very different from the structure of the corresponding dichotomized variables." (25 footnotes, 26 references)

757.   Reynolds, H. T. "Some Comments on the Causal Analysis of Surveys with Log-Linear Models." *American Journal of Sociology* 83, no. 1 (July 1977): 127-43.

Several log-linear models for the analysis of categorical data and the effects of collapsing variables are discussed, along with three subtopics including the treatment of continuous data as if they were discrete, collapsing variables for convenience, and the analysis of recursive systems. Reynolds concludes that a researcher has to be "pessimistic about using categorical data-variables that have in effect been collapsed – to detect causal structures." The use of discrete data may not necessarily solve measurement problems. Log-linear analysis does not solve every measurement challenge, as shown in the highly misleading results explored in the causal analysis of surveys. (9 footnotes, 57 references)

CODING

758.   Frisbie, Bruce, and Seymour Sudman. "The Use of Computers in Coding Free Responses." *Public Opinion Quarterly* 32, no. 2 (Summer 1968): 216-32.

The challenge of precoding natural-language responses to open-ended questions is addressed. The National Opinion Research Center (NORC) was the site for work on adapting the General Inquirer (GI) system developed at Harvard University. A brief history of the GI system is presented. The system is similar to a thesaurus, with words grouped by similarity and dissimilarity. The study undertaken at NORC involved 540 respondents who spoke some 35,000 words. The manner in which responses were coded is described in terms of how a human coder would respond to list information, as well as how a computer would address the task. The following section deals with complex language analysis using Key Word in Context (KWIC), a system developed by IBM. Another area of interest to Frisbie and Sudman was whether computer content analysis could explore "latent dimensions" in the answers provided. In this study the system was unable to differentiate concepts, an experience the researchers describe as "disappointing." (8 footnotes)

759.   Muehl, Doris, ed. *A Manual for Coders: Content Analysis at the Survey Research Center, 1961*. Ann Arbor, MI: Survey Research Center, Institute for Social Research, University of Michigan, 1961. 43p.

The Survey Research Center (SRC) at the University of Michigan was established 1 July 1946 by Rensis Likert (formerly of the Division of Program Surveys, U.S. Department of Agriculture) and staff. The term "coding" is used at SRC to mean content analysis, and is the process of reducing verbal responses to numerical representations. This manual discusses content analysis including standard code conventions, the types of coders and how to use them, coding challenges, and standard operating procedures. General survey procedures are covered, with discussion of study design, sampling, questionnaire construction, interviewing, coding, and results tabulation and analysis.

760.   Schooler, Kermit Koppel. "A Study of Error and Bias in Coding Responses to Open End Questions." Ph.D. diss., University of Michigan, 1956. 89 leaves. [*Dissertation Abstracts International* Order No. 0018648; *DAI* 16, no. 12 (July 1966): 2542.]

Ten coders employed by the Survey Research Center at the University of Michigan were selected, with each person coding the same one hundred questionnaires. The survey dealt with political behavior in the 1952 election. Interviews had been conducted in which open-ended question responses were recorded. Schooler wanted to determine if the coders would tend to interpret the material according to their own attitudes on the issue, and if the coders' expectations of probable frequency would influence categorization. It was found that the coders' own attitudes did not have an impact on the results, but probability expectations were an "important source of bias." Further, probability expectation increases as ambiguity increases. The most ambiguous task involved the use of the entire interview to categorize personality characteristics (such as rigidity) of the respondent. Schooler reports that "expectancies of the observer are a source of distortion at all levels of judgmental complexity." References are provided.

761.   Sidel, Philip S. "Coding." Section 2, Part B, Chap. 9 in *Handbook of Marketing Research*, edited by Robert Ferber, 2/178-2/199. New York, NY: McGraw-Hill Book Company, [1974]. (various pagings)

The term "coding" is defined as the "procedure of classifying responses and entering the codes on the questionnaire or on another form." In structured question formats the response categories appear on the questionnaire form. Open-ended quesions record the respondent's own words which are later coded and analyzed. Sidel discusses the use of extensive codes (which "includes a separate category and code for every distinguishable different response"), and empirical codes ("the technique of collecting and coding numerical data . . . in full, original numeric form"). The primary rule of code construction, which states that categories must be all-inclusive and mutually exclusive, is outlined. Coding instructions and the use of a codebook are described. Postinterview editing and coding are discussed in terms of administrative procedures, the choice of coding forms, and the conversion to machine-readable format. Quality control is considered, with discussions of accuracy and coding error. (13 references)

762.   Woodward, Julian L., and Jack DeLott. "Field Coding versus Office Coding." *Public Opinion Quarterly* 16, no. 3 (Fall 1952): 432-36.

Reported is a "very simple" and "limited" experiment in which the efficacy of field coding and office coding of an open-ended question is compared. Advantages and disadvantages of each procedure are reviewed. Two questions are addressed: (1) Does the common pretest yield enough complete information to construct a satisfactory precode for field classifying? and (2) Will the results produced from field coding be significantly different from those obtained from office coding? One question was selected from a regular Roper survey. The field interviewers alternately used two forms of a questionnaire which produced two closely matched samples of two thousand individuals each. The first form used eight precoded categories plus space for verbatim answers. The second form allowed space only for recording verbatim answers plus a "don't know" box. Two experienced office coders processed the questionnaires by recoding one-half of each of the two samples. The two processes yielded different results. The interviewers tended to classify answers into the precoded categories more frequently "than office coders classify into corresponding categories in the office code." Further, when the precoded form was available, there were fewer don't know answers. Possible reasons for the findings are offered and discussed. (3 footnotes)

763.   Woodward, Julian L., and Raymond Franzen. "A Study of Coding Reliability." *Public Opinion Quarterly* 12, no. 2 (Summer 1948): 253-57.

The experiment took place in the coding room of Elmo Roper's office in New York City. Three different open-ended questions (the first from a *Fortune* Survey) were coded separately by three different coders (and also recoded by one of them). The coders used information from 730 questionnaires on which the previous coders' answers were covered. There was a high degree of agreement among all four codings. However, there were substantial differences in some of the coding, leading the authors to conclude that "the objectivity of coding must differ with the subject matter of the code." There were also some differences among the coders. The authors characterize the experiment as being a "first step" in coding reliability research. Although the results are viewed as insufficient to be "conclusive," they do highlight the need for both well-trained coders and well-constructed codes. (1 footnote)

ERRORS

General

764.   Alwin, Duane F. "Making Errors in Surveys: An Overview." *Sociological Methods & Research* 6, no. 2 (November 1977): 131-50. [Reprinted in *Survey Design and Analysis: Current Issues*, edited by Duane F. Alwin. Sage Contemporary Social Science Issues, no. 46. Beverly Hills, CA: Sage Publications, 1978. 156p.]

This paper serves as an introduction and overview to a collection of articles appearing in this issue of *Sociological Methods and Research*. The seven papers in this issue deal with survey errors. The Alwin overview covers a range of topics including completion rates, sample coverage, locating respondents in longitudinal research, response rates, item nonresponse, weighting to adjust for noncoverage and nonresponse bias, interviewer variability, question structure and sequence, methods of administration, and respondent errors. (1 footnote, 132 references). The following entries have been selected from the volume, with individual annotations found at the indicated item number.

"Question Wording as an Independent Variable in Survey Analysis." (Schuman and Presser - Item No. 325).

"Modest Expectations: The Effects of Interviewers' Prior Expectations on Responses." (Sudman, Bradburn, Blair, and Stocking - Item No. 403).

"The Treatment of Missing Data in Multivariate Analysis." (Kim and Curry - Item No. 775).

"Response Error in Earnings Functions for Nonblack Males." (Bielby and Hauser - Item No. 689).

Two studies from the collection have been excluded from this bibliography – one by Lloyd Lueptow which is based on a self-administered questionnaire, and the other by Gideon Vigderhous, a foreign author.

765.   Deming, W. Edwards. "On Errors in Surveys." *American Sociological Review* 9, no. 4 (August 1944): 359-69. [Reprinted in *Sociological Methods: A Sourcebook*, by Norman K. Denzin, 320-37. Methodological Perspectives, edited by Richard J. Hill. Chicago, IL: Aldine Publishing Company, 1970. 540p.]

Deming has classified thirteen different factors which can affect the usefulness of a survey. The article consists of a separate discussion of each of the following: (1) variability in response; (2) differences in the mode of interviewing (telephone, long schedule, and so forth); (3) interviewer bias; (4) bias due to the sponsoring organization; (5) questionnaire design errors; (6) changes to the universe in which the survey was completed prior to the release of the results; (7) nonresponse bias; (8) late report bias; (9) unrepresentative selection of the survey date resulting in bias; (10) unrepresentative selection of respondents' bias; (11) sampling error and bias; (12) processing error; and (13) interpretation error. Deming observes that any presentation of data should be accompanied by a discussion of the errors and difficulties encountered with the survey. He states that while errors will occur, accuracy of a useful level can be achieved. Deming suggests that "both the accuracy and the need for accuracy" may have been overestimated. (24 footnotes)

766.   Gonzalez, Maria E., Jack L. Ogus, Gary Shapiro, and Benjamin J. Tepping. "Standards for Discussion and Presentation of Errors in Survey and Census Data." *Journal of the American Statistical Association* 70, no. 351, pt. 2 (September 1975): 5-23.

This special supplement to the *Journal of the American Statistical Association* is a revision of Technical Paper 32 (*Standards for Discussion and Presentation of Errors in Data*) issued in March 1974 by the Bureau of the Census. The bureau developed this document to address the limitations of estimates due to sampling, response, or other nonsampling errors. Divided into two parts, the first presents a policy on error information, followed by part two which provides methods of presenting error information. There are three appendixes which include six pages of multiple tables and graphs. (16 footnotes, 6 references)

767.   Wells, William D., and Joel Dames. "Hidden Errors in Survey Data." *Journal of Marketing* 26, no. 4 (October 1962): 50-54.

Using the results of one hundred middle-income "housewives" who were contacted through a door-to-door canvass and interviewed at home, the researchers sought detailed information on the accuracy of the reporting. The questions concerned which brand of instant coffee, if any, was present in the home. If the respondent answered "yes," the interviewer asked the brand name, and similar questions for a variety of products. Then the exact weight or size was asked, which usually required the respondent to go to examine the item. The interviewer then followed and was able to verify the accuracy of the brand claims. The errors were examined to determine if a pattern was present. Exaggerators and understaters were identified. The errors which did occur were "relatively small." Response-style bias was discussed as playing a role only if the conditions were opportune. (7 footnotes)

Control

768.   Hyman, Herbert. "Processing, Estimating, and Adjustment of Survey Data: Control of Error in Editing, Coding, and Tabulation." Chap. 8 in *The Pre-Election Polls of 1948: Report to the Committee on Analysis of Pre-Election Polls and Forecasts*, by Frederick Mosteller, Herbert Hyman, Philip J. McCarthy, Eli S. Marks, and David B. Truman, 221-24. Social Science Research Council, Bulletin no. 60. New York, NY: Social Science Research Council, 1949. 396p.

The control of error by Crossley, Gallup, and Roper in each of the three areas of editing, coding, and tabulation is discussed. Covered are issues such as who did the editing (full-time versus part-time employees), punching methods used for coding (in-house versus contract checks for consistency), and accuracy checks for tabulation (again, whether in-house or contracted out). Hyman concludes that the "net effect of any errors in editing, punching, and tabulation on final predictions was almost certainly negligible." (1 footnote)

769.   U.S. General Accounting Office. *Better Guidance and Controls Are Needed to Improve Federal Surveys of Attitudes and Opinions: A Report by the Comptroller General of the United States*. General Accounting Office Report No. B-181254. "GGD-78-24." [Washington, DC]: General Accounting Office, 15 September 1978. 72p. Microfiche. [SuDoc GA1.13:GGD-78-24]

Many federal agencies conducting attitude surveys and public opinion polls are lacking in expertise to perform or review these surveys. The General Accounting

Office (GAO) identified 209 public opinion polls at six agencies and reviewed five in detail. The poll results should have enjoyed limited use, according to the GAO, as each survey contained "serious technical flaws." Problems were noted in sampling limitations, the length and complexity of the questionnaires, and inappropriate projections based on an extremely low response rate. Other issues observed include the reluctance to make changes to a survey questionnaire once considerable time and effort have been invested. As a result, items submitted to the Office of Management and Budget for review may have already been submitted for contract awards or be far along in the development process. Recommendations for overcoming these challenges include the following: (1) amend the "Standards for Statistical Surveys" to incorporate guidance on contracting for statistical surveys; (2) develop and implement a system for ascertaining which surveys require early review; (3) establish criteria for determining which polls and surveys need to be monitored and reviewed during the implementation phase; and (4) provide postreview of poll and survey data to ascertain whether the inferences and conclusions drawn are appropriate based on the data gathered. Agency comments expressed concern which governmental unit would have responsibility for the reviews. Some agencies maintained that it should be the initial agency which is responsible for the review (early and past), with the Office of Federal Statistical Policy and Standards approving such functions, and subject to external audit. Nine appendixes contain a series of letters to and from Comptroller General Elmer B. Staats.

Measurement

770.   Andersen, Ronald. "The Effect of Measurement Error on Differences in the Use of Health Services." Chap. 13 in *Equity in Health Services: Empirical Analyses in Social Policy*, edited by Ronald Andersen, Joanna Kravits, and Odin W. Anderson, 229-55. Cambridge, MA: Ballinger Publishing Company, 1975. 295p.

The book in which this entry is a chapter deals with a comparison of the use of health services among groups which have been defined by age, income, residence, and racial characteristics. Andersen provides a framework for determining the degree to which the differences among these groups "might be affected" by social survey measurement error. The analysis revealed "relatively few major difficulties in estimating differences by race, age, income, and residence." Neither the validity of the assumptions nor the sources of error (sampling biases and nonsampling noncoverage biases which could impact groups such as young male African Americans and migrant workers) were examined or measured in this study. The presentation includes consideration of variable error and bias measurements including standard errors, nonresponse biases, field bias, and processing bias. The findings cover the data for hospital admissions, hospital days, percent seeing a physician, mean number of physician visits, differences among the subgroups, and for each of the four characteristics considered. (6 endnotes with 131 references at book end).

771.   Asher, Herbert B. "Some Consequences of Measurement Error in Survey Data." *American Journal of Political Science* 18, no. 2 (May 1974): 469-85.

A number of estimates are presented of the amount of measurement for some standard face sheet items in two survey data sets collected by the Survey Research Center (1956-1958-1960 American panel data) and by Jennings-Niemi (1965 socialization data). Asher defines "measurement error" as "any deviation from the true value of a variable that arises in the measurement process." The effects of measurement error on correlation coefficients are determined using the multiple-indicator approach, as well as an observations-over-time strategy (both of which use path analysis techniques). It is concluded that random measurement error may have a major impact on the studied coefficients which would give rise to misleading inferences. The section dealing with causal models of measurement error uses advanced statistics. (27 footnotes)

772.   Neter, John. "Measurement Errors in Reports of Consumer Expenditures." *Journal of Marketing Research* 7, no. 1 (February 1970): 11-25. [Reprinted in *Readings in Survey Research*, edited by Robert Ferber, 84-117. Chicago, IL: American Marketing Association, 1978. 604p.]

"Measurement errors" are defined as "the difference between the response obtained in a survey and the 'desired response,' the one that would have been obtained with the best measurement procedure available." Measurement errors are put in mathematical terms at the beginning of the article. Methods for collecting consumer expenditure data and methods for evaluating measurement errors are considered next. Measurement error is examined by causal categories in the following areas: (1) recall errors; (2) telescoping errors; (3) reporting load effects; (4) prestige errors; (5) conditioning errors; (6) respondent effects; (7) interviewer effects; and (8) reporting instrument effects. After each area has been addressed, Neter discusses the implications that the information presented has for survey design. Instrument, questionnaire, and telephone effects, and recording versus recall are considered. Pertinent studies relevant to each section are cited in the bibliography. (48 references)

Psychological

773.   Hastorf, Albert H., and Hadley Cantril. "Some Psychological Errors in Polling – A Few Guides for Opinion Interpretation." *Journal of Educational Psychology* 40, no. 1 (January 1949): 57-60.

The issue of "why" an individual holds an opinion, and whether or not that person will act upon that opinion are the questions which motivate this research. The authors note that an opinion must be understood in light of the individual's past experience, and that knowledge may serve as the basis for a prediction, but that determining whether an individual will act on an opinion requires insight into whether the event will affect the individual personally. In order to understand opinions Hastorf and Cantril maintain that there must be an understanding of the group identifications and loyalties of the individuals. In this case the authors recommend supplementary survey data with more complete case studies. (1 footnote)

Reporting

774.   Schroeder, Larry D., and David L. Sjoquist. "Survey Reporting Errors and Class Income Interval Definitions." *Social Science Quarterly* 56, no. 4 (March 1976): 715-20.

The rounding of reported incomes from cross-sectional surveys using grouped data is examined. If income is grouped by "class intervals" and the respondents round income to the "class boundaries," it is "possible that analyses which employ grouped data may be sensitive to the definitions used to define the class intervals." Therefore, the definition used to determine income classes becomes significant when evaluating class means. The authors utilized the class intervals found in the *Current Population Reports* (*CPR*) and explored the question raised by using the data from the 1966 *Survey of Economic Opportunity* (specifically the national random sample portion) which incorporates the same questions used by the census for the *CPR*. (11 footnotes)

INCOMPLETE AND MISSING DATA

775.   Kim, Jae-On, and James Curry. "The Treatment of Missing Data in Multivariate Analysis." *Sociological Methods & Research* 6, no. 2 (November 1977): 215-40. [Reprinted *in Survey Design and Analysis: Current Issues*, edited by Duane F. Alwin. Sage Contemporary Social Science Issues, no. 46. Beverly Hills, CA: Sage Publications, 1978. 156p.]

Survey researchers often choose either a listwise or a pairwise deletion as a means of dealing with missing data, and then continue to interpret results with the usual statistical means. The purpose of this paper is to review and organize the procedures available for dealing with missing data. Kim and Curry consider the nature of the missing data, listwise and pairwise deletion, the estimation of missing values, and the estimation of missing values without iteration. The options are not rated as to which is more or less useful. The foregoing concern multivariate cases. References are made in the conclusion to resources which discuss other variable possibilities. (13 footnotes, 52 references)

776.   Lansing, John B., and A. T. Eapen. "Dealing with Missing Information in Surveys." *Journal of Marketing* 24, no. 2 (October 1959): 21-27.

Four types of missing information are discussed, along with techniques which can be employed to deal with the challenge. Missing information may include missing dwelling units, nonresponse, incomplete interviews, and incomplete families. Missing dwelling units may be created through sampling errors. In the case discussed here, the 1958 *Survey of Consumer Finances* was compared with Census Bureau data. The survey figure for households was slightly larger than that of the census data. Weighting is discussed in the section on nonresponse, including variable sampling fraction, methods, and effects. In the incomplete interviews section Lansing and Eapen discuss choices between adjustments and two stages of assignment procedure. A system of weighting was used to compensate for incomplete families. (2 footnotes)

777.   Lehnen, Robert G., and Gary G. Koch. "Analyzing Panel Data with Uncontrolled Attrition." *Public Opinion Quarterly* 38, no. 1 (Spring 1974): 40-56.

Panel designs use repeated interviews with the same respondents. Lehnen and Koch, using three-wave panel designs for seven race and occupational categories, analyze citizens' preferences for Hubert Humphrey, Richard Nixon, and George Wallace. Data were collected in Florida and North Carolina. Partial candidate preference information was available from some, while for others the data were incomplete. A discussion of the supplemented marginals method for dealing with incomplete panel data is presented. The supplemented marginals models are combined, with the authors noting the effectiveness of the approach for time-based data. It is observed that the "level of choice" for the candidates in the 1968 election was determined by the "net political preferences" – not the proportion of the actual vote. Advanced statistics are used. (7 footnotes)

INSTRUCTIONAL MATERIALS

778.   Davis, James A. *Elementary Survey Analysis*. Prentice-Hall Methods of Social Science Series, edited by Herbert L. Costner and Neil Smelser. Englewood Cliffs, NJ: Prentice-Hall, [1971]. 195p.

This textbook, designed for use in sociology research methods courses, is intended to teach the user how to start from raw data and progress to a statistical report. Beginning with a discussion of variables, each successive chapter adds layers of complexity, as follows: two-variable relationships, three-variable relationships, three variables followed by causal systems ("the relationships among all pairs of variables in a set"), four variables, and finally "(Too) Many Variables." The volume includes a three-page index.

779.   Hirschi, Travis, and Hanan C. Selvin. *Principles of Survey Analysis*. 1967. Reprint. New York, NY: Free Press, a Division of the Macmillan Company, 1973. 280p. [The book was originally published under the title *Delinquency Research: An Appraisal of Analytic Methods*. New York, NY: Free Press, 1967. 280p.]

There are two intended audiences for this textbook: scholars in the areas of delinquency and criminology, and students in research methods courses. Hirschi and Selvin cover methods of analysis and critique the empirical research on delinquency. The volume, also a source for essays on the major topics in methodology, is divided into four parts: "The Nature of Methodological Criticism"; "Causal Analysis"; "Multivariate Analysis"; and "Conceptualization and Inference." The authors maintain that as of 1967 there had not been a comprehensive book on analysis. In 1968 the book won the C. Wright Mills Award for the best book in the field of social problems. Each chapter concludes with endnotes. A six-page index is included.

780.   Sheth, Jagdish N., ed. *Multivariate Methods for Market and Survey Research*. Chicago, IL: American Marketing Association, 1977. 388p.

This volume, a development of a workshop held at the University of Chicago, is designed for use as a textbook. Some twenty-seven writers contributed to the collection which deals with specific multivariate techniques. A brief technical description is supplied, along with the application of the techniques to market and survey research. Subjects covered include Automatic Interaction Detection analysis, latent structure analysis, and conjoint measurements. The collection is broadly divided into the areas of functional multivariate methods, structural multivariate methods, and computing aspects. The volume has a nine-page index and thirty-nine pages of references.

781.   Weisberg, Herbert F., and Bruce D. Bowen. *An Introduction to Survey Research and Data Analysis*. San Francisco, CA: W. H. Freeman and Company, 1977. 243p.

This is a textbook with questions posed in each chapter and answers provided at the end of the volume. Divided into two parts, survey design and data analysis, the first part describes how surveys are conducted, and the second discusses statistical reports and data. The design chapters include a discussion of the following: (1) the nature of survey research; (2) sampling; (3) questionnaire design; (4) interviewing; (5) coding; and (6) survey interpretation. The data analysis chapters cover these topics: (1) an introduction to analysis; (2) the use of computers; (3) single-variable statistics; (4) interviewing; (5) measures of association; (6) statistical controls; (7) changing variables; (8) interval statistics; and (9) research reports. Forty suggested readings are included, as well as footnotes throughout the book.

RELIABILITY

782.   Broedling, Laurie A. "On More Reliably Employing the Concept of 'Reliability'." *Public Opinion Quarterly* 38, no. 3 (Fall 1974): 372-78.

Broedling discusses some of the meanings of the term "reliability" in survey research and the resulting conceptual confusion. The uses of the term are divided into two major categories: "those pertaining to reliability as an index of sampling error variance and those pertaining to it as an index of measurement or response-error variance." The bases for the varying usage are discussed, suggestions are made on ways to increase the clarity of the terminology, and explanations are offered as to why the same term has been employed for the two different concepts. Because of terminology problems, adequate attention has not been paid to conceptualizing and measuring all types of error variance in a survey. Researchers are advised to be aware of the effects of measurement variance. The use of the term "precision" is suggested to mean sampling variance, and "psychometric reliability" to denote measurement variance if there is a possibility that "reliability," used alone, could be misunderstood. The term "statistical reliability" could be used to mean statistical significance. (16 footnotes)

783.   Coughenour, C. Milton. "The Problem of Reliability of Adoption Data in Survey Research." *Rural Sociology* 30, no. 2 (June 1965): 184-203.

The data used to examine the issue of adoption were taken from Ohio farmers surveyed in 1957, resurveyed in 1959, and then surveyed for a third time in 1962. The study provides information on the reliability of present survey methods and the impact of unreliability on selected research objectives. The "diffusion period" became progressively longer with each survey, a satisfactorily reliable rank order of adopter was not achieved, and the desired "innovativeness scales" and efforts to "determine relationships between earliness to adopt and other characteristics of farmers were seriously hampered." The survey data dealt with the adoption of 2, 4-D weed spray and Decon or Warfarin rat control (reliable estimates of the mean year of adoption for these products were found). However, reliable survey data were not produced for Clintland oats or soil tests. Three areas are suggested for changes in survey research. (49 footnotes)

784.   Deming, W. E. "Some Criteria for Judging the Quality of Surveys." *Journal of Marketing* 12, no. 2 (October 1947): 145-57.

Deming divides samples into two types (probability and judgment), defines the terms, and then exposes the similarities and differences of the two approaches. Validity, reliability, bias, and sampling variability characteristics are considered. A partial list of biases is presented, including a discussion of bias in the selection process, automatic selection, and the control of nonresponse. Misconceptions in bias control are outlined, as well as misconceptions regarding the computation of sampling errors. The possibility of automatic selection is discussed, with the difficulties delineated. Deming closes with observations on the costs and reliability of government and other statistics. (10 footnotes)

785.   Ferber, Robert. "On the Reliability of Responses Secured in Sample Surveys." *Journal of the American Statistical Association* 50, no. 271 (September 1955): 788-810.

A study considering the variability in response of different family members to the same question is described. Specifically, the research focuses on the consistency of the responses of different family members to questions concerning a variety of family characteristics including income, family size, purchases, planned purchases, and so forth. Between late 1951 and the first six months of 1952, a randomly selected sample of 237 families was interviewed in Champaign-Urbana. This group represented a response rate of 43 percent from the original 556 families approached. The results indicate that (1) one family member's attitudes and expectations do not necessarily represent those of other family members, (2) one family member's knowledge of the purchases or purchasing plans of other family members is incomplete, and (3) various family members will have differing information on the family's status and characteristics. Ferber suggests that at least two family members should be interviewed to determine family characteristics and status, and that unless all family members can be interviewed, individual statements on attitudes and expectations should be viewed as one individual's opinion. (17 footnotes)

786.   Ferber, Robert. "The Reliability of Consumer Surveys of Financial Holdings: Demand Deposits." *Journal of the American Statistical Association*
61, no. 313 (March 1966): 91-103.

The presence of response and nonresponse errors in relation to demand deposits
reports in consumer surveys is examined. Ferber maintains that this study represents the first time that the measurement of nonsampling errors in individual
consumer reports was undertaken. Two consumer panels were used in the study.
The files of cooperating financial institutions were available, without the knowledge of the respondents. The challenges of trying to monitor demand deposits is
explained, with major changes and fluctuations common. Ferber found that response and nonresponse errors can "influence substantially" the accuracy of the
data. The results from the surveys showed that respondents tended to understate
the actual balances. Reports of balance changes were "grossly inaccurate." Ferber suggests that overall the survey results "possess a fair degree of reliability" –
more so than reports of time deposits and personal debt. The study was part of
the Consumer Savings Project of the Inter-University Committee for Research
on Consumer Behavior. (4 references)

787.   Ferber, Robert. "The Reliability of Consumer Surveys of Financial Holdings: Time Deposits." *Journal of the American Statistical Association* 60,
no. 309 (March 1965): 148-63.

The level of response and nonresponse errors experienced in the reporting of
time deposits found in two consumer financial surveys is considered. The means
and size of distributions of accounts are found to contain "substantial errors,"
suggesting that confidence intervals calculated from the data are "badly distorted."
Respondent characteristics and aspects of the questionnaire approach are cited
as factors. Results of four similar studies are summarized as part of the concluding remarks, along with an outline of six findings from the current research (the
first of which acknowledges that at times the understatement of time deposits
exceeded 50 percent). Advanced statistics are employed. The studies undertaken
for this article were conducted by the Inter-University Committee for Research
on Consumer Behavior as part of the Consumer Savings Project. (14 references)

788.   Lehnen, Robert G. "Assessing Reliability in Sample Surveys." *Public Opinion Quarterly* 35, no. 4 (Winter 1971-72): 578-92.

The research applies psychologists Campbell and Fiske's "multitrait-multimethod
matrix" approach to sample survey data (Campbell, Donald T., and Donald W.
Fiske. "Convergent and Discriminant Validation by the Multitrait-Multimethod
Matrix." *Psychological Bulletin* 56 [1959]: 81-105.). The technique, originally
intended to assess the validity and reliability of psychological tests and methods,
requires "the computation of a large matrix of correlations between responses to

different items under varying methods of application." The study data were obtained from a national sample of 1,504 adult Americans who were interviewed on public policy questions during March 1966. In addition to open and closed questions there were ninety-seven statements on the survey instrument. These were administered by use of the card-sort technique in a ninety-minute interview. The fifteen policy areas studied indicate "considerable variation in item-method reliability." However, those items designed to measure views on open housing, integration of schools, and full employment show item-method reliability that is seen to be comparable to that of psychological tests. Lehnen believes the technique is applicable to sample surveys. Recommendations are offered to political scientists who are conducting research in the area. (18 footnotes)

789.   Ridley, Jeanne Clare, Christine A. Bachrach, and Deborah A. Dawson. "Recall and Reliability of Interview Data from Older Women." *Journal of Gerontology* 34, no. 1 (January 1979): 99-105.

The recall and reliability of interview data from females between the ages of sixty-six and seventy-six concerning their marital and fertility histories are discussed. A sample of 211 was selected as part of a pilot for a national survey; a random sample of fifty of the original respondents was reinterviewed by telephone and asked selected topics from the questionnaire. Questions covered the date and number of marriages, births, and other fertility events. Exact answers were provided an average of 90 percent. The study results suggest that recall ability and reliability have a "relatively minor effect" on the retrospective reports of older females. (2 footnotes, 14 references)

790.   Rose, Arnold M. "Reliability of Answers to Factual Questions." *Ohio Valley Sociologist* 31, no. 4 (June 1966): 14-18.

A study of voluntary associations in the Twin Cities (Minneapolis and St. Paul, Minnesota) provided an opportunity to test the reliability of factual information as provided by the association leader. Ninety-one organizations were involved, with interviewing conducted by trained graduate students. While there were varying levels of reliability depending upon the information requested, the overall level was low. The study results are compared with the work of the Survey Research Center (University of Michigan), the American Institute of Public Opinion (Gallup) Poll, and the National Opinion Research Center, each of which found three significantly different percentages for individuals who claimed they belonged to one or more voluntary associations. Rose notes that for each poll organization the question wording, interviewing, and sampling procedures were different, but what was reported was supposedly the same "factual characteristic." Studies replicated rarely reach the same conclusion. Rose recommends that "facts" be viewed with a "critical attitude." (3 footnotes)

791.   "These Public-Opinion Polls: How Do They Work? Are They Reliable?"
        Changing Times 10, no. 8 (August 1956): 34-36.

After a few introductory paragraphs, the article assumes the form of answering
specific questions such as, "Do people really say what they think?" There are
just over a dozen questions addressed, varying in response length from a single
sentence to multiple paragraphs. Topics covered include sample size, sample
selection, question wording, poll accuracy, the 1948 polls, and poll reliability.
Four major points regarding the failure of the 1948 polls are covered.

792.   "They Predict How People Will Vote: Election Time and the Pollsters
        Are in Full Cry. How Much Faith Can You Put in Them? A Few Tips
        on How to Stay Skeptical." *Changing Times* 26, no. 7 (July 1972): 13-15.

The article first discusses sample size. Seven questions dealing with the issue of
poll reliability are posed and answered. The questions raised are designed to
assist the reader to evaluate poll results. The reader is asked to consider these
elements: who sponsored the poll; who conducted the poll; who and how many
were interviewed; what questions were asked; how many interviewers conducted
the poll; when and where were the interviews conducted; and are the results
based on the entire sample. Ways to determine the margin of error (a chart previously published by the Gallup organization) are shown in tabular format.

793.   Warner, Lucien. "The Reliability of Public Opinion Surveys." *Public Opin-
        ion Quarterly* 3, no. 3 (July 1939): 376-90.

The article begins with a discussion of probable error in surveys. Warner divides
possible sources of error into three types: definitional, psychological, and mathematical, concentrating almost exclusively on the latter. Examined are random
sampling, determinants of opinion, controlled sampling, weighting, sample size,
and reliability of whole versus parts. It is emphasized that factual empirical
checks (such as elections and other tests) are necessary to determine the accuracy of a survey. Warner states: "There is great need for the testing of survey
methods against a 100 per cent of the population of a limited area." Mathematical formulas are used throughout to illustrate the concepts. (1 footnote)

REPLICATION

794.   La Sorte, Michael A. "Replication as a Verification Technique in Survey
        Research: A Paradigm." *Sociological Quarterly* 13, no. 2 (Spring 1972):
        218-27.

The term "replication" is defined as a "conscious and systematic repeat of an original study." A paradigm is developed containing the following parts and subparts: (I) retest replication: (1) confirmation retest; (2) validity retest; (3) data measurement retest; and (4) stability retest. (II) internal replication: (1) multiple independent samples; and (2) single samples. (III) independent replication: (1) empirical generalization; (a) validity; (b) extension; and (c) specification. (IV) theoretical replication: (1) theoretical generalization; (a) inter-societal; and (b) intra-societal. Replication adds to the verification of findings, methods, and theories through updated data. The author believes that such an undertaking should go beyond merely confirming previous efforts; it would add new knowledge as well. (39 references)

SECONDARY ANALYSIS

795.   Hyman, Herbert H. *Secondary Analysis of Sample Surveys: Principles, Procedures, and Potentialities.* New York, NY: John Wiley & Sons, [1972]. 347p.

Secondary analysis of survey data is defined as "the extraction of knowledge on topics other than those which were the focus of the original surveys." Obstacles and benefits of this approach are considered in the introduction. The following chapter considers secondary analysis by the primary analyst, secondary analysis incorporating primary data, and secondary semianalysis. Subsequent chapters cover approaches to secondary analysis, social categories and groups, studies of fundamental phenomena, and studies of change. The final chapters deal with age comparison and cohort analysis in the examination of long-term change and cross-sectional studies. A list of seventeen international data archives is provided. Each chapter contains extensive footnotes. A fifteen-entry "credits" section includes the books and periodicals cited.

VALIDITY

796.   Belloc, Nedra B. "Validation of Morbidity Survey Data by Comparison with Hospital Records." *Journal of the American Statistical Association* 49, no. 268 (December 1954): 832-46.

The challenge for validation of illnesses lies in the fact that only if a condition is medically attended is such a process possible – and many illnesses are not reflected in school or work absence. The study described validates survey findings against hospitalization records. San Jose, California, was the study site, with hospitalization reports ranging from the preceding seven to eleven months, which were then checked against the records of five hospitals. Belloc found that the household sample surveys were "sufficiently accurate" to be used in place of hospital record data. Comprehensive checks of overreporting and underreporting of illness are not an option due to the difficulties noted above. Nearly half of the underreporting was from individuals who had experienced multiple hospital admissions, but who had reported at least one other hospitalization. (18 references)

797.   Clausen, Aage R. "Response Validity: Vote Report." *Public Opinion Quarterly* 32, no. 4 (Winter 1968-69): 588-606.

Response error in vote reports occurring during the 1964 election is studied. The Survey Research Center (SRC) at the University of Michigan conducted the review, comparing estimates of voter turnout and division by political party vote with Census Bureau data and official voting records. Response error is defined as the "proportion of professed voters whose reports are not confirmed by the official record check." Estimates of voter turnout have regularly been 12 to 13 percent higher than the population figures. The overreport is not due entirely to sampling error. Clausen discusses both visible and hidden discrepancies between official and SRC estimates of voter turnout. The samples of SRC and the Census Bureau studies are compared in tabular form, broken down by sex, education, age, and race. The challenges of determining the actual vote from the official record are recounted. Difficulties include vote records which had been destroyed, and registrars who either by law or by protectiveness would not provide access to the records. Respondents were classified on a ten-point chart, with some elements being the following: not registered, vote recorded, and no record of vote. The 1,450 respondents who were interviewed before and after the 1964 election are charted accordingly. Assuming a high degree of accuracy of both the official records and the reports on those records, and factoring out nonvoter respondents, Clausen calculated an invalidity rate of 6.9 percent in the respondents' reports of election day turnout. Three hypotheses are suggested to explain the average in the report for Johnson, with the sample vote of 67.5 percent as compared with the actual population vote of 61.5 percent. A further explanation is offered by the "stimulus" hypothesis, in which individuals are stimulated to vote as a consequence of preelection interviews. Such individuals are "generally less interested and less informed about political affairs than those who would have voted, interview or no." Clausen maintains that this hypothesis helps to explain both voting turnout and proportion of the presidential vote, as well as "the overestimate of the Democratic proportion of the two-party vote for president." [See Item No. 806 for a 1979 replication of this study.] (9 footnotes)

798.   Connelly, Gordon M. "Now Let's Look at the Real Problem: Validity." *Public Opinion Quarterly* 9, no. 1 (Spring 1945): 51-60.

This article points out how validity problems have been overlooked and under-estimated, perhaps in favor of attention to sampling procedures and reliability of results. Validity, according to Connelly, is negatively affected by several factors: (1) when readers "interpret the specific response apart from its own stimulus," that is, a misinterpretation of the meaning of a question; (2) when poll questions do not adequately reflect objective behavior being measured; (3) believing that respondents must think clearly and logically; and (4) writing questions incorporating "unmasked prestige" factors. The author uses a routine but controversial question by the National Opinion Research Center (NORC) to illustrate the above points. The question received considerable discussion at the time and asked how respondents felt about Japanese people living and working in the United States, and whether they have "as good a chance" at postwar employment as white people. The NORC question is discussed at length because it shows "so many angles of validity and because validity of questions both needs and deserves far more attention." (16 footnotes)

799.   Dollard, John. "Under What Conditions Do Opinions Predict Behavior?" *Public Opinion Quarterly* 12, no. 4 (Winter 1948-49): 623-32.

Dollard discusses some of the "social and cultural factors which tend to sustain the validity of surveys, and also various other factors which tend to make people's opinions unreliable indices for predicting their behavior." Three social situations – origin, test, and criterion – influence the validity of a verbal response made in a survey. Seven "conditions" are offered to explain the relationship between what an individual may feel and her/his subsequent behavior. The conditions are described first in a commonsense statement, followed by a technical statement. Examples of each are included. The technical statements are in terms of behavior theory, as well as the three social situations. Dollard believes that better estimates of validity could be made if certain classes (for example, neurotics, apathetic people, and poor verbalizers) could be omitted from samples. Likewise, validity can be increased under certain applications of the origin, test, and criterion sitations. (6 footnotes)

800.   Ferber, Robert, John Forsythe, Harold W. Guthrie, and E. Scott Maynes. "Validation of Consumer Financial Characteristics: Common Stock." *Journal of the American Statistical Association* 64, no. 326 (June 1969): 415-32.

The Federal Reserve Board *Survey of Financial Characteristics* was conducted in 1963. A sequel, employing the same interviewers with identical field and data processing procedures, was conducted by the Bureau of the Census. The purpose of the study was to evaluate the degree to which individuals appropriately report holdings of common stock. The results show that nonreporting of stock ownership is "substantial," thereby creating a major source of bias. The stock holdings of nonrespondents were much larger than those of respondents. One technique suggested to improve the results is to interview all family members as a way to deal with "the problem of poor memory and lack of knowledge." The authors maintain that while nonsampling variance is likely to continue, analytical models are in the process of being developed to detect and correct these errors. (6 references)

801.   Link, Henry C., and A. D. Freiberg. "The Problem of Validity vs. Reliability in Public Opinion Polls." *Public Opinion Quarterly* 6, no. 1 (Spring 1942): 87-98.

Two questions are posed: (1) "Do public opinion polls furnish a valid index of the course of political action which people really want?" and (2) "How can the polls be made into more meaningful expressions of preference for certain public policies?" The Psychological Barometer, a nationwide poll of public opinion and buying habits, was begun in 1932 by the Psychological Corporation, of which Link is vice-president. Questions from the barometer are used to highlight reliability and validity issues. The classical laws of chance are seen as applicable to polling. The Gallup Poll is used to indicate the need for knowing, for reliability purposes, the size and distribution of a sample. Four tests of the validity of polls are election results, purchasing behavior, public attitudes and actions, and tests of knowledge. The fact that a study "calls for answers in terms of objective behavior raises a presumption in favor of the validity of its results." The authors describe the "cancellation" technique (or method of "residues") as an attempt to establish validity on a verbal level. Behavior is seen as the basic criterion for validity. (4 footnotes)

802.   Manfield, Manuel N. "AAPOR Standards Committee Study of Validation Practices: Pilot Study on Designs, Introductions, Questions, and Practices." *Public Opinion Quarterly* 35, no. 4 (Winter 1971-72): 627-35.

A special subcommittee of the Standards Committee of the American Association for Public Opinion Research (AAPOR) was established at the annual conference in 1967. Manfield, the sole member of the subcommittee, was charged with the responsibility of investigating and, possibly, developing new guidelines for validation methodology. This article reprints his report to the AAPOR Standards Committee. Data, gathered by means of mail questionnaires completed by forty-seven companies, showed that validations were used almost entirely for "policing," rather than for evaluating, the fieldwork of interviewers. Manfield delineates and evaluates the two commonly used validation designs – the "investigation-oriented" design and the "extension-oriented" design. Among other things he criticizes the introductions used, the questions asked, and the effects on both the respondent and the interviewer of the present validation practices. Manfield

concludes with nine recommendations for "more effective and more useful validation methodology" with the goal of "safeguarding the good will of the public."

803.   Manfield, Manuel N. "The Status of Validation in Survey Research." In
        Current Controversies in Marketing Research, edited by Leo Bogart for
        the Market Research Council, 61-85. Markham Series in Marketing. Chi-
        cago, IL: Markham Publishing Company, 1969. 164p.

Validation refers to the process of determining whether and how interviews
were conducted. Manfield believes that independent checks on the interviewer
and checking with the public can often be counterproductive. Instead of directing efforts toward monitoring honesty, the author maintains that it would be
wiser to educate data collectors in the "why and how of their functions." The
article explores undesirable validation practices, the current status of validation,
and fabrication in data collection. Further sections cover interviewers, supervisors, and field directors. The current practice is for supervisors to validate at
least 10 percent of the interviews for which they are responsible. Concerns include the implied distrust of interviewers, the view that respondents may come
to distrust interviewers, and the "unreasonable" hours at which some of the validation calls are being placed. (14 footnotes)

804.   Max, Alfred Raymond. "Basic Factors in the Interpretation of Public
        Opinion Polls: An Attempt at Assessing the Degree of Reliance to be
        Placed upon Figures Released by Private Polling Agencies on Current
        Social and Political Issues." Ph.D. diss., American University, 1941. 239
        leaves. [Not available from *Dissertation Abstracts International*.]

Almost fifty years ago, Max suggested that sociological applications, rather than
political ones, would be the "most promising" uses of the "new science" of public opinion polling employing scientific samples. The dissertation was written
only five years after George Gallup's pioneering work and presents the issues of
the evolving discipline. One area of consideration was the relationship between
"commercial organizations" and "scientific institutions." A call is made for cooperation, shared knowledge, and peaceful coexistence. The concept of a board,
controlled by the government, merging nonprofit and commercial polling organizations is suggested. The 1940s was a time in the United States in which
government boards were being instituted for a wide variety of social concerns.
Instead, the National Opinion Research Center was established, and continues to
this day. Most of the dissertation covers the qualitative concept of cross section,
with additional chapters devoted to question wording, interviewing techniques and
their impact on poll validity, and the qualitative approach to opinion measurement.
References are provided.

805.   Parry, Hugh J., and Helen M. Crossley. "Validity of Responses to Survey Questions." *Public Opinion Quarterly* 14, no. 1 (Spring 1950): 61-80.

The article, part of a series on validity, covers three topics: two current concepts of validity, a selective literature review in narrative form on the subject, and a presentation of numerous results of a survey in Denver. The two concepts delineated by the authors are predictive accuracy and validity as a matter of interpretation. Differing definitions and uses of the terms are discussed. Studies are reviewed from several sources: commercial research (the Magazine Audience Group); government research (especially Bureau of the Census publications and the War Department's *The American Soldier*); medical and related research (such as the Kinsey Report); and political research (the 1948 election). The Denver Validity Study of 1949 was carried out at the University of Denver's Opinion Research Center. The results of the study showed that the validity of even simple "factual" responses was questionable. Invalidity was shown to often follow social pressures. Respondents tended to exaggerate their participation in elections, to inflate their charitable contributions, and to claim to have a library card and a valid driver's license. Despite problems, however, invalidity is not seen as "inevitable." (31 footnotes)

806.   Traugott, Michael W., and John P. Katosh. "Response Validity in Surveys of Voting Behavior." *Public Opinion Quarterly* 43, no. 3 (Fall 1979): 359-77.

The findings of a study are provided which validated the reported registration and voting behavior of respondents in a national election study. The work of Clausen [Item No. 797] is reviewed. Traugott and Katosh attempt to replicate Clausen's procedures in this investigation. The validity of respondents' self-reported voting behavior in the 1976 presidential election was assessed in terms of demographic characteristics of the 2,882 respondents and the extent of their participation in a survey panel begun in 1972 to the 1976 National Election Study by the Center for Political Studies. The other survey instrument was the U.S. Bureau of the Census's Voting Supplement to the November 1976 *Current Population Survey*. Results indicate that there was a significantly higher turnout rate in association with the number of interviews in which a respondent had participated, the significant interview effect appeared to be cumulative, and there was a significant amount of overreporting. Evaluated are three alternative social-psychological models concerning the effects of preelection interviews. They are the stimulus, the alienation, and the self-concept hypotheses, with the first being confirmed by the research. It is concluded that "researchers using the survey method with panel designs should be sensitive to the effects of their method on the behavior which they are trying to measure." (19 references)

807.   Vidich, Arthur J., and J. Bensman. "The Validity of Field Data." *Human
        Organization* 13, no. 1 (Spring 1954): 20-27. [Reprinted in *Human Or-
        ganization Research*, edited by R. N. Adams and J. J. Preiss, 88-204.
        Homewood, IL: Dorsey Press, 1960. 456p.]

Errors and misinformation are categorized in four ways: purposeful intent, temporary role of the respondent, respondent psychology, and involuntary error.
Each of these areas is examined in terms of evaluating the reliability and validity of the information secured. The particular impacts that these possibilities
pose for anthropologists are discussed. Census and survey approaches to data
gathering are considered. Polls and surveys are determined to be valuable for
probing "relatively simple areas of choices," such as presidential polls or radio
and television polling. According to Vidich and Bensman, depth studies of communities or institutions require alternate techniques. Basic anthropological fieldwork is compared and contrasted with surveys involving large samples. (32 footnotes)

808.   Weaver, Charles N., and Carol L. Swanson. "Validity of Reported Date
        of Birth, Salary and Seniority." *Public Opinion Quarterly* 38, no. 1 (Spring
        1974): 69-80.

Prior research on the topic, especially surveys emanating from the government
(such as the 1950 and 1960 Censuses of Population and Housing), is briefly
reviewed. The authors believe the validity of date of birth and salary is very important since "these data are frequently used as indices of broader social characteristics." The sample survey involved telephone interviews with a random
group of six hundred firefighters and police officers employed in San Antonio,
Texas. The information gathered was compared with personnel office records.
Of the total group 339 interviews were completed; there were forty-five termi-
nations. Due to irregular working schedules, 216 were never found at home
when the calls were made, and there were some refusals. The following are
some of the findings which emerged from the study: (1) of the 321 responses
concerning date of birth, 295 were accurate, with 13 overstatements and 13 understatements; (2) the oldest age groups (age fifty and older) showed the highest
rate of inaccuracy; (3) there were 277 inaccurate responses having to do with
salary, with 235 overstatements and 42 understatements; (4) the variations in
reported salary were also age related; (5) the older the respondent, the more apt
s/he was to understate salary; and (6) of the 313 responses gathered for seniority, 199 were accurate, with 63 overstatements and 51 understatements. Implications of the wide variations in the degree of accuracy of the variables examined are discussed. It is concluded that invalidity is a "specialized" phenomenon, and that "the direction and magnitude of inaccurate response are structur-
ally associated with the characteristics of respondents." (13 footnotes)

809.   Weiss, Carol H. "Validity of Welfare Mothers' Interview Responses." *Public Opinion Quarterly* 32, no. 4 (Winter 1969-70): 622-33.

A validation study of responses made by African-American welfare mothers was conducted. All were New York City residents receiving public assistance in 1966 who had been interviewed by the National Opinion Research Center in a study of the use of health services. From a total of 1,002 women, validation data on registration and voting were available for 549. No "general trait or condition" of response error was found. The data did not support the view that welfare mothers would provide interviewers most unlike themselves a more biased, idealized story. Weiss observes that "status-similar interviewers who interact with respondents on a personal basis tend to get biased answers." Task involvement, rather than personal involvement, is recommended for interviewers. (14 footnotes)

810.   Weiss, David J., and Rene V. Davis. "An Objective Validation of Factual Interview Data." *Journal of Applied Psychology* 44, no. 6 (December 1960): 381-85.

The sample consisted of ninety-one people with physical disabilities from the Minneapolis-St. Paul, Minnesota, area. The original sample was two hundred, with more than half unavailable due to residence change, refusals, and other reasons. Experienced interviewers from a polling agency were used, with thirty-nine interviews answered by the people with disabilities and fifty-two interviews completed by an adult relation. Validation of personal information and the individual's disability were obtained from the Division of Vocational Rehabilitation and the Employment Service. Another source was through the employers. The results show that information obtained from adult relatives was as valid as that obtained directly from the people with disabilities. Validity varied by the nature of the questions asked. It is suggested that surveys seeking factual information do need to be validated. Weiss and Davis question the reliance on interviewer rapport as the only validation approach. (9 references)

WEIGHTING

811.   Advertising Research Foundation. *A Comparison of Estimates from the Nights-at-Home Formula with Estimates from Six Calls*. New York, NY: Advertising Research Foundation, 1961. 63p.

The foci of the discussion are the advantages and limitations of weighting responses obtained from one and two calls when accounting for individuals who were not at home when an interviewer visited. The estimate used is referred to as the "nights-at-home" formula. The formula estimates were compared with data from a six-call survey which recovered 86.5 percent of the original sample. The two-call weighted estimate came closer than the one-call estimate. Appendixes include the estimates with and without recovered refusals, the questions used, and the sampling tolerances. (3 footnotes)

812.   Fuller, Carol H. "Weighting to Adjust for Survey Nonresponse." *Public Opinion Quarterly* 38, no. 2 (Summer 1974): 239-46.

Fuller considers the assumptions underlying the use of statistical weighting to adjust for nonresponse in sample surveys, as well as the implications for survey researchers using weighting techniques. Topics addressed include the following: (1) the distinction between judgment and probability samples; (2) proportionate and disproportionate sampling; (3) weighting with and without follow-up procedures; and (4) calculating nonresponse bias in proportions. A procedure used by the U.S. Bureau of the Census, and the Politz-Simmons method (for use with interviews when recalls are not included), are reviewed. Many comments apply particularly to mail surveys. It is concluded that "when the returns of respondents who are judged to be similar to the nonrespondents are multiplied to adjust for nonresponse, population estimates will be biased to the extent that the weighted returns differ from those that would have been obtained from the nonrespondents." Nonresponse bias can best be avoided by obtaining a complete follow-up (100 percent return) from a random sample of those not responding. (22 footnotes)

DISCIPLINE-ORIENTED STUDIES AND APPLICATIONS TO SPECIFIC AREAS

ASSOCIATION

813. Bywaters, David R., and Richard A. Hamilton. *How to Conduct Association Surveys.* Prepared for Foundation of the American Society of Association Executives. Washington, DC: Foundation of the American Society of Association Executives, 1976. 64p.

A brief outline of survey research history begins this volume, followed by a review of the major data collection methods (personal and telephone interviews, and mail questionnaires). In planning a survey the authors recommend identifying study objectives. Suggestions are made as to how to structure the chosen data collection device. Brief observations are provided on issues such as question wording, question type, pretesting, and interviewer training. Basic sampling methods are outlined, with a discussion of probability sampling, stratified random sampling, cluster sampling, and nonprobability sampling. Statistical analysis is covered, including measures of central tendency, frequencies, and cross tabulations. The book closes with comments on how survey data can be reported to the association members. The appendix provides six sample questionnaires. A seventeen-entry bibliography is included.

BUSINESS

814. Blankenship, Albert B., ed. *How to Conduct Consumer and Opinion Research: The Sampling Survey in Operation.* The American Council Series of Public Relations Books, edited by Rex F. Harlow. New York, NY: Harper & Brothers Publishers, 1946. 314p.

Twenty-six authors wrote the twenty-three chapters included in this three-part volume. Part 1 deals with surveys reported to business and industry. The subjects covered range from psychological concerns to public relations work and research involving advertising and radio, as well as editorials. Part 2 concerns surveys reported to the government and includes governmental use of research for information problems, survey use in the census, with consumer research, and by the Department of Agriculture. Surveys reported to the public and trends in public opinion research are discussed in part 3. In each section the authors describe the depth of the work pursued, as well as the characteristics of the results achieved. The following chapters have been selected from the volume, with individual annotations found at the indicated item number.

Part 1,   Chapter   2:   "Market Description – Quantitative and Qualitative." (Lockley - Item No. 27).

           Chapter 15:   "The Survey Applied to Editorial Problems." (Ludeke - Item No. 893).

Part 2,   Chapter 22:   "Attitude Surveying in the Department of Agriculture." (Campbell - Item No. 72).

Part 3,   Chapter 23:   "Trends in Public Opinion Research." (Alderson - Item No. 46).

815.   Bogart, Leo. "Use of Opinion Research." *Harvard Business Review* 29, no. 2 (March 1951): 113-24.

This article reviews the uses of "opinion surveys" by businesses, based on the experience of Standard Oil Company (New Jersey). Areas discussed by Bogart include the organization of research activities along the continuum of centralized to decentralized; the use of surveys to study broad currents as well as specific issues; surveys for communications concerns, attitude measurement, and political purposes; and surveys for determining popular images. Other areas of survey use are to determine sources of criticism, to conduct surveys in foreign countries for use by company affiliates in those locations, and for research involved in preparation for advertising. The article covers the use of survey results and means of gaining acceptance of surveys by company executives. Bogart closes with a consideration of professional standards. (1 footnote)

816.   Chamber of Commerce of the United States of America. Public Affairs Department. *Surveys as Tools for Interpreting Business.* Washington, DC: Public Affairs Department, Chamber of Commerce of the United States, [1975]. 29p.

The chamber guide is intended as a basic introduction to surveying. Researched and prepared by Donna C. Dodenhoff, public affairs assistant, the document includes the following chapters: "The Communications Challenge to Business"; "The Interpreting Business Survey"; and "Surveying in the Community." Part of the discussion is divided into four phases. Phase 1 considers the basic steps in conducting a survey. Phase 2 is devoted to numerous ways of preparing the written survey report. Phase 3 discusses how to implement and interpret a business program, and phase 4 offers suggestions on how to conduct a follow-up survey. Appendixes provide some sample surveys, glossaries of terms, and a sixty-entry further reading section.

817.　　Gray, Robert D. *Manual for Conducting an Employee Opinion Poll.* Bulletin no. 36. Pasadena, CA: Industrial Relations Center, California Institute of Technology, 1966. (various pagings)

As of 1966, the Industrial Relations Center (IRC) of the California Institute of Technology had conducted seventy surveys of forty-three companies covering 165,000 employees. IRC Director Robert D. Gray, along with L. Robert Sorensen and Gloria M. Fowler, published a 1953 version of this volume titled *Conducting an Employee Opinion Poll by Questionnaire.* The current publication includes questionnaires used by Walt Disney Productions at Disneyland, Southern California Gas Company, and United California Bank. The manual covers the following areas: (1) polling methods; (2) types of questionnaires; (3) contents of specialized questionnaires; (4) who should conduct the poll; (5) distribution and processing of the questionnaire; (6) reporting of results; (7) summary of steps taken; (8) costs; and (9) poll follow-up. Ten exhibits, containing examples of questionnaires, a cover letter, and estimates of cost, are included.

818.　　Hansen, Morris H., William N. Hurwitz, and Margaret Guerney. "Problems and Methods of the Sample Survey of Business." *Journal of the American Statistical Association* 41, no. 234 (June 1946): 173-89.

The article begins with a review of some fundamental considerations in sample designs, followed by a discussion of the difficulties found with the use of sampling in the business arena. Population characteristics and resources available to sample business activities are reviewed. Retailers are divided into two categories: those that are a part of existing lists, and the rest. A mathematical presentation explains how to cope with the sample of large stores, followed by the unlisted smaller stores. Hansen and the other researchers describe an estimation method using the 1940 *Census of Retail Trade.* Cost studies, sampling errors, and challenges from the fieldwork may cause modifications and variations in the size of the sample selected (and may give rise to regional or statewide samples). (8 footnotes)

819.   Hartwell, Dickson. "Business Asks the Public How It May Serve Best: Business Needs to Know Public Opinion No Less Than the Politician and through Scientific Surveys Is Finding Out." *Nation's Business* 28, no. 5 (May 1940): 26-28, 106-9.

The methodology of random sampling is explained, followed by a discussion of the qualities of a good interviewer. The article describes interviewing as "dull work," and one prominent organization admits to "100 percent turnover among its interviewers every year." Graduate students are recommended for the task. Hartwell distinguishes between publicly published polls which appear in newspapers versus those which businesses commission and keep private. Poll information is considered in relation to any propaganda value, as well as the possibility that polls may influence public opinion. The concept of the "faked" survey is discussed.

820.   Robinson, Claude. "Measuring Public Opinion." *Savings Bank Journal* 20, no. 4 (June 1939): 33, 78-79.

The works of Gallup and Roper are referred to as examples of the application of statistical methods to "objectify our appraisal of public trends." Robinson, president of the Opinion Research Corporation, discusses the collection of facts, rather than the following of hunches. The *Literary Digest* experience is reviewed, along with how opinion trends are determined. Also covered are polling on presidential actions during Roosevelt's attempt to restructure the Supreme Court, and Robinson's recommendations as to how polling could be applied to the depositors of the organizations which subscribe to the *Savings Bank Journal*.

821.   Roper, Elmo. "Sampling Technique in Surveying Occupations." *Occupations* 19, no. 7 (April 1941): 504-6.

Using the *Fortune* Survey sampling controls (geographical location, place size, sex, age, occupation, and economic level), Roper developed a procedure for determining by occupation when the likely employment opportunities were going to occur. The sampling procedure involved visits to 2,500 companies, with 1,000 of these being revisited some six months later. The companies employed four or more people, with a total employment of 400,000 to 500,000. The poll has two main purposes: to determine what a successful company looks like in terms of employees' age, sex, and experience, and to gain the opinions of employees on a variety of subjects including new skills needed, trends, and better educational methods. (1 footnote)

822.   Smith, James D. *Methodological Issues in the Collection of Financial Data: Problems and Recommendations.* Prepared for the Office of Assistant Secretary for Planning and Evaluation, Department of Health,

Education and Welfare. Contract number HEW-100-76-0179. Cambridge, MA: Abt Associates, 1977. 230p.

The purpose of this contribution is to identify the challenges which occur in the survey research process when attempting to determine financial information. The arena for the discussion is large government questionnaires. Problems considered include failing to obtain a response from sample units, questionnaire inadequacy leading to measurement errors, lack of motivation on the part of respondents, poorly identified recipient units and accounting periods, and the manner of data collection. Additional areas covered are sampling problems, data processing and imputation, and linkage of field data with administrative records. Major sections deal with nonresponse problems, locus of response problems, and response errors related to components of income, expenditures, assets, and liabilities. Twenty-five tables and four figures are provided, along with a sixteen-page bibliography.

823.   Smith, Lee. "The Boom in Polls: In the Wake of Their Resurgence, the Public-Opinion Pollsters Are Counting Businessmen among Their Biggest Clients." *Dun's Review* 103, no. 4 (April 1974): 49-53, 128, 131.

Smith reviews the business polling units of large well known public opinion organizations, as well as those private polling organizations which have grown into sizable companies. The companies discussed include the Opinion Research Corporation (ORC) of Princeton, New Jersey, headed by Claude Robinson; Daniel Yankelovich, Incorporated; Louis Harris and Associates, Incorporated; and the Gallup Organization. Syndicated studies by ORC, Yankelovich, Harris, the Roper Organization, and Gallup are discussed. The increasing costs of polling are noted, with some explanations provided. Focus is directed to the challenge of asking questions, with Harris advising: "You have to know what you are after." Cheating interviewers seem to be a problem common to all polling organizations. Various solutions are suggested.

COMMUNITY

824.   Blake, Brian F., Ned Kalb, and Vernon Ryan. "Citizen Opinion Surveys and Effective CD Efforts: One Objective of a Survey May Limit the Effectiveness of Another Objective." *Journal of the Community Development Society* 8, no. 2 (Fall 1977): 92-104.

The "CD" in the title refers to community development. The thrust of the article is that there are a number of possible objectives to be pursued in CD, each of which requires a different survey design. These survey objectives are discussed, beginning with a section which asks the reader to consider the problems and priorities. The second objective calls for identifying the positions of crucial local organizations, which includes the topics to be considered and the nature of the survey respondents. Objective three is titled "Enhancing Support for Locally Initiated Community Improvement Efforts," and objective four is maintaining the residents' sense of community as desirable and fulfilling. The authors believe that no single multiobjective survey could adequately address all of the areas reviewed above. Therefore, it is suggested that one or more of the objectives be separated in order to be successful in the other areas. The article contains a conclusion and addenda. (7 footnotes, 23 references)

825.   Burke, John G. *Community Attitudes Survey.* Community Program Development & Management Series, no. 21. Tallahassee, FL: Department of Community Affairs, Division of Technical Assistance, 1978. 16 leaves.

This document is designed to provide standard procedures for developing and implementing a community attitude survey. Topics covered include designing the questionnaire; distributing and collecting; tabulating; interpreting and reporting the results; and follow-up. A sample survey form is included. There are two lists at the end of the pamphlet, one for "dos" and the other for "don'ts." The lists are designed to provide new survey researchers with highly specific instructions to improve both the quality of surveys and to avoid pitfalls. The document was developed in Tallahassee, Florida, as a result of a number of requests from local officials for assistance in the development of community surveys.

826.   Chambers, Merritt M., and Howard M. Bell. *How to Make a Community Youth Survey.* American Council on Education Studies, edited by Clarence Stephen Marsh, Series 4, American Youth Commission, vol. 3, no. 2, January 1939. Washington, DC: American Council on Education, 1938. 45p.

The basic steps in how to make a community youth survey are divided into preparatory plans, conducting the survey, and presenting the results. Section 1 deals with developing the idea, sponsorship, funding, the survey budget, inexpensive methods, and the survey staff. Section 2 covers interviewer training, editing and coding, representative samples, data tabulation, and nontabulated responses. Chambers and Bell discuss report writing, graphics, publication, and follow-up in section 3. An appendix contains the eighty questions in the "Maryland Youth Survey Schedule No. 1." A thirty-three-item bibliography is included.

827.   Cohen, Mark W., Grayce M. Sills, and Andrew I. Schwebel. "A Two-Stage Process for Surveying Community Needs." *Journal of the Community Development Society* 8, no. 1 (Spring 1977): 54-61.

The first stage of the process is to determine the problems faced by the community, followed by stage two in which the prevalence and severity of the problems are ascertained. The initial step is conducted using open-ended interviews seeking as wide a range of discovery as possible. The second step uses closed-ended interviews utilizing items obtained from the first step. This approach is a means of reducing questionnaire bias and should provide the investigators with a clearer view of the needs of the community. (2 footnotes, 13 references).

828.   Jackson, John S., III, and William L. Shade. "Citizen Participation, Democratic Representation, and Survey Research." *Urban Affairs Quarterly* 9, no. 1 (September 1973): 57-89.

The two objectives of this article are to show how survey research can be used as a form of citizen participation, and to compare the citizen participation activists of the city to the community as a whole. The comparisons include socioeconomic characteristics, political attitudes, and the general orientation of both groups toward the community. A modification of the Cataldo card-sorting technique was used to measure citizen response to sixty alternative programs, policies, and projects. The authors found that the "citizen participant" views the city as an agent of change rather than as a service producer, which is the opposite view held by the average citizen. The article extensively reviews other literature in the area of citizen participation. (7 footnotes, 27 references)

829.   Josephson, Eric. "Resistance to Community Surveys." *Social Problems* 18, no. 1 (Summer 1970): 117-29.

In 1967 a pilot survey of adolescent health was undertaken in the Washington Heights (Harlem) health district of New York City. For the study 122 interviews were completed, along with medical examinations conducted during the summer for about half the group. Beginning at the end of 1967, the plan was to interview as many as one thousand adolescents ages twelve to seventeen. A protest began shortly after the main project was underway. An unfavorable report appeared in the *Amsterdam News*, a local newspaper. A meeting was held at a local church with seventy-five in attendance. Media attention grew to radio-broadcast discussions and a story in the *New York Times*. Josephson advises the following actions as a means to address concerns raised in the community: (1) screen interviewers very carefully; (2) establish community participation through an advisory committee; (3) overcome perceptions of threat caused by the survey topic; (4) explain the value and utility of the research; (5) assure privacy of information; and (6) communicate that the results of the study will be of value to the community. (9 references)

830.   Stark, Stephen L. *Conducting Community Surveys*. Community Education How To Series. Midland, MI: Pendell Publishing Company, 1976. 39p.

This manual on how to conduct the community survey is divided into sections dealing with the philosophy behind surveying, the organization, and the mechanics. The organization section addresses the questions of who, what, and when. The mechanics section covers writing the instrument, publicity, training, and tabulating results. Stark has created a list of ten suggestions for successfully completing the survey, including the following: "act on the findings." The appendix has examples of a questionnaire and four surveys. The publication also provides examples of a record sheet, a survey worksheet, and a list of survey procedures which includes interviewing suggestions. (2 references).

831.   Swander, T. Lester. "Let's Make a Survey – Effective!!" *Family* 16, no. 9 (January 1936): 284-85.

A number of principles are outlined for community organizations planning a survey. These include the following: (1) a definite and practical objective is needed for the survey; (2) agency approval should be obtained; (3) agency participation is important during the planning and conducting of the survey; (4) competency of sponsoring committees is necessary; (5) the conference approach is recommended for "group thinking" as a means of obtaining cooperation; and (6) the survey should lead to both data and action thereon. A series of seven points is made concerning needs which surveys are unable to meet and what must be done in these cases. Surveys are not (1) planning substitutes, (2) substitutes for weak leadership, (3) able to achieve social change without disturbing the status quo, (4) able to generate, alone, coordinated programs, (5) alternatives to time needs for adjustments to change, (6) useful unless appropriate interpretation accompanies the process and data analysis, and (7) alternatives to adequate financial support from a community.

832.   Wolf, Eleanor P. "Some Questions about Community Self-Surveys: When Amateurs Conduct Research." *Human Organization* 23, no. 1 (Spring 1964): 85-89.

The community self-surveys referred to here are those in which "the research itself is conducted by non-professionals." Issues raised include violations of ethical practices ("community self-surveys violate such standards constantly"), and the possible effects of asking questions. Various forms of bias are discussed, including topical bias, oversimplification bias, and commitment bias. Additionally, the problem of overinterviewing is considered. Some of the possible problems associated with amateur "researchers" are cited as potential causes of increased refusal rates on interviews, and unreturned questionnaires. The risks to professional research efforts are reviewed. (18 footnotes)

ECONOMICS

833.   Brady, Dorothy S., and Faith M. Williams. "Advances in the Techniques of Measuring and Estimating Consumer Expenditures." *Journal of Farm Economics* 25 (May 1945): 315-44.

The challenges of measuring income are presented, with a definition of income provided, followed by a discussion of farm income, wage and salary income, and other types of monetary income. Nonmoney income is also covered. Biases in reporting income receive consideration. Methods of data collection are reviewed, namely, account keeping versus schedule interviewing. The option of short- versus long-schedule formats is discussed. The authors maintain that the above-described test surveys, conducted in 1944, were the first "systematic" tests which could be summarized in quantitative terms. Expenditures are defined, and the breadth of coverage explained along with a scheme for classification. Brady and Williams discuss the measurement of savings and consider how to estimate total consumer expenditures. The presentation closes with a view to the importance of understanding consumer expenditures both in the United States and for the rest of the world in the post-World War II era. (21 footnotes)

834.   Katona, George. "The Function of Survey Research in Economics." In *Common Frontiers of the Social Sciences*, edited by Mirra Komarovsky, 358-75. Glencoe, IL: Free Press and Falcon's Wing Press, [1957]. 439p.

"Microeconomic distributions" are described as data gathered through the fact-finding approach of economic surveys. Sample surveys conducted by the Bureau of the Census are cited, with unemployment statistics noted as one example. Studies of economic behavior and economic attitudes are covered, beginning with those which address the effects of income change. Other topics discussed include the effects of liquid asset holdings and inflationary forces. Katona views the "most important single contribution of survey research to economics" as "the integration of attitudinal and motivational data with the study of economic processes." In a section describing the values and limitations of survey research in economics, Katona outlines key points made earlier in the presentation, including the observation that "the main function of survey data is to understand and predict short-term changes in economic behavior." Survey research is described as ascertaining "relatively superficial or surface character" patterns of motivation, with some doubt as to whether "deep-seated, elusive motives" will be reachable. A discussion follows of how economics can be integrated with other social sciences. The role of social psychology is considered along with the field of economic psychology (which utilizes economic theory as well as social-psychological theory). (2 unnumbered footnotes, 11 references)

835.   Katona, George, Lawrence R. Klein, John B. Lansing, and James N. Morgan. *Contributions of Survey Methods to Economics*, edited by Lawrence R. Klein. New York, NY: Columbia University Press, 1954. 269p.

The data used in this volume have been gathered annually since 1946 as part of the Economic Behavior Program conducted by the Survey Research Center (a division of the Institute for Social Research of the University of Michigan), specifically the *Survey of Consumer Finances* for the Board of Governors of the Federal Reserve System. In the first chapter Lansing presents survey concepts and discusses income, savings, and consumption. Repeated interviews and reinterviews are explained. Katona discusses the functions of survey research in the second chapter which deals with variability as found in consumer behavior. Klein considers the principles of estimation from survey data in chapter 5 and addresses the challenge of prediction in chapter 6. (Chapter 1 - 7 footnotes; chapter 2 - 11 footnotes; chapter 5 - 22 footnotes; and chapter 6 - 7 footnotes)

836.   Lamale, Helen Humes. *Study of Consumer Expenditures Incomes and Savings: Methodology of the Survey of Consumer Expenditures in 1950.* Study of Consumer Expenditures, Incomes and Savings. [Philadelphia, PA]: University of Pennsylvania, 1959. 359p.

The historical setting and significant technical and administrative procedures are described. The 1950 survey was conducted in ninety-one urban areas in cities from 2,500 to nine-plus million. Reports were obtained from 10,791 families and 1,698 single consumers. The sampling units were selected by the U.S. Bureau of the Census, and the data were collected by and for the U.S. Bureau of Labor Statistics (BLS). Potential respondents received a mailing indicating that a BLS representative would call, and that participation was voluntary and without remuneration. An average family which agreed to cooperate received one interview lasting approximately eight hours. A staff of 1,065 interviewers was needed. The pay rate was $1.27 per hour. Sampling nonresponse and response errors are discussed. On average nonresponse was about 20 percent, ranging from 3 to 33 percent. Wage and salary information were most accurately reported, with income from interest, dividends, and rent significantly underreported. The 1950 data are compared with data from other sources. The analytical uses of the data in social welfare, economics, and market research are outlined, as well as for the *Consumer Price Index* and place-to-place comparisons. The study, conducted by the Wharton School of Finance and Commerce in cooperation with the BLS, was funded by a grant from the Ford Foundation. The first part consists of eighteen volumes of statistical tables of expenditures; the second part involves academic studies using the data. Almost two hundred pages of the methodology volume is comprised of appendixes covering a variety of subjects including survey forms, dwelling unit samples, characteristics of the cities selected, and summaries of expenditure surveys from 1888 to 1950. The volume includes a six-page index and numerous footnotes numbered individually on each page.

837.   Lansing, John B., and James N. Morgan. *Economic Survey Methods.* [Ann Arbor, MI: Survey Research Center, University of Michigan], 1971. 430p.

The authors became aware that no available volume addressed the needs of staff training, graduate teaching, and research sponsors as to what constitutes a good study design. This multipurpose textbook covers the following topics: (1) the historical development of surveys and appropriate and inappropriate uses of economic surveys; (2) survey design; (3) sampling challenges with economic surveys; (4) data collection methodology; (5) data preparation for analysis; (6) analysis; and (7) the financing, organization, and utilization of survey research. Each chapter has footnotes (provided as chapter endnotes), and at the end of the volume there is a six-page bibliography of books and articles published by the staff of the Economic Behavior Program of the Survey Research Center.

838.   Morgan, James N. "Contributions of Survey Research to Economics." In *Survey Research in the Social Sciences*, edited by Charles Y. Glock, with contributions by John W. Bennett, et al., 217-68. New York, NY: Russell Sage Foundation, 1967. 543p.

In a review of economic survey research Morgan discusses household surveys, other economic activities of households, and business behavior. The use of survey data in economics is described in the following areas: (1) behavioral theory; (2) short-run changes in behavior; (3) middle-range changes in behavior; (4) with structural models; (5) long-term changes; and (6) testing economics hypotheses. Methodological developments, problems, and prospects are considered, with sections dealing with the accuracy of validity of data, methods of analysis, the economic problems of survey research, the new sources and types of survey data, and areas for further study. A chapter summary is provided. A 157-entry bibliography is included. (72 footnotes)

EDUCATION

839.   Brieve, Fred J., and Aubrey P. Johnston. "Surveys for Local Education Agencies: Theoretical and Practical Considerations." *California Journal of Educational Research* 24, no. 2 (March 1973): 78-92.

Beginning with a consideration of why a survey should be conducted, the authors explore some of the purposes and limitations of survey research, along with considerable discussion of the various stages of planning involved. An eight-point planning safeguard guide is provided. The article closes with a section on interpreting data and using the results as management tools. Brieve and Johnston do not believe that the survey should be used as a "decision-maker in its own right." Rather, the decision should be in the hands of the administrator who may be able to make wiser decisions with the use of survey research. (7 footnotes, 6 references)

840.   Cornell, Francis G. "Sample Surveys in Education." *Review of Educational Research* 24, no. 5 (December 1954): 359-74.

The literature on sample surveys in education is reviewed, covering the years from mid-1951 through mid-1954. The nature of survey sample design is addressed, along with alternative sample designs. Survey errors are discussed, with special attention directed to the works on nonresponse. U.S. Bureau of the Census and education surveys are considered. The author examined the pertinent literature indexed in the "usual sources." Excluded are master's theses and doctoral dissertations, as well as many specialized studies. Cornell believes that survey sample methodology is being underutilized in the field of education. Sample survey methods deal with the issues of determining how many or how much (the challenge of enumeration). (1 footnote, 60 references)

841.   Cornell, Francis G., and Eugene P. McLoone. "Design of Sample Surveys in Education." *Review of Educational Research* 33, no. 5 (December 1963): 523-32.

The authors maintain that the field of education is not in the forefront of research into the methodology and application of sample surveys. Sample survey methods are designed to ascertain how many or how much – in other words the challenge of enumeration. The article, containing a review of the literature from late 1960 to late 1963, begins by discussing nontechnical sources and continues with the development of statistical theory. Sections are titled "Use of Available Lists in Sampling Procedures," "Sampling as a Means of Identifying Information in a Census," and "Teacher Surveys." A list of seven possible limitations or errors in educational surveys concludes the article. Specific studies discussed include Project Talent (conducted by the American Institute for Research and dealing with characteristics of schools and their effects upon students), and Furno's study [Item No. 843] which statistically evaluated the Cost of Education Index. (68 references)

842.   Eastmond, Jefferson N. *Conducting Public Opinion Surveys in School Systems: A "Do-It-Yourself" Activity for Project NEXT STEP*. Next Step

[series]. Salt Lake City, UT: Worldwide Education and Research Institute, 1971. 39p.

This booklet is designed to enable local school districts, Parent-Teacher Associations, or other educational units to conduct polls, with pupils or volunteer groups as the data gatherers. Eastmond provides sections on school needs assessment by polling, sample size determination, the poll instrument, and tabulating and interpreting the results. Appendixes include a statistical formula, a table of random numbers, and an example of poll data for a selected school district. Footnotes are included.

843.   Furno, Orlando F. "Sample Survey Designs in Education – Focus on Administrative Utilization." *Review of Educational Research* 36, no. 5 (December 1966): 552-65.

Furno's article reviews the literature on sample survey design in education found between December 1963 and 1966. The surveys are drawn from four periodicals with varying dates for each, within the time frame noted. The journals are the *American Educational Research Journal*, the *Journal of Educational Psychology*, the *Journal of Educational Research*, and the *Review of Educational Research*. Considered are 292 articles, with 61 perceived to be primary sources for use in this review. Furno wrote the article for school administrators who had little or no background in survey research, but who nevertheless must use survey research data as a basis for decision making. The entire gamut of the field is addressed, from probability theory to data collection and analysis. The nontechnical treatment contains examples found in the referenced literature. (67 references)

844.   Gallagher, Donald R. "Learn Citizens Opinions through Surveys: Surveys Can Be Helpful in Learning What Citizens Think about What Educators Are Doing with Tax Dollars." *Journal of Educational Communication* 1, no. 5 (March-April 1976): 20-25.

The specific need Gallagher describes is for school administrators to understand what citizens think about the way schools are using tax dollars. A series of eleven questions are posed before a survey can be undertaken, such as what questions should be asked, should an outside agency conduct the survey, and what would be the optimal time to conduct the survey. The issues of sampling, how to interview, and designing the questionnaire receive attention. A table compares and contrasts the advantages and disadvantages of four types of data collection, namely, the personal interview, the telephone interview, the drop-off/pick-up questionnaire, and the mailed questionnaire.

845.   National School Public Relations Association. *Feel Their Pulse: A Guide to School Opinion Polling.* [Washington, DC]: National School Public Relations Association, [1956]. 48p.

Seven chapters guide the reader through a series of how-to steps accompanied by a number of humorous graphics. The chapters consider these topics: (1) a school that has tried the polling approach; (2) the reasons why one might wish to poll; (3) the desirability of getting professional assistance with polling; (4) the questionnaire versus the interview; (5) question wording; (6) sampling; (7) interpreting results; and (8) the time required to appropriately conduct the poll. The chapter on wording provides a checklist of fourteen points to consider, and the last chapter lists twelve steps to follow from initiating the pilot study through implementing the findings. The appendix contains five examples of questionnaires. (10 references)

846.   Nunnery, Michael Y., and Ralph B. Kimbrough. "Public Opinion Polling." Chap. 4 in *Politics, Power, Polls, and School Elections*, 59-102. Berkeley, CA: McCutchan Publishing Corporation, [1971]. 174p.

The volume is intended as a textbook for the training of school administrators at the college or university level. Nunnery and Kimbrough have prepared what they hope will be a "guide or chart for skillful leadership in politics." Chapter 4 covers poll purposes; sample selection; data collection; instrument type; organization and conduct; number, cost, and value of polls; and the use of poll data in school elections. Nine footnotes are provided, as well as nine suggested readings.

847.   Orlich, Donald C., Patricia A. Clark, Nancy M. Fagan, and Gary A. Rust. *Guide to Sensible Surveys.* Olympia, WA: Research Coordinating Unit, Washington State Commission for Vocational Education, 1975. 162p. Microfiche. (ED 112 017)

This manual, designed for vocational educators, provides the basics for constructing questionnaires and conducting interviews. The nine chapters cover the following topics: (1) data collection techniques; (2) question writing; (3) forced-response questions; (4) coding; (5) preventing biased results; (6) conducting the survey; (7) data tabulation; (8) statistical analysis; and (9) planning and preparing the report. Examples are provided throughout. The appendixes include three model questionnaire formats. A two-page index is included, along with twelve references.

848.   Peach, Larry. "How to Take an Honest District Survey." *American School Board Journal* 159, no. 12 (June 1972): 29-30.

Peach suggests obtaining a list of all voting-age residents in the school district, and, if that is not available, conducting a house-to-house canvass in the district to generate a sample. The author favors the interview approach, rather than mail questionnaires which will produce returns of 40 to 50 percent and likely to be biased in favor of those already interested in the district's schools. Question format is discussed. A warning is provided to use "utmost discretion" with questions so as to avoid antagonizing or offending. Community involvement in the survey is stressed, as is the need to train interviewers to be friendly, firm, and impartial. Peach recommends the simplest form of results reporting – that of percentages of respondents. The results can be "translated readily into feasible, specific plans of action or change" by the school district staff. (2 footnotes)

849.   Pittillo, Robert A., Jr., and William G. Katzenmeyer. "Specifications for a School District Survey: Here Is One Way to Insure That a Survey of Your District Will Not Be a Waste of Time and Money." *School Management* 15, no. 4 (April 1971): 34-35.

Issues surrounding the retention of an outside consulting team to conduct a school district survey are explored, and the rationale for choosing such an approach over internal options is covered. The authors list nine points which should be included in the survey contract: (1) the definition of the survey scope; (2) the minimum sources of input; (3) the survey time schedule; (4) the role of the board of education; (5) the preliminary report details; (6) the final report procedure; (7) the format and number of copies of the final report; (8) the total cost; and (9) the actual survey staff working on the project. These specifications are designed to avoid inadequate results, financial waste, and loss of confidence by staff and community. Pittillo and Katzenmeyer describe how one school district successfully followed the above specifications.

850.   Roaden, O. Paul. "Surveys – Valuable Tool for Planners." *American School & University* 37, no. 9 (May 1965): 23-25, 27.

A survey is defined as "an inventory and evaluation of the factors that determine the existing conditions in a specific school or school system." Three types are identified as the educational survey, the plant and facilities survey, and the comprehensive survey, with the latter being basically a combination of the first two types. Roaden discusses four approaches to conducting surveys: self-surveys; the use of the services of a university survey; the use of a private consulting firm; and self-surveys under the direction of a qualified university survey team or private consulting firm. Costs are based on the nature, scope, and depth of the survey, as well as on the size and complexity of the school system.

851.   Stark, Nancy. "How Schools Can Listen to the Community." *American Education* 7, no. 6 (July 1971): 8-11.

Inforet (an acronym standing for "information return") is an approach to polling which includes the use of professionals, data processing equipment, and volunteers. Developed for the Oakland County (Michigan) schools, a one-time poll cost about $250 in 1971; a nine-month survey program cost about $2000. Approximately 3,600 individuals can be questioned in the nine-month survey program, and a trained volunteer working for fifteen hours can achieve 95 percent reliability. Both school records and voter registration lists are utilized as the basis for samples. A proposed schedule for Inforet use over several years is included.

852.   Thomas, John H., Stuart C. Smith, and John S. Hall. *Polling and Survey Research*. Analysis and Bibliography Series, no. 17. Arlington, VA: National School Public Relations Association; Eugene, OR: Oregon University, ERIC Clearinghouse on Educational Management, 1973. 20p. (Clearinghouse Accession no. EA 005 328; ERIC Document no. ED 087 083.)

Intended as a source of practical information for schools conducting surveys, this document provides a review of some of the advantages and disadvantages of surveys and the steps involved in conducting them. The choice of the survey method over other alternatives is considered, followed by questionnaire construction and data analysis. Three examples are described in the following locations: Lincoln, Nebraska; Oakland, Michigan; and Santa Clara County, California. Although the eighty-one-item bibliography focuses primarily on the literature relating to education, it also contains general citations relating to statistics, analysis, interviewing, and questionnaire construction, as well as citations to some resources which discuss the topic area in broad terms.

853.   Trow, Martin. "Education and Survey Research." In *Survey Research in the Social Sciences*, edited by Charles Y. Glock, with contributions by John W. Bennett, et al., 315-75. New York, NY: Russell Sage Foundation, 1967. 543p.

The nature of survey research as covered in education research methods textbooks is discussed, along with the role survey research plays in educational sociology. Major types of surveys are explained, as in descriptive, explanatory, and "pseudo." The advantages and challenges of survey research in education and problems with using survey research with teachers and administrators are described. Also reviewed are areas for future survey research in education and the relevance of survey research to educational practice. A seventy-six-entry bibliography is provided.

854.   Walker, Helen M. "Poll-Taking and Educational Research." *High Points* 31, no. 1 (January 1949): 5-7.

The first part of the article differentiates between quota sampling and random sampling. It is reported that all opinion polls are using quota sampling even though the experts are aware of the "dangers" of this approach. Random sampling is described as a method using a mechanical device which "precludes all conscious choice." The second portion of the Walker article applies similar sampling concerns to the area of educational research, with the observation that some of these studies do not even "stratify the universe." More testing and government aid for research are suggested.

GOVERNMENT

855.   Campbell, Angus. "The Uses of Interview Surveys in Federal Administration." *Journal of Social Issues* 2, no. 2 (May 1946): 14-22.

Survey research is reported to have been widely used by the federal government during World War II. The need by the government to assess the public's attitude led to a significant increase in fact-finding services. Campbell reviews these areas as (1) ascertaining how well the public is informed, (2) determining the success of government information campaigns (such as the War Bond Drives), (3) planning the implementation of new programs, (4) ascertaining public attitude on government actions and specifically why the attitude is held, (5) determining how the public feels about proposed action, (6) reporting public activity, (7) assessing public intentions, and (8) determining if there are actions which the government should be undertaking in order to meet unfulfilled needs of the public. Campbell expresses concern that a peacetime economy and government may not support research to the degree as experienced during the previous five years.

856.   Daneke, Gregory A., and Patricia Klobus-Edwards. "Survey Research for Public Administrators." *Public Administration Review* 39, no. 5 (September-October 1979): 421-26.

The purpose of this article is to provide an overview of survey research for those individuals engaged in administrative policy development. The authors foresee a time when surveys might become the normal approach when considering the planning, evaluation, and negotiation of programs and policies. A study is cited showing that 50 percent of those surveyed (in cities over 100,000 and counties over 250,000) had used some form of survey. Daneke and Klobus-Edwards consider reasons for survey use reluctance, including the fear that surveys may be change agents. Strategic planning, and input and output analysis, are discussed. General guidelines are provided, including an eight-point list of suggestions for the construction of the survey instrument. The authors also cover format and sampling techniques. Analysis using cross tabulation, comparison of mean responses, and regression concludes the review. (6 footnotes, 17 references)

857.   Owen, Raymond E. *A Survey Manual for State Legislators.* Pittsburgh, PA: University Center for International Studies, University of Pittsburgh, 1975. 69p.

The manual, designed to serve as a brief guide to enable state legislators to conduct valid low-cost surveys, is divided into three chapters. Chapter 1 introduces the topic of surveys, discusses samples, and closes with the practical steps necessary when using sampling techniques. Chapter 2 deals with types of interviews; questionnaire construction; question form, type, and order; and the importance of interviewer training. In chapter 3 Owen discusses the compilation and analysis of results, including a section on ethics. The five appendixes cover a checklist of steps to be followed in sample creation, the "dos" and "don'ts" of interviews, suggestions for data analysis, a random numbers table, and a sample questionnaire. There are no references included, although three works are cited in the preface for more in-depth reading.

858.   Robinson, James A. "Survey Interviewing among Members of Congress." *Public Opinion Quarterly* 24, no. 1 (Spring 1960): 127-38.

The period considered is 1957 to 1958 (the Eighty-fifth Congress). The article reviews the procedures used in obtaining interviews, the difficulties encountered in scheduling appointments, and the failure to obtain responses to certain questions. Interviews were conducted with a sample of one hundred reelected representatives and senators as part of a larger study. The interviewers used were three graduate students in political science (only one of whom was somewhat experienced), and five political scientists, each having experience in interviewing Washington officials. Congressmen were initially contacted by mail to explain the purposes of the research. A follow-up telephone call to a secretary requested a thirty- to forty-five-minute appointment. In some cases repeated callbacks (about 3.3 average per respondent) were necessary. The interviewers eventually secured eighty-six of the one hundred interviews sought (a figure said to compare favorably with those of other surveys). Nine interviews had to be conducted with staff members; five interviews were discarded. Robinson reviews some of the differences between journalistic and survey interviews. In spite of the obstacles, answers were eventually obtained for 90 percent of the questions (again a number comparing favorably to other sample surveys). It is concluded that "in terms of time and effort the cost of securing the interviews will be relatively high, but results should be acceptable." (15 footnotes)

859.   Saroff, Jerome R., and Alberta Z. Levitan. *Survey Manual for Comprehensive Urban Planning: The Use of Opinion Surveys and Sampling*

Techniques in the Planning Process. SEG Report no. 19. College, Alaska: Institute of Social, Economic and Government Research, University of Alaska, 1969. 143p. [Distributed by the U.S. Department of Commerce/National Bureau of Standards, Clearinghouse for Federal Scientific and Technical Information, Technical report no. PB 184 004.]

There are two parts to this study. The first consists of a case study of housing and the environment in Providence, Rhode Island. The second is a manual dealing with techniques and analysis in survey research. The case study is discussed in successive chapters which cover background, research design, fieldwork, and results. The methodologies chapters address research design, sampling, questionnaire construction, data collection, data processing, and preparation of the final report. Areas of research into which this study delved are opinions on the quality of public facilities, reasons for moving, issues concerning the Urban Renewal and Model Cities programs, and an evaluation of social welfare programs. Eleven tables, two diagrams, and two appendixes are provided. (49 references).

860. *Survey Research Methods for Planners.* The Second Annual Summer Institute in Environmental Planning and Design, no. 8. Sponsored by the College of Environmental Design and Continuing Education in City, Regional, and Environmental Planning, University Extension, University of California, Berkeley. Berkeley, CA: University Extension, University of California, 1976. 228 pages with various paginations.

Number 8 of this series consists of twenty-one reading selections utilized at the Second Annual Summer Institute in Environmental Planning and Design held 21 June to 9 July 1976. The sixth reading in the volume, authored by George Y. Glock, is titled "A Brief History of Survey Research." Glock contributes two other items of relevance to this bibliography: paper number 8, "Variations on the Cross-Sectional Design," and paper number 15, "Survey Design and Analysis." Earl R. Babbie's study titled "Three Examples of Sample Design" is the tenth selection in the volume.

861. U.S. Congress. House. Committee on Government Operations. *State Department Public Opinion Polls: Hearings before a Subcommittee.* 85th Cong., 1st sess., 21 June, 1, 8, 9, 10, 11 July 1957. Washington, DC: U.S. Government Printing Office, 1957. 351p. [SuDoc Y4.G74/7:St2]

The testimony and statements of fourteen individuals are recorded. Clyde Hart, director of the National Opinion Research Center (NORC), and Paul Sheatsley, the eastern representative of NORC, were present to answer questions as to how NORC conducted State Department polls. Hart is questioned about the specifics of the NORC sampling approach in which he describes area probability sampling. A detailed NORC document, "Description of Stratification of Primary

Sampling Units, Selection of Sample Areas, and Allocation of Cases," is part of the record. (A fuller account, reproduced from hearings before a Senate committee in 1953-54, appears in the appendix.) Further questions from the committee concern the topics and wording of actual NORC survey questions – especially loaded and leading questions. At issue is the nature of the data that were gathered concerning foreign affairs, and the question as to whether NORC was aware that the State Department was using the information to "formulate foreign policy in relation to the granting of foreign aid." No other individuals from the polling community addressed the committee. Numerous letters and statements from seventeen individuals are part of the record, as well as the testimony or statements of sixteen individuals over the six-day period.

862.   Webb, Kenneth, and Harry P. Hatry, with contributions from Louis H. Blair, et al. *Obtaining Citizen Feedback: The Application of Citizen Surveys to Local Governments*. [Washington, DC]: Urban Institute, [1973]. 105p.

Designed for use by city and county governments (especially for those units conducting regular annual surveys), this guide presents an outline of the major areas of concern. The document begins with a review of the uses of citizen surveys, and is followed by a chapter expressing the dangers and pitfalls of the approach. The authors then address survey procedures, costs and funding sources, and organizational alternatives in the management of surveys. Recommendations are suggested for individual local governments, associations, foundations, and state and federal governments. Six appendixes provide examples of a questionnaire, a cover letter, and a table showing sample size versus precision. A forty-three-item bibliography is included.

863.   Weiss, Carol H., and Harry P. Hatry. *An Introduction to Sample Surveys for Government Managers*. Report no. UI-72-108-65. Washington, DC: Urban Institute, March 1971. 47p. Microfiche. (ED 111 077)

The nature, implications, and costs of sample surveys are explored in light of their potential uses by government managers. Most of the attention is focused on the environment in which government employees are the respondents. Considered are the steps in a survey, the advantages of conducting government-sponsored research (as compared with university or private organization sponsorship), and the costs involved at each phase of the process. Weiss and Hatry cover accuracy, data confidentiality, the avoidance of sensitive questions where possible, and interviewing in low-income minority areas. Personal interviews, mail surveys, and telephone surveys are separately addressed in the report. Demonstrated are cost comparisons among samples of four hundred, five hundred, and one thousand interviews. (15 references)

HEALTH AND MEDICINE

864.   Andersen, Ronald, Judith Kasper, Martin R. Frankel, and Associates.
         Total Survey Error: Applications to Improve Health Surveys. National
         Opinion Research Center Series in Social Research; Jossey-Bass Social
         and Behavioral Science Series. San Francisco, CA: Jossey-Bass Inc., Pub-
         lishers, 1979. 296p.

The validity and reliability of data collected in a large national survey covering
health care use and expenditures are explored. The project undertaken cost in
excess of one million dollars to collect and analyze the data. Verification is estimated to have used about one-third of the resources, causing the total data collection time to be extended by approximately eighteen months. The following
writers contributed to the volume: Ronald Andersen, Martha J. Banks, Virginia
S. Daughety, Martin R. Frankel, and Judith Ann (Dellinger) Kasper. Some of
the eleven chapters were written by as many as three authors, with several contributors responsible for more than one chapter. The volume is divided into four
parts covering the overview, estimates of survey error, alternative approaches to
improve survey estimates, and a summary and implications. In the first part the
authors discuss a model of total survey error which uses Leslie Kish's classification of sources of bias and variable error [Item No. 192]. The researchers found
that the assumption that respondents in health surveys generally underreport is
incorrect, with many examples cited showing the opposite. It is reported that bias
correcting in social survey estimates could go "either way," as it has been shown
that respondents both overestimate and underreport by using an estimating
technique based on "usual behavior" when asked to recall information from as
long ago as one year. There are three appendixes: "Calculation of Bias"; "Example of Adjustment Factors When One of Them Lies Outside of a Desired Range";
and "Definition of Variables and Variable Frequencies." The volume includes a
four-page index. (74 references)

865.   Breslow, Lester. "Uses and Limitations of the California Health Survey
         for Studying the Epidemiology of Chronic Disease." *American Journal
         of Public Health* 47, no. 1 (January 1957): 168-72.

The uses of the California Health Survey with respect to the epidemiology of
chronic disease include the following: (1) providing a demographic description
of the population, including patterns of its household composition, occupation,
income levels, racial characteristics, age, sex, and marital status; (2) portraying
the overall picture of community health; (3) adding to the knowledge base dealing
with diseases; (4) determining how health services are used; (5) creating lists of
patients for more detailed epidemiologic study; and (6) generating data on the
causes of diseases. The limitations include the fact that the survey data on diseases
which occur infrequently do not permit useful observation to be made (10,000

households were included). In addition, the survey's exclusion of the institutional population removed high levels of chronic disease (125,000 Californians were institutionalized with over one-third suffering from chronic mental illness). The overall purpose of the survey was to ascertain the incidence of disease, with needs determination as the goal.

866.   Calver, Homer N., and Otis T. Wingo, Jr. "Public Opinion Measurement as an Instrument in Public Health Practice." *American Journal of Public Health* 37, no. 4 (April 1947): 426-30.

The purpose of this article is to alert public health officials that opinion measurement "approaches an exact science" and has definite advantages. The authors outline some of the mandatory requirements of survey work, such as the representativeness of the sample, as well as the adequacy of the number of respondents. Also discussed are the qualities of the interviewers and the timing of surveys. National survey results can be used for newspaper stories and to provide guidance to local health programs. A list of ten uses for locally conducted health surveys is provided. (3 references)

867.   Cannell, Charles F., Floyd J. Fowler, Jr., and Kent H. Marquis. *The Influence of Interviewer and Respondent Psychological and Behavioral Variables on the Reporting in Household Interviews*. In *Vital and Health Statistics: Data Evaluation and Methods Research*. Public Health Service Publication No. 1000, Series 2, No. 26. Washington, DC: U.S. Department of Health, Education, and Welfare, Public Health Service, National Center for Health Statistics, March 1968. 65p. [SuDoc FS2.85/2:2/no.26]

Inaccuracies in interviews have long been a concern for researchers. This study examines the respondents' and the interviewers' reactions to the Health Interview Survey. The following are some of the findings which emerged: "(1) respondent feelings, level of information about the survey, motives, attitudes, and perceptions are not directly related to health reporting behavior; (2) interviewer attitudes, preferences, styles of interviewing, or expectations as measured here are not related to the reporting of conditions she obtained from her respondents; (3) respondent demographic characteristics showed no important systematic associations with the reporting index"; and (4) "the higher the level of behavioral activity in the interview the better the overall reporting on the part of the respondent." A total of 412 respondents were observed and reinterviewed. Four appendixes are included, the last of which provides the interview observation form (fourteen pages). Also included are twenty-four footnotes and a six-item bibliography.

868.   Feldman, Jacob J. "The Household Interview Survey as a Technique for the Collection of Morbidity Data." *Journal of Chronic Diseases* 11, no. 5 (May 1960): 535-57.

The household surveys discussed here are considered primarily in relation to how they benefit medical research. The advantages of surveys are discussed in terms of sampling, including quality and the breadth of data which can be collected. More than half the article addresses inaccuracies of diagnoses found in interview surveys. The nature of a "true diagnosis" is considered. The impact of single-visit surveys versus periodic visits is presented, with the benefits of the latter having a greater likelihood of respondents recalling conditions. The choice between having every member of a household interviewed versus the use of "household informants" is related. The use of informants produces a lower number of clinically determined conditions being reported. Feldman debates the issue as to what level of specificity should be utilized for diagnostic categories. Medical research would need specific diagnostic categories, while surveys tend to seek "global assessments." Standards of agreement are observed whereby the respondents' remarks are matched with the appropriate clinical diagnosis, as well as standards of diagnostic validity in which physicians verify the accuracy of the conditions relayed in the interviews. The challenge of the underreporting of medical conditions is presented, noting that the adequacy of the data may vary considerably depending upon the disease in question. The author sees no alternative to the survey for collecting data on attended and unattended acute illness, and therefore believes that the technique will continue to be used. (Unnumbered footnotes and 84 references)

869.   Guernsey, Paul D. "The Modern Public Opinion Poll: A Means of Defining and Appraising Community Health Education Problems." *American Journal of Public Health* 32, no. 9 (September 1942): 973-78.

Guernsey introduces the topic by describing a typical interview environment, and then proceeds to explain why poll data can be useful in the community health education field. Several examples of poll results are provided. Polling techniques are briefly described, with the caveat that representative cross-section sampling is more important than the number of respondents interviewed. Also highlighted is that the results present opinions only from the time that they were collected. Guernsey observes that the cost of polling is not prohibitive. (1 reference)

870.   Marquis, Kent H., Charles F. Cannell, and Andre Laurent. *Effects of Reinforcement, Question Length, and Reinterviews on Reporting Health Events in Household Interviews.* Ann Arbor, MI: Survey Research Center, September 1971. 82 leaves.

Respondent selection was conducted by using randomly chosen African Americans from two census tracts in Jackson, Michigan. The tracts contained "intact white families" of moderate income, with a small proportion of individuals over age sixty-five and a high proportion of native-born citizens. A sample size of four hundred was used for the original interviews. The study results show that different interviewing procedures are effective for different respondent education groups. For individuals who did not complete high school, reinforcement "significantly increased accuracy of reporting," with long questions and reinterviews tending to reduce it. With high-school graduates the opposite effects were found. The highest average accuracy for the high-school graduates was found in the reinterview using long questions and no reinforcements. The experimental treatments did not affect the high reliability of chronic conditions and symptom reporting. The reliability of physician reports was "reasonably high." Consistency was not shown on the quantity of information collected as a product of the experimental treatment utilized. The authors note that the sample studied is not typical of the U.S. population, but that the results nevertheless show that "small variations" in questions or reinforcement procedures yield variations in the quality of data. (6 footnotes, 16 references)

871.   Miller, Marvin L. "Survey Fatigue: It's Killing Your Market Research!" *Medical Marketing* 21 (April 1962): 3-8.

Survey fatigue is responsible for creating a "pool of disgruntled nonrespondents" and "survey-conditioned yes-men," according to Miller. Three categories of "survey-resistant strains of M.D.s" are described. Causes include overexposure to surveys and unnecessarily large samples. These ten "don'ts" are outlined: (1) operate a survey which is really designed to remind the doctor of a product; (2) use surveys actually designed to get a salesperson in the office; (3) "burden" the doctor with "nothing in return"; (4) use incompetent interviewers; (5) have the interviewer pose as a patient to gain access; (6) call after hours or request that the call be returned; (7) have interviewers stay too long; (8) ask ambiguous or embarrassing questions; (9) ask questions designed to "produce promotional statistics"; and (10) validate by telephone (Miller recommends mail). Solutions to these challenges include requiring market research organizations to exercise restraint, creating enforceable controls, developing survey techniques which are "more productive and less annoying" to the respondents, and starting an educational program for physicians which highlights the benefits of surveys to them.

872.   Nisselson, Harold, and Theodore D. Woolsey. "Some Problems of the Household Interview Design for the National Health Survey." *Journal of the American Statistical Association* 54, no. 285 (March 1959): 69-87.

The National Health Survey Program is a continuing sample survey collecting data on the incidence and prevalence of illness and injury, disability, hospitalization, the use of medical and dental services, and related subjects. The survey uses a staff of about 140 interviewers. The survey was pretested in Mecklenburg County, North Carolina (including Charlotte), with a one thousand household sample. The following challenges were addressed: (1) whether to accept proxy respondents (accepted, but under certain conditions); (2) the control of interviewer error and bias; (3) the use of checklists and probes; (4) underreporting and misreporting of events during a specified time; (5) definitional problems with the beginning and end of episodes of illness; (6) improving detail and reducing response variability; and (7) the validity of the prevalence measures provided for specific chronic diseases. The Charlotte pretest demonstrated that checklists were useful. A two-week recall period was used for most illness, medical, and dental data. Separate "attacks" of chronic illnesses were not counted. Codability improvements were made. Data from previous surveys and the Charlotte pretest are used to explain how decisions were made. More objective operational definitions were developed to reduce response variability. Pending further data availability, many of the decisions selected reflect judgment. (21 references)

873.   Samuels, Robert, Sidney M. Stahl, and Alan Sparkes. *Problems of Sample Survey Research on Health Related Issues.* Studies in Health Care, Report no. 2. Columbia, MO: Section on Health Care Studies, Department of Community Health and Medical Practice, School of Medicine, University of Missouri, 1970. 54 leaves.

Samuels and the coauthors discuss the pretesting of questions and interviewer training. Examples of specific technical problems with a health-related sample survey are provided. During the winter of 1967-68, two sample surveys were conducted to determine the health characteristics of the population of the state of Missouri. This publication seeks to identify challenges with sample surveys which are specific to the health field. The problems discussed are in the areas of the collection and interpretation of sample survey data. The designing of appropriate questions is one area cited as needing further research. (31 references)

874.   Suchman, Edward A. "The Survey Method Applied to Public Health and Medicine." In *Survey Research in the Social Sciences*, edited by Charles Y. Glock, with contributions by John W. Bennett, et al., 421-519. New York, NY: Russell Sage Foundation, 1967. 543p.

The survey method is placed in the context of the "increasingly close relationship between the behavioral sciences and the fields of medicine and public health." The nature of survey research in public health and medicine is explained. The major applications of the survey method are outlined, including ecology and etiology, variations in response to illness and the maintenance of health, and health professions and organizations. Suchman maintains that there are "probably more surveys being made in this area [health survey research] than in any other professional field." Specific survey uses reviewed include morbidity; social epidemiological; public information, attitude, and behavior; and health needs, resources, and utilization. The chapter has a conclusion and a 312-entry bibliography. (242 footnotes)

875.   Tayback, Matthew, and Todd M. Frazier. "Continuous Health Surveys, a Necessity for Health Administration." *Public Health Reports* 77, no. 9 (September 1962): 763-71.

The continuous monthly household survey conducted in Baltimore is described. Specific information needs of the local health administration included innoculation status of children, knowledge of respiratory diseases, information on mobility, and a determination of attitudes on subjects such as smoking, day care, and the use of health department services. The survey involved 100 households (about 300 persons), with annual data on approximately 3,600 persons from about 1,000 households (allowing for 15-person incompleteness due to refusals, not-at-homes, and so forth). The Polk city directory was used to generate the household addresses after the Bureau of Biostatistics from the Baltimore City Health Department had provided an independent sample. Interviewing was conducted by staff nurses. Excluding original survey design and increased staffing costs to interpret the data, the survey cost $10,000 for the field operation, sample selection, editing of returns, and preparation for data analysis. The department uses survey data for planning and assessment. (3 references)

876.   U.S. National Center for Health Statistics. *Health Interview Survey Procedure, 1957-1974.* In *Vital and Health Statistics: Programs and Collection Procedures.* Public Health Service Publication No. 1000, Series 1, No. 11. U.S. Department of Health, Education and Welfare, DHEW Publication No. (HRA) 75-1311. Rockville, MD and Washington, DC: U.S. Department of Health, Education and Welfare, Public Health Service, Health Services and Mental Health Administration, National Center for Health Statistics, 1975. 153p. [SuDoc HE20.6209: 1/11]

Seventeen years of procedures are traced, with information provided on history, technical aspects, and questionnaire development. The National Center for Health Statistics conducted the first Health Interview Survey in July 1957. Statistical design, estimating procedures, reliability of estimates, and errors due to sampling variability are discussed in the technical section. Most of the publication addresses the questionnaire format, the basic questionnaire, and supplements to it. The 1957 survey included approximately 36,000 households, with each interviewer assigned an average of 12 households. Bureau of the Census data were used to generate the sample. Sequential changes to the questionnaire are not presented in favor of a topical consideration – beginning with social, economic, and demographic characteristics. The document provides examples of the questionnaire as it appeared through the years. The 112 pages of appendixes cover the rotating supplements, the one-time or single supplements, definitions of terms, and checklists for selected chronic conditions from 1969 to 1973. (19 references)

877.   U.S. National Center for Health Statistics. *Health Survey Procedure: Concepts, Questionnaire Development, and Definitions in the Health Interview Survey. Concepts of Morbidity, Disability, and Utilization of Medical Services and Facilities; Questionnaire Development, Fiscal Years 1958-64; and Definitions of Terms Used in Statistical Reports.* In *Vital and Health Statistics: Programs and Collection Procedures.* Public Health Service Publication No. 1000, Series 1, No. 2. Washington, DC: U.S. Department of Health, Education, and Welfare, Public Health Service, National Center for Health Statistics, May 1964. 66p. [SuDoc FS2. 85/2:1/no.2]

Questionnaire development during the fiscal years 1958 through 1964 is reviewed, along with a presentation of the statistical design and explanations of the concepts used in the survey, such as morbidity, disability, and the use of medical services and facilities. The questionnaire is described, the interview structure is discussed, and the time references made in the interview are considered. The document explores the nature of the social, economic, and demographic characteristics sought. Questions are noted which require recall of illness and injuries, and those which deal with hospitalization. Also covered is the manner in which some questions are asked on a rotating basis and questions which are asked only once. Twenty pages are devoted to the various questionnaire formats used, including the basic format and the supplementary questions addressing specific topics. The survey terms used are defined and discussed in an additional twenty pages. A four-page index to the terms is provided. (1 footnote)

LABOR UNIONS

878.   Sheppard, Harold L., and Nicholas Masters. "Union Political Action and Opinion Polls in a Democratic Society." *Social Problems* 5, no. 1 (July 1957): 14-21.

The particular union considered here is the Detroit United Automobile Workers. A sample of 156 members was selected through an area probability approach in 1956. A number of topics were included during the interviews, with some of them dealing with the issue of unions in politics. The authors found that on the closed-end question nearly half the sample opposed the use of union dues for political education. However, on the open-ended question only 9 percent cited "unions as organizations that should not be allowed to give money to parties and candidates." Sheppard and Masters suggest that decision makers "exercise responsibility" in the use and evaluation of polling techniques, and be sensitive to "varying degrees of acceptable research and interpretation." (3 footnotes, 5 references)

LAW

879.   Barksdale, Hiram C. *The Use of Survey Research Findings as Legal Evidence.* American Research Foundation Publications. Pleasantville, NY: Printers' Ink Books, 1957. 166p.

The use of survey research data as evidence in judicial proceedings and administrative hearings is examined. In the second chapter each step of the survey research procedure is discussed, including preliminary investigation, hypotheses, design, data collection, processing, analysis, results presentation, and the types of errors which are possible. Barksdale then places survey research within the legal framework, discusses early legal applications, and follows with applications in the mid-1950s. The legal requirements are explained, along with the experience of practitioners. The author closes by observing, "The course has been charted. Increasing use of survey evidence seems certain." Eight pages of references and a three-page index are provided.

880.   Deming, W. Edwards. "On the Presentation of the Results of Sample Surveys as Legal Evidence." *Journal of the American Statistical Association* 49, no. 268 (December 1954): 814-25.

Deming addresses the challenges which statisticians face when testifying in courtroom settings. The article concerns probability samples only and focuses attention on the situations of direct testimony and cross-examination. During direct testimony, the statistician will probably need a prepared statement. Although the statistician will provide information about the precision of the survey results, comments will not be made concerning their usefulness. Deming observes that the statistician may have to deal with preconceived ideas about sampling, and he recommends "patience, truth, and simple language" when explaining sampling procedures. Precision, accuracy, and standard error are discussed in terms of the manner in which these areas may be approached in cross-examination. The fixed nature of the standard error and its interpretation in a procedure of sampling are stressed at the conclusion of the article. (2 footnotes)

881.   Geiser, Robert L., and Roger W. Newman. "Psychology and the Legal Process: Opinion Polls as Evidence?" *American Psychologist* 16, no. 10 (October 1961): 685-90.

The use of polls by regulatory or administrative agencies at both the state and federal levels is discussed. One reason that polls are used by agencies is that cases are heard before a board of "specially trained and experienced experts" who decide the advisability and relative weight of the evidence. Polls have been used in jury trials in cases of change of venue decisions. Other areas for potential uses of polls in the legal process include libel and slander, moral issues, and capital punishment. Geiser and Newman offer specific instructions on how to conduct surveys and prepare for the presentation of their results for use in cases under litigation. Questions are provided which will be asked of the pollster. The issue of the hearsay rule is introduced, and the possibility of having to have interviewers and respondents testify is acknowledged. The potential biasing effect of this if told to respondents is cited. The authors believe that the uses of polls as legal evidence is "largely untapped." (2 references)

882.   Payne, Stanley L. "Simple Surveys for Legal Evidence." *Journal of Marketing* 24, no. 4 (April 1960): 74-76.

Pretests, probability samples, large interview staffs, and machine tabulating should be avoided for the purpose of presenting marketing research in court. Payne recommends using data which appear as though "almost anyone could have done it!" Also recommended is the use of the word "test" instead of the word "survey," leading to such marketing phrases as "brand description tests," "label reaction tests," and "confusion tests." Overall, simplicity is the key. The sampling method and the number of issues addressed should be easy to understand, with brief questionnaires of four or five questions. All other usual precautions should be followed with respect to record keeping, interviewing, and so forth. (2 footnotes)

883.   "Public Opinion Surveys as Evidence: The Pollsters Go to Court." *Harvard Law Review* 66, no. 3 (January 1953): 498-513.

The terms "public opinion poll" and "public opinion survey" are used interchangeably, and refer to the "use of questionnaire-interview techniques to determine public opinion or knowledge." The article draws upon Parten's *Surveys, Polls, and Samples* [Item No. 45] for a review of polling techniques. Issues surrounding the hearsay rule and the problems this poses for surveys as evidence are discussed, along with the probative value of surveys. Court concerns with defects in polling technique are cited. A section on tactical problems explains what information attorneys need to have available to them when using surveys (such as the complete record of the survey methods used). Also discussed are three areas in which surveys can be used: change of venue cases; immigration, naturalization, and deportation cases; and legislative and quasi-legislative proceedings. The article closes with the observation that in 1953 the rule on the admissibility of poll evidence had not been clarified. (103 footnotes)

884.   Sherman, Edward F. "The Use of Public Opinion Polls in Continuance and Venue Hearings." *American Bar Association Journal* 50, no. 4 (April 1964): 357-62.

The use of public opinion polls to provide proof of community prejudice in hearings for continuance and change of venue had achieved a considerable degree of acceptance by 1964. The author writes that appellate hearings had accepted polls as evidence for some time. The article begins with a discussion of procedures governing motions, followed by a consideration of two legal cases where surveys were used, admitted as evidence, but where the motion for changes of venue was denied in both cases (Bloeth and Estes). Sherman then reviews numerous polling techniques which lead to accurate results: size of the sample, phrasing of the questions, cross section of the community, statistical techniques, and trained interviewers. The author believes that poll results appear "deceptively simple," but nevertheless require careful attention to each of the areas described above in order to continue to be useful tools in court cases. (28 footnotes)

885.   Tepping, Benjamin J., and Warren J. Wittreich. "Sample Surveys for Legal Evidence." *Journal of Marketing* 25 (October 1960): 57-59.

An article by Payne, "Simple Surveys for Legal Evidence" [Item No. 882], suggests that simple tests be used as legal evidence. Authors Tepping and Wittreich disagree and explain why they believe that sample surveys are the appropriate approach. One argument as to why not to use sample surveys is due to the difficulty of explaining probability sampling in court. The authors argue that the case of *U.S. v. E.I. duPont de Nemours and Company* demonstrated that probability sampling and related issues can be successfully presented. (2 footnotes)

886.   Waterbury, Lester E. "Opinion Surveys in Civil Litigation." *Public Opinion Quarterly* 17, no. 1 (Spring 1953): 71-90.

The admissibility of consumer surveys in civil litigation is uncertain, with the court's reception "highly unpredictable." Waterbury discusses the case of *Elgin National Watch Company v. Elgin Clock Company* (1928) 26 F. (2d) 376 (D.C. Del.) and subsequent cases dealing with admissibility issues. Decisional law on admissibility is discussed with three cases cited: *U.S. v. 88 Cases [Bireley's Orange Beverage]* (1951) 187 F. (2d) 967 (C.A. 3); *People v. Franklin National Bank of Franklin Square* (1951) 105 N.Y.S. (2d) 81 (N.Y. Supreme Court, Nassau County); and *S. C. Johnson & Son, Inc. v. Gold Seal Company* (1950) 40

Trade-Mark Rep. 347 (Patent Office, Examiner of Interferences), affirmed (1951) 90 U.S. Pat. Quar. 373 (Patent Office, Commissioner of Patents). Waterbury maintains that the consumer opinion survey "will become the standard method of presenting opinion evidence." One solution to some existing problems is to have both parties agree to have a survey conducted, thereby eliminating some or all of the design disputes. The survey planner is called as an expert witness, with cross-examination possible. One issue that is not clear is how much of the survey work material should go to the jury for their review. (34 footnotes)

887.   Zeisel, Hans. "The Uniqueness of Survey Evidence." *Cornell Law Quarterly* 45, no. 2 (Winter 1960): 322-46. [A section of Item 887 appears in *Public Opinion Quarterly* 23, no. 4 (Winter 1959-60): 471-73, with the title "Survey Interviewers as Witnesses."]

The presentation begins by explaining the type of survey being considered. Zeisel refers to "public opinion poll surveys." A brief discussion follows of the use of U.S. Census data as evidence, with the remainder of the article considering surveys. The author then discusses sampling principles, challenges with the accuracy of sample measurement, how the law views sampling error, and the issue of surveys as hearsay evidence. Whether survey respondents should be called as witnesses is considered – with Zeisel suggesting that this would be inadvisable. The circumstances are reviewed which might make a survey inadmissible, such as a survey inappropriate to the issue at hand, an inadequate sample, and issues surrounding the conditions of the interview. An argument is made for having expert testimony to accompany the introduction of a survey as evidence. The article concludes with a summary of the safeguards necessary to permit survey evidence. (75 footnotes)

LIBRARY

888.   McDiarmid, E. W., Jr. *The Library Survey: Problems and Methods*. Chicago, IL: American Library Association, 1940. 243p.

Chapter 1, titled "The Survey Method," covers the determination of the purpose of the survey to be conducted, the various options available for use in libraries, what criteria should be used, and planning. McDiarmid outlines the following primary methods for collecting information: (1) observation; (2) interview – expressed as "conversations with people"; (3) analysis and criticisms – achieved by examining the existing written record; (4) questionnaires – defined as "written replies to certain queries"; and (5) checklists – marking prepared lists of statements or opinion. In chapter 10 the author discusses preparing the report and disseminating the findings in which tables, graphs, "pictorial statistics," and pictures are described. Options for publicizing the results are outlined. The eight chapters in between consider these applications of library survey methodology: (1) community; (2) finance; (3) administration; (4) personnel; (5) collections; (6) use; (7) determining potential users; and (8) multilibrary survey research at the regional, state, and national levels. A twenty-three-page appendix provides examples of forms. The second appendix consists of a 174-entry bibliography which includes references to individual library surveys, aspects of library service, specific tools to assist in the conduct of survey research, and miscellaneous entries. The book chapters are footnoted throughout.

MASS MEDIA

889.   Bonafede, Dom. "Polling." *Washington Journalism Review* 1, no. 4 (September-October 1978): 34-39.

This article places polling as it is used in newspapers and to some degree in television. The first recorded newspaper poll was conducted in 1824 by the *Harrisburg Pennsylvanian* in Wilmington, Delaware. The subject was voter preference in the presidential election, a race which was won by John Quincy Adams. The media of the late 1970s had no set format as to how polling studies were conducted. The various ways in which newspapers conduct their polling are by (1) hiring outside commercial firms, (2) relying on commercial pollsters, (3) purchasing a polling organization (for example, the Gannett chain buying the Lou Harris organization), (4) purchasing syndicated studies such as those from Gallup, and (5) varying combinations of the above. Bonafede discusses the range of views held by newspaper personnel, and notes that polls are receiving ever greater use by newspapers. The article contains an insert on Barry Sussman, the *Washington Post's* polling specialist, and another insert with nine suggested titles for potential pollsters.

890.   Cantril, Albert H. "The Press and the Pollster." In *Role of the Mass Media in American Politics*, edited by L. John Martin, 45-52. *Annals of the American Academy of Political and Social Science*, edited by Richard D. Lambert, vol. 427. Philadelphia, PA: American Academy of Political and Social Science, September 1976. 194p.

At the time of this article Cantril was president of the National Council on Public Polls (NCPP). Cantril writes that the intellectual origins of polling are found in sociology, psychology, and statistics. The "Fourth Estate," namely the print and news broadcast media, have actively supported polling since 1824 when the first "straw poll" was conducted. The media have placed certain requirements on pollsters, including brevity (one thousand words or no more than one minute of air time), topicality, timeliness (causing most polling to be conducted by telephone), clarity, and broad appeal. Challenges in the way in which polls are reported are discussed, including a consideration of errors, and failures to appropriately represent the nature of the findings. Reference is made to the disclosure standards of the American Association for Public Opinion Research and the NCPP. (3 footnotes)

891.   Eiselein, E. B. *Some Thoughts on Survey Research.* Tucson, AZ: Department of Radio-Television and Radio-TV-Film Bureau, University of Arizona, 1977. 11p.

The introduction describes ratings and opinion polls as examples of descriptive surveys. Eiselein then proceeds to discuss various types of surveys, beginning with the mail survey. Borrowing from Erdos's book (Erdos, Paul L., with the assistance of Arthur J. Morgan. *Professional Mail Surveys.* New York, NY: McGraw-Hill, [1970]. 289p.), the advantages and disadvantages of mail surveys are listed. The same procedure is followed for telephone and field surveys. The author points out that "man-in-the-street" and "shopping center" surveys have no scientific validity, even though these are widely used in broadcasting. The publication concludes with a list of five essential requirements of a survey, as well as the questions which should be posed when reporting survey results (such as who sponsored the survey, who was interviewed, and so forth). (29 references)

892.   Greenberg, Allan, and Daniel Lissance. "The Accuracy of a Journalistic Poll." *Public Opinion Quarterly* 19, no. 1 (Spring 1955): 45-52.

The *New York Daily News* has conducted twenty preelection polls over the past twenty-six years on voting for mayor, governor, and president. The newspaper claims a high degree of accuracy (nineteen correctly predicted polls out of twenty prior to 1953). Greenberg and Lissance select one poll – the 1953 mayoral race – for analysis (a similar analysis was made of the 1950 mayoral poll for comparison purposes). It was found that although the winner was correctly predicted, the percentage of votes was overestimated by nearly 11 percent. A 10.6 percent error was found for 1950. The authors rule out certain errors such as the size of the turnout, the sample size, or the closeness of time of polling to the election date. However, a systematic error was found to be present, possibly due to invalid polling procedures and analysis techniques. Since the *Daily News* claims to be "scientific," and because it has considerable influence in the community, it is urged that its methods and data be made available for detailed study. Accepted standards, such as those formulated by the American Association for Public Opinion Research, should be applied to the methods in order to benefit the entire public opinion polling field. (10 footnotes)

893.   Ludeke, H. C. "The Survey Applied to Editorial Problems." Part 1, Chap. 15 in *How to Conduct Consumer and Opinion Research: The Sampling Survey in Operation*, edited by Albert B. Blankenship, 188-208.

> The American Council Series of Public Relations Books, edited by Rex
> F. Harlow. New York, NY: Harper & Brothers Publishers, 1946. 314p.

An editorial problem which existed at *Country Gentleman* is documented, along
with the steps which were taken to address the problem through the use of a
survey. A number of issues were identified, such as the following: (1) Should
artwork or photographs be used? (2) Should article length be reduced? and (3)
Are newly added sections being read? One thousand interviews were to be conducted from among the two million copies distributed to readers on a monthly
basis. Interviewing locations were selected on the basis of regions containing 3
or more percent of the subscribers, with fifteen such regions representing 80
percent of all subscribers. Numerous examples of survey findings are provided,
along with the actions which were taken based on the research results.

894.   McCombs, Maxwell, and G. Cleveland Wilhoit. "Conducting a Sur-
        vey." Chap. 5 in *Handbook of Reporting Methods*, edited by Maxwell
        McCombs, Donald Lewis Shaw, and David Grey, 96-122. Boston, MA:
        Houghton Mifflin Company, 1976. 340p.

An outline is presented of how a journalist should conduct a survey. McCombs
and Wilhoit begin with the interview, and explore cost, response rate, and the
kinds and numbers of questions to ask. Social desirability bias and the representativeness of the respondents are covered. The authors cite the need for the survey to address the "focal question." Questionnaire development follows, including the nature of the question mix and the pretesting of the survey to ensure reliability and validity. Interviewer selection is discussed, with observations regarding accuracy, completeness, and the avoidance of interviewer errors. Data analysis and the preparation of information for use in reporting concludes the chapter,
along with a section on the presentation of tables. (10 footnotes)

895.   Meyer, Philip. *Precision Journalism: A Reporter's Introduction to So-
        cial Science Methods*. 2d ed. Bloomington, [IN]: Indiana University Press,
        1979. 430p.

Meyer begins chapter 6 on surveys (pages 115-43) by describing the elements that
constitute a systematic survey, and moves to a discussion of survey sampling. A
table of sample sizes is presented. Different question forms are considered, namely the open and closed varieties. The challenges with each are reviewed, with the
observation that the "agree/disagree" response option is a simpler format. Meyer
suggests that journalists new to survey research use experienced interviewers to
avoid the training required for beginners. Field tests are discussed as a way to reduce unforeseen problems. The author identifies a checklist of areas in which the
survey researcher can expect to be able to explore: (1) opinions; (2) attitudes
(involving both direction and intensity); (3) changes in attitude; (4) personality; (5)

knowledge; (6) behavior; and (7) background variables. External checks are enumerated, one of which involves the interviewer rating the respondent, thus permitting evasive or uncooperative respondents to be compared with others for systematic differences. Internal checks for consistency and panel surveys are briefly covered. The need for flexible computing – especially for journalists seeking "deep-probing" surveys – is noted. In chapter 7 (pages 144-63) Meyer reviews public polls, starting with a discussion of the early history beginning in 1935 with the "pioneers in systematic opinion sampling," and tracing the work of George Gallup and Louis Harris. How journalists can create their own surveys is the subject of chapter 9 (pages 191-213), with discussions of sampling, question writing, precoding, and interviewing. The analysis and presentation of survey data are covered in chapter 10 (pages 214-45).

896.   Patrick, William Lawrence. "Network Television News and Public Opin-
         ion Polls." Ph.D. diss., Ohio University, 1975. 249 leaves. [*Dissertation
         Abstracts International* Order No. 7610314; *DAI* 36A, no. 11 (May 1976):
         7030.]

Divided into five major sections, the dissertation includes a history of public opinion polls, the results of personal interviews with network news personnel and pollsters, the purpose and methods of the research, and recommendations for the use of public opinion polls by network television news. The network news personnel include executives in the network news divisions and producers of news programs. The pollsters included are those whose national public polls are regularly used by the networks. Patrick explores the questions of how and why networks use polls and what impact they are having on programming. The level at which polls are authorized and how they fit within corporate networks are analyzed. The author hypothesizes that "poll material is utilized not only as news content but also as an input to the news decision-making process." Patrick's findings indicate that polls "serve as agenda-setting devices shaping the editorial stance of some news and public affairs presentations." Another finding is that television networks rely "almost exclusively" on telephone sampling and interviewing. Three major critics of public opinion polls, the news, and their relationship are discussed. The three critics are Herbert Blumer, a sociologist; Herbert Schiller, a professor of communications; and Daniel Boorstin, a historian [and former Librarian of Congress]. Patrick suggests further study in the area of the impact of polls. References are provided.

897.   Wilhoit, G. Cleveland, and Maxwell McCombs. "Reporting Surveys and
         Polls." Chap. 4 in *Handbook of Reporting Methods*, edited by Maxwell
         McCombs, Donald Lewis Shaw, and David Grey, 81-95. Boston, MA:
         Houghton Mifflin Company, 1976. 340p.

A checklist of ten questions which journalists should ask is presented. These questions consist of the following: "(1) Who sponsored the survey? (2) Who was interviewed – that is, what population is being described? (3) How were the persons selected for interviews and what was the sample design? (4) How many persons were interviewed? (5) How accurate are the results? What is the estimated size of the sampling error? (6) Who were the interviewers? (7) How were the interviews conducted? (8) When were the interviews conducted? (9) What were the actual questions asked? and (10) How are the data tabulated and analyzed?" Each question is explained and elaborated upon. The American Association for Public Opinion Research (AAPOR) Standards for Disclosure include these eight points: (1) sample size; (2) sponsor; (3) base of results; (4) timing of the interview; (5) how the respondent was contacted; (6) definition of population; (7) exact wording of question(s); and (8) error allowance. During the 1970 congressional elections, twenty-four metropolitan dailies were studied – only one news story adhered to all eight AAPOR standards. A *Miami Herald* story showing these disclosures is reproduced. Also shown are two stories about a *Playboy* "survey." (6 footnotes)

POLITICAL PSYCHOLOGY

898.   Hyman, Herbert. "Surveys in the Study of Political Psychology." Chap. 12 in *Handbook of Political Psychology*, edited by Jeanne N. Knutson, 322-55. Jossey-Bass Behavioral Science Series. San Francisco, CA: Jossey-Bass Inc., Publishers, 1973. 542p.

Hyman reviews a number of ways in which surveys describe and explain the political behavior of individuals, considering individual differences, relevant variables, and political character. The opening remarks to this chapter indicate that surveys are playing a crucial role in the advancement of knowledge in the area of political psychology. Hyman traces the development of the approach in the field of political psychology. Questionnaire design and surveys as experiments are discussed. Political action, knowledge, beliefs and attitudes, and character are addressed in terms of how survey researchers have worked with the challenges in each of these areas. Hyman observes that through trend, comparative contextual, and cross-national surveys, the varying political institutions' impact on individual psychology would be open for study. However, the author observes that "psychological data in abundance in ordinary surveys tell us of man's sensitivities and satisfactions under a particular political order." (References are provided)

POLITICAL SCIENCE

899. Likert, Rensis. "The Sample Interview Survey as a Tool of Research and Policy Formation." In *The Policy Sciences*, edited by Daniel Lerner and Harold D. Lasswell, with the editorial collaboration of Harold H. Fisher, Ernest R. Hilgard, Saul K. Padover, Ithiel De Sola Pool, and C. Easton Rothwell, 233-51. Hoover Institution Studies, no. 1. Stanford, CA: Stanford University Press, 1951. 344p.

The sample interview survey is described as a combination of recent developments in the areas of sampling, interviewing, research design, attitude measurement, content analysis, and motivational theory. This type of survey involves systematic interviews with a sample of respondents. Information on attitudes and opinions is gathered, as well as personal information such as age and education. Knowledge or misinformation, experience and behavior, and motives for their attitudes and behavior related to the topic are obtained. Likert explains how sample interview surveys differ from polls by noting a series of shortcomings: (1) the use of quota sampling in the 1948 presidential polls; (2) the use of error formulas designed for probability samples on samples using the quota method; (3) the use of arbitrary adjustment; and (4) the interpretation of "don't know" answers. Additionally, little effort is made to determine what respondents mean, and to use that information in the interpretation of the data gathered. Examples of sample interview surveys, as well as some suggestions for future uses of the technique, are provided. (36 references)

900. McClosky, Herbert. *Political Inquiry: The Nature and Uses of Survey Research.* [New York, NY]: Macmillan Company, [1969]. 163p.

A number of issues are explored, including when surveys should be used to investigate political phenomena, how survey technology has contributed to political inquiry, and the role of surveys in moving political science from a documentary field to one more systematic and empirical in nature. In chapter 1 McClosky reviews and evaluates the major contributions of surveys to political science. The following two chapters are basically research monographs which are included to illustrate applications of the survey research method to areas that previously could not have been systematically explored, and also to illustrate the explanatory, theoretical, and descriptive purposes of surveys. Chapter 2 deals with foreign policy, while chapter 3 covers anomie. All three essays are reprinted from other sources and contain footnotes. The first chapter, with 151 entries, is the only chapter to contain a bibliography.

901. McClosky, Herbert. "Survey Research in Political Science." In *Survey Research in the Social Sciences*, edited by Charles Y. Glock, with

contributions by John W. Bennett, et al., 63-143. New York, NY: Russell Sage Foundation, 1967. 543p.

The nature and types of surveys, survey methods, and the science of politics are explained. The substantive contributions of surveys are covered, with the discussion ranging from public opinion, to psychology and politics, to comparative and international studies, with an additional half-dozen areas in between. New applications for survey research are considered, including political leadership, internal party affairs, relation of belief to action, and historical and trend analysis. McClosky comments on how surveys have contributed to theory. The limitations of political surveys, as well as the problems involved in their use, are reviewed. A 134-entry bibliography is provided.

POLITICS

General

902.   "Bad Samples and Political Polls." *Science News* 94, no. 8 (24 August 1968): 179.

This article is designed to highlight some of the statistical challenges faced by those organizations involved with presidential polling. Angus Campbell, director of the Survey Research Center at the University of Michigan, advises that the range of error implied by Gallup, Harris, and Roper is in reality larger. Additionally, the samples used in presidential polls are small and not truly random. In order to reduce the error rate to within 1 percent, a 5,000 member or greater sample would be required. The average political poll described has between 1,200 and 1,500 people. Also, polling organizations use corrections to adjust for individuals who are not home when the interviewer visits. Herbert Hyman of Columbia University indicates that when a political race is close (that is, within three or four points), the political polls considered would not be useful in forecasting the election outcome.

903.   Benson, Edward G. "Three Words." *Public Opinion Quarterly* 4, no. 1 (March 1940): 130-34.

The American Institute of Public Opinion conducted an experiment in June 1939. From a national sample of the voting public, 3,054 individuals were selected and divided into smaller groups. They were queried on the meaning of three words: "radical," "liberal," and "conservative." It was found that (1) the term "conservative" was the easiest to identify, (2) about half of the respondents were able to define one of the three terms to the satisfaction of the interviewer, (3) it was impossible to ascertain the knowledge of the three terms for about one-seventh of the cases, (4) the remaining two-fifths had no answer or responded with incorrect definitions, and (5) voters in upper-income groups were the most successful in identifying the terms. Respondents were asked, prior to the definition question, to identify themselves as being radical, liberal, or conservative. About one person in fifty classified herself/himself as radical, and there was considerable variation in self-classification between those familiar with the terms and those who were not. The results of a question linking the three terms, income level, and 1936 voting patterns (that is, Republican or Democrat) are also given. (1 footnote)

904.   Bower, Robert. "Public Opinion Polls and the Politician." In *Parties and Politics: 1948*, edited by Charles C. Rohlfing and James C. Charlesworth, 104-12. *Annals of the American Academy of Political and Social Science*, edited by Thorsten Sellin, vol. 259. Philadelphia, PA: American Academy of Political and Social Science, September 1948. 207p.

The purpose of this article is to focus attention on areas in which polls are underutilized or not used at all, as well as to make some observations concerning the role of polls in political life. In the discussion of poll reliability Bower maintains that polling experts have solved the problem of sampling. He proceeds to discuss the "enigmatic 13 percent" – the individuals who change their minds after they have responded to an opinion poll ("last minute changer[s]"). The author considers the effect of polls on voters, reviews voting apathy, and comments on the use of polls to ascertain the attitudes of minority groups and to determine which media approach is effective. Politicians are just beginning to use polls to decide which issue to focus on in campaigns, but little use by politicians in office is noted. Polls as producers of the bandwagon effect are essentially dismissed, citing a study showing that 44 percent of those interviewed had never heard of polls. The value of repeated interviews (the panel technique) is seen as useful in tracking opinion changes on issues. (14 footnotes)

905.   Deming, W. Edwards. "Good Statistical Surveys Are Not Accidents, and There Are No Bargains: Government Research Authority Says Clients Can Assist in Improving Research by Taking More Interest in Methods." *Printers' Ink* 226, no. 5 (4 February 1949): 34-35, 48-50.

To some degree this article is a statement of reassurance to users and consumers of surveys following the outcome of the 1948 presidential election in which the major pollsters misforecast the outcome. Deming, who was a sampling adviser to the Bureau of the Budget, Executive Office of the President, describes the steps involved in a survey, namely, definition of the universe, the questionnaire, the sample, and results interpretation. As the author observes, predicting is not a phase common to all surveys. Quota sampling is distinguished from probability sampling, with the latter using rules to select respondents and to determine estimates for the universe. (3 footnotes)

906.   "The Facts about Political Polls." *U.S. News & World Report* 77, no. 15 (7 October 1974): 34, 37.

In the question-and-answer format *U.S. News and World Report* addresses twenty issues regarding political polls. The questions asked range from the accuracy of polls, to how interviews are conducted, to the accuracy of telephone polls. A variety of polling authorities are called upon to consider these questions, including Gallup, Harris, the National Council on Public Polls, Yankelovich, and Sindlinger, as well as other organizations and individuals. A separate section of the article discusses the mistakes made by the *Literary Digest* and the mistaken poll predictions of the 1948 presidential election.

907.   "How Good Are Election Polls? Exclusive Interview: An Expert's Size-Up." *U.S. News & World Report* 49, no. 15 (10 October 1960): 64-68.

Richard M. Scammon, a political scientist and director of elections research for the Government Affairs Institute (a nonprofit organization), is interviewed on polls and voting trends. The five pages of text are presented in the question-and-answer format. The 1960 presidential election was drawing closer as this interchange was recorded. A wide range of topics are covered, including the following representation: (1) range of error; (2) private polls; (3) people who change their minds; (4) undecided voters; (5) margin of error; (6) polls as estimates of popular vote rather than electoral votes; (7) how payment is made for political polls and public polls; (8) voter turnout; and (9) the success of polls in providing both private and public information needs.

908.   Likert, Rensis. "Why Opinion Polls Were So Wrong: Outdated Methods Used, Survey Expert Says." *U.S. News & World Report* 25, no. 20 (12 November 1948): 24-25.

Likert, director of the Survey Research Center at the University of Michigan, begins by explaining the errors of the *Literary Digest* poll in the 1936 presidential election, and follows by observing that the polls in the 1948 election all used quota sampling. Likert explains how the process works and what the shortcomings are for the procedure. Persons in the low-income category were underrepresented by 12 to 20 percent. The undecided voters were an unusually large percentage of potential voters. Another challenge was to determine actual voter turnout as distinct from respondents' statements of intent to vote. An alternative mode of operation is suggested, namely, sampling based on area (or geographical control) in which the households are preselected by the polling organizations to be representative of the population. Improvements in questions which go beyond "yes" or "no" answers are recommended – questions which address the respondents' reasons for candidate preference. The changes have been used successfully by government and academia for the last ten years. The results of nine major polls versus actual results for the 1948 election are shown in tabular format.

909.   Louviere, Vernon. "Pollsters Are Off and Running, Too. Political Pulse-taking Will Focus on the Electorate's Attitudes toward Pocketbook Issues." *Nation's Business* 67, no. 11 (November 1979): 53-59.

The section titled "Checking the Answers" advises the reader that, according to Albert H. Cantril, president of the National Council on Public Polls, "less than 3 percent of the interviewers who complete their training ever turn up as cheaters." The cheating referred to here involves the interviewer simply filling in bogus answers to survey questionnaires without actually interviewing respondents. Louviere discusses the challenges that pollsters face with their clients, such as bringing bad news of unfavorable poll findings to politicians who are not always open-mindedly responsive to the suggestions that their pollsters may propose. Most of the issues raised in the article are the frequently addressed ones, for example, the nonvoting public, the business of polling, changing political strategies in light of polling advances, and some of the specific political issues likely to be in the public's eye in the 1980 presidential election.

910.   Mann, Martin. "How Those Political Polls Work . . . and How Good Are They, Anyhow?" *Popular Science* 177, no. 4 (October 1960): 132-35, 236-38.

The article is arranged in the question-and-answer format, with Mann supplying both. The effort is to address commonly asked questions about polls. Issues considered include the following: (1) sampling; (2) respondents who answer polls but do not vote in elections; (3) the size of voter turnout; (4) lying and "face-saving falsehoods"; (5) the undecided voter; (6) reasons why polls can be incorrect; and (7) the accuracy record of the Gallup Poll. In the response to polling errors, Mann addresses the "inescapable margin of error" of polls which makes close elections difficult to predict (with the 1960 Nixon-Kennedy election cited). Additionally, the polls count popular votes, but the president is chosen by the Electoral College. Further, polls are a measure of opinion before the election, with the possibility that voters will change their minds.

911.   Mazo, Earl. "The Intelligent Woman's Guide to Political Polls." *McCall's* 92, no. 1 (October 1964): 80, 82, 84.

Mazo reviews the range of political polling beginning with recent examples. News polls are differentiated from the confidential variety. Sample size and selection, question wording, and bias are discussed, along with an outline of the

Literary Digest "poll" of 1936. Pretesting, intensity scales, undecided voters, respondent lying, and poll "adjustments" are other topics covered in an effort to
explain the "whys" and "hows" of polling methodology. The polling margin of
error is cited as one of the reasons close elections are difficult to impossible
to forecast. Additional issues, such as the degree of trust that can be placed in
polls, are addressed.

912.   Perry, Paul. "Certain Problems in Election Survey Methodology." *Public
        Opinion Quarterly* 43, no. 3 (Fall 1979): 312-25.

The historical background of the use of sampling theory is explained, beginning
with the "so-called straw poll" of 1824. The work of Gallup, Roper, and Crossley in the 1930s is discussed, followed by developments through to 1950. Perry
reviews sampling and sampling error, with the note that rates of refusal are higher
than they were twenty years ago. The use of the secret ballot and the issue of
response validity are addressed. The author outlines the approaches needed to minimize the number of undecided voters. A discussion of direct questioning, measuring likelihood to vote (including a table), and the evaluation of late preelection trends complete the text. (7 footnotes, 11 references)

913.   "Political Pulse-Taking: How the Pollsters Do It." *U.S. News & World
        Report* 73, no. 16 (16 October 1972): 26-28.

The Gallup Poll and Sindlinger and Company are compared. George Gallup uses
door-to-door interviews for the Gallup Poll; Albert E. Sindlinger utilizes long-
distance telephoning for data collecting. Gallup retains primarily women, working part-time, as the interviewers in some 350 precincts, while Sindlinger has
women telephone interviewers who call 487 counties using 800 telephone directories to randomly select names. For every 1,000 calls, an average of 600 interviews are completed on the initial attempt, 50 are refusals, and 350 do not answer. Both Gallup and Sindlinger question individuals who say that they are
registered and that they plan to vote. Several pages of actual responses appear
– first those that the Gallup Organization has collected, followed by responses
collected by the Sindlinger Company.

914.   "Polling: Growth Industry with Problems." *U.S. News & World Report*
        86, no. 10 (12 March 1979): 85-87.

Polls are described as "measuring the public's mood" but which still on occasion produce "terrible mistakes." In particular, an Iowa senate race between incumbent Dick Clark versus Republican Roger Jepsen is cited. Although Clark
was shown by a survey to be ahead by a safe margin, Jepsen won. Similar defeats
by incumbents in Massachusetts and New Hampshire are documented. Advertising researcher Ellen Sills-Levy describes surveys used in marketing as "insurance

policies" when contemplating new products. George Gallup is quoted in relation to the problem of "when only 37 percent of the electorate votes," the real challenge is to identify the 63 percent of individuals who are not going to vote. Burns Roper is described as being concerned about the many people who do not tell the truth about their voting behavior, thus befuddling even the best screening techniques available. The author(s) observe that Harris, Roper, and Gallup no longer conduct political polling for candidates due to the inability or unwillingness of candidates to pay/afford quality polling research, as well as the risks associated with trying to appear impartial to the general public. Albert Cantril expresses concern about sweeping conclusions which are drawn from limited data, especially by those working for the news media.

915.   "Pollsters Follow Business' Lead." *Business Week*, no. 1595 (26 March 1960): 29-30.

The major pollsters have all initially developed their professional skills in the market research arena. Pollsters today usually work for particular candidates, for political parties, or for others who need the results for their own use. Results are used as strategy tools rather than as predictors. Daniel Yankelovich describes the average American voter as "lacking confidence in his ability to evaluate issues, chooses instead the candidate whose personality image inspires the most confidence." Social Research, Incorporated, of Chicago, studied the criteria for selecting presidents. The key factors are "friendliness and warmth – approachable in manner – should have convictions, but not so unrelentingly as to seem an 'angry man' – sincere, trustworthy – reasonably energetic in pursuing public goals." Continuing challenges for pollsters include the "don't know" vote, individuals who change their minds, and those who do not turn out to vote.

916.   Roll, Charles W., Jr., and Albert H. Cantril. *Polls: Their Use and Misuse in Politics*. New York, NY: Basic Books, [1972]. 177p.

Describing the press and mass media as "the Fourth Estate," Roll and Cantril suggest that polling is a candidate to become "the Fifth Estate." Chapters are devoted to unfortunate as well as meaningful uses of polls in politics. Poll reliability, procedures, interpretation, and the place of polling in a free society are considered. Each of the seven chapters is followed by endnotes. Closing the volume are one-and-a-half pages of acknowledgments and a six-page index.

917.   Rowse, Arthur E. "Political Polls." *Editorial Research Reports* 2 (12 October 1960): 745-62.

The changing roles of public opinion polls and the use of polls to determine whether to enter primaries and in campaign strategy are discussed. Also considered are the influence of polls on candidacies, their effect on preconvention tactics, and their impact in past presidential contests. In the second section Rowse covers sampling, sample size and margin of error, poll accuracy in predicting elections, and criticism of syndicated poll performance. The bandwagon effect, national polls versus state primaries, and the issue of the benefit of polls to "good government" are reviewed in the third and final section. (27 footnotes)

918.   Salmans, Sandra, with Bureau Reports. "A Primer on Poll-Taking." *Newsweek* 87, no. 1 (5 January 1976): 16-17.

Several Gallup and Harris polls which produced opposite results were the stimulus for the writing of this article. The questions pitted Gerald Ford against Hubert Humphrey, and Ronald Reagan against Hubert Humphrey. *Newsweek* took this opportunity to review some polling basics, including sampling, the questions, interviewing, and analysis. Gallup conducts an average of five interviews in each of 300 geographic areas across the United States, while Harris conducts ten interviews in each of 150 locations. Both Gallup and Harris utilize personal interviews (telephone interviews are said to have a "built-in Republican bias" against the poor and the transient young). Data are weighted to adjust samples to conform with U.S. Census statistics.

919.   Scammon, Richard M. "Polls, Pollsters and Politicians in '60." *New Republic* 142, no. 14, issue 2368 (4 April 1960): 19-24.

The two types of polls – public and private – are identified, followed by observations on polling basics such as samples, question wording, interviews and interviewers, analysis and weighting, and error measurement. The nature of private political polling is discussed, with reasons as to why a candidate would pursue this option. The bandwagon effect is reviewed, noting that the poll results versus the actual vote in the 1948 election should have dispelled this notion. The costs of private polling are related to the overall costs of campaigns. The reliability of polls is covered. Scammon observes that polls "cannot lead, or act, or do," but they may come closer to the "popular feeling about the Presidency than either primaries or the national conventions."

920.   Wheeler, Michael. "Political Polling: The German Shepherd Factor." *Washington Monthly* 8, no. 2 (April 1976): 42-50.

Adapted from his forthcoming book *Lies, Damn Lies, and Statistics* [Item No. 114], Wheeler raises a number of concerns which he believes are either overlooked or not given sufficient attention. These include the following: (1) personal interviewers frequently work for two or more polling firms; (2) home interview refusal rates are 20 percent or more; (3) interviewers often ask "piggy-backed" questions from multiple clients of the polling firm in sessions that can last between one- and one-and-a-half hours or more; (4) the "fundamental weakness" of polls is their "agree/disagree" simplistic format leading to meaningless results; (5) interviewers may fabricate data; (6) respondents lie to poll interviewers; and (7) though the "theory of polling is scientifically sound, the actual practice is not." The "German shepherd factor" refers to the unwillingness of interviewers to enter properties where such dogs are present, thereby adding an additional segment of the community not polled.

Bandwagon

921.   Baumol, William J. "Interactions between Successive Polling Results and Voting Intention." *Public Opinion Quarterly* 21, no. 2 (Summer 1957): 318-23.

The issue focused upon deals with whether poll results have an impact on voting. Bandwagon behaviors (switching to the candidate with the high vote) and underdog behaviors (voting for the low-vote candidate) are discussed. Successive repolling is said to have an impact on voter intentions. Baumol uses graphs to show the predicted vote plotted against the public's intended vote, and poll results plotted against voter intention. These mathematical presentations are designed to indicate the ultimate results of repolling. Baumol's work indicates that with a sufficient number of polls, bandwagon effects will be minimized. Underdog effects are possible when predicted votes for a candidate oscillate. In both cases a certain number of polls could "conceivably" determine the outcome of the election. (4 footnotes)

922.   Fleitas, Daniel W. "Bandwagon and Underdog Effects in Minimal-Information Elections." *American Political Science Review* 65, no. 2 (June 1971): 434-38.

The study undertaken was to determine whether the publication or dissemination of preelection preference polls might affect voting behavior by stimulating bandwagon and underdog phenomena. The results "clearly demonstrated" that poll results alone are insufficient to induce bandwagon or underdog identifiers to change their votes. The experimental election sample consisted of 625 students at Florida State University who were in the basic American government course during late 1969 and early 1970. A minimal-information election is described as having low voter issue awareness, low candidate party identity, and low or no voter information on the candidates. Generally such elections stimulate little interest or voter turnout. (10 footnotes)

923.   Gallup, George, and Saul Forbes Rae. "Is There a Bandwagon Vote?" *Public Opinion Quarterly* 4, no. 2 (June 1940): 244-49.

Several examples are used to distinguish the motivations of the politician, as opposed to the average voter, to join the bandwagon rush to support a leading candidate. To test the theory that bandwagon psychology influences the voting electorate, the authors analyze data from sample surveys conducted by the American Institute of Public Opinion. The surveys were conducted in 1938 in five states: Kentucky, Georgia, South Carolina, Maine, and Maryland. No support for the theory was found in the first four states, and only in Maryland was the vote for the leading candidate "so slight as to be insignificant." Likewise, bandwagon psychology is shown to have little validity in a presidential preference study and in one involving issues. Gallup and Rae conclude that "the impact of events and the everyday life experiences of the mass of people . . . are the determinants of political attitudes and actions." (1 footnote)

924.   Klapper, Joseph T. *Bandwagon: A Review of the Literature.* [n.p.]: Office of Social Research, Columbia Broadcasting System, 1964. 80 leaves.

These two questions are investigated: (1) Do election results broadcast in the eastern United States affect the vote in Western states where the polls are still open? and (2) If bandwagon effects occur, what evidence is there for them? The study conclusion is that "there is no absolutely conclusive evidence that the broadcasting of election returns or the publication of poll results does or does not affect the subsequent vote." No empirical data were found to address the first question posed. Three approaches were followed: (1) studying the literature back to 1940 and earlier; (2) discussing issues with voting experts and research directors of polling agencies; and (3) searching the Roper Public Opinion Research Center files. Claims of poll effect are considered, along with polls on polls and the issue of postelection bandwagon. Studies of voting behavior are reviewed in terms of responses to polls and "voting determinants and the last minute vote." (46 references)

925.   Simon, Herbert A. "Bandwagon and Underdog Effects and the Possibility of Election Predictions." *Public Opinion Quarterly* 18, no. 3 (Fall 1954): 245-53.

The research focuses on the question of whether it is possible for published election predictions to be confirmed – even in those instances when there are reactions to the predictions which can, in themselves, change the outcome of the predicted event. Simon defines bandwagon and underdog effects and uses the case of a preelection poll to show that correct prediction is possible only if the pollster privately adjusts the results for publication effects prior to publishing. Through several examples (including Brouwer's "fixed-point" theorem), Simon shows that it is "always possible *in principle* to make a public prediction that will be confirmed by the event." Some practical problems arising from making predictions are examined, and the theoretical conditions under which prediction might or might not affect results are discussed. (3 footnotes)

Campaigns

926. Campaign Associates, Inc. *The Role of Polling in Your Campaign.* Wichita, KA: Campaign Associates Press, 1978. 20p.

The volume consists of a series of nine contributions by the following authors: (1) Roderick Bell, "New Polling Technique Evaluates Campaign Alternatives"; (2) Clifford Levy, "Research Techniques Can Be Adopted for Political Campaigns"; (3) Marvin Dicker, "Research Is the Key to Winning Primaries"; (4) William R. Hamilton, "Check Out Your Pollster, Then Use His Results"; (5) Eugene Declercq, "Two Significant Trends Noted in 1976 Polling"; (6) Gary Hong, "Here's Where to Go for Opponent Research"; (7) Jeff Wainscott, "Don't Neglect Opponent Research"; (8) Gayle Essary, "Election Results Prove Reliability of Survey Data"; and (9) Paul Lutzker, "Research Is a Key Element in Fund Raising." The format used in all but the Hong entry is that Campaign Associates, Incorporated, poses a question, and the author-respondent provides the reply. The selections included in this item are designed to supply practical guidance for those individuals operating a political campaign research program.

927. Declercq, Eugene. "The Use of Polling in Congressional Campaigns." *Public Opinion Quarterly* 42, no. 2 (Summer 1978): 247-58.

The 1974 campaigns for the U.S. House of Representatives are the ones chosen for consideration. Declercq examines the role of public opinion polls – specifically where and how polling was used, as well as the factors influencing their use. Both congressional representatives and their staffs were contacted for a total of 421 offices, and nearly complete interviews were achieved in one hundred cases. Questions focused on the type of campaign conducted, when and how frequently polling was carried out, how it was conducted, what kind of information was gathered, and how the information was used for campaigning purposes. It was found that races that involved polling were very competitive, well financed, conducted by younger nonincumbents, and carried out in districts with Republican orientation. The average number of polls conducted per candidate was 2.5. Polling was done far in advance of the election, with the questions being issue-oriented. However, candidate standing was emphasized in later stages. Three main factors were found to determine how polling was used: the party affiliation of the candidate, how much was spent, and whether professional pollsters were used. Further exploration must be made to determine if differences exist between the campaigns of losing candidates and those of the winners. Also, research is needed to examine if study findings apply to city, county, state, or national elective offices. (3 footnotes, 8 references)

928.   Dexter, Lewis Anthony. "The Use of Public Opinion Polls by Political Party Organizations." *Public Opinion Quarterly* 18, no. 1 (Spring 1954): 53-61.

The presentation begins with a discussion of the effects of polls on campaigns. The negative impact of both overconfidence and the opposite, created by high-and-low popularity polls, is cited. Candidate popularity polls are stated to be of little use so far as campaign strategy is concerned. Dexter makes some proposals for useful polling, including polls concentrated in key precincts. He observes that although many polling organizations are now increasingly repeating their own questions, they are not repeating those of other organizations. As is noted, question wording may be very difficult to determine. The author suggests that the Committee on Regional Polls of the American Association for Public Opinion Research be responsible for indexing and codifying the questions. The next topic covered deals with addressing the need for polls to answer the "why" question: "Why do people vote as they do?" Dexter believes that a nonprofit organization should be established, paid for by tax-deductible contributions, that would enable members of Congress to be up-to-date on the public's reaction to a variety of issues. (10 footnotes)

929.   Glass, Andrew J. "Pollsters Prowl Nation as Candidates Use Opinion Surveys to Plan '72 Campaign." *National Journal* 3, no. 33 (14 August 1971): 1693-99, 1702, 1704-5.

The nationally published polls by Gallup and Roper are discussed, with brief historical notes on both. The major political campaign polling firms are identified for each party. Senator Hubert H. Humphrey discusses his experience with polls during his 1968 presidential campaign and his 1970 senatorial campaign. Sampling and sampling error are explained in a separate box under the heading "Establishing the Tolerances." The relationship between pollster and politician is reviewed from the standpoint of ethics. Glass also considers polling techniques, with sections on costs and timing, sample methods, and the challenges of the nonpolitically sensitive conducting political polls.

930.   Harris, Louis. "The Use of Polls in Political Campaigns." Chap. 17 in *Politics U.S.A.: A Practical Guide to the Winning of Public Office*, edited by James M. Cannon, 253-63. Garden City, NY: Doubleday & Company, 1960. 348p.

Harris outlines some of the major advantages polls have over other methods. These include the following: (1) a cross section of voters are asked for their opinion; (2) voters and nonvoters can be distinguished; (3) the opinions and intentions of voters are heard directly; (4) nondirective depth-interview technique permits "people of all levels of articulation" to be heard; (5) polls combine the interpretative, qualitative methods with statistics; (6) they are nonpartisan; and (7) polls present results that can be analytically compared with past results. Harris discusses the trend toward private polling. The most effectively utilized political polls are those which (1) are taken early for results application, (2) are completed for the candidate rather than the party, (3) maintain confidentiality, (4) have the results written in prose, and (5) are fully discussed among candidate, manager, and pollster. Harris reviews the polling results through ten recent elections.

931.   Javits, J. K. "How I Used a Poll in Campaigning for Congress." *Public Opinion Quarterly* 11, no. 2 (Summer 1947): 222-26.

Representative Javits discusses the use of a special survey, conducted for him by Elmo Roper, during his first attempt at public office. Javits was elected to represent the Twenty-first District of New York in the U.S. House of Representatives, Eightieth Congress. The district covers the west side of Manhattan Island. Javits wanted to determine how close his views were to his potential constituents, as well as what people felt were the most important issues. The results are presented along with an explanation of how they were used. Javits writes that the "opinion poll has proved invaluable as a gauge of popular sentiment on a wide number of important issues."

932.   Smolka, Richard G. *The Use of Polls in Political Campaigns*. Practical Politics Booklet, no. 5. New York, NY: Robert A. Taft Institute of Government, 1975. 21p.

The Robert A. Taft Institute of Government provides seminars for elementary- and secondary-school administrators and teachers. Smolka is professor of government at the American University. Divided into four parts, this booklet covers the use of polls, polls and campaigning, and analyzing poll results. Topics discussed in the use of polls in political campaigning section include political climate determination; ways to ascertain opponents' shortcomings; how to dramatize a candidate's standing; the candidate's image; and how polls help to identify important issues. (18 footnotes, 8 references)

Election Prediction

933.   Crossley, Archibald M., Stuart C. Dodd, J. E. Bachelder, George H. Gallup, and Henry J. Kroeger. "Causes of the Disparity between Poll Findings and Election Returns." Chap. 15 in *The Polls and Public Opinion:*

> *State University of Iowa, Iowa City*, edited by Norman C. Meier and
> Harold W. Saunders, 159-99. New York, NY: Henry Holt & Company,
> [1949]. 355p.

Crossley begins with an in-depth analysis of why the Crossley Poll showed Harry
Truman with 44.8 percent of the vote three weeks prior to the election, and why
Truman actually received 49.5 percent of the votes cast for president. Dodd,
director of the Washington Public Opinion Laboratory (WPOL), discusses the
different poll techniques used, particularly in sampling, by the various organizations attempting to predict the outcome of the presidential race. Bachelder,
codirector of WPOL, reviews the differences between area and quota sampling
and those who voted in terms of rural versus city, age, sex, and education. Gallup
observes that poll accuracy needs to be evaluated over the course of poll history,
namely from 1935 to 1948. Gallup notes that polls should have been taken at the
last minute. Kroeger, director of the research department of the *Des Moines
Register and Tribune* and the Iowa Poll, discusses the special circumstances of
other candidates running for elections in 1948 and their influence on the voters
in relation to whom they voted for president. Meier, one of the volume's editors,
and Paul F. Lazarsfeld provide remarks in response to the above presentations.

934.   Felson, Marcus, and Seymour Sudman. *The Accuracy of Presidential
        Preference Primary Polls*. Faculty Working Papers, no. 196. [Urbana, IL]:
        College of Commerce and Business Administration, University of Illi-
        nois at Urbana-Champaign, 1974. 9 leaves.

This working paper examines the record of state polls in predicting the outcomes of presidential preference primary elections. Polls conducted during the
week of the primary elections are better at predicting than polls completed earlier. Results from primaries in 1968 and 1972 are examined. These indicate that
state polls have "generally been reasonably accurate in predicting primary results." Primary results are taken from information reported in the *New York
Times*. The average difference between actual results and those of the final poll
was about 4 percent. The sample size used was four hundred voters likely to
vote in the primary. Telephone interviewing is the typical mode. The authors conclude by observing that early prediction of primary elections is difficult because
of rapid changes of a candidate's position within the field of other candidates'
places in the race.

935.   Felson, Marcus, and Seymour Sudman. "The Accuracy of Presidential
        Preference Primary Polls." *Public Opinion Quarterly* 39, no. 2 (Summer
        1975): 232-36.

Analysis of the state primary polls of the 1968 and 1972 elections shows a "reasonably accurate" record of prediction. Accuracy is affected by the amount of

time between the poll and the election, as well as by the shifting attitudes of the voter. The figures in table 1 show about four percentage points average difference between the final poll and the primary election results of each participating state. Felson and Sudman discuss the major differences. The primary poll accuracy record is shown in table 2. (The indexes of dissimilarity range from 4 to 57 percent, the mean being 18 percent.) The data indicate that the fewer the number of days before the election that a poll is conducted, the more accurate will be the prediction. The McGovern-Muskie contest is used as an example to show that polls can also indicate trends in the "relative strengths" of candidates during pre-convention campaigning. The authors reiterate the need for timely surveys.

936.   Field, Harry H., and Gordon M. Connelly. "Testing Polls in Official Election Booths." *Public Opinion Quarterly* 6, no. 4 (Winter 1942): 610-16.

To investigate criticisms that sampling surveys on social and economic issues do not reflect the "true opinions" that people would reveal if they could vote on them, the National Opinion Research Center (NORC) conducted an experiment in Boulder, Colorado, with the cooperation of the University of Colorado. Permission was obtained from appropriate officials for NORC to enter polling stations requesting voters to vote on a special ballot. Questions dealt with a national sales tax, old-age pensions, and a world union. The final sample included 1,224 voters. The opinions of the sample were compared with the opinions on identical questions of all voters of Boulder on election day. Results show that on three questions the sampling survey "proved capable of ascertaining public opinion...with a reasonable degree of accuracy." The outcome of two political contests was "virtually perfect" with respect to the predicted versus the actual vote. The article concludes with discussions on the value of the sample survey, possible reasons for discrepancies, and principal shortcomings. (8 footnotes)

937.   McCarthy, Philip J. "Processing, Estimating, and Adjustment of Survey Data: Use of Nonsurvey Data in Preparation of Estimates." Chap. 8 in *The Pre-Election Polls of 1948: Report to the Committee on Analysis of Pre-Election Polls and Forecasts,* by Frederick Mosteller, Herbert Hyman, Philip J. McCarthy, Eli S. Marks, and David B. Truman, 210-21. Social Science Research Council, Bulletin no. 60. New York, NY: Social Science Research Council, 1949. 396p.

At issue is the attempt to balance the sample proportions with those found in the known population and to use quota controls to better represent all the variables, thereby improving the election predictions. Gallup considered education level as such variable, with a "voting intention" table provided. Roper also used the educational variable, but he combined it with a geographic component. State-level predictions by Gallup and Crossley are discussed. McCarthy observes that the

Gallup Organization was the only one to use "data external to the survey in the preparation of estimates from a quota sample." (1 footnote)

938.   Mann, H. B. Correction to the paper "On a Problem of Estimation Occurring in Public Opinion Polls." *Annals of Mathematical Statistics* 17 (1946): 87-88.

This entry corrects an incorrect statement, along with a numerical error. The error was brought to Mann's attention by J. W. Tukey. [See Item No. 939 for the original presentation.]

939.   Mann, H. B. "On a Problem of Estimation Occurring in Public Opinion Polls." *Annals of Mathematical Statistics* 16 (1945): 85-90.

The example considered deals with determining the number of votes which will be cast for a presidential candidate. The poll taken to address this question produces the estimation of the number of electoral votes. The properties of this estimation are what Mann presents using advanced statistics. The poll is considered to be a random or stratified random sample, and bias created through inaccurate answers is not addressed. (3 references)

940.   Nolan, William A. "Are Election Polls Reliable? Predicting Votes a Hazardous Undertaking." *Social Order* 2, o.s. 5 (October 1952): 339-44.

The distinction between polling and prediction is clarified, followed by a discussion of sampling technique, the limits of statistics, and the margin of error. Nolan covers representativeness, area versus quota sampling, and interviewer bias, with further discussion of the difficulties of predicting and the usefulness of polls. The value of polls to government, lobbyists, and pressure groups is briefly considered. The author suggests that opinion polls might be more useful in determining "what the American people know and do not know about vital political issues." Polls are viewed as being able to render positive service to democracy and to the future of the free world. (27 footnotes)

941.   Perry, Paul K. "Gallup Poll Election Survey Experience 1950-60." *Public Opinion Quarterly* 26, no. 2 (Summer 1962): 272-79.

The Gallup Poll election survey procedures consist of the following: (1) using sampling areas which are probability samples of election precincts; (2) completing the final survey in the week of election day; (3) using intention-to-vote questions and election interest project turnout ratio; (4) ranking respondents on scale of likelihood to vote; (5) employing the turnout ratio to determine how the vote will be divided based on those most likely to vote; and (6) implementing techniques to "minimize" the undecided. In the 1956 and 1958 elections Gallup used a split sample in which half the respondents were openly asked their voting preference and half used the secret ballot. In the 1960 election all of the respondents used the secret ballot box procedure. Perry indicates election breakdowns from 1950 through 1960 showing actual results compared with survey results, indicating standard error, and highlighting the "effect of the progressive elimination of likely nonvoters and the use of the secret ballot." (3 footnotes)

942.   "Pollsters: The Voters Still Elude Them." *Business Week*, no. 1211 (15 November 1952): 43-44.

Business Week reports the discrepancy between what each of the three major polling organizations predicted would be the outcome of the 1952 presidential election with the actual results. While Archibald M. Crossley, George A. [*sic* H.] Gallup, and Elmo Roper all correctly reported Eisenhower in the lead, the percent of the vote underforecast was as follows (in the same order as above): 8 percent, 8.8 percent, and 6.4 percent. Equally noteworthy, the undercount of the Stevenson vote was as follows: 2.3 percent, 4.6 percent, and 7.6 percent. The undecided voters (reported as 9.9 percent, 13 percent, and 14 percent by the above three organizations) seem to have been the challenge for the polling companies. Each organization expressed confidence that missing the margin of victory will not damage their market research efforts which are based on "what people do, not what they think" (as one market researcher is quoted to say).

943.   Roper, Elmo B., Jr. "Forecasting Election Returns: How Accurate Are the Polls? A Study of the Methods Employed Will Guide You in Forming Your Own Conclusions." *Review of Reviews* [New York] 94 (October 1936): 58-59.

Statistical sampling requires three elements in order to be valid and accurate: (1) the sample size needs to be adequate; (2) the sample should be representative; and (3) appropriate methodology should be followed in conducting the sampling process. The inadequacy of the *Literary Digest* in fulfilling these caveats is described. The differences in approaches pursued by the American Institute of Public Opinion (AIPO) poll, the *Literary Digest* poll, and the *Fortune* Survey are outlined. AIPO combined mail surveys for upper-income individuals, with personal interviews for lower income and the young; the *Literary Digest* used millions of mail surveys; and *Fortune* used personal interviews exclusively. About forty million will vote from seventy-five million eligible voters. The polls which used statistical techniques indicate that President Roosevelt is ahead in the popular vote.

944.   Seymour, Gideon, Archibald Crossley, Paul F. Lazarsfeld, and George Gallup. "Should Public Opinion Polls Make Election Forecasts? A Symposium." *Journalism Quarterly* 26, no. 2 (June 1949): 131-44.

Three months after the 1948 presidential election upset, three major polling figures and one newspaper editor gathered to discuss whether pollsters should remain in the forecasting business. The vote was three to one in favor, with Crossley being the lone dissenter. Crossley believes that pollsters should be doing
more trend analysis. The symposium reported in this article brought together
Seymour, vice-president and executive editor of the Minneapolis *Star* and the
Minneapolis *Tribune*; Crossley, president of Crossley, Incorporated, New York;
Lazarsfeld, director of the Bureau of Applied Social Research, Columbia University; and Gallup, director of the American Institute of Public Opinion, Princeton, New Jersey. Virgil M. Hancher, president of the State University of Iowa,
presided. Each person spoke individually on the topic, followed at the end by a
question-and-answer period open for all speakers to respond. (2 footnotes)

945.   Smith, Charles W., Jr. "Measurement of Voter Attitude." In *Meaning of
         the 1952 Presidential Election*, edited by James C. Charlesworth, 148-55.
         Annals of the American Academy of Political and Social Science, ed-
         ited by Thorsten Sellin, vol. 283. Philadelphia, PA: American Academy of
         Political and Social Science, September 1952. 252p.

An outline of early poll history is presented, including mistakes of the *Literary
Digest*, the less-than-accurate early state-by-state electoral vote predictions of
Gallup and Crossley, and the "Dewey landslide of pollsters and journalists" in
1948. Smith discusses academic views of the 1948 election, considers the influence of the polls, compares poll reliability, and takes "specific hazards" into
account. The views of political leaders are reviewed, as well as the issue of when
voters do, in fact, decide how they will vote. (15 footnotes)

946.   Suchman, Edward A. "Socio-Psychological Factors Affecting Predic-
         tions of Elections." *Public Opinion Quarterly* 16, no. 3 (Fall 1952): 436-
         38.

As a result of the public opinion polls' failure to predict the 1948 presidential
election, pollsters are analyzing their mistakes and searching for techniques to
improve their performance for the 1952 election. In addition to the more obvious reasons (such as sampling and interviewing procedures), Suchman believes
there are social and psychological factors that affect predictions. At the center of
his research is the question why a respondent says s/he will vote in a particular
manner and then actually votes for a different candidate at the polls. Suchman lists
twenty factors, grouped into five major categories. They are listed in such a way
as to show when the lowest validity will be present. The factors relate to the voter in relation to the specific campaign (interest, degree of concern and knowledge); to certain personality traits; to pressures on the voter (such as propaganda);
to the campaign itself (the candidates, the issues); and to national and international affairs.

947.   "What Do You Think? And What Will You Do about It: That's What
         Public Opinion Polling Aims At. And the Techniques of Predicting
         Elections Are Becoming a Valuable Tool in Finding Out How to Run
         Any Organization." *Business Week*, no. 1057 (3 December 1949): 37-38,
         41-42, 44, 46.

Rensis Likert and Angus Campbell were members of the Institute for Social Research (ISR) at the University of Michigan. Likert was director of the institute,
and Campbell was director of the Survey Research Center, a part of ISR. The
interview format of the article addresses a variety of topics including the 1948
election outcome, the danger of taking the expression of those polled at face
value, and the possibility of bandwagon effects as a product of announcing poll
results. It is noted that poll results do not imply that policymakers "ought necessarily to follow the majority vote in any particular survey."

Presidential Polls

1936

948.   Crossley, Archibald M. "Straw Polls in 1936." *Public Opinion Quarter-
         ly* 1, no. 1 (January 1937): 24-35.

The presentation recounts the polling experiences of the major organizations
during the 1936 presidential campaign. The *Literary Digest* results are examined
with the reasons for their failure analyzed. Also considered are the Gallup Poll,
the Crossley Poll, and the *Fortune* Survey. Crossley outlines the essential elements
which polls need in order to obtain accurate results and discusses controlled
quotas and how the Gallup Polls are conducted. "Survey points" – dominant factors which influence large blocks of voters – are described. The article closes with
a look to the future of polls. After the 1936 elections, many media sources criti-
cized polling, lumping the less than adequate and the more accurate into a single
category. Crossley suggests that polls truly offer the legislative representatives
the opportunity to have "government *by* the people."

949.   Gosnell, Harold F. "How Accurate Were the Polls?" *Public Opinion Quar-
         terly* 1, no. 1 (January 1937): 97-105.

Gosnell refers to the Crossley Poll, the Gallup Poll, and the *Literary Digest* polls as
"straw" polls. A state-by-state comparison of the results of all three are compared with actual election results. The comparison shows that in 1936 none
of the polls came "very close to the popular pluralities." In another table the
percentage plurality errors are displayed, state by state, for the 1936 presidential

election. An analysis follows as to why each polling organization failed to provide a more accurate reading of the election. (10 footnotes)

950.   "Landon, 1,293,669; Roosevelt, 972,897. Final Returns in *The Digest's* Poll of Ten Million Voters." *Literary Digest* 122, no. 18, whole no. 2428 (31 October 1936): 5-6.

The final returns of the *Literary Digest's* poll are included as a record for the numerous references made to the poll through the early literature of polling. A table indicates votes for Landon and Roosevelt broken down by state. Figures on reported voting behavior during the 1932 election are also included, broken down by party and whether individuals voted or failed to reveal that information. The results show Landon with 1,293,669 votes and Roosevelt with 972,897 votes. The article cites previous successful presidential election predictions as grounds for confidence in the accuracy of the data provided.

1940

951.   Cantril, Hadley. "Do Different Polls Get the Same Results?" *Public Opinion Quarterly* 9, no. 1 (Spring 1945): 61-69.

Cantril makes the point that identical questions asked at approximately the same time are necessary for comparison purposes. The results of four independent polling organizations are compared in five ways: (1) the American Institute of Public Opinion (AIPO) and the Princeton Office of Public Opinion Research (OPOR); (2) AIPO and the *Fortune* Poll [*sic*]; (3) OPOR and *Fortune;* (4) the National Opinion Research Center (NORC) and *Fortune*; and (5) OPOR and NORC. For this study twenty-one questions were selected. These are reprinted in the article and deal primarily with public opinion on Wendell Willkie, President Roosevelt, and Thomas Dewey and the presidential elections of 1940 and 1944. There were also several questions on World War II. The average difference between the results was 3.24 percentage points. The highest agreement occurred for questions asked during the same ten-day interval and for questions involving purely political issues. Cantril believes these results show a "highly creditable performance" for the polls under consideration. Polling organizations are urged to make their data available for more frequent comparisons. (2 footnotes)

952.   Crossley, Archibald M. "Methods Tested during 1940 Campaign." *Public Opinion Quarterly* 5, no. 1 (March 1941): 83-86.

Crossley, president of the national research organization of Crossley, Incorporated, describes several new techniques used by the company in the 1940 presidential election (Roosevelt versus Willkie). Since previous test polls and studies indicated clear winners in twenty-nine states (only the extent of leadership would be shown by further polls), the methods were employed in only nineteen states considered pivotal. The most significant change involved the distribution of the sample, placing "full reliance upon cross-sectioning the population of voting age." Variables taken into account included undecided voters and those who tended to shift their opinions. A series of follow-up questions was used to determine more accurately the intentions of the undecided voter. In addition, asking voters when they had reached a decision seemed to have an important impact on the prediction. Other checks included the use of callbacks, secret ballots, and tabulations by cities and towns. On the basis of all the new techniques, Roosevelt was correctly predicted to be the winner.

953.   Katz, Daniel. "The Public Opinion Polls and the 1940 Election." *Public Opinion Quarterly* 5, no. 1 (March 1941): 52-78.

Katz compares and contrasts the methods and results of three polls on the 1940 presidential election: Gallup (the American Institute of Public Opinion); the *Fortune* Survey (conducted by Elmo Roper); and Crossley, Incorporated (Archibald Crossley). All three organizations, which are well established in the polling field, agree on predicting a close election, a Roosevelt victory, and in over-estimating Republican strength. Katz reviews five possible sources of error, only some of which were operational in 1936. These include the difficulties of estimating how many voters will turn out, setting up an accurate cross section of the population, defects in the measuring instrument, the problem of the uncommitted voter, and the role of trends and shifts in public opinion. Katz concludes the following: (1) even though the 1940 polls underestimated Democratic strength, their predictive performance "compares favorably with predictive measurement in the social sciences"; (2) the polls' failure to represent the lower-income population and attempts to correct for last-minute changes in opinion contributed to constant error; (3) the interview technique, as opposed to the mail ballot, was far superior; (4) "unorthodox" methods (from remote secondary factors) of prediction are as yet unproven; (5) the Gallup method is superior to the *Fortune* method; and (6) the "less tinkering" with the original data yields a greater chance of correct predictions. Katz completes his article by posing three questions focusing on research problems in public opinion measurement. (6 footnotes)

954.   Roper, Elmo. "Checks to Increase Polling Accuracy." *Public Opinion Quarterly* 5, no. 1 (March 1941): 87-90.

Roper reviews how changes of opinion, and reasons for the changes, were measured in some of the 1940 preelection polls conducted for the *Fortune* Survey. Two experiments are reported: one in Erie County, Ohio, an area very strongly in favor of Willkie, and one in Missouri where Roper tried to "coordinate positive and negative reasons for opinion." Certain states were determined to be "barometric" areas, and surveys were conducted in St. Louis and Alameda County,

California. The framing of the national survey questions was based on the study of the preliminary ones. In a final test two independent national surveys of five thousand interviews each were made. On some surveys an attitude scale was used in addition to the usual "yes" and "no" questions. The scale offered four possible answers which provided a gradation of opinion. All tests and checks were seen as assisting in polling accuracy. (1 footnote)

1944

955.   Benson, Edward G., Cyrus C. Young, and Clyde A. Syze. "Polling Lessons from the 1944 Election." *Public Opinion Quarterly* 9, no. 4 (Winter 1945-46): 467-84.

Benson is statistical director of the American Institute of Public Opinion (AIPO), and the coauthors are his associates. This article discusses the polling lessons to be learned from the 1944 election. Specific areas of concern include area sampling, the secret ballot, and a voter turnout study. The AIPO "pinpoint" method of "extensive family coverage of a cross section of small election districts selected in the central office" is discussed. The secret ballot, as well as the regular personal ballot, was used by AIPO in national elections. The turnout issue is twofold: (1) how large will the vote be; and (2) is there a difference between those who will vote from those who will not. A study regarding these questions is presented. (12 footnotes)

956.   Katz, Daniel. "The Polls and the 1944 Election." *Public Opinion Quarterly* 8, no. 4 (Winter 1944-45): 468-82.

Katz has previously reviewed the poll performance of the presidential elections of 1936 [Item No. 54] and 1940 [Item No. 953]. He finds a repeat in 1944 of the polls' "very creditable" record of 1940, in spite of the new challenges of manpower shortages, military voting, and a shifting population due to wartime conditions. In 1944 Roper (for the *Fortune* Survey) named the popular vote with only 0.2 percent error. Crossley (Crossley, Incorporated) and Gallup (the American Institute of Public Opinion or AIPO) made errors of 2 or 3 percentage points in the state-by-state predictions. As in 1940, the errors were made in underestimating the direction of the Democratic vote. Due to the fact that no radical changes in methodology had been made from the previous election, Katz believes that increasing skill was used in manipulating existing techniques. The polling methods of five polling organizations are reviewed: the *Fortune* Survey, the Princeton Poll, the National Opinion Research Center Poll, the Crossley Poll, and the Gallup Poll. Also covered are the pros and cons of quota-control sampling, Roper's use of attitude scales, and Crossley and Gallup's state-by-state predictions. Following the Katz article are comments by E. G. Benson of AIPO which criticize Katz's discussion of the Gallup Poll. (5 footnotes)

1948

957.   Chase, Stuart. "Are the Polls Finished?" *Nation* 167, no. 23 (4 December 1948): 626-29.

The reasons for the pollsters' error in predicting the winner of the 1948 presidential campaign are analyzed. In 1936 Roper and Gallup were the first pollsters to engage in applying sampling theory to measuring public opinion in elections. Through the 1936, 1940, and 1944 elections accurate forecasting had earned polling considerable public attention. An examination of the 1948 experience shows that although the poll results may have been accurate for the date they were collected, these results were not useful in predicting what attitudes would be weeks or months later. In other words, attitude position changes were not reflected. The "don't know" category was 15.4 percent – the majority of which voted for Truman. Additionally, millions of individuals who were expected to vote chose to stay at home. Most of those who stayed at home were Republicans. Chase maintains that pollsters are making "unwarranted predictions about voters' actions."

958.   Committee on Analysis of Pre-Election Polls and Forecasts. Social Science Research Council. "Report on the Analysis of Pre-Election Polls and Forecasts." *Public Opinion Quarterly* 12, no. 4 (Winter 1948-49): 599-622. [Reprinted in *Supplement to Reader in Public Opinion and Communication*, edited by Bernard Berelson and Morris Janowitz. No. 10: *Methods in Public Opinion Research*, 584-93. Glencoe, IL: Free Press, 1953. 611p.]

The committee reached seven conclusions regarding the 1948 election forecasts: (1) "pollsters over-reached the capabilities" of 1948 polling methodology in predicting a winner without "qualification"; (2) more careful data analysis and review of past oversights would have assisted in the prediction of a closer race; (3) sampling and interviewing errors, as well as errors in forecasting related to undecided voters and late voter shifts, were made; (4) the sources of error had occurred in 1940 and 1944; (5) errors in each step of the polling process will have to be addressed; (6) the way in which poll results were provided to the public led to an overly optimistic interpretation of their accuracy, followed by the opposite after the election; and (7) the outcome of the preelection forecasts have no bearing on the "accuracy or usefulness of properly conducted sample surveys." The report discusses the complexity of preelection forecasting and compares election results with the forecasts. The nature of the principal sources of error is covered along with specific evidence of sources of error. The committee observes that the report deals only with the technical aspects of preelection polling, rather than with issues such as fraud or "sell-out." (5 footnotes)

959.   "The Great Fiasco." *Time* 52, no. 20 (15 November 1948): 66.

The various major polling organizations' reactions to the 1948 election results are briefly outlined. Gallup, Roper, and Crossley are considered, along with some of their evaluations as to the causal nature of the incorrect predictions. Errors cited include the lack of polling right up until the election, the assumption that voters would not change their positions as the election drew near, and that undecided voters would "split about the same way the 'decided' votes were." In 1948 the survey industry employed about ten thousand individuals and conducted some $25 million worth of business. The cancellation of some Gallup newspaper subscribers, and the general attitude of the public toward the pollsters' unanimous errors, were seen as threats to both the continuity and the growth of the industry. Photographs of Gallup and Roper appear with the article.

960.   "How Right Are the Polls?" *U.S. News & World Report* 57, no. 12 (21 September 1964): 33-36.

The article focuses on the poll results of the 1948 presidential election and provides a large graphic displaying the four races from 1948 to 1960. Each candidate's position in the polls is traced from early to late September, the same for October, and then the final poll and the actual vote percentages are shown. George Katona, director of economic research at the University of Michigan's Survey Research Center, is interviewed with the text in question-and-answer format. A broad range of issues are addressed, including sample size, the amount of time spent interviewing a respondent, the use of private polls by politicians, and the use of the public release of favorable results and the concealment of unfavorable results.

961.   "How the Election Polls Went Wrong: The Pollsters Couldn't Read Their Own Figures, and Their Sampling Method May Have Been Wrong." *Business Week*, no. 1002 (13 November 1948): 25-26.

The 1948 presidential election polls and the reasons for their errors are discussed. It is pointed out that in the case of Roper, 15 percent of the responses were "don't know." An assumption was made that the " 'don't knows' would split about even between the major candidates." It was not known as of the writing of this article if, in fact, that was the case. The issue of quota sampling versus probability sampling is discussed, with the note that Gallup, Crossley, and Roper all used quota sampling for the 1948 polls. Probability sampling is advocated, with the Bureau of the Census and the Advertising Research Foundation given as examples of users. In response to the question as to whether the 1948 results negatively affected market research activities, the article points out that commercial surveys involve facts and actions, rather than issues of future intentions.

962.   Lasswell, Thomas, and Edward McDonagh. "Presidential Polls: One Year After." *Sociology and Social Research* 34, no. 2 (November-December 1949): 97-103.

Seven implications for quantitative research in the social sciences are suggested as a consequence of the failure of the 1948 preelection polls. These are as follows: (1) the necessity of a representative sample; (2) the acceptance of quantitative findings as static; (3) the careful designation and delimitization of the study subject; (4) the careful selection of instruments and interviewers; (5) the full awareness of the qualities of the subject under study; (6) a warning against using empirical interpolation and unwarranted postulates; and (7) the importance of primary fact publication, along with appropriate explanation. Lasswell and McDonagh raise a series of questions about the 1948 polls and seek to answer them using Gallup data, among others, as compared with the actual election vote. A figure clearly shows the degree to which the poll results differ from the November 1948 election returns. (14 footnotes)

963.   Likert, Rensis. "The Polls: Straw Votes or Scientific Instruments?" *American Psychologist* 3, no. 12 (December 1948): 556-57.

A number of reasons for the failure of the polls in 1948 are identified, including (1) the use of the quota sampling method instead of area or probability sampling, (2) the mistaken use of error formulas computed for probability samples for use with quota sampling, (3) the introduction of pollsters' individual judgment to make arbitrary adjustments, and (4) the interpretation of the "don't knows," or uncertain answers. Other observations include the idea that motivational forces should have been explored, as well as concerns related to the attitude intensity toward both the candidates and the issues raised. Inadequate training and supervision of interviewers are also cited. Likert maintains that the polls operated more "like straw votes than scientific instruments. They have relied on rule of thumb methods and historical relationships rather than objective, precise methods." The author believes the additional cost of the suggested alternatives is the reason to date why poll organizations have not changed their approaches. (4 footnotes)

964.   Likert, Rensis. "Public Opinion Polls: Why Did They Fail? A Leading Authority Assays Their Weaknesses and Suggests Some Tested New Techniques That Would Improve Their Accuracy." *Scientific American* 179, no. 6 (December 1948): 7-11.

The article is a response to the errors of the presidential election forecasts of 1948. The shortcomings of quota sampling are discussed, along with the weighting correction attempted by the polling organizations. The types of bias that arise from quota sampling are reviewed, with the better approach of probability sampling (or area sampling as it is referred to) suggested as an alternative. Area sampling is believed to provide a greater degree of accuracy. Likert continues the discussion with a consideration of interview difficulties. The secret ballot technique is described as one way to attempt to encourage respondents to be frank, unrestrained, and assured of confidentiality. The problems of different word meanings for different respondents are addressed. Some possible solutions include the "fixed question-free answer" method of interviewing, open questions, questions employing an indirect approach, and the use of a series of interrelated questions covering the same issue from a variety of approaches.

965.   Mosteller, Frederick. "Measuring the Error." Chap. 5 in *The Pre-Election Polls of 1948: Report to the Committee on Analysis of Pre-Election Polls and Forecasts*, by Frederick Mosteller, Herbert Hyman, Philip J. McCarthy, Eli S. Marks, and David B. Truman, 54-80. Social Science Research Council, Bulletin no. 60. New York, NY: Social Science Research Council, 1949. 396p.

Eight methods for measuring errors in election forecasts are outlined. National forecasts from 1936, 1940, 1944, and 1948 are compared using the actual vote, as compared with the predictions of Crossley, Gallup, and Roper. Errors in state forecasts are reviewed, covering the same years, but comparing only the forecasts of Crossley and Gallup. Persistence forecasts are contrasted with polling forecasts. (The persistence approach – a crude mechanical forecasting scheme used as a lower limit of what can be expected from polls – holds that last election forecasts will "persist" to the next election.) The electoral college system is discussed. Mosteller concludes that the 1948 results were not "out of line" with those of previous elections, that the degree of error may occur again in future elections, and that more research in every phase of polling is required to reduce errors. (4 footnotes)

966.   Mosteller, Frederick, Herbert Hyman, Philip J. McCarthy, Eli S. Marks, and David B. Truman. *The Pre-Election Polls of 1948: Report of the Committee on Analysis of Pre-Election Polls and Forecasts.* Social Science Research Council, Bulletin no. 60. New York, NY: Social Science Research Council, 1949. 396p.

This bulletin contains the studies on which the Committee on Analysis of Pre-Election Polls and Forecasts of the Social Science Research Council based its report of 27 December 1948. The committee undertook the task of evaluating the technical procedures and methods of interpretation used by public opinion polling organizations in attempting to predict the outcome of the 1948 presidential election. Appendix A reprints the full report of the committee. S. S. Wilks served as chairperson. The following entries have been selected from the volume, with individual annotations found at the indicated item number.

"Development of Election Forecasting by Polling Methods." (Stephan - Item No. 63).

"Measuring the Error." (Mosteller - Item No. 965).

"Interviewing and Questionnaire Design." (Hyman - Item No. 131).

"Processing, Estimating, and Adjustment of Survey Data: Treatment of Undecided Responses." (Marks - Item No. 665).

"Processing, Estimating, and Adjustment of Survey Data: Use of Non-survey Data in Preparation of Estimates." (McCarthy - Item No. 937).

"Processing, Estimating, and Adjustment of Survey Data: Control of Error in Editing, Coding, and Tabulation." (Hyman - Item No. 768).

"The Undecided Voter." (Marks - Item No. 666).

967.   Politz, Alfred. "The 1948 Election Forecast – A Useful Disaster." *Printers' Ink* 225, no. 7 (12 November 1948): 36c-36f.

The major point that Politz makes is that the election forecast disaster of 1948 is a great opportunity for "population research" to move ahead into scientific methods of conducting research, as compared with the invalid approaches of the past. Politz divides these approaches into three discussion areas: the sample, analysis, and social issues. In the sample section the problems with quota samples used until, and including, the 1948 election are discussed. Under analysis, the failure of many voters to go to the polls on election day is considered, as well as the distortion this creates when these individual's opinions are included in opinion poll results. The social issues section covers the "menace to the democratic procedure" when "unscientific guesses" are reported to the public, possibly causing voters to refrain from voting because they believe that the outcome is a foregone conclusion.

968.   "Report on the Holes in the Polls: Market-Research Techniques Still Basically Sound. So Are Properly Conducted Election Polls. Seven Recommendations Made." *Business Week*, no. 1010 (8 January 1949): 56-58.

As a consequence of the errors of Crossley, Gallup, and Roper in forecasting the 1948 presidential election, a committee was appointed by the Social Science Research Council to investigate the causes and to make recommendations. The committee chair was Samuel S. Wilks, serving with committee members James P. Baxter, Philip M. Hauser, Carl I. Hovland, V. O. Key, John Hopkins, Isador Lubin, Frank Stanton, Frederick F. Stephan, and Samuel A. Stouffer. The errors were traced to sampling, interviewing, and forecasting what people will do – based on what they say they will do. Quota sampling is singled out for criticism. The committee made seven specific recommendations: (1) improve sampling methods; (2) investigate further the area of sampling; (3) perform additional research in social psychology and political science; (4) advise the public of poll limitations; (5) call for greater cooperation among poll researchers on reliability and methods; (6) institute training programs for students of polling; and (7) provide election statistics more expediently to the public.

969.   "Why Opinion Polls Were So Wrong." *U.S. News & World Report* 25, no. 20 (12 November 1948): 24-25.

Aspects of polling error are discussed as related to the failure of all the major polling organizations in the presidential election forecasts for 1948. Rensis Likert, director of the Survey Research Center of the University of Michigan, explains his analysis of the difficulties. The two major problems deal with quota sampling and interviewing. Using quota sampling, the pollsters experienced the consistent bias of underrepresenting lower-income individuals by 12 to 20 percent. Additionally, the undecided vote was unusually high, and the pollsters underestimated the voter turnout. Interviewing beyond "yes-and-no" answers is recommended as a means to determine issue attitudes, thereby providing data on possible voter turnout. The major pollsters are admonished for not using sampling based on area or geographical control and for not using sophisticated interviewing techniques. It is pointed out that area sampling and newer interviewing methods have been in use for nearly ten years in government and academic polling units.

1952

970.   "How Pollsters Plan to Redeem Themselves." *Business Week*, no. 1173 (23 February 1952): 22-23.

After the disastrous 1948 polling record, each of the major pollsters plan changes which they believe will prevent a recurrence. Gallup thinks that pollsters should be reporters, rather than forecasters. The major area of modification seems to be with sampling. Although Gallup will move from quota to "pinpoint" sampling, quota sampling will be maintained as a secondary method. Additionally, Gallup plans the use of filter questions to deal with the voter who is undecided or who has a change of opinion. Crossley plans to refine his quota sampling, to conduct a telegraphic poll, and to poll close to the election. Roper intends to research what the voter is thinking about, rather than who the voter is going to vote for.

971.   "Polls as Election Guides: Errors Appear Again." *U.S. News & World Report* 33, no. 20 (14 November 1952): 32.

The 1952 presidential election proved to be very challenging for Gallup, Crossley, and Roper, all of whom missed the Eisenhower landslide – even though they had picked the correct winner. Each poll reported between 10 and 13 percent voter undecided/noncommitted. The outcome of a record presidential election in which the polls failed to come closer to the final outcome has caused many to question polling. In fact, this article reports that newspaper editors and farm-belt magazines and newspapers came closer to predicting the election outcome than did the major polls.

972.   "Presidential Polls." *Newsweek* 40, no. 6 (11 August 1952): 60.

The 1948 presidential election aftermath for the polling operations of Gallup and Roper is discussed. Gallup lost subscribers to his news service (twenty-five from one hundred), and Roper lost commercial accounts. Several reasons have been suggested as to the cause of the incorrect prediction: (1) voters changed their minds at the last minute; (2) undecided voters were inappropriately disregarded; and (3) polling was not continued close enough to voting. For the 1952 election Gallup has developed questions designed to determine the "leaning" of the voter, even when "don't know" is the answer to the direct question of who the individual will vote for. Roper plans to present all the data he collects, and suggests how he thinks it should be weighed. Readers of Roper's Monday column in the Herald Tribune Syndicate and viewers of his NBC television program will be allowed to decide who will win.

1960

973.   "How Polls Helped Candidates: Applying Marketing-Research Techniques to Politics – Both Candidates Used Polls in Choosing Campaign Tactics. Now Pollsters Want to Find Out Why the Election Went the Way It Did." *Business Week*, no. 1631 (3 December 1960): 34, 36.

The aftermath of the 1960 presidential election is reviewed, and the polling methods of Claude Robinson, the Republican's pollster, and Louis Harris (of Louis Harris and Associates, Incorporated), the Democrat's pollster, are discussed. Kennedy asked Harris to conduct an examination as to why he won and how it happened. Robinson began a reinterview program to determine if people voted, who they voted for, and why. Additionally, the Rockefeller Foundation funded the University of Michigan's Survey Research Center to reinterview the same sample interviewed in the 1956 and 1958 elections. Robinson is quoted as saying, "This election showed that there is no essential difference between the merchandizing of politics and the merchandizing of products." Both Robinson and Harris served as route finders on the campaign map.

974.   "Pollsters Counter Critics' Attacks." *Business Week*, no. 1620 (17 September 1960): 34, 38.

During January 1960, for the first time in election year polling, the lead between two candidates (Nixon and Kennedy) changed five times, prompting Senator Albert Gore (D.-Tenn.) to propose a congressional investigation. The article focuses on the polling errors of the 1948 election and efforts to overcome them. The change from quota sampling to random sampling is discussed, along with some interviewing modifications. The Gallup Poll has instituted a "time-place" pattern of interviewing in which the interviewer follows a specific sequence of home visits at defined time periods (late afternoons, evenings, and weekends). Gallup is cited as stressing that polls measure opinion only as of the time of the interview, and that only the popular vote is measured.

1964

975.   "The Battle to Call the Winner: Networks Leaned Hard on Both Pollsters and Computers in Reporting California." *Business Week*, no. 1814 (6 June 1964): 24-26.

The discussion provides some background as to how presidential primaries are handled by pollsters and the news media. The 1964 California presidential primary is the main focus, with frequent references to the experience of the 1960 race. Paul Perry of the Gallup Organization is quoted as saying that polls "are really reports of an existing situation," which is why pollsters maintain that their numbers are in no sense predictions. The 1948 election is cited as an example of where pollsters stopped polling too early, thereby missing the last minute shift in voting. In 1964 networks were still in the business of calling elections while voters were still going to the polls. Archibald M. Crossley, George Gallup, and Elmo Roper are credited with having started the era of modern presidential polling during the 1936 election campaign. The Crossley Poll ceased publication in 1952. A brief discussion is included as to how pollsters select voting precincts using census data. As of 1964, the Gallup Organization did not participate in polling for primaries, considering them too risky.

1968

976.   "The Polls and the Pols and the Public." *Newsweek* 72, no. 2 (8 July 1968): 23-27.

The 1968 preconvention campaign is described. The article proceeds to outline the major elements of a poll and discusses them in terms of their development to date, beginning with the sample which has undergone a transition from quota sampling to a "random-precinct" system. In the question format section five types of questions are discussed: validation, filter, closed-end, open-end, and semantic differential. Interviewer technique is covered, followed by poll analysis. The volatility of primaries is reviewed, along with a number of criticisms of polling, including the charge that politicians just reiterate what the polls say the people want. (1 unnumbered footnote)

977.   "Polls: Confusing and Exaggerated." *Time* 92, no. 6 (9 August 1968): 19.

At issue are the unusual circumstances of significantly divergent results from Gallup, Harris, and Crossley with respect to the preconvention Republican standings in 1968. George Gallup, Jr., described it as a "credibility-gap problem." In June 1968 the National Committee on Published Polls had been formed to publicize standards for opinion surveys. Harris persuaded George Gallup, Jr., and Archibald Crossley to issue a joint public statement which essentially combined the results of all three organizations as though they were one, and released a revised statement of predicted outcomes. The different approaches of Gallup and Harris are discussed, with some doubts expressed as to the worthiness of "race-horse surveys" in which the electorate changes from one week to the next. The press is described as exaggerating the importance of polls.

Private Polling

978.   "Can Pollsters Deliver the Votes? Opinion Samplers Agree They Can Influence Voters and Help Candidates. But Pre-Convention Brouhaha over Republicans' Chances Shows Prophecies Can Change with Alarming Speed." *Business Week*, no. 2032 (10 August 1968): 50-52, 54.

Discussed here is polling – specifically political polling – as a business. The argument is made that political polls are designed to influence voters and to help candidates, but not necessarily to predict election results. Syndicated polls are designed to promote either private polling services or marketing research services. Gallup's highest weekly fee of $350 for syndicated polls is to the *Philadelphia Bulletin*. Harris, Gallup, and Crossley are named as the recent founders of the National Committee on Published Polls, an organization designed to establish standards, to serve as a clearinghouse for poll results, and to respond to difficult questions about polls posed by the press or the general public. Political polls are sometimes commissioned by individuals or groups interested in supporting a candidate as a means of determining strengths and weaknesses. In 1968 it was estimated that there were about two hundred firms active in political polling, with an average pretax profit of approximately 10 to 12 percent.

979.   Harris, Louis. "Polls and Politics in the United States." *Public Opinion Quarterly* 27, no. 1 (Spring 1963): 3-8.

Harris breaks with past practice and chooses to discontinue his role (and the role of Louis Harris and Associates, Incorporated) of conducting polling for candidates and political parties. In a recently signed six-year contract, he and his firm will conduct election research for CBS. Harris writes that the private pollster should begin one year before the election, and should be polling on a continuing basis. Three areas in which polls can be useful for candidates include group breakdowns (such as racial and religious patterns), what the electorate thinks of the candidate as a public figure, and the definition of the issues. Harris sees private political polling growth as continuing, with the pollster serving as a member of candidate strategy meetings. He maintains that poll leaks are the exception, and the first obligation is to "report truth as we see it."

PUBLIC RELATIONS

980.   Lindenmann, Walter K. "Opinion Research: How It Works; How to Use It." *Public Relations Journal* 33, no. 1 (January 1977): 12-14.

Discovering that 90 percent of the population does not know something about a problem is not sufficient information so far as Lindenmann is concerned. He suggests a series of questions – motivation, explanation seeking, and depth – which should be asked. Planning the research is discussed, and the types of research are explained. The various uses of particular types of survey techniques are reviewed, with attitude research described as ideal for academicians and opinion research well suited for politicians. A six-point research study checklist is presented, with suggestions for various aspects of the planning process. The article is designed to assist the public relations person faced with the decision as to which information-gathering approach to follow.

981.   Moynahan, John F. "Opinion Research: To Solve a Problem, to Grasp an Opportunity." *Public Relations Journal* 19, no. 6 (June 1963): 26-27.

Three benefits of opinion surveys are in management planning, in directing the public relations effort toward the characteristics of the audience, and in providing a base against which employee attitudes could be compared with future results. Moynahan notes the value of raw survey data as critical to solving problems in public relations. A seven-point planning program is discussed, and examples of the use of survey research in public relations are provided. Polls and the dissemination of their results are seen as important to the country as a means of keeping the population informed, which is perceived by the author to be of great value. The technical benefits polls provide to public relations efforts are noted.

982.   Robinson, Edward J. *Public Relations and Survey Research: Achieving Organizational Goals in a Communication Context.* ACC Business Series, edited by Stanley F. Teele and David W. Ewing. New York, NY: Appleton-Century-Crofts, Educational Division Meredith Corporation, [1969]. 282p.

There are three parts to this textbook. The first places public relations in the context of the communication model. Part 2 describes survey research in a "nutshell," and the third part presents seven cases demonstrating the use of survey research. Part 2 is divided into six chapters, the first of which relates survey research to other means of obtaining information. The following chapter describes the survey research process. Subsequent chapters define the purpose; identify the population and sample; explain how to use the data collection instrument; discuss the training of the data collection staff; and describe ways to analyze and interpret data. A section on the use of survey research in a public relations program is included. The seven cases presented cover a variety of environments, such as military, corporate, association, and council. A three-page index is provided. Footnotes are used throughout.

RELIGION

983.   McCourt, Kathleen, and D. Garth Taylor. "Determining Religious Affiliation through Survey Research: A Methodological Note." *Public Opinion Quarterly* 40, no. 1 (Spring 1976): 124-27.

The National Opinion Research Center's (NORC) Continuous National Survey (CNS) asked the questions, "What is your religious preference? Is it Protestant, Catholic, Jewish, some other religion, or no religion?" In 1974 NORC conducted another survey, the Catholic School Study, which asked the question, "What is your present religion?" The latter study took as its sample all those who gave Catholic as their religious preference in the CNS surveys. However, in interviewing this sample, forty-five cases (5 percent), assumed to be Catholic by their stated preference, replied that they were actually not Catholic. Eventually, four hypotheses were delineated which might be responsible for the different responses to the two forms of the religion question. The authors conclude that (1) interviewer or coding errors were not the cause of the inconsistent answers, (2) hypotheses can be constructed that provide plausible explanations for most of the inconsistencies in the responses, and (3) the form of the question used by the Catholic School Study, which asks for present religion, seems to be more accurate in determining religious affiliation and should be used instead of a religious preference question. (2 footnotes)

984.   Schroeder, W. Widick. "Measuring the Muse: Reflections on the Use of Survey Methods in the Study of Religious Phenomena." *Review of Religious Research* 18, no. 2 (Winter 1977): 148-62.

The "foundational problems" which are present in each of the steps of survey research are discussed. These include the following: (1) the "ambiguity of linguistic symbols," and the predominance of "forced option response" formats in the study of religious phenomena; (2) how the causal past relates to the emerging present; (3) the issues surrounding the relationship of isolated parts to the whole; (4) the "ahistorical and egalitarian biases" of survey research and the fact that results dealing with the "average" assist in the comprehension of the "dominant sustaining ethos," but fail to speak to the "emerging future"; and (5) "larger generalities" cannot be derived from questionnaires and interviews. Schroeder illustrates the last point by citing the pervasiveness of religious institutions in America and the impossibility of holding the phenomena constant in an independent/dependent causal analysis study. (23 footnotes, 27 references)

SOCIAL SCIENCES

985.   Campbell, Angus, and George Katona. "The Sample Survey: A Technique for Social-Science Research." Chap. 1 in *Research Methods in the Behavioral Sciences*, edited by Leon Festinger and Daniel Katz, 15-55. New York, NY: Holt, Rinehart & Winston, 1953. 660p.

Numerous types of survey design are discussed, including the unweighted cross section, the weighted cross section, contrasting samples, successive cross sections, and reinterviews. Types of data studied are personal, environmental, behavioral, and the various levels of information, opinions, attitudes, motives, and expectations. Additionally, Campbell and Katona cover modes of analysis, including comparing different parts of the sample, linking behavior and attitudes, studying motivations, and making predictions. A written flowchart of the survey is presented. Survey reliability and validity are considered, along with survey limitations in the areas of precision and adaptability. Three tables are provided, as well as a fifty-item bibliography.

986.   Crespi, Leo, and Donald Rugg. "Poll Data and the Study of Opinion Determinants." *Public Opinion Quarterly* 4, no. 2 (June 1940): 273-76.

A differentiation is made between the poll administrator and the social scientist. The poll administrator is described as one whose role is to report public opinion on issues of the day. By contrast, the social scientist seeks to understand that opinion, determine its genesis, and decide whatever relationship there may be to group or institutional affiliation or to personal views. The samples used for polls are those that will best reflect public opinion, not necessarily the samples that social scientists would select for data sought for their studies. It is observed that polls should be used with caution when trying to seek determinants of opinion. Some steps are suggested when using poll data for this purpose.

987.   Glock, Charles Y., ed., with contributions by John W. Bennett, et al. *Survey Research in the Social Sciences*. New York, NY: Russell Sage Foundation, 1967. 543p.

The twenty-one-page introduction by Glock provides a brief history of survey research, describes the character of the study, and places the work within the context of the social sciences. The first two chapters deal with present uses of survey research in sociology and political science. Chapter 3 discusses present and potential use in psychology. The fourth and fifth chapters cover economics and anthropology – areas which have been slow to implement survey research. Chapter 6 deals with misconceptions about survey research in the field of education and how these have caused difficulties for researchers. The seventh chapter outlines the lack of insight in the area of social work to best utilize survey research, while the final chapter discusses evolving uses in public health and medicine. All chapters have extensive footnotes and bibliographies. The volume includes separate name and subject indexes. The following entries have been selected from the volume, with individual annotations found at the indicated item number.

"Survey Design and Analysis in Sociology." (Glock - Item No. 989).

"Survey Research in Political Science." (McClosky - Item No. 901).

"Contributions of Survey Research to Economics." (Morgan - Item No. 838).

"Education and Survey Research." (Trow - Item No. 853).

"The Survey Method in Social Work: Past, Present, and Potential." (Massarik - Item No. 989).

"The Survey Method Applied to Public Health and Medicine." (Suchman - Item No. 874).

988.   Likert, Rensis. "The Sample Interview Survey: A Fundamental Research Tool of the Social Sciences." In *Current Trends in Psychology*, edited

by Wayne Dennis, et al., 196-225. [Pittsburgh, PA]: University of Pittsburgh Press, 1947. 225p.

The sample interview survey gathers information from a sample of respondents through systematic interviews which ask attitude and opinion questions, as well as questions concerning personal characteristics such as age, education, knowledge, and misinformation on the topic under consideration. The respondents' experience and behavior are related to the issue question and also to motives underlying their attitudes and behavior. Likert places this approach in the context of previous survey techniques and that of public opinion polls. The interview method, the sampling approach, the interpretation, and the applications of sample interview surveys are presented. Information is provided on the potential and actual use of the method by psychologists, economists, and public and business administrators. Utilization by government and communications, as well as by the United Nations, is explored.

SOCIAL WORK

989.   Massarik, Fred. "The Survey Method in Social Work: Past, Present, and Potential." In *Survey Research in the Social Sciences*, edited by Charles Y. Glock, with contributions by John W. Bennett, et al., 377-422. New York, NY: Russell Sage Foundation, 1967. 543p.

The earliest uses of surveys in social work are described, along with the changing survey concept and obstacles to the use of the survey method in social work. Recent applications of the approach are considered, including the client as focus of survey research and social work's professional, occupational, and organizational matrix as focus of survey research. Massarik addresses a number of areas in which the potential of survey research could be extended in the field of social work, namely, by (1) carefully evaluating if a survey is the right method for the task, (2) deciding on the most useful sampling unit, (3) using fieldwork – "one-shot" or "multi-shot" surveys, (4) incorporating greater flexibility in analysis and reanalysis, and (5) viewing the survey report as the beginning of a process, especially in community planning. An eighty-five-entry bibliography is provided.

SOCIOLOGY

990.   Glock, Charles Y. "Survey Design and Analysis in Sociology." In *Survey Research in the Social Sciences*, edited by Charles Y. Glock, with contributions by John W. Bennett, et al., 1-62. New York, NY: Russell Sage Foundation, 1967. 543p.

Beginning with basic survey design, Glock discusses the cross-sectional survey in terms of marginal tabulations, time-bound association, and time-ordered association. Variations of the cross-sectional design are covered, including over-representation and the following designs: contextual, sociometric, and parallel sample. Studies of short- and long-term change are presented with the focus on trend and panel studies. It is noted that although the cost of survey research has restricted its use, new uses for existing data may partially address this situation. An eighty-five-entry bibliography is provided.

991. Lee, Alfred McClung. "Sociological Theory in Public Opinion and Attitude Studies." *American Sociological Review* 12, no. 3 (June 1947): 312-23.

Lee suggests, based on sociological theory, shortcomings in the following areas of polling procedures: (1) purposes of polls or surveys of opinion – selection of issues and prediction of probable behavior; (2) development of schedules; (3) selection of interviewers; (4) training of interviewers; (5) selection of samples; (6) interview situations; (7) analyses of results; and (8) social and societal consequences of polling. It is noted that to date psychologists, semanticists, statisticians, journalists, and account executives have been the primary professionals involved with public opinion polling organizations. Lee seeks to avoid the theoretical problems associated with special interest sponsorship or privately subsidized research. (52 footnotes)

992. Schwartz, Mildred A. *Survey Research and the Study of Change.* Chicago, IL: National Opinion Research Center, University of Chicago, December 1965. 110p.

The use of survey data as sources of information for the study of social change is explored. Data from public and private agencies were considered, with the focus directed to data collected from nongovernmental bodies such as newspapers, magazines, books, films, radio, and television. Fifty-two studies are reviewed, each of which is annotated in an appendix. Annotation length ranges from 36 to 219 words per entry – with an average length of approximately 100 words. The treatment of time, along with the data sources, are covered as part of the study summary. Schwartz explores some of the ways that survey data have contributed to the item considered. Methodological challenges created by the use of accumulated data are discussed, with designs for the study of change contemplated. Some of the other areas covered are the availability of questions, sampling, statistical concerns, differential bias, mechanisms for classifying questions, and trend data interpretation problems. Study designs considered include trend, quasi-cohort, quasi-experimental, prediction, and stage comparison. Models of the treatment of time discussed include the sequence of events and the time series. (72 footnotes)

993.   Sudman, Seymour. "Sample Surveys." In *Annual Review of Sociology*, vol. 2, edited by Alex Inkeles, James Coleman, and Neil Smelser, 107-20. Palo Alto, CA: Annual Reviews, 1976. 436p.

Recent developments in the uses of surveys are summarized, particularly basic research and as input for public policy decisions. Sudman discusses the major methodological developments in the collection and analysis of survey data and considers legal barriers, rising costs, and related challenges with sample surveys. The use of survey research in articles and books in 1945, 1960, and 1974 is shown (major sociology publications are the source). Survey archives, interactive computer analysis, telephone surveys, threatening topics, and machine-readable formats are all covered in the methods section. In the section on problems Sudman discusses refusal rates, the 1974 Federal Privacy Act, the Freedom of Information Act, and cost issues. (35 references)

SPECIAL TOPICS

AUDITING

994.   Advertising Research Foundation. *Standards and Procedures for ARF Audits of Syndicated Survey Research.* New York, NY: Advertising Research Foundation, 1979. 8p.

The contents of the booklet, prepared by the Research Auditing Council of the Advertising Research Foundation, cover five general auditing standards, four standards on coverage, and four standards of reporting. Four auditing procedures are considered: the measures and variables used; the consistency between the current study and the preceding one (if one exists); the accuracy and precision; and the mathematical treatments applied to the raw data. The audits are designed to determine the value of the syndicated service to the users' individual needs.

CONFIDENTIALITY

995.   Assembly of Behavioral and Social Sciences (U.S.). Panel on Privacy and Confidentiality as Factors in Survey Response, Committee on National Statistics, National Research Council. *Privacy and Confidentiality as Factors in Survey Response.* Washington, DC: National Academy of Sciences, 1979. 274p.

Funded by a National Science Foundation grant, the American Statistical Association brought together a group of social scientists and survey methodologists to investigate whether concerns about privacy and confidentiality are contributing to the difficulties of conducting surveys, and whether this poses a "threat to the continued use of surveys as a basic tool of social science research." The purpose of the panel was to generate empirical evidence, as the literature to date consists of individual observations and unsupported judgments. The panel set out to determine if the proposed techniques would be useful with respect to determining the public's attitude and behaviors on assurances of confidentiality. Two nationwide surveys were conducted. The panel reached eleven recommendations on research methods and eight recommendations for census and survey procedures which are summarized in the first chapter. These recommendations are addressed in the following four chapters dealing with the survey, response behavior, small group discussions, and a review of the research experience. Few people believe that confidential census records are truly confidential, and many believe that survey results are "affected by deliberate dishonesty of sponsors, researchers, or respondents." Appendixes contain the forms used, notes, and survey validation materials. A twenty-four-page bibliography is included. Chapter 5, the research experience, has a thirty-two-entry bibliography.

ETHICS

996.   American Association for Public Opinion Research. "Code of Professional Ethics and Practices." *Public Opinion Quarterly* 24, no. 3 (Fall 1960): 529-30.

In the preamble to the Code of Professional Ethics and Practices, members of the American Association for Public Opinion Research (AAPOR) pledge to support sound practices in the profession, to maintain high standards of scientific competence, and to reject assignments not in accord with the principles set forth in the code. Part 1 of the code is titled "Principles of Professional Practice in the Conduct of Our Work." It relates to matters of methodology and urges that care be used in setting up the research design, in gathering and processing data, and in interpreting and describing the results of a research project. Part 2, "Principles of Professional Responsibility in Our Dealings with People," addresses issues relating to the public, to the client or sponsor of the research, and to the profession. Sections deal with confidentiality, truthfulness in describing the methods used, and appropriateness of the research assignment in relation to our limitations. Membership in AAPOR is not to be used to certify professional competence. Ideas and findings from public opinion research are to be disseminated as freely as possible.

997.   King, Arnold J., and Aaron J. Spector. "Ethical and Legal Aspects of Survey Research." *American Psychologist* 18, no. 4 (April 1963): 204-8.

Sample surveys have been used as legal evidence since 1940. The issues raised in this article deal with the manner in which that evidence should be provided. The problem is that the hearsay rule evidence that is admitted must be subject to direct and cross-examination. In the case of surveys this could mean identifying respondents and causing unwilling individuals to be subpoenaed, clearly posing a challenge since respondents have been assured confidentiality and anonymity. The authors ask the following questions: (1) Should the respondents' names be kept confidential? (2) Should the respondents' names be released without restricted use? and (3) Should the respondents' consent be sought and restrictions be placed on the use of the names? A specific case involving the Borden Company in which a survey was admitted as evidence is discussed (3 *Trade Regulation Reporter* 20, 466 Commerce Clearing House). (7 footnotes, 1 reference)

998.   Manheimer, Dean I., Glen D. Mellinger, Robert H. Somers, and Marianne T. Kleman. "Technical and Ethical Considerations in Data Collection." *Drug Forum* 1, no. 4 (July 1972): 323-33.

The article reviews the techniques used to generate 90 percent cooperation from a sample consisting of approximately two thousand male students at the University of California at Berkeley. The survey was part of a longitudinal study of changing life styles and values. The following topics are discussed: anonymity, interviewers, pretesting, community support, respondents' cooperation, and reliability and validity. Drug use, academic and career development, personal well-being, and social commitment or alienation are some of the areas covered in the survey. The authors wanted to create a study of direct benefit to the students, and therefore they plan to discuss publicly the results of the data analysis. The article closes with a review of why longitudinal surveys are useful in studies of drug use.

999.   Tremblay, Kenneth R., Jr., and Don A. Dillman. "Research Ethics: Emerging Concerns from the Increased Use of Mail and Telephone Survey Methods." *Humboldt Journal of Social Relations* 5, no. 1 (Fall-Winter 1977): 64-89.

The primary ethical concern of the Tremblay and Dillman article is seen to be the "risk of infringing on the privacy of respondents to an unnecessary degree." Other issues include unkept promises and lack of adherence to voluntary participation approaches. Tremblay and his colleague discuss the use of invisible ink to identify questionnaires, and telephone interview forms with the name and address supplied. The practices of using certified mail and calling unlisted telephone numbers are addressed. The latter are considered invasions of privacy and counter to the "voluntary" spirit of ethical surveying. The issue as to whether survey respondents are harmed as a result of participating remains unexplored.

The authors maintain that ethics must be given "fundamental consideration" in the research design. (40 references)

LEGAL SETTING

1000.   Frankel, Lester R. "Restrictions to Survey Sampling – Legal, Practical and Ethical." In *Perspectives on Attitude Assessment: Surveys and Their Alternatives*, edited by H. Wallace Sinaiko and Laurie A. Broedling, 54-67. Champaign, IL: Pendleton Publications, 1976. 242p. [This book was first published as Technical Report, no. 2 by the Smithsonian Institution.]

The advent of the use of sampling in surveys (beginning in the 1930s) is discussed, along with a consideration of nonsampling errors – including nonresponse and interviewer error. Response rate, with attention to its decline in the early 1970s, and the nature of legal restrictions to surveying are reviewed. It is noted that survey results can be subpoenaed as well as the respondents (unlike census data where anonymity is guaranteed by statute). Locations which prohibit interviewing are mentioned, along with communities which charge a per-day fee for interviewing (basically a license). Frankel addresses the challenge of the not-at-homes in a section titled "Practical Issues." The differing functions of market sample surveys in relation to surveys sponsored by government agencies are observed. The review of ethics in survey work deals with the violation of the rights of respondents. Issues such as invasion of privacy, informed consent, disturbing the peace through telephone or personal interview attempts, and deception are addressed. In the last section Frankel considers alternatives to the survey. Observation, the randomized response technique, guaranteed anonymity, and confidentiality are topics briefly reviewed. (19 references)

POLLS AND DEMOCRACY

1001.   Gallup, George. *Public Opinion in a Democracy*. Stafford Little Lectures. [Princeton, NJ]: Published under the University Extension Fund, Herbert L. Baker Foundation, Princeton University, 1939. 15p.

This published lecture demonstrates the connection made by Gallup between public opinion polls and democracy. Gallup speaks of the cross-section survey and discusses the reliability of opinion surveys. Discounted is the so-called bandwagon vote – created when people know who the most popular candidate is and vote for that person simply to be on the winning side. Another concern which is dispelled is the notion that once a majority view is known, debate will be stifled or stopped. Gallup views polls as a benefit to government representatives since these individuals will now have a "truer measure of opinion in their districts and in the nation." The wisdom of the "common people" has been questioned as a source for decision making. Gallup argues that "great faith" can be placed in the "collective judgment or intelligence of the people." The author suggests that as a result of wide ownership of radio and large newspaper circulation, the entire nation has become like the New England town meeting. The nation's views are measured through the "process of the sampling referendum."

1002.   Gosnell, Harold F. "The Polls and Other Mechanisms of Democracy." *Public Opinion Quarterly* 4, no. 2 (June 1940): 224-28.

Public opinion polls are systematically compared with initiatives, referendums, and recalls. Polls are described as having the advantages of being national in scope and yet small in sample size, being relatively inexpensive, and having great flexibility. Polls are also cited as being capable of reaching groups that are not part of the official electorate (such as minors, aliens, and those lacking legal residency status). Among the disadvantages are that respondents do not know the question ahead of time and may respond with answers based on "half knowledge and intuition," bias may arise from the investigators' presentation style, and the question selection may lead to biased responses. (6 footnotes)

1003.   Nelson, Allan Dwight. "Political Implications of Modern Public Opinion Research." Ph.D. diss., University of Chicago, 1962. 489 leaves. [Not available from *Dissertation Abstracts International*.]

This dissertation contains eleven chapters, three of which have a direct bearing on public opinion polls. In chapter 1 Nelson discusses the general character of public opinion research, covering basic elements and practical claims. Chapter 3 deals with public opinion polls and representative democracy. The subjects of tyranny, preferences, and strategies are reviewed. Chapter 10 considers the question of public opinion research as an instrument of democracy. Each chapter mentioned provides a lengthy discussion of the issues. The foundations of opinion polling are discussed, with considerable effort exerted to explain, query, and theorize on such topics as "values" in public opinion research, cognitive elements of opinion, the public's interests, and democratic "requirements" in relationship to scientific "values." Nelson's conclusion is twenty-four pages, ending with a call for opinion researchers to "give closer attention to our heritage of political theory." He also states that "it is likely that only the relatively simple and trivial facts of human existence can be known with the degree of certainty that the opinion researchers are wont to claim (at least by implication) for their findings." References are provided.

PROPAGANDA USE

1004.   Doob, Leonard W. *Public Opinion and Propaganda.* 2d ed. Hamden, CT: Archon Books, 1966. 612p.

All but the last chapter and the appendix of the second edition are the same as the 1948 text. The volume is devoted to the salient issues of the late 1940s. In the preface to the second edition Doob comments that the word "propaganda" has been replaced by value-free terms such as "communication" or, more recently, "information." There are a number of chapters dealing with polling. These include discussions of sampling, polling mechanics, evaluation, and intensive measures in chapters six through nine and cover over one hundred pages of text. The notes for each chapter are grouped together in the references section at the end of the volume. Cumulatively, there are 119 notes for the four chapters directly covering polling.

PUBLIC REACTION

1005.   Hartmann, Elizabeth L., H. Lawrence Isaacson, and Cynthia M. Jurgell. "Public Reaction to Public Opinion Surveying." *Public Opinion Quarterly* 32, no. 2 (Summer 1968): 295-98.

Two questions were asked of one thousand Americans in an area probability sample in June 1966. The study attempted to determine the extent of public dissatisfaction with public opinion polling. The questions asked how frequently people had been interviewed and whether they considered the questions objectionable. Data in table 1 indicate that 35 percent of the respondents reported having been polled. Table 2 shows sex, age, income, and area breakdowns. Of the 35 percent polled, 80 percent reported no objection, 13 percent refused to answer objectionable questions, 5 percent answered objectionable questions, and 2 percent did not respond; 18 percent voiced invasion of privacy (primarily against income questions). The authors discuss three issues not considered by the present study: (1) nothing is known about the 15 percent of the original sample who refused to participate; (2) attitudinal changes over time; and (3) overall reaction to polling in general as an invasion of privacy, as opposed to objecting only to specific questions. (1 footnote).

REGULATION

1006.   Gallup, George. "On the Regulation of Polling." *Public Opinion Quarterly* 12, no. 4 (Winter 1948-49): 733-35.

Gallup writes in response to the many who call for government regulation of polls. He observes that this call has been heard for twenty years and will probably be raised in the Eighty-first Congress. Gallup believes that such regulations would favor established organizations, as they would all be able to meet "almost any" set of regulations imposed. Additionally, Gallup writes that defining a poll "is an almost impossible task." He favors self-regulation, with full disclosure of polling methods to appear with all published polls. (A duplicate of every Gallup Poll ballot ever collected is on file at Princeton University for the use of qualified individuals.) Gallup believes that some standard of truth and accuracy – such as basing criticism on facts – should be followed by poll critics. The use of entire batteries of questions and open questions are mentioned as ways of weeding out wholly uninformed respondents and for determining the nature and intensity of respondents' opinions. (1 footnote)

1007.   Meyer, Philip. "Truth in Polling: Poll Takers Are Adopting New, Stricter Standards of Disclosure – But the Reform Cannot Work Unless Reporters Ask the Right Questions." *Columbia Journalism Review* 7, no. 2 (Summer 1968): 20-23.

As a means of introducing a mechanism to gauge the "truth" of polls, the American Association for Public Opinion Research has produced standards of disclosure which call for public opinion polls to report the following: (1) identity of the survey sponsor; (2) exact question wording; (3) definition of the population sampled; (4) sample size, and with mail questionnaires, the number who responded; (5) allowance for sampling error; (6) "identification of findings based on parts of the total sample"; (7) interview format: in-person, telephone, street corner, or mail questionnaire; and (8) timing of the interview as related to an event that might have affected the responses. Congressman Lucien Nedzi (D.-Mich.) is described as having written a bill which would require results and methodology of published polls to be filed with the Library of Congress. An example is presented of how some poll results were used in a less-than-honest way.

1008.   Nedzi, Lucien N. "Public Opinion Polls: Will Legislation Help?" *Public Opinion Quarterly* 35, no. 3 (Fall 1971): 336-41.

The article recounts Representative Nedzi's (D.-Mich.) unsuccessful attempt to introduce in the Ninety-first Congress a bill to require certain disclosure of information by pollsters. The bill was the first piece of federal legislation to address this subject since 1943 when Senator Gerald Nye (D.-N. Dakota) proposed "regulation" for polls. Nedzi's 1968 bill called for a congressional investigation of polls with the goal of increasing poll data reliability and establishing standards for the industry. Nedzi was "concerned about the possible mischief polls can cause." The author presents five examples of how some politicians have been "abused" by the polls. He concentrates on the 1966 case of *Citizens for Ferency v. Market Opinion Research.* Market Opinion Research, the defendant, argued and received dismissal on the grounds that the company's polling methods were a "trade secret" and therefore protected against disclosure. Several reasons are given as to why disclosure is desirable, and seven questions are posed as substance for congressional hearings. The article concludes with a summary of the Nedzi bill which would have required the following information from pollsters: (1) sponsor of the bill; (2) sampling method; (3) sample size; (4) time frame involved; (5) questions asked; (6) method for acquiring the data (telephone, mail, face-to-face interviewing); (7) number of respondents contacted; (8) number not contacted, and number of nonrespondents; and (9) poll results.

1009.   Pekkanen, John. "The Abuses and Fears of Polling Power." *Life* 65, no. 3 (19 July 1968): 62, 62B.

Reference is made to two hundred ongoing polls which demonstrate little agreement as to how a poll should best be conducted. Pekkanen compares and contrasts the results of Gallup and Harris, with Gallup providing little interpretation of results beyond the percentage breakdowns, and Harris insisting on some interpretation. The American Association for Public Opinion Research is mentioned as having adopted a set of standards which call for the public release of the poll methodology used to obtain results. The "truth-in-polling" bill introduced by Congressman Lucien Nedzi (D.-Mich.) in the House of Representatives is discussed. The bill calls for "data on a poll" to be filed with the Library of Congress within seventy-two hours after public release. Gallup is in favor of the bill, Harris is opposed, and Burns Roper would prefer that the problem be solved without federal legislation, although he is "not sure that it can be."

1010.   "Pollsters and Journalists." *America* 119, no. 9 (28 September 1968): 239.

Congressman Lucien Nedzi (D.-Mich.) is reported to have written a bill which would require the results and methodology of published polls to be filed with the Library of Congress. The American Association for Public Opinion Research (AAPOR) has adopted standards of disclosure for its polling members. Additionally, AAPOR states that published surveys should include eight items: (1) identification of the survey sponsor; (2) exact question wording; (3) definition of the population sampled; (4) sample size and number of respondents in mail surveys; (5) an allowance for sampling error; (6) identification of findings based on parts of the total sample; (7) nature of the interviewing format – telephone, mail, street corner; and (8) timing of interviews in relation to other events. These measures are designed to assist the reader to judge the value of the poll.

1011.   "Public Polls: Variance in Accuracy, Reliability." *Congressional Quarterly Weekly Report* 29, no. 38 (18 September 1971): 1927-34.

A number of election instances in which polls have had negative effects due to inaccuracy are discussed. Bandwagon effects and inadequate disclosures are considered, along with efforts to regulate polling. Also reviewed is Representative Lucien N. Nedzi's (D.-Mich.) bill H.R. 5003 covering poll disclosure requirements which was introduced in the Ninety-first and Ninety-second Congresses. Polling methodology is outlined, with the personal, telephone, and mail approaches explained. Probability sampling, sample size, weighting, timing, questioning methods, and repeat visits are described. As the "biggest" names in polling, Gallup and Harris are considered on a separate page, with their organizations' approaches compared and contrasted. The last four pages of the article present published polls by state, along with their techniques and results for the 1970 political campaigns.

1012. U.S. Congress. House. Committee on House Administration, Subcommittee on Library and Memorials. *Public Opinion Polls. To Provide for the Disclosure of Certain Information Relating to Certain Public Opinion Polls: Hearings on H.R. 5003.* 93d Cong., 1st sess., 19, 20, 21 September, 5 October 1972. Washington, DC: U.S. Government Printing Office, 1973. 260p. [SuDoc Y4.H81/3:Op3]

These hearings concern the "Truth-in-Polling-Act" which would require those conducting public opinion polls involving federal office or which deal with any political issue "the results of which are intended to be and are disseminated to the public through the mail or through interstate commerce" to file certain information with the Librarian of the Library of Congress within seventy-two hours after the results are made available. Eight points of information cover the following: (1) name of the poll requester; (2) method used in the sample; (3) sample size; (4) dates of the poll; (5) questions asked; (6) methodology used; (7) number contacted and responded, number contacted but with no response, and number not contacted; and (8) results of the poll. The information is to be publicly available. Punishment for failure to comply is established with a maximum of $1000 fine or thirty days incarceration, or both. Twenty individuals appeared before the subcommittee, many reading prepared statements before being questioned. An additional seven individuals had prepared statements submitted for the record. Those testifying during the four days of the hearings included, among others, Angus Campbell, Albert H. Cantril, Mervin Field, George Gallup, Louis Harris, and Burns W. Roper.

HUMOR

1013.   Barrett, Francis D., Jr. "The CANIS Method of Reducing Bias in Survey Research." *Journal of Marketing Research* 9, no. 3 (August 1972): 329-30.

The issue of whether the respondent is being truthful during the interview is explored. Barrett maintains that existing approaches of asking related questions to ascertain whether similar attitudes are expressed are not sufficient, as most respondents are "too sophisticated to be duped by such a naive method." As an alternative, Barrett suggests weighing the truthfulness of the response by observing the respondent's dog. A truthfulness scale is presented, with the range being from a very truthful response in which the dog licks the owner's face, to a very untruthful response in which the dog bites the respondent, with the midpoint shown by a motionless dog. Attention is given to the manner in which appropriate dog-respondent samples are to be drawn. The primary interviewer challenge seems to be recording both the respondent's answer as well as the dog's reaction. Barrett closes by observing that he is exploring the possibility of eliminating the human respondent and interviewing the dog exclusively.

APPENDIXES

APPENDIX A: ACRONYMS

AAPOR	American Association for Public Opinion Research
ABC	American Broadcasting Company
ACC	Appleton - Century - Crofts
ACD	Rockwell - Collins Automatic Call Distribution Telephone System
AIPO	American Institute of Public Opinion
AIS	Attitude Information System
ANOVA	Analysis of variance
ARF	Advertising Research Foundation
ARI	Audience Research, Incorporated
ASCII	American Standard Code for Information Interchange
BLS	Bureau of Labor Statistics
BRS	Behavioral Research Survey Services
CATI	Computer-Assisted Telephone Interviewing
CBS	Columbia Broadcasting System
CD	Community Development
CNS	Continuous National Survey
CPO	Commercial public opinion
CPR	*Current Population Reports*
CPS	*Current Population Survey*
CRT	Cathode ray tube
CV	Certainty value
CW	Conventional wisdom

DAS   Detroit Area Study
DK   Don't know

EBCDIC   Extended Binary-Coded Decimal Interchange Code

FACT   Field Audit and Completion Test
FCC   Federal Communications Commission
FM   Frequency modulation

GAO   General Accounting Office
GI   General Inquirer

HIS   Health Interview Survey

IBM   International Business Machines
Inforet   Information return
IRC   Industrial Relations Center
IRSS   Institute for Research in Social Science
ISR   Institute for Social Research

KWIC   Key-Word-in-Context

MBS   Mutual Broadcasting System

NBC   National Broadcasting Company
NCHSR   National Center for Health Services Research
NCPP   National Council on Public Polls
NORC   National Opinion Research Center
NSR   Nonsubstantive response

OI   Open-ended interviews
OPOR   (Princeton) Office of Public Opinion Research
ORC   Opinion Research Corporation

PCS   Permanent Community Sample
POQ   *Public Opinion Quarterly*
PP   Piggyback phenomena
PSU   Primary sampling unit

RADAR   Radio's All-Dimension Audience Research
RAND   Research and Development [Corporation]
RDD   Random digit dialing
RE   Response error
RGB   Rotation group bias

RL	Response latency
RRM	Randomized response model
RRT	Randomized response technique
SEG	Institute of Social, Economic and Government Research
SIR	Statuses of Investigator and Respondent
SMIS	Survey Methodology Information System
SMSA	Standard Metropolitan Statistical Area
SRC	Survey Research Center
SRL	Survey Research Laboratory
SVTI	Standardized Video Taped Interview
TDM	Total design method
TIMBO	A computer program written in FORTRAN and used with files of frequencies for behavior codes
UCLA	University of California at Los Angeles
UQM	Unrelated question model
USDA	U.S. Department of Agriculture
WATS	Wide Area Telecommunications Service
WPOL	Washington Public Opinion Laboratory
YMCA	Young Men's Christian Association
YWCA	Young Women's Christian Association

APPENDIX B: SOURCE JOURNALS

The numbers following each journal title refer to item numbers in the text.

Advertising Age, 450, 647
Agricultural Economics Research, 158, 703
America, 1010
American Anthropologist, 508
American Archivist, 12
American Bar Association Journal, 884
American Behavioral Scientist, 5, 169, 551, 743
American Education, 851
American Journal of Community Psychology, 560
American Journal of Hygiene, 431
American Journal of Political Science, 683, 771
American Journal of Public Health, 161, 557, 572-73, 576, 578, 865-66, 869
American Journal of Sociology, 263, 366, 400, 419, 441, 489, 677, 749-50, 756-57
American Political Science Review, 922
American Psychologist, 881, 963, 997
American School & University, 850
American School Board Journal, 266, 848
American Sociological Review, 162, 296, 328, 515, 547-48, 582, 745, 754, 765, 991
American Sociologist, 730
American Statistical Association Bulletin, 483
American Statistician, 66, 713
Annals of Mathematical Statistics, 938-39
Annals of the American Academy of Political and Social Science, 115, 890, 904,

Harvard Law Review, 883
High Points, 854
Human Behavior, 264
Human Organization, 145, 223, 228, 286, 505, 663, 807, 832
Humboldt Journal of Social Relations, 999

Industrial Marketing, 129
Industry Week, 144
International Journal of Aging and Human Development, 510
Items – Social Science Research Council, 189, 399

Journal of Abnormal and Social Psychology, 285, 323, 356, 369
Journal of Advertising Research, 88, 213, 246, 249, 255, 288, 290, 302, 341,
    406, 522, 586, 652, 662
Journal of Applied Psychology, 56, 123, 212, 295, 306, 321, 345, 417, 493, 577,
    596, 620, 630, 643, 661, 679, 810
Journal of Black Psychology, 507
Journal of Broadcasting, 230
Journal of Business, 694
Journal of Business Research, 238
Journal of Chronic Diseases, 868
Journal of Consulting Psychology, 394, 488
Journal of Criminal Justice, 636
Journal of Educational Communication, 844
Journal of Educational Data Processing, 118
Journal of Educational Psychology, 773
Journal of Educational Sociology, 74
Journal of Experimental Education, 187, 737
Journal of Farm Economics, 589, 599, 833
Journal of Gerontology, 299, 511, 789
Journal of Health and Human Behavior, 287
Journal of Higher Education, 600
Journal of Home Economics, 525
Journal of Leisure Research, 585
Journal of Marketing, 102, 107, 135, 146, 149, 166, 170, 179, 181, 203, 289,
    309, 311, 316, 333, 342, 352, 370, 388, 429, 433-34, 437, 444, 453, 485, 495,
    517, 527, 529, 555, 558, 601, 603, 619, 642, 649, 672, 767, 776, 784, 882, 885
Journal of Marketing Research, 16, 156, 231, 237, 247-48, 250, 252-54, 256,
    259, 279, 293-94, 298, 339, 348, 350-51, 386, 405, 454, 459, 462, 523, 528,
    554, 563, 608, 612, 629, 653, 706, 711, 716, 720, 722, 735, 772, 1013
Journal of Negro Education, 221
Journal of Personality and Social Psychology, 458, 460-61
Journal of Social Issues, 47, 132, 136, 401, 475, 503-4, 751, 855
Journal of Social Psychology, 376, 481, 595, 622

301, 303-4, 307, 310, 313-14, 320, 322, 330, 336, 338, 346-47, 354, 357-58, 360-64, 367, 371-73, 382-85, 387, 389-91, 393, 395, 397-98, 402, 414-15, 422-23, 427, 430, 432, 438, 442, 446-47, 455, 476, 478, 482, 484, 486, 490-91, 496-98, 502, 506, 513-14, 516, 519-21, 533, 537-39, 541, 543, 546, 549, 553, 565, 570, 581, 590, 597-98, 602, 609, 613, 615-16, 618, 625-26, 628, 632-35, 640-41, 650-51, 657, 659, 664, 670-71, 675, 680-82, 686-87, 692, 698, 705, 714-15, 718, 723, 728, 740, 744, 748, 752, 758, 762-63, 777, 782, 788, 793, 797-99, 801-2, 805-6, 808-9, 812, 858, 886-87, 892, 903, 912, 921, 923, 925, 927-28, 931, 935-36, 941, 946, 948-49, 951-56, 958, 979, 983, 986, 996, 1002, 1005-6, 1008
Public Relations Journal, 980-81

Quarterly Journal of Studies on Alcohol, 353

Research Quarterly, 211
Review of Educational Research, 840-41, 843
Review of Religious Research, 984
Review of Reviews, 943
Rural Sociology, 300, 644, 783

Savings Bank Journal, 820
Scholastic, 55
School Management, 532, 849
Science Digest, 318
Science News, 902
Scientific American, 964
Social Biology, 638
Social Forces, 646
Social Order, 940
Social Policy, 260
Social Problems, 829, 878
Social Science Quarterly, 292, 392, 501, 774
Social Science Research, 128, 315, 592
Society, 86
Sociological Methodology, 324, 684
Sociological Methods & Research, 127, 325, 403, 499, 689, 700, 712, 764, 775
Sociological Quarterly, 614, 623, 794
Sociology and Social Research, 60, 291, 312, 654, 658, 962
Sociometry, 54, 198, 225, 305, 377
Survey Research, 233, 531

Television Magazine, 215
Time, 167, 959, 977
Trans-Action, 119

APPENDIX C: PRINT AND CD-ROM SOURCES

Print

ABC Pol Sci: A Bibliography of Contents: Political Science and Government
Access

Bibliographic Index
Book Review Digest
Book Review Index
Business Periodicals Index

CIS Index to Congressional Publications and Public Laws
Communication Abstracts: An International Information Service
C.R.I.S.: The Combined Retrospective Index Set to Journals in Political Science
C.R.I.S.: The Combined Retrospective Index Set to Journals in Sociology
Cumulative Book Index
Current Index to Journals in Education (CIJE)

Dissertation Abstracts International

Education Index

Historical Abstracts

Index to Legal Periodicals
International Index

International Political Science Abstracts

Library Literature

Monthly Catalog of U.S. Government Publications

National Union Catalog

Psychological Abstracts
Public Affairs Information Service Bulletin (PAIS)
Public Opinion Quarterly Index 1937-1982

Readers' Guide to Periodical Literature
Resources in Education (RIE)

Sage Public Administration Abstracts
Shelflist of the Library of Congress
Social Sciences & Humanities Index
Social Sciences Citation Index (SSCI)
Social Sciences Index
Sociological Abstracts
Statistical Reference Index
Subject Guide to Books in Print

United States Political Science Documents (USPSD)
Universal Reference System – *Political Science, Government, and Public Policy*
  Series

CD-ROM

ABI/Inform 1971-
AGRICOLA 1970-

Encyclopedia of Associations (Gale) current release
ERIC 1966-

GPO on Silver Platter July 1976-

Medline 1966-

PAIS International 1972-
Psyc Information 1967-

Sociofile 1974-

APPENDIX D: ORGANIZATIONS

Academy of Political Science (APS)
475 Riverside Drive, Suite 1274
c/o Demetrios Caraley, President and Executive Director
New York, NY 10115-1274
(212) 870-2500
Year Founded: 1880

American Academy of Political and Social Science (AAPSS)
c/o Marvin E. Wolfgang, President
3937 Chestnut Street
Philadelphia, PA 19104-3110
(215) 386-4594
Year Founded: 1889

American Association for Public Opinion Research (AAPOR)
c/o Marlene Bednarz, Administrator
PO Box 1248
Ann Arbor, MI 48106-1248
(313) 764-1555
Year Founded: 1947

American Association for Public Opinion Research
Central New Jersey Chapter
The Gallup Organization
c/o Laura Kalb, President

47 Hulfish Street, Suite 200
Princeton, NJ 08542-3709
(609) 924-9600
Year Founded: 1977

American Association for Public Opinion Research
Midwest Chapter
c/o Richard M. Perloff, President
Cleveland State University
Department of Communication
Cleveland, OH 44115-2407
(216) 687-5042
Year Founded: 1975

American Association for Public Opinion Research
New England Chapter
c/o Ellen Boisvert, President
Dudley Research
14 Front Street
Exeter, NH 03833-2737
(603) 778-1583
Year Founded: 1994

American Association for Public Opinion Research
New Jersey Chapter
c/o John Zeglarski, President
Ronin Corporation
103 Carnegie Center, Suite 303
Princeton, NJ 08540-6235
(609) 452-0060
Year Founded: 1977

American Association for Public Opinion Research
New York Chapter
c/o Dr. Robert S. Lee, President
Pace University
Lubin School of Business
One Pace Plaza
New York, NY 10038-1598
(212) 346-1823
Year Founded: 1978

American Association for Public Opinion Research
Southern Chapter

c/o Robert Oldendick, President
University of South Carolina
Survey Research Laboratory
Institute for Public Affairs
Columbia, SC 29201-3633
(803) 777-8157
Year Founded: 1978

American Association for Public Opinion Research
Washington/Baltimore Chapter
c/o Maria Elena Sanchez, President
Agency for Health Care Policy and Research
2101 Jefferson
Rockville, MD 20852-4908
(301) 594-1400
Year Founded: c. 1953

American Political Science Association (APSA)
c/o Catherine E. Rudder, Executive Director
1527 New Hampshire Avenue NW
Washington, DC 20036-1527
(202) 483-2512
Year Founded: 1903

American Psychological Association (APA)
c/o Raymond D. Fowler, Chief Executive Officer
750 1st Street NE
Washington, DC 20002-4242
(202) 336-5500
Year Founded: 1892

American Sociological Association (ASA)
c/o Felice Levine, Executive Officer
1722 N Street NW
Washington, DC 20036-2981
(202) 833-3410
Year Founded: 1905

American Statistical Association (ASA)
c/o Barbara A. Bailar, Executive Director
1429 Duke Street
Alexandria, VA 22314-3402
(703) 684-1221
Year Founded: 1839

Association of Social and Behavioral Scientists (ASBS)
c/o Dr. Jacqueline Rovse, Contact
American University
Department of History
4400 Massachusetts Avenue
Washington, DC 20016-8038
(202) 885-2461
Year Founded: 1935

Council of American Survey Research Organizations (CASRO)
c/o Diane K. Bowers, Executive Director
3 Upper Devon Belle Terre
Port Jefferson, NY 11777-1224
(516) 928-6954
Year Founded: 1975

International Survey Library Association (ISLA)
c/o Everett C. Ladd, Jr., Executive Director
Roper Center
PO Box 440
Storrs, CT 06268-0440
(203) 486-4440
Year Founded: 1964

Midwest Association for Public Opinion Research (MAPOR)
c/o Prof. M. Mark Miller, President
University of Tennessee
3370 Communications Building
Knoxville, TN 37996-0330
(615) 974-4452
Year Founded: 1977

National Council on Public Polls (NCPP)
c/o Sheldon R. Gawisen, President
205 East 42nd Street
Room 1708
New York, NY 10017-5706
(212) 986-8262
Year Founded: 1969

Roper Organization
c/o Burns W. Roper, Chairman
205 East 42nd Street, 17th floor
New York, NY 10017-5706

(212) 599-0700
Year Founded: 1933

World Association for Public Opinion Research (WAPOR)
c/o Prof. Valarie Lauder, Contact
University of North Carolina
School of Journalism and Mass Communication
CB-3365, Howell Hall
Chapel Hill, NC 27599-3365
(919) 962-4078
Year Founded: 1946

INDEXES

AUTHOR INDEX

The numbers following each entry refer to item numbers in the text.

SELECTIVE KEYWORD INDEX
STOP WORDS

Age

Analysis

Bias

Data

Face-to-face

Face-to-face interviewing

Female

Finding

Interview

Interviewed

Interviewee

Interviewer

Interviewing

Male

Men

Method

Methodology

Opinion

Opinion Poll

Poll

Public opinion

Public opinion poll

Question

Questionnaire

Reliability

Research

Researcher

Respondent

Response

Result

Sample

Sampling

Survey

Survey research

Technique

Telephone

Telephone interview

Telephone interviewer

Validity

Women

SELECTIVE KEYWORD INDEX

A stop-word list of highly cited terms (those not posted in the index) appears on the previous page. The numbers following the keywords refer to item numbers in the text.

347, 473, 515, 522, 529-30, 536,
555, 562, 564, 569, 591, 593-94,
598, 619, 652, 656, 676, 703, 709,
784, 817, 823, 851, 862-63, 869,
894, 919, 929, 993
Cost-benefit analysis, 559
Cost control, 120, 470
Cost data, 492
Cost differentials, 180
Cost effective, 552, 587, 606
Cost estimates, 179, 711
Cost functions, 605
Cost issues, 554
Cost of Education Index, 841
Cost of living, 408
Cost options, 452
Cost reduction, 243, 596
Cost savings, 561
Cost studies, 818
Cost-variance function, 175
Couch, A. S., 626
Could, 318
Council environment, 982
Council of American Survey
  Research Organizations, 706
Council of Planning Librarians, 15,
  365, 449
Counseling, 552
Country club samples, 129
Country Gentleman, 893
Country of origin, 502
County, 143
County governments, 862
County probation offices, 658
County voter-registration files,
  658
Court, 883
Court cases, 884
Courtroom settings, 880
Cover letter, 817
Coverage, 184
CPO, 50
CPR, 774
CPS, 407, 477, 689

Credibility, 110-11, 114, 118, 743
Credibility gap problem, 977
Credit offices, 658
Crespi, 113
Crider, 659
Crime, 395
Crime characteristics, 721
Crime Code, 239
Crime overreporting, 721
Crime rates, 239, 700
Crime records, 721
Crime victimization, 234, 240
Crime victims, 538
Criminal justice agencies, 240
Criminal victimization, 636
Criminal victimization surveys,
  721
Criminology, 721, 779
Criss-cross directories, 658
Criteria, 769, 888
Criterion situations, 799
Critical, 580
Critical attitude, 487
Cronbach, L. J., 626
Crop estimates, 116
Cross-classify, 756
Cross cultural methods, 507
Cross-examination, 880, 886, 997
Cross-national comparisons, 3
Cross-national surveys, 898
Cross-pressures, 367
Cross-racial interviewing, 372
Cross section(s), 77, 804, 930, 985
Cross-section sample survey, 168
Cross-section sampling, 53, 869
Cross-section survey(s), 23, 1001
Cross-sectional design, 860
Cross-sectional studies, 795
Cross-sectional survey(s), 478,
  774, 990
Cross tabulations, 813
Crossley, [Archibald], 46, 51, 54-
  55, 57, 59-60, 63, 69, 178, 188-89,
  343, 399, 665, 768, 912, 937, 942,

Irritated respondent, 544
Irritation, 488
IRSS Technical Papers, 708
Irvington, 284, 482
Isolated, 644
Isolationism, 272
Isolationist, 357
ISR, 147, 947
Issue awareness, 922
Issue consistency, 283
Issue voting, 310
Issues, 991
Italians, 609
Item content, 283
Item design, 139
Item embarrassment, 425
Item location, 299
Item-method reliability, 788
Item phrasing, 292
Iteration, 775

Jackknife repeated replication, 156
Jackson, 870
Japan, 47, 376
Japanese, 376, 798
Jargon-free language, 114
Jefferson, 82, 96
Jennings-Niemi, 771
Jepsen, Roger, 914
Jewelry store, 101
Jewish, 641, 983
Jewish-looking interviewers, 369
Jewish names, 369
Jews, 224
Job analysis, 429
Job Corps, 504-5
Job criterion, 429
Job evaluations, 429
Job performance, 340
Job satisfaction, 582
Jobs, 485
Johns Hopkins Hospital, 573
Johnson, [Lyndon B.], 797
Jokes, 488

Jossey-Bass Behavioral Science
  Series, 898
Jossey-Bass Social and Behavioral
  Science Series, 280, 684, 864
Journal code list, 13
*Journal of Abnormal and Social
  Psychology*, 449, 626
Journal of Applied Psychology,
  137, 680
*Journal of Educational
  Psychology*, 843
Journal of Educational Research,
  137, 843
Journal of Marketing, 137, 351,
  708
Journal of Marketing Research, 16-
  17, 32, 244, 350, 708, 717
Journal of Social Psychology, 449
*Journal of the American Statistical
  Association*, 15-17, 137, 708, 717,
  725, 737, 741, 766
Journalism, 63, 74, 82, 96, 471
Journalism professor, 82, 97
Journalism Quarterly, 15
Journalistic interviews, 858
Journalistic poll, 892
Journalistic presentation, 46
Journalists, 193, 894-95, 897, 945,
  991, 1010
Judgment(s), 27, 30, 79, 122, 135,
  453, 488, 751, 872, 963, 995
Judgment-making process, 538
Judgment samples, 784, 812
Judgment sampling, 158
Judgment selection, 188
Judgmental problems, 402
"Judgments of the Comic," 488
Judicial proceedings, 879
Jury, 886
Jury trials, 881

Kaiser Foundation Health Plan, 574
Kansas City, 594
Kansas Radio-Television Audience

Studies in Health Care, 873
Studies in Public Opinion, 317
Study of Consumer Expenditures, Incomes and Savings, 836
Study time, 447
Stupid, 433
Subclasses, 337
Subcultural norms, 581
Subjective analysis, 327
Subjective data, 663
Subjective methods, 347
Subjective states, 313
Subjectivist research, 122
Subjectivity, 334
Subpoena, 1000
Subpoenaed, 997
Subpopulations, 175
Subquestions, 361
Subsamples, 194
Subsampling, 157, 161, 191, 561, 712
Subscribers, 893, 972
Subsidized, 991
Substantive bias, 702, 708
Substantive variable values, 701
Substitutions, 72, 203
Subtleties, 314, 507
Subtlety, 401
Suburbs, 612, 627
Successful interviewing, 469
Successive cross sections, 985
Successive polling, 921
Successive recalls, 710
Successive responses, 703
Successive-sample technique, 481
Sudfeld, Walter H., 410
Sudman, 232
Suggestion(s), 305, 601
Suggestive phraseology, 261
Suggestive phrases, 266
Suggestive words, 266
Sunday editions, 82
Superficial analysis, 141
Superficial opinions, 645

Superficial patterns, 834
Superficiality, 585
Superficially held, 674
Superfluous questions, 347
Supervision, 27, 196, 346, 407, 498, 500
Supervisor(s), 98, 239, 341, 446, 454, 500, 506, 575, 803
Supervisor-subordinate relations, 471
Supervisory rating(s), 418
Supplemented marginals, 777
Suppress facts, 441
Supreme Court, 820
Sureness, 674
Surface character, 834
Surface rationalizations, 269
Surgery, 546
Surname, 654, 658
Survey abuses, 393
Survey analysis, 138, 778
Survey archives, 993
Survey benefits, 142
Survey-conditioned yes-men, 871
Survey Data for Trend Analysis, 2
Survey design, 138, 140, 837, 990
Survey evidence, 887
Survey fatigue, 871
Survey industry, 959
"Survey Interviewers as Witnesses," 887
Survey limitations, 142
Survey method(s), 17, 132, 874
Survey Methodology Information System, 17, 244
Survey methodology literature, 17
Survey of Consumer Expenditures, 836
Survey of Consumer Finances, 419, 776, 835
Survey of Economic Opportunity, 637, 774
Survey of Financial Characteristics of Consumers, 800

About the Compiler

GRAHAM R. WALDEN is Assistant Professor, Reference Librarian and Collection Manager, in the Information Services Department of the Main Library at the Ohio State University. Previous publications include *Public Opinion Polls and Survey Research: A Selective Annotated Bibliography of U.S. Guides and Studies from the 1980s* (1990); entries for *Psychology Today* and *U.S. News and World Report* in *American Mass-Market Magazines* (Greenwood Press, 1990); an article on polling sources in *Reference Services Review* (1988); and over 30 book and serial reviews in multiple journals.

ISBN 0-313-27790-7

90000>

EAN

9 780313 277900

HARDCOVER BAR CODE